ANZAC
SONS

MATESHIP, BRAVERY AND SACRIFICE

ANZAC SONS

MATESHIP, BRAVERY AND SACRIFICE

BIG SKY PUBLISHING
www.bigskypublishing.com.au

ALLISON MARLOW PATERSON

*To my father Noel Marlow (1937-2020) – thank you for walking
in their footsteps with me, and always being by my side.*

This revised edition published 2022
First published 2014

Big Sky Publishing Pty Ltd

PO Box 303, Newport, NSW 2106, Australia

Phone: 1300 364 611

Email: info@bigskypublishing.com.au

Web: www.bigskypublishing.com.au

Cover design and typesetting: Think Productions

National Library of Australia Cataloguing-in-Publication entry (pbk.)

Author: Paterson, Allison Marlow

Title: Anzac Sons: Mateship, Bravery and Sacrifice
           Allison Marlow Paterson.

ISBN: 9781922615459 (paperback)
           9781922615640 (ebook)

A catalogue record for this
book is available from the
National Library of Australia

Front cover image: Kandahar Farm dressing station, the 3rd Australian Division field dressing station,
on the afternoon of 7 June 1917 during the Battle of Messines (AWM E00482).

Back cover image: Dead and wounded in the railway cutting, Broodseinde Ridge, 12 October 1917
(AWM E03864).

CONTENTS

PREFACE

Anzac Sons is an account of the Great War experiences of five brothers drawn from a collection of over 500 letters written to their families at home. The letters, penned by my grandfather and four of his brothers, were sent from the training grounds of Victoria, from Egypt, England and the battlefields of the Western Front — Pozieres, Bullecourt, Messines, Menin Road, Passchendaele, Villers-Bretonneux and the village battlegrounds of 1918. The narrative that runs through these letters not only provides an insight into the experiences and suffering of a family, but also into the tragic deaths of their friends and the impact of such events on the small Australian community they called home. The letters also reveal much about the young men themselves — their motivation for enlisting, their fears and their grief. The story of their family and the way its members coped with the tragedy that ultimately consumed their lives forms a strong undercurrent to this narrative and reflects the experiences of families the length and breadth of the nation.

In their original form, some of the letters are crumbling, torn and stained. Most are written in pencil, now faded with the impact of time. The transcriptions in this book are as accurate as possible and each letter is presented as it was written. Occasionally the sentiments expressed have not stood the test of time and may even be offensive to some readers. If this is the case I apologise. These letters should be read in the context in which they were written — as personal letters addressed to loved ones almost 100 years ago in what was a different age, entirely removed from the sensitivities of the modern age. I have preserved all emphases from the original letters, including any underlining, as these illustrate the emotions at the heart of these words. Occasionally I have included an interpretation and these interjections will be indicated as such, employing the usual practice of enclosing them in square brackets [interjection].

I am responsible for any errors of fact in this volume. My thoughts and reflections on what happened to my ancestors have been refined and developed by my research, by careful reading of their letters, discussion with family members, my own recollections and memories and the experience of days spent traversing the battlefields of the Western Front. On many occasions I express an opinion which I only wish could be clarified by those involved.

A FEW TECHNICALITIES:

Allan Marlow enlisted with his Christian name spelt Allan. Inexplicably he later changed the spelling to Allen. To avoid confusion I have chosen the earlier spelling of Allan.

In my narrative I have adopted the metric system of measurement rather than the imperial. The letters contain imperial measurements as used at the time:

1 mile = 1.6 kilometres
1 yard = 0.91 metres
1 chain = 20.1 metres

The Australian currency system was based on the old British system of 12 pence to a shilling and 20 shillings to a pound:

1 pence (penny) written as 1d
12 pence = 1 shilling (or a bob) written as 1s or 1/-
20 shillings = 1 pound written as £1

Australian soldiers were paid six shillings a day, more than the average worker, and were the highest paid regular soldiers in World War I. Early in the war the Australian recruits were often referred to as 'six bob a day tourists' by critics who believed that the Australians would not see any action. The soldiers later adopted this term for their own use in a piece of bitter irony. Nonetheless, many troops made the most of their opportunities to see the sights of North Africa and Europe. If a soldier had dependants he was required to allocate at least two shillings to his family. One shilling was deferred for payment on discharge.

When Australia adopted the decimal currency in 1966, one pound was exchanged for two dollars, with one shilling valued at ten cents. As a comparative guide to values, to post a letter or buy a loaf of bread cost approximately 1½d in 1916. In a letter dated July 1917, Charlie complains that a peach in France costs 10d, almost the value of six loaves of bread and the approximate cost of a dozen eggs in Australia at the time.

AUSTRALIAN MILITARY STRUCTURE

In 1916, I Anzac Corps consisted of the 1st, 2nd and NZ divisions under British General William Birdwood, who also commanded all Australian forces. II Anzac Corps comprised the recently formed 4th and 5th divisions under British Lieutenant General Alexander Godley. In July 1916, when II Anzac arrived on the Western Front, followed later by the 3rd Division, the formation was reorganised. I Anzac Corps then comprised the 1st, 2nd and 4th divisions and II Anzac the 3rd, 5th and New Zealand divisions. Generally, each division was commanded by a major general and comprised three infantry brigades, three artillery brigades, a headquarters and field engineers. A brigade, commanded by a brigadier or brigadier general, was then divided into battalions of between 800 and 1000 men. A battalion, under the command of a lieutenant colonel or colonel, was divided into four companies. Each company was commanded by a captain and comprised four infantry platoons. A platoon was commanded by a lieutenant and divided into four sections commanded by a corporal.

ACKNOWLEDGEMENTS

We owe an enormous debt of gratitude to the men and women who sacrificed so much in the Great War. Not only are we indebted to those who served, but also to their families who suffered the traumatic loss of loved ones both on the battlefield and in the permanent scars of those who returned. Their experiences were horrific and heartbreaking.

My sincere thanks to all who researched and wrote on the history of World War I, and whose work is essential to any understanding of this immense conflict: Charles Bean, Eric Fairey, Bill Gammage, Lyn McDonald, Patsy Adam-Smith, Peter Stanley, Les Carlyon, Peter Pedersen and all those listed in the recommended reading list at the end of this volume. I acknowledge the important work of the Pyramid Hill and District Historical Society and their excellent publications associated with the *Pyramid Hill Advertiser*. Margaret Williamson and Helen Stevens of the Pyramid Hill Historical Society provided valuable assistance and generously shared their prolific knowledge of the Pyramid Hill and Mologa area. I am grateful to the curator of the Bendigo RSL Museum, Mr Peter Ball, for sharing his knowledge of the 38th Battalion and allowing me access to the photos of the Grinton Collection. I could not have gained an understanding of the Great War without the extraordinary work of the Australian War Memorial and the team at the National Archives of Australia and their superb online databases.

I would also like to thank those who assisted me so much during my visits to the Western Front. The Cardoen family of Varlet Farm in Poelkapelle, Belgium, greeted me with enthusiasm, warmth and fabulous fresh-baked bread from Passchendaele. Military historian Martin Pegler and his wife, Kate, of The Orchards at Combles in France, extended their wonderful hospitality and patiently answered my many questions, providing clear explanations of often complex concepts. My thanks also to Dr Brendan Nelson whom I met briefly at Tyne Cot and whose kind words at what was a significant point in my research I found extremely encouraging and inspirational.

Meeting Dr Brendan Nelson at Tyne Cot Cemetery (author photo 25 April 2011).

I am grateful also to Mr Dave Elley who has cured my love affair with the comma and is now working on my verbs. Dave spent many hours not only on the mechanics of my writing, but also in providing direction when I experienced the inevitable 'Where to from here?' Mrs Kaye Bence of Tarragindi kindly offered me her late husband's entire collection of C.E.W. Bean's *Official History of Australia in the Great War of 1914–1918*. It proved an invaluable resource and I thank her for her extraordinary generosity.

I also owe much gratitude to my family. I am grateful to my grandfather for the few memories I retain, and to my beautiful grandmother for the conversations, the crochet and the cream lilies. Significantly, I owe eternal gratitude to my great-uncle Jim for choosing to keep this extensive collection of letters. My thanks extend also to the later generations — to my wonderful parents, Noel and Joan Marlow, who preserved the letters, saving them from destruction, and then answering so many questions while encouraging me all the way along my journey. I thank my children for tolerating the many hours I spent sitting in front of a computer screen and my husband, Rob, for his endless patience and support, for providing the right word when I could not find it, and for volunteering to drive on the wrong side of the road in Europe. Thanks also to my cousin, Kevin Marlow, for contributing letters and photos kept by my grandmother and to other family members, friends and colleagues who helped along the way. Their answers to my myriad questions, their support and encouragement meant a great deal to me. My dear uncle and godparent, Allen Marlow junior, also deserves my grateful thanks. He generously answered endless queries and waited with anticipation while I tried to pull this work together. Sadly, I did not finish in time. He was one in a million and we all miss him.

I would also like to thank the team at Big Sky Publishing, including Diane Evans, Denny Neave and Sharon Evans, whose dedication to the preservation of our history ensured that the story of the Marlow brothers would be told. Much appreciation also to designers Pat Kan and Chris Nesci for their patience and creativity. I also owe an enormous debt to Cathy McCullagh, a very patient editor whose skill and insight transformed a rather unwieldy manuscript into a book.

I dedicate this work to Sarah, Charles, Jim, Charlie, George, Allan, Percy and Albert Marlow. We are now the custodians of the Marlow legacy, a responsibility I bear with a deep sense of the great honour bestowed on me.

To the men and women who served and their families — we will not forget.

PROLOGUE...
THE BEGINNING
THE WESTERN FRONT

BELGIUM

18.7.17
Dear Mrs Marlow

It is with the greatest regret that I write because it is to offer our deep sympathy in the sad loss of your son. It seems so hard when you have four sons at the front & your anxiety cannot be realized by us who are in it. Your son was in a dugout which was hit direct by a big shell & it killed and buried five men. We have been subjected to severe bombardment during the past week and I am sorry to say yesterday one shell snatched from us two officers, two sergeants & your boy who were taking refuge from flying fragments of shell. It is the most awful calamity which has befallen us since we came to France. Accept the sympathy of us all in this your sad bereavement. What else can we offer? We also express our determination to go on & revenge the death of our mates & your son which this war has so cruelly taken from you. He was a good brave lad & is sadly missed by all who knew him. Your other boys are feeling the loss but taking it bravely.

I beg to remain

Yours Respectfully
RW Gollan Lieut

FRANCE

Nine months later:

27-4-1918
My Dear Jim,

Well dear Jim it breaks my heart to write this letter. Our dear [brother]
*was killed yesterday morning at 5.30. The bullet killed him instantly and
he never spoke a word. I had just left him and gone down the trench to see
the other lads when I was called back. Oh Jim it is awful. He is buried in
a nice cemetery a good way behind the line. I attended the burial with a
lot more … Oh I do hope he is the last. What awful lot of trouble we have
had in a few months. Jim I do hope you all bear it the best you can. It has
broke me up properly … Tell dear mum & dad to try and bear up as well
as they can …*

Jim Marlow had six brothers, one died in infancy, the other five served
on the bloody battlefields of the Western Front. This is the story of a
family torn apart by the tragedy of the Great War.

MOLOGA, VICTORIA
THE 1970S

It was an era when most young schoolchildren like me had little
concept of war. Life was relatively simple and secure in a world far
from strife and trauma. The Great War, World War II and Korea were
now historical events. Vietnam, to many children whose brothers had
not been called up to serve, was a place discussed by adults, or a name
mentioned in black and white television news reports from which they
were bustled away. It was a negative place not suitable for the ears of
children. Iraq and Afghanistan were yet to come.

It was also a time when a generation of small farmers left their land
and their homes to their younger descendants. As their twilight years
approached, these ageing men and women, many the survivors of two
world wars and the Great Depression, farewelled their homes and a
lifetime of memories for the security and services offered by local towns.

My great-uncle Jim Marlow was a bachelor. The eldest son of Charles
and Sarah Marlow, he had lived on his farm, just north of Mologa, all
his life. Jim's parents had bought the land in 1892. In 1881, his father,

Charles Marlow, had left his home in the tiny village of Drayton in Leicestershire, England, at 24 years of age and had sailed to distant Australia aboard the SS *Cuscoe*. His motives were unclear, and we can only surmise that Charles sought a better life than that which an industrialised England could offer the son of a country carpenter. He disembarked at Port Phillip Bay, travelled north by train to Inglewood, caught a Cobb & Co. coach to the hamlet of Durham Ox and then walked the remaining distance — some 20 kilometres — to the fledgling township of Pyramid Hill. As he trekked across the flat, scrubby plain, he must have wondered at the stark contrast his adoptive land presented to the rolling green hills and closely settled villages of his native Leicestershire.

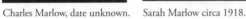

Charles Marlow, date unknown.   Sarah Marlow circa 1918.

With land opening up for selection, Charles quickly found work as a surveyor's assistant on land and rail surveys between Pyramid Hill and Kerang. In 1888 he married Sarah Mahoney, born near Castlemaine in 1862. For a few years they lived west of Pyramid Hill, just a few kilometres from the farm where I spent my childhood. In 1892 Charles purchased the original selection of Mr William Brown and here the couple established their farm, north of Mologa township, fronting Bullock Creek, with the Terrick Terrick Forest Reserve on the high ground to the east overlooking their land.

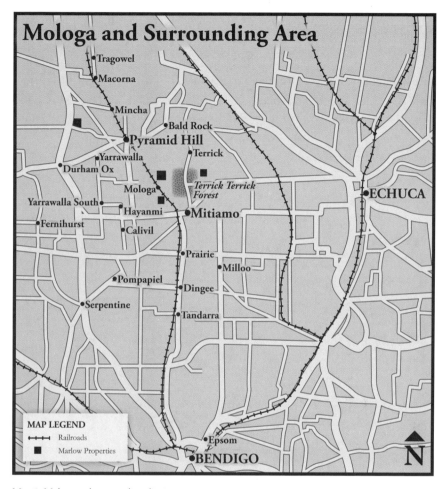

Map 1: Mologa and surrounding district

When the Laanecoorie Weir burst its wall in 1909 and sent a torrent of water flooding across the central Victorian plains, it washed away many of the early mud and straw homes — 'Egyptian brick' buildings as they were commonly called. The residents of the young and vibrant railway township of Mologa, adjacent to Bullock Creek, had no warning on that sunny Saturday morning of 21 August when the devastating wall of water engulfed them.

When the floodwaters receded, little remained of the home built by the original selector and in which Sarah Marlow had raised her children. The family stoically began again, this time building a new timber home, wisely perched on stumps, of which they were justifiably proud and which endowed them with a renewed sense of optimism for the future. With six sons —the seventh, Frederick, died in 1895 at the age of four months, the same year that Sarah gave birth to twins — the family's new dwelling must have been alive with the noise and raucous good humour of adolescents soon to be renowned for their practical jokes, strong community spirit and warm, endearing personalities.

Sarah Marlow and her youngest son, Albert, at their new home circa 1912.

The eldest son, Jim, was destined to inherit the farm, and he worked the land with his father. Jim's younger brother, Charlie, was employed as a carpenter with a local builder. During harvest season he assisted his uncle, George Mahoney, on his property at nearby Fernihurst. The third brother was George Tennyson, affectionately known as 'Geordie' or 'Ten', who also worked on the family farm. The twins Percy and Allan were making their own way: Allan was employed at McKay's General Store at Pyramid Hill, while Percy helped his maternal aunt and uncle on their farm at nearby Hayanmi. In 1914, when the dark years of war descended, the youngest son, Albert, was almost 16 and labouring on the family farm at Mologa.

No-one could have predicted what 1914 would bring. It was certainly not the life that Charles and Sarah had envisaged as they toiled to deliver their sons a legacy greater than that which Charles had been destined to inherit in the depressive class structure of Victorian England. The ensuing years plunged the family into the darkness of despair which cast its shadow over millions of families across the world. When the darkness lifted, the grief remained, a generational legacy that could never be erased. It was left to the survivors to rebuild the dream.

Just a few kilometres up the railway line from Mologa towards the little town of Mitiamo was yet another family farm. This was the small holding where my father spent his childhood. This property was owned by my grandfather who had purchased the land in the early 1920s and began to build a home for his new wife. He toiled laboriously, fashioning handmade mud bricks which were to form the walls that would enclose his family in safety and comfort. Above the front door, written in coloured glass, was the name given to his labour of love: 'Passchendaele'. As a young child, I didn't look up. I didn't notice. I didn't ask why. Forty years later, I wish I had. Such is the regret that comes with the hindsight of decades.

My father took over the running of the original Marlow property from his Uncle Jim in 1971. Dad later bought the property for cropping, while continuing to produce sheep and cattle some 30 kilometres away, west of Pyramid Hill, at my mother's family farm, the property which was our home.

My great-uncle Jim packed his bags and shut the door on the family home that his younger brother Charlie had helped his parents to build. In doing so he left behind more than memories. Already in a state of disrepair, the house was frozen in a moment in time, a poignant reminder of a period when small rural townships thrived, community spirit abounded and allegiance to the mother country was unreserved and unquestioned. Furniture, clothing, crockery and ornaments, even the food in the pantry — all were abandoned.

It is at this time that my memories of the home begin; they are few, but those I have are clear. Ink pens and bottles, a bullet-shaped letter opener, writing paper and glasses adorned the dining table; mirrored wardrobes with beady-eyed fox furs hanging lifeless, their gaze accusingly following any intruders; iron beds with grey-striped mattresses, torn by the family of possums that had made the old house their home and covered with the droppings of swallows that flitted about through broken windows. Old trunks and cupboards crammed with books, photos, cards and letters — hundreds of them. 'Most from your Grandpa and his brothers,' my father told us, 'from the war.' So many yellowed, torn envelopes, kept for so long. It meant little at the time.

My most vivid recollection is of rooms which I eventually refused to enter. Like most young children my imagination knew no bounds. I was convinced there were ghosts. There was a sense of emptiness and sadness that engulfed this old home, the warmth of its early years was long gone, replaced by the chill of lonely abandonment and the heaviness of saddened souls. Looking back, I wonder whether perhaps there was more to my imagination than I realised.

It is within the walls of this home that this story begins. Over 500 letters and postcards along with mementos and photos of the Great War were uncovered in an old wardrobe, cupboards and trunks that Jim had left behind. These precious treasures were once close to being destroyed. Opportunistic thieves, scavenging antique furniture from abandoned homes across central Victoria, were remarkably thwarted by a matter of minutes in their attempt to burn the timber home to cover all trace of their activities. My father arrived late one afternoon to the lingering smell of cigarette smoke and old newspapers piled high in the centre of the living room clearly ready to ignite. The thieves escaped. Was this the hand of fate at play or the intervention of the ghosts of a young girl's imagination?

These precious memoirs are now safely stored, the catalyst of a lifelong dream to honour forebears who today can tell their story in their own words. This is the story of a family with six sons who survived the rigours of childhood illnesses at a time of high juvenile mortality and the dangers of life on the farm when accidents were commonplace. This was a family in which five sons took up arms and ventured willingly into the horrific conflict that we now know as the Great War of 1914–1918.

James (Jim) William Marlow, born 30 September 1889. The eldest son, he attempted to enlist but was rejected.

Charles (Charlie) Edward Marlow, born 29 June 1891, was the fourth to enlist after twice being rejected. He joined the 38th Battalion.

George (Geordie or Ten) Tennyson Marlow, born 8 October 1892, was the first to enlist. He joined the 7th Battalion before later transferring to the 2nd Light Trench Mortar Battery.

Allan (later Allen) Sharp Marlow, born 10 December 1895, was Percy's twin brother. They signed up together, joining the 38th Battalion.

Percy Place Marlow, born 10 December 1895, was Allan's twin brother. They had consecutive regimental numbers, 119 and 120, and joined the 38th Battalion.

Albert Wilfred Marlow, born 25 November 1897, was the youngest and last son to enlist, his earlier attempts having been rejected. His parents eventually signed the form allowing him to enlist. He also joined the 38th Battalion.

2011

In 1924 Jim took the long sea voyage to Europe to walk in the footsteps of his five brothers who had gone to war. Eighty-seven years later, in 2011, I embarked on the same journey to France and Belgium with my father and my husband. It was a pilgrimage which, at times, proved overwhelming. The idyllic and peaceful fields of today belie their former existence as the battlefields on which thousands and thousands of men met their deaths. The relics of war abound, many stacked in the yards of the local farmers: shell casings, wire and chunks of broken metal. There are the hundreds of graveyards that scar the verdant fields. There are imposing memorials with thousands of names of the dead and missing, lost to the fields of Flanders and the hell of the Somme valley.

We came to find the graves of my great-uncles and tread the places where they gallantly gave their lives in the shocking carnage of 1914–1918.

This is their story …

PART ONE
1914 TO 1915

ONE
TAKE UP OUR QUARREL
WITH THE FOE …

AUSTRALIA

It was not unexpected. While most rural Australian families waited for the newspaper or their local grocer to confirm the latest news, the British declaration of war on Germany came as no great surprise. The immediate chain of events that catapulted Europe into what would be a devastating conflict had been initiated by a Serbian nationalist's assassination of the heir to the Austrian throne, Archduke Franz Ferdinand, and his wife on 28 June 1914. Initially, many Australians did not recognise the significance of the event; however as further reports filtered through over the following days, their interest was kindled and talk began. Within a few short weeks a war like no other had erupted.

Austria declared war on Serbia on 28 July. The dominoes fell. Within a week, all the major European powers except Italy were at war. Germany, under the leadership of Kaiser Wilhelm II, threw the full weight of its support behind Austria, as would the ailing, corrupt, financially bereft Ottoman Empire (modern-day Turkey) once German diplomacy reaped its rewards. Russia, however, keen to maintain an interest in the Balkans, mobilised its forces in support of Serbia.

On 1 August Germany declared war on Russia and, two days later, delivered the same declaration to France. On 4 August German troops invaded neutral Belgium en route to France. The Triple Entente, an alliance of mutual support between Britain, France and Russia, was immediately invoked and Britain, in accordance with her alliance obligations, declared war on Germany.

Australia, while recently independent, remained a loyal member of the Commonwealth. In 1914 Australia boasted a tiny population of less than five million consisting largely of British immigrants or their descendants, most with strong ties of allegiance to the mother country. Australia was also acutely aware of the close proximity of the colony of German New Guinea and the nearby islands of the Bismarck Archipelago to its northern shores. The German presence in the Pacific posed a threat to the young nation.

Australian men, eager for adventure, enticed by the lure of income in time of drought and inspired by the fervent patriotism of the era, rushed from the remotest corners of the young Australian nation, flocking to major enlistment centres in large numbers. Many were devastated when rejected — not tall enough, not broad enough, bad teeth, poor eyes, too old, or not old enough. Some persevered and travelled to other centres where the recruitment and medical officers were not quite as particular. Nonetheless, the volunteer Australian soldiers of the first contingent to sail in support of the Empire were the fittest and strongest young men the tiny population could boast. Labour Prime Minister Andrew Fisher famously declared that Australia would commit herself 'to the last man and the last shilling'[1]. In hindsight, Fisher's words were a chilling prophecy of the appalling attrition of young men that was soon to unfold.

For the Marlow brothers, the declaration of war brought some dilemmas. Soldiers were required to stand at least five feet six inches tall, boast a chest of 34 inches and be aged between 19 and 38. Percy and Jim knew they would not meet the initial physical requirements, both a good two inches shorter than required. Charlie and George reached the requisite height, but had obligations to the family farm or to assist other farmers in the local area. It was approaching harvest time — the busiest time of the year for the farming community. Crops stunted by drought still required harvesting. Percy's twin brother Allan was working at McKay's store at Pyramid Hill, a job he valued and which paid well. Both Percy and Allan were not yet 21, the required age for enlistment without parental consent. Albert was not quite 16 and fully aware that his parents would not consent to his enlistment. With talk that the war would be over by Christmas, they waited with thinly disguised impatience.

THEATRES OF WAR
THE WESTERN FRONT 1914

Across Europe, the chill of war descended quickly. German forces immediately marched their way through Belgium following plans carefully prepared years before. The Schlieffen Plan had been devised in 1905 and was ready to be enacted in the event of simultaneous declarations of war against France and Russia. The plan involved a lightning-fast advance of German troops through neutral Belgium followed by rapid victory over French forces. At its core were the premises that Belgium would not resist invasion, that Britain would not declare war in support of Belgium, and that France would fall within the estimated six weeks it would take Russia to mobilise its forces to assist the French. With France under German rule, the Kaiser's army could then move swiftly to defeat the Russian forces in the east.

But Germany had seriously underestimated its neighbours. A stubborn Belgium stoically resisted the invading army while British troops were swiftly deployed across the English Channel. French troops, assisted by the British, made a stand on the Marne River, fighting to save Paris from the German menace. By the end of the bloody Battle of the Marne on 12 September 1914, the attacking German forces had been driven back to the northern reaches of France. There the race to gain control of the crucial ports of the English Channel continued until November 1914 when the First Battle of Ypres reached its agonising conclusion in the teeth of the European winter. Despite enormous casualties, the Allies had prevented German forces taking the vital French ports. North of Ypres, the Belgians opened a lock to create a flooded, stagnant no man's land that blocked the German invaders' access to the critical coastal region. The mobile war had ended, the troops dug into a complex maze of fortified trenches which cut its way for over 700 kilometres from Nieuport on the Belgian coast to the Swiss border. This enormous front line, the infamous Western Front, was to remain largely deadlocked for the next four years.

THE EASTERN FRONT AND SOUTHERN EUROPE IN 1914

In southern Europe, Germany's allies, the Austro-Hungarians, had marched on Serbia, only to have their attack rebuffed by determined Serbian forces. On the Eastern Front, Russian forces surprised the Germans, attacking East Prussia on 17 August 1914. While Russian casualties were immense — an entire army was lost while the other retreated — Germany had been forced to open a second front. The division of German forces between the two fronts had a significant impact on the successful implementation of the Schlieffen Plan. Despite this, the Allies were dealt a powerful blow when the Ottoman Empire (Turkey) joined the German-led Central Powers in October 1914. The poorly equipped Russians were unable to access Allied supplies through traditional land-based supply routes; the seaborne supply routes via the Mediterranean Sea and the strategically vital Dardanelles were likewise closed. British plans to reinforce their Russian ally and control the region would soon result in the first commitment of Australian forces to battle.

ON AUSTRALIA'S SHORES

The Australian Imperial Force (AIF) was raised as an expeditionary force specifically designed to fight abroad. It was to be an army of volunteers and would remain so for the duration of the war. Initially, a small corps of some 2000 men, the Australian Naval and Military Expeditionary Force, was rushed to the German-held colonies of the Bismarck Archipelago and German New Guinea to the north of Australia. German wireless stations were destroyed, forcing the German colonists' surrender to the Australians by mid-September. It was here that the young nation suffered its first military casualties of the war: six men were killed in the fighting and four wounded. There would be another four long years of devastating warfare and unimaginable casualties to come.

THE FIRST ANZACS

By the end of October 1914, volunteers from every state had assembled at King George Sound in Western Australia. A contingent of New Zealand troops joined the Australians and, on 1 November, the men who would become the first Anzacs sailed in convoy for the Middle East. Within a week a distress call had been received from the Cocos Islands; the *Emden*, a rogue German cruiser creating havoc in Malay and Indian waters, was approaching Direction Island. The warship *Sydney* detached from the convoy and engaged the *Emden* in a brief but decisive battle. The *Emden*, having suffered heavy damage, was forced aground and many of her crew surrendered.

With the ocean now clear of the threat posed by the *Emden*, the Australian convoy continued on its voyage to the ancient lands of the Middle East. In the desert sand close to the fabled pyramids of Egypt, the volunteers of the AIF were drilled and instructed for four long months. This was a time in which the young Anzacs developed their celebrated reputation for a unique Australian spirit and, notoriously, their contempt for British officers and the class structure on which the British army based its concept of discipline. The Anzacs were to become renowned for their irreverent sense of humour and their highly developed concept of natural justice — the ideal of a 'fair go'. They were resourceful and tough, courageous and fiercely loyal, and they were prepared to give their lives for their mates. From this point, the Australian army would forge its own iconic image as an army of citizen soldiers, volunteers who had little time for polish and pettiness.

February 1915 arrived and, while rumours of impending departures to an unspecified theatre of war were rife, it was not until April that the Australians set sail, crossing the Mediterranean Sea en route for the Dardanelles. It would be here, on the fabled and ancient Greek battlegrounds, at the narrow entrance to the Sea of Marmara, that the Allies would attempt to capture the Gallipoli peninsula, held by well-entrenched Turkish troops. The defenders were thinly ranged along the heights above the shoreline and they were determined to protect their homeland. The straits, known as 'The Narrows', had been mined;

lines of floating mines were anchored throughout the narrow passage that led to the Sea of Marmara. The attempts of the combined British and French fleet to capture the Dardanelles had come to naught, yet this was critical to the planned Allied invasion of Turkey, the key to supporting Russian forces by carving a supply line through to the Black Sea ports.

On the morning of 25 April 1915, the first wave of Anzacs clambered over the sides of their transports into rowboats towed by steam pinnaces. It was 2.35 am. By 4.15 am they were approaching the beach. Dawn was beginning to break, casting a pale light on the faces of the silent men. While most had some sense of the historical significance of their landing, they could not have known that a campaign that would ultimately end in defeat would become the stuff of legend, the failed invasion celebrated as marking the birth of the Australian national character. However the military blunder that was the Gallipoli campaign would cost the lives of over 8700 Australians while some 19,400 were wounded. It would be a nine-month ordeal that would earn the 50,000 Australians who endured the rigours of Gallipoli a reputation for indomitable courage, initiative and fierce loyalty.

While the Marlow brothers did not witness the horrors of Gallipoli, they watched with increasing impatience as the list of killed and wounded grew. Local boys such as Bert (Robert) Wishart of the 9th Light Horse Regiment wrote letters home, many published in local newspapers. Prior to his enlistment Bert had played football with Macorna, a rival Australian Rules Football team to that of the Marlow sons. Seventy years after he rushed to enlist on 17 September 1914 in the wave of excitement that had greeted the declaration of war, he laughingly suggested that I could have asked my grandfather what a fast runner he had been. His older brother Rex (Reginald) had served in the 38th Battalion with the Marlow brothers. Rex died as the result of a gunshot wound to the abdomen on 28 May 1917 during a raid on enemy trenches near Ploegsteert Wood, Belgium.

Bert was sent to Gallipoli with the 9th Light Horse Regiment, 3rd Light Horse Brigade, landing on 16 May and spending six arduous months on the rugged peninsula. Fortune smiled on him in the infamous attack on The Nek on 7 August — he was in reserve and watched in horror as waves of Western Australian and Victorian men were mown down by Turkish machine-gun fire in a miscalculated assault on strongly fortified enemy trenches. Bert's good fortune continued when, just a few weeks later, half his regiment was killed or wounded in the attack on Hill 60[2]. In late November, those men who had endured six months on Gallipoli were sent to Lemnos Island for a period of rest. Bert was one of only eight original members of his 500 to 600-strong regiment who had survived that first six months. All the other members of his regiment had become casualties — killed, wounded or evacuated with illness. While Bert rested at Lemnos, Britain's Minister for War, Lord Kitchener, visited Gallipoli for the first time at the behest of the War Committee. He ordered the now-famous evacuation from Turkish soil.

For the men who had fought the Gallipoli campaign, retreat was not easy to digest. Many had left their youth, ideals and particularly their mates on the craggy spurs and in the scrub-choked valleys of the Gallipoli peninsula. For some, having endured months of deprivation and despair, the sorrow outweighed the relief. Bert was among the ranks of the disillusioned. He had seen the horrific sights of war. He had dodged injury and death. The initial patriotic fervour which had driven his enlistment had been lost in the rugged foothills of Gallipoli.

He spent Christmas Day aboard a transport ship sailing to Egypt:

It was Christmas Day, 1915, we were on a boat coming from Lemnos back to Egypt ... I was twenty, we'd literally been kicked off Gallipoli, and I can remember saying to myself, "Whyever have we come 8000 miles to fight the Turks, to try and take Turkey from the Turks, I said what has it got to do with Australians?" I thought we deserved to be kicked out ... we had no right to be there, it was because some Archduke or somebody in Austria had been killed, what has it got to do with us? I just couldn't see it, I'd seen so many of my mates that were killed and I thought goodness me what is it all about? It was a terrible waste of young men ... I thought at the time we were supposed to end all wars ..."[3]

Bert Wishart went on to fight in the desert campaign in the Middle East, being wounded in the Allied assault on the Turkish outpost of Magdhaba on 23 December 1916. He recovered from the gunshot wound to his thigh and returned to his regiment in time for the 4th Light Horse Brigade's historic charge at Beersheba which led to the fall of Gaza. Bert was the first to leave his home town of Macorna and the last to return, eventually arriving home in November 1919. It was on the farm in the company of his widowed mother, sisters, younger brother and later, his wife Hilda, where peace and the daily rhythms of farm life gave him the opportunity to rebuild his life. He died at Kerang, Victoria, on 21 October 1988 at the age of 93.

MOLOGA, AUSTRALIA, JUNE 1915

By June 1915, Jim, Charlie and George had decided that they would join the 'fair dinkums', the men who were now enlisting despite the ever-increasing casualty lists appearing in the newspapers. For many it remained a grand adventure, although the lists of names could not mask the reality. This was an industrial war, men pitted against new technology capable of dreadful destruction, of shocking carnage on a scale never before encountered. The 'fair dinkums' knew there was more to this war than adventure and six bob a day.

Charlie was soon disappointed. It was not his turn to fight for king and country. The attestation paper clearly records why he was rejected:

AIF Attestation Paper of Persons Enlisted for Service Abroad

Charles Edward Marlow June 14th 1915

24 yrs Farm

Medical Officer – Owing to bad teeth cannot be accepted otherwise very good

But bad teeth would not keep Charlie from the war for long. Jim was also unsuccessful. Despite the lowering of the minimum height in July to five feet two inches, he was rejected because of his poor eyesight.

George was accepted immediately and now faced the prospect of going to war without his brothers. He enlisted on 12 June and was appointed to the 6th Reinforcements of the 21st Battalion just prior to his departure on 1 October. He was just short of his 23rd birthday. George was soon training in Bendigo and Seymour and then, to his disgust, at the Broadmeadows Camp on the outskirts of Melbourne. The appalling living conditions at Broadmeadows had resulted in a high rate of illness and the camp had been closed in May. However, by the following September, conditions had improved sufficiently for the camp to reopen in time to welcome a new batch of recruits.

15th September 1915
Bendigo
Dear Charlie,

Just a few lines to let you [know] *that I am leaving this camp on friday morning for Broadmeadows to join the reinforcements. We just got word that the rest of my company are to go from here and some out of the other companies, 36 of us altogether. They sent 100 away last week and 50 on Tuesday so there is not many of us left. We have to pass the doctor yet, it would be a bugger to be bumped out now. They are putting a lot into reinforcements now. I don't know when we will be sailing they are going to send a lot away this and next month. Some buggers took my military pants on Monday afternoon. 50 men went away tuesday morning to join the new brigade, I would like to have got in it. I suppose you are having some rain it has been raining here heavily and is very cold and rough. I will write soon as I know my new address. I suppose you have got over your holiday.*

I remain
Geordie

Less than a week later George wrote again, telling Charlie that he had arrived at Broadmeadows:

21st September 1915
Dear Charlie

Just a few lines to let you know how I am getting on. We arrived here last friday afternoon. It is a B of a place too, not half as good as Bendigo camp, in fact it is not as good as Seymour. It rained like Hell here last night and we are up to our boot tops in mud and sticks like _____ to a quilt, you wouldn't believe what it is like, and the wind it would blow a dead horse over there is no timber to break it. I don't know why they made a camp here, they would spend millions of money here then it would be no good. The only thing that is any good is the huts, they are bonzer huts too. There are 50 of us in each but we might be shifted out into tents but I hope not. The different churches have fine big buildings here. I went to the Church of England last night, the parsons sermon was on the language of the camp, and it is pretty tough I can tell you. Nearly all of us that came from Bendigo broke camp on Saturday afternoon and went into Melbourne and got back about 12 at night, the sentries don't say anything they just let you walk through. The city was just full of soldiers. There are a lot of returned soldiers in the city. I see in the papers that Frank Penglase's brother is coming back. Archie Bailey and Andy Erikson are here in the same reinforcements as me. I am in the 6ᵗʰ reinforcements of the 21ˢᵗ battalion. You can address the letters to the YMCA. I have just been in to get my photo taken. How did the football turnout come off, was my photo there in time. I went over to the light horse to see Bert Gibson [cousin] *but they are all on final leave and supposed to sail next Saturday. I got no idea when we will be going. I wouldn't like to be here long. I went out to see Sharp's* [family friends] *on Saturday I didn't know Mrs Sharp was up home. One of the military airships flew over the camp on Friday. Well I will close now hoping all are well.*

I remain your loving brother
Geordie

A few days later, George arrived home on his final leave. Mr Bill Fyffe, local farmer and Sunday School teacher, and the Marlows' closest neighbours, the Jones family, organised a farewell for George. In small rural communities the support of neighbours was highly valued and the community of Mologa was no exception. As well as being devoted members of the Church of England congregation of St Luke's, the Marlow, Fyffe and Jones families were always prepared to lend others a hand.

Mologa 25ᵗʰ Sept, 1915
Dear George

On behalf of Mologa Friends I have much pleasure in inviting You, with your Parents, and brothers, to a Farewell Social and Presentation to yourself, in the Mologa Hall, on Monday evening 27ᵗʰ Sept at 8.30.

I remain
Yours Faithfully
William Fyffe
Hon Sect.

The hall was crowded that evening as the community gathered to farewell one of its own with patriotic songs and speeches. The following day the family hitched the horse to the wagon and drove George into town where friends waited at the railway station. Sarah farewelled her son with a mixture of pride and apprehension. Perhaps he promised he would return. It was a promise made to loved ones all over the Empire and it kindled a sense of hope which often left families unprepared for the trauma of a death and the empty place left by those buried on distant shores who would never come home.

Broadmeadows
Sept 30ᵗʰ 1915
Dear Mother

Just a few lines to let you know that I arrived here last night. We got word that we are sailing on Tuesday next at about 3 oclock in the afternoon on a mail boat. I think it is the Moldavia. We were sent away in a special train as soon as we had breakfast this morning to the Williamstown rifle butts for practice and never got back till late we have to wait up tonight to make out our pay sheets and they are giving us our rifles tonight. I went out to Cheyne's on Tuesday and to Mahoney's they did not know me at Mahoney's. Bert Gibson sailed on Monday.[4] Send Albert out to Charlie to tell him when I am going he said he was coming down and I don't know that he will be able to see much of me he could see me at the railway siding at the Port

Melbourne pier. Georgie Gibson saw Bert off he walked with him from the Port Melbourne station to the pier but they tell us that we are going right up to the pier in the train but if he intends to come down I could meet him either out here at the camp or next Monday evening or under the clocks at Flinders station that night. I might not be able to get into the town as they have to issue us with our uniforms and clothes yet. I [cannot] write any more now as I have to go back to the lines. The safest way for Charlie to meet me [is] at the end of my lines the 6th of the 21st is marked up at the end of our huts.

I remain
Your Loving Son
Geordie

Albert sent word to Charlie who was camped on the eastern side of the Terrick Terrick Forest clearing the family's new block of land. Charles senior and Charlie caught the train to Melbourne to farewell George who left Australia aboard the mail ship *Moldavia* on 5 October 1915. Charlie wrote home from Melbourne to tell his mother of his brother's imminent departure.

Melb
Dear Mother

Just a few lines we all got down all right and went out to Broadmeadows yesterday and saw Geordie but he could not get off as they were issuing the soldiers their kits etc. but he got off that night and came into Melbourne with us we had tea in here. He did not get the telegram till Sunday morning, on Saturday he was out at Williamstown Rifle Butts and put up the highest score against all his company. He has got tiptop mates they are a lively lot, they sail tomorrow by the Moldavia, it is a mail boat and calls at all the ports so he should have a long way better time on it than on a transport. Well I will have to close now.

I am Yours etc
Charlie E

MOLDAVIA, AT SEA, OCTOBER

Moldavia
Wednesday
Dear Mother, Father & Brothers

Just a few lines to let you know how I am getting on. The sea is fairly calm so far but there are a lot sick yet I think I will be alright. Downie has been very sick all the night. It is good on deck but when you get down below it makes you feel a bit funny. We got through the heads last night about six oclock it was a bit rough going through. We got bonzer tucker on board. 4 meals a day, there are 16 of us at each table and two of us have to go orderlies each day to get the meals and wash up. We have hammocks to sleep in, they are just the thing. I slept as sound as a rock. Nearly all darkies on this boat, they are tricks too. One of the lady passengers gave out about 80 packs of cards to the soldiers, we don't see much of the passengers. I don't think we will get any drill on board. We don't know where we are going yet, one of the officers said we would most likely know when we get to Perth, we get to Adelaide tomorrow "Thursday" morning at 6 oclock. There is a big steamer not far off us now. I will close as I have nothing to write about.

So goodbye with love to all
I remain
Geordie
<u>*Later*</u>
We have just reached Port Adelaide and have just been told our address for Egypt.

Pte G. T. Marlow
2748
6ᵗʰ reinforcements
21ˢᵗ Battalion
Intermediate Depot
Egypt

To Charlie, he added:

… Well we are a fair way out on the water now. We passed through the heads at 6 oclock last night but I did not notice it, slept too sound, there

were a lot sick last night and this morning. I am alright so far but it is calm today … When we got up this morning we could just see a steamer in front of us, we passed within half a mile of it at dinner time and can hardly see it now, it is just 6 oclock so we must be going fairly fast but it was going fairly slow for a while something went wrong with one of the engines. We have just passed another ship it is going the opposite way to us, we are supposed to get to Adelaide tomorrow morning at 6 oclock, they say we are going to be let off for a while. We are going to be allowed anywhere on the boat after we leave Adelaide. It has been a nice sunny day most of us went up on deck and laid down in the sun and had a sleep … We haven't seen much of the passengers yet but one of the ladies came down and gave out cigarettes and playing cards. Another one is going to give out prizes for tugowar. They have just told us what our address would be in Egypt you will find it on the back of this paper. There is a concert on tonight. It is very muggy down below that is what makes them sick …

The Moldavia
Sunday 10th
Dear Mother, father & Brothers,

Just a few lines to tell you how things are going. We stopped in Port Adelaide for 12 hours, they only let 50 off there they are going to leave some off at every port. It was fairly calm when we left the port but it gradually got rougher and last night it was very rough and is today too, the waves come sweeping over the hurricane deck it is a great sight from on deck looking over the water, some of them slept on deck last night and got wringing wet with the waves. Some of the poor devils are very sick. I have not been sick yet I think I will be right now, I rather like it. Downie is very sick. They started to give us some drill but the officers are too sick to go on with it. We were supposed to have Church Parade this morning but [it] is too rough. We get into Fremantle to[morrow] morning at about 6 oclock. I suppose you have my other letter by now. I not too sure about that address being right they don't seem to know where we are going yet, most of them put their address this way Name & number 6 of 21 Abroad. It wont be too good going back on the camp tucker again after we leave the boat. We get real good meals. Some of the passengers gave out a lot of chocolates and cigarettes to us. This is all the news this time.

I remain your loving son
Geordie

Later
Tuesday 12th

We arrived in Fremantle this morning at 7 oclock. We are nearly a day behind time on account of going straight against the rough sea. I think they are going to leave us off for awhile.

Sunday 17th 1915
RMS Moldavia
Dear Mother, Father and Brothers,

Just a few lines hoping all are well as I am at present. Well they let all of us off the boat at Fremantle for four hours, we had a good look around the town, it is not a bad little place, the streets all narrow and seem fairly busy some of the men went to Perth it is about 11 miles from Fremantle. The people told us that the last lot of troops that went through played up something terrible they all jumped off the boat without leave and the guard put the bayonet in two of them. One of our fellows was put off at Fremantle, he had the measles. There is another in the hospital with pneumonia and last night they said he was dying. Well since we left Fremantle it has been very calm, I don't think there have been any more sick, the trip seems to be doing me good, I am 13 stone now. We are in the hot climate now for this last four days I sleep up on deck now it is very close down below. We all have had our hair cut as short as we could get it; we do look tricks now. We wear short nicks, we got orders to cut the blues off just above the knee all we wear now is the flannel nicks and white hat. They have started to do the vaxinating I have not been done yet. The passengers gave us a great concert last night, they had everything fixed up nicely and at the interval they shouted all the troops drinks, it cost them £12-10/. Most of the performers were actors going to England. They have been very good to us they have given us a lot of eatables and smokes. They *have started boxing tournaments and are giving prizes to the winners in the different weights and are giving prizes for the best tugowar team. We get a little drill now and have to wash our part of the boat out every day and do guard duty. We are supposed to reach Colombo that is the next port on thursday it is 8 days sailing from Fremantle but we might reach there on wednesday as we are going over the limit rate, she is supposed to do 15 knots an hour, yesterday we travelled 360 miles nearly 16 knots an hour, she has had to gain a day we lost going to Fremantle in the rough weather. The 50 devons "British troops" get off at Colombo, all of us have given something each to them and have collected £7-10/- this morning for them in about an hour some of the officers and one of the lady passengers gave about £4, they only get 1/1 a day each. We have been paid twice since we left, a pound each time. There will be some of my wages sent home soon 4/- a day, see that it comes, and those photos. We had a church service this morning. We got some good war news yesterday by wireless, that the allies had sunk some warships and a lot of merchant ships and that the Germans are losing 20 and 30 thousand [soldiers] a day in France, this is the first war news that we have heard. We have been told what our proper address will be. If you have written any letters I think I will get them with that first address I gave you. I was just called away from writing this letter to get vaxinated, but it is supposed to hurt a little in a few days time if it takes. I hope you have got those other two letters that I wrote. I suppose you have started the harvest by now. Well I will have to close now. We have to post all the letters on board by tonight so I cant get any stamps.*

With love to all from Geordie

The following day, George penned a letter to Charlie in which he provided a little more information than he had been prepared to share with his parents:

… Well they let all of us off at Fremantle and we had a good look around the town, it is not a bad little place, we had four hours there. Some of the men went to Perth it is not far from Fremantle. Everyone lined back at the boat in time to sail, some came back a bit merry. The people in the town told us that the last lot that went through played up something terrible. They

all jumped off the boat with their rifles and bayonets and went into the shops and helped themselves. Two got the bayonet in them through breaking through the guards. The people there gave us a great rally off when we were leaving. Just after we got out of the port things were only middlen between some of the infantry and light horse men, the beer began to make them talk it seems some of the men reckoned the light horse were trying to run the show and fists were flying all roads it was good amusement for us that were looking on. The sea has been very calm since we left the west none sick at all. We have the measles on board and one chap is supposed to be dying of pneumonia. We are supposed to reach Colombo wednesday 20th after 8 days sailing from Australia. I don't know whether any of us will be allowed off there. We get some drill each day now and some have to go on guard each day and night. We have to wash our part of the boat out each day, it wasn't much of a game when the last meals were all over the floor but there is none of that now. We had a great concert given us on Saturday night by the passengers, the performers were mostly actors who are going to England, they shouted us drinks at the interval. The passengers are also given prizes for the winners in the boxing tournament, a prize for the different weights. There has been some good goes, it is starting again this afternoon … We have been vaxinated, I don't think it is going to take on me, I was only done yesterday and today you wouldn't know it was done …

Wednesday 20th
We got to Colombo tonight. We have to post all our letters on board by 8 o'clock tonight so I cant get any stamps. This is all the news so goodbye with love to all from

Geordie.

The journey to Colombo was incident-free, with *Moldavia* anchoring in the Ceylonese (Sri Lankan) harbour along with scores of other steamers and warships busy loading coal and tea before continuing on to Bombay (Mumbai), India. George was suffering from the tropical heat and preferred the cool of the night air on deck. *Moldavia* arrived at the port of Bombay en route to Aden (Yemen) and her final destination, Egypt.

RMS Moldavia
Wednesday 27th
Dear Albert

Just a few lines to let you know how things are going. We arrived in Bombay on sunday 24th. *We stopped about 30 chains out on the water from the town, there is no pier there everything had to be brought to the boat on tugs. We took on a lot of stuff there. All of the tugs and boats are worked by the darkies, the women even work on the coal boats and it is terrible hot and dirty work too, a white man would not last half an hour with them. The black crew got off the boat there and a fresh crew came on, they seemed pleased to be going off. They would not give anyone leave to go ashore but over two hundred of the men jumped on a motor boat and made the crew fetch them ashore, one of the bridging train men got on a wheel and a light horseman started the engine and some did the stoking and away they went, they had about an hour to look around, they sent word after them to be back by eleven o'clock and all of them but 3 came back in time and the 3 have been left behind they will most likely have to stop in the barracks for a fortnight, One was a sergeant he will lose his stripes. A Major belonging to the English army brought them back he said we should all have been let off. All of the men that were on the Osterlg (the last boat that went through) were let off and 50 of them were left behind. The officers said they were going to make it hot for them going off the boat without leave but there hasn't been anything said since. I like a dam fool stopped on board. They said Bombay is a very nice place it looks nice from the boat. There are forts all along the front of the town we saw a search light flash out at night. The niggers came over to the boat selling fruit, best bananas and oranges I ever tasted 1d for oranges and 6d a dozen for bananas they could sell them a lot cheaper. It was a bit of a luxury to get a feed of fruit we cant get any on board. We stopped a day longer in Bombay than what we should have done. One of the pipes burst when they were lifting the luggage aboard, and they had to put something in one of the engines. The next port is Aden I think they will let us off there. We have the measles and mumps on board, two were put off at Bombay with the measles. It hasn't been so hot since we left Bombay nearly everyone got a heat rash on them while it was very hot. Send the addresses of some of my relations when you write. Well I will now close hoping all are well as I am at present. I remain your loving brother*

Geordie

There is a yarn that we might be sent to England but I think it is like the rest of the yarns.

Later
Thursday 28th 1915
Wed Nov 3rd (Egypt)

We are supposed to reach Aden tomorrow morning. They say it is not much of a place, we have to coal up there. We wont be long now before we are in Egypt we get there about the 2nd of November. We had a concert last night, we gave one of the lady passengers a present, she has been very good to us, always giving us something, so we arranged to give her a present worth about £5, about 3d a man. I have been paid twice since I came on board, two pounds altogether. I was going to post this letter at Aden but they told us it would not get home any [faster] than if we waited till we got to Egypt. I will write again soon.

We have arrived in Egypt safely on Wednesday the third of November

ZEITOUN CAMP, EGYPT, NOVEMBER

In one of many entries made in lead pencil in his small, leather-bound notebook, George now added his arrival in Egypt to the details of his voyage:

Pte George T Marlow
Reg. No. 2748
6th reinftns 21st Batt sailed from Australia in the Moldavia 5th Oct 1915 transferred to 7th Batt
Sailed from Port Melbourne 5th Oct on the Moldavia
Arrived at the Suez on the 3rd November 1915
Rifle No 30997

To this he gradually added pages of addresses of fellow soldiers, family and friends, pay calculations and notes from the various training schools he had attended. He recorded brief details of his movements, simply noting the names of places and battles with no insight into his emotions at the time. His letters home became the repository for his personal reflections. He composed a lengthy letter to his mother in which he described his first experiences in Egypt:

Yeitoun Camp[5]
Sunday 7th November 1915
Dear Mother

We arrived here in camp on the third of November at 8 o'clock pm. We got off the boat at Suez and caught a train there and landed here after seven hours ride. We had a very decent trip right through, after leaving the station it was very barren looking country but got better as we went on. We stopped at different stations going through and got some fruit and water melons. The huts they live in out of the towns would amuse you they are made of mud and are only about 5 or 6 feet high and all cramped up together, how they can live in them I don't know, a white man would die within a week of fever, the fowls camp up on top of them. It is a great place for maize and sugar cane and other green stuff but mostly maize, especially around Cairo you can go for miles and see nothing but green paddocks of it. We could not see all the country going through as it was dark but what we did see didn't look too bad. We passed three hospital trains with Australians and Indians on board. We only had half a mile to walk from the station to the camp, they soon fixed us up with blankets and something to eat, we were put in huts but have been shifted since into tents. They have special huts for all the troops to have their meals in, we all sit down to tables and do it in style. The tucker is much better than at Broadmeadows, we get curry and rice for breakfast the dinner is much the same with a little of different kinds of vegetables and some preserved fruit. We get up at half past five in the morning and go out at half past six and do bayonet drill till breakfast time half past 8 we get a cup of tea and biscuit just after we get up. We go out again at 9-30 and come back at 11 and have an hours spell, go out again at 12 and drill again until 1 o'clock and then have dinner, we go out again at 2-30 and come back again at about 5-30, but if on a rout march might not get back until 7 or 8 o'clock, but they seem to have done away with a lot of the long rout marches, we have had one march so far, we went about 10 miles one afternoon. It is supposed to be winter here now but it is just about the same as what it is in Australia now, we are lucky to get here in this time of the year, it must be terrible hot in the summer time. It is a bit heavy drilling on the sand. At night it gets very cool and early in the morning it gets very cold. We got half a day off the day after we came into camp, we went into Cairo, it is about 7 miles from here, it only costs half a piastre (that is 1¼ d) to go there. I know all their coins it was a bit awkward at first, we lose ¾ on every shilling coin, ½d on every 3d piece but with a gold coin we get a little over the value. Their coins are ½ piastre 1¼d in our money, 1 piastre 2½d, 2 piastre 5 and 10 and so on. The worst of their money we get such a lot of coins for a quid. We can get nice soft drinks and ice cream here but the beer and whisky is not safe to be drunk, but I think they can get the English drink. Well Cairo is not much of a place it stinks like the devil I wouldn't live here if I was paid to, I did not think it was as bad a place as it is. It is just swarming with people, all sorts arabs, Egyptians and I think there are a lot of Turks there too, you don't see many white people only a few French. One of the lady passengers that came across with us, a doctors wife invited all of the troops that came across on the Moldavia to come to the pyramids with her today and other places and she was going to pay for everything, my word she was good to us coming across she spent pounds and pounds on us. I did not go I wanted to write these letters as the mails leave here tonight. They only keep the men here three or four weeks now so I might be gone by the time you get this letter. I haven't seen anyone that I know yet but one of my mates and I are going over to another camp this evening about a mile away, the heleopilis [Heliopolis] camp. There are a immence lot of troops in camp here, they say if you get up on the pyramids you see nothing but military camps. There are men from everywhere, Australians, English, Scottish, Canadians, Indians, Maiors [Maori New Zealanders] and all sorts. The Maiors are a fine stamp of fellows and real nice chaps too. Well I suppose everyone are very busy with the crops now, I hope they turn out well. Well I will now close, it is dinner time here and I suppose you will just about be going to bed. I write again in time to catch the next train so goodbye hoping all are well as I am at present. I remain your loving son

Geordie.

Writing to Charlie the same day, George was a little more forthcoming with his impressions of his new surroundings:

… It was very barren looking country till we got a long way from Suez station, then it gradually got better small plots of maize along the line but around Cairo it is nothing else but maize, there seems to be plenty of water, big channels running full. We stopped at some of the stations coming through, and as soon as the train stops the arabs are around you in dozens trying to sell you fruit and different things. They have very little huts that they live in only a few feet high, this is out in the country. Some of them are terrible crooks they would try and sell bad fruit and beat you for money, most of the men didn't know anything about their money, but one chap that had been over before told some of us all about it. Some of the men made it a bit lively for them at one of the stations we had to stop there half an hour and they took the fruit off them and jumped on their donkeys and had a ride around, by jove it was funny. We passed three hospital trains with australians and Indians on board. They tell us they don't send them home now like they use to do, they have to be crippled up now before they will send them home. The camp is only half a mile from the station and about 7 miles from Cairo. We were put in huts when we got here but we are now in tents, it is not near as good, there are twelve of us in each tent, it is too many. Every thing gets covered in sand it is inches deep and so loose and as for marching it is a bugger. We have all our meals in mess huts and have tables to sit up to, the tucker is not bad but is generally covered in flies. It is supposed to be winter here now but it is dam hot, must be terrible in the summer time, the nights get very cold. We have to get up at 5.30 in the morning, go out to drill at 6.30 for two hours bayonet drill, we have to do it different here to what they have been doing in Australia it is much easier, we had a sergeant major from England showing us how to do it, I would like to be as good as him … They showed us how to dig ourselves in, we have to dig ourselves in in 20 minutes here. We all have to do some trench digging and put in about a week at the rifle butts at shooting. We have had one long march so far, we left the camp at 3 o'clock and got back again at 7.30, I think we must have went 10 or 12 miles, there were a lot of us the whole reinforcements for the sixth brigade. It is terrible dusty marching through sand, I would not like to be here long, we will be gone to the front by the time you get this letter,

they only keep the men here three or four weeks now, they are sending them to the front in thousands every week, 5000 left the night we came in and they were only in camp here 3 weeks and they are sending them over from Australia very fast, 2000 came into camp last night, I think there will be something great doing soon. I haven't been to the pyramids yet but they say when you get up on them you can see nothing but military camps, there are troops from everywhere here, the maoris are fine fellows. The water here is not too good, it causes the diarrahea the returned chaps tell us it is one of the worst enemies of the dardanelles, they say it is very cold there at present. We got half a day off the day after we came in so we went into Cairo, a chap that one of my mates knew showed us all around the town, well I thought it was a fairly bad place but I had no idea that it was as bad as it is, it is something terrible, by jove it would open your eyes, they will say anything to you … [page missing]

Perhaps there is a reason for the missing page in which George was ready to describe to his older brother exactly what 'they' would say. There are some suggestions that, at any one time, there were over 30,000 prostitutes working in Cairo alone. Many Australian men were repatriated to Australia when the temptations of Cairo left them with venereal disease. Their war records were clearly stamped 'V.D.' and all pay would cease. While procuring a prostitute was not illegal, contracting venereal disease was considered a military offence as the soldier was then unfit for front-line service. Once the AIF moved to England and the Western Front the practice of returning men to Australia was discontinued. As soon as they were considered well enough to fight, the men were sent back to the trenches. The records of the Marlow sons have no such stamp; perhaps they chose to heed the advice of the padres and doctors who routinely lectured the soldiers on the dangers of commercial sex. Many men ignored the warnings, some naïve, others simply reckless. The afflicted presented a very real problem to military authorities as venereal disease depleted the fighting force and Australia had the dubious honour of the highest rate of VD of the Allied forces.[6]

Dear Mother

Just a few lines to let you know that I am alright. I have not got any news, it is a half holiday every saturday here and most of the men have gone out. I did not go out today as I had a lot of letters to write and we don't get much time for writing other days, it is always dark when we come in from drill the sun sets very early here. I am thinking of going to see the pyramids tomorrow. It was open camp when we came here first but now we are not supposed to go without leave well in fact there is not much to see if we should go out only that I would like to go to some of the other camps I might strike someone that I know. They are a bit stricter here some of our chaps are doing C.B. [confined to barracks] *already.*[7] *I don't know where we are going yet there is a yarn that they are going to take the troops from the Dardanelles and sending them to Salonake* [Salonika]. *The war news that we have been getting here has been pretty good. They say the turks are coming to make another attack here in Egypt. Well I will now close hoping all are well.*

I remain your loving son

The mails close here every sunday night, I will write again next week. We were inspected by the General yesterday morning. The Bridging Train men that came over with us left here for the front this morning.

Just where the reinforcements were to be sent was a hotly debated topic. England, France, Gallipoli and, as George mentions, Salonika (Thessalonika) in Greece, where British and French troops had been rushed to assist Serbia against a Bulgarian invasion — all were rumoured as possibilities. The uncertainty led to frustration among the men and George quickly became exasperated with the monotony of drill, sand and bad food. The town of Heliopolis, on the outskirts of Cairo, provided some relief. Constructed in recent years, it had originally been designed to rival Monte Carlo with gambling facilities, accommodation and entertainment parks, but had been refused the required gambling licence. Nevertheless, it represented an oasis in the sands of Egypt. The Palace Hotel, now converted to a hospital for the wounded from Gallipoli, contained 3000 beds. A short distance from the hotel, the skating rink, haunted house and other entertainment facilities of Luna Park were no longer bringing enjoyment to tourists, also converted to a medical facility capable of accommodating 2000 patients.

Yeitoun Camp
Sunday 14th Nov 1915
Dear Charlie

Just a few lines to let you know that I am alright. I suppose you will know the chaps in the photo you met them at Broadmeadows. Jim Gritton the tall chap that I mentioned to you went straight into the hospital to be operated on for rupture. He was bad on the way over and the doctor on board told him he would have to be operated on here or be sent back, he is getting on alright so far. One of my mates from my tent was sent to the hospital yesterday he has the diptheria. I think I pointed him out to you in Broadmeadows his name is Bill Leask he comes from near Leongatha he knows old Jim Haw. They are a lot stricter here, a lot of my company are doing C.B. already. I was going out to see the Pyramids today but have to go on guard at one of the stations, they have guards on the tram cars and every where. They have pickets to go round to all the houses every night and hunt the men home. There are a lot of troops shifting from here to another camp today. Well I have no more news this time, the mails leave here every Sunday night so I will write again next week.

I remain your loving Bro
Geordie

Nov 17, 1915
Yeitoun Camp
Dear Charlie

… Well I have been here a fortnight today. It hasn't been so hot this week. I haven't felt so good in the stomach this last two days, I think it is the tucker, too many maggots in it, a lot of us paraded today before the Heads for more and better tucker. Three of us went into Helopilis last night to see Gritton in hospital. I got quite a surprise to see such a fine town after seeing Cairo. Such fine big buildings you wont see one low building and it is a

very clean place. You wouldn't believe what a fine place it is. The buildings in Melbourne are not a patch on them of course it is a new town. But you wouldn't think so by the size of it. We saw a big church my word it is a lovely building. Nearly all the French people are in Helopilis. You don't see any of the slum. The fifth reinforcements of my battalion are going to the front next week, they only came here a week before us, it is hard to say where they will send us. They have sent 120,000 Australians and New Zealands to the front up to now and there must be a good many in camp here, the cities are just swarming with them of a night. A lot from New Zealand came in this week, the Maiors are the boys that can drill. We had a march last night and finished up with an attack. We are getting all kinds of drill here and plenty of extended order drill making short quick rushes and flopping down on the sand and digging ourselves under cover it is every bit as bad as real hard work, we are always covered in dust when we come in. This is all the news this time.

I remain your loving Bro
Geordie

21.11.15
Dear Mother

Just a few lines to let you know I am sending a little box with some silks in, they are registered so you ought to get them safely nearly all the boys send some home, they are supposed to be the best silks you can get, there is a cushion cover, a table centre to put a flower pot on, a scarf, handkerchief and a lace. It has got a little cooler here now, the nights are fairly cold, I am still in the tents but half of our company have been shifted into the huts, it is warmer of a night in the tents. We did not go out to drill one morning it was too dusty but an officer back from the front gave us a lecture instead, he says they get a lot better tucker at the front than what they get here. I have been into Heliopilis it is a very nice place, much different to Cairo, there are some wonderful buildings, the Palace Hospital is a tremendous big place and is something lively inside, three of us went there to see a chap who has been operated on, he was crook coming over on the boat and the doctor told him he would either have to be operated on here or be sent back to Australia, he is getting on alright, a lot of my company has been sent to the hospital they reckon it is like home in there. The town is full of troops of an evening and it is just the same in Cairo. There is trouble along the Suez again, the turks are coming up to have another go there were 3 lots of light horsemen left here last night to go there. I don't know whether Bert Gibson would be among them I haven't seen him yet …

[continued on photo]

… This photo is three of my mates & myself. You have seen two of these in Bendigo. The one standing up in the centre is the chap … There were 10 of them picked out of the ranks for M.P. but they need not stop at it. We go to the Butts for shooting this week, we have to stop there for 3 or 4 days. There have been a lot of New Zealanders come into the camp this last week. It tried to rain here this morning but all we got was a mist, there is a slight mist every night. This mail leaves Egypt on the 24th so I suppose you will get it by xmas. Well I have no more news this time. Hoping all are well as I am at present.

I remain your loving son
George

Just a few days later, George sent the same photo home to Allan:

George on left, George Downie standing centre, the other men are unknown.

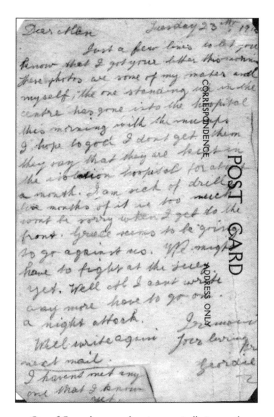

One of George's postcards written typically in pencil.

Tuesday 23 No 1915
Dear Allan

Just a few lines to let you know that I got your letter this morning. These photos are some of my mates and myself; the one standing up in the centre has gone into hospital this morning with the mumps. I hope to god I don't get them they say they are kept in the isolation hospital for about a month. I am sick of drill, five months of it is too much wont be sorry when I get to the front. Greece seems to be going to go against us, We might have to fight at the Suez yet. Well Al I cant write anymore have to go on a night attack. Will write again next mail. I remain Your loving Bro
Geordie
I haven't met any one that I know yet.

Yeitoun Camp
Sunday November 21ˢᵗ 1915
Dear Charlie

Just a few more lines before I close this letter up. An officer from the front belonging to my battalion gave us a lecture on the war in the Dardanelles, it was very interesting. He spoke on how to use the bombs and hand and rifle grenades, he says the trenches we have to go in are only 50yds away from the turks at the most and some are only 20, the turks used to throw bombs and the australians used to throw them back again, he warned us not to try that now because the turks don't throw them now till just before they explode and we have to throw a blanket or a coat over them. Each side are sapping [tunnelling] all the time he says you can hear the turks digging sometimes, the Australians are advancing under ground by digging tunnels and then make a trench and dig the top off it, he says there is a hell of a lot of hard work to do it sounds very <u>healthy</u> what he says about the fighting but I don't care how soon I get there, and I don't think it will be very long either, we are going to the butts tomorrow and they never stop much longer than a week after that, they take a note of each ones shooting to pick out the best that's for sniping, in the quick firing we have to get 10 shots in half a minute, we have to load up and all in that time. One of the snipers in the 21ˢᵗ Batt. at the dardanelles has got 142 turks altogether and is still going strong they take enough tucker to last them for 3 days and go out and snipe they don't be shooting all the time, sometimes they have to wait a long time for a shot, this officer said that this sniper whom is halfcast from Victoria is a wonderful good shot, he has been awarded the D.C.M. and made a sergeant. The lice are very bad at the front, they only have one lot of clothes the others are left at Alexandra, they go down for a swim sometimes but are always fired on by a big gun which they cant find but they think it is on a train and comes up and down every day. Most of the returned chaps seem to think they will never take the dardanelles now they reckon they would have had a good chance at the start if they had more men there. The officer was telling us that the tucker is better at the front than it is here but there is a terrible lot of sickness. There is trouble at the Suez again the turks are coming up to have another go, there were three lots of light horse left here last night to go there. Things seem very serious in the Balkans and the Greeks are inclined to go with Germany, they reckon if they do there will be an outbreak here because *there are a lot of Greeks and Turks in Egypt. This officer that was giving us the lecture says there are spies here because when he left Alexandra for the front there were a lot of head officers on board and they were torpedoed and the boat went down and a lot of officers and men were drowned. There were about six boats altogether and the submarines let all the others pass, he reckoned they knew which boat the heads were on.*

I remain your loving brother
Geordie

The mail leaves Egypt for Australia on the 24ᵗʰ the mails leave about once a fortnight but they leave the camp once a week. I have sent a parcel with some silks in, I hope they get it it is registered so it ought to be safe, nearly all the boys send something home. I was into Heliopilis yesterday. I don't think Downey will be going to the front, he has taken on a job of M.P. I think he is afraid he wont be able to stand it, he has got terrible thin since he left Australia, and being young makes the difference, this officer said that a lot of young men get nervous and get a jumping feeling …

Tuesday 23ʳᵈ Nov 1915
Dear Mother, Father & Brothers,

Just a few lines to let you know that I got your letter and Allans today and was pleased to get a letter as it seems such a long time since I got one. The mails leave Egypt for Australia tomorrow but they have left the camp yesterday so I am writing this one and chance it may get away alright, and am giving it to a chap to post in Cairo tonight they close tomorrow morning. I would go in and post it myself but we have to drill tonight we don't do any drill this afternoon but we have tea at half past 4 o'clock and go out at 5.30 and our company and a couple of others have to attack another lot of troops, we are supposed to attack with the bayonet and not fire a shot, the other side fire with blank cartridges it will last about three hours, we get these one night every week, I like it alright because we get all the afternoon off and get a chance to write some letters. Am very sorry to hear that Blossom is dead, you will be short of horses to do the harvesting. I think all the best Australian horses are over here, they look bonzer, I seen some working the artillery this morning by jove they do work well. You never said whether you are getting my pay or those photos, dad has the receipt for them, I have plenty of money on me. Tell Chrissie

Alford that I never got her letter but I might chance to get it over here as a lot of the boys got letters today that were addressed to Broadmeadows. I hope you get the little box of silks safely, they do some wonderful good work with the silks and all by hand, the shops in Heliopilis are just full of fancy work. Be sure and let me know what reinforcements Amos [Haw] and Ray [Leed] are in and also Charlie Cockcrofts [Cockroft] and if you can find out I might chance to meet them at the front. I would like to meet my cousin there. I intended to get the addresses of all my relations in England before I came away. Downey, the chap from N.S.W. has gone into hospital today, he has the mumps there has been such a lot of my company get them, I hope I don't get them not that they are painful in any way but I would lose my company, he is the third one of my mates that has gone into hospital since we came here. It is hard to say where we will go yet, we might have to go to the Suez yet, it is not far from here, they have sent men from here to dig trenches there and are sending loads of sandbags there everyday. It seems as though Greece are going to be against us after all, I think there will be hell to do here if they do come against us there are a lot of Greeks in Cairo and I think they would get hell too, the people are all much alike and look a soft and childish lot, but the real Egyptian look much different. The arab are big and strong looking people, they wear long dresses just the same as a woman but they are just like big kids. They are building a very big brick place in this camp to show pictures in, there is no amusement in this camp and to go into Cairo now we have to get a pass but we can go to Heliopilis without a pass. The heads reckon the troops were beginning to own Cairo, I don't blame them either some of the places want burning down, I haven't been in there for over a fortnight and haven't got to the pyramids yet I was going there sunday but my mates got put on fatigue work so I wasn't going by myself. Well I might have to draw this letter to a close it will soon be time to go out to drill again. You all will have a lot of work with the harvest I hope it turns out well. I will bring that piece of heather that my cousin sent to the front with me it might bring good luck. This is all the news this time will write again next mail. It leaves in a fortnight's time. So goodbye with love to all.

I remain your loving son
George
Tell Al I received his letter, was going to write again to him but have not time.

DECEMBER, MOLOGA

As family and friends at Mologa were busy bringing in the harvest, dealing with the routine of daily life and preparing for Christmas, the situation on the other side of the world was becoming increasingly grim. Lord Kitchener had finally recognised the futility of the Gallipoli campaign and the evacuation plan was now in place. Over 80,000 men, 5000 horses and 200 heavy guns were quietly withdrawn from Gallipoli without alerting the enemy. These men and their equipment were now on their way to Egypt.

In Europe, the Western Front remained deadlocked in the line of trenches that ran through France and Belgium from Ypres to the Swiss border, while in Eastern Europe the German-Austrian offensive had taken Warsaw and the Allied Russian army had been forced to retreat. In southern Europe, despite the landing of Allied troops at the Greek port of Salonika to boost the flagging Serbian forces, the combined strength of Austria and Germany and their new ally, Bulgaria, proved too powerful. By October Serbia had been defeated. Italy joined the Allied forces in May 1915 creating another deadlocked front along border regions with Austria-Hungary. In the Middle East, the threat of a Turkish invasion of Egypt looked increasingly likely.

It was in this menacing climate that the Australian Prime Minister, Billy Hughes, while promising another 50,000 Australian soldiers to the British High Command, launched an aggressive enlistment campaign, completing a war census that listed some 244,000 Australian men as statistically, though not necessarily medically, eligible to enlist. Individual appeals were sent to those identified. Pressure came not only from official sources. The 'Order of the White Feather' was established in England in 1914, its purpose to encourage women to send or present a white feather, the traditional symbol of cowardice, to men of eligible age who were not in uniform. It was a practice that quickly spread to other nations, including Australia.

It is unclear whether white feathers ever reached Mologa; however, this small community was rife with conflicts of its own as the following letters written to George from Mologa reveal. The first correspondence is from Aileen Lowrie, Head Teacher at the Mologa East State School between 1913 and 1915. The second letter from Charlie describes tension in the community over the fundraising activities of the Red Cross. Aileen's public farewell was the event that saw the genesis of the conflict.

SS 1836 [State School]
Mologa E
Dec 15th '15
Dear George,

I spent last night with your mother. While there I read your letter which was indeed very interesting George. You were as usual very unselfish when you preferred to write to those at home rather than take the opportunity of that treat which the lady so very kindly provided. But I am sure you would be repaid if you could only see how pleased your dear mother is to receive your letters. The part where you were describing Cairo tickles me and before I go any further I must ask you if you are speaking from experience when you say "Cairo stinks like the devil" – have you ever been close enough to the latter to find out? Well George, Christmas will soon be here. Only two days now until "knock-off" time for me. I will throw up my old hat and jump on it I can assure you. I suppose you would have heard about poor Alan having his collar bone broken on account of falling from the motor-bike. Your father was up on Monday when he was getting on splendidly. You know he is back at McKay's as overseer. He said that if he had been at the war and popped over a few Germans before such a thing happened there would have been some honor about it but as it is it ain't no good. A young fellow who had been Kitchen boy at M Kelly's in Pyramid was drowned in the weir last Saturday afternoon. He was about 18 I am told. Mrs Wm Townsend senior came home again today. She went to Bendigo and underwent another operation and they say she is cured – but that remains to be seen.

Albert and Jim are up to their eyes in work with the harvesting. They miss you they are quite pleased with the way the crops are yielding. Jim's vegetable garden looks so nice. We had both potatoes and French beans from it for tea last night and I did enjoy them. The tomato plants are just laden with fruit but they are not quite ripe yet. Billy Williams has a great garden - turned Chinaman altogether. I believe he has been selling tomatoes for some time. I must not forget to tell you about the stir which Mrs Rankin's maid created just recently, she got this girl from Bendigo about a fortnight ago & I must tell you that she appeared just what she proved to be. Well, to begin … Mrs Rankin went in to change the maid's bed & in so doing found towels, handkerchiefs, tea-towels, empty soft drink bottles & quite an assortment of lollies. Then she went to Jack's money box and found it empty. They accused her but she flatly denied. They then sent for Mr Brown, but during the meantime she escaped towards Mitiamo but was held up at the cattle yards by his worship, she got away in a pair of Mrs Rankin's shoes too.

Evening

I saw Alan this evening – he came down by train. His shoulder is getting on splendidly & he is as cheeky as ever he was. I am wondering what my new school Nth Blackwood will be like. I'll get there quite soon enough though I am sure. Well, George, old boy, I think I must really stop or you'll tire of reading. A Merry Christmas & a Bright & Prosperous New Year is my heartfelt wish for you. I wonder if you will have a meal of "Turkey" or will it be "germans".

Kindest regards & very best wishes for good luck & God speed.
From your old friend
Aileen V Lowrie
Mologa

Sunday 12th
Dear Geordie,

Just a few lines today I wrote to you last Sunday and I am not doing anything today so I thought a few lines might go alright we are still stripping I have finished Mahoney's. My share was 584 bags of wheat and 160 bags of oats so I have not done to bad the crop averaged a little over 8 bags wheat and 16 bags of oats. I think we will be finished by Christmas our crop is yielding about the best in the district it is beating them home here. I am sending you the Christmas Number of the Australasion.[8] I am not sure whether it is allowed to go or not but I will chance it I cannot get it today myself as it is

Sunday but I am getting Albert to get it on Monday and address it to you I hope it will reach you alright I believe Tom Gray has not received a letter from Australia at all he has written to Mr Jones. There was hell to pay in Mologa last night over a send off to Miss Lowrie. G. John is secretary and some of them wanted a red cross sale there also and Mrs Johnnie P. put a notice up at the station about it and never consulted George about it and he called a meeting and then the fun began Jack Delaney told him he was the meanest man in Mologa and that he ought to be tarred and feathered and there was trouble all round and the johns got a knock out so they are going to have a sale of gifts as well as the send off. I believe Miss Lowrie has written two letters to you and Pearl was going to write last week this is the fifth letter I have written we have not got a letter from you for about a fortnight now I suppose by this you are in Egypt what do you think of that place I suppose the sand and flies go some it is very hot here this last few days. I told you in my last letter that Allan got his collar bone broken he has gone back to McKays he is not home today but he is getting on alright again. Have you got any idea when you will be going to the front the war does not seem to be nearing a close at all yet Australia is going to send another 50, 000 yet I do not know where they are going to get them from they will soon have all the men from here. Well I hope you are getting on all right and the rest of the chaps remember me to those I met especially Archie Bailey tell them I wish them good luck. Well I will draw to a close this letter will go on the "Moltan" I hope you get all my letters I write nearly every boat, I will now say goodbye Geordie and Good luck and a happy and good new year a good time and a safe return I am your loving brother.

Charlie E. Marlow

In the context of the life of a soldier, the pettiness that Charlie describes will have caused some amusement, and George will probably have enjoyed Aileen's gossipy news of home. However, her words are laden with meaning. Allan had spoken to her of his injury and its less than glorious cause. His reference to the honour of a wound incurred in front-line service is the first indication that he was planning to follow his older brother to boost the numbers of the AIF. By the time George received the letter in late January, Allan's shoulder had healed and his plans were well underway.

ZEITOUN CAMP, EGYPT, DECEMBER

In the lead-up to Christmas, George struggled to cope with his distance from home during what was an important traditional family celebration. He was now not only writing lengthy letters home, but also sending numerous postcards with views of Egypt and greeting cards with Christmas wishes. One simple card, bought from the AIF Gifts Store at the Savoy Hotel in Cairo, bears the outline of a boomerang on which are written the words 'I go out to return'. An irony existed in the original verse which mocks the hope of return:

… Our lands of freedom over the sea,
Our homes and our bright blue skies,
The sweeping plains and the dear green trees;
We would give our lives and soul for these
And we'll fight to the last man dies.

This was a Christmas card featuring appropriately patriotic words, although I doubt it brought great comfort or joy to its recipients. For many families the poem would come to represent the realisation of a feared prophecy.

December 4 1915
Yeitoun Camp
Dear Albert,

Just a few lines to tell you that I don't think there will be any more Australians sent to the Dardanelles till after the winter, that will be feb. or march. Lord Kitchner has just been over there and now they are going to send the Australians back to Egypt and put Canadians in their place as they are used to the cold climate. There are some back already, they will have to make some fresh camps I think this one is full right up now. I think they are going to send us back to the Suez, as the Turks are going to make another attack, it will be a proper one this time as they have built a railway up towards the Suez, they tell us that when they attacked before they were about 200,000 strong but had to go back as they had no way to bring provisions up. We might be formed into a new brigade, there is a yarn to that effect. I received your letter also one from Charlie. It is very cold here in the night now but is warm in the day time. On the first of December it was field day. A big crowd of us left here after breakfast, bringing our dinner with us and marched out over the desert had dinner and made an attack on another lot that went out before us, it is a bit tough charging up sandy hills, we arrived back at the camp in time for tea. The next night we had another attack and Friday we went for a rout march, by jove there was a string of us about a mile long in fours. I went to the Pyramids last sunday and climbed right up to the top of them, it takes a fair while to go to the top but they are worth climbing, get such a bonzer view, but it is a wonderful affair, how they got such amense blocks of stone up there, and is built so well. I went inside apart of the way but was too hot and crowded to look right through it all, have to crawl a long way in before you come to a chamber, my word it is worth seeing I intend to go in again some other time and look right through them, it took an hour to go out and an hour to come back. We passed the zoo and gardens going there they say they are well worth seeing I have not been there yet, we also crossed over the Nile it has a bonzer bridge over it. The Mena camp is right close to the pyramids and also the hospital. A lot of the chaps in my company are getting the mumps, there are three gone out of my tent to the hospital with them, two of them are mates of mine they are kept there for about five weeks. Well I have no more news this time. Hoping all are well as I am at present.

I remain your loving Bro
Geordie
There are some more mails coming in tomorrow.

Sunday Dec 12th, 1915
Dear Mother and Father,

I received the letter from you and Jim also one from Charlie and from Auntie Etta. I hope Dad has got rid of his rash by now, one of the chaps in my tent had a rash on him much like the one Dad gets. I am very sorry to hear about Beat Saville being dead it must have been very sudden. Glad to hear the crops are so good. Tom Jackman has just landed here, he says the crops are looking splendid. I suppose Amos and Ray will soon be here, *now that they have had their final leave. There were a lot of men come in lately, the new brigade and about 1200 remounts have just arrived here. They will have a big crowd of troops here now that they are not sending anymore to the Dardanelles till after the winter, a lot have been sent back some have gone into hospital with frost bites. They have just had a tough fight at the front, we heard that the Turks mined two companies 23 and 24 and blew them up a bit and that the Australians won it back and also took some hill and 3 miles of railway, a lot of wounded have arrived here at the hospital. There were four companies took part in it the 21, 22, 23 and 24, and one of the men in my company got a cable from his father in Australia telling him that it is rumoured in Melbourne that the 6 of the 21st were in it, so it shows you how yarns get about. We might have to fight here yet, we have all been formed up into a battalion ready to go in case we should be wanted. They say that the Turks have built five railways up towards the Suez, the British are building a big railway now. If we don't have to fight here it will be a long while before we go to the Dardanelles. I heard that little Tom Lowe has gone back to Australia and that big Tom is in a London hospital. Charlie Cockcroft is in the hospital with the mumps, I got a letter from Downie who is in there too, saying that he happened to mention my name and Charlie heard him, no-one is allowed in there, or I would go and see him, Downie says he is alright and as fat as a pig. A lot of men go out looking for beads and different things each sunday, there has been a city buried many years ago, it is only half a mile out from the camp, it is part of our drilling ground, there was supposed to have been a great battle fought there once and is covered with deep holes full of bodies, all that can be seen now are bones. There is a chap in my company, his name is Bush he says he knows Dad he used to go up to Dripps for his holidays, he comes from Moonee Ponds.^{9} Well I havent much news but will be writing again next week to Jim. I hope you are getting all my letters. They have mail bags in Cairo by the thousands but cant sort them quick enough. I will now close hoping all are well as I am at present.*

I remain your loving son
George

They are wanting horse drivers, stretcher bearers and boot makers here now.

In his letter to Charlie, George typically included more detail:

… I suppose you have heard about the 2 or 3 companies of Australians being blown to atoms out of the trenches, we heard here that there were about 600 killed and 1000 wounded and that the attack was at that Lonesome Pine … A lot of the wounded have come in to the hospital from this last attack, those that saw them say that they look terrible wrecks … The returned chaps here don't think there is much chance of taking the Dardanelles. None of them are anxious of going back to the front … Ken Laird had just left here for the front when we arrived here and young Hill from Calivil has only just left here too but I suppose they will both be back again soon because since Kitchener has been over there they are sending them back again … We were getting very little tucker here for a while but are getting more now. The lice are very bad, they call them sand lice they are about as big as dog fleas they give us hell at times …

16/12/15
Yeitoun Camp
Dear Jim,

Just a few lines to let you know that I got a letter from you yesterday also the one last week from you and mum. There was another lot of letters given out today but nearly all of them had been addressed to the Broadmeadows camp. I thought I might get that one from Chris, but no luck. I have received 4 from home, 2 from Charlie & 1 from Allan. One of my mates that has been with me ever since we left Bendigo says that he went to school with some of the Alfords, the elder ones, ask them do they remember him, his name is L [erased]. Glad to hear that dad is getting better again. You will have a lot of work this harvest and wont have too many horses either. Must have had a great feed of peas, we get some here in the stew but they are hard ones, they are picked too late. They grow a lot of vegetables and fruit here, there are some big gardens with orange trees in them and other fruit trees. I don't know what to write about, we are not allowed to say much now all the letters are to be handed in unclosed and are censored now. Yesterday it was field day we left the camp at 8am and took our dinner with us and marched out over the desert and attacked another party of troops we all had blank cartridges to make it a little like real, we arrived back in time for tea, we don't get out this afternoon till 5 o'clock and go out on a night attack till 8pm, tomorrow afternoon is a rout march. The new brigade and 1 200 remounts have arrived here and some other troops came in last night, one lot is the 7 reinforcements of the 21 Batt. They are getting very particular here about the way to dress and so on. We are to keep hair cut short and to shave every day and have to wear our tunics all the time while we are drilling and it is dam hot with them on from about 10 am till about 3pm then it gets a little cooler, at night it is very cold and there is generally a thick fog in the morning. I suppose Amos and Ray will soon be here now, Charlie Cockcroft is in the hospital with the mumps I haven't seen him yet. Tom Jackman is here in the remounts, they are mostly old chaps and the rejects. Well I have no more to write about this time so will close hoping all are well. I remain your affectionate Bro.

George

Christmas arrived and departed with little fanfare. It was probably the first Christmas that 23-year-old George had spent without the company of his family.

Dec 31ˢᵗ 1915
2748
6 rfms 21 Batt
6 Inf Bgde
A.I.F.
Egypt

Dear Charlie

… I don't know what your Christmas was like but it was a fairly quiet one here that is in the camp but in Cairo things were lively. We had a flash dinner salmon and bread & jam but in the other camps they got a fairly good dinner, there were a mob of geese round by the cooks the day before xmas but I think the sergeants got them. We were given xmas boxes but no billies but all the troops in the other camps got billies and boxes, in the boxes were were 2 packets cigarettes, 2 cigars 1 tin tobacco and some post cards,

I heard that we might get billies New Year's Day, tomorrow. I believe that one chap got a £10 note in his billy. I went into Cairo in the afternoon and into Heliopilis in the evening, it was lively in Cairo in the afternoon and evening I cant tell you what happened as these letters are censored now. I am going to see the Zoo tomorrow. I went to see the gardens on xmas day they are got up very nice I think they look lovely. Well I suppose you have seen it in the papers about the troops being withdrawn from the Dardanelles, a lot of them are here. I met Tom Gray the other night he has been over in the trenches for about 2 months he was only kept here for a fortnight, he looks thin on it, he said he had been crook over there with the mumps and something else. He says Les Whitfield, Ryans and all the Mitiamo and Pyramid light horse chaps are back in the Heliopilis camp with him. I am going over one day to see them. Ray Leed and the others must be here now Archie Bailey said he met Dennie Hardiman. I see by this morning's paper they are going to make it compulsory in England and call up the single men first so I suppose they will do likewise in Australia. The light horse and some British troops are fighting on the Western Frontier Egypt. It seems they are having a very severe winter in Russia. I am on guard duty today at the detention guard the prisoners, there are 15 of them here with a barb wire fence around them, we are getting a lot of guard and picket to do here, I was on picket on Sunday night in Cairo, we have to march up and down the streets with a red & white arm band around our arm, each company get it to do, they have pickets on the trams stations and in the streets etc. I am very sorry to hear that you hurt your foot, it will be a bit awkward for awhile with all the work to do, but hope it will soon be better. You remember Downie the tall chap from N.S.W. that is with me, well he just came out of the mumps hospital after being there for five weeks and was only out 2 days and was sent back into one of the other hospitals I haven't heard what is the matter with him yet but he has a bad cold and coughed up a cup full of blood he has had no luck since he joined up the military. Evans is still in the mumps hospital. Young Gale the married chap is alright but often says he wishes he was home, there are a lot that way, I am quite satisfied here but wish they would send us to the front somewhere, it is monotonous drilling every day. It is a lousy joint here they are crawling all over us at times especially in this guard tent where we are today. Jim Gritton that I pointed out to you in the theatre in Bendigo has been crook nearly all the time since we came here he went under an operation but they didn't do him any good and is in there again, it is a rupture of some kind. I don't think I have lost any weight I weighed in Cairo the other day and went 13 stone, so am not doing too bad although we were not getting enough tucker but is a bit better now but I cant tackle the curry stew they give us for breakfast. A fellow wants to be a sergeant they get good tucker. I ought to get a letter anytime now from Pearl [Charlie's girlfriend], I have written about four to her.[10] I believe Eddie [cousin] enlisted again but didn't pass.[11]

I hear there are a lot to be married up there soon what has come over them all. The government are getting a bit hot 'aint they, putting the price on the wheat and buying it themselves. I am glad they are getting my pay alright. The letters from Australia are not censored I got yours the day after xmas. I don't want any money although we are always broke before every pay one shilling a day don't go far here and if you were to send money I might not get it because we might be going at any time but where I know not. They are holding sports here on Sunday I don't think I will be bothered going. We had a drop of rain here on xmas eve only about 30 points they say it is the third drop of rain that has fallen here since the first Australians came. Well I have no more this time so will close hoping all are well as I am at present. Wishing George, May & family and yourself a merry and prosperous new year.

I remain your loving Bro
George.

As the sick and wounded soldiers from Gallipoli began their recovery in nearby hospitals, their mates made the adjustment to camp life after months clinging to precarious positions surrounded by unburied corpses, living with the constant fear of attack and being shelled day and night, even on the beaches at Anzac Cove. For the new recruits, the reality of war was clearly visible in the maimed and emaciated Gallipoli veterans. Although George remained keen to escape the monotony of drill and to see some action, for others such as 'young Gale', the initial enthusiasm with which they had enlisted had turned to regret and a longing for home.

PART TWO
1916

TWO
I WISH THEY WOULD SEND US OFF SOMEWHERE OUT OF THIS …

MOLOGA, AUSTRALIA, JANUARY 1916

The lists of casualties from Gallipoli sent shock waves through the young Australian nation. For many, despite their unswerving loyalty to the mother country, the appeal of fighting for king and country had been undermined by the awful cost in life and limb. Many families quietly prayed that the war would end before their sons were old enough to enlist. However, the recruitment campaign continued relentlessly and the prospect of conscription was now being openly discussed by a government desperate for men. Britain, faced with a recruiting crisis, introduced conscription in late January.

It was inevitable that more sons of Sarah and Charles Marlow would go to war. The harvest was completed, Allan's shoulder had healed, the papers and posters all demanded it, and even the Church of England voiced its support for the war. Charlie attempted to enlist a second time and was once again rejected. But this time he was referred to the local dental board, a dental service established to treat problem teeth and ensure that conditions commonly referred to under the broad banner of 'bad teeth' would not prevent otherwise fit and healthy Australian men from seeing active service. Allan now arrived home with the news that his medical examination had declared him fit for service. With the original physical height requirement of 5 feet 6 inches now relaxed to 5 feet 2 inches, Allan's twin, Percy, at five feet 3 inches, also managed to scrape through on 15 February, just four weeks after Allan.

While the prospect of the twins marching off to war together was cause for celebration for many in the little community, I doubt Sarah Marlow met the announcement with any sense of joy. She may certainly have been proud of her boys, but her loyalty must have been divided and her heart heavy. However it is unlikely that the twins' enlistment would have been openly questioned in a household characterised by a strong allegiance to England and its church. While Sarah may have found some consolation in the fact that her eldest son, Jim, had been rejected on the basis of poor eyesight, she was destined to be the proud and stoic mother of three patriotic and brave soldiers. Surely that would be enough — no-one could expect more from her and her sons.

YEITOUN CAMP, EGYPT, JANUARY

On the first day of the new year, George put pen to paper, clearly disappointed with the quality of the celebrations that marked the festive season:

Jan 1st 1916
2748
6 reinforcements 21 Batt
6 Inf Brigade AIF
Egypt
Dear Mother, Father & Brothers,

Just a few lines hoping all are well as I am at present. It is New Years Day here, they have just given us a couple of oranges and apples each. I thought we would be given a billy but no such luck we never got any in this camp for xmas and in all the other camps they did and got a good dinner too, all we got was salmon and bread and jam. I suppose you are thinking that I am in the trenches by now, we were told when we arrived in Egypt first that we would be gone in three weeks but we are still here ... In my letter to Jim I was telling him there is a chap along with me that used to go to school with Alfords, the elder ones, I closed the letter up and forgot to finish his name, the name is Lousada, he asked me to ask you to ask Alfords if they remember him, he has two brothers over here, or on their way back from the trenches. They are holding sports on sunday in the Abbasive camp, some of the men are out running getting in form. I suppose they will be making it compulsory [conscription] *in Australia soon as they are doing in England. Downie just came back from the mumps hospital and has gone back to another one now he had a bad cold he has got very thin since he left Australia ...*

While George was revelling in his new experiences in Egypt, including the pyramids and the aircraft of the fledgling Flying Corps, he remained eager to discover just where and when he would eventually enjoy his first taste of action. He wrote of his mates, particularly Downie, who had been readmitted to hospital and was gravely ill with possible tuberculosis. By now George had realised that his friend was unlikely to recover and his letter is tinged with concern. This would be the first of many new friendships that would be lost in the months to come.

Egypt Jan 18th 1916
Dear Mother, Father & Brothers

Just a few lines to let you know that I am alright and am having a good time at present. My company are all on guard at the different hospitals we have to do a week of it, each company gets it, our company was on a while back but I wasn't on. I am on guard at the Sporting Club Hospital it is a convalescent Hospital. It is a very nice place all the paths have nice trees and hedges planted on each side of them, it looks lovely. There are a lot of soldiers here and nearly all of them are camped in huts. Lorrie Johnson is in here I met him last night while I was standing at the door of their mess hut keeping them back till the bugle went and when they were going in I spotted him he don't look too good on it, he says he has been in the hospital nearly all the time he has been in Egypt and they don't know what is the matter with him. It is like a home here we don't get many hours guard a day to do, and a bonzer bed to sleep in and the tucker is first class such a change to in the camp I think we will all break out in pimples by the time we are finished here. The company that was here before us tried to get another week of it but wasn't successful. You wouldn't believe what a lot of traffic there is in [and] out of these hospital camps. The tram line from Heliopilis to Cairo runs right along side here, I was on guard along the tram line by the hospital last night and the trams seem to go all night long, the trams run on the same sort of line as the trains, a hospital train just went now to the Palace Hospital with wounded and sick men on it. It is nothing but the buzz of the aeroplanes just here, the Flying Corps camp is only a few chains away and the aeroplanes are going up and down all the time. You remember Downie the tall chap from N.S.W that I pointed out to you in Bendigo he is being sent back to Australia also another chap I have known well ever since we left Seymour, there are about five of my company altogether. Downie has just come out of the mumps hospital and was only out 2 days and we went on a rout march and it seem to settle him and went into the hospital that night, the doctor says he has consumption [Tuberculosis] and he looks very much like it too he has got very thin, just like a skeleton now. I am very sorry for him he was such a nice chap. I am afraid he is done for now, they were supposed to leave here today. I answered your last letter about Al having an accident. I suppose you are getting my letters and that silk I sent. I hope Allan is getting better. Ray Leed and I went out to the Pyramids last Sunday week and went right through them also climbed them this is my second trip to them, when coming back we called in at Heliopilis and met Amos Haw in there he looks real well I also met Young Erickson. These troops that just came in on the train have just arrived back from Lemnos Island they have been there in the Hospital for a long while, the red cross wagons have been flying about like the devil shifting the men into the different hospitals some came in here. I got no idea when we will be going to the front there don't seem to be much doing at the present. Well I hope the crops have yielded well and [you] are getting a good price for the wheat. One chap here got a letter from home saying that they have stopped recruiting in Australia. I haven't met Bert Gibson yet, Lorrie Johnson said today that he heard that he got wounded over in Tripoli. It might not be true, so don't tell his mother, some of the light horsemen were sent over there just after I landed here. Well I have no more news this time so will close hoping all are well as I am at present, with best wishes to all.

I remain your loving son Geordie

The latest furfie we heard is that we are going to France but of course we hear such a lot of them here, don't know whether to believe it or not. Send the address of my relations in England, might chance to get there.

Nineteen-year-old George Downie was invalided home in late January and eventually recovered from his illness.[1] In 1923 he signed for the Victory Medal which was issued to all soldiers who had served. If Downie had indeed suffered from tuberculosis, he was fortunate to still be alive. These were the days before the advent of antibiotics and the effective treatment of bacterial infections. In the hospitals of Egypt, the makeshift tents on the Western Front, in the best medical facilities in England and across Europe, men were dying not only as a result of the conflict, but also from secondary bacterial infections. Weakened by their wounds, often festering in the filth of the trenches and no man's land, exhausted from days and weeks in wet dugouts where sleep and nutritious food were equally rare, the bodies of the sick and wounded had little protection against the ravages of infection.

Just where the Australian troops were to be sent remained a topic of hot debate. George refers to 'the latest furfie', a term often used to describe the rumours that quickly spread throughout the camps. The troops would gather around the water carts exchanging news and gossip which rapidly became 'the latest furphy'. The water tanks perched on the carts were boldly labelled with the manufacturer's name: J FURPHY & SONS.

Reinforcements arrived from Australia, the Anzac troops returning from Gallipoli were reorganised, and those drilling in the dry desert sands of the Egyptian camps waited with growing impatience for their turn to strike at the foe. The reorganisation saw the two AIF divisions increased to four, the additional divisions formed by splitting the old divisions in two and making up numbers with the newly arrived reinforcements. Five Australian infantry divisions were raised in this way. British General William Birdwood commanded I Anzac Corps which comprised the 1st and 2nd Australian divisions and the New Zealand Division. The 4th and 5th Australian divisions formed II Anzac and were commanded by British General Alexander Godley. The 3rd Division, under the command of Australian General John Monash, was being raised in Australia and consisted of those troops recently enlisted. The Anzac Mounted Division comprised the Australian Light Horse regiments and New Zealanders who would remain in Egypt to provide protection against expected Turkish incursions.

On 23 January, mounted troops were deployed to fortify the Allied position east of the Suez Canal and prevent Turkish troops in Palestine crossing the Sinai Desert and entering Egyptian territory. Soon after, additional infantry divisions were sent to the canal to reinforce and relieve the mounted troops.

In Europe, the need for Anzac troops to fortify the Western Front had become urgent. On 21 February German Chief of the General Staff General Erich von Falkenhayn launched an unprecedented artillery bombardment which targeted the fortress city of Verdun in the north-eastern sector of the French front line. Verdun and its forts had guarded the eastern approach to France for centuries and formed a crumbling bastion, a traditional symbol of strength. Falkenhayn's plan was to hit one section of the line with massive firepower, his objective to bleed 'France to death'.[2] While the determined French were staunchly holding the line, an influx of fresh fighting men was desperately needed to stem the German advance.

As rumours heralding a move to France began circulating within the camps of Egypt, George was enjoying the mild winter climate and making the most of time free from drill or duty to write home to his family and friends. At the same time, as George describes, discontent in the camps continued to grow.

Egypt Jan 21ˢᵗ 1916
Yeitoun Camp
Dear Charlie

… I am having a good time this week, we are on guard at the Sporting Club Hospital, it is a convalescent hospital, there are 20 of us here altogether, the rest of the company are on at the other hospitals, we have to do a week of it altogether. It is different to doing guard at the guard tents, we only do about 24 hours altogether for the week so don't lose any sleep over it. I wouldn't mind if they left us here until we go to the firing line. We get the same tucker as the hospital staff, it is good too, such a change from the camp tucker. Yesterday the staff complained about the dinner and brought in the orderly officer to see it, they ought to go into the camps for a day or two and would have something to taught [talk] about. All the hospitals are let by contract to the French people for supplying the food and you cant beat the French cooks. There are a lot of men in the wards some very bad cases of

frost bite from the Dardanelles. Most of the returned chaps have a very poor opinion of the Tommies as fighters they have a better opinion of the turks and say they are very fair fighters. We see plenty of aeroplanes flying here they are camped just a little bit away, they came over to the hospital and gave a concert it was very good they come once a week. We are having some bonzer weather here now, it is winter time but the days are nice and sunny it is cold at night. I see by today's paper that all the reserves in the Egyptian army are called up. Half my company have been sent down near the canal, they picked out all the worst of the companies and sent them away, things have been very lively in Cairo lately, and they reckon that is the reason they were sent away, they are not in any fighting but are drilling just the same as here, they say it is a b____ down where they are, a lot of them are sleeping out in the open, not enough tents for them all. It is rumoured here that we are going to France, it is quite possible that they will send all of us over there and leave Tommies and Indians here, of course it is too cold there yet. I see they are calling for another 50,000 more men in Australia, I suppose there aint many enlisting there now. Downie and Grittons the chap I pointed out to you in the pictures that night, are on their way back. Lorrie Johnson is here in this hospital, he says he is going back to his unit today. Well Charlie I hope the crop has yielded well and that you get a good price for the wheat. I will now close with best wishes to you all.

I remain your loving Bro
Geordie

Send the addresses of the relations in England if the others haven't sent them, I might have a chance of getting to England.

A week later, George wrote to Charlie's girlfriend, Pearl:

... I received five letters yesterday the first since Christmas I have been looking out for a letter from you. Charlie said you were going to write I hope you have got mine, it is a luxury to get letters here ... There are a lot in the hospitals hopping about on sticks some have got some bad frost bites at the Dardanelles, they are all back from there now. Les Whitfield and all those other chaps are back here in Heliopilis they had a fairly rough time of it towards the finish. I got no idea when we will be going to the firing line. I

wish they would send us off somewhere out of this it is sickening drilling day after day. There cant be many men in camp in Australia now, I see by the paper that they are wanting another 50,000 we heard here that they had stopped recruiting for a while, I suppose there werent many enlisting while the harvest was on. One of my mates is on his way back to Australia I think there are four out of my company gone back altogether and two have died here lately. General Birdwood inspected all of us last week ...

FEBRUARY

Sunday, Feb 6th 1916
Dear Mother, Father and Brothers,

I received your last letter on the 29 Jan also 2 from Charlie, 1 from Auntie May and 1 from Miss Lowrie, they had been written on the 13th and 21st of December, they are the only letters I have received since the day after xmas there must be some gone astray somewhere because auntie Etta, Sharps and Allan had been writing regular. A lot of our mail had been sent down to the brigade down on the desert near the canal and it is rumoured here that they destroyed what didn't belong there. Well I hope you have been getting mine I have been writing regular but the worst of it here we never know when the mails leave Egypt. I suppose Al's shoulder is better again, I met a young fellow from Pyramid he didn't tell me his name he had Pyramid written on his hat, so I spoke to him, he knew who I was straight away and was telling me about Allan getting hurt. He is in the same battalion as me but the 8th reinforcements. Jack Jamison is in the same lot as him, they are camped in tents right alongside our huts. They were telling me that Bill Hesens and one of the Hogarths are going to enlist, I think they will have to come. Frank Donaldson that used to play football with Calivil is here he is in the 7th reinforcements of the 21st Batt. I often see him. Archie is a Lance Corporal now, stripes are not much good here because as soon as we join the original Battalion they all lose their stripes. I have met a lot of chaps that were in my company at Bendigo they have just arrived here. Ray Leed has been getting the Pyramid paper sent from home when he is finished with them he gives them to me then I pass them on to Archie ... about sending things over, you address them the same as the letters but I don't think it would be wise to send any now as we might not be here much longer than a month well it is about time they shifted us out of this. I don't think there will be any fight in the canal after all, according to the paper we get here, so I think we will be left here until the winter is over in the other fronts and that we will be either sent to France or Salonika. This is a lovely place to sport the winter it is no wonder that such a lot of people come here for the winter, the days are nice and sunny but the nights are cold, it is gradually getting hotter coming on summer again soon. I went into Heliopilis with Reg Evans last night, Dad and Charlie met him at Broad meadows, he wanted to see his sister she is a nurse, we got wet through coming home my word it did come down we have had such a lot of rain here lately, nearly all the huts leak they are not made to keep the rain out, I noticed in one of the paper[s] that they got a lot of recruits in the month of January, they are making it compulsory in England now. Well I suppose that you will all be having a spell now that the harvesting is finished. They must have had a very lively meeting over Miss Lowrie send off. My word the lucerne plots in the irrigation look lovely it seems to grow very fast, they cart a lot of it away on the camels. Every morning before breakfast our company goes for a fast walk of about four miles past the lucerne plots and will always see the niggers carting it away I think some of them work all night. They have a lot of wells put down and pump the water out with horse works but they have a bullock or cow in them and go all day and night it is fairly slow of course there is the irrigation channels too for watering they don't seem to run much water down them in the winter time but in the summer they are always full. They don't have the ground fenced off here only round the roads and there it is a hedge fence and the way they feed the stock is have a rope around their heads and tied on a peg or else they stand there and mind them. We got a surprise today they gave us our xmas puddings for dinner that we should have got on xmas day it was just the thing, the tucker is better now than what we used to get. Well I have not much news this time so will close hoping all are well as I at present with best wishes to all I remain your loving son and brother.

Geordie
That chap from Pyramid is <u>Millar</u>.

Later news

We have just been warned to leave here in four days time for active service. I wont be able to write so often now but don't worry I will write when ever I get a <u>chance</u>.

George

George was probably already aware of his next destination. I suspect his underlining of the word 'chance' is an attempt to beat the censor, hoping that his family will understand that the Australians were bound for the Western Front in France rather than the Macedonian Front at Salonika in the east where Germany, Austria-Hungary and Bulgaria had now defeated Serbia. In his next undated letter, as he describes the reorganisation of the Australian forces, he spells out the expected destination quite clearly, although a sense of uncertainty remains.

Egypt
Yeitoun Camp
Dear Mother

Just a few lines to let you know that we are leaving here in the morning to go down on the canal and that all the Australian troops are being formed up afresh again into different battalions they say that they are mixing the ones that have seen fighting with the new ones and have the battalions half of each, we the 6 of 21 are forming the seventh battalion, Ray Leed is going in the 58 Batt. and Jack Jamison and young Millar from Pyramid are in the 60 Batt they are splitting the old Battalions up all roads, they are forming a lot more Battalions now, and before they only had them up to the 32 Batt., so I think we will go to France later on, or they wouldn't be making such alterations, it will be a long while before we get any letters, in fact we are not getting any now I have only received 5 since xmas, we were getting them very regular before xmas, but it doesn't matter much as long as all are well. I haven't much time at present as we have to pack up our things. So hoping all are well as I am at present.

I remain Your loving son
Geordie

Give the others my new address

My address
2748
Pte G. T. Marlow
7 Batt
2ⁿᵈ Brigade A.I.F.
On Active Service Abroad
Send the addresses of my relations in England

As George packed for the welcome move from the heat and dust of Egypt, he jotted in his notebook a list of items to be stored in his kitbag and those that would remain in his pack. On the following page he recorded his movements since 12 June:

> In kit bag
> 1 Drawers, 1 singlet, 1 boots, 1 abd Belt, 1 Breeches, 1 hair brush, 1 service jacket, 1 towel 1 flannel Shirt, socks
> In Pack
> Shaving outfit, Laces, Tooth Brush, Knife Fork & spoon, comb, cap comforter, socks, field dressings, cord jacket, towel, Great Coat Housewife
>
> Enlisted on June 12ᵗʰ 1915 went to camp 28 June Went to Seymour August 10
>
> Bendigo to Broadmeadows Sept 5 Sailed from P. Melb. Oct 5 Arrived at Suez Nov 3 and went by train to the Yeitoun Camp and later went to Aredrome camp and then went back to Yeitoun and left there on Feb 24ᵗʰ at 8 am and arrived at Serapeum 2pm.

SUEZ CANAL, MARCH

The reorganisation was now almost complete and George was on active service, positioned along the Suez Canal as a reinforcement to D Company, 7th Battalion, 2nd Brigade of the 1st Division. The men of the 1st Division had moved to the front line in January, digging trenches and building roads, railways and pipelines in a 19-kilometre stretch close to Serapeum. They were preparing for an expected attack by Turkish forces now relieved of the defence of the Dardanelles and moving inexorably south. George next wrote home on 2 March, the day on which a desert sandstorm, blowing for the third day, completely enveloped sections of the trenches.

March 2ⁿᵈ 1916
Dear Mother

… Well it is very rough here today with the wind and dust and is also getting very hot I suppose it is getting a bit cooler over there now. Well I told you in my last letter that we were leaving the Yeitoun camp and going into new Battalions, well we are a long way from Yeitoun now and are in D Company Seventh Battalion Second Brigade Abroad, that is my address now. Ray Leed is in the 57 Batt Archie Baillie is in the same Batt. as me, he has joined the N.C.O. school to try for stripes. Well Mother we are not allowed to say anything about where we are or what we are doing, so I don't know what to write about, so will close hoping all are well as I am at present.

I remain Your Loving Son
Geordie

A fortnight later, George wrote to Charlie of his rapid return to Cairo from Serapeum to collect some money his family had cabled. He expresses his surprise at the news that Allan has enlisted.

March 17ᵗʰ 1916
Dear Charlie

Just a few lines hoping all are well as I am present. I received word from the Anglo – Egyptian bank in Cairo saying that you had cabled some money to me, having shifted from Yeitoun before the letter reached me and being such a long way from Cairo I thought it was all up with the money but I saw the captain of my company about it and he told me to put in for leave and would try and get it through for me and it was successful so I reckon I was lucky, I got two days as would be unable to do it under that time. I got on a train at a siding called Serapeum at 8 oclock last night and arrived in Cairo at 1 oclock this morning I managed to get a bed but when I got up I was covered in lumps from flea bites. Well I have just been to the Intermediate Base depot and the bank to fix up the papers and have drawn the money £6. You can fix it up out of my pay which I hope is coming along alright. You would be surprised to see what a crowd of men go into the bank to draw money some cable for as much as £20 at a time. We cant buy anything down where we are only a tin of fruit now and again, no drinks of any kind we only get one of those water bottles full of water every day and have to wash ourselves and all out of it, and it is very hot down there and sand up to our necks, we are right over the canal in Arabia and have the trenches about 10 miles out from the canal, all of our brigade have been relieved from the trenches and the light horse are in them now and we are camped right on the edge of the canal now we get a swim about twice a week but have to go down in full fighting order, it is a bonzer place for a swim about 100yds across. You would be surprised to see what a lot of boats go through. It is a very rough place for horses they seem to be getting very poor. Well Charlie I think we will be shifting from there very soon perhaps within a week, it is too hot to fight there now I hope they send us to a cooler place this time. We were inoculated yesterday and have to be done again and are being fitted up with all the leather equipments and I believe they are going to get new rifles and different kind to what we have, when we shift. Amos Haw is in the same brigade as me and I often have a yarn with him, he says he received a letter from Rene saying that they haven't received a letter from him yet he asked to tell you to tell his people that he is alright, she said that four more have enlisted from Mologa, including Allan, it was news to me as I haven't received a letter from anyone for months but hope to get some with my new address as I told you all in my other letters that I am in the 7 Batt now. You can show them at home this letter or tell them the news. Well Charlie I will now close thanking you very much for sending the money.

I remain your loving bro
Geordie …

Tell Allan to write and send his address when he is about to leave as he wont know till just before he is leaving, what letters I write to him you could send to him in camp. Send the address of my relations in England when you write also say if they received those silks. I am writing this letter in the YMCA in the Gardens Cairo, it is very hot but not as hot as in Arabia. When we left Yeitoun our kit bags were sent to the Base, they never told us that they werent going with us, so all the clothes that we have had are what we have on us, you can guess we werent lousy a bit, so I am going to buy new socks and other things today.

While ordinary soldiers heard only rumours of their move to the fields of France, those in command were rapidly organising their embarkation. On 13 March the men of the 2nd Australian Division began to embark from Alexandria and were soon followed by the remaining battalions of I Anzac Corps. At this point, I Anzac consisted of the 1st, 2nd and NZ divisions under General Birdwood, while II Anzac, comprised the 'new' 4th and 5th divisions under Lieutenant General Godley. By July 1916, when II Anzac arrived on the Western Front, closely followed by the 3rd Division, the structure of I Anzac Corps had changed again, now comprising the 1st, 2nd and 4th divisions. II Anzac consisted of the 3rd, 5th and NZ divisions.

As George waited for word of his impending departure from Egypt, he took a moment to record his movements in his notebook:

Sunday 12 March
Church parade in morn swimming parade in the afternoon
Thursday 16 March
Drill in morning enoculation in afternoon
March 16 on leave to Cairo arrived back at Serapeum on the 18th
March 19 visited by Prince of Wales 1916
Monday 20
General muster & inspection taking note of shortages.

BENDIGO, AUSTRALIA, MARCH 1916

In Australia, the formation of the 3rd Australian Division was now well in hand. The 38th Battalion was raised on 1 March 1916 on the outskirts of Bendigo, the new battalion training grounds entirely subsuming the

Epsom Racecourse. The 38th Battalion was part of the 10th Brigade, 3rd Division, under the command of Lieutenant Colonel C.H. Davis.

Among the 38th Battalion's initial intake were twins Percy and Allan Marlow, their regimental numbers 119 and 120 respectively. They were immediately sent to the machine-gun section as Lewis gunners. The Lewis automatic machine-gun was light and relatively portable compared to the larger Vickers gun. First used by the Belgians in 1914, it had proven efficient and lethal, capable of firing 500 to 600 rounds per minute, and could be operated by a lone gunner if required. Lewis gunners worked in a team, usually of five men, with supplies of ammunition and spare parts carried in the field. The gunners remained constantly on the move to avoid being registered by enemy artillery fire. The Lewis gun was a weapon of industrialised warfare and vital to defending trench systems from attacking enemy forces. Allan, after years of hunting rabbits in the paddocks and along the creek at Mologa, was a skilled marksman and soon to become the number one gunner.

Allan and Percy and their 38th Battalion mates boarded the train at Mologa for the three-hour journey to Bendigo. They were about to begin their lives as soldiers of the AIF. The local newspaper that served the community of Mologa reported their departure:

> Messrs T Alford and C. Fyffe, the first recruits for the new army from Mologa, left here on Monday morning and would go into camp in Bendigo on that day. On the 1st March they will be followed by Messrs A Marlow, P. Marlow, J Townsend, E Johnson and W. Street. All have been prominently connected with the Mologa Football Club and other entities of a social nature in the district. Along with those who have gone, Mologa may be proud of these young men who are about to take part in the Empire's great struggle.[3]

Over 100 years on, I cannot help but wonder whether, had these brave young men been able to envisage the true horror of war, they would still have enlisted. Perhaps they would have preferred the ignominy of receiving a white feather to the nightmare of trench warfare. It is more likely, however, that the strong sense of duty, the patriotic fervour and the relentless propaganda would have combined to stir their souls and provide them the requisite courage for the ordeal that awaited. The passing of time has robbed us of the opportunity to ask.

While the early weeks of drill kept the boys busy, they still found time to visit family and friends in Bendigo, including the family of Charlie's girlfriend, Pearl Clee. Despite the early bravado and thrill of military life that permeated the boys' letters home, Sarah Marlow was clearly anxious for her sons, particularly Allan, who had suffered poor health as a child and who she considered might not cope with the tough life of a soldier. Sarah's concerns were quickly justified as many of the new recruits fell ill, a significant number isolated with meningitis. The men were later confined to camp to contain the epidemic. In his letters Allan does not mention the increasing rate of illness to his parents, pointedly asking Jim not to reveal to those at home that his mate Tom Alford was now in hospital. Allan was already protecting those he loved from the reality of his experiences; like many of his fellow soldiers his true feelings would be concealed in humour and ironic understatement.

Military Camp
Bendigo Monday 6-3-1916
Dear Mother Father and Brothers

Well Mum I enjoy this life first rate so do the other lads. Well they are rocking the drill into us. We got the rifles today so it looks like if somethings doing. Our Officers are all first rate men you could not better them don't matter where you go. There are about 1100 men in camp now and another 600 coming in this week so things will be pretty lively soon. We are still up in the grandstand but we are shifting to B company tents tomorrow thank god as the grandstand is very draughty and things seem to be so unsettled up there but still the life is lovely. Well mum when you write still address the letters to Z Company because I am not sure whether we will be going away to Melbourne this week or not. It puts a lovely feeling through you when you see about 1000 men marching and the band playing I often think if only I could get at the b___ germans.

Well mum I got a letter from Jim and one from a friend in Pyramid and by hell they were welcome too. Jim has not been to good according to his letter. We all went to Bendigo on Sunday. Percy and I went to Gibsons but I only stayed a little while but Percy stayed till late. I went to Clee's for tea. They are bonzer people. I really did enjoy myself. The old man and I did have some fun. Well as for Annie I simply love her I think she is of a lovely disposition. At 9 oclock I left for camp but not a dam move could I take till I had supper. Then mum and dad and Annie and I went to [the] fountain and then they bid me good night.[4] I must go up there every time I come into Bendigo so they say and by hell I am going too when ever I get a chance. It is simply lovely to have a place like that to go to. I am taking Percy with me next time too. There is nothing to go into Bendigo without you having some friends to see. I do like old dad he is a great one to laugh. Well mum you have heard enough about now as for the camp. The tucker is not the best and it is scarce at present on account of us new recruits being in Z Company. Z Company consists of men who cannot get on with their drill and new recruits. We are all in B Company but have our meals with Z Company on account of there being no tents for us but we will be shifted tomorrow. There must be about 50 chaps here that I know – and it seems like home with one or two exceptions. Well mum I expect a letter from you tomorrow this is about the 16 letter I have wrote all together now. There is boxing here tonight but I am too busy to go. I will drop a line every day while there is something to write about. Well mum we have all had a bit of trouble at night but are over it now. There [are] any amount of amusements here such as concerts boxing bobs coits and billiards. In the day time one really has no time to think of anything but drill. I am going to drop Jim a line now. It is raining now but we are quite safe so goodnight mum. I hope you are all well as it leaves us now at present.

I remain Your Loving Son
Allan S

Pte A S Marlow
… Percy is busy writing in the Salvation tent but I don't know who to_____.
Tell Albert I will drop him a line.

Bendigo
Tuesday 7-3-16
Dear Albert

Well Albert things are progressing well I have just stopped laughing I am sure I laughed for about 20 minutes at Peter Owens. He went to salute an officer very smartly and he gave himself a hell of a hit on the nose. It was so funny. They rocked the drill into us today very solid. About 120 men came into camp today and there is a hell of a crowd here now. I got mum's and your letter today. If you come down Thursday come out to the camp on Friday you can get in at 4 oclock. We will be in Bendigo Saturday and Sunday that is if I am not on bloody guard it looks like if I am going on but never mind it is all in the game and the game must be played. Well Albert there is a concert here tonight but I am too busy writing. Alby Windridge is here in camp just camped by us. I suppose things are quiet up there. I also got the paper you sent. I am quite settled down to this life now and I like it [in] town. Well Albert the lights are about to go out so goodnight. Will write tomorrow. I am writing to George tomorrow.

I remain
Your loving Brother

On the same day, Percy also wrote home, describing his increasing adjustment to life as a soldier:

Bendigo
7th

Dear Mum & Dad

Well I am still alive, hoping you are the same. We are just enjoying the luxuries of camp life, we got our residence in the grand stand, sleeping between the seats, the other night one of the springs broke. Well Mum it is a good life a bit stiff for a start but it will be all right after a while. We get bread and jam for tea boiled beef for breakfast stew or curry for dinner, not a bad course is it. It would make you laugh to see us at meals, we look like a lot of tramps. There don't seem to be any more coming down from up that way. I suppose their feet is too cold. We get off of a Sunday and half a day

Saturday We got to march in next Saturday. Well Mum I think I have told you all the news. So I am your loving son

Percy

A little over a week later Allan and Percy were making arrangements to come home:

16-3-1916
Dear Jim

I received your welcome short note today. Sorry to hear that your head has been bad again. Well Jim I think it to be certain that we will be up Saturday morning and will leave about 3 oclock on Sunday as the car will have to go around to Streets and Townsend place but some of you go to the post office Saturday morning and if I am coming I will send a wire so don't forget to go to the post about 10 or half past but I think it a cert that we will be home. But tell mum and dad not to put their weekend holiday off for me. Well I am tip top and the other boys have recovered from their inoculation but, next week will be a bugger on account of us to be vaccinated. Well Jim this is a hurried note as I want to catch the post you will get this tomorrow. We had an easy day again today. Tom Alford is in the hospital but don't say a word to any one but them at home. I have not seen Albert since Sunday.

All the news so goodbye
I remain your loving bro
Allan

Bendigo
27-3-16
Dear Mum

… We went into Bendigo on Friday night but things were very quiet and we came back to camp early. We also went into Bendigo on Saturday afternoon – it was very quiet too. We were looking for Albert but he went to the Ballarat Picnic and came back the same night. We saw him on Sunday but he went out to tea somewhere both he and Percy. Sunday was a bad day here it was terribly dusty and windy. We were inoculated on Friday we had

a double dose but never affected us a slight bit. Albert is coming out to camp tomorrow and is coming home on Wednesday I will give him a parcel of clothes to fetch home. Percy and I are putting in for leave next Saturday and if we get it I will go straight to Pyramid. Mother we do not get much time to write now as we have to go out on night parade every night now it is to keep the lads out of town when they have not [got] leave. I received a letter from Georgie yesterday but he did not have much news. Well mum Percy, Les and I volunteered for the reinforcements that H Johnson was in but they would not give us a transfer from the machine guns we were terribly wild about it I can tell you. We tried very hard to get away. Tom and Charlie did not like the idea of going away so soon. They were very down on it. Well Mum ever since we came down here it has been nothing else but shifting, we had another shift today it is no good to us and we told the lieut that today. I believe they are giving the lads a send off tonight. Write and tell me all about it. I think we are sure to get away next Saturday. Percy has just told me that Auntie Florrie is coming down next Friday I suppose if she comes he wont go down but put in for leave the following Saturday. Well Mum this is all the news today but will write again to morrow. I am writing to Geordie to morrow. I also got a letter from Charlie. Well mum goodnight

I remain your loving son
Allan
Same address
Please excuse writing and mistakes

As Allan wrote to his family describing the plight of his friend Tom Alford, he could not have predicted that, just a few days later, he would also find himself hospitalised along with another neighbour, Les Townsend. The meningitis epidemic was now out of control and the restless soldiers were soon quarantined in camp.

Bendigo
Thursday
Dear Jim

Just a few lines to let you know, all is well Allan is not as good as last time, I wrote, I was going to write last night but he seemed pretty crook his tem was 102 and I thought I would wait till this morning and if he was worse I would phone up, but he is a bit better. Les [Townsend] was brought to the Bendigo hospital last night he was very bad, and after he went to the doctor, they kept him in the tent for about ¾ of an hour, before they took him away, it is rotten the way they treat crook men. We have not heard what is the matter with him. We were out to the range yesterday and Les should have fell out before.

We tried to get on the phone last night so as Townsends would hear at the dance but it was to late. Well I am trying to write this in the tent and I have no time so will close

From your loving brother
Percy

Once recovered, Allan wrote home:

Dear Mum
Just a few lines to let you know that I am pretty well. I came out of the hospital today and I was [not] sorry either as the treatment was something awful. We got boiled rice for breakfast stew for dinner bread & jam for tea. They were nearly taking me into the Bendigo hospital with Les only my temperature fell. Poor old Les looked bad but I rung the hospital up today and they said he was getting better. Well Mum there was another case of meningitis yesterday and the sickness is getting worse. Percy wrote 2 or 3 letters up to you while I was in hospital. It is a terror the camp been closed on Saturday and Sunday. Tell Charlie I will write to him on Sunday. We have no idea when we are sailing of course we hear a lot of rumours. If you see any of the Townsends on Sunday tell them I am writing to them. I have no drill to do this week. I always go over and make toast for myself every mealtime while I am off duty now and it is just the thing too. We were issued with our seakit today. Well Mum news is scarce so I think I had better close I write again on Sunday all the rest of the lads are as well so goodbye for the present. Have you got the photos yet

I remain
Your loving son
Allan

Bendigo, Sunday 1916
Dear Mum

Another few lines again today to let you know that we are well. Ted Bennits went into the hospital yesterday. Bill and Les are still in the hospital. I received your welcome letters. I also got the hamper yesterday by the amount of goods they sent one would really think that we are staying here for 12 months. Talk about a hamper it was bonzer. It took 2 of us to carry. There were all sorts of things in – cakes fowls pastrie sauce sausages milk apples pears and goodness knows what and we being under isolation nothing could have been more acceptable. I bring Billy Street and Ted Bennits some every day. I don't know who it is all from so I am sending a letter of thanks on behalf my tent mates and myself to the Pyramid advertiser. Mrs Gamble packed [a] Box of cakes and things for us so I will also send her a letter thanking her. Well Mum things have got to a bad state down here with the sickness, there is a terrible lot [of] it. Our colonel is in the Bendigo hospital sick. Major Henderson is also isolated in Melbourne as a meningitis carrier. They say they never seen a worse case than his and he will never get with us. Our O.C. [officer commanding] told us today that we are going to shift camp. The rest of the camps that the battalions are in are also isolated so goodness knows when we will get away. I wish they would send us away at once. The lads are playing up at the main gate today they reckon that they are going out and the guard are using ball Ammunition so if they get out things will be a bit mixed. They are hooting the guard and calling them everything and the poor devils can not help it. If I was on guard I am dam sure I would not stand it. I don't know what they want to go out for as everything is very comfortable here especially when you have a hamper in front of you. I have about 12 letters to write so I have my work cut out. We were out on church parade this morning and it was very good. Have you found the sheep yet. Percy had the earache very bad the other night but he got his ear syringed out and he is better now. My cold is absolutely better now and I don't think I ever felt better. Well mum we got another uniform yesterday we have everything ready for sailing I am buying a new pair of military boots here as the other ones hurt my feet terribly I will send them up to Albert he [may] want to get them mended at the toes but they are a bonzer pair of boots. I will send them up at once if we are allowed send parcels away. I will also put a testament in the boots as I don't want it because I had one given to me …

Tuesday 1916
Dear Mum

Well Mum it is a long time since I got a letter from you. I am better than ever now but Will Street went into the hospital to day and I think they are taking him in Bendigo as he is pretty bad. Well Mum we shifted camp yesterday we shifted on to the parade ground and I think it will check the sickness a lot. I rung up about Les to night and they told me he is getting on splendid. I wrote to Townsends on Sunday. Well Mum how are things up Mologa way. How are the crops. They say we are not sailing for another 3 weeks. We are bound to be up again before we go anyhow I hope so. This camp being closed is a terror and the tucker seems to be very much off too. I can tell you when it opens again I am going to have a big feed. We get bread and jam for dinner now … We have to gargle twice a day now. We go to bed about 7 oclock every night. Ted Bennitts is fighting in the heavy weight boxing to morrow night. Tell me if any of the Townsends are in Bendigo. How are the Johnsons getting on. Well Mum we heard to night that the camp will be open next Sunday I hope so anyhow. Well Mum this is all the news to night so goodbye for the present and I hope you are all well.

I remain your loving Son
Allan

THREE
THE GUNS DO ROAR AT TIMES …

FRANCE

As the winter snow thawed on the Western Front, the Allies were now spread the length of the line with the Belgian army holding some 30 kilometres north of Ypres to Nieuport on the coast. The British army (including the dominion troops of Canada and India) held 130 kilometres from Ypres to the village of Albert in France. The French held the remaining 600 kilometres to the Swiss border.[1] A zigzag line of trenches snaked its way across the countryside with networks of communication trenches linking the front to the rear supply areas. Since November 1914, following the German failure to break through in the First Battle of Ypres and again after Second Ypres which had commenced three days before the Gallipoli landing on 22 April 1915, the whole front had been deadlocked. It was in this second bitter battle for the Belgian city, a German offensive which British and Canadian forces had repelled, that German forces first used poisonous chlorine gas as a new and deadly weapon of war.

With the Russian army driven back on the Eastern Front, German forces concentrated their effort on the French fortress of Verdun, launching their attack on 21 February 1916. The battle raged until December of that year and cost over 300,000 casualties on each side, French and German.[2]

The embattled Allied forces were soon to be reinforced by the 40,000 Australian and 18,500 New Zealand troops of I Anzac, now en route to the Western Front. But the voyage across the Mediterranean to Marseilles on the southern coast of France was not without its hazards as enemy submarines actively searched for targets. The hapless transport *Minneapolis* was lost on its return voyage from Marseilles. All Australian transports were now on full alert and, in the event of a submarine sighting, were prepared for action.

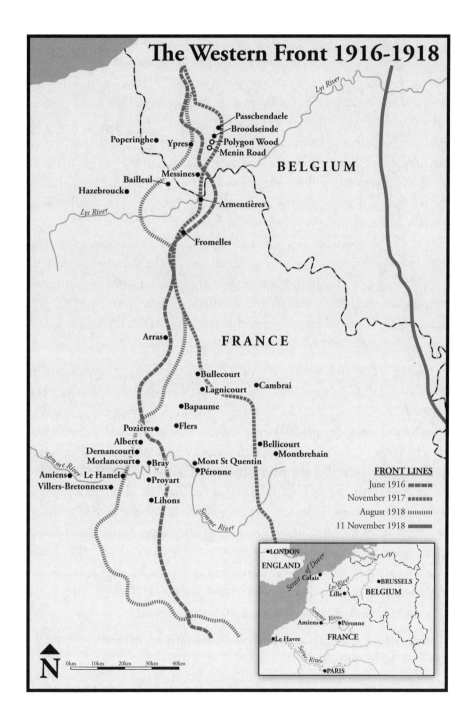

Map 2: The Western Front 1916–1918

George disembarked at Marseilles on 31 March and immediately began the cramped 58-hour rail journey north, following the valley of the River Rhone. Despite their confined and often uncomfortable conditions, the troops marvelled at the beautiful spring countryside of southern France. After the hot, featureless sands of Egypt, the sight of blossoming orchards, rows of vineyards and fattened sheep grazing in the lush pastures of France was met with delight; this was a landscape at which to marvel, particularly for those troops who, like George, were farmers by occupation. During their occasional stops for tea and coffee, the troops were met by local women and their daughters whose husbands, fathers, sons and brothers were in the northern reaches of France repelling the invading army. As the trains passed through the picturesque villages and verdant fields, workers stopped to wave, clearly displaying their appreciation for the Australian contingent which had arrived to help them in their hour of need. The new arrivals bolstered French hope that the slaughter of their men would cease and the tide turned against the German invader.

Bypassing Paris and with the weather turning bleak, the Australians travelled on to Calais on the northern coast and then inland where the troops from the 1st Division disembarked and, following an exhausting 30-kilometre march, reached their billets in the villages surrounding Hazebrouck, a small railway centre in French Flanders some 27 kilometres from the front line. The division was allotted to the British Second Army under the command of General Sir Hubert Plumer. Plumer's army was holding the front with French and Belgian troops on either side. Billeted on farms in barns and huts surrounding the village of La Créche, the soldiers enjoyed helping the country people, particularly 'Madame' whose husband and sons were at the front. The locals sold beer, coffee, chocolate and eggs to the appreciative Australians. The estaminets, or local cafes, maintained a lively trade in beer and wine.

George wrote letters home describing his arrival in France and also jotted in his notebook:

> Left Serapeum on March 25th for Alexandria & left there on Monday 27th & arrived at Marseilles on Friday 31st and left there at 9 o'clock P.M. & arrived at La Creche on April 3rd

His letter reveals more of his journey and his transition to a chilly northern France now in the midst of the winter thaw. While relatively safe in billets well behind the front line, George could hear the roar of the guns as he prepared for his first experience of the trenches. His letter reassures his family that they need not be concerned if he writes less frequently as he doubts he will have many opportunities to write once he reaches the line. He was soon on his way forward, his ears already ringing from the roar of the guns and his body tensed in anticipation of the battles to come. Before long he would be an experienced soldier who could determine the direction of an enemy bullet simply by its sound, would understand intuitively when to take cover from artillery fire and recognise the sounds of the shells that signalled when it was time to rush for a gas mask.

France
April 4ᵗʰ 1916
Dear Mother, Father & Brothers

Just a few lines to let you know that I am now in France but the name of the place I don't know but they call it French Flanders, in fact we are just about in Belgium. We left Serapeum down on the Canal on Saturday 25ᵗʰ of march at 8 oclock in the morning at [and] arrived at Alexandra at 5 oclock on Sunday morning and went on board the Megantic a big white star liner she was a bonzer boat, she carried 2000 of us, the 7 and 8 Batts. We remained on the boat all day Sunday and left there on Monday morning and after sailing for 5 days we arrived at Marseilles, for the first 3 days the sea was very calm and as smooth as a board, but after that it got rough and at night it blew like the devil, I was on submarine guard and there were men sick all over the boat, I was right up on top and had to hold on to the railing to keep up as the boat was rocking and the wind was blowing that much but I never felt a bit sick. Well after we got off the boat at Marseilles we got on the train there and travelled for 3 days and 3 nights. Nearly all the fields here are worked by the old men, boys and the women and most of the people are in mourning. It is much different here to Egypt. I found it fairly cold at first but am getting used to it now. They tell us that there was a foot of snow here about 3 weeks before we landed here. We are not in the trenches yet but not far from them, can hear the guns going off quite easily, I don't know what time we are going in but have to be fixed up with every thing, we are not allowed to say much about the place or what we are doing. Don't expect many letters as I wont be able to write very often. A few days before we left the canal we got a big bag of mail the first I had got for months, I got 20 letters altogether and they had been all over Egypt most of them had been written in Dec and Jan. but there are still a lot somewhere. I got 4 from home, 4 from Charlie, 2 from Allan, 1 from Percy and the rest from Gibson, Cheyne, Clees and Sharps. I never got the Australasian. I suppose Al and Percy are in camp by now as you say they are enlisting, I might chance to meet them some time if they get in the same brigade as me. I will give you my address again D Coy 7 Batt 2 Brigade [crossed out but legible] *I have just been told we are not allowed to put our addresses in, but if you have got my other letters you will have my address. Well I don't think there is any else I can say so will close hoping all are well as I am at present with best wishes to all*

From
Geordie

The embroidered card George sent home to his father.

France
Dear Father

Just a line to let you know I am well hoping all are the same. It is fairly cold and has been raining. We are camped in the farm houses and small huts here, there are a lot of houses and small villages here and the people are mostly farmers but seem to be on a small scale. Well we are not allowed to say anything about our doings so will close

From your loving son
George

Training began immediately the men arrived in Flanders and the Australians were surprised to find the farming community going about their daily business so close to the front line. In some cases, schools remained open only two or three kilometres behind the line. With the early crops just emerging, the Australians carefully avoided walking through the fields so as not to trample the young shoots. Much of their training consisted of long marches, lectures and practical experience with gas warfare, while selected men were sent to trench mortar, sniping and bombing schools. The troops were issued with new clothing and the claustrophobic flannel gas helmets and goggles impregnated with chemicals designed to protect soldiers from this new and insidious form of warfare. Steel helmets were used in the front-line trenches and passed to incoming units as they arrived to take over the line.

Writing to Charlie, George warns his older brother not to enlist. He is closer to the bitter reality of warfare and can feel the earth tremble from the guns; he has seen the wounded and maimed — the results of massed shellfire. While acknowledging that conscription in Australia was all but certain, he is adamant that offering three brothers was enough sacrifice for one family.

France
Dear Charlie

… I suppose by the time this letter reaches you, you will know that we are in frogland where the pigs root for sunshine. We are not allowed to say what

time we arrived here or where we are so I cant tell you much. It is very cold here and is raining nearly every day so makes things a bit miserable ... on our train ride we saw a lot of the country and towns, of course it is all small villages here, houses all along the line and all are made of brick and stone with tiled roofs also thatched ones. All the fields are worked by the old men, women and boys, it seems fairly good ground but so very hilly. They are big cockies here one and two horse teams but the machinery they use is very light and like what they used in the olden times the only up to date machine that I have seen yet is a McCormick binder. Back a bit from here they grow a lot of hops there must be a lot of work with them as they have a devil of a lot of poles up about 20 feet long and very close together, and on the first part of our journey they seem to go in for fruit and vegetables, on our way through we passed fairly close to Paris. Well we are not in the firing line yet, well not in the trenches but could be easily shelled the airplanes were having a great go a couple of days ago and a piece of shell dropped along side one of our huts. We are 4 miles further on than what we were at first. Some of our officers and N.C.O.'s have been out to the trenches to see how things are fixed up so I suppose it wont be long before we go in, some of the Australians are already in them. I met Sam Crossman the other night he is in the ammunition column, he looks real well. We are billeted in huts and houses and when we reached here I was surprised to see all people going about their work just behind the firing line as if there was no war on. Just before we left the canal we got a big bag of mail ... as you say Percy & Allan are going to enlist I suppose they will be in camp by now. You were asking in one of your letters about you enlisting I think with Percy and Allan there will be enough of us in it, let some of those other cold footed fellows come ... Archie Bailey is still hanging to it, he went into the Non Cons school while in Egypt and qualified for a corporal but hasn't got any stripes yet but will have a chance when some of the other corporals get put out of action. There are about 6 chaps from Cohuna way in my company. My address 2748 D Coy., 7 Batt, 2nd Brigade A.I.F. Abroad. We are only allowed to put our address in the body of the letter, they have funny ideas in the military. Well it is raining again, they say it is spring here now I don't know what it must be like in the winter, just before we arrived here there was a foot of snow on the ground, one day when we were moving out further it started to snow. The first mail *that our battalion has got here has been delivered today but there were none for us that transferred from the 21, 22 and 24 Batts, and they say according to their letters that it is almost certain to be compulsory in Australia soon. That mail that we got at the Canal is the only one that we have got since Xmas, those that always belonged or came as reinforcements to the 7th Batt, get their letters regular. Well Charlie don't expect many letters as I wont be able to write, I wrote a letter to them at home about a fortnight ago from here. The guns roar like the devil and mostly in the evening and morning some of them shake the houses right back past here. Well I think I will now close hoping all are well*

I remain your affectionate Bro
Geordie

We can get a feed of eggs and coffee here. The women come round selling buns & chocolate. They are mostly refugees. I hope the case of apples turn out lucky. I didn't get the paper.

In early April, the 2nd Division (I Anzac Corps) moved forward to take over a 16-kilometre section of the front line from east of the village of Armentieres to the Sugarloaf salient, a German position which projected into the Allied line on Aubers Ridge near occupied Fromelles.[3] The 2nd Division was commanded by English-born Major General James Legge, a Sydney University law graduate. The 1st Division, including George's 7th Battalion, marched through rain and snow on 14 April to reach 'the Nursery', so named as it was a relatively quiet sector, ideal for new arrivals.[4] The 1st Division moved into reserve to the south of the 2nd Division. George was about to experience duty in the line for the first time.

In the front-line trenches, the troops 'stood to' for an hour at dawn and again at sunset. During 'stand to' the men stood below the parapets with their rifles loaded and their bayonets fixed, keeping watch across the barbed wire into no man's land, ready for an enemy attack. Dawn and dusk were considered the most likely time of attack and 'stand to' was a practice that continued throughout the war. At night, men would venture into no man's land on listening patrols to gather intelligence or to search for the dead and wounded. Before dawn, rations, ammunition and trench fortification materials would be brought up from the busy rear areas on divisional wagons and delivered to the battalion quartermaster. A fatigue party delivered the supplies to the front lines via the complex network of communication trenches that traversed the fields. Owing to the boggy conditions in Flanders, the trenches were sandbagged breastworks with wooden duckboards at ground level to allow drainage, but which by now were rotten and collapsed. Troops were regularly withdrawn to farms and villages for rest and British canteens, communal baths and delousing facilities were available. Working parties also laid underground telephone lines at night. By the end of June, the 1st Division had dug 24 kilometres of cable trench. Night patrols were also sent into no man's land to reconnoitre enemy positions and repair any sections of damaged barbed-wire defences.

As George adjusted to life in the trenches, he wrote to Allan who, while hoping soon to embark, remained in camp at Bendigo. Given the usual delay in the delivery of letters from the front, Allan was unlikely to have received his brother's letter prior to his departure. George had now experienced the trauma of trench warfare and seems to accept that death is inevitable, commenting: 'There hasn't been many of our troops killed yet.' He was witnessing the stark truth of the carnage first-hand and this hardened attitude characterised his way of coping.

Dear Allan

Just a few lines to let you know how I am getting on, I don't know whether it will reach you before you sail as you said you were going into camp on the 1ˢᵗ March. I picked up a Bendigo paper over here and noticed that Percy had enlisted and passed so I suppose the both of you will be going in together so if you should be lucky enough to get in the second brigade I will stand a good chance of meeting you both over here, the four battalions in my brigade are the 5,6,7 and 8 Batts. I don't think you will see Egypt, you will be dam lucky if you don't, I think you will either go to England or straight to France. Well when we first landed here it was very cold and rained nearly every day but now it is getting warmer. There hasn't been many of our troops killed yet, the guns do roar at times, last night our guns were letting a few go and my word they did make a row. Well Allan the censor is very strict here so I cant tell you anything. Just before we left Serapeum down on the Canal we received a lot of mail, the only I have received since Xmas I got two from you one dated 26 Dec the other 2ⁿᵈ Jan, it is only us that were transferred from the 21 Batt that are not receiving the letters but soon I ought to get some with my new address. I haven't seen Amos since we have been here but used to see him often at the Canal he says Charlie Cockcroft isn't in the 5 Batt so I don't know where he can be, he came over as reinforcements to the fifth. Dave Fyffe and Vic Winterbottom are stopping a long while in camp. I hope you receive this letter. I hope they send the addresses of my relatives in England as I stand a chance of getting a trip over there after being in the firing line a certain time. Well Al I will close now hoping all are well, so good luck and goodbye

George

On 20 April George volunteered to transfer to the 2nd Brigade's 2nd Light Trench Mortar Battery. The light trench mortar was a recently developed rapid-fire gun labelled the Stokes mortar after its inventor, and was used by the infantry in the front line; four mortars were allocated to each battalion, one for each company. The Stokes was a carefully guarded secret, its use strictly rationed so as to retain the element of surprise and increase its effectiveness in forthcoming Allied offensives. As the last days of April drew to a close, the arrival of Commander-in-Chief Sir Douglas Haig to inspect the 2nd Brigade signalled the move to the front-line trenches at Fleurbaix, just a few kilometres from a village named Fromelles.

MOLOGA, APRIL

In Mologa, the family was preparing to farewell both Allan and Percy. In nearby Pyramid Hill, where Allan had worked at the store and volunteered in the fire brigade, he was given a rousing send-off as reported in the *Pyramid Hill Advertiser*. During his speech, the local fire brigade captain strongly advised Allan to choose an Australian bride. At the time, Allan was courting a young lady from Pyramid Hill and the advice, delivered in a very public forum, may have caused some discomfort to the young man. As the war dragged on, his later letters reveal a cooling of his courtship. The impact of war infiltrated all facets of life in countless ways and young love was not immune.

Farewell to Soldiers

A large number of the district soldiers being on the final leave from Bendigo and other camps last week-end, there were a good many farewell gatherings on Saturday and Monday evenings.

At Pyramid Hill

The populace assembled in the Victoria Hall to bid adieu to Privates J.R. McDonald, W.S. McKinnon, Alan Marlow and Frank Dee … Mr E. Lyndon Smith gave an address. We of this fair, sunny land, he remarked so far away from the scene of conflict, could not fully realise the mighty struggle that was shaking Europe to its foundations; but there were continual reminders of the terrible war being waged in the coming and going of their soldiers and the other daily preparations for participation in the fight; and more especially, as was fitting in the departure of their fellow-citizens who had joined the Australian forces. If Britain failed in the struggle the consequences would be more serious to Australia than many realised. The record of enlistments in the Gordon Shire, as revealed by the Chairman was very good … They all heartily wished success to the men at present leaving, a safe and prosperous expedition and a safe return. He congratulated them in the part they were playing…

FIRE BRIGADE VALEDICTORY

Later in the evening Private A Marlow, who was a member of the Pyramid Fire Brigade when he enlisted, was entertained by that body at Mrs Finemore's dining rooms, and a very fine spread was prepared by the proprietress. Capt. Cardillini was in the chair, and the comestibles having been enjoyed, he addressed the company in regard to Private Marlow's work as a fireman. He had proved there that whatever he took in hand he did well and was always keen on making it a success. In his travels and while engaged in duties he was now undertaking, he had no doubt he would prove to be what he had been with them – a man. They had heard of marriages being contracted in England by Australian soldiers, but he hoped that if Private Marlow ever thought of looking for a wife he would choose an Australian as a bride. An Australian; his mother had reared him; and he could not do better than follow his father's example by choosing one here. He was assured that Private Marlow would acquit himself well. The President, Mr Seales, spoke of the courage shown by Private Marlow, who was the second of the family to volunteer; and hoped he would be spared to be amongst them again. He also complimented guest on his fire brigade work. Fireman T. Kelly said he had been to demonstrations with Fireman Marlow and found him keen in his work, always doing his utmost in assisting his team in the hope of winning a trophy. He wished him a safe return.

Mr M.D. Grant, one of the Brigade auditors, said he was pleased at the stand taken by their friend, Alan Marlow. His work as a fireman evidenced that if occasion required he would be quick at machine gun operations. The Australians who had already been in the fighting showed they were made of the real stuff, and that had a good effect on those following. The experiences abroad had a beneficial effect on men who got through safely. He heartily wished Private Marlow a safe return ... Private Marlow expresses his high appreciation of their sentiments and the memento. He assured them that when he went abroad he would never forget his connection with the Brigade, which was one of his most pleasant associations. He thanked them most sincerely[5] ...

So went the stirring farewells, the public accolades, the rousing applause and the wishes for a safe return. For those who had yet to enlist, the pressure was mounting.

Decades on, I wonder whether Sarah knew just what Albert was planning on that April day when he caught the train with his neighbour Will Jones to spend a few days in Bendigo. Albert's bold move, lying about his age in order to enlist, was often discussed in our family. His enlistment details provide some explanation. At 18 Albert was officially too young to enlist, as parental approval was required from the age of 19 until the young man turned 21.[6] If not for a surviving section of a letter, the story of Albert's enlistment would have remained a mystery. It seems that sometime in April Albert attempted to enlist without parental approval, telling the recruiters that he was 21. It was not the first time, and Albert and his friend Will were once again 'thrown out', a perceived injustice in the minds of the colluding pair who had heard of boys as young as 14 who had enlisted and died for king and country. No doubt it was a relief to Sarah that Albert's application had been rejected; with Allan and Percy's final leave just around the corner, three boys in France was enough, and her family could never be accused of not doing its duty.

Allan wrote home to Charlie of the incident, the first page of his letter missing:

… I believe Will Jones and Albert got thrown out I knew they would. I met Jim Gibson in Bendigo last night. I believe things are only middling at the shop. I intend to go through to Pyramid on Saturday. Our bugle has just gone for night parade so I will finish it when we come in. Well Charlie we have just come in off night parade it is now about 9-30 and the buggers are rousing about the candle being alight. We are going to Port Melbourne on the 24th of this month for certain. I will tell you all the news on Sunday.

I remain Your loving Brother
Allan
We are well hoping all are the same.

While Albert's family may have been pleased that he had been refused enlistment, this young country boy, for whom a trip to Melbourne was a highlight, was bitterly disappointed. His brothers were off on their grand adventure and many of his mates had now enlisted. He felt compelled to join them and he was determined somehow to achieve this. Perhaps if Albert had read Allan's following letter his resolve may have weakened. Having been transferred to the camp at Port Melbourne and arriving in the dark, Allan woke to discover what he later scathingly christened 'Port Hell'.

Port Melbourne
Thursday
Dear Mum and Dad and Brothers

Well Mum we arrived here at last. We left Bendigo by the 3.15 train in the afternoon. We could not get away sooner as we could not get our kit sooner. We got to North Port at 9 oclock as we waited there for our kits. Then we had to march out to the camp about 1 mile and a half it was terribly dark and no one seemed to know the track. The road was terribly wet we got out here about 10 and had bread and jam for tea and then slept in a bit of a hut. This morning when I woke up I could have shot myself. I was that disgusted you never saw such a camp in all your life. It is rotten cold stinking smokey wet camp, no canteen only a bit of a thing run by two tramps no post office no writing room and no paper in the camp to write. I had to walk about a mile to night to buy a pad and now I have no stamps. The dam place seems to be surrounded by sea what I can see about it and talk about cold it is a bugger. And the ground is sopping wet. The tucker is something awful I will give you [an] idea of what we get ½ loaf of bread and 1 tin of jam between the 8 of us isn't that awful. Well mum when Charlie comes down send that black and white jersey of mine with him I will not want it before. I heard to night that we sail on the 14th and we go to Aldershot so that won't be too bad. The camp is in complete darkness at night time. Well mum I never want another final leave one is enough for me. Well mum I think I have told you all the news. We are going into Melbourne on Saturday for a good feed. Well mum I will now close hoping you are all well as it leaves us at present. I will write to morrow again

I remain your loving Son
Allan

Tell Charlie I will wire him when we will sail
Don't send any tucker down as we might not get it
Excuse writing as it is that dam cold
Address Pte AS Marlow
Machine Gun Section
38th Battalion
Port Melbourne

I suspect Allan's desire to 'never have another final leave' refers to being the centre of attention at another public farewell as reported in the local newspaper:

MOLOGA

On Monday evening in the Mologa Hall a large crowd assembled in spite of the weather, to bid farewell to three departing soldiers, namely, Ptes W. Street, L. Townsend, and A. Marlow. The three soldiers returned home on final leave on Thursday last, all looking well after their passing … The following soldiers have gone from this district and have received presentations – Prs. J. Ryan, T. Gray, G. Marlow, A. Haw. J. Leed, P. Fyffe, C. Fyffe, T. Alford, E. Johnson, W. Street, F. Townsend, A. Marlow, P. Marlow, J. Price, P. Ryan.[7]

In a portrait taken in Bendigo, Allan and Percy stand in front, while the man on the right is Les Townsend. In the centre is Ewen Johnson and on the left is possibly Bill Street.

MELBOURNE, MAY

Despite hopes of sailing promptly, Allan and Percy remained in the bleak camps of Port Melbourne for the month of May. Their departure was delayed while illness ravaged the troops and meningitis remained a constant threat.

Port Melbourne
Monday night
Dear Mum & Dad

Well Mum I am dead tired I have a job to write I am that tired. We left the camp this morning at 9 oclock and went into Melbourne to march. We met the Bendigo Seymour Ballarat Broadmeadows battalions there. Then we marched all over Melbourne with full kits up it was a fair terror. There was about 5000 of us all to gether, it was a very nice sight for those who were looking on but not nice for us. I never saw such a crowd in my life before. We got a slice of bread and jam at 3 oclock for dinner and then we came out to the camp and had tea. Well Mum I will be glad when we get out of this camp because it is a fair terror. You have no idea what it is like. I went up to buy 12 stamps tonight and all I could get was one … I like the machine-gun work there is no bally marching with it but I do not like this camp. Les has been crook ever since his final he has a terrible bad cold but is nearly better now. On Sunday we went out to Geelong on the boat. We left at 11 and got back at 7. It was a bonzer trip. We did not get sick at all. Next Sunday we are going out to Sharp's. We are sailing about the 14 allright our Lieut told us it would be one day next week anyhow I will wire you for certain. Well Mum this is all the news to night. We had our photos taken on Saturday at Kalma.[8] *They cost 20/- a dozen with an enlargement. We also had our photos taken on Saturday in one of those joints where they take them in 5 minutes I will put it in but tear it up. I weighed with my full equipment on today I was about 12 stone. This is all the news hoping you are all well as it leaves us at present.*

I remain your loving son
Allan

Percy in centre, Allan on right at the rear, standing is possibly Les Townsend.

Percy also wrote to express his displeasure at the conditions in the camp at Port Melbourne:

Port Melbourne
2nd Tuesday
Dear Mum Dad & Jim

I suppose you have been expecting a letter from me, but I did not seem to get time, the look of this dam place takes some getting over. Well Mum we are getting on nicely, I do not like the camp it is an inconvenient place quite different to Bendigo, the cook house is about a mile away. We are not far from Port Melbourne pier the ground has been tip with the rubbish of Melbourne and the sand out of the Yarra. We were on a march through Melbourne yesterday, four battalions were marching, we were going nearly three hours, the streets were packed. We went to Geelong Sunday it was a calm day and we had a good trip, there was a large crowd aboard the boat. I do not care much about Melbourne. There is a guard on here at night some of them started coming in late so they had to put on a guard. There are several transports in now. I wish we were going on them but I don't think we will be going till next week anyhow. We have a good tent that is the only dam thing good about this place, it was very windy to day and the sand would blind you. Well Mum I hope you are not worrying about us … Well Mum news is scarce so I will draw to a close.

From your loving son
Percy

Port Hell
Tuesday night
Dear Jim

Just a few lines to let you know that we are first rate but it is dam cold here at nights. We paraded for another blanket last night but could not get it. We only have 2 so you will know what its like at Port Melbourne with 2 blankets … Have you had any rain up there are you finished cropping yet. I like the machine gun work I think it very interesting and it will be more interesting when we put 500 rounds a minute into the B- germans. By hell the bullets do go some it makes you laugh to see them lobbing into the bank. Well Jim they have no system of running a camp down here talk about a mess up it is awful at times. Bendigo is worth a 100 of this one in all ways. Well Jim I think we will be going next week all right. They [say] we are sailing on the Loonich [Runic] and she is at Sydney now 2 transports sailed out today and there are four left there now we can see them quite easily from here as we are only ¼ of a mile away. We are going over to them on Saturday. On Sunday we are going to Sharps. Send their address again will you. Well Jim the measles are broke out in the camp also 130 cases of meningitis at Broadmeadows …

Port Melbourne
Wednesday Night
Dear Mother

Just a few lines to let you know that we are all well. We are in guard here to night. It is showery here to night but I don't think there will be much rain. It has been very cold here all day. Have you had any rain up there yet. I suppose every one is looking out for it. There is a transport leaving here tomorrow morning. It consists of machine gunners and artillery men. We are getting on first rate with guns. It is most interesting work. Well mum

I have not heard any more about going next week. I heard in camp to day that you and dad were coming down to see the boat out. The Townsends are coming down I believe. Well Mum news is very scarce but will always drop a line to let you know that we are well …

St Kilda Beach
Sunday 6th
Dear Mum

Well Mum you can see by the top address that we are on St Kilda Beach this morning. We came down here for a hot bath and we struck a YMCA tent for soldiers. So we are here having a cup of coffee and letter writing. The ladies here are very good to us you could not wish to meet nicer people. There is a reading and writing room here too. We came into Melbourne yesterday afternoon and stayed in all night. We went to a picture and show play at the Tivoli it was very poor. Well mum things are still the same at the camp very cold at night the tucker seems to be a little better but still plenty of room for improvement. On Saturday afternoon we had to go through our tests for the machine gun. We are passed. We have to mount the tripod, fix the gun on, load her get the range and fire in 57 seconds to. I can tell you we have to go some. We have to dismount her in about 25 seconds. I like the gun work. After we had all gone through our tests there was a go between all the squads for the championship. A chap from Kerang named Jack Hewitt and I were picked for it and we got 2nd place for mounting her and dismounting her.

Well there is no use you sending anything down to us as they say we will be going next Friday or Sunday of course we are not sure but will let you know for certain at a latter date. I would not live in Melbourne for £10 a week I think it is a terror of a place. I have not struck anyone I know yet. We all knock around together. This afternoon Percy and I are going out to Sharps but we will [not] stay long. How are things up at Mologa. Things must be very dry up there. I suppose you are looking for rain. Well Mum this is all the news today but will write to morrow. So I will now close hoping you are all well as it leaves us at present.

I remain your loving Son
Allan

Percy and Allan's dislike of the city and their displeasure at being stuck in camp was clearly growing. For country boys used to farm life and the pleasure of their mother's cooking, life at Port Melbourne was utterly miserable. Time spent learning to use the machine-gun provided their only relief. Percy wrote:

Port Melbourne
Monday
Dear Jim

I received your welcome [letter] *today and was extra pleased to hear from you; you forgot to tell me how the girl was, which I suppose you have. In reference to that question you asked whether I see any nice girls such as sometimes you see in Mologa, I do not know who you mean. You were complaining about the dry weather, well I suppose you could do with some rain, as so down here, we got a few showers, the only time we got too much was one night, we were on guard. It is a b_ of a game on guard Jim, two hours walking about. Well Jim we got another blanket tonight, it was through our Officer we got it, I tell you it was a b_ cold some nights, could hardly sleep. I suppose you got a wrinkle or two on Sunday. Albert would be in his element, tell us how things went.*

I like the guns all right, we were shooting today, it is interesting by jove she does rattle. We fired ten rounds the first time, and twenty the second time, it does shift them.

We were in Melbourne on Sunday, it was a quiet time, I am about sick of Melbourne. Les and All were in Melbourne today getting teeth out, I think I will try and get off, I have one or two bad teeth. You seem anxious to know whether they send anyone from Mitiamo to Mologa. I would not mind if they sent the Ganger daughter, down here. Well Jim I am writing this in the tent it is a cow of a place laying on the floor ...

Port Melbourne
Friday
Dear Mum Dad & Jim

... It has been a cold day down here. I dam near got frozen last night they do not give us enough blankets. Allan Les and Bill have gone into Melbourne, I

did not feel to anxious to go I had a few letters to write; there used not to be any guard down here, but some of them started coming in next morning so they put on a guard. There were some troopships go from here the other day. Some of the troops came from Broadmeadows I do not know whether Jack Price was with them or not. We will probably be going to Sharpes Sunday, it will probably be our last Sunday in Melbourne. There is a kid come round every day selling fruit pies, they are very good, the canteen here is run by outsiders it is not near as good as Bendigo. We had to pull our tents up today and take the boards out to let them dry underneath. I suppose you could do with some rain now. They are not near so strict about the tents here as in Bendigo some of them here have bags. Well Mum I think I have told you all the news so I will close

From your loving son
Percy

FRANCE, MAY

While the men of the 38th Battalion looked forward to their departure from Port Melbourne, the troops of the 1st Division remained in trenches in the Fromelles-Fleurbaix area south-west of Armentieres. They were rotated out of the line for a few days' rest and then returned to the front. On their left was the 2nd Division and further on were the New Zealanders. In the Somme valley, 100 kilometres to the south where the French and English lines met, the Allies were preparing for a major offensive. To distract enemy attention from the Somme, the Allies began shelling the enemy lines around Armentieres.

On 5 May the Australians were south of the Bridoux salient, an area of the front that had been the target of heavy German shelling since the end of April when a devastating enemy artillery bombardment had opened. As soon as the barrage ceased, German soldiers wielding bombs, daggers and revolvers stormed the Australian line in the first trench raid the 2nd Brigade had experienced. Raids were a tactic used by both the German and Allied armies to infiltrate enemy defences. Specially trained raiding parties were withdrawn, drilled and rehearsed for their role in planned small-scale attacks in which gathering intelligence, demolishing defences, killing enemy soldiers and taking prisoners were the prime objectives. The raids were sent in under cover of artillery fire or alternatively, and more often as the war progressed, in covert actions, often at night, when stealth was the key to the raiders' success. Australian soldiers built an enviable reputation as proficient and tenacious raiders.[9]

As the German artillery strafed the Bridoux salient, the Australian troops stoically endured the heaviest bombardment they had experienced at the front. The 20th Battalion was holding the salient at the time and lost four officers and 91 men killed or wounded while 11 were taken prisoner. Two of the precious Stokes mortars fell into the hands of the German raiders, an embarrassing and alarming loss to the battalion.[10] For the Australian soldiers it marked the beginning of their deadly experience of war on the Western Front.

Of this day George would simply record in his diary:

Fleurbaix Bombardment Friday May 5th

A fortnight later he wrote home from the trenches. He revealed nothing of his experiences and appeared indifferent to the shelling, writing from his dugout with the air of a seasoned veteran. In his card to his mother he did not mention the German shells, describing instead the Allied bombardment of German lines and how lovely the countryside now appeared as summer approached. Regardless of the reality, his instinct was to protect his mother from the grim reality of war. Sarah's sons would continue to write reassuring words as the war raged.

France
May 22

Dear Albert, It is fairly quiet along our trenches, the Germans are putting a few shells over just at present I am writing this in the dugout, two of us sleep in it. I am in the trench mortar battery it is a small gun for firing bombs we be in the trenches along with the infantry. I will give you my address again. 2748 Light Trench Mortar Battery 2nd Brigade Headquarters 1st Aust Division. Any letters that have been addressed to the 7 Batt I will receive alright but with this address I will get them quicker. Hoping to get a letter from some of you soon. I remain your loving Bro

George
Has Al & Percy sailed yet

France
Dear Mother

Just a card to let you know I am well hoping all are the same. It is nice weather here now and all the trees are sprouting out, everything looks lovely. Our guns were bombarding the germans heavily last night. I have written to Jim and hope you get my letters. So goodbye with love from

George

Two days later in his letter to Charlie, George's indifference to shellfire appears as an acceptance of fate; life had now become a game of chance:

France
May 24th
Dear Charlie

… We are having nice weather here now everything looks splendid, it is a great country for grass, everything grows so thick and high of course there is no stock on it to keep it down, it seems a great pity that such a fine country should be blown about as it is. It is not too bad in the trenches, where we are there are a few bombs and shells flying now and again, of course you never know when one is going to lob on top of us just got to take our chance. I am in the trench mortar battery now it is a small gun for firing bombs, we [will] be along with the infantry just the same, we have been giving them a few bombs and nearly always get some back. There seems to be a big battle on our right as we can hear the guns going day and night. I haven't seen Amos for a fair while and don't know where Charlie Cockcroft is. I think Ray Leed must be in Egypt yet he is in the 58 Batt. You remember I told you in other letters that I met young Miller from Pyramid in the Yeitoun camp well I noticed in a paper that he is seriously *ill, we very seldom get any papers to read and would be glad if you would send the Pyramid paper, wrap about 6 up together and send them, I never got that paper you sent at Xmas time …*

MELBOURNE, JUNE

As Allan and Percy waited impatiently for their departure they could not imagine what George was now experiencing in his position at the front. His letters home revealed little; they were censored and were weeks, often months reaching their destination, sometimes never arriving as ships were sunk by German submarines in the North Atlantic. Newspaper reports were censored, details were manipulated and Australian actions were generally reported as British. Only the casualty lists provided some measure of the truth.

As the meningitis epidemic continued to plague the formation of the 3rd Division, the men of the 38th Battalion underwent a stringent medical examination. All those considered to be in good health shifted camp to Campbellfield on 5 June in final preparation for departure. Allan's assessment of his latest accommodation differed little from his view of the camp at Port Melbourne.

Cambellfield
Wednesday
Dear Mum

Well Mum you will see by the top address that we are in a new camp. We got orders Monday night that we had to shift camp to Broadmeadows. We got up at 4.45 Tuesday morning and packed up. It was raining and I can tell you things were pretty sloppy, anyway we were examined before we left. Anyone with a sore throat and cold were left behind. Only young Kerr and the lads that were in the hospital were left behind. We boarded the second troop train about nine and got out to a station here about 4 o'clock. Then we marched about 1 ½ miles to the camp and it was very late when we got fixed up or I would have wrote last night. Anyway Mum the camp was very very dirty and we [were] all day in, the whole battalion, cleaning it up and it is not finished yet. The tent floors were something disgraceful you would think pigs slept in the tents. We were only issued with 3 single blankets but I got to work and got 3 more. We are not under isolation here but the camp is very poor. Anyway we will be going soon, I believe we are getting another final [leave] anyway I will be up. We can see the Broadmeadows camp from here it is only ½ a mile away. I got 5 letters today. The ones you addressed to Bendigo came in today. I believe Les has had one or two bad turns again. I don't think he will get with us and I am sorry too. Billy Street's feet are very cold he says straight out he does not want to go. He says everyday, he wished to God that he did not enlist: and poor old Les is just the opposite. Well mum we have a firm Lieutenant he is proper white man, he says he will look after us at the front. He treats us well here. Mum I want you to write to Kirby the jeweller in Bendigo and get those compasses Charlie give us we left them there to be inscribed and of course we have been under isolation and could not get them. Well Mum we will go to Sharps on Sunday. I will write again to morrow night so goodbye for the present.

I remain your loving Son
Allan

… We got our cakes down with us. They are a bonzer lot of cakes. I could fancy I could see Mrs Gamble. Tell Jim to put a nice letter in the Pyramid paper from me and on behalf of the rest of the lads thanking the Mologa people for their kindness. Tell him to stretch it out well…

After returning from his final leave, Percy wrote home:

Thursday [15 June]
Campbellfield
Dear Mum & Dad

Just a few lines to let you know, I arrived here all right, I got down about quarter past five, it was a long tiresome trip, I slept well that night. Well Mum we are going Tuesday we might be going aboard Monday, but as far as we hear it will be Tuesday morning. Peter Owens is not back yet, he sent a wire, I did not hear what was in it. I suppose you saw Les he is supposed to come back to night. Albert Brookes is transferred to our section, it was not its full strength. The Governor General was out yesterday, he presented the colours they are very pretty, there was a fair crowd out from Melbourne. We were supposed to go on a night march tonight but the doctor advised it not thank God he was right for once. We have to go for a bath to morrow, it will be all right. We have to come back Saturday night, I don't know why they want it. Well Mum news is scarce so I think I will close

From your loving son
Percy

Percy reveals little of his feelings now that his departure was imminent. By contrast, the prospect of travelling to England was clearly an adventure for Allan as he wrote to his mother to reassure her once again that he would always be safe.

Friday night [16 June]
On Town
Dear Mum,

… we are well and happy. We go on board Monday thank God. I believe we are going to England, Wont we have a fine time. We are going out to Sharps to morrow but wont stop long. I am not to keen on going but anyway I will fulfil my promise. Yes Mum we got another hamper today Les brought it down. We are not working to hard now. Just getting ready for embarking. I don't [think] *the war will last long now the Russians are smashing them up some. I am going to the train to morrow night to meet Charlie. Well mum don't worry of us I can assure you will be always safe and will be good boys. Well mum I have told Albert all the news but I will drop you a line on Sunday so goodnight Mum*

I remain
Your Loving Son
Allan

Charlie travelled to Melbourne to say his final farewell to his brothers and to pass on small gifts which Sarah and Charles hoped would bring some comfort to their sons as they embarked on their long journey. Allan and Percy made the most of their final days in Australia before they wrote their farewells to their family.

Commonwealth Hotel Melbourne, Sunday
Dear Mum & Dad

… Charlie gave me that parcel I thank you Mum for it and dad and Mum, for the money. Well we are off on Tuesday it's a good job isn't it. We met Charlie and Joe at the camp yesterday we were just coming in and they were going round the camp we weren't expecting to see them till night. It was a bad day yesterday, we went to Sharps we got a great welcome she had a nice tea for us, I enjoyed myself. When we came back we intended to go to the theatre but it was too late. Well Mum I think I have told you all the news so I will close from your loving son

Percy

Commonwealth Hotel
Melbourne Sunday
Dear Mum and Dad

Well mum you will see by the top address where we are staying. Joe Dee and Charlie Les and Frank are here with [us]. *Joe and Charlie came out to the camp yesterday morning and we all came in together. Charlie Percy and I went to Sharps yesterday morning and had a good time she had a bonnie tea for us and we left about 7 oclock. I promised to go back today to take Lily for a walk but I don't know whether I will go or not. Mum thank you for the money. I am sure we will have a good time when we get to our destination. Lily gave me another pair of socks and two pair of socks. Tell Jim I think she will be his sister all right. The old dame looks very young. They have a very nice place there. Lily is a very flash little thing now. Well Mum I think I have told you all the news but will write first chance so goodbye mum till I get back again. No need to worry we will always be safe and will return back very soon.*

I remain
Your Loving Son
Allan

Melbourne
Sunday
Dear Albert

Just a few lines to let you know that we are well. Joe and Charlie came out to the camp yesterday morning and we came in with them. Well Albert we are going on board to morrow. So I suppose it wont be too long before we are sick. Well Albert don't forget to write you will get a letter from me. I wish you had come down and we could have a good time here. Well Albert I will say goodbye to I see you again. Remember me to all.

I remain your loving Brother
Allan
Goodbye Albert old cockie

As the time for departure drew near, I doubt the youthful optimism of the twins and their efforts to reassure their mother, while noble in intent, could diminish the growing anxiety that Sarah experienced. The divided emotions of pride and apprehension as mothers waved goodbye to their sons surely brought fear of their potential loss. This goodbye could prove to be their final farewell ...

On Tuesday 20 June, HMAT *Runic* slid slowly away from Port Melbourne pier. As the ship moved out into the bay, the streams of coloured paper ribbon thrown on board by friends, family and sweethearts who bid the men of the 38th Battalion farewell were gradually severed.

AT SEA, JUNE

While many of the troops suffered from seasickness on the journey across the Indian Ocean to South Africa, Percy and Allan were more fortunate, feeling quite at ease with the rocking motion of the ship. While boredom could easily have dampened their spirits, daily drill, church services, boxing and wrestling matches kept the men entertained. Allan's enthusiasm for his adventure had yet to wane.

Dear Mum and Dad

Well Mum we are well out on the ocean at last. Percy and I are having a bonnie time we have not been sick yet but there are hundreds sick. The sea is very ruff and it is showery now and again and very windy. Last night was a wild night but it is not a bit cold. Oh Mum there are a terrible crowd of the boys sick, one does feel sorry for them. It is a bonnie sailing boat we are in.

When it gets ruff she side rocks and pitches a treat. Dad would know what that is like. I reckon that is the best joke of the lot. We get splendid tucker on board and we sleep in hammocks above the tables. I always stop on the top deck all day they say that is the best too. I got a letter from Albert this morning Percy got a letter from someone too. Well Mum I have no news to tell as we see nothing but water. Now that I have hung out so long without getting sick I think I will last the rest of the journey. We do not know where we are going. I am putting in for leave next Saturday I think I will get it. Well Mum this is all the news for the present.

I remain
Your Loving Son
Allan S
Did you fix up about the photos.
My teeth fit lovely. Thanks for the money.

Percy also wrote of settling into the routine aboard the *Runic*, albeit displaying rather less enthusiasm than his brother:

At Sea
Dear Mum and Dad

Just a few lines to let you know I am still alive, we are well out at sea now, there is water everywhere you look. It is very hot today just like Summer it has been mostly cold days since we started. We have had nearly all calm weather since we left, except a few days after we started it was rough then, I was not sick, there were a good few sick. Well mum I would like to see a paper now, it seems a long time since we seen one. We get fairly good meals on board butter and cheese twice a day and porridge for breakfast, soup for dinner. I was terrible hungry for a while after we came on, the sea seems to make you hungry. We have to do some work; drill from nine till twelve, and two till four, not very hard. We had washing parade the other day. I had a big wash, it is a great job, I think if I was to make my living at it, I would starve. We have not passed many ships, only one was close. There is boxing contests and other amusements on board. There is not much room for anything on board, such a lot of men on. I saw a whale the other day he was a big one and he looked very pretty; I don't think there is no news to tell it is very scarce on here. We have to go to church tomorrow, we will have to be in uniforms, we mostly drill in blues …

In a note to Jim, Percy added:

… the tea is not as good as in camp, it has a funny taste. We had church parade yesterday, we had to come out in uniform, we are in blues in the week. There has been a lot of wet days since we left, it is miserable on deck when it is raining. It was very hot a few days ago, but it is cool again. It is very hot down below when it is hot. We sleep in hammocks, I do not care very much about them I would sooner have the boards. We have not passed many ships, one we passed was very close, we could see the passengers on board. There is not much room for drill on board, we have some every day, it is mostly an easy time. There is a boxing contest on today. I might go and have a look at it. I suppose you are having a good time with the school teachers; has it come on to rain any time you have been there. You will be well into the ploughing now. Has Charlie any intentions of going by what he was saying to me he has. Well Jim news is scarce on here, it is a terror without any papers. Well I think I have told you all the news so I will close.

From your loving brother
Percy

FRANCE, JUNE

In an attempt to relieve pressure on the embattled French forces at Verdun, and with an eye to breaking the stalemate on the Western Front, the Allies refined their plans for an offensive in the area of the Somme River. In late June, Australian and New Zealand battalions launched trench raids on German lines at Armentieres, hoping to exhaust the enemy in preparation for the Somme Offensive. These raids were designed not only to inflict casualties, but also to gather information, take prisoners and scout the German defences to assist in the preparation for the 'big push'. German forces answered with ferocity. George wrote to his mother as the German artillery pounded the Allied trenches:

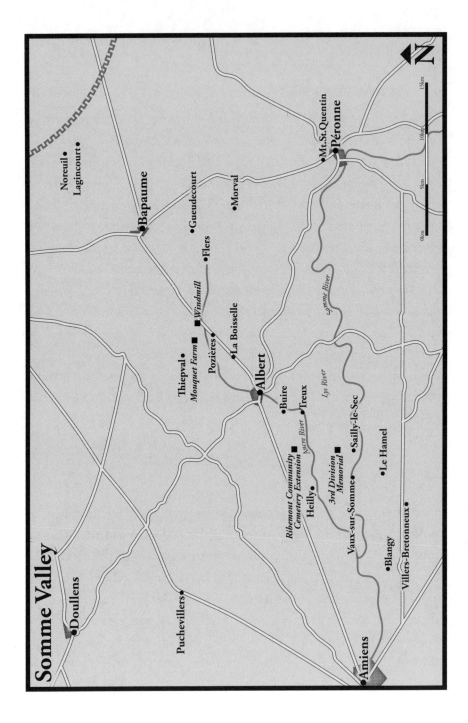

The Somme Valley

France June 2nd
Dear Mother

… I don't know whether this letter will catch this mail but I have written other letters and posted them before I got your letters. It is nice for Allan and Percy and the others to get in the Machine Gun section together I suppose they will have sailed by now, I haven't had any letters from Al since Xmas. Tom Alford and the others didn't stay long in camp I suppose they will have to finish their training over here. I suppose you know that Hughie Wales and Clift are sick in the hospital. I was very sorry to hear that young Miller died I noticed in a paper that he was ill. The last I saw of him was I think on the 22nd Feb he was quite well then I used to have a yarn with him every night, I haven't received any letter from his mother yet, Jack Jamison was looking very wretched then, there were a terrible lot of men getting sick while in Egypt of course it was a rough shop, don't worry about me I haven't had an hour's sickness since I left and I am quite happy here. I haven't met Amos since we left the desert. Arch Bailey is well. I was pleased to know that you got those silks, I sent them on the 25th Nov and I thought that you hadnt got them. I was surprised to hear that Bert Gibson is back home. Well there is some heavy bombardment going on. I will write again soon, hoping all are well.

I remain Your Loving Son
George
The letters I got were written in Feb, March and some on the 3rd April. Never got the parcel Charlie sent.

Like many Australians with relatives in England, George was keen to secure leave to visit his father's family whom he had yet to meet. His cousin, Clem Payne, had enlisted in the British Royal Navy. The Royal Navy's Grand Fleet had engaged the German High Seas Fleet in the Battle of Jutland which lasted from 31 May until 1 June 1916. Over 200 warships pounded one other with heavy losses on both sides. The German fleet finally disengaged and escaped, signalling the end of the largest naval battle of the war. German policy then focused on avoiding further engagements with the Royal Navy, pursuing instead the devastating submarine campaign which was creating havoc in the English Channel with hundreds of merchant ships destroyed. Similarly, the English blockade of German ports was having a crippling effect on the German economy.

France June 8th
Dear Father

… I received about a dozen letters about the first of the month they are the first I have received while being in France and only the second mail since Xmas. Jim sent the addresses of Lee's and Wilson and I have written to them and ought to get an answer from them soon.[11] I have been looking forward to getting leave to England but now it is cut down only one out of the Battery to go each fortnight for 7 days before it was one each week for 9 days leave so my turn is that far off that it isn't worth bothering about, had it not been cut down I would have got away in Sept. Five out of the Battery have been and they say they have had glorious times over there. Some of the chaps that have been wounded here are over in some of the hospitals in England. You will have had the news about the great naval fight I wonder if Clem Payne would be in it, there has been great losses on both sides but I think our fleet came out on top it ought to help to bring the war to an end sooner. The first news was in the Germans favor and there was great rejoicing in Berlin, they put up a notice in front of their trench about it and at the bottom they had "Poor England" I believe now they are keeping it quiet in Berlin about all their losses, there are great battles going on here and on the Russian front. It is alright for Al and all the others to be in the Machine Guns together. I told you before that I am in the Trench Mortar Battery now this is my address 2748 2 A/2 Light Trench Mortar Battery 2nd Inf Brigade Headquarters 1st Australian Division France. I haven't heard anything of Charlie Cockcroft for months I think he must have been transferred to the 7 Batt. I haven't met Amos since we have been here, I think I saw Gordon McKay one day going along in the Transport Column. Well dad there is not any news as we are not allowed to say where we are etc. So I will now close hoping all are in the best of health.

I remain
Your loving Son
George

Have you seen the Anzac books yet they are dead funny.[12]
Excuse the writing

In early June the troops received news of the death of Lord Kitchener,

Secretary of State for War. Kitchener had been aboard the warship *Hampshire,* on his way to discussions in Russia, when the ship struck a German mine near the Orkney Islands. The report of Kitchener's death was met with disbelief across the Commonwealth while the men at the front were dismayed at the passing of a man regarded as a fine old soldier.

France
Sunday June 11th 1916
Dear Mother

… We are back from the firing line now having a bit of a spell I don't know how long we will be having, it is not a bad little place where we are, I was at a small picture show last night, there are two here one is run by the soldiers club and the other is run by the Y.M.C.A., they charge ½ a franc to go in, that is 5d and are very good, fancy going to pictures behind the firing line. I told you in last letter that I received some letters but haven't got the parcels yet perhaps they will turn up soon. Fancy Lord Kitchener going down it was sudden wasn't it, we didn't believe it when we first heard about it. The Germans must have known he was going to Russia, we often hear a lot of rumours here like we heard a few days back that they had captured the Crown Prince and all his staff at Verdun, there is still heavy fighting going on there, the germans have gained a little but paid very heavily in losses for it, the Russians have taken a lot of Austrian prisoners and are still pushing them back, I wouldn't be surprised to see the war over by Xmas now that the fleets have had a great fight and ours came out on top, it ought to make a great difference …

France
June 17th 1916
Dear Charlie

Just a few lines to say I received one of the parcels a couple of days ago, it isn't the one that was sent on the first of March as it would have been addressed to the 21 Batt, this had the right address D Coy 7 Batt the other one I suppose has gone astray. The tin was in good order. I was wondering whether you sent it or Jim as the address was his writing it contained cake, pudding, tin sardines, socks, handkerchief, lollies and smokes they are always pretty safe when sent in a tin and wrapped in cloth, funny getting the tin and no letters, the letters that I got which I told you in my last letters came by the boat that left on the 4 April that is the latest letters that I have got but I believe there is some letters in now at the Battalion post office so perhaps I will get some more soon. I wrote to my cousin in England Flo Wilson but have had no reply yet …

There were no further letters from George during the remaining weeks of June. On 19 June the 1st Division marched to Neuve Eglise (now Nieuwkerke) on the Belgian border and then on to Ploegsteert in Belgium, to the north of Armentieres. The 2nd Brigade moved into the line on the night of 23/24 June. This was a well-worn sector which was regularly subjected to gas attack, artillery and mortar fire and plagued by the presence of enemy aerial surveillance. From his notebook we know that George had been on the move with the brigade and in the final days of the month he was positioned to the north at Messines, on the southern end of the embattled Ypres salient. He noted briefly:

Messines front

June 27, 28, 29, 30th

Possibly in the trenches at Messines, George wrote the words of a popular and sentimental song, *Little Grey Home in the West*, scribing them carefully in pencil as if to commit the words to memory. Written in 1911 by D. Eardley-Wilmot and Hermann Lohr, it was one of many songs that boosted morale and patriotism throughout the war years:

When the golden sun sinks in the hills, and the toil of the long day is over, though the road may be long in the midst of the song I forget I was weary before. Far ahead where the blue shadows fall I shall come to contentment and rest and the toils of the day will be all charmed away in my little grey home in the west. There are hands that will welcome me in, there are lips I am burning to kiss. There are two eyes that shine just because they are mine, and a thousand things other men miss. It's a corner of heaven itself though its only a tumble down nest. But with love brooding there, why, no place can compare with my little grey home in the west.

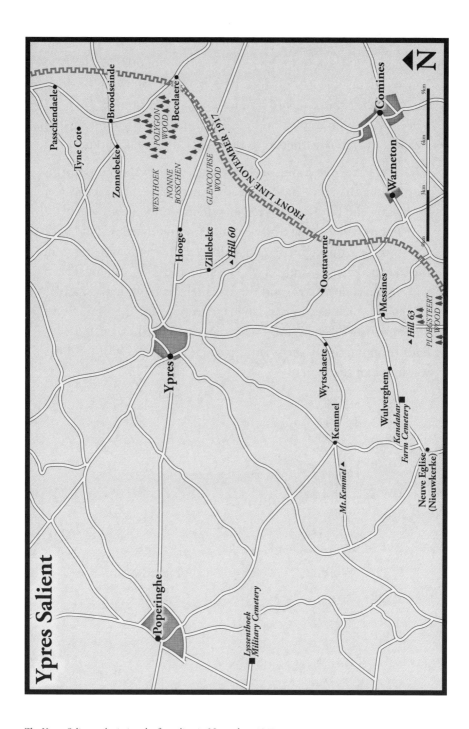

The Ypres Salient - depicting the front line in November, 1917.

On long route marches and in the trenches, numerous adaptations of these songs would entertain the soldiers and lighten the gravity of their darkest moments. George obviously enjoyed the following version, for he also took the time to record it in his notebook. *Little Wet Home in the Trench* is blackly humorous and clearly amused this young Australian soldier who was now hardened to the reality of trench warfare:

> I have a little wet home in the trench which the rain storms continually drench. There's a dead german close by with his feet to the sky, and he gives off a terrible stench, underneath in a place of a floor there's a mass of wet mud and some straw, and Jack Johnsons tear through the rain sodden air over my wet home in the trench. There are snipers who keep on the go so you must keep your nappers down low, and the star shells at night make a dance of a light which causes bad language to flow, for then bully beef and biscuits we'll chew, for its days since we tasted a stew, but with hails dropping here, there is no place to compare with my little wet home in the trench.

FOUR

'THEY LOOKED LIKE MEN
WHO HAD BEEN IN HELL'[1]

ENGLAND, JULY

With II Anzac Corps now in France, the training camps in Egypt were dismantled and the few remaining men sent to England on 29 April 1916. AIF Administrative Headquarters was now housed in the Wesleyan Methodist Training College at Horseferry Road in London's Westminster district. The training camps for reinforcements were established in green fields near Salisbury, some within sight of Stonehenge.[2] Once the men from the 3rd Division arrived, they would begin their training at the huge Larkhill complex. Nearby Perham Downs housed command depots for men who were recuperating from their wounds and accommodation for troops who had regained their fitness and were awaiting their return to units at the front. Servicemen still unfit after six months and awaiting repatriation to Australia were accommodated at Weymouth.

As Percy and Allan continued their journey across the sea, units from the 3rd Division under Australian General John Monash and reinforcements for both Anzac Corps began to arrive at the training grounds of Salisbury Plain. Monash was a civil engineer, born in country New South Wales and educated at Scotch College in Melbourne. He had commanded the 4th Brigade at Gallipoli and was to prove an extremely capable commander in the very different warfare that characterised the Western Front. Unlike the traditionalists, Monash understood this new form of conflict. In 1918, he became commander of the combined Australian forces and was knighted in the field. Monash was to become one of Australia's most respected Great War commanders.

While the fledgling 3rd Division would not leave Larkhill for France for some weeks, reinforcements from command and training depots were sent to replace losses at the front. Having departed Southampton, the transports carrying reinforcements crossed the English Channel, mindful of the ever-present threat of German submarine attack. It was a tense, anxious journey for the troops. Disembarkation at Etaples on the French coast was met with relief despite the prospect of action promised by the next stage of the journey.

FRANCE, JULY — THE FIRST BATTLE OF THE SOMME

The first day of July was chosen for the largely British attack against the German lines on the Somme River to the east of the ancient city of Amiens, where the lines of the British and French forces met. The 'big push' involved 120,000 Allied soldiers advancing on a front that stretched almost 30 kilometres. The entrenched German lines had been subjected to a massive seven-day bombardment considered sufficiently intense to cut the wire and destroy German entrenchments, promising a straightforward advance for the Allied troops. The push was designed to relieve the pressure on French troops at Verdun and aimed to capture not just the strategically vital ridge on which the village of Pozieres was perched, but also break through to the market town of Bapaume, some 13 kilometres in front of the British lines and occupied by the Germans since August 1914.

The roar of the massive artillery barrage was heard as far away as the shores of England, and the soldiers prepared for their advance. They would be attacking at 7.30 am — in broad daylight — on a beautiful summer's day. Despite the intensity of the barrage, in which over 1.6 million shells had been fired, the barbed-wire defences had not been cut and the three rows of deep enemy trenches with concrete fortifications, enormous bunkers and pillboxes had withstood the bombardment, allowing the German troops to survive the maelstrom. The British artillery had not achieved the expected devastation of the enemy lines and the Germans were primed and waiting.

British soldiers clambered from their trenches, in some cases ordered to walk towards the enemy lines with one-minute intervals between units.

Inevitably they were cut down by the machine-gun fire of the Germans, now emerging largely unscathed from their underground fortresses. The units were continually ordered forward despite the carnage. The slaughter also continued. Those wounded who could move stumbled or crawled back to their lines; others died a dreadful death in no man's land amid the cries of their wounded comrades.

To the south of the British advance, the French artillery had successfully paved the way for its assaulting infantry and their objectives had been attained. The British were slaughtered in their thousands. On the first day 19,240 British soldiers were killed and another 38,230 wounded.[3] It would be Britain's bloodiest day of the war. In a little over a fortnight, 100,000 men would be listed as killed, wounded or missing.

* * *

FRANCE 2011

Ninety-five years on we drive through the picturesque French countryside with our guide, military historian, writer and authority on the history of sniping, Martin Pegler. We stop at a cemetery. Close to a wall, a large unexploded shell, freshly uncovered from the surrounding fields, stands in silent menace. We walk along a section of the British jumping-off line at Serre Sheffield Park, just north of Beaumont-Hamel, on the northern end of the Somme battlefield. The memorial here is dedicated to the Accrington Pals, a regiment comprising groups of friends from Accrington in East Lancashire, England. Of 720 Pals who advanced in the opening phase of the Somme battle, 584 were listed as killed, wounded or missing. Signs point to other nearby cemeteries and memorials.

We look up the slope towards a small cemetery perched on the edge of the ridge. It was up this slope that the British soldiers were ordered to walk, into the face of machine-gun fire that cut them to pieces. It is a delightful spring morning; the sky is clear, the larks singing. We listen as our guide reads a surviving soldier's account. His words cut to the heart as we stand on the soil that today hides the dreadful truth of a senseless slaughter. The sustained attack in the face of clear disaster is beyond our comprehension; the futility is inconceivable.

FRANCE, JULY

By 5 July, the Australian 1st and 2nd divisions had been relieved in the trenches south of Armentieres by the 4th and 5th divisions and were now further north, close to the Belgian town of Messines. They were preparing for an attack, a diversion designed to draw German troops to this sector. The 2nd Brigade moved into the front line, remaining there for a fortnight. On 7 July the planned attack on Messines was abandoned and I Anzac Corps was ordered to proceed immediately to the French city of Amiens, some 140 kilometres south of Messines. The Australians were to provide reinforcements to support the Somme Offensive where the attempt to take Bapaume had failed in the face of devastating casualties.

George penned a hurried letter to his brothers just prior to the move south:

July 3rd, 1916
Dear Allan & Percy

I am dropping you a few lines in chance that this letter might reach you, if it should would you drop me a few lines straight away and let me know where you are and what you are doing. I have had a letter from Albert saying that he thought you would be sailing about the 1st May so I suppose by now you are in this part of the world. This is my address 2748 2 A/2 Light Trench Mortar Battery 2nd Inf Brigade Headquarters, this address will find me, we are not allowed to say what part of the firing line we are in of course you know that I am fighting in either France or Belgium and have been under some heavy bombardments lately if you get any war news you will see that we have made some advances on this front I have just come out of the front line again and it was very lively this time you wouldn't believe what it is like when all the guns speak well lads I wont say much this time as you mighten get this letter. Albert said that you were in the 38 Batt. I have been expecting some letters from you but I haven't had any since Xmas, have only had two mails since Xmas. Well lads I will close, good luck to you all and I hope it is all over before you get in the firing line. Goodbye from your loving Bro

George
Remember me to all the lads.

I am not attached to the 7 batt now but am in the trenches with them, this is what I am in, is small guns for firing bombs it is not very safe work in the trenches. I picked up a paper here and noticed that the 10 Brigade was going to march through Melbourne on the 1ˢᵗ May, I don't think the war will last much longer. Well lads I hope you do better than me for letters I have only had 1 dozen since I arrived in France and I have been a long while here now.

Goodbye and Good luck to all.

Several of George's letters also appeared in the *Pyramid Hill Advertiser*. Recipients would often forward letters of interest to their local newspaper to share the news of their loved ones with the community. It was not a practice that appealed to the Marlow brothers and in later correspondence they implored their parents not to publish any of their letters. In this remarkable letter from George he writes of the mocking threats exchanged between the Germans and Australians across no man's land and of being surprised by a German deserter. He explains that the infantry preferred not to be located near the trench mortar and machine-gun teams, known as 'suicide clubs' for their ability to draw enemy fire. George, however, had acquired his own brand of front-line fatalism, concluding that location or role was irrelevant; to survive or to be killed was a matter of fate.

> Pte. G.T. Marlow, writing to his brother in Mologa from France, says – At last I have received some letters, the second mail since Christmas, and am pleased to hear that all are well; but those papers you sent have not arrived yet. They would be a luxury. I am in the Brigade Trench Mortar Battery. They asked for volunteers out of my company; only three of us stepped out; we had only five days of instruction, and then they gave us a bit of an examination. The infantry chaps did not like us firing at first but they don't take much notice of it now, as Fritz always fires back to blow us out. We give Fritz about two to one, so things are pretty lively at times. When their artillery starts shelling our trenches ours always retaliates; the bombarding is nearly always done at night, and sometimes the trenches get badly blown about. One night

after they had finished the bombardment, we thought we were going to charge, so every one of us got his head and shoulders up above the parapet and gave them five rounds of rapid rifle firing and, in a new favourite army phrases, invited them to have a go next morning. They had a notice up that they were stopped by the "scum of the earth". Another night they put up a notice that peace would be declared on the 15th of that month, but before that they were going to have the ground between our trenches and theirs strewn with Australian dead. I think they will get a lively time if they try it on. The machine gunners and trench mortar battery are called the "suicide club", as they reckon it is not too safe. But if one is to be killed it does not matter what he is in. The other night we had a visit from a German deserter. When he got close to the parapet he asked if there were any Melbourne lads there. Someone said Yes. So he came up and told us that he used to live in Melbourne. We also took some prisoners. I was looking forward to a trip to England, but now the leave is altered my turn is so far off, that is not worth bothering about it now. I have been in the army 12 months and have not had an hour's sickness. I was sorry to hear young Miller from Pyramid was dead. I noticed in the paper that he was ill. The last I saw him was on the 22nd February. He was quite well then. I used to have a talk with him every night.[4]

July 5th 1916
Dear Mother, Father and Brothers,

… I don't know whether you will receive these letters as it is rumoured here that they are stopping all letters from going for a while as there is big things doing now, you will see by the papers that we are pushing old Fritz back I think he is out for a lively time, with the Russians advancing also the Italians and there attacks on Verdun have been a failure, I think it will be all over before Xmas. Our artillery is to good for them also the aeroplanes when we first arrived here Fritz's planes used to be always hovering about but now very few come over if they do ours are soon after them, I have seen several brought down, it is a great sight to see them come down, our

men are very plucky in the planes, they are nearly as thick as flies now. I wrote a letter last week saying that we were in the trenches again and in a different place this time in Belgium this time before we were fighting in France and it is much hotter in this place; I have been under some very heavy bombardments they kept it going every night for a week in a lot of places the trenches were blown down flat with the ground, but we came off very lucky, we used the gas and got good results, you wouldn't believe what it is like when all the guns roar as there are thousands of them around where we are, nearly all the bombardments are done in the night time and when they start in the night is turned into day by the flash of the guns. The firing line here is much different to where we were before it is hilly and thickly timbered in places, you wouldn't think there was a war two miles behind the firing line, the people go about their work the same as in peace time, they have some nice crops here and are all out in ear, every house that is left standing is turned into a shop of some kind, they sell mostly postcards, smokes, chocolates etc. can get a feed of eggs in nearly every farm house, 3 eggs, one cup of coffee and a piece of bread and butter for 1 franc that is 10d. That is very reasonable, I reckon there has been more eggs eaten here since the war started than what was ever eaten before especially by the Australians, the people must be making their fortune out of us. They have stopped all leave for us to England and also for the Tommies while the big move is on … I think you had better not send any more parcels and papers to me as I haven't received a paper yet and have only got one of the parcels and not getting the letters regular it beats me where they got to. One of the chaps got an Argus today dated the 10th and there was a lot in it about us landing in France, my word they kept it back a long time because we have been here over 3 months and the second division arrived here before us, and we went into the firing line the beginning of the second week in April, we have done well with the raiding parties. I wrote a letter to Allan today and addressed it Machine Gun Section, 38 Batt I doubt whether he will get it, but I think he must be in England. I will now close with best wishes to all

From George

George appears to have been completely unaware of the disaster that had unfolded to the south on the Somme and into which he was soon to be thrown. In England and across the Commonwealth, the reports were vague and generally positive; censors prevented war correspondents revealing detail that could be valuable to the enemy or detrimental to the morale of those at home. It would be years before the extent of the disaster was reported with any accuracy.

MOLOGA, JULY

As the month of June drew to a close, Charlie made another attempt to enlist. He travelled to Bendigo and visited his girlfriend, Pearl Clee, whose family had shortened the long days for Allan and Percy when they had first arrived in the central Victorian city. On 29 June at the age of 25 and, having fixed the problems with his teeth, Charlie was deemed fit for active service. While listing his father as next of kin on the enlistment form, Charlie added that this listing was 'not to be construed as in the nature of a will'. Charlie and Pearl had other plans.

The news of Charlie's enlistment travelled swiftly north and, as the new month opened, Albert's sweetheart, Myrtle Stone from nearby Calivil, wrote to Albert with news of her own brothers who had recently enlisted and of the impact Charlie's enlistment would have on the Marlow family. Unlike George, who suggests to his family that the war will be over before Christmas, Myrtle was far less optimistic.

Calivil South
July 1ˢᵗ
My Dear Albert

Just a few lines hoping you are well, I suppose you think I am never going to write but I have not had a chance Alma as [has] gone home so now I can write without her prying into it, well Charlie has passed I suppose your mother will be upset over it it is too bad on her so many of her boys going. It's a pity the war don't end but it looks as if it will last a while yet. I suppose you have had plenty of rain now we have had a lot here too wet to plough new ground, Joe is out of the hospital Jimmie was in for two days, we got a letter from him last night he said he was still isolated they would of liked to get home today but could not get out. Joe went up to Bendigo last Saturday. There was a Euchre party & dance in the Calivil South school last Friday week mother won the 1ˢᵗ prize & Alma the booby. There was a Euchre & dance at Jarklan last night we did not play, we were too, there was not many there the roads are so bad, there is going to be another there on Tuesday I think I will be booked for playing that night it is for the Hospital Queen Funds its no treat sitting so long playing these cold nights. Dolly Rowe is getting better now I am glad she is the boys came home to say good bye to them but had to turn & go away again. We got a letter from Jim Johnson last week written 7ᵗʰ May he was then well he a [has] been in France 3 months, did you hear from George I hope he is alright yet. Have you got Allans and Percys photos yet don't forget I am to have one of each. Most likely Jim & Joe will be home next Sat so you ought to try & get over if you are not too busy you could come on Sat & stay all night they would like you here while they are home. I just wish you were here next Friday to go with us to Bramleys they sent word over today that they are having a party it is Fannys 21ˢᵗ birthday I think it will be fun to see Mrs B fussing around I suppose Mary will be able to entertain the company with her usual performances & the old woman will wind up with God be with you. Well Dear Albert I will close with love from your affec girl

Myrtle
XXXXXXXX

Life continued as usual in the tiny community while locals rallied behind the war effort with dances and gatherings to raise funds for the various organisations which had sprung up to support their young men. Myrtle was kept busy providing the musical entertainment. Her brothers, Jim and Joe Stone, were both farmers. Joe was 20 years old and embarked with his brother in February 1917, both allocated to the 14th Battalion. Joe later wrote a remarkable letter describing the sinking of the *Ballarat* and his rescue off the coast of England. He was gassed on 20 May 1918 and returned to his family at Calivil in April 1919.[5] Jim was 21 when he enlisted. He fell ill when he arrived in England and was hospitalised with pneumonia, convalescing until May 1918 when he finally moved to the front line. On 9 July he was shot but recovered to rejoin his battalion on 1 October 1918. He returned to Australia a few days before Christmas in 1919.[6]

In late July, the Mologa community of the Church of England decided to honour the service of its young men with the unveiling of an honour roll. The Reverend Plumtree delivered an address which included the expectation that these men would also have their names engraved on an 'Immortal Honour Roll in Heaven', as reported in the local newspaper:

Mologa – Honour Roll Unveiled

On Tuesday evening a special service was held in St. Luke's church, in connection with the unveiling of an Honour Roll. There was a large congregation and the service was most impressive. After the singing of Kipling's Recessional "Lest we Forget" the Rev. H. Plumtree gave an earnest and inspiring address on the words, "But rather rejoice because your names are written in heaven" Luke 10.20. The preacher said that the disciples were soldiers of Jesus Christ, and their names were written in heaven because, it is their country, for they are only pilgrims and strangers here; also because they are precious in their master's sight. The unveiling of the Honour Roll this evening means that some men have heard their country's call, and they are away in a strange country; while they are away we place their names on an Honour Roll, because their lives are precious to us. The names on the Honour Roll represent an individual life, history, experience, and destiny; this means that if our names are written on an earthly Roll or on the Heavenly Roll of Honour, we must live up to the reputation which is involved upon us. There are no Honour Rolls for the shirker, and pleasure seeker; for these there will be shame and disgrace. Only those who are faithful, who live the purest lives and make the greatest sacrifices in the world, will be recorded on the Honour Roll; whether it be in heaven or on earth. There is a joy in having the name on the Honour Roll; it is a cause of pride to the parents and a great joy to the faithful soldier. As a soldier will make a great effort to have his name mentioned in a dispatch or in history, even at the risk of losing his life; so all Christian men and women should seek to have their names written on the Immortal Honour Roll in Heaven. Before concluding his address Mr. Plumtree unveiled the Honour Roll, reading out the names of the soldiers who had left the church.

Pte. Geo. Tennyson Marlow
Pte. Amos H. Haw
Pte. Allan Sharp Marlow
Pte. David Leslie Townsend
Pte. Percy Place Marlow
Pte. John Theodore Price
Pte. David Wilson Townsend[7]

I cannot help but wonder whether the 'Immortal Honour Roll in Heaven' was divided into Allied and Axis soldiers for, according to both, God was on their side. Such was the propaganda, the stirring words delivered from pulpits in the small townships and in the cities across the world.

As the propaganda increased in intensity, so too did the pressure on young Australian men and their parents. Jim and Albert sat in the congregation while honour was bestowed on their brothers; the eldest and the youngest had been rejected. Enlistment conditions had now been relaxed and it is possible that Jim could have been accepted to serve in some capacity. Albert, however, required his parents' consent. As the family sat on the wooden pews on a cold winter's evening, Sarah and Charles must have proudly read the names of their sons, yet also felt the weight of the Reverend's words. Albert was frustrated. He was not about to wait another two and a half years until parental consent was no longer necessary. The war could well be over by then.

AT SEA, JULY

As their names were proudly being unveiled in the tiny church at Mologa, Percy and Allan were now two weeks into their journey across the Indian Ocean. Allan's excitement was palpable, he was soon to see exotic places of which he had only heard and read. For a young man from the country for whom a trip to the city was a rare treat, to journey across the world was an improbable adventure.

July 5th 1916
Somewhere at Sea

SS Runic
My Dear Mum & Dad

Well Mum we are enjoying ourselves tip top time. None of us have been sick yet, a terrible lot of the boys have been sick, this is the best time ever I had. We go on parade every day now, but we don't do such a great lot talk about eat mum, I can eat something awful and we get terrible good tucker. Well Mum I am going to post this letter at Durban or Capetown. We don't know exactly which place we are calling at. Now mum I will start and tell you what we have done and what we have seen right from the day we embarked. Well mum we left the pier on that Tuesday about 1 o'clock and about 5.30 we got to the heads, there a pile of boats pulled up along side our boat and took away mail. I did not know that they would be doing it so soon or I would have wrote to you. Well Mum we got our hammocks issued to us at 6 o'clock that night. They hang from each floor of the deck above it, and I can tell you they was some fun that night when we were going to bed, but they are first class to sleep in and I sleep right on the outside near the porthole and it is just the thing. We first sailed it was a bit cold now the weather is warmer and it gets a bit stuffy in the night, mind you, we are exceedingly lucky to be where we are because we are on the top deck and we will appreciate it when we get into the tropics. We get up at 6 in the morning I always get up early so I can get a wash before the crowd gets there, Mum I know you wont credit that because I was generally a wee bit fond of the bed, but it is a fact. Anyway after we wash it is 7 o'clock, then it [is] breakfast we get porridge stew, or curry and coffee. Then we are all cleared out from down below, to the top deck, so that the orderly can wash up. And scrub the floor, at nine o'clock we go on parade till 12 then it is dinner time, we get soup roast meat and pudding for dinner. Then at 2 oclock we go on parade again till 5 then it [is] tea time, We get bread butter jam and cheese for tea, then at 8.30 we got to bed. Well mum you will be wondering why we did not write before but it is because we never called at any ports. The one that we are going to now will be the first one, and as I said before I am not sure what one it will be. We was on the boat two days when I got a letter from Albert I can tell you I was pleased to get it. Last Sunday week we could see West Australia at a big distance and [a] few whales, porpoises and numerous other sea birds and animals. We get boat drill here in case of mishaps. We have had [a] lot of rain since we have been on board and few rough nights and days. There is canteen on board tobacco and cigarettes are very cheap, just about half the price to what they are in Victoria. There is a barbers shop here too. We have boxing and wrestling matches too, so things are pretty lively. It is a very clean boat there are about 2 000 soldiers on board also a very valuable cargo, such as motor cars and terrible lot of wheat and a lot [of] valuable cargo. We do not pick up our escorts until we get to Africa, I thought we were going to have them from Australia but it not so. Well mum I started this letter last Wednesday and I am finishing it today Sunday the 9th. Well mum we got up this morning and we had bacon and liver for breakfast, but the tucker has been a bit crook lately, not near so good as before. We went to church about 10 oclock and it finished at 11 oclock. We hold the church parades on the top deck. I looked at the watch at 10.30 and by the time in Australia it was 5.30 so I suppose you were all busy at tea. I have been all over the boat except the stoke hole and I am going down there today. I am playing in a big euchere tournament tonight. If I should win it would be worth about £5. Well Mum I think I have told you all the news so I hope you get this letter. We are getting off at Cape Town. They tell us it will be for four days. They are going to give us a big route march there. We arrive there Wednesday night or early Thursday morning. Well mum and Dad I will say goodbye for the present and I hope you are all well as it leaves us all at present.

I remain
Your Loving Son
Allan S

Frank Penglase is on the boat too. We have not been a bit sick yet. I would not mind if I was a sailor I simply love the water. The weather is getting a bit warm now. We are going to have some very ruff weather now as we are near Africa. It is getting ruff now. Mum I am pleased to say that we are going to England. Well that is what we hear.

As usual, Percy was less enthusiastic than his twin brother. The weather was disagreeable, he was missing the newspapers and he hankered for a decent cup of tea:

At Sea
Sunday
Dear Charlie

... Well Charlie we get good meals on board, a bit of a change from camp, we get porridge in the morning and soup at dinner time, it substitutes for tea then. The only thing I don't like is the tea it has a funny taste. We have sixteen to a table; for a start there was a few sick and it made a lot for what was left. Brookes has been fairly crook he was in the hospital for a couple of days with sea sickness. We have drill on board, start at nine and knock off at half past four, we have a fairly easy time, there is not much room for drill it is amusing sometimes, we will be doing physical jerks, and the boat will roll and over a lot will go. There was church parade today, all had to come out in uniforms; through the week it is blues. Well Charlie news is scarce. I suppose you are having a good time today, I would give anything to see a paper now. There is not much amusement on board not much room for anything ...

Your loving brother
Percy.

Meanwhile, Allan outwitted the censor with his reference to Uncle Arthur, a veteran of the Boer War – a significant clue to the ship's next port of call:

At Sea
11.7.16
Dear Albert

... I played in euchre tournament last night and won it. We have to go on parade everyday but we don't do such lot of work. We are calling at a port in a couple of days and I hope to see Uncle Arthur there.[8] *How are the crops looking. Have you finished working out at Bob's yet. Well Albert news is scarce as we are not allowed to say much. Have you heard from Georgie lately, I hope we meet him over there. We are not allowed to say where we are going but we can form a good idea all the same. I suppose you are still going down South Calival way. Remember me to them all next time you go. How do they take it about us going. Is Charlie still thinking of having another cut. This boat is a very good sailing vessel. We are in for a bit of ruff*

weather now. There is a canteen on board and you can get drinks, biscuits, tinned fruit and tobacco and cigarettes …

The sight of land after three weeks at sea aroused great excitement among the troops aboard the *Runic*. As the ship sailed into Table Bay in South Africa, the prospect of leave and, for many, the opportunity to set foot on and explore the scenery of a new country, was greeted with raucous enthusiasm. For five days the Australians enjoyed the sights of Cape Town, appreciating the kindness of the locals, including the 'pretty girls'.

Capetown
Dear Albert

Well Albert we are having a fine time here. We have had a good look around the town and the district surrounding it. The scenery around the cape is lovely. We had a motor car and we motored around the hills etc. We went to a theatre the other night and it was very poor. I don't think I have heard anything worse and it cost 3 /- to hear it. The streets of the town are very narrow and not too clean. The town itself is full of blacks. On [censored] we went for a march to Rosebank it is a very pretty place. It is about a 5 mile march. The ladies of the district out there gave us a bit of a picnic. They did not know we were coming until we were half way out. Anyway we had a fine time. Well Albert I will tell you more news next time, as I have posted a lot of letters home and I hope you get them. I also sent a cable home. How are things around Mologa. I suppose the crops are good. We had a bonnie trip over here. None of us have been sick but Peter Owens is in the hospital. He is pretty crook. Les in the hospital with bronkitus. I would not say anything to the people if I were you. Well Albert we are moving out shortly. Well Albert I say goodbye for the present. Hoping you are all well as it leaves me at the present.

I remain
Your loving brother
Allan

From Durban and Cape Town, Allan sent home picture souvenirs on which he had described his experiences. He rode in a rickshaw, visited noted places of interest and delighted in the beautiful scenery. The young ladies also inspired him to write 'I never saw such pretty girls'. It is clear that Allan was determined to take advantage of the opportunity to become a 'six bob a day tourist'.

FROMELLES, FRANCE, JULY

As the 38th Battalion prepared to depart Cape Town and George was moving south to Amiens, the Australians of the 5th Division were about to launch an assault. This was to be a diversionary action, designed to keep German troops pinned down in the north and away from the Somme front, and would involve the Australians in their first full-scale attack on the Western Front. An infantry advance to the north close to Armentieres was to proceed despite an earlier unsuccessful attempt. These troops were now to take the high ground of the heavily fortified Sugarloaf salient on Aubers Ridge, a position which allowed German observers a clear view of the Allied lines. The Australians would attack towards the village of Fromelles, close to the area of the front in which George had been positioned at nearby Fleurbaix just a few weeks prior.

The 5th Division, led by Major General James McCay of Victoria, now faced the prospect of launching its first action on the Western Front.[9] The newly arrived Australians of II Anzac Corps were relatively unprepared. The artillery of both the 4th and 5th divisions, which largely consisted of rapidly trained men from the inexperienced troops in Egypt, was to provide the preparatory artillery bombardment. The 5th Division and the recently arrived British 61st Division were to advance on Aubers and take the village of Fromelles, almost two kilometres behind the German line. Australian Brigadier 'Pompey' Elliott of the 15th Brigade warned of impending disaster; the troops were inexperienced and the quality of the artillery support was highly questionable. The German soldiers were well-trained and battle hardened, protected by strong defences with a clear view of Allied preparations; they had been in this section of the line for months and knew the area intimately. Against the odds, the Allied attack was ordered to proceed.[10]

On 19 July at 6.00 pm, in full daylight, with some three hours before dusk, the attack was launched. German artillery fire had already bombarded the troops as they waited in the trenches for zero hour.

The bombardment had killed or wounded many Australians even before the signal to go over the top. The dead choked the trenches. Elliott's 15th Brigade was decimated while trying to cross a distance of 400 metres toward the Sugarloaf salient. Those of the 8th and 14th brigades who reached no man's land were easy targets. Those troops not rescued by courageous survivors were left to die in agony where they fell; over five nights the Australians continually risked their own lives to rescue their mates.

Fromelles was a disaster. Australia suffered 5533 casualties in what was to become known as the bloodiest 24 hours in Australian military history. Over 1900 men had been killed, almost 1300 with no known grave. Some 470 men were to spend the rest of the war in German prison camps. It was a military disaster on a grand scale. In some of the most brutal fighting of the entire war there was one notable and later notorious survivor, a German lance corporal named Adolf Hitler.

With the heavy toll of casualties, the 5th Division was incapable of offensive action for some months following Fromelles. The survivors were demoralised and the failed attack would haunt Pompey Elliot for the rest of his life. He committed suicide in 1931.

POZIERES, FRANCE, JULY

The troops of the 1st Division had been hurried by train to billets in the villages north of picturesque Amiens, 90 kilometres south of Fromelles. They were now preparing for their part in supporting the Somme Offensive. George kept a list of the villages in which he had been billeted or close to where he had served in the trenches. It now read:

Godewaersbelde
La Creeche
Bertham
La. Haalobean
Erquinham
Fleurbaix S
Sailly

Neuve Eglise
Messines S
Bailleul
Doullens
Berteaucort
Flesselles
Rainneville
Sealvillers
Albert S

He was soon to include yet another village, a name which was to become synonymous with living hell: Pozieres.

Colonel Carl Jess, commander of the 7th Battalion (2nd Brigade), informed his men that they would shortly be in 'a hot spot'.[11] To assist the artillery to identify Australians in the upcoming attack, each man stitched a piece of pink cloth to the back of his tunic. The target of their interest was soon revealed: the village of Pozieres.

Pozieres was perched on the crest of a hillside astride the main road between Albert and Bapaume, protecting the German-held village of Thiepval and critical to Allied success on the Somme. All along the Western Front, the German troops commanded the high ground, building massive concrete bunkhouses and observation posts from which Allied movements could be easily monitored; it was up these slopes that Allied troops must now advance. From Pozieres along the ridge to Thiepval in the north and Guillemont in the south, the enemy had a commanding view of the Allies to the west. The magnitude of the battle for this crucial German stronghold had shattered the once quiet village of Pozieres. It was littered with broken tree stumps and surrounded by German wire defences on which the bodies of English soldiers had remained tangled since their attempts to capture the village at the opening of the Somme battles on 1 July.[12] It was here that the 1st Australian Division was to create its own legend, albeit a bloody and bitter one.

The 1st Division marched through the town of Albert, past the shelled basilica of Notre Dame de Brebières, and beneath the symbolic golden statue of the Virgin Mary and baby Jesus which once stood on a tower high above. Having been struck by shellfire, the statue now hung precariously on an angle, secured from falling by Allied engineers. The Australians called her Fanny Durack after the 1912 Australian Olympic swimmer and gold medallist. The men fighting on the Somme had heard the legend that the fall of the statue would mark the end of the war. Sadly, when it finally fell in early 1918, struck by British artillery following the Germans advance on the town, the prophecy was not fulfilled; the war would continue for another eight long months.

As darkness fell on the night of 22 July, George's 2nd Brigade was positioned in the reserve area of Sausage Valley to the south-west of the ruined village of Pozieres.

Enemy shells and shrapnel burst around the men as their fellow brigades moved forward into front-line positions. Their task was to take Pozieres Trench which protected the southern approach to the village. In a leap-frogging action, the battalions were then to move on and reach the main Bapaume-Albert road running through the centre. Simultaneously, to the south-east, British divisions would attack towards Guillemont. A massive artillery bombardment commenced and was visible from over 30 kilometres away. The German reply was equal in intensity and laced with phosgene and tear gas.

Soon after midnight, the 1st and 3rd brigades advanced on the ring of enemy trenches which surrounded the pulverised remains of Pozieres. The artillery barrage had achieved its objective. The shell-shocked Germans were quickly overrun and the Australians rushed through the trench into the remains of the village, where shattered homes had been further reduced to rubble. The Australians held the village throughout the day, fighting off enemy attempts to reclaim the ground they had lost. As the sun rose on 23 July the Australians reached the centre of the village following some of the most courageous fighting yet on the Western Front. In capturing the village, the Australians had created a salient which projected into enemy territory. German infantry and artillery could now enfilade their position from three sides. Later the following day, the men of the 2nd Brigade moved forward from their reserve position. George, part of the 2nd Light Trench Mortar Battery responsible for firing the Stokes mortar, pushed forward into the haze of smoke and dust.

Desperate German attempts to recover lost ground were repelled over the next four days in the face of intense artillery bombardments and enormous loss of life. The embattled Australians took cover in shell holes as the ground shook with deafening explosions. Troops were killed, concussed or blown apart, buried alive, dug out and buried again as the ceaseless shelling raged about them and the earth rocked under the might of the German artillery. Wounded and dead men lay in the blinding smoke and dust of an inferno that raged both day and night.

On 26 July the commanders of the 7th and 8th battalions sheltered in a captured fortification known as 'Gibraltar'. So named by the Australians, 'Gibraltar' was a heavily fortified German concrete observation post that covered the approach to Pozieres, protruding some three metres above the ground with deep chambers beneath. Against the odds the commanders established telephone contact with the headquarters of the 2nd Brigade. Lieutenant Colonel Jess of the 7th implored his headquarters for reinforcements:

> It has been impossible to construct adequate trenches owing to the pulped nature of the ground. Those that were constructed N.E. of Pozieres are wiped out, and men are so dazed that they are incapable of working or fighting. Consider relief imperative as we could not resist attack if this is the preparation of it. 6th and 8th Battalions endorse this.[13]

Relief came with the entire artillery of the 1st Division concentrating its power on the German front line. A deadly artillery battle continued until late into the night. The troops were exhausted. The effort of fending off continuous counter-attacks under such intense fire while desperately trying to dig in had shattered the fighting force. They were surrounded by the bloated bodies of the dead, covered in their blood and exhausted by the constancy of battle. The eager fighting force had been reduced to a disillusioned and traumatised group of exhausted men:

"They looked," wrote a sergeant (E.J. Rule) of the 4th Division, which watched the 1st pass into a rest area, "like men who had been in Hell … drawn and haggard and so dazed that they appeared to be walking in a dream and their eyes looked glassy and starey". When they reached bivouac in Vadencourt Wood, and had washed, shaved and rested, they were strangely quiet, far different from the Australian soldiers of tradition. They resembled rather boys emerging from long illness, many lying quietly apart in their blankets, reading books, smoking, or writing home letters.[14]

As the taking of Pozieres had been the only successful action along the 11-kilometre attacking front, the German counter-attack was focused on Pozieres Ridge.[15] Nowhere were the bombardments as fierce as those that targeted Pozieres. On 27 July, as the 2nd Division completed its relief, the casualty list of the 1st Division reached over 5000 killed or wounded. George's brigade had lost 1136 men including eight officers.[16]

AUGUST

In the days leading up to the beginning of August, the 2nd Division fared no better than the 1st, adding another 6846 killed, wounded or missing to the casualty lists, the heaviest loss suffered by any Australian division in one tour on the Western Front.[17] The task of the 2nd Division was to drive further north and take the highest point of the battlefield, Hill 160, a strategically vital observation point where the Germans had converted the brick ruins of a seventeenth-century windmill into a defensive blockhouse. The windmill sat to the north, just off the road to Bapaume. In this action, the Australians would also seize the old German trench lines known as OG 1 and OG 2, strongpoints to the east of the village.

On 29 July, under cover of darkness, the 2nd Division pushed forward. The men were decimated. The belts of barbed wire had not been cut by the artillery bombardment as accurate sighting had not been possible in the haze of dust which had engulfed the ridge. Men died entangled in the barbed wire while others succumbed to clouds of gas. Those who survived were ordered to dig in and construct jumping-off trenches closer to the German line. The 2nd Division was to take the windmill and capture the OG lines at all cost. Remarkably, the depleted and exhausted force, albeit now assisted by more accurate artillery fire, achieved its objectives and, by 4 August, the Australians looked down on the valley, easily detecting signs of enemy movement. The ultimate objective — Bapaume — was clearly visible in the distance.

As the 4th Division under British General Sir Herbert Cox prepared to relieve the remaining soldiers of the 2nd, German artillery unleashed a heavy bombardment which thundered down on the heights of Pozieres. There were few fighting men left to relieve; many had been killed or suffered dreadful wounds and the survivors were shell-shocked. Pozieres was described by many as 'hell on earth'.

By 6 August the 4th Division was in its jumping-off position in old German dugouts where the men were trapped by the relentless artillery fire. The next morning the Germans advanced, gaining ground and capturing some 40 men from the 48th Battalion. Lieutenant Albert Jacka, a 22-year-old forestry worker from Wedderburn who had worked in the Terrick Terrick Forest above Mologa, and who had won Australia's first Victoria Cross at Gallipoli, was sheltering in a German dugout with his platoon. Two Germans rolled bombs into the entrance of the dugout, killing two of the Australians and prompting Jacka to lead his surviving men in a charge from the shelter. Once outside the dugout, they discovered a large group of Germans marching their prisoners back to the enemy line. In the heavy fighting that ensued, Jacka's men and the prisoners overcame the Germans and, despite most being wounded, they took fifty Germans prisoner, recaptured that part of the line and effectively turned the tide of the battle. Witnessing the attack by Jacka and his men, other small groups of Australians sheltering in nearby trenches and dugouts rushed to take on the Germans in a deadly hand-to-hand fight. Jacka was badly wounded — shot seven times — but recovered to be awarded the Military Cross for this courageous action.

Withdrawn from the line, George marched back beneath the leaning virgin. The church had been transformed into a dressing station where medical teams tended the wounded as best they could. George simply wrote in his notebook, 'Heavy Bombardment July 22 to 27 Pozieres'. When he next found the time to write to his family he chose not to describe the horror of Pozieres to his brothers — perhaps it was beyond words. His first letter after Pozieres was brief and guarded. He had survived, but this battle was not over. He was unaware that, across the field, one kilometre north of Pozieres, was the heavily fortified position of Mouquet Farm which had to be taken, once again, at all costs.

August 1ˢᵗ 1916
Dear Allan & Percy

Just a few lines to find out where in the world you are you must be over in this part of the world by now. Charlie sent your addresses to me, they tell me you have been delayed from coming before, through the meningitis breaking out, you are lucky in one way to miss as much of this "Big Push" as you can because I can tell these are terrible battles here where we are advancing I wont say much as you might not get this letter, am sorry to say that Arch Bailey got badly wounded in the advance Amos is alright, I havent seen Harry Burrows he is in the 6ᵗʰ Batt. Tom Alford and the others will soon be joining the 6 Batt now I have just received a letter from you and one from Percy dated May 11 it is the first one from you since Xmas. My address 2748 Light Trench Mortar Battery 2ⁿᵈ Inf Brigade Headquarters. They are small guns for firing bombs we be in the trenches with the battalion just the same. Well boys should you get this letter drop me a line straight away and let me know whereabouts you are. Remember me to all the other boys hoping all are well as I am at present.

I remain
Your loving Bro
George

As George wrote home, Archie Bailey was on his way to England. Archie, a carpenter who lived at Pompapiel, a short distance from the Marlows, had enlisted in July 1915. He had been shot in the face and arm at some point during the dreadful days of 22–25 July. While he survived Pozieres, he was wounded again on four separate occasions. On 25 February 1917 he was evacuated with severe gunshot wounds to his left leg and sent to England where he remained until July when he rejoined his unit. On 20 September 1917, at the Battle of Menin Road, he was again wounded in the left leg; he recovered in England and returned to the front in December. Archie was awarded the Military Medal for his courageous action on 9 August 1918 at Lihons, east of Villers-Bretonneux. As the 1st Division battled its way towards the village, Archie's commanding officer was killed in fierce fighting and he took control of the platoon. Archie's platoon captured two enemy machine-guns and their crews.[18] During this assault he was wounded in the left arm and was once again hospitalised in England. This brave soldier returned to Australia in February 1919 and was destined to marry and live to the age of 81. He died on 21 September 1968.[19]

Amos Haw – wounded by gunfire in April 1917.

Harry Burrows was a local farm labourer from Tandarra who had also enlisted in July 1915. He recovered from wounds suffered on the first day of August 1916 and continued to serve on the Western Front until his return to Australia in July 1919.[20] Amos Haw, a 24-year-old farmer from Mologa, was wounded by gunfire in April 1917; he returned to the front nine months later and, in the last months of the war, was in England training others in the techniques of gas warfare.[21] Tom Alford was also a farmer from the local area who joined up in March 1916 and was to arrive in France in late September. He was allocated to the 59th Battalion of Pompey Elliott's 15th Brigade (5th Division).[22] Tom frequently wrote candid letters home to his mate Jim Marlow until his return in May 1919.

William Thomas (Tom) Alford standing. Written on the back of this photo is 'Tom Bray', possibly 5335 Thomas Bray of Goroke, Victoria, who was killed on 4 February 1917.

MOUQUET FARM, AUGUST

The Australians were immediately ordered to push forward along Pozieres Ridge and take the underground defences of Mouquet Farm, a kilometre further to the north of Pozieres. Mouquet Farm had been transformed into a German stronghold, the cellars extended to accommodate hundreds of men and fortified with logs and concrete. Secret entrances allowed rapid entry and exit. Perched on the ridge that runs from Thiepval through Pozieres and south to Guillemont, it was a fortress that protected the village of Thiepval.

The line of attack to the farm was on a narrow frontage which allowed the Germans to enfilade the Australians from the front and flanks. British forces were to attack on their left. Over a period of a week, the 4th Division lost 4549 men, advancing on the farm in the face of withering machine-gun and artillery fire. They were relieved by the men of George's 1st Division on 16 August. It was a rainy, misty day, the churned-up ground now muddy and slippery. Since the division was last at Pozieres Ridge, the front had moved forward a mere 450 metres. Despite the arrival of reinforcements, the 1st Division was at two-thirds of its full strength. While the troops were rested and re-kitted it is unlikely that they were ready to endure more of what they had received at Pozieres. By 22 August, once the division had been withdrawn and the roll called, another 2650 men had been killed, wounded or were missing. Little ground had been gained and what had was a pulverised wasteland strewn with the bodies of Australians who had died in a torrent of murderous fire from the stronghold of the farm. The 2nd Light Trench Mortar Battery comprised some 50 men of whom over a quarter were now casualties.[23]

George had once more cheated death or a serious wound. The piece of heather his cousin had sent him was still bringing good luck. His notes briefly recorded, '2nd Stunt August arrived at Contalmaison [village 2 kilometres south of Pozieres] August 15 Tuesday left 21st.'

The 1st Division was now utterly exhausted. The 2nd Division was again sent to attack this most formidable of positions. In the final days of August, with the 2nd Division suffering the loss of a further 1270 men, the 4th Division returned to the fray and, in desperate fighting, broke through into the remains of the farm on the rain-drenched night of 29 August.[24] The Germans emerged from their underground defences. But the tenuous position could not be held and the surviving Australian soldiers were forced to retreat.

Eventually, on 5 September, when the Australian forces could no longer continue, the 4th Division was withdrawn to be replaced by the Canadian Corps. In 19 attacks over a period of seven weeks, the

Australians had incurred 23,000 casualties to capture just 1500 metres of ground. A total of 6741 Australians had been killed.[25]

The ruins of Mouquet Farm were eventually captured by British forces on 26 September. Having first taken Thiepval, the British chose a broader frontal attack rather than continuing from the rear on the narrow salient which had led to the decimation of the Australian lines.

On the spot where the Pozieres windmill once stood, a memorial has been built which marks the area of less than one square kilometre which, as official historian Charles Bean so aptly remarked, 'marks a ridge more densely sown with Australian sacrifice than any other place on earth'.[26] Thousands of Australians were listed as missing at Pozieres, wounded and left to die. It was often too dangerous to collect the dead; blown to pieces in the massive artillery bombardments, they simply disappeared, their bodies never recovered, lost to the fields of France. The soldiers who survived would never forget the carnage, the horror, the hell that was Pozieres.

* * *

The Leaning Virgin of Albert today (author photograph taken 27 May 2011).

FRANCE, 2011

Australian pilgrims are drawn to Pozieres to reflect on the sacrifice of the thousands of men who lost their lives on this once insignificant patch of earth. We begin by navigating our way to where the golden statue of the Virgin Mary proudly towers over the bustling community of Albert. George will have gazed on this sight as he marched towards the battlefield. Today a new statue (the other disappeared, possibly broken up and souvenired) stands erect, towering above Albert. Beneath the basilica is the entrance to a 230-metre-long tunnel used as an air raid shelter during World War II but now housing the Somme 1916 Museum. This collection brings to life the reality of trench warfare with audio and visual displays and relics of the devastation that shattered the town.

We plunge beneath the basilica, down a steep set of stairs and make our way through the tunnel amid the array of memorabilia. Eventually we emerge in a picturesque park and, as we turn to retrace our steps through the city to our starting point, we look up at the golden statue standing proudly above Albert. On the wall of a building in front of the basilica is a mural, a scene from 1916 in which three Allied soldiers march beneath the toppling statue as smoke billows from the town below. Today, the new statue rises above this scene, a reminder of the resilience and determination of the Allies and the residents of the town who were later to rebuild their community.

The Lochnagar Crater on the approach to Pozieres (author photograph taken 26 May 2011).

We continue our journey towards the village of Pozieres on the Roman road from Albert. As straight as it is, the road undulates; the old trenches beneath the bitumen have gradually subsided and the road has collapsed with them. We turn off the main road, through the village of La Boisselle and stop opposite the enormous Lochnagar Crater, the remains of one of ten Allied mines detonated on 1 July 1916, the opening day of the Battle of the Somme. Thousands of men, English and German, were killed here. It is 90 metres across, 30 metres deep and is at the head of Sausage Valley, or Sausage Gully as the Australians called it, from which the troops made their approach to Pozieres. We walk around the rim and try to make the leap from 2011 to 1916, to imagine how the countryside looked — the sights, the sounds, the smells. I wonder what George was thinking as he encountered this enormous crater and as he picked his way past shattered wagons and guns, past the wounded in the aid posts, past the bodies of the dead and into the inferno he could see and hear on the ridge beyond.

Flags mark the site of the windmill. In the centre on the horizon is Mouquet Farm, to the left is Thiepval. There were some 23,000 Australian casualties on this patch of earth and its surrounds in seven weeks (author photo taken on 26 May 2011).

Back on the road from Albert we approach Pozieres and pause at the memorial to the 1st Division. The information board reminds us that the division lost 5285 dead or wounded here. Nearby is a viewing platform from which we look across the battlefield and its surrounds. From this point it is possible to understand the value of Pozieres to the German forces. The town of Albert is to the west. Swing around to the right and the dominating Thiepval Memorial to the Missing of the Somme is visible on the skyline and a little further to the right is Mouquet Farm. Today it is quiet, with only an occasional vehicle on the road behind us to break the silence. There are skylarks singing far above, the undulating fields are golden and green and the wheat is shimmering in the sunlight. A farmer has planted new trees that will eventually obstruct the view to Thiepval, the ground over which so many Australians succumbed in such a small area. Close by are the remains of 'Gibraltar', the German blockhouse that stood some three metres high, captured by the 1st Division on 23 July. It was from this point, three days later, that Lieutenant Colonel Jess sent his urgent message to headquarters.

The AIF memorial at the entrance to Mouquet Farm (author photo taken on 26 May 2011).

We drive through the village to the site of the windmill and walk to the mound where the fortified structure had stood since 1610, over the ground where so many Australians fought and died. We stand on the high point. It is 26 April 2011. The mound is covered with small Australian flags and an occasional Aboriginal flag, flapping wildly in the wind, Australians paying homage to their brave forebears. Beyond, just visible on the horizon, are the silhouettes of Mouquet Farm and, further on, the imposing Thiepval memorial. The land in between is a patchwork of brown fallow and the green shoots of young crops. Every year, across this verdant pastoral ground, the bones of the missing are disturbed as the farmers plough their fields. The detritus of war — shells, bullet casings, pickets, wire and more — are continually uncovered and piled in the corners of fields. It was here that George carried the Stokes mortar into battle, preparing to fight for his life.

FIVE
I THINK THERE ARE ENOUGH OF US HERE NOW …

FRANCE, AUGUST

A few days after George was withdrawn from Pozieres he again wrote to his enlisted brothers. Now free of his filthy and bloodied clothes, rested and fed, he is a little more forthcoming about his experience than in previous letters. He describes the extent of the German fortifications and warns of the role that chance plays in survival. He is obviously concerned that four brothers on the fields of France is tempting fate; he expresses his displeasure that Charlie has now signed up.

August 26th
Dear Allan & Percy

A few lines to say that I have received a card and a letter from you and was pleased to learn that all are well I would have written before but we were in the firing line when I got the card and received the letter yesterday but have been on the move the past few days. My word it was hot and lively where we were as we are not allowed to say much about it, you wouldn't believe what it was like a man is lucky to come out of it alive, Archie Bailey and Harry Burrows were wounded in the first stunt. Harry is only slightly wounded I believe, as I inquired at his company but Archie got some bad knocks about the head, face and arms he is in one of the hospitals over there so he is alright, both Amos and I came out of it alright. I haven't heard anything about Charlie Cockcroft and Ray Leed but the division that they are in was not round in the Big Push. You would be surprised to see the place now where all the fighting has been going on, and to see how the germans have been prepared, the dugouts are something wonderful just like houses underground and are 40 and 50 feet deep and one room above the other well lads we are going into a different front this time and hope it is better than the last, I have seen a lot of France and Belgium since I have been here. My word you chaps are lucky getting over there instead of going to Egypt don't be in a hurry to get into the fray. There is a rumour that our leave to England is going to start if it does I might get over there before you leave I suppose Tom and the others will not be long there. I have had some letters from home lately, they tell me Charlie has enlisted and passed I think there are enough of us here now without him coming. Your Auntie and the others must have been pleased to see you. Remember me to all the boys, drop a line every week. I will write as often as I can, hoping all are well

George

Charlie Cockroft and Ray Leed were not in the 'big push' that was Pozieres, but this did not mean that they were safe. Ray Leed was 21 years old when he left the family farm near Mologa and joined the 57th Battalion of Pompey Elliott's 15th Brigade. He was killed near Armentieres in an action prior to the Battle of Fromelles on 15 July 1916.[1] Charlie Cockroft was also a farmer from the local area. He enlisted in July 1915 and served in the 58th Battalion, 15th Brigade. He was wounded three times, the first at Fromelles on 19 July when he was shot in the arm. On the third occasion in 1918, while in England and on the mend, he was listed as absent without leave on a number of occasions. The charges were eventually dismissed; perhaps it was considered that he had good cause as he was married in London on 30 November 1918.[2]

The day after George wrote to Allan and Percy, he also wrote home to his mother. He again expressed his disappointment that Charlie had enlisted and his frustration that other eligible men in the Mologa district appeared unwilling to risk their lives. After Pozieres, George knew that the chances of four brothers surviving the dreadful carnage were slim.

August 27th
Dear Mother

… before you receive this letter you will be alarmed at not getting any letters well I haven't had much time to write as we have been in this Advance and shifting about etc., well it was very lively you wouldn't believe what it was

like, some of the battles are the greatest that have been fought here every inch of the ground is ploughed up with shells, well Amos and I were lucky enough to get out of it without a scratch but Arch Bailey and Harry Burrows were both wounded in the first stunt, I didn't see Archie but I believe he got some bad wounds, Harry is not too bad, I enquired after him, Archie is in England at present and is doing fairly well, we have shifted again and are going into a different part of the line this time, we are not allowed to say much about it. Well the boys have arrived in England I had written two letters to them and they got them just after they arrived and Al wrote to me straight away and has also written another letter he said they have had four days leave into London and that they went out to Leicester my word they are lucky to be sent over there, Tom Alford and the others are also over there but I suppose they will soon be sent here to reinforce the battalion. I met Jack Gallagher here a few days ago he is in the artillery and had been sick in the hospital. And Charlie is going into camp I think there are enough of us here now without him coming, it is time some of those around there woke up. I got a letter from Miss Lowrie saying that she has got another school ...

I remain your loving son
George

As George wrote home he was en route to the Belgian border, marching through French villages until a train arrived to take the men to the Belgian village and soldier's retreat of Poperinghe, a vital Allied centre 13 kilometres to the west of Ypres in unoccupied Belgium. Nicknamed 'Pop's' by Allied soldiers, it was a place of refuge where they could visit shops and restaurants and be entertained at a theatre or dancing hall. A period of rest at Pop's represented a brief interlude in which some sense of normality could be restored. The most popular venue was Talbot House and Concert Hall, a club established by army chaplains Phillip Clayton and Neville Talbot in the mansion of a hop trader and banker who had fled Belgium. Today the building has been preserved as it was at the time of the war. George did not stay at Poperinghe but would return in 1917. Instead the Australians marched on to the shattered town of Ypres, arriving on 29 August. The battlefields to the east of the town were now a quagmire as the autumn rains fell.

MOLOGA, AUGUST 1916

On the first day of August, Charlie swore his oath of allegiance and was appointed to the 3rd Reinforcements of the 38th Battalion. He would be joining Allan and Percy as members of the 3rd Division. As he quickly organised his financial arrangements, his letters to his mother revealed nothing of his intention to propose to his girlfriend, Pearl Clee.

Bendigo
1ˢᵗ August 1916
Dear Mother,

I have opened a joint account in the Bendigo State Savings Bank which I enclose a form for your name just under mine, by this you will be able to pay in or draw out just the same as I can. I open with 1 pound I have the book here which I will leave with Pearl post the form back to the bank. I am in a devil of a hurry.

From
Your loving son
C.E. Marlow

The local newspaper promptly acknowledged Charlie's enlistment:

> *Mr C E Marlow, of Mologa, who has been accepted for active service, went into camp on August 1. He previously enlisted 13 months ago, but the teeth regulations at that time did not permit him to be accepted. Five sons of the family have now offered their services to their country, 4 of whom have been accepted.*[3]

Charlie was preparing to fight his own personal battle. He and Pearl were to marry. Revealingly, he does not mention this to his mother; rather he keeps his discussion to the daily routine, making no mention of his young love. While later he explains to his mother that he expected no opposition, his silence regarding his intentions may indicate that he was not as confident as he wanted his parents to believe. He evidently expected a negative reaction from his family and he was justified.

Bendigo
Wednesday 2nd 1916
Dear Mother,

… I am in the same tent as one of the Miles's from Kamarooka he is a cousin to the Miles' at Yarrawalla. We get plenty to eat any amount of tucker here including a plum pudding for dinner. I sent up a letter yesterday about the Savings Bank business which you were to sign and send back to the bank. I have met all the boys from about Mologa and Pyramid. Young Jim Baker is in this camp, it has been a miserable day down here today raining nearly all the time it is raining here now like blazes. I paid Mr Walker for the teeth on Tuesday and White Bros are fixing up that clock for Jim, I will send it up next week, I think I will be going into Bendigo on Sunday, the camp is a good way back from the old one but you can get right through the old camp and right across the racecourse it is a short cut as round the road is a good bit further. I am in "C" Company so when you write address my letters Pte C E M, "C" Company Military Camp Bendigo. There is not a great number of men here now, there was a lot went away the day I came in, I saw Hughie Martin last night he expects to go about the 16th August. Well I think I have about ran out of news so I will draw to a close hoping all are well as I am at present.

I am
Your loving son
C.E.

With the uncertainty of departure, Charlie wasted no time and the wedding plans were rapidly prepared. At home on the farm, the family received their invitation. The suddenness of the announcement angered Charlie's father and, in the days leading up to the wedding, debate raged within the family circle.

> *Mr & Mrs Clee present their compliments to Mr & Mrs Marlow and request the pleasure of your company at Heywoods Coffee Palace on the 19th August to celebrate the Marriage of our daughter Pearl with your Son Charles*
>
> *Ceremony at One PM at St Pauls Bendigo*
>
> *14/8/1916 RSVP*

Friday, 11ᵗʰ Aug, 1916
Dear Mother

I received your letter today dinner time also one from Jim yesterday which I answered I was very sorry indeed to learn that you were all up in arms so much about us getting married I thought that was a matter that only concerned myself as I am old enough now to know what to do and besides I have always kept myself and had to work hard for what I have got. Pearl said that she did not expect me to leave her any of my money if I was killed and I think that is what they are so much out about I wrote to Pearl about it and was to see her tonight, but we have to march into Bendigo so I will not see her till Sunday and then we will see what we intend to do. I did not think that any of you would mind in the least, I spoke to the officer about leave and he got me leave and we were to be married next Saturday. Pearl has got her dress or rather is getting it and we had everything fixed, but I will see about putting it off if possible, but I reckon that the boss and them had no right to interfere, if we do get married I may get into the N.C.O. school, but if not I intend to get away the first chance I get which will be soon. I have written to George for money and have written to him before but have not got a reply up. I reckon that it is a hard knock to us and I can tell you I feel it. Otherwise I am getting on splendid I like the drill more every day it is very interesting. One of the officers says they will have conscription within a month as there are no one enlisting and there is not many in camp they have shifted us to different tents and it is rumoured that the camp is to be divided into two parts one for the volunteers and one for the conscripts well I have to go to drill now so will close hoping to have an answer from you early next week.

I will now say goodbye
Hoping all are well as this leaves me
I am your loving son
Charlie E

The wedding proceeded despite strong Marlow family disapproval and the young couple were married. With Charlie in camp, the opportunity to share their lives as newlyweds was restricted to brief visits when leave was granted. Such visits were few as Charlie's period of training in Australia was cut short. The need to replace casualties in the line was now urgent. Within five weeks Charlie was on his way to England while the raging debate over conscription continued to exacerbate the deepening social chasm.

Charlie and Pearl Marlow on their wedding day.

Bendigo
Sunday [27.8.16]
Dear Mother,

Just a few lines I received your letter yesterday I am getting on alright I got leave from 2pm on Saturday till 11pm on Sunday night that is not too bad we have had a very easy time since I came back, we marched into Bendigo on Friday night and got away at the Masonic Hall we were supposed to go in but I cleared, it was a play but half of the boys cleared down the street there was a terrible crowd of people in town that night I met Jim Mahoney but I did not see any of the Gibsons and I have had leave about 3 times since I came back I do not know if I will be able to get into Bendigo next Sunday as I am afraid I will have to go on guard. I was picked for guard on Thursday night along with 8 others but they only wanted three so the officer said that the men that were dressed best and the cleanest looking he would let them off so I got out of it and was not sorry either. There is one of the Roberts from Durham Ox in my company he is a nice fellow, that young Miles that was with me was robbed of his pay £3/15/- the night after he was paid and was fined £1/15/- for staying over his leave so that is a bit rough on him. I do not know when I am sailing but I do not think it will be inside a fortnight. Well I will close hoping all are well as I am at present so goodbye mum I am your affect son CE

Pearl wishes to be remembered to all
I saw Townie down the street Friday night but was not talking to her.

Unlike those of his brothers, Charlie's farewell was a hurried affair on the siding of the Mologa railway station. The controversial issue of conscription was mentioned by Councillor Jones in his farewell speech and Charlie carefully responded that duty to his country and helping his brothers was his motivation. A public airing of personal differences was avoided.

Mologa – Farewell to CE Marlow

On Tuesday afternoon before the departure of the train the residents of Mologa assembled at Mologa railway station to bid farewell to Pte. C.E. Marlow and made a presentation of a gold medal. Mr Fyffe, president of the farewell committee made the presentation and in doing so spoke at some length, first of all congratulating the departing soldier on his recent marriage. He trusted he would have the pleasure of seeing Pte. Marlow return safely to live amongst them, and assured him of a hearty welcome back. He paid a high tribute to Pte. Marlow as a young man of the district who had worked hard and bore an excellent character … Mr R. Jones, J.P., said Pte. Marlow was an industrious young man and a credit to Mologa. In the football field he was never found wanting, and he felt sure he would be the same at the front. The speaker also touched on conscription he asked his hearers if it was fair that four sons in one family should go, while in another not even one had enlisted. Pte. Marlow in response said when he went into camp he was taught to stand still and say nothing so they would excuse him for a short stay at home. He said he thought it was his duty to go and fight for his country and help his brothers and comrades at the front. He thanked them one and all for the congratulations and kindly remarks and the nice gold medal, which he would value to his life's end. Three cheers were then given for Pte. Marlow, followed by more cheers for the Marlow family ...[4]

LARKHILL, ENGLAND, AUGUST

While the battle for Pozieres raged across the channel, the men of the 38th Battalion first sighted England's shores on 10 August. Allan and Percy disembarked at Plymouth and travelled through the green pastures of England en route to Larkhill Camp, Salisbury Plain. Arriving at midnight, the brothers saw little of their new home until morning when the expanse of the soldier city with amenities and huts nestled in the rolling fields was unveiled. The nearby village of Amesbury provided entertainment with a YMCA hut and cinema helping to relieve any boredom in the few idle hours. Four days' leave was granted and the Marlows followed the majority of their fellow Australians to London then immediately continued further north to Leicester to surprise their father's family with their unannounced but very welcome arrival.

Allan wrote to George:

England Friday
11 August
Dear Georgie

Well Georgie old cockie I received 2 letters from you today and by jove I was pleased to get them. I never even dreamt of getting any so soon. Well Georgie I am pleased to hear that you are well. You must be having a pretty ruff time over there. I believe you chaps have been hit about a bit. Well Georgie it wont be long before we will be with you. We landed here last night at 2 o'clock. We disembarked at Plymouth at 2 o'clock yesterday. We had a great trip over we were 7 weeks on the water, but we had a very narrow escape. Well when I left home everyone was well. We are in a good camp here it is at Salisbury Plains. Well I will send you a letter on Sunday. We are all well. The boys wish to be remembered to you ...

Percy took the time to write a long letter to his parents. He had much to tell of his first impressions of England — the countryside, the sights and meeting his relatives for the first time. The twins were already capitalising on the opportunities and seeing the sights was a priority.

Amesbury
20 Aug
Dear Mother & Dad

Just a few lines to let you know I am still alive, we are in England at last, it took us seven weeks and two days to come over, it was a lovely trip, I was not sick although the trip was a good one. The meals were rotten they were good at the start but after the first week or two they were not fit to eat. We had a bit of a guard duty to do, we were on a gun on the ship, there were twelve of us altogether on the gun, she was a big one. We landed at Plymouth but we could not see what the place was like, the camp we had to go [to] was eighty miles from Plymouth, it was four oclock in the morning before we got to bed. It was a lovely trip from Plymouth the country is pretty all layed out in little fields, and enclosed by blackberry, the lanes are very narrow hardly room for two carts to pass. The camp were [where] we are is not a very nice place, no towns near it. The village of Amesbury is not far away it is not much of a place not very many people there. We got four days leave, we went to London it is a nice place, the streets are crowded Allan & I went to Leicester it is about a hundred miles from London, it took us two hours to go there it is a nice place, we did not have much trouble finding our relations in Leicester. When we got to Paynes, Aunty and Ethel were at the pictures, the lady next door made us go in and she went to the pictures and told Aunty; they got a great surprise when they got back. There was only Auntie and Ethel there, the others were at Drayton – Ethel is about eighteen or nineteen she is a nice girl. They told us about Leicester and one or two good tales about Dad. The next day we went with Aunty to Drayton, we got there about ten it was a long walk to Aunt Charlotte[s] place on the way there we saw where Grandfather was buried and cannot think of the place where Aunty lives, it is not much of a village.[5] While we were there we saw our Aunt Edith she walked six miles to see us, we saw Ida also, you would hear Jim talking about her, and a lot of other cousins Flo Wilson was the only one we did not see, she was away on holidays. They made a great fuss of us. We came back to London on the Wednesday and had a look round in the afternoon. The next day we went for a trip round London and by jove it did rain, we saw the Tower of London it is a very nice place and to St Pauls it is a nice place also. We had to go back to camp that night, it was about two when we got back and I was not a bit tired. We are going to go to Salisbury one week end. I just got a letter from Charlie and Albert and Aunty Etta. Well Mum we got a letter from George the other day he did not have much news. Well Mum we are going for a walk to the village blacksmith today so I think I will close.

From your loving son
Percy

As the brothers settled into weeks of training, thoughts of home were never distant. Persistent rain did little to alleviate their longing for the familiar countryside of Mologa, although Second Lieutenant O'Donnell, Commanding Officer of the Machine-Gun Section, did his best to ensure that his men were satisfied with their new environment. Regular leave on Saturday and Sunday afternoons provided opportunities to catch up with old neighbours and friends in nearby camps.

Lark Hill
Amesbury
20-8-16
Dear Albert

We were all through these buildings they are of course very ancient but very interesting when you have a guide to tell you all about them. We seen some lovely scenery in London but would not live here for anything I have posted you all a lot of letters I received yours but was not at all pleased, you would know that too.

Goodbye Albert
Brother Allan

On 23 August Allan sent a number of postcards home which his cousin had given him in Leicester, using some to write his news:

Amesbury
Lark Hill Camp
Wednesday 23.8.16
Dear Old Albert

Well Albert I hope you and all at home are well. I never felt better in all my life. The other boys are well too. I got another letter from you yesterday I was so pleased to get it. This is the only one I got from home. I also got one from Lily Sharp and one from Ida Payne and Flo Wilson. I have not got the paper yet, but I believe they are in London.

By hell skins are a big price now, couldn't we play hell with them. I am pleased to hear you are having a good season over there. I thought Charlie would enlist, but I think he should have stopped at home, as we are well presented. There is one thing about it when he sails they are bound to send them here somewhere, and it is a good home compared with Egypt. I don't think the war will last much longer now. You must be having a good time out at bobs.[6] We will have a good time out there after the war. The rabbits will get hell I can tell you. We get splendid tucker here now and plenty of it. We have got a bonzer officer. He is the boy to stick to you. I like our new machine gun. With the Lewis Gun we have to go into the front line of trenches. The Vickers machine gunners go in the 2nd and the maxim gunner go in the 3rd line. We have to drill a treat here, it is not a pleasure trip we are on. We have had a good deal of rain since being here. We might go into the trenches anytime now. Has conscription come in yet. I am always wondering if you got my cable from Cape Town and also my letters from here. I posted the parcel over. The brooch is for mum, pipe for dad, cigars for Jim and cigarette case for you. I don't know whether Percy sent anything or not. Well Albert old cockie, I don't care how soon we go to the trenches. I do hope mum is getting my money. Tell her she can have what she likes of it and one of you can have what you like. I am sending you some postcards what Ida Payne sent to me, they are no good to me here. Oh Albert I have wrote such a lot of letters. I will also send you over some English papers. I have a few farthings in my pocket. I will send them over. Jim will be playing hell with that new plough now. I suppose he is singing better than ever now. How much crop have you put in this year; considering being a good one you will have your work cut out in the harvest time. By hell you all miss me at the bag sewing. Too true says you. Well Albert that was a good rumour about us being back at Campellfield. As I said in my other letters we had a terrible lot of sickness coming over. We buried 2 at sea and had over 200 cases of measles etc...

To his mother Allan added his thoughts on the upcoming harvest and the lunches she always prepared that he knew he would miss.

... Well Mum I believe you are having a good year over there, and I am pleased too. I wouldn't mind being there for the lunches, as that was the place where I could shine isn't that so A few hot scones and tea was what I liked, anyway we will still get them after the war. I put all Sunday in in writing letters so I hope you get them. Also the little present. I hope you like it mum. Well dear mum don't worry over us as we are enjoying ourselves and I don't think it will be long before we are home so goodbye mum till we meet again.

I remain
Your Loving Son
Allan

To his father he suggested:

... I can tell you I might get leave to go home and sew the bags ... I like the climate over here it agrees with me. Everything looks lovely here. After the war dad I will take you over this way and show you around, But I told you I would not live here, Australia for me. It was the best move that ever you made to go to Australia. Well Dad I am writing such a lot of letters to you all, as you will excuse the writing. Well dad goodbye till we meet again I hope you like the pipe. I thought it was the best thing I could buy you so I hope it suits. It is supposed to be a good one but they come the bluff on us ...

I don't think the war will last much longer ...

At Larkhill, the reports from the battlefields were finally bringing hope. In Europe, news that Romania had joined the Allies was met with jubilation as was the news that Australian and New Zealand forces had repelled the Turkish advance on Romani and that Egypt was, in the short term, secured. Allan wrote home of the positive news from France. Ironically this was the same day that the 4th Division was forced to retreat from Mouquet Farm. The 'latest in the paper' was a long way removed from reality.

Amesbury
Letter no.1
Lark Hill Camp
29th-8-16
Dear Albert,

… You are having some bonnie rains over there you will have a great harvest no doubt. It is just the same here raining practically every day, and it makes everything so miserable. On Saturday we went around to Salisbury to see the town, it is a place a bit bigger than Bendigo but not as nice a place. There are some terrible old place[s] there. There is a beautiful cathedral there, It is the oldest one in England. We were all through it. We also went through the gardens. We got back to the camp about 1 oclock that night. Well on the Sunday Les [Townsend] *Percy and I and 2 other chaps went over to see Charlie* [Fyffe], *Tom*[Alford] *and Hughie* [Johnson], also referred to as Ewen and Uhun] *at Perrim Downs. We motored over after church parade and came back in the trains. The boys look well. Hughie was off to France this morning* [Tuesday]. *He seemed to be glad to get away I only wish I was getting away too. Today they have taken 45 men out of each company to make reinforcements up. I really think there will be no 38th Battalion soon. I think it will be split up into reinforcements. Things seem to be going well over in France now. Roumania will shake the huns up. In todays paper things are good. We always get the latest in the paper here. To morrow we are going out on the rifle range, the next day we are going out on a route march, so you can guess we will be going some but it doesn't matter a dam we know it is all in the game. Tomorrow night I am going over to see Dave Glass. I think they are moving off soon. If I only knew how long it would be before the 38th went into action and I knew it would be long, I am off into some reinforcements, buggar it all I think I am fit now to have a cut. I have no letters from Georgie but I had 2 or 3 from England. Well Albert old*

boy you must be having a lovely time out at bobs. Tom Alford showed me a photo of Pearl Saville to me on Sunday he had just got it. It was some stile too. She just looked tip top. Well Albert I hope you get my letters all right ... Don't forget to tell me how all at home are. Though I am a long way away I never forget you all. Well Albert old boy I will say goodbye.

I remain
Your loving brother
Allan

Frustrated with training and anxious to get to the front, Allan was willing to forgo the brotherhood of the Bendigo battalion for the chance to show his worth. Percy's main concern however, was the monotony of the wet English autumn.

Lark Hill
29 Aug
Dear Charlie

I received your ever welcome letter yesterday and glad in a way to hear you have enlisted although, I think there is enough of us in it. We have not heard from Geordie lately, I don't know whether he could have got our last letters. It is terrible wet here lately, it seems a buggar of a place for rain. I don't know what it will be like in winter time. We went to Salisbury last Saturday afternoon, we could only get leave for the afternoon it is not a bad place, it is bigger than Bendigo. On Sunday we went over to Perron Downs, where Charlie Fyffe and Tom, Johnson, it is about twelve miles from us, we went in a motor, it was a wet day. Uhun is leaving for France this morning, Charlie and Tom are not going, Tom has been a bit crook. We get plenty of drill now, it is a sticky place here when it is raining much. Well Charlie I suppose you had a taste of the stew by now, its good isn't it. We have not had any shooting out of the Lewis guns yet. We will have an idea of the trenches before we leave here, B Company had 48 hours in them, it is raining a lot of the time. We got inoculated yesterday it was a buggar for about 24 hours, it was ten times as strong as we [had] in Australia, Well Charlie I think I have told you all the news so I will remain

your loving brother Percy

Allan wrote to Jim of his discontent but also his pleasure when Albert's mate from Mologa arrived at Larkhill:

30-8-16
Dear Jim

Well Jim old boy how the devil are you ... I am getting fat as the devil and ugly with it. I am getting my photo taken so I will send them over to you ... The lads don't know when they are going but they are sending them away in hundreds now. I wish to God I could get away. We are being going some lately. This is the place where you [get] it rocked into you, but it is all in the game. They tell us all the more work we get, will help us to get back to Australia, anyway that is their b- tale. We went out to the range on Friday and went through our musketry. We all done pretty good shooting. We will be going down to the range any day to do our shooting with the machine guns. I am dying to shoot with them, According to our paper here the machine guns are doing good work at the front and I hope we hold our end up with them. The boys are doing some big route marches lately, but we have missed them up to date and I am sure we don't want any either. We have had a terrible lot of rain here lately and it makes everything so miserable. They are having a very wet harvest here but they seem to work away just the same. I am finishing this letter on Sunday 3rd Sept. Well Jim we all went down to a little village called Andover on Saturday. It is not much of a place, but I thought it might be a nice little place. Percy and W. Street got leave to go to London so they can come back tonight. Anyway Jim I was busy writing letters to you today when Jack Price came along we did get a hell of a shock. Anyway I put the afternoon in with Jack and I am a little bit behind with my letters now. Well Jim Jack does not look to well. He has been in the hospital for a month and has just came. He put a week in Egypt but did not think to much of it. I am going to try to get him into the 38th Battalion and I think I can do it too. He does not think too much of the reinforcements he is in. You can tell his people about that but don't tell them about him not looking too well. Well Jim Charlie Fyffe came over to see us on Saturday but we were down at Andover. He never sent us any word to say that he was coming or we would have stopped home. Well Jim I hope we [are] over in France by the time you get this letter. I have not got any more letters from Geordie. I hope I soon get some more letters from home. Don't forget to tell me if you got my letters and cable from Capetown. I am anxious about them …

I remain your loving brother
Allan

Charlie Fyffe has gone to France this morning. Don't forget to tell Mrs Price and Mrs Fyffe Alford and Johnson that we met the boys.

Hurrah Jim

Writing home to Albert, Percy remarked on the surfeit of nice girls in London. Many dominion soldiers found new friends, girlfriends and lovers during their English leave. While the intentions of many of the ladies on the streets of London were not always admirable, there were others who were genuinely concerned for the welfare of the soldiers who were so far from the comfort of their homes.

Lark Hill
31 Aug
Dear Albert

… We are still in England and will be here for a while. It has been raining like b- here lately, I don't know what it will be like in the winter time. You have had bad luck with the rain, not been able to go and see the girl, you will be able to have a good time now, that I am not there to watch you. Well Albert I see a few girls now and then, they are easy to get in London some nice girls there …

Your loving brother
Percy

THEATRES OF WAR, SEPTEMBER

In France the Battle of the Somme continued into its second phase. On 15 September at Delville Wood, east of Pozieres, Haig's secret weapon, the tank, was used for the first time. While initially terrifying the enemy troops, the tanks were slow and largely ineffective with only nine of the 49 'Willies', as they were nicknamed, reaching the German lines before breaking down or becoming easy targets for artillery fire.

British, Canadian, Scottish and New Zealand forces advanced towards Bapaume, taking Courcelette, High Wood and Flers, then later Thiepval, Combles, Morval and Gueudecourt. The ultimate objective of Bapaume was not reached before the dreadful Somme winter began to descend. Incessant rain began to fall, the shattered ruins of villages and fields turned to mud and shell holes filled with putrid water. The Battle of the Somme was grinding to a halt; the stalemate had not been broken. While Allied forces had gained some 11 kilometres of ground, the cost was beyond comprehension. Over one million Allied and enemy soldiers had become casualties. Of these, 146,000 Allied soldiers were listed as killed or missing.

In the east, the mobile Russian offensive had gained much ground while the German offensive at Verdun had stalled. The optimism of the brothers that the Allies were wearing the German forces down is evident; however, as the September rains turned the battlefields to mud and the European winter set in, the enemy position strengthened. Russian forces were demoralised by an influx of German reinforcements, Romania struggled and the Italian front, like the Somme, was deadlocked.

BELGIUM, SEPTEMBER

The Australians had withdrawn to the relative quiet of the Ypres sector, the 1st Division rotated through the trench line north of the Ypres-Comines Canal, in the vicinity of the infamous Hill 60 site which was to become well known to the Australians in 1917. Here they were told to prepare for the winter and this is where the soldiers expected to remain during the approaching cold months. They began digging and fortifying trenches and raiding enemy lines while reinforcements, fresh from training in England, began to arrive to boost the division's depleted numbers.

Writing home, George addressed his letters as 'France'; however, he was now positioned just over the border in Belgium. George may have been attempting to inform Charlie of his location as he mentions that the trenches are 'noted for one thing here'. Perhaps George is referring to the Ypres salient, notorious for the first use of gas by German forces on 22 April 1915.

France
Sept 6ʰ 1916
Dear Charlie

I received a letter from you, mother and Albert yesterday also one from cousin Ida telling me about Al and Percy going to see them and what a surprise she got when her mother sent her a telegram saying that she was coming home with two Australians. You say you have enlisted and passed, you will have fair idea of camp life by now, it is about time some of them you mentioned woke up and enlisted. You ought to try to get in some reinforcements to the second Brigade, I don't think there is much chance of me seeing the others as they are in a different division to me I could claim them and get them in my Brigade but as they have such a lot of mates from home I wouldn't think of it. I don't think they will see much fighting this year as it is coming on winter, it has been raining here this last few days they say this month is generally very wet and we are into the winter by next month and last till about march. We have had some good news lately that Roumania is fighting on our side and that the Russians are taking prisoners in ten(s) of thousands and where we were fighting last month we advanced a good bit, my word it was very lively on the Somme the fighting was the fiercest since the war broke out talk about shells every bit of the ground was ploughed up you wouldn't believe it. Archie Bailey and Harry Burrows were wounded in the first stunt that we were in there, Amos and I are alright. Tom Alford and the others are in England, lucky aren't they. You seem to be having a lot of rain over there. I am getting the letters regular now I wrote to them at home last week, don't send any more papers as I haven't received one yet they don't bother about them. I saw a letter in the Bendigo paper from a chap over here. He wrote just after we arrived here, he had in it that it was a picnic here to the Dardanelles I bet he don't think so now the fight we just came out of was worse than any fight at the Dardanelles. We are on a different part of the firing line now the trenches are good here but it is noted for one thing here. Well Charlie I have no more news so will close hoping you are well as I am at present

I remain
Your Loving Bro
George

I hope you have better luck with the second ticket

The following day he wrote to Albert:

September 7th 1916
Dear Albert

… I told you in my letters that I received the both parcels one took 5 months to reach me, don't send any more papers as I haven't got one yet they give them away to anybody they want stirring up about it, I would like to get the one with the piece about K. Lairds death in it, I didn't know he was dead, tell me what he died from when you write. You need not send those addresses any more as I have all the lads addresses also the English addresses. I have written to Al & Percy several times and have had two letters from them. I had a letter yesterday from Cousin Ida saying that they were out to Leicester to see them. I wrote to Charlie yesterday also to Mother last week and will write to Jim in a few days time. I am doing a lot of writing this last week as I have had a good chance to write since we came out of this <u>Advance</u>. This is a picnic here where we are now to where we just came from but is a great place for mines and gas. I am not in the front line at present but soon go in and relieve the other part of the Battery. I am going to drop a line to Jack Price to see if he has joined the Batt. yet. Tom Alford and some of the others might have to go into the 58 Battalion as some of the reinforcements that come from the sixth have to go to the 58 Batt. Amos is alright I often have a yarn with him, I told you in other letters that Arch Bailey and Harry Burrows were wounded in the <u>"Big Push"</u>. Well Albert news is exhausted so will close hoping all are in the best of health as I am at present.

I remain Your Loving Bro
Geo.

While George described life in the trenches protecting Ypres as a 'picnic' compared to the hell of Pozieres, the regular clouds of gas and the constant shell and mortar fire continued unabated, not only in the front line but also in the rear support areas. George wrote in a letter home of his surprise at the death of Ken Laird. Ken was a 27-year-old farmer from nearby Calivil who had enlisted in July 1915 and served in the 22nd Battalion.[7] He married just prior to leaving Australia and had survived the tough Gallipoli campaign. In the early hours of 2 July

1916 Ken was guarding an ammunition store behind British lines near the busy staging post of Bailleul, north-west of Armentieres. He was hit by a long-range shell and severely wounded. Ken died in the field ambulance as it struggled through congested roads to seek treatment for the wounded Australian.[8]

September 12th
Dear Jim

Just a few lines to say that I received a letter from you, Charlie and Allan also my first Pyramid Paper with the piece about Ken Laird's death and the Honour Roll, I suppose Charlie's name will be down on it by now. Allan said in his letter that Jack Price is in England and has been in the hospital sick and does not look to well, Dave Glass is also there, he said Ewin & Charlie have left there for France so when we go out of these trenches I will have a look through the 6 Batt. for them but they might be sent to the 58 Batt as some of the reinforcements that come for the 2nd brigade have to go the 15 brigade. Bert Gibson has got his discharge and they call him the returned "Hero" I don't think he saw a shot fired, if he had been through the fighting here he would have room to talk. You don't seem to have got my letters telling you that I received both parcels although one was travelling for about 5 months. Well Jim I started to write this letter two days ago but had to stop well since then I received a letter each from Charlie, Albert and Aunt Lizz. Dated 1st August, I have received a lot of letters lately. I hope you like the new plough it will be much quieter. I often see Amos and have a yarn with him. We do a lot of Mortar work here when Fritz fires his bombs over we give him about twice as much back. Well Jim I will now close hoping all are well as I am at present.

Your aff. Bro
George

Bert Gibson enlisted in June 1915 and was allocated to the 13th Light Horse Regiment. Soon after arriving in Egypt he was kicked by a horse and the resulting injury proved so severe that he was invalided back to Australia and discharged in February 1916. He married later that year but was recalled for special duty at the AIF Depot in Cape Town, where he served from March to November 1917.[9]

George also found time to pen a letter to his parents:

… You mentioned about sending money, well I have had money all the time I have been in France and being in the trenches so often don't get the chance to spend it, it would come in handy if I got leave to England but there is no such luck so you need not send any, but take £15 out of my pay and buy yourself something. Charlie is lucky getting such good tucker in camp we do fairly well here … I was very sorry to hear about Ken Laird and Donaldson that used to play with Calival I used to see him in Egypt very often, he was camped along side us there, I suppose there are others that have been knocked in the same place as we were fighting. I had a letter from Al saying that [they] have no word of shifting yet but said Ewan and Charlie had left for France and that Jack Price has been sick in the hospital. I don't think they will see much heavy fighting before the winter and doubt if they see any, we do a lot of firing bombs here, have just finished having a bit of a duel with Fritz. Do you know how Ray is getting on I think he was with Campbell that got wounded. Has Vic Winterbottom left yet. Well I have no more news so will close hoping all are well as I am at present.

I remain
Your Loving Son
George

P.S. be sure and buy yourself something out of that money

Robert Campbell (photo courtesy Pyramid Hill Historical Society).

George was yet to hear that Ray Leed had been killed near Fromelles almost two months before while Robert Campbell was recovering from a gunshot wound to the head. Robert had been Head Teacher at Mologa Central School when he enlisted at the age of 22 and, like Ray, he had been sent to the 57th Battalion. He returned to the front on 10 November 1916. Thirteen days later he was reported killed in action.[10]

George wrote to Allan and Percy describing the recent casualties:

… It is rumoured here that your division is being split up for reinforcements for the others that are here, but must be a furfie as you say you have no word about shifting, if you should try and get into this brigade. Did I tell you that Ken Laird has died of wounds he was in the 6th Brigade Trench Mortar also Donaldson that used to play football with Calival has been killed and his brother had a leg blown off and Campbell the school teacher and a son of Pentreath's has been wounded they were telling me about these chaps in their letters from home, we only here [hear] of the ones that are in our own brigade, Amos is well he is only a little way along the way from me. We do a lot of bomb firing here it gets lively at times. Well boys I don't think you will see much fighting this year as it will soon be winter and things will be at a standstill then we are preparing for the cold now, it will be very miserable here…

While George was expecting a miserable winter, he could not have foreseen that this would be one of the worst European winters on record.

ENGLAND, SEPTEMBER

Throughout September, Allan and Percy enjoyed moments of respite from training and continued to find opportunities to familiarise themselves with their father's homeland. But thoughts of their own birthplace were never too distant. The twins frequently wrote home, anxious for news and to send updates regarding George and their friends and neighbours.

Amesbury
Sunday 3rd September

My Dear Mother and Father

...Well mother just as I am getting a good start again after Jack Price has gone Dave Glass has just come to see me so I am finishing this letter off on Monday night. Well, Jack Price came down to see me on Sunday afternoon so I can tell you that I had a hell of a shock. He is camped about 2 miles away from us. I am often going down to see the poor devil, I feel sorry for Jack on account of him being away on his own. I am going to do my best to get him into the 38th Batt and I think I can do it. He has just come out of the hospital. He had measles and numonia. He does not look too well on it. Well mum Percy and Will Street got leave to go to London on Saturday they came back Sunday night. They had a pretty decent time. The rest of us lads went down to Andover to see the town there. It is not a bad little place. I think I have seen most of the sights around about our camp now. Well Mum I am terribly pleased to night, do [you] know what happened, I got a letter from Georgie, this is the first since I wrote to him, he got my letters all right and good many from home. He said he was well. Him and Amos came out of the trenches together. He said he had not seen Ray Leed or Charlie Cockcroft, he said their division was not in the Big Push. He also said they were shifting to where the fighting was not so heavy. He said he heard they were going to be sent to London for a holiday. I only hope he is, as I would like to see him. He said in his letter that Harry Burrows and Archie Bailey had been wounded. Well mum dear it is raining here again today. All the battalion bar us have gone for a two day route march, so you can see we are lucky to be M Gun Section. Mum everything over here is good we are all happy - I expect a letter or two from you in a few days. Jack Price is getting a lot of letters he says. He has not had his 4 days leave in London yet but expects to go this week. We get a good many letters from Leicester and our other relations. There has been some big zeppelin raids in London lately. They brought a big one down on Saturday night. So things were very exciting. Well dear mum and dad I think I have told you all the news, so I trust and hope you are all well as it leaves me and the rest at present,

Goodbye I remain your loving son
Allan S

Charlie Fyffe and Hughie Johnson have gone to France. Tell their people that we met all the Mologa boys that have gone lately. They all look well.

I have been wondering if you got my cables and letters from Cape Town. I do hope so.

It is getting very cold here now
We get pretty good tucker now.

To Jim, he briefly mentioned Charlie's wedding:

... The 2/38 have just come in so Charlie wont be long. I have not got any letters referring to the wedding ... You will be busy with the crops by the time you get this letter. They say we are in for a cold winter. I will send my photo by next mail. Give my love to your girl that is if I know her ...

German airships known as Zeppelins were frequently used for bombing raids across England and were responsible for killing and injuring many civilians and causing widespread damage. The raid Allan refers to occurred on the night of 2/3 September, a Saturday night. Sixteen airships crossed the English Channel under cover of darkness. A 19-year-old British pilot took to the air and shot one of the zeppelins in the early hours of Sunday morning. As further letters describe, the pilot was awarded the Victoria Cross for his bravery. In 1917, German long-range heavy bomber aircraft, Gotha Bombers, were to cause greater loss of life and destruction as they targeted the busy port of Folkestone, various army camps and, in a daring daylight raid, were responsible for the death of children attending a London school.

Percy was in London the night the Zeppelins set their sights on the city:

... We went to London last Saturday, there was a zeppelin raid in London while we were there, it was two oclock in the morning, when they came we did not see them, we slept too sound, they were firing at them and they brought one down. Well Jim we have plenty of drill now, not near as bad a time as the infantry, they get plenty of marching, news is scarce at present I only hope to hear about your marriage any day now ...

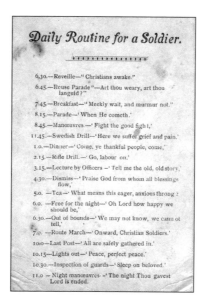

Allan's card, 'Daily routine of a soldier', which he sent to Albert.

Allan scribbled a quick note to Albert on the back of a postcard and, a few days later, wrote lengthy letters to his brothers in Australia:

"Daily Routine for a Soldier"
No.3 Letter
Lark Hill Camp
Amesbury
Tuesday 5 September
Dear Albert

Well Albert old boy this is our daily routine so you can see we are kept going. The battalion has just arrived home from their route march. The poor devils look tired. We are going through our machine gun tests on Saturday. I think we ought to do well enough. Well Albert when you write don't forget to tell me all the Mologa news etc. I am sending over some English papers to you.

I remain your loving Brother
Allan

Bye Albert old boy
No word of going to the front
I have just got Pyramid paper

Amesbury
Lark Hill Camp
8/9/16
Dear Jim

… Well Jim you are having a wet year over there alright. It must be delaying you with the plowing and I suppose it inconveniences you as regards going to see this new girl of yours. Jim you are dead mean every time you write, you never mention her name so next time you write please do mention her name. Well Jim we were inoculated the day before yesterday and by hell it gave us blazes. We went out on parade yesterday, but had to come in again. We heard that there was a route march today so some of us malingered out of it. It is the first time ever I malingered but we cant be too cunning in the army. I saw Jack Price again the other night, he is still on light duty and is going into London today. I am finishing this letter Sunday 10th. Well Jim my arm is alright now and I am on duty again. On Saturday a few of us went to a place called Whitchurch but it [is] a very poor place and we did not stop long. On Sunday morning Percy, Les and a few more of us went over to a place called Stonehenge. I am sure you have read about it in History. This afternoon I am busy writing letters, but a few of the lads have gone to Salisbury. Well Jim yesterday we saw a big mob of German prisoners. They got out of the train at Amesbury and were marched out into our german prison in the camp. They were the biggest men I ever saw. They were as fat as pigs. We have to travel in 3rd class carriages, but the b- germans travel in first class carriages. We have a terrible lot of them in the prison out here. About 3 weeks ago a nurse down at the prison went into prison to dress the wounds of one of them and the b- got the stuff she had in the bowl and threw it over her face and it blinded her. She called out to the chap that was on guard and he was an Australian. He came in and bashed him to pieces now he is in the clink and is to be tried. Yesterday they took the reinforcements out of our battalion and they went to Perim Downs. Things are very quiet here today. I think I will be going to London next Saturday. Only 2 a week are allowed to go. The fare to London from here is 14 /- but we go for 7/-. Les seems to be getting better now; but does not [look] to well on it yet. Well Jim I hope you and all at home are well as it leaves me at present. Remember me to your new girl whoever she might be. Jim let me know by return of post who she is …

To Albert he added:

... I had a terrible job to read Etters letter and all the news Lily Sharp had was that they had not got any letters from me yet and that she had just finished washing her hair. Well Albert old boy I don't suppose it will be long before you will be cutting hay. It don't seem anytime since last harvest ... I am glad you like your job on the cutter, the only job I would like on it, would be the boss ... I am sending those Pyramid papers onto Georgie, he will get them in 4 days from here. He had a very interesting letter in it. Jack Wales must have had a great welcome home. It is very funny the pub in Pyramid being isolated. Hu Martin wouldn't like that would he. Auntie Etter said in her letter about a ghost chasing a girl in Bendigo. I expected something like that from her. I think she delights in these b- ghosts. I suppose Charlie knows what camp life is like by now. I supposed you cursed the rain up dale when you could not go to see the girl no doubt it must be a bit of a b-. Does it delay Jim too. He never says in his letter who his girl is. I wish I knew... I saw Jack Price again last night, he is still on light duty and is going into London today. I wish I was going too. London is a lovely place for a holiday but for nothing else. I have just read in the paper when poor old Jacka has died of wounds.[11] *Yesterday there was 2 700 Australians put out of action. The poor Australians are in the hottest of fighting. Ted Bennitts is pretty crook with lumbago. He does not look well at all but don't say a word. They split our battalion up the other day they took 50 out of each company for reinforcements but now they have brought them back. There were a lot more Australians come in the other day. They say they are going to shift us out of here for the winter. They tell us it is a fair brute in winter time ...*

Jack Price was a neighbour and classmate of Albert. He was also a keen member of the Mologa Football Club. On his 18th birthday he persuaded his parents to sign his enlistment papers and was allocated to the 46th Battalion. Allan, believing that Jack needed the support of familiar faces, would soon attempt to have him transferred to the 38th.

On 10 September Percy and Allan spent much of their day writing home to each family member. Percy wrote to his parents of his visit to 'marvellous' Stonehenge, also telling them that the 3rd Division was to be inspected by the Commander-in-Chief of the British Home Forces:

… We went to the Stonehenge this morning, it is marvellous how the big stones were brought there, it is very interesting to see it … General French is coming out here tomorrow, I am sure he will be struck with the 38th Battalion …

Allan wrote a lengthy letter to his mother:

Sunday 10.9.16
My Dear Mum

… We are having a lot of rain over here and I hope it keeps like this for a while. Sometimes when you get up in the morning it is lovely, and perhaps in a couple of hours it is raining like billy o. Well mum I am glad you got my cable but then you wrote you never said when you got it and where it came from … It is very funny about all the rumours of our boat going down, well mum they said it was in this mornings paper that she was sunk in the Mediterranian. I got a very interesting letter from Georgie. I write to him every week I am sending the Pyramid papers over to him.

I think I am going to London next Saturday. I was very sorry when I heard about Ken Laird. I had only just finished reading his letter in the pyramid paper when I got your letter. Well mum we are having a good time here. We get plenty of work and we get pretty good tucker. I knew that young Falconer of Mincha. Les has had a bad back. The doctor said it was lumbago. He seems to be pretty right now. Ted Bennitts has had a very bad back. When I go to London I am getting flannels as they say it is terrible cold here in the winter. I have not had a cold since I left Australia. Mum I have never felt better in my life. I am getting my photo taken so I will send them over …

I remain
Your Loving Son
Allan S

I don't think we are going to France for a long time
All the boys are well.

MOLOGA, SEPTEMBER

As the Australian winter ended and the Somme casualty lists revealed the tragic results of the battle, the Australian people were consumed by the raging debate over conscription. A significant drop in recruitment following Fromelles and Pozieres now meant that Australia could not supply the 80,000 men required over four months to replace Australian losses and to strengthen its battalions.[12] England had demanded the compulsory service of its sons in January 1916, while in New Zealand conscription was introduced in August. Australian Prime Minister Billy Hughes had recently returned from England and France. Despite widespread opposition within the Labor Party he announced a referendum on 28 October to settle the question of conscription once and for all.[13] Hughes was so confident that the referendum would support the introduction of conscription that he ordered a call-up of all unmarried men between the ages of 21 and 35 for home service prior to the vote, ensuring that these men would be ready for overseas service once conscription was introduced.[14]

In Mologa, Albert arrived home requesting that his parents sign the form providing their consent to his enlistment. While he would not turn 19 until November, he would be accepted by the Bendigo recruiting office at 18 years 10 months (the minimum age of 18 was not introduced until May 1918). Parental consent duly provided, Albert was certified fit at Royal Park in Melbourne on 18 October 1916, one month before his 19th birthday. I suspect it was with great reluctance that Sarah had agreed to provide her consent. Sarah and Charles probably expected the Conscription Bill to pass and that their youngest son would soon be conscripted regardless of their wishes. The burden of that day was to last Sarah a lifetime.

Bendigo
Tuesday
Dear Mum,

I got your letter today, and was glad you signed the papers. I couldn't possibly get home tonight, as I'm going to Melb tomorrow, and will be back on Thursday or Friday. I will be home on Friday or Saturday. Charlie is in town today, in Fatigue duty, pulling down a building. I was out at the camp last night and he came with me, He is coming in again tonight. I am going up to Ettas now. Fancy Martin Kelly dying. I heard about an hour after he died.

I remain your loving son
Albert

On the same day, Charlie wrote to his mother:

5th Sept 1916
Dear Mother

Just a few lines in a hurry this morning I was in Bendigo last night and did not write I am getting on alright and we do not know when we are going, Albert passed yesterday he was out at the camp last night there are a lot of men coming into camp now. I think they must be frightened of conscription which I think will be in about November and they are going to give the soldiers a vote. I have not seen the Gibsons since I came back but Pearl saw Florrie on Parade yesterday. I got leave last week from 2pm Saturday till 11 oclock Sunday night. I put in for week end leave but they would not grant leave to anyone. They are holding the Railway Picnic on the 16th September I think I will be here for that because they have got posters up everywhere about the sports which are only for the soldiers. Well Mother I will say goodbye from me and Pearl hope all are well as I at present.

I am your affect. son.
Charlie

… We quite forgot to send up those photos with Albert, Pearl thought of them and went up to the station to give them to Albert but the train was just going out as she got there, however we will send them up or wait till some of you are down they are fairly heavy so would cost a bit to post up … I believe they are starting another class for the N.C.O. I do not know whether the 3rd 38th will be given a chance in it if so Horris Whinfield and I are going to have a try, which will last for a month. Harry Street did not pass in the old class and may be having a try in the next one. Bert Whinfield passed. I have got leave from two oclock today till 11 oclock tomorrow night, I saw Wilson Townsend last night he said he had a good mind to go home today but I do not know whether he went or not …

At Mologa, Charles Senior had received word that his young nephew, Harry Marlow of the British 1st Essex Regiment had been wounded, possibly at Beaumont-Hamel in the opening days of the Somme battles.

Little is known of the extent of his wound and the circumstances in which he was wounded, although Harry certainly survived his wounds. He was discharged in October 1917.

Cousin Harry Marlow of Leicestershire who served on the Somme with the British 1st Essex Regiment.

A few days after Charlie's letter, on 14 September, General Birdwood was appointed Commander-in-Chief of the AIF. The news was welcomed across the nation. 'Birdie' was a popular commander and had a reputation for fairness and a keen interest in the welfare of his troops.

3rd 38th Batt
Bendigo
Sep Wed 14th 1916
Dear Mother

Just a few lines I got your letter yesterday also one from Arthur, well I am getting on alright, and I believe we are sailing on the 25th Sept. We will be here for the Bendigo Picnic and will take part in the sports which is only for the soldiers, nearly all the men in the camp will be sailing together so I will have a chance of seeing the other local boys going over. Pat O'Brien is in the 4th 38th also Harry Street and Bert Winfield. I was sorry to hear about Harry Marlow being wounded, and you spoke about another Marlow in camp, there is not another Marlow in camp as far as I know it was a fellow from Maldon that asked me if

I was related to the Marlow at Bagshot so there must be plenty of them about. I am afraid I will not be able to get up again before I go if I can get leave I will. The heads are getting down on leave now they will not allow us out at night as often as they used to, I was into Bendigo last night and intend to go in tomorrow night and I think we will get off early on Saturday. There is Church Parade here tonight and it was also on last Tuesday I went it was very good Captain Canon Percival is the preacher. Wilsie Townsend was fined 10/- for being away and Jack Sinclair was fined 3-/- for 3 days Harris Wingfield was away half a day and was fined 5/- …

… we marched through the street on Friday night and in our blue and white hats we were very dry when we got back I managed to get a drink on the road and an old lady brought out a bucket of water for us which was soon emptied. I gave those photos to Dad to bring up I gave one to Auntie Ettie we were up there last night and heard the news of course, Bert was not up for the picnic. Florries boy is in the Machine Guns in Seymour Camp. I did not see any of The Cheynes yesterday. Auntie Ettie said they were coming in. Herbert Street is still very bad in the Bendigo hospital. Jack Sinclair was up to see him this morning. Joe Stone went up with him and also to see the doctor he has been a bit off this last few days. I think we are going on the 25th of September so I don't think there will be any chance of getting up again … Well mum I will draw to a close hoping all are well as I am so goodbye I am your affect. son.

Charlie
My number is 2133

LARKHILL, ENGLAND, SEPTEMBER

As Charlie's departure drew near, Allan and Percy continued to find time to write from the camp at Larkhill to their family and friends at home. While this meant that their news was often repeated, it confirmed that their thoughts were never far from home. Their older brother Jim was causing them some degree of frustration as he continued to hint at the identity of his latest girlfriend while never providing quite enough information for his younger brothers, in particular Percy.

Lark Hill
11 Sept
Dear Jim

Just a few lines to let you know I am still ticking, we are still in the same place. You did not say who she was, I am very interested to hear who she may be. Well Jim there was a big air raid in London, about two weeks ago, we were there at the time, but did not see it, it was too early in the morning, about two, they were firing at it from the guns, one was brought down by an aeroplane, the airman got a VC for it … General French was here today. I did not get near him, he had a big guard. We had to fall in a bit of a speech, from a salvation bloke, today, I did not hear much of it I went to sleep. We are going to have a football match here Saturday with the 37th Machine Gunners it will be a great game. Well Jim I think I have told you all the news so I will close.

From Your Loving Brother
Percy

Allan wrote to Charlie not only of his disgust at seeing the German prisoners transported in first class carriages, but also of his growing frustration that he had not yet reached the front:

Amesbury
Lark Hill
Monday 11th-9-16
Dear Charlie

Well Charlie I hope you and all at home are well as it leaves me at present I received your most welcome letter, well Charlie you know what camp life is like now. I was saying to [the] boys that I reckon you will be sailed by the time you get this letter. Well Charlie we are having a good time, we are getting plenty of work, the tucker is pretty good but by god it is getting pretty cold at nights I don't know what it must be like in the winter time. Well Charlie you all are bound to be sent here somewhere it is nothing but camps all around here. I have not got any more letters from Georgie, but may get one any day. I believe they are taking all the boys out of the trenches in France. The poor devils [have] been getting hell lately. They are taking them out so they can reorganize. Well Charlie we went to a little place called Whitchurch on Saturday. It was not much of a place, anyway we were not sorry to get back. Next Saturday if we get leave we are going to London. When we got to Amesbury to go to Whitchurch a train load of german prisoners came in. They are big fat buggars. They travel in first class carriages but the poor Australian has to travel 3rd. They brought them down to a prison camp here we have a lot of them here. Well Charlie I hope you have a good trip over, you have my address so write at once and I will come and see you, if we are not gone, but I wish to god we were in it somewhere. I am getting tired of training. Well Charlie old boy I am bustling like hell with this letter to catch this mail. I will write you a longer one next mail, but there is absolutely nothing to write about.

So goodbye Charlie till we meet

I remain
Your loving Brother
Allan

Percy had made his own assessment of the German soldiers:

… There was about two hundred Germans brought here, they are about a mile from us, they are enclosed in a barb wire enclosure, they look as if they have not been starved. They are big men, not a very nice body to run against …

Allan composed a lengthy letter to Albert after receiving very welcome correspondence from his younger brother and, it would seem, a rather surprising letter from an old girlfriend in an earlier delivery:

… Well Albert I received your most welcome letter, it was the only letter I got. I was rather disappointed but I suppose I will get a lot next time. Well Albert we are having a good time here, but it is getting terrible cold. This morning was the coldest morning ever I felt. There is a brigade sports on today but I am not going. I have just finished my washing and now I am busy writing letters to catch the next mail. Well Albert you seem to be having a good time on the cutter, but I suppose you will have a much better time when you get out to Listers, but I suppose you wont be there long

before you have to go home. I am finishing this letter Sunday 17th-9-16. Well Albert we had a good time since last Thursday. On Friday we went out to the range and on the Saturday we had a foot and kit inspection and a washing parade and in the afternoon the 38th MG Section played 37th MGS football and we beat them. Well Albert on Wednesday night I went down to see Jack Price but he had come up to our hut and so I went down again on Friday night. He is camped about 2 miles away. I thought I could [get] Jack into our battalion I could have too but he is on a draught that is going away before Saturday week, therefore they wont let him out of it. So he says he will be contented where he is. I expect him down today. Well Albert I got a bonnie mail yesterday. I will tell you who I got letters from, one from each Mabel McNeilly, Annie Clee, Mum, Eileen Braddish and Charlie. Mabel McNeilly wrote me a nice letter and is sending me some socks and by hell Albert I got a surprise when I got Eileen's letter. It is a long time since I heard from her. She got my address from Pearl Saville. It was a bonnie letter and wants me to write every mail so I am doing so. Well Albert you are having a good year over there, you will have to work some in the harvest time. I suppose it wont be long before you will be having a good time at the Pyramid Show. Between suicides and accidents things are not going to well about the surrounding districts. A good many of the boys around the districts are getting wounded or killed. I believe Alf Ferris and Will Guinnane are in this camp now and I believe there are any amount of the boys in the camps about. Albert Bowman from Leitchville came over to see us last Sunday. He said he has been over here 6 months and has only got 6 letters since being over here. I have got no more letters from Georgie, but he sent us a letter the other day, that Jim had wrote to us, and posted it to Georgie so Jim must be very much in love. Well Albert I have a devil of a lot of letters to write this mail. I am writing to the Pyramid advertiser explaining my trip up to the present. Well Albert I hope all at home are well as it leaves us at present.

Goodbye Albert
I remain
Your Loving Brother
Allan

Eileen asked me for a photo of me so will you send her one of mine in civilian clothes I think Jim or Charlie have two you will fix that up for me. You write and say that I asked you to send it on to her. I am sending her one of me in uniform

Address – get Pearl Saville to address it[15]

Allan put pen to paper championing the benefits of being a Lewis gunner:

Sunday
17-9-16
Dear Charlie

… We are very lucky to be in the Machine Gun, we don't get half the work that the infantry get. I like the Lewis Gun they are very easy to learn. We are going out to the ranges next week to do some shooting with the gun. There are a terrible lot of the boys I know about the camps. I was trying to get Jack Price into the battalion but it was too late on account of him being in a draught that is going away next week. He looks well on it now. I never felt better in my life before. There is one thing this country suits us alright at present, but by hell they say it is terrible cold in the winter… This is where you will be sent for a cut. All the boys are well, but for W.S. [Will Street] I cannot make him out at all. We played the 37th M Gunner football on Saturday and we defeated them. They started to make it a bit willing at the last, but we were equal to them. It is starting to rain here now. The war is looking much better according to the paper this morning

In Allan's letter the same day he implored Jim not to marry before he returned to Australia:

… I never felt better in my life. We are having a good time here, we have not been working too hard this day or two. In fact we are having a picnic to the boys in the companies. They are the poor devils that have to work … We had a great game of football on Saturday We played the 37th M.G. and we beat them. It was getting a bit willing toward the last, but still all the same we could have mixed it with them. Well Jim you must be having a roaring time. Not too much work to do. Look at the time you must have had out at Bobs. It is a holiday resort at any time. Jim you never tell me who this new girl is. Jim do tell me. I often wondered if it was Winnie Price. If it is not her it is

Mollie Gamble, but Jim whatever you do don't get married before I get back. Percy got a letter from Charlie he seems to like the camp life alright. Percy got a letter from Auntie Florrie and she says that mum is worrying over us. If she only knew how comfortable we were it would be alright and we all as happy as if we are going to a picnic. For God's sake Jim what ever you do don't you go. I write to Georgie every week but I never got any letter this week from him. I am sending all the papers on to him. I can tell you what a fine thing if we could all get together, but I don't suppose there is any luck. Everything is going well with the war in this morning paper. Things are not so good as your paper say so.

Will Guinane and Alf Ferris are over here I believe they are coming up to see us tonight. We have any amount of friends. I have had a lot of the Cohuna district boys over to see me. I wish to God we were going to France. Not another word have we heard about going. Georgie sent me over a letter that you had wrote to us and posted it to him. Will Street is very quiet I can't make him out at all. Well Jim you could never guess where I am writing this letter. It is too roudy in the hut. So Les and I rigged up a table in a little dugout about 100 yds from the hut. So here we are writing in peace and quietness. Well Jim I think I have told you all the news so I will ring off hoping all are well.

Goodbye Jim
I remain
Your Loving Brother
Allan
Kind regards to your young lady.

Concerned that his mother was worrying too much, Allan advised his eldest brother not to enlist; another son going to war would cause his mother even greater anxiety. Allan was unaware that Albert was in camp at Bendigo waiting to be accepted. His hope that the brothers could serve together in the same battalion had not included his little brother. The same day he wrote to his mother in conversational and reassuring language, attempting to make light of his situation and persuade her that civilian life could be just as risky as that of a soldier. The casualty lists told Sarah a very different story.

Sunday 17-9-16
My Dear Mum

*Well Mum I hope you and all at home are well as it leaves me at present.
I received your most welcome letter. I also got others which you will read
about in the other letter. Well Mum we are having a good time here. We
have been having sports and football kit inspection and feet inspection
and washing parades. But oh I did do a big washing. I have not a dirty
thing now. We get hot water to wash with but still it is no joke. Mum
when I come back you wont have to do my washing I am too good at
it now. In fact I've a bit of a mind to take washing in, but when you
come to think of it, I have come to be a soldier and not a washer man so
I think I will leave it alone. Well Mum I have met such a lot of boys I
know Alf Ferris and Will Guinane are here now they are coming down to
night. Jack Price has just come down and he has just gone over to see Will
Stevens. He is going away next week so I cannot get him in the battalion.
He is well again. Well mum dear things have not been going to well about
the districts lately between men getting killed and suicides a man is far
better here. Well Mum Les and I rigged up a table in a dugout about
100 yds from the hut and it is here where we are writing. It is too noisy
in the huts and I have such a lot of letters to write. I got a letter from
Miss McNeilly it was very acceptable. She is sending me a couple of pair
of socks. It is very good of her. I am writing to her to night. Well Mum
you will have a lot of work to do now that the cows are in and it wont be
long before you will be in harvest too. Well Mum after this is all over you
ought to go for a good holiday to the seaside. Here at night it is that cold.
I am getting some woollen flannels. Mum who is the new girl of Jims, he
never says who she is. You will soon have the Pyramid Show to go to. That
was a day that I was always looking forward too. Do you remember the
time that I bought those fancy flowers for my coat. I think they are still
home. I will never forget it. I don't think you will either. Ha wasn't it fun.
I didn't think so then but I do now. Charlie seems to like the camp life
alright. And his girl came to our place. I will never forget the last time she
came. Mum I got such a nice letter from that little girl of mine that used
to live at Mologa. She said that her uncle had met Amos Haw over there.*

*I write to Georgie every week and I send those Pyramid papers on to him.
Well Mother dear I always [write] every week to you all and I hope you
get all my letters. Never worry over us mum we are well and happy and
according to this mornings paper the war will not last much longer. Well
Mum goodbye for the present. I do hope you get my parcel alright.*

I remain
Your Loving Son
Allan S

Allan mentions more soldiers from the local area arriving on the
training grounds of Salisbury Plain. Alf Ferris was 31 years old when
he left the farm at Terrick Terrick to enlist in the 60th Battalion in
March 1916. After the 1917 battles at Ypres he was seconded for
duty with the 5th Division Horse Clipping Depot. He returned to
Australia in July 1919.[16] Will Guinane of nearby Mincha enlisted at
the same time as Alf and they served together in the 60th Battalion. A
34-year-old farmer, Will was wounded at Bapaume on 12 May 1917.
His wound was severe and, as he was no longer fit for duty, he was
discharged the following March.[17] Will Stevens was also a farmer and
lived at Sylvaterre, where he enlisted at the age of 22. He was shot in
the chest on 19 July 1917 but recovered to return to C Company of
the 38th Battalion on 12 October 1917, a day of disaster for the 38th.
Will eventually returned to Australia in September 1919.[18]

Tom Alford, who was about to leave England to reinforce the 59th
Battalion of Pompey Elliott's 15th Brigade, dashed off a hurried note to
Jim to acknowledge that he had received a letter from Mologa and to
tell him that his time on the Western Front was about to begin.

Perham
Sept 21st
Dear Jimmy,

*I received your welcome letter yesterday. I was glad as I am off to France on
Saturday. Well I've had a pretty good time in England taking it alround so
Hurrah*

From T Alford

While continuing to reassure his mother that he is well, Allan's letters are now laced with nostalgia and a tone of intimacy. His sentences frequently begin with 'Mum', as if he longed to be sitting opposite her at the kitchen table enjoying a cup of tea and chatting over the latest news. He does his best to provide reassurance to his mother, yet reveals a longing for family and the comforts of home.

My Dear Mum

… we have been on march. We had a march past our divisional officer [General Monash] *the other day, and since then we had a march past the King, it looked very nice. There was 40 thousand of us altogether but the only fault it was a wet* [day]*. Well Mum I got a terrible shock when I heard that Charlie was married. I never thought he would be doing it before he left. He ought to be over here soon now if he sailed when you said he was. I have only got one letter this mail so far that was from Albert. Percy only got one too and that was from Hilda. The other boys have not got any yet, so they must be in camp somewhere. I hope I get them so I can see about the wedding … We are going into the trenches next week for 5 days, that will be nice too. I don't think they are going to shift us from here before winter and I don't think the war will last much longer. They are taking a lot of prisoners lately. I was in London last Saturday and we could hear the shells dropping when the Zeppelin raid was on. They made a terrible row and I would have liked to have seen it, but it was about 1 or 2 oclock in the morning. They tell us we are going to get another 4 days leave if so we are going to see our other relation. We have had letters from them all and I can tell you we are kept writing. I have not had a letter from Geordie lately but ought to get one any time now. We are getting splendid tucker now. I had my photo* [taken] *in London on Sunday so I will send them over soon, I expect them today … I hope you have a good time at the show I shall write another letter this mail and tell you if I got your letters. I hope you get my parcel alright.*

… I feel lovely I never felt better in my life. This climate agrees with me. I have not had a cold or an hour sickness of any sort since being here. About the flannels mum well I was going to get some but I have worked a good

scheme and are getting two good ones from our Quarter master. We are having a lot of rain here again. You will see by Albert letter what a time we had at the trenches. It was raining all the time but I enjoyed it it just reminded me of when I was [young] and use to paddle in water. Mum I have just finished my Sunday dinner and this is what we had Roast beef, and a plum duff. I always have a cut of toast every meal. Yesterday when I was in the cook house toasting some the cook roused on to me and told me I was not going to make a b- rest home of this place. So I only told him I only came 3 times a day and that made him worse, but anyway I was back again today. It don't trouble me. Well mum they tell us they are going to give us another 4 days leave if so that will be great. I am on the look out for Charlie he ought to be here soon. We have just finished a bombing course but you cant beat the machine guns. We don't get half the work the other boys do. Mum I was sorry to hear about the boys getting wounded. I have got 2 letters from Georgie since last Saturday and he is getting mine too. So that is first rate. Mum I am sending you my photo it is not much but you will be pleased to get it just the same. Mum when you go to Bendigo again I want you to get your photo taken and send me one. Mum I would like one. Send me one of dad too then I will have the lot. Mum I am glad you are having a prosperous year. Auntie Ette could not have got my Cape Town letters but all the same I wrote. I have wrote thanking Miss McNeilly for the socks. Mum you can thank her personally to for me. Mum they are lovely there is no kid about it. Lily Sharp has sent a pair too but I have not got them … Mum I am going to write to different others. But Mum you cant rely on getting 4 letters at home every mail as I write 4 letters to home every week. Mum I hope you have got my parcel. Mum I hope you like the brooch and I hope the others like the present. I did not know what Jim would like. Mum I have found a few little relics here and I will send them home. I found a great coin in the ground the other day. I tried to get a bit of stone henge but I could not break it off. There are some bonnie flowers here. I wish I could send you a cutting. Our battalion colours are red and purple. One of the boys got a table centre made of them and they are very pretty. If I can get one I will send you one. Well dear mother I think I have told you all the news so I will close with love.

From your loving son
Allan S
Mum what ever you do don't worry over me I am well and happy as well.

As Allan and Percy received the news of their brother and his bride, the young couple was preparing to be parted. With the likely assurances of return, Charlie farewelled his wife of just five weeks and embarked on the *Shropshire* on 25 September. Thousands of kilometres away at *Shropshire's* destination, further news of the unexpected union and of Charlie's departure was eagerly anticipated as Allan wrote to Albert:

Sept 27 1916
Amesbury
England
Dear Albert

Well Albert I received your most welcome letter but it is the only one I have received this mail, but expect more tomorrow. Well Albert I nearly dropped dead when I read that Charlie was married. I never dreamt of him getting married before he went to the war. In your next letter tell me all about it. We have been going very solid this last week or two. We have been out route marches and shooting a terrible lot. We had a 15 mile route march and field operations the other day. Last Thursday we had a march past General Monash our division officer and today we had a march past the King. There were about 40 thousand of us altogether, and it was raining pretty well all the time. We were all out there yesterday practising the day before … Last Saturday 3 of us got leave to go to London and we had a fair time. Percy could not go as he had been before. Percy and Les have gone down to a place called Andover today, they have to be back tonight.

Well Albert we went through our machine gun tests the other day and I passed easy. Yesterday we went through our machine gun tests at the range. There is only 7 or 8 of us that get our 1ˢᵗ class machine gun certificates as on the whole the shooting was not too good. The possible was 75 and I got 70. Percy done very crook. He only got 15. When they give us the certificates

I will send it home. I have not had a letter from Georgie for a long time. I have only got one letter this mail so far. I am anxious to get mums letter to see about the wedding. No doubt it was a shock to Percy and me. If he sailed when you said he was to sail he will soon be over here. All the boys seem to be up on final leave together. Ralph Alford is a dam fool to try again. Well Albert we are working very solid lately. Next Tuesday we are going into the trenches for 5 days, so that will be nice wont it. We are getting splendid tucker now. They say we are going to be billeted out for the winter. That is that we are going to stop at peoples places, but I would sooner be here because here a man is sure of getting plenty and good tucker. In your next letter tell me about Charlies wedding in case I don't get anymore. Well Albert old boy I think I have told you all the news. I am sending you some papers and postcards.

Well Albert goodbye
I remain
Your Loving Brother
Allan S

AT SEA, SEPTEMBER

As Allan was writing home to Albert, Charlie was aboard the *Shropshire*, en route for England and the training grounds of Salisbury. Like Allan he was anxious to reunite all the brothers on the Western Front in the belief that they should fight together.

27th Sept
At Sea
Dear Mother, Father & Brothers,

Just a few lines to you today. I am writing this in case we pass a mail boat or have a chance of posting this, well I am getting on alright now, but the first two days I felt a bit off in the stomach I lost part of me tea one night but put it down to my cold I started to cough and up it came, but now I am very pleased to say that I feel splendid and am enjoying the trip first rate, the sea is very calm especially this last few days, we get splendid food on board and plenty of it. W. Crossman J. Sinclair Wilsin Townsend G. Humbert, L.

Cant Tom Roberts and G. Collison are on board with me they were all a bit sick but are quite well again in fact I think a bit of a heave do not do us any harm. We were paid the day we came on and can get almost anything at the canteen on board, there is all sorts of amusements on board and we have a little drill now and again to give us exercise. We are not allowed to say anything about where we are going or the nature of the ship. I wrote to Pearl and told her to tell you that she heard from me if she got the letter, so in case she did not get it and you get this one you could let her know that you heard from me. If at any time you want to find out any thing about any of us write to the Secretary Department Defence Melbourne, we were told to tell our people about this. My address is No 2123 Private C. E Marlow 3rd Refs 38 Batt 10 Inf Brigade A.I.F. England. There is a splendid band on board and also other kind of music, including a piano. I have heard for certain that I being the oldest brother can claim Geordie and get him into my battalion, so when I get abroad I will write to him and see if he is willing to join us. I believe I will see Uncle Arthur on the way over and will let you know later how he is getting on. Just a few lines today as I believe we can post this today I am feeling splendid and enjoying the sea air, the sea is not rough yet, it surprises me to see how calm it is to what I thought it would be. Well I have no more news so will say goodbye hoping all are well as I am,

So goodbye I am your affect son
Charlie

SIX
I NEVER THOUGHT YOU WOULD LET HIM GO …

THE WESTERN FRONT, OCTOBER

As the weather deteriorated with the approach of the European winter, George remained in the Ypres salient in Belgium where the 1st Division continued to rotate through the front-line trenches.

October 1ˢᵗ 1916
Dear Albert

Just a few lines to let you know I am well hoping all are the same. I received a letter from you a few days ago saying that Charlie was married and that he was about to sail he didn't stop long in camp, I didn't think that he was going to be married before he left. I had a letter from Percy today they are still in England, perhaps Charlie will get there before they leave. Well we have just come out of the trenches, I was only out a day and was writing a letter here in the Y.M.C.A. and the corporal came over and said they wanted some of us to go back again to take part in a raid so I went and was there 3 days, it turned out very successful, we gave them a great doing with bombs. We have just arrived back and am going my hardest writing letters as the mail closes tonight. We are camped in huts here not far behind the firing line there are a Y.M.C.A. and a Picture Show here so it is not too bad. Well it is coming on winter here now the time is put back an hour today, I believe we are to have two blankets this month. I have just found out that Charlie Fyffe and Ewin Johnson are in the 6 Batt. here and that they joined the Batt. while we were in these last trenches. I am going to look them up as soon as possible. I don't know how long we are out for, don't think it is for long. The fighting on this front has been very successful lately. Well Albert I have a lot of letters to write so will have to close, hoping all are well.

I remain
Your affectionate Bro
George

The raid George mentioned was a highly risky foray launched in the darkness of 30 September. Clad in balaclavas and with blackened faces, 80 men crawled towards the enemy lines, their mission to take prisoners and collect intelligence. The raid was hailed a success and a number of members of the raiding party decorated for their bravery.

Eighteen-year-old Jack Price, who Allan had been attempting unsuccessfully to have transferred from the 46th Battalion to the 38th, had now reached France. He wrote to Albert with indignation after an earlier letter had been censored, while also hoping that Albert's parents would follow his own in consenting to his friend's enlistment.

France
Tuesday Oct 3rd 1916

Dear Albert

A few lines to let you know that I got two letters from you last Saturday. I was pleased to hear that you are all well. I wrote to you yesterday and put in a song about the Kaiser. I have just been up to the orderly room over the song and also parts of the letter. I did not think there was any harm in sending it to you but I believe I was lucky to get off the way I did. The Officer who censured it said he would let me know in time to catch the mail, if I wanted to go with another letter, so I thought I might as a man never knows his luck when he goes up to the firing line. I hope your father and mother will let you go if you pass when you enlist this time. I was up to see Allan and Percy the night before I left England, there wont be many of you left if you come over too. I suppose I will get to the firing line soon now or I hope so as you get sick of camp … Well laddie I don't seem to have much to write about and it is nearly dinner time so I will close by wishing you all the best of health and luck.

From your sincere pal
Jack Price

France
Monday October 16/10
Dear Albert

Just a few lines to catch the mail for good old Australia. It is a bonzer day over here today and we have no drill. I have just come off a fatigue party all the same. We are going to get our vote today on conscription and I think will win easy enough here. I got four letters from home on Saturday night. I have not had any from England since I came here I don't know where they go to. We get issued with plenty of cigarettes over here but they are not much good. We play banker for cigarettes sometimes and I won a lot that way. I was marked an efficient soldier this morning. My mate went into the observation tent yesterday with a bad cold but I hope we get away together. He knows that Collison that used to be at Durham Ox and Salter that used to play football with Calivil. There has been a lot of fights about here lately. We had one in our tent the other day but one fighter spent too much time on the ground. I got down to the village the other day with the chap from the Officers mess for some things. All the townships are out of bounds from our Division. The permanent men can get a pass allright. We get our meals in big mess huts here and the tucker is pretty good lately. Well Albert I must bring this to a close with kind regards to you all from your sincere pal

Jack Price

While Jack was hoping soon to reach the firing line, further north in Belgium, George had returned to the front line near Hill 60. He noted with discontent on 8 October that he had spent his 24th birthday in the trenches. Hill 60 was a small rise in the landscape that afforded significant advantage to the enemy forces who held the area, particularly the snipers who posed a constant threat to the soldiers moving about those trenches that were in range.

October 12th, 1916
Dear Jim

As I am sitting in the dugout I thought I would drop you a few lines but have no news to tell you but am well and that's about the main thing. I wrote to Dad and Albert a few days ago we were out for a few days spell then, it was my birthday the other day so kept it up in military style by going into the trenches that day. We are not allowed to say what part of the line we are in but are in where there has been much heavy fighting but isn't bad at present, while we were out I often used to see Amos, Charlie [Cockcroft] and Ewin they have just joined their Battalion but Tom hasn't joined up yet they don't seem to fancy it at all. I am well used to it now, Ewin was telling me that he is getting a lot of letters, Charlie and I went to a concert one night, Ewin wouldn't come, he didn't seem to shift from the camp, Charlie is just the same talk for a month without stopping young Charlie Wales is with them also I saw Harry Burrrows he is back again was only slightly wounded. I got Mother's letter saying that she got my letter about receiving the parcel well I told you a long while ago that I got both parcels although one was travelling five months it was as good as gold when I got it. Well Jim I will now close hoping all are well,

I remain
Your affectionate Bro
Geo

You remember me telling you about that chap named Lousada that said he used to go to school with the Alfords at Warragul he was killed up on the Somme, he was a great mate of mine up till he went to the 21 Battalion.

The first of the Field Service postcards George sent from the trenches.

George now sent the first of many government-generated Field Service postcards that the Marlow brothers posted home to their family from the front line. While designed to bypass the censor and thus speed mail delivery, Field Service postcards represented their own form of censorship, with soldiers crossing out pre-printed lines which did not apply, leaving only the words officially supplied. While far more impersonal, they were popular with weary soldiers or those with little time to write before the mail closed as a means of briefly reassuring their families that they were alive and well and that letters from home had been received.

NOTHING is to be written on this side except the date and signature of the sender. Sentences not required may be erased. If anything else is added the post card will be destroyed.

I am quite well.

I have been admitted into hospital

sick— and am going on well.

wounded and hope to be discharged soon.

I am being sent down to the base.

I have received your letter dated_____ telegram,,_____ parcel ,,_____

Letter follows at first opportunity.

I have received no letter from you lately. for a long time.

Signature only. G. J. Marlow

Date 18/10/16

[Postage must be prepaid on any letter or post card addressed to the sender of this card.]

(93871) Wt. W3497-293 4,500m. 8/16 J. J. K. & Co., Ltd.

Field Service cards were both a means of censorship and rapid communication.

The soldiers of I Anzac Corps were astonished when they were suddenly ordered to leave the Ypres sector and return to the devastated Somme front. They were to prepare for an attack that would finally secure the higher ground of Bapaume. Now reinforced after the disaster of Fromelles, the 5th Division went into the line at Gueudecourt. The 1st, 2nd and 4th divisions were soon to follow. At the same time, as the Australians were en route from Ypres to the Somme, the weary soldiers were required to cast their vote in the impending conscription referendum.

As November approached, autumn rain turned the shattered battlefields into a sea of mud. Trenches were filled with muddy water, roads and routes to the front line became impassable, exhausted troops sank into thick mud with every step, cursing as they pulled their feet from the morass. Standing up to their knees in mud in the trenches, the troops were to endure a bitter winter on the Somme. The conditions were compounded by the cold weather that was now descending. The incidence of trench foot quickly soared and the front-line troops were instructed to massage whale oil into their feet to protect them from the debilitating condition.

George was camped at Montauban, some nine kilometres from the Gueudecourt front. He had grown increasingly concerned as he waited to hear from his mate Ray Leed. When the opportunity arose he set off to find Ray's battalion, but could not locate his mate. The bad news was to come to George from Mologa. He was distressed to discover that Ray had not been the only Mologa boy killed. On 15 July as the 5th Division had moved forward in preparation for the disastrous Fromelles attack of 19 July, Ray and his mate Pat Ryan had both lost their lives. They were buried close to each other at Rue du Boix Military Cemetery, Fleurbaix, five kilometres from Fromelles. Pat was 23, a farm labourer who had enlisted in July 1915 and transferred from the 22nd Battalion to the 57th in February 1916. While training in Egypt, his parents had been notified that their son was listed as dangerously ill with pneumonia; just six months later, they were to receive the worst news of all.[1]

October 25th
My Dear Mother,

Just a few lines to say I am well hoping all at home are the same. I haven't time to write a letter. Well today I was over to Ray Leeds Battalion inquiring for him but no one knew anything of him, it is the first time I have been anywhere near his division since I have been in France, well I got a shock when I got back to my unit there was a letter from you dated September 3rd saying that he and Pat Ryan had been killed, I told Amos, he is about 100 yds from me, there are only us two that have escaped so far. Charlie Fyffe, Hughie Johnson and Charlie Wales are well. I got a letter from Jim today and got 6 others a few days ago dated August 27ᵗʰ. I suppose the parcel will be along any day. It is wet and muddy, we have had some frosts. I will write some letters when I get the chance.

Goodbye
George

Jack Price was now with the 46th Battalion and had experienced the perils of the front-line trenches. He now understood that luck played a considerable part in the survival of the soldier on the Western Front. He wrote to Albert, describing some of the hazards of service that came not from the enemy lines ...

France
Monday, October 30/1916
Dear Albert

Just a line or two to let you know that I am still well. I hope you are all the same. I had a card from Allan yesterday morning. It is the only mail I have got since I joined up the Batt. I joined the Batt about 2 weeks ago up in Belgium and am in the C Company so that will be my new address. The Reinforcements all got their letters allright when they join the Batt. There is another Jack Price in my Company but a different Platoon. We shifted down here to France the other day and are billeted in a village. We get a lot better treatment since we joined up plenty of cigarettes and some gift stuff. Things were fairly quiet up at the last place but I think they will be a bit different next time we go in. I was on guard the other day and our orderly got a punch in the nose. They are a rough mob some that you strike over here in the clinks. We have been out on a route march this morning and doing some Battalion drill. How is Mologa getting on. I suppose Ralph Alford will be just about leaving by now. What Battalion is Geordie attached to now. He must be very lucky to get this far allright. By what they say he is among those that went through a bit. Allan and them are lucky to be so long over the other side. I hear that they have had 6 days kings leave lately. Well Albert I think I will close by wishing you all a merry Xmas and a happy new year from your old pal.

Jack

ENGLAND, OCTOBER

In England, the men of the 3rd Division continued their training in the techniques of trench warfare: night training attacks, sleeping in the trenches and bomb-throwing were just some of the activities listed on the schedule. Allan and Percy, unaware that their youngest brother had enlisted, were anxious for Charlie to arrive prior to their departure to France and keen to pass on news of their comrades and Australian successes. As the month drew to a close the prospect of their first Christmas away from their family prompted early messages of Christmas and New Year wishes to ensure the long mail journey did not cheat their loved ones of their thoughts.

Percy penned a number of letters in which he, like Allan and George, voiced his surprise that Charlie had chosen to marry:

Lark Hill
Sunday 1 Oct
Dear Albert

… Well Albert we had the King out to see us; he reviewed the troops, and then we had a march past, it took an hour and half for all the troops to go past, his arm must have been tired, we were not marching in fours but twenty wide. It was a terrible wet day, it made it miserable. I suppose you would see it in the paper it was all the third division, and all the reinforcements. Well Albert I got quite a surprise when you mentioned about Charlie being married, I never thought it was coming off so soon, good luck to him … Lets know who Jim's tart is, he is always talking about the new one. I hope you are having a good time with Myrtle lets know if its coming off soon …

Dear Mum and Dad

… We had the King out to see us last week, I was not talking to him, he had a very wet day. There was a big crowd of men, when they were all lined up. The King reviewed the troops and then there was a march past, it looked all right. We have had some nice weather lately, just like spring time, they are still carting in hay over here, they have enough men

with one wagon, to do two or three in Australia. We are going out to the trenches next week, for five days they have trenches here like those in France, about three miles from the camp, it will be very good. We got a letter from George yesterday, he was well, when he wrote he was having a rest. You have a daughter now. I got quite a surprise when I heard I never thought it was coming off so soon …

5 Oct
Dear Mum and Dad

Just a few words, I have no news, we are getting plenty of rain, I do not think it will ever stop. We had a letter from George, he says it is terrible wet, he was saying he met Gordon McKay. Well Mum I will not be sorry when we go to France the camp life gets sickening…

Lark Hill
8th Oct
Dear Jim

Just a few lines Jim, but I don't know what I can tell you. Well Jim Charlie has broke the ice, you will not be long after by your advance; don't you think he was silly to break his independence so soon. We had a lovely trip out to the trenches this week, they were out at the back of the camp, about four miles, it rained all the time we were going out, and while we were there. The first night we had tents to sleep in, but the next night was a night attack, and it did not rain a little bit; we were out till five in the morning, I can tell you it was good. The trenches were all chalk, and we were white when we came out of them. It is all chalk after you dig down about eight inches, it is funny how things grow. We have been on bomb throwing this last few days, its very interesting we had the mills [hand grenade] …

Allan sent Albert a studio photo recently taken in London. Inside this envelope was also a newspaper clipping from *The Argus* describing the Australian role in the taking of Pozieres. The reader could be forgiven for thinking that Pozieres had been a pleasant afternoon sports meeting.

Allan in London.

New York, Aug 7

American correspondents, writing from the Western battle-front, praise the gallantry and mettle of the Australians at Pozieres. They point out that the Allies bombardment was so complete that it destroyed all the German defences, shelters and entanglements. The Australians with the Sussex Regiment, then advanced, and captured six lines of trenches north-west of Pozieres without striking a blow. They carried a large work at the intersection of Thiepval road, continuing their vigorous advance towards Thiepval. The operation was the most brilliant in the Somme offensive, and resulted in the position being carried rapidly and with certainty. At one point the bombardment had buried some German machine-gunners. In one counter-attack the Germans found their retreat cut off by the British fire, and the Germans threw up their hands. They were taken prisoner, and the Australians unconcernedly dug themselves in in their new positions under a sweltering sun.[2]

8th October 1916
Dear Old Albert

… Well Albert we are still enjoying ourselves. In my last letter I told you we were going into the trenches on the Monday. Well on Monday it was raining like mad, but at 9 oclock we all started off. We had to march out about 4 ½ miles to the trenches still raining like blazes, we went into them for about an hour then came out for dinner. Then we went back again still raining Albert, till tea. We had tea then they told us we had to sleep in tents, anyway that was not to bad. They put 15 of us in a round tent but still that was better [than] out in the pouring rain. We got up at 6 had breakfast then went in the trenches again, it was still raining. We came out for dinner then we went back again. We had a big night attack and got to bed at 5.30 in the morning. It was still raining like mad. All the time we were in the trenches the MG Section never dug any trenches but the other lads did. We had breakfast about nine and we never went back till 1 oclock. It was dreadful in the trenches but the rain had ceased. The doctors got together and took us out at 2.30 and we came home. We were supposed to stop for five days but we have to go out again. Albert it just reminded me of when we were kids when we used to play in the water. By hell we had a pack to carry out there too. We had a spare pair of boots shirt singlet cardigan jacket socks underpants waterproof and over coat. Well Albert we have just finished a course of bomb throwing. It is not a bad game but you cant beat the machine gun. I got a letter from Jack Price the other day he is in France but not in the firing line. He says it is good over there where he is. Well Albert you are going to have a good year alright and I am glad of that. I have got my photo but it is rotten all the same I am sending you all one. Percy and I are going to be taken together one of these days. Our officer just came into the hut and wants our section all taken together so I will send one home. Well Albert they tell us they are going to give us another 4 days leave, so that will be good. I am looking out for Charlie now he will soon be here. I was sorry to hear about the boys getting wounded but I suppose it cant be helped. Well Albert I think I have told you all the news so I will close hoping all are well as it leaves me at present. Hoping all you are the same.

Goodbye Albert

I remain
Your Loving Brother
Allan

No word of making a move yet. It is raining here today.

A week later Percy wrote to his parents:

Lark Hill
15 Oct
Dear Mum & Dad

Well Mum we are still alive and still in England. We are going to the trenches for a few days next week. I hope it does not rain, like it did last time we was out there. The voting is tomorrow there will be a lot voting against conscription, if it comes in, it will cause a stir. We had a brigade stunt this week, we were advancing as in battle and then it ended up in a sham fight, we camped for dinner near a wood, there was a bee hive near where we stopped, of course we had some of the honey it was very good. We saw plenty of hares and pheasants, I would have liked to had a gun. Sunday is a very quiet day, nothing to do but to write letters. We had a letter from Geordie he was out of the trenches for a spell, he met Charlie Fyffe and Uhen Johnson they are joining his brigade. Tom Alford was not with them. We have not heard from Jack Price lately. Well Mum news is terrible scarce. I think I will close wish love to all from

Your Loving Son
Percy

Allan also wrote to Albert and his parents:

Sunday 15-10-16
Dear Old Albert,

Well Albert this is the second letter to you that I am writing for this mail and I hope you get them both. We expect a mail tomorrow, Well Albert this is the coldest day that ever I witnessed in my life, oh it is a brute. The other day they issued us with straw bunks and pillows and it makes a big difference too. Last week we were out on field operations and I thoroughly enjoyed it. We were out in some lovely fields and there was a few steep hills to climb. Talk about hares, I never saw so many hares in my life before I tell you it brought back old memories when we used to shoot the b_. They tell me if a man shot a hare over here they would dam near get hung for it. Well Albert we are off to the camp trenches again on Tuesday morning until Friday. I hope it don't rain again, but it looks very much like it. If ever it looks like rain here you can depend on getting it. Well Albert we are going to move at last thank God. Our Colonel told us last night that we are going to move to France and we would be going sooner than we expected. Well Albert it is time we made a move. I have been in the army 8 months and I reckon I am fit for the fray. The boys over in France reckon we are cold footed. They reckon we are holding the front line of trenches at Lark Hill. Albert I will tell you why we have been so long. Now none of the other boys have trained for open warfare and we are doing a lot of it. Now they reckon by the time we get there we will have a lot of open work. I got another letter from Geordie yesterday. He is well and has met Hughie [and] Charlie over there. Well Albert I thought I had finished studying but have not yet. On Saturday O'Donnel our MG Officer picked 4 of us to go through a course of scouting. In the day time we are on the gun, and at night time we have to go out scouting for the enemy. You see we have listening posts out and we have to go out to them at night to listen what the enemy is doing and we have to send word back to our officer what is going on. We have to learn the dot dash business and we carry these machines with us. When we got over here they cut all this out, but now the 4 of us have to learn it. There is none of the other boys from our way in it. Every company has its own scouts as well. Well Albert I done my washing yesterday. I washed 1 shirt underpants singlet and 5 pair of socks and handkerchiefs. I have got it up drying. I rather like washing now when I go back I think I will do my own. I don't know for certain Albert anyway we will see…

I never felt better in my life.
We have no word of the 3/38 landing yet but they ought to be here soon
All the boys are well
I got Lily Sharps socks they were very nice …

While, after eight months of training, Allan was convinced that he was ready for the Western Front, Monash was keen to ensure that the men of his division were well prepared for what was to come. The teasing by men of the older divisions concerning the length of time the 3rd Division had spent in camp was common in inter-division rivalry. But talk of being 'cold footed' would not rest easy with Allan and his mates who were anxious to reach the front.

On his return from trench training, Allan penned a lengthy letter to his mother:

Saturday 21-10-16
My Dear Mum

Well Mother dear I received your most welcome letter. I got eleven letters altogether. I got 2 mails at once the end of August letters and September letters. I also got your photo mum. You don't know how delighted I was to get it. I was often wondering how long it would be before I got one. I was glad to hear that you are well. Now Mum in my last letter I told you that we were going to the camp trenches on the Tuesday till Friday. Yes we went and I will tell you about it. We left the camp on the Tuesday morning. It was raining but not near so bad as usual. Well we marched out about 5 miles to a terrible big cockies place where they billeted us. We had dinner then fixed up our bunks for the night. All the boys slept in the sheds but our officer got us up in a loft. By jove we were comfortable. He slept with us too. Well Mum by the time we done this it was tea. We had a real good tea had a smoke and went to bed. We got up at six in the morning had breakfast and done practically nothing for the day. Well on this night Wednesday we were supposed to get up at 2 oclock and go on a stunt to the trenches. Well everyone of us even the officer slept in and never heard the others going off. We woke up about 6 and then he said we better make a good job of it and sleep on till 7.30. There was not one of us that was sorry we missed it. Well after breakfast we done gun drill for the whole day. Well at 8 oclock on the night (Thursday) we had to move off to the trenches and put the night in there. By jove talk about cold it was a brute. At 11 oclock we had to make a charge, oh it was lovely I don't think. We got back at 12.30 and laid down in our dugout but we could not sleep as it [was] a freezer. About 600 yds from the trenches was a wood where the cooks were camped and I could see some beautiful fires there. I watched for a long time to see if I could see any officer about and could not see any and so at 2.30 I sneaked out of the trenches with one of the boys down to [the] fire. I stopped at the first fire there was only about 6 at it. The cooks gave us some hot coffee and it was a treat. We saw a chap sitting on a box and who should it be but the officer. He seemed to feel the cold worse than anyone. He reckoned it was a b-. He had been sitting there for 2 hours and then wasn't warm. He didn't abuse the Kaiser a bit. We were not long there before Percy and the rest of the boys came. He seen them coming and said here comes the whole b- section. He said if there coming I had better go back and hold the trenches while they were getting warm and off he went but was not there long before he was back again. Some of the boys went back again but a lot of us stopped till day break. We came out of the trenches at 12 oclock on Friday and marched back to camp. We had a real picnic to what we had last time. Today (Saturday) I have been doing my washing. We had to return our old stuff and get new stuff in its place. I have got 4 of those shirts new underpants and socks and singlets. I have a lot of socks now. I am using the new flannel shirts as flannels, they are better than the one you bought as they have sleeves in them. Well dear Mum I am busy writing letters again this afternoon but Percy and Will Street have gone down to Amesbury. Peter Owens is in the hospital. He is going under an operation. He has got tonsilitis. All the other boys are well. Mum I have never been the slightest bit crook since being here. In fact I never felt better. But mum it is terrible cold and it is only autumn here yet. Charlie is not here yet but ought not be long now. I was glad you got my cable. You ought to be getting my letters wholesale now. Mum we have been here 10 weeks now and I have never missed in writing to you one week. So Mum I hope you get the letters alright and also the parcel. I hope you like the brooch alright. Mum I was terrible sorry to hear about Ray Leed and Will Hare.[3] *It is bad luck …*

The following day Allan wrote to Albert. He had received word that his youngest brother had enlisted and was quick to berate him for not heeding his advice not to sign up:

Sunday 22-10-16
Dear Old Albert

Well I received 2 of your most welcome letters. I was pleased to hear that all are well and we are the same. I was out in the trenches when I got all the letters, quite a lot of them. Well Albert you are having a great year over there, and we are having a beautiful cold one here. Oh it is a brute and it is only autumn yet. What it will be like in the middle of winter I don't know. I never felt anything like it in my life. Well I don't think we will be here for the winter, as we have heard a lot of rumours to France, I hope it is so, as I think it is time we went. I had a letter from Jack Price yesterday. He is in France but not in the firing line. He said he had a couple of letters from you. I have been getting all yours and papers. By jove they were welcome. I was reading about the first hare shoot in the Bendigo paper. Where G.J. got top score. I would like a hare shoot now. You must have had a fine time the second time you were out. Well Albert I heard that you went and enlisted again. What did I tell you before I left. Albert you were foolish you know. There is enough of us in here now. Charlie ought to be [here] soon that [is] if he sailed when you said the 7th. I got [a letter] from him and one from your <u>sister</u>. Charlie told me about the hearty reception he got when he got home what a beaut he must have got. We got issued with new underclothing gloves etc on Saturday … When you write tell me what sort of a time you had [at] the picnic and the Pyramid show. I voted for conscription here the other day not many here voted for it but I think it is the best thing I know of. By hell it would hit G.J. up wont it. He wont like leaving the girls. I believe he is going strong. Well he is welcome to them. It is a wonder they are not out hare shooting for themselves this year… The war is going well now but our boys are still getting knocked about. I was sorry to hear about Ray Leed getting killed … You know Gus Ryan well he has [been] sick ever since being over here and was sick all the way over. He went under an operation here but is still crook, I think they will send him back again. Well Albert they tell [us] they are going to give us another 4 days leave. I hope they do it will be very welcome I have [not] started my course of dot dash yet as we were out at the trenches, you will see what sort of a time we had at the trenches by mum's letter. Well Albert I think I have told you all the news so I will close hoping you are all still well.

Goodbye Albert
I remain

Your Loving Brother
Allan

It was alright Jack McKay getting stuck you done alright out of it. I supposed he enjoyed it. Albert thanks for sending me the wallet it will be very acceptable. I have not received it yet, but I got the rag. I was sorry to hear that you have a bad cold. Well Albert I never felt better in my life. I have put on some weight since being here. I am glad you got my cable. Well Albert old boy I think I have told you all the news.

So Goodbye
Have a look at the letters that I sent Mum
Please excuse scribble and blot I dropped my pen Albert

The next day, Percy wrote to his parents:

Lark Hill
23 Oct
Dear Mum & Dad

Well Mum, I received your photo, I think it is very good, you look a bit worried. We were out at the trenches when it came, we had a good trip out there this time, we were billeted for two days at a barn, they had a big sale there, while we were there, it was very amusing to see them selling. We slept in a hay loft, it was nice and warm, we were supposed to have a night attack but we never heard the alarm, so we missed the joke, I was not sorry. We put a day and a night in the trenches, it was very cold. Well mum conscription seems like as if it is going to come in, it will make a stir among the cold feet. It is very amusing here the people think we are conscripts, because we wear the badge in the front of our hats, all the brigade have to wear there hats that way.[4] We are getting revolvers instead of rifles, all the machine gun section will get them. We are going through a twelve days course, we go through everything, that we have learnt; drill we had just after we came in camp we are doing. We are expecting our few days leave after the twelve days course. It was very sad about Ray Leeds, they will feel it very much. Bob Leeds came over with us, but he is not here now, he must have gone to France, he was not in our battalion. Well Mum, that was a great letter of Charlie Fyffe's, it must have took him some time to write it, I think I have told you all the news so I will close.

From your loving son
Percy

As Percy describes, even in the photos that Sarah sent to her sons, he could recognise the signs of her growing concern. Five of her children had now left the security of their home and the safety of Australia. Her anxiety was evident to those who knew her well. Allan wrote to Albert to ensure he would seek to be allocated to the same battalion as his brothers. Having all the brothers together in the one battalion was one means to ease Sarah's apprehension.

… I have just come back from Amesbury. Les and I went down, oh it is a brute of a town. It is only 1 ½ miles away and since being here I have only been down twice. Well Albert I wish you hadnt passed for the war I think there is enough of us here now. You seem to have a good time in Bendigo. Good luck to you too. Well Albert we are having a 12 day stunt now. They are giving us a general touch up of all the work we have done and then we are going away I believe. And I wont be sorry either. They tell us they are going to give us another 4 days leave too. I hope it is true too. Well Albert if you get through allright you are bound to be sent to England. If you do and Charlie is here, you get with him. Now Albert don't forget. You will be able to do it too and then in the end we will be all together with the exception of Geordie. Well Charlie isn't here yet but I hope he gets here before we go away. Albert when you come here you will find London etc the dearest b-place God ever made. You want to beat them down a treat. I never saw a place like it in my life. Beat the b- down. Now Albert don't forget to get with Charlie. If Charlie is here you apply for a transfer at once. You write to Charlie or see him and get him to work for it too. Well Albert news is b- scarce. All the boys are well. Well Albert by the time you get this letter it will be Christmas. Well Albert I wish you a very merry Christmas and a happy new year and if you get through allright I hope you have a good trip over. As soon as [you] lob write to me at once … Well Albert old boy I will say goodbye hoping if you get through to see you over here.

I remain
Your Loving Brother
Allan

Writing to his mother, Allan reassured Sarah that he would soon be home to once again enjoy the delightful lunches she routinely brought to the paddocks during harvest time:

… The other night we all went up to a play it was not too bad. It was first one that ever I have been too since our arrival here. Well mum you will be very busy by the time you get this letter. You will be cutting up lunches. That what I used to look forward to when I used to be up to my neck in work out in the fields. As long as the lunch came I was right. We don't get any lunches here mum but I will have plenty when I go back. In my other letter I was telling you that I used to toast myself some bread in the cook house. Well Mum there was too many on the game at last and we all got stopped. We are getting good tucker here and you get a good appetite too. Mum I am sending you Albert Brooks photo he gave it too [me] yesterday. I suppose Percy sent you his photo. I sent some of mine up to Leceister. Mum I was delighted to get yours. I wrote to you asking you to send me one, so you will see what a pleasant surprise I got. I never got a letter from Geordie this week. I suppose he never had time to write. I have wrote to him to day and I have been posting a few of my letters to him in case he didn't get any. I also sent him my photo. He gets my letters regular. Mum many thanks for the Christmas tin it will be very nice. We will get it alright mum. Mum there is no need to worry over us. We are alright and having a good time. Really mum I never felt better in my life. This climate agrees with me but all the same mum I would not live here for anything. Mum tell Jim I am sending him over my diary of my trip over. He can read it too. The notes are very brief and they are wrote in lead pencil. I want him to read them to you so you see what sort of trip we had, and what the sea was like each day. I have a little note book in my wallet that will do me, there are a lot of addresses in the diary, but I have got them all copied out … I got a letter from Jack Price this week. He is well and is still training in France. I think it is a good way from the firing line. Well Mum I think our brigade ought to do good work at the front if we only have good leaders, as we are well trained and we have a big artillery and more machine guns than any other brigade that has gone to the front. Well dear mother I think I have told you all the news so I will say goodbye for the present. Hoping all are well. Dear Mum I wish you a merry Christmas and a happy new year.

I remain

Your Loving Son
Allan S…

A Merry Christmas and a happy new year to you mum

Percy also wrote to his parents and to Jim. He openly expressed his surprise that his parents had signed Albert's enlistment papers but falls short of rebuking his family. His opinion is clear, however: there were already enough Marlow sons doing their duty and Albert should have stayed at home.

Lark Hill
Oct 29
Dear Mum & Dad

Well Mum, we are just the thing, I have no news, I wrote to you to catch a mail that went a few days ago. We do not know when we are going away. I am ready to go anytime. Jim says in his letter that Albert has enlisted, I never thought you would let him go. It has been raining a lot here this last week, we had lectures while it was raining on gas helmets, and bombs; of course we were inside. Well Mum I have no more news so I will close

From Your Loving Son
Percy

Lark Hill
England
29/10/16
Dear Jim

Well Jim, news is scarce but I will try and tell you some, we are having some wet weather lately, I suppose you are having hot weather over there now, you will be into harvest now, you will miss Albert, he says he has enlisted, I never thought they would let him go, I think there is enough of us gone. You were asking did I get letters from Flo and Paynes I get letters from all of them, it keeps them writing. You talk a lot about that girl in Bendigo but you never say anything about her name. I would just like to watch you. Conscription seems like it is going to come in, it will cause a stir among the cold feet "eh Jim", I see by the papers they tried to shoot Hughes, it will give him a bit of a fright.

We had a lot of lectures this last few days, mostly on bombing and gas helmets, bombing is very interesting Jim, they make a scatter when they burst. The gas helmets are funny when you get them on the first time, they are something like a bag over your head when you see anyone with them on. I am a real church goer since I came over here, we have to go every Sunday, there is no way out of it. We have got new clothes for all our worn out ones, we have a list of what we got to take to France, we have to carry it in our pack, our kit bag does not go to France, I do not think it will be long before we go. Well Jim I had a letter from Flo Wilson she said it was splendid that five of us has enlisted.

Well Jim I think I have told you all the news so I will close
From Your Loving Brother Percy

MOLOGA, OCTOBER

With Albert in camp, Charles, Sarah and Jim were now managing the farm alone with the harvest looming. Albert planned to take some leave to assist in those vital weeks when the wheat was ready and their year's work had come to fruition.

Bendigo
Monday 1916
Dear Mum

Just a line to say I came into camp this afternoon There were five came in. Billy Taylor and a lad from Pyramid and I and two others. The lad from Pyramid used to work at Bob Newton's. We got issued with our sleeping rig out, four blankets and a water proof sheet, and a piece of hessian. We had bread and jam and black coffee. It didn't go too bad. I was up at Rowe's for dinner yesterday and was up to the hospital yesterday to see the Stone boys. Jack Gibson and I went up to Mahoneys after tea. We had a good time up there. Aunty and Hannah were at Church. We got plenty of music up there. I was asked up there next Sunday afternoon. I got a pass to go home last Sat. I left Gibson's at 20 to 12 and hurried all the way and got up to the station at 3 minutes to 12 just in time to see the train going off the station. We have got to get examined in the morning before we get our blues.[5] There is talk of sending all the men from here to Royal Park on Wednesday so I may have to go there. I don't know yet what my address is, so address it care of Gibson's. Well Mum this is all so I will close hoping all are well.

I remain Your Loving Son
Albert
Melb
Wed evening
Dear Mum,

Just a few lines to let you know I shifted down here this morning. We left Bendigo at 9 oclock, had to get up at 5.30. All the men left the camp this morning for Royal Park. Two of my mates got left behind, but I got picked out among 8 others to load all the equipment. So I had to come down here. I got examined again yesterday morning. Bill Taylor got kicked out he couldn't pass the eyesight test. I got inoculated yesterday morning and my arm is still stiff. I haven't done any drill yet. We were all yesterday morning getting our kit, and in the afternoon they told the four of us to do what we liked, so I went into Bendigo at four oclock, and was up to Gibsons for tea, and we went to the pictures. We got down here at 1 oclock and loaded up the equipment and we were ages waiting for the lorry to load the next. It is five oclock now so we haven't done much today.

I remain
Albert
Pte A Marlow
B/Co
4/38 Batt
Royal Park

Royal Park
Thursday
Dear Mum,

Just a few lines to say I am going on well. We got out to this camp last night at about 6 oclock, and it was as wet as blazes, but it is dry again now. It dries up very quick. We unloaded the equipment last night and our corporal shouted us to town to the theatre. We had a great time. I never laughed so much in all my life as I did yesterday. We get up at 6.30 here, and have stew for breakfast, then at dinner, we have roast mutton and for tea tonight we had bread, jam and cheese. The bread is lovely here, quite fresh, in Bendigo it was as stale as blazes. The tucker is better here than in Bendigo, and there is plenty of it. It is a very big camp, and there is a hell of a crowd here. About 100 new recruits came here today. I done my first real drill today. The sergeant had a dozen of us to drill, and when he finished told us, we were the smartest men he ever drilled. There is a big canteen here, and seems to be plenty of amusement at night. There is a concert tonight. I think I will go if I finish writing letters in time. This is much better than in Bendigo, but I would sooner be there all the same. Eight of us sleep in one tent here. They are all decent fellows. I sleep fairly well on the boards. All of our company who have not had final leave had to step out at roll call, so I think I will get final leave soon. Nearly all the volunteers in Victoria are in this camp. A lot came here today from the Domain camp. I think I will be vaccinated soon as a lot out of our company were done today. Harry Street is in the same company as me. We got dismissed at half past four this afternoon, and get half an hour a day smoke-o besides about two hours standing easy. Well Mum, I will ring off, as I have more letters to write. Don't forget to write. Excuse scribble.

I remain
Your Loving Son
Albert

I got two letters and two packets of books and postcards from Allan, and a letter from Percy. Did you get any from Geordie

Royal Park
Sat 1916
Dear Jim,

Just a line to let you know I am still here and like it tip-top. I got leave till tomorrow night but I got tired of walking about the town, so I came back to camp. I am going to the zoo tomorrow. 30 out of our company had to stay in camp to look after the lines. There are some damn thieves here, I haven't lost anything yet but a lot have. This is a great camp. Miles ahead of Bendigo. The tucker here is good. We have a mess in each tent, and two go mess orderlies each day. There is about 3 000 men here and you have a job to get a wash in the morning. I have a cold bath every night before tea. We had church parade this morning. All the Protestants have theirs together. The Catholics fall out but don't make much difference. I am applying for weekend leave to Bendigo next Sat. I couldn't get right home so I am trying to get that far. Well Jim, this is all this time

I remain Your Loving brother
Albert

Albert's final leave came suddenly. He made the journey home from Melbourne, little suspecting that, on his return to his company, embarkation would be scheduled for the following day, 20 October, when the men would board the *Port Lincoln*. The desperate need for reinforcements demanded their immediate move to England for training.

Albert returned to Mologa for his farewell which was reported in the *Pyramid Hill Advertiser*. The article also describes the family's attempt to delay Albert's departure. The harvest was about to begin and Albert was needed on the farm.

Private A. W. Marlow farewell

On Tuesday, 11th October, the friends of Pte. A. W. Marlow met together in the Mologa Hall to bid him farewell prior to his departure for the front. Private Marlow, the youngest member of the family, 18 years of age, had been in the camp only 10 days, and in that short time military life improved him so much that he appeared to have grown ... Mr. W. Fyffe occupied the chair, and on the conclusion of the programme made the presentation of a gold medal to the departing soldier. In doing so he spoke at some length and referred to the fine qualities Private Marlow possessed, and instanced his readiness to assist in preparing for, or promoting any worthy social function happening to be on the tapis, altogether, a youthful, useful member of the community. Mr. and Mrs. Marlow in giving their fifth son had done much for their country. In conclusion the chairman expressed the hope that Mr. Marlow, along with his brothers, would return safely ... Pte. Marlow in responding thanked his many friends for coming to see him that night, and for the nice medal presented to him, which, if he safely returned, he would proudly wear … Three cheers were then given for the Marlow family.

Pte. Marlow left by the afternoon train on Wednesday, when a number of friends assembled to see him off. On behalf of Pte. Marlow, Cr Jones endeavoured to get leave granted to him for part of the harvest only. It was thought that four sons having gone they would stand a good chance. Cr Jones forwarded a letter to Mr. Angus, M.L.A., who sent it on to Mr. Sampson, M.H.R, who in turn interviewed the Defence Department. The result was that word was received that it would be favourably considered. A few days passed and Pte. Marlow came up on final leave. Cr Jones wired to the Defence Department, who then granted the leave asked for. By this time Pte. Marlow was back in camp getting his sea kit ready for sailing. His parents received a post card announcing the fact that in an hour's time he would be marching to the boat. He need not have gone into camp till the 28th October. However, as he wished his leave to be during November he decided to go to camp a month earlier, thinking that by doing so he would have a better chance of leave, as his purpose was honest and his mission to fight for his country well meant …[6]

Thursday morning [19 October]
Dear Mum,
Just a few lines to let you know that we are going to embark this morning and are sailing tomorrow. We had to get up at 4.30 this morning. I got here about 12 last night. They roared me up a bit about staying away, but I don't think I will be fined. I got the surprise of my life, when I heard we were going today. We are just getting issued with our sea kit, no time to write any more, so goodbye.

Your loving son
Albert

There is a photo of mine at Kalma's, a full length one, you had better get it and get some off it, I have no time to get it taken again.

The postcard Albert sent before he embarked.

With only an hour to spare, Albert quickly wrote to his mother before leaving Australian soil, writing on the back of a photo postcard taken in Melbourne. The youngest and last of Sarah's sons to leave for war was now on his way. The photo is haunting. Despite the uniform, his staunchness and resolve, Albert looks every inch the young boy farewelling his devoted mother as he sets off on a great adventure.

Friday
Dear Mum

Just a line or two before I sail We are going to march to the boat in about an hours time, and are sailing about 1 oclock. I never had time to get my photo taken, You had better write to Kalma and ask him to send that one (in full length) up, and get some taken off it, You had better get 1 dozen and 1/2 and pay for them out of my allotments.

I will write a list of those to send them to, Well Goodbye mum,

From your loving son
Albert

One more loving son was about to depart. Like those before him, Albert was keen to ensure that his family had a handsome photo of himself in uniform. For families farewelling their men a photo was akin to an insurance policy, reassurance that their brave soldier would never be forgotten in the event he did not return. While the Marlow family assembled a large collection of photos, it proved little insurance against wounding or death, nor against the concern that Sarah and Charles Marlow must surely have felt with five sons now on active service.

SEVEN
A LOT OF THE MEN THOUGHT THEIR LAST DAY HAD COME

AT SEA, OCTOBER

Charlie was now almost two weeks into his journey on the *Shropshire* and heading towards South Africa as his reference to Uncle Arthur reveals:

Sunday at Sea [8 October 1916]
Dear Jim,

Just a few lines today we are not allowed now to put the date but today is Geordie's birthday. I am getting on alright but my cold still hangs to me it is getting better now I used all the medicine that I got in Bendigo so now I go to the hospital dispensary and of course get it for nicks, I wrote home about 7 or 8 days ago and have also written to Pearl and Arthur & George our letter box closes on Thursday next as I will be seeing Uncle Arthur in a few days we are following the same course as Al and Percy. There are a lot on board that I know and nearly all of them have been a bit seasick. I said in my last letter that I felt a bit sick the second day out but since I feel splendid. Les Cant is in the hospital and also George Humbert and that young Miles that was in camp with me, they have got measles or influenza we get war news every day now by wireless according to if things are going good. I went to church parade this morning there is 2 Protestant and one Catholic Chaplain on board. There is a canteen on board but I could not get any ink so I had to write with a pencil, we get good food on board and plenty of it, the tucker here is far better than in camp. I suppose Albert is in camp now the two Stones didnt come as they were in the hospital. I hope to be able to get to some of the relations for christmas. Willie Crossman is down on our deck he belongs to Castlemaine lot I see all the Mologa boys every day Jim Baker is also on board. They have all sorts of games on board and a good band and a concert every Saturday night. I suppose by the time you receive this you will be harvesting and I suppose the crop will be pretty good, we don't see much crop out here for water ...

South Africa Durban
Oct 16th 1916
Excuse the type but I write this somewhat under difficulties.
Dear Mother,

Just a few lines to let you know that I am getting on alright my cold has completely gone I had to go on guard on the ship one night and being out in the fresh air all night done me the world of good and ever after that I slept up on top it is very healthy sleeping up in the sea air, so now I felt better than I have ever felt in my life. We landed in Durban at 4 oclock on Sunday Oct 15 and got leave from 5 oclock till 10 pm that night we were marched in the town and dismissed, I was out with Tom Roberts from the Ox [Durham Ox] and Bill Crossman we had tea and a good look round and today Monday we had a march for about 2 miles this morning and after dinner we were marched in the town and dismissed and we are allowed out till 11 oclock tonight so that is not too bad.[1] I am writing this in a place called Wesley Hall it is something like a Methodist Church in Australia, they give all the soldiers and sailors tea and coffee and sandwiches cake and fruit including tomatoes free to all there are ladies waiting on the tables all day long I am sure I don't know how they do it for nothing. I am sure this is the best place I have struck since I have joined the army they have also a band playing here tonight and they supply the writing paper free in fact they are only to pleased to do anything for the soldiers, they gave us a great reception as the boat pulled in. There are about 1700 men on board and we had great weather coming over it was as calm as the bullock creek. I felt a bit sick the second day but it was my cold I think that made me sick if it is rough I will not be sick I think I have gained weight for I can eat like a horse, things are very dear I sent a little present to Pearl it was a tea strainer I hope she gets it alright I registered it so she ought to get it I also wrote to her telling her that I sent it. I believe we will call at Cape Town for a day or two and I think we will be leaving tomorrow. I have written to you before and to Jim and to all the relations in Australia. Well mother I will draw to a close, do not worry over me as I am alright and getting on fine I hope all are well at home if Albert is in camp show him this note so goodbye all.

I am your loving son
Charlie

South Africa
Cape Town
21st Oct 1916
Dear Albert

Just a few lines to let you know that I am still alive and today we are in Cape Town we are not allowed off so far and I believe we will not be getting off here at all we had a great time in Durban we got there on the Sunday night at 4 oclock 15th Oct and left on the Wednesday morning at 7 am, it is a very nice town and we had a real good time it rained while we were there, but here we cannot see much from the boat there are a lot of ships in the harbour at present the table top mountains look very nice with the clouds on top of them they are very high if you come this way you will see them we followed close to land all the way from Durban the coast is very pretty especially near Cape Town we pulled in at 7.30 last night and it is very cold here today. I do not know when we leave but I think it will be today sometime. I hope this note will reach you alright I suppose you will be on the job when this reaches you be sure and try and get in the 38th. I believe we are bound straight for England now and this is our last port of call, I wrote to Jim and Mother and also to Pearl I hope they are all getting on alright. I am enjoying the trip first rate and feel splendid my cold has got alright. I am writing this and will throw it overboard to the South African soldiers to post so excuse the type as I have not much time. I hope you have a good trip over and hope to see you there so I will close for the present so goodbye and good luck.

I am your affectionate
Charlie

Charlie was later surprised to discover that Albert was now steaming westward aboard the *Port Lincoln*, following the same route as the *Shropshire* across the Indian Ocean:

At Sea
21ˢᵗ Oct-16
Dear Mum,

Well we are out on the sea now. We left Royal Park yesterday morning and went onto the pier at 9 oclock and then waited there till two oclock. We then went on the boat and sailed at a quarter past two (Friday). There was a hell of a crowd at the pier and there was some sad hearts there when we left. All the men seemed to take it all right. We had to get up at 5 yesterday morning. I had nothing to eat from 6 oclock on Thursday night till 7 oclock on Friday night, so you can see I did a bit of a starve. And the tucker I had last night wasn't much good for an empty stomach. We got butter on board, I think the tucker will be good when we settle down a bit. We anchored just inside the heads last night and are still here. I think we will be moving off shortly. There will be a few sick when we go, I bet. I got a bit of a surprise on Wednesday night, when I heard we had to sail next day. I went to the C.O. and told him that I had applied for harvest leave, and he said it was too late. He said if I had not stopped away without leave, he might have fixed me up. Then I tried to get it with Gil Hansford, but it was too late too. I would have liked to stop another week longer as I had no time to get anything. We got leave from a quarter to six on Thursday, so I went into town and got a wristlet watch. I didn't have time to get anything else. I never got any notepaper, but I think I can get some at the canteen when it opens. We slept on hammocks last night, they are not bad, but I think I would rather have the boards. Well Mum I don't know if you can read this as I am writing this on the boards. I don't know if you will get this before we get to Cape Town but I heard the mail was leaving the boat at Queenscliff so I will close, hoping all are well,

I remain
your loving son
Albert

Don't worry about me, I am in the best of health and spirits.
Send a photo to Dolly Rouse 23 Chum St Golden Square

If you don't get that full length photo from Kalmas, write and ask Myrtle for it. I told her to call for it. If you get it you had better order 18 and pay for them out of my allotment – don't forget. These are the ones I want you to send photos too Auntie Etta, Annie, Liza and Florrie, Myrtle Stone, Myrtle Saville, Winnie Price, Mollie Gamble, Ralph Alford, Pearl Saville and anybody else you like, I think Mrs Stone wanted one too.

At Sea
25th/10/16
Dear Mum, Dad and Jim

Just a line to let you know I am not too bad now, I have been a bit sea-sick … the smell on the 2nd deck was enough to turn any fellow off. I felt crook when I went on the boat and the smell settled me. We had terrible rough weather and the boat rocks like hell. The only thing I ate was pears preserved which I got at the canteen. It is a rotten boat, and there is no comforts on it. The canteen is about as big as our dairy, and a trap door to get things through, and it is closed half the time. My mate managed to get some lemonade for me, and a few biscuits, I got a writing pad a while ago, but have got to wait till tomorrow for envelopes. On Sat and Sunday nearly every man on board was sea-sick, it was horrible to see the poor devils. The sharks done a hell of a business. The boat travels very slow, we will pass near [censored] tomorrow or tonight, but I don't think we will call in there. We will be in calmer water tomorrow. It has been terrible rough so far, and a lot of the men are still sick. I never had a decent feed until today. The tucker is getting better now. I often fancied some before, but the smell of the 2nd deck used to finish me. There was bully beef for tea, and I was as hungry as blazes, so I got some onions out of a bag and had a feed. I had to go down a while ago and have another feed, and I could eat some more now. I think the trip will be real good from now on, but a day or two ago, I did not give a damn if the boat sank or not. You have to buy your own notepaper on this boat, they don't supply you with anything here. We get butter on board, and plenty of salt so I am right. I never got any of those letters you wrote to the camp, but I got one from Bert Gibson asking me to go to his wedding, but I was too late as it was on the day I left Mologa … There was a fair few on Bendigo station to see me off, also a few at Mitiamo. Lily Stone gave me three khaki handkerchiefs and some oranges …

At Sea
Sunday 29/10/16
Dear Mum, Dad and Jim,

Well I am still going strong and enjoying this life a treat. We called in close to a port on Thursday night, but not close enough to get off. We only stopped there a few hours. I am feeling tip top now, and am getting as fat as mud, so my mates say. I have got a bonzer appetite ... My word the tucker is a change after Royal Park. We don't have so much amusement on board, No music, but there is plenty of singing and boxing. We had a C of Eng church parade this morning. About ¾ of our company are C of England. There are a terrible lot of boys in our company. There is 11 at our mess table and 6 of us are under 19 and two under 21. There is no news on board so I will finish this some other time. –

Nov 2nd

Well Mum, we are having a good trip. The sea is lovely and calm. We saw a few whales yesterday. Things are livening up a bit now. We are having a sports meeting on board on Tuesday. I am in the potato race and the "onion and bucket" race. Each company has to have 6 men in each event. We are having a separate potato race for our company tomorrow. The winner gets 5/-. We have run off some of the heats. I won my heat. We are going to run off tonight. There is about 8 of us left in it. I got vaccinated the day before I sailed, and it is just starting to take now. It is getting a bit sore. We expect to get to a port in a weeks time. I will write from there if we get off. It is the place where Allan sent the leaves from. We haven't heard yet if the referendum passed. Well Mum this is all this time so I will close hoping all are well as it leaves me at present.

I remain Your Loving Son
Albert

We are going to do drill soon but it wont be much, as there is no room. Don't worry about me Mum, I am quite well and in the best of spirits.

In the last days of October, Australians went to the polls and voted in the conscription referendum. Conscription was rejected, defeated by

72,476 votes from a total of 2,247,590. The issue had clearly divided the nation. Victoria, Tasmania and Western Australia voted in favour, while the remaining states were firm in their rejection. Australian soldiers also voted for conscription with 72,399 in favour while 58,894 rejected the proposition.[2] While it was a blow to the campaign of Billy Hughes, the veteran politician would not give up easily and the conscription debate looked set to continue.

It is difficult to know how the mothers of soldiers such as Sarah Marlow might have voted. Her youngest son's departure prior to the conscription vote and her allegiance to the staunchly pro-conscription Church of England may have prompted a 'Yes' vote consistent with the majority of Victorians. On the other hand, she may have sought to spare other mothers the anguish that she must have felt watching her boys depart. As the war entered its third year, reinforcements were needed more than ever to fill the places left by the dead and wounded. Despite Jim's earlier rejection by the medical officer, it was still possible for the last of Sarah's sons to be called up as the casualty list continued to grow.

THE BATTLE OF THE SOMME ENDS, NOVEMBER

As the bitter winter began to bite in earnest, the opposing armies on the Somme front continued their attempts to break through.[3] Australian troops were sent in at both Gueudecourt and Flers, but the attacks were bogged down in the mud and all movement stalled in the morass that was no man's land. Enemy trenches were briefly captured and held but then abandoned. British High Command eventually accepted that no significant gains would be made and the big guns fell silent in the now devastated Somme Valley. In some sectors the front line had not moved while in others between 11 and 13 kilometres of territory had been gained at the cost of over 600,000 Allied casualties, of whom 150,000 had been killed or were listed as missing.[4]

As relative quiet descended on the Western Front, raids and small attacks into enemy territory continued while the troops struggled in the personal battles with more immediate enemies: mud, frostbite, trench foot and the plague of rats that invaded the trenches and ventured into no man's land to forage among the bodies of the dead. Wooden duckboards began to arrive to line the base of the trenches and provide solid footing along the routes to the front. Fatigue parties were kept busy improving the appalling conditions under which the soldiers were required to live and fight.

Albert's friend Jack Price, who had hoped that Albert's parents would consent to his enlistment, was blithely unaware that his old school mate was now on his way to England. Jack wrote of helping the local farmers harvest their mangolds, a type of beet used largely to feed stock. This young man from the country had enjoyed being a 'cockie' again.

France
Sunday November 5th 1916
Dear Albert

I got another letter from you yesterday and was glad to hear that you were all well. It is Sunday afternoon over here today and things are a bit quiet. We are billeted in a village a few miles back but I think we will be going further up to-morrow. It is a fortnight since we left the last front we were on. When you write again tell me what Battalion Geordie is attached to and I will try and find him. I suppose it is fairly warm over your way by now. You will be taking on a bit of bag sewing again this year I suppose to get hold of some £ S.D. to have a good time on. Charlie's old job would suit you allright only I suppose you are wanted at home. We were cockies again yesterday pulling mangolds and heaping them up. It was a nice change and not a bad job at all. By what I hear Allan and Percy are over in this country now just arrived. I have just been down for a tin of 3 castles. They are 1 franc 75 centines for a tin of 50. I think I will soon have forgotten the English coinage. Well boy I want to get my hair cut this afternoon so I will close with best wishes to you all.

From your sincere pal
Jack Price

Allan and Percy had yet to reach France, while George remained on the deadly Somme front close to Pozieres. On 1 November he moved into the front line at Dernancourt where machine-gun fire and artillery regularly swept the trenches. On 6 November they were relieved and some days later were treated to the luxury of a hot bath, albeit one in which many weary soldiers had already bathed their filthy bodies. On 19 November George wrote to his mother telling her that he had been promoted in the field — he was now a lance corporal. His expression of disappointment that Albert had been granted permission to enlist will not have eased the apprehension that Sarah was enduring.

France
November 19
Dear Mother & Father

Just a few lines to let you know I am well hoping all are the same. I have just come out of the trenches again so have missed one mail and it was the xmas mail, we were in the lively part again and was raining nearly all the time so there was plenty of mud about, while we were in Charlie Fyffe and Charlie Wales were wounded but don't know how bad I passed them in there one day that was the last I saw of them, they had a short turn in the firing line only about a month. Amos and Hughie Johnson are both well I was with them the other night we often see one another. You seem to think that Allan & Percy are here fighting well I had a letter from them about a week ago, they were still in England then and were well. I also had a letter from Charlie saying that he had arrived in England. I am getting your letters regular the last were written on the 24 September and one from Jim written on the 25 saying that he was down in Melbourne seeing Charlie off, I have had several papers one with poor old Ray's photo in. I had a letter from Theo. Phillips also give him my proper address he had it addressed to the 7th Battalion. I received that small parcel which I thank you very much for. I was surprised about you letting Albert come away there are enough of us here now. Well we had a surprise two mornings ago when we got up to find snow on the ground but it wasn't so very cold. Well I have a lot of letters to write so I will close. Wishing you all a happy New Year.

I remain
Your Loving Son
George

Later

Just received a letter from Allan & Percy, written on the 16 of this month saying that they hadnt left England yet also saying that they had a letter from Charlie and are going to look him up. I am a Lance Corporal now and in charge of a gun and crew, I think I told you before that we have small guns for firing bombs from our trenches into the enemies. Hughie Johnson told me that George Leed is in his Battalion and he didn't know Ray had been killed. Will be writing to Jim in a few days time.

So Goodbye
George

While George's luck was holding, his friends were less fortunate. Charlie Fyffe, a 23-year-old local farmer, had been serving in the 6th Battalion. He had enlisted in March 1916 but returned to Australia in July 1917 having been badly wounded on 11 November 1916.[5] Farm labourer Charlie Wales from Bald Rock near Mologa was also a member of the 6th Battalion, having enlisted in January 1916. He was wounded in the leg on 22 September 1916 and remained in England convalescing until April 1917 when he returned to France. He was killed in the village battles of 1918, shot in the chest on 9 August near Lihons, some 20 kilometres east of Villers-Bretonneux.[6]

AT SEA, NOVEMBER

Charlie wrote to his family describing his journey as the *Shropshire* steamed up the west coast of Africa:

Sea
Dear Mother, Father & Brothers

I am writing you a few more lines today as the mail box closes very soon, yesterday we crossed the equator so you can guess that it is very hot here the boys kept up the old custom of ducking everyone under the taps and showers, and I can tell you there was some water flying. They would catch a man and put him under clothes and all, of course our clothes on board are the blueys and every man that got drenched joined the mob, and at times things were a bit fast some of our chaps showed fight, however they did not get me, we can get a drink of water on board as cold as ice and there is ice on the pipes that lead to the tank. It will not be long now till we reach the other side and I think I have a good chance of seeing Al and Percy there also I think I will stand a good chance of seeing some of the relations over there. They had a 1/- sweep on board for the Melbourne Cup and I won a 5/- consolation prize, we have been paid £1 since we have been on board. There was a splendid concert on board last night some of the items were very amusing, it was the best concert we have had since we left Victoria. There was also a good boxing contest last night one had a job to get near the ring for men. The weather has been calm all the way since we left Cape Town, in fact the trip all the way over has been grand. Tom Roberts and Les Cant and Bill Crossman are in the same deck as me I have got in good with a lot of fellows the Major said that the people of Durban thought we were the best troops that have passed through there. Well I suppose this will reach you somewhere near Christmas, so I wish you all a merry Christmas and a happy new year and hope the crop turns out well. I will write to you as often as I can when I get the other side, I have written a good few letters home and hope they all have reached you. I will now draw to a close hoping all are well as I am at present

So I will now say goodbye
I am Your Loving Son and Brother
Charlie

… Tell me how the conscription business is getting on I saw in the paper where 60,000 odd had registered … We get war news by wireless every day.

While writing to his parents and Jim describing events on board, Charlie's letter to Albert also includes a dose of big brotherly advice. However, Charlie's main concern was still the security of his money, as the AIF was not immune from petty pilfering. By the time his letter reached Mologa, Albert was nearing the shores of England.

… there are some very good singers on board also some good violin players, when you come over you ought to bring your mouth organ. Also you want to get a good money belt get one for your arm and put surplus money in it also have one as a belt round your waist to have cash that you need in it you want to take great care of your money belt when you are in a crush

watching anything and at all times, remember if your money is gone your done, some fellows will get at the back of a man in a crush and cut his belt with a razor, that is why I say to have one on your arm also, and another thing don't lend money to anyone unless you know you are sure of getting it back. I lent money here and had a job to get it back …

Sea Nov, 6th 1916
Dear Mother Father & Brothers

I am writing you a few lines before we land so as to be able to post them as soon as possible, we will land in about 4 days from now, after a grand trip we called at a place called Dakar at Cape Verde on the coast of Africa for a Gun it is about 1000 miles north of the equator … we landed at Durban on the 15th Oct, and landed at Cape Town on Oct 20th and landed at Dakar on Thursday Sept 2nd. I am feeling real well and have enjoyed the trip first rate so far the sea has been very calm tomorrow I think we will be going through the Bay of Biscay.

I have written to Al and also to Geordie and will write to Percy and the relations in England I think I will be able to see some of them as far as I know. I have so far no idea where Al and Percy are, we get war news every day by wireless. Nov 8th Bay of Biscay Later News, you will see by now that we are in the Bay of Biscay it is very rough, last night was the roughest night we have had, we have our life belts on all day in case of submarines but I think we are pretty safe, we are not allowed up on deck now for long if we are up on the decks we have to get behind deck houses, away from view, we are not doing any drill now and having a real good time down below playing games etc.

Arrived safe mail closes in a few minutes will write later. I am at a place called Bovington Camp near Wool in the County of Dorset.

I am Your Loving Son
Charlie

LARKHILL, ENGLAND, NOVEMBER

Having received a generous delivery of mail from Australia, Allan spent most of his Sunday writing replies:

England
Sunday 5-11-16
My Dear Mum

Well dear mum I got your most welcome letter dated 18 Sept I got 4 letters altogether 3 from home and 1 from L Sharp. I was pleased to hear that everything is looking well ... About us being in action is a perfect rumour but it wont be long now as we are on the move now ... I got a letter from Georgie last week. He is well. He said Amos Haw is only about 100 yds from him. Well Mum I have been on the look out for Charlie every week but every letter I get is that he is not sailed yet ...

To Albert he included a note concerning the conflict at home over Charlie's wedding:

... I went over to Perrin Downs yesterday to Joe Cocking but he had gone to France again. I believe he was on leave from the trenches. Albert what a time you must have had at Calival. The fuss over C- wedding seems to have quitened down a bit now. What a good job too.

The boys' cousin, Ida Payne, wrote to her Uncle Charles from Leicestershire. Ida and their other relatives would provide a link to home which the boys would value; when in England they invariably travelled to Leicestershire or Devon to enjoy the company of their English family. Ida's letter describes how life has changed in England since the war began.

33 Green Lane Road
Leicester
Nov. 5th. 1916
My Dear Uncle,

I was so pleased to receive a letter from you ... I like to write to the boys as often as I can for I know how a letter is looked forward to when they are in the trenches. When I received your letter we had already met two of your boys and fine boys we thought them too. We are expecting to see Charlie almost any day now. I have not had a letter from Allan this week but he was expecting him to land a fortnight ago. I hear from George pretty regularly. Ethel writes to Percy and I to Allan. Percy & Allan sent us their photos last week. We thought they were very good. George has been hoping to get leave for some time now but has not managed it yet. Allan tells me that Albert has joined now, so you will only have Jim left. I hope for your sake that he wont have to come & I hope & trust all your dear lads may be spared to come safely home to you. My brother Clem is knocking about the Red Sea somewhere. He has been in one or two fights with the Turks & Arabs & was wounded once but we did not tell Mother so she knows nothing about it, but he is alright so far. He had a very narrow escape in one of the North Sea battles. Harry Marlow was badly wounded in France & has been in hospital for some time. He never writes to any of us. Friends are more to him than his relations. Neither he nor his sisters take after the Marlows. They all have their Mother's temper & disposition. Uncle Ted's son is in the "Blue Cross". He looks after sick & wounded horses & has been out in France for some time. Am glad to say we are all pretty well & up to now have got on fairly well. Mother has had to turn out to work as things are so dear, it costs twice as much to live now as it did before the war. The war has not touched us much in other respects. We have not had the horrors of Belgium & France. The only things that can harm us are the Zepps. We have escaped them so far in Leicester but they have been over Corby twice. Aunt Edie was about scared to death. They dropped about 40 bombs near there during the last raid, but luckily they all fell in fields & no damage to speak of was done. I have a piece of one of the bombs that fell there. The holes were seven yards across and about 4 feet deep. It is not safe to go out at nights. The streets are kept in total darkness & we get heavily fined if our windows show any lights. But the darkness has saved us from the Zepps so we cheerfully put up with it. Mother sends her love & says she expects your boys will think their Aunt Lizzie is a funny woman. She told them some fine tales I can tell you. Aunt Edie is inclined to be dosy & Aunt Charlotte is rather shy but Mother is the saucy one of the family I tell her. She keeps everyone alive. Aunt Annie is very nice but is very prim & proper & one always has to be on best behaviour with her. Well, think I must close now. I will write again soon. Hoping this will find Auntie & Jim & yourself all quite well & not feeling too lonely. With love to all.

I am
Your loving niece
Ida Payne

Charlie arrived at Plymouth on 11 November. He travelled to Bovington Army Base at Wool in Dorset and immediately tried to send word to his brothers who were some 80 kilometres to the north. In the frozen English training camps, Allan and Percy were eventually reunited with their older brother and eagerly received news of home and of Charlie's wedding. In mid-November the three young soldiers from Mologa were to see their first snow.

The twins wrote home with pleasure at the prospect of being reunited with Charlie.

Wednesday Night 16.11.16
My Dear Mum

… Well Mum we have finished our 12 day stunt and I am not a bit sorry either. We have had nothing but instructions lately. We have everything ready for the front now. They tell us we are going on Tuesday. So that is not to bad. I got a letter from Charlie to day and oh mum I was pleased to hear he has just landed and is [in] *a camp called Bovington and where it is nobody seems to know but I am doing my best to see him on Sunday. He said he had a great trip over. I got another letter from Geordie. He is well and still going strong. I get letters from the Aunt's and cousins every week. Flo Wilson sent us some socks cakes and cigarettes last week, it was very good of her. Tell Albert I got his wallet and the Pyramid papers. Mum I will lose all my letters in answer to the first we wrote on the Arabic. I am not sure but I think that will be the boat they are on. It is bad luck. I would love to have got them. I hope you get the parcel all right.*

… Now Mum I want you to go for a holiday to Melbourne or anywhere after harvest. Now you can take as much of that money as you like the more the better and have a good time. Now Mum when you write don't say that you didn't have a spell that's no good mum I mean it and you must go. If you don't I will be annoyed …

Percy wrote of his reservations, aware that his departure for France was imminent:

Friday 16/11/16
My Dear Mum & Dad

… Charlie is over here now, he landed this week, he is not here, we are going to see him tomorrow, he's about sixteen miles from here. Young Cocking and Clauss were over last night, they look real well. Cocking has put ten months in the firing line he got wounded in France, and got sent to Belfast, he had a good time he was then sent to Fairfield a hospital near London and now he is in Rollestone about three miles from us, he has to go away tomorrow. Clauss is quite deaf he expects to go back, but I do not think he will. We are going away on Tuesday, all our kit bags have gone away, I am sorry when we go, it will take some time to shift the Division. We had four days leave, we went to London, and we had a good time, it was very foggy while we were there, It will be xmas soon, we will have a different time to last year. Well Mum it's a good life soldiering, have a few reserves some times. I think I have told you all the news so I will close.

From Your Loving Son
Percy

Within a few days Percy had been reunited with Charlie. Percy then wrote to Jim describing his brother's visit and, in contrast to his letter to his parents, he tells Jim that he hopes to be in France soon to break the monotony of life at Larkhill.

19 Nov
Dear Jim

Well Jim, just a few lines to let you know, we are still alive, well Jim we are having snow for the first time, it has been going a day and a night. The place just looks like what you see it in the pictures, there are snow fights every where, it hardly safe to move out side. Well Jim Charlie is over here, we went down to see him yesterday, he looks real well on it, he is a good way from here. There are a good few chaps from up that way with him, they will not be long before they are with the 38. We expect to go away soon, all the letters have to be censored, so I cannot tell you much about us. I am not sorry we are going away, it is monotonous here. Well Jim we had four days leave, we went to London it was very foggy while we were there, but we had a good time. We had a letter from Geordie he was saying that it was hot over there, he was well when he wrote young Charlie Wales is wounded, he went there with Charlie Fyffe. Joe

Cocking and Clauss were here the other night. Cocking has had a long run in the trenches, he put ten months there. Hugh Martin is in the 38 now, he was in the second of the 38 and they were transferred to us, to make strength. Well Jim, you were asking about the girls, but I do not know anything about them, to shy to speak to them. You had <u>some</u> time at Jones by your letter, but Jim was it really Eva; hows the girl in Bendigo. I reckon you ought to get married, it near time you made a move Jim, because she cannot wait to soon. How's Nelly and Bill getting on I hear they are doing well. You have had some rain Jim, it ought to do a lot of good. Well Jim I think I have told you all the news so I will close

From Your Loving Brother
Percy
Give all the girls my love Jim

… It will take some time to shift the Division across, they are always saying when is the 3ʳᵈ Division going to declare war, you can bet it will give them a surprise when it gets to France, for most of the men are sick of here. Dave Glass is in this Division. Hugh Martin is in the 38 now, he came over in the 2ⁿᵈ reinforce 38 and they were transferred to make up strength …

Joe Cocking was 23 years old when he enlisted in January 1915. He originated from Castlemaine but worked at Pyramid Hill as a bootmaker. A member of the 21st Battalion, he was wounded on 26 August 1916 and, as Percy described, Joe was shipped to Belfast and then returned to recuperate at the camps near Salisbury. He rejoined his unit on 12 May 1917 and returned to Australia in August 1919.[7]

Charlie wrote:

Hurdcott Camp
Nov, 19ᵗʰ 1916
Dear Father, Mother & Brothers,

I am writing a few lines to let you know that I have shifted from Bovington Camp, Wool, to Hurdcott Camp Salisbury Plains we arrived here on Friday and I met Al and Percy on Saturday and I think they will be over today. I am 15 miles from where they are. I wrote about half a dozen letters and sent nearly as many wires before we could arrange to meet the O.C. of my company would not let me off so that made it worse and then we were shifting, I wrote to them as soon as we got to Wool but they were away on their 4 days leave, I arrived here about a week to late or they could have come to Bovington Camp anyhow I saw them yesterday they both look real well and are getting on alright I gave them 3 sovereigns and sent one with them for Geordie. I also saw Hughie Martin Bill Street Les Townsend Albert Brooks Hughie Martin is in the 38th now and they are going to France very soon and will train there for a while and then go into action. I got a letter from Ida Payne she gave me a great invitation to go up there when I get my 4 days leave which I think will be at the end of this week so I intend to go there we will have to go to London and then to Leicester. Al and Percy were up and saw them all, it has been very cold here this last few days it has been snowing here this last day or so, yesterday was the first snow that Al and Percy saw since they have been here. They have been issued with a new kind of boots and a new hat and all new underclothing. I wrote to Geordie when I came here first and expect an answer this week Al got a letter from him last week he is getting on alright, I am sending him a tin of cake and cigarettes etc. This is the third letter I have written to you since I have been in England, I saw Horris Wingfield yesterday he left about a week after me he is in the 6/60 Batt. Wilsie Townsend and Jack Sinclair and Jim Baker of the 5/60 are still at Bovington Camp and I think they will be going to the front very shortly. Everything here is very dear. Al says it is the same in London. When Albert comes over tell him to bring at least £10 and get a belt for his arm like mine and one for his waist, and tell him to be very careful of his money and things on the boat. When I was coming over a lot of fellows lost their money belts and things through carelessness. Well I hope you are all well as I am and hope you get all my letters. I will write again after I get my leave. I suppose you got my cable alright. Well I will say goodbye for the present

I am your loving son & brother
Charlie

AT SEA, NOVEMBER

As George and the latest contingent of Australian reinforcements were safely disembarking on the shores of England, Albert's transport was just a few weeks behind. His journey was not as calm, comfortable or uneventful as that which Charlie had enjoyed:

At Sea
Nov 9ᵗʰ – 16
Dear Mum, Dad and Jim,

Just a few lines today before we call at port. All the letters have to be in by tonight, so we must be getting near land. It is 3 weeks tomorrow since we sailed. All the men are writing letters. We cant buy envelopes on board, and the Y.M.C.A. man only gives us a few. Well, we have had a good trip so far, and there is a little more fun now. There has been two real good fights this week. They fought till they dropped. We had a great concert here on Friday night. The sports were held yesterday and Tuesday. I was on guard from 8 am on Tuesday till 8am on Wednesday, and so I had to pull out of the sports, as I was too tired after being up all night. The potato race was not run till Wednesday. I got wet through when I was on guard, so did not fancy running in the sports. Our company won the tug-of-war. There was great excitement over it. The tucker on board is not too good (censored). We had sausages for breakfast this morning and they were lovely. I only ate five. But some days we get stew twice a day, and it is rubbish. We get hardly any jam or butter now. Plenty of bread but nothing to put on it. Everything at the canteen is terrible dear. I never buy anything there, as it's a waste of money. It is pay day. We get a shilling a day on board and the other shilling when we get off the boat. We get paid every 10 days. I will draw about £2.15 when we get over and I have £3 put by in reserve, so I have plenty of money. Besides there is the shilling a day we get on board. Well Mum I will write when we get to port …

Albert took the opportunity to write a lengthy letter frankly describing his experiences of life on board. He planned to beat the censor by posting his letter by civilian mail at Durban:

Letter No 4
Port Lincoln
At Sea
Friday 10ᵗʰ 16
Dear Mother, Father and Jim,

Just a few lines to tell you a little I couldn't tell you in my other letters. We are supposed to call in at Durban tomorrow or Sunday, and if I get ashore I will post it there, so it wont have to be censored. Well to start with, we are the advance guard, yet they stuck us in the worst part of the ship, we are in the 3rd deck, and it is a buggar of a place. There is very little fresh air down here, and the first few days on board it smelt awful, and was enough to make anybody sick. The tucker at first wasn't fit for pigs, but it is a lot better now, though some days it is not good at all. We get the stew twice a day sometimes, and it is rubbish. We hardly ever eat it. There are rumours about that we are going to be put off at Durban, but I don't think there is any truth in it. There are 1200 men on board and a lot of them are kids. When we called at Fremantle, we put off 3 cases. One man fell down a ladder and broke his legs, so he was put off. Also two others that had diptheria. There are a few cases of measles on board now. We have got some rotters of men in our company and they are as dirty as pigs. We also have two officers in our company. The C.O. was terrible cut up that day we sailed from the pier. A lot of the men took it bad. They were all right till the band played "Auld Lang Syne", then they cut up a treat. A few of the men out of our company are wanting to go back. I think there will be a few desert at Durban, and a good job if they do, as they are only a lot of wasters. I don't know what they will be like when they get to the front. When we were going from North Melb to the boat, one fellow jumped out of the train, and I believe he was killed. Another chap tried to jump overboard when we were on the boat a few days. He threw his boots over, and was just going to jump over the rails when two chaps caught him. We haven't got room on the boat to turn round hardly. We cant get notepaper or envelopes on board, and everything at the canteen is dear as hell except cigarettes and tobacco. It doesn't pay to smoke on board as there are too many hummers [cadgers]. We have just had tea, and have got orders about going ashore, so we must be getting off right enough. The men are as excited as blazes over it. I will finish this letter when I get ashore. There is great fun after "lights out". The men get yelling out like sheep, and you would think they were a big mob to hear them. After we pass Cape Town the boat will be in darkness and we will have to use our life belts as pillows. I don't know if we will be calling at Cape Town but I think we will be. We are not allowed to say much in our other letters, so if I have anything _special_ to say, I will write it in the envelope, so you always want to be careful opening them. Some say we will not be going to England, but I think we will be. It will be a long trip yet, as this boat only does 13 knots an hour. There is a terrible lot of gambling on board. I will number all my letters from this out, this is No 4, you will know then if you are getting all my letters. If you get my photos taken off don't forget to give them to those I told you too. You can pay for them out of my allotment. I hope you are getting all my money alright. I am going to make a will on my paybook, you can make one that way; if I go out you will have no trouble to get my money then. Well Mum I am enjoying this life a treat, and don't mind the tucker a treat, sometimes it is real good and other times it is rotten, but I don't mind it at all. I am getting as fat as mud. I have got an enormous appetite, and am nearly always last at the table. There is a young Ross on the boat. He knows Allan well, he used to be a porter at Pyramid. I met him in the train that day I was going down to Bendigo to enlist. I had a yarn with him today. He is a bonza chap. I have got some decent mates on board. There is another porter on our table. He knows Uncle Jim Mahoney and Uncle Tom. Well Mum I will say goodbye for the present. Sunday morning – well we have had very rough weather yesterday, the roughest we ever had, a lot of the men got sick again, but I was all right. We slackened down to 2 knots an hour at yesterday dinnertime, and have been like that till this morning. We can see the land now, we are going at full speed now. I think we will be able to get in today. We could not get in yesterday as it was too rough –

Monday morning. Well Mum we arrived into Durban pier Sunday at about 12 noon. We were let off at 1 o'clock for a march, but we only went a few miles. We had to march in about 6 inches of sand. We came back to the boat at about 4.30, but were not let off. We are going to get off at 1 oclock this afternoon. There are dozens of niggers around the boat, selling fruit. It is very cheap here, and they are doing a great biz. It is a change to get a bit of fruit. The harbour here is very pretty, and there are a lot of boats in at present. There is a range of hills about 600 feet high running for miles around Durban. It is covered with scrub and flowers and looks very pretty. We had to march along at the foot of these hills and the niggers have poultry farms against the rocks. The niggers are busy coaling the boat now. I think *we will be leaving here Tuesday morning. We might be calling at Cape Town. Well Mother I will write a town [letter] when I get in the town. We are allowed out till 10.30 tonight, this is all this time, so I will say goodbye, hoping all are well as I am at present.*

I remain
Your Loving Son
Albert

Monday 13/11/16
Dear Mum,

Just a line to let you know I am well. We got leave off the boat at 1 oclock and have to be back at 10.30. I am having a look round Durban. It is a very pretty place. There are a mob of soldiers about. There is two transports in besides ours, also a hospital ship with 300 men going home. I had a great ride in the ricksha a while ago, the niggers can travel some

Goodbye
Albert

At Sea
Thursday Nov 16th 1916
Dear Mother, Jim and Dad,

Just a few lines to let you know I am on the ocean again. We left Durban at noon on Tuesday the 14th and are making towards Cape Town now, we expect to get there tonight or tomorrow. I think we will be getting off there, so I will be able to post it without it being censored. We had a good time at Durban, but not half long enough. I sent a few cards from there. I did not have time to get much, but outside it is lovely. We could ride free on the trams or trains, and we had free meals at the Y M C A. My mate and I went into a hotel for dinner, and the niggers were waiting on the tables. I had a feed of soup, then some rump steak, they are awful slow, but it was a flash place, all the same. We ordered pudding, but got tired of waiting, so we walked out and had a free dinner. Half of our fellows did not pay for their meals there. I had 3 lunches at the Y M C

A. I had tomato sandwiches and it was free. The place was crowded. I forgot to say that we were anchored across the bay from the town, so all off the boat, went across to the town side on a barge. We were all lined up then and marched to the Town Hall. It is about 2 miles from the pier. We were then dismissed and it was about 2.30. We had to wait about 2 hours for the barge to take us across. I got a bit of a surprise in Durban, I thought we would be able to get fruit cheap there, but they were awful dear, grapes 1/-6 lb apples 3s each oranges 1 d each. At the pier the fruit was fairly cheap, but the people told us not to buy fruit off the niggers as they were "rooking" us. The Durban people are very nice, and the girls are respectable. I never saw a soldier with a girl. The last lot of soldiers that were there played up top-ropes, and at first the people would hardly look at us. They said that the name of Australia fairly <u>stunk</u> in their nostrils. There was no beer sold to soldiers and some of them were wild about it too. A few of them managed to get some and stopped all night in town. The M.P.'s went to get them next morning, and brought 3 of them back. They were half drunk, and just as they got on the boat, they jumped overboard. The boat was anchored in the bay, and they bought them over on a motor boat. The three men swam towards the motor boat, but the boat moved away from them. Then they waited till the three of them got exhausted and then picked them up. The guard had a hell of a job to lock them up. They are being tried today for desertion. Two of our company deserted at Durban, besides men from other companies. We left Durban at 12 noon on Tuesday and could see land all the way till this morning. There are also two boats near us now. One is a very big one and going to Cape Town. I think it is a troopship. There were 5000 Australian troops at Durban on Monday, also, a lot of Tommies and South African Inf. There were Tommies out of 29 different regiments. I was talking to some of the Essex Regiment. The Tommies are going to India and German East Africa. They are very quiet chaps, different to the Australians. It is rumoured that we will be at Cape Town for three days, I think we will be getting off there. Well I will finish this in time to post it at Cape Town if we get there. They got a newspaper called the "Port Lincoln Lyre" printed in Durban, it is all lies but it is a fit funny. I am sending you one. They gave us one each. Don't lose it _____

Friday

Well Mum we got into Cape Town at 2 oclock this morning and they took us off the boat at 9 oclock for a march. We marched out away from the town about 4 miles. We did not go near the town at all. It is a very pretty place. The town is between Table Mountain and the sea. Well Mum, I do not think I will be getting off at all. I am trying to get this posted on the pier, this is all so I will close hoping all are well.

I remain
Your loving son
Albert

Albert's letter was posted in Cape Town and the newspaper was sent with the letter. Soldiers were invited to submit their writing to the *Port Lincoln Lyre*, a publication designed to amuse and entertain during the long weeks of travel across the sea.

Albert continued his voyage to England and, on the day he turned 19, he began a journal-cum-letter to his family documenting his eventful passage up the west coast of Africa. The *Port Lincoln* had struck trouble but worse was to come.

Port Lincoln
26/11/16
Dear Mother, Father & Jim,

Just a few lines to let you know I am tip-top. We left Cape Town on Friday the 17th Nov. I wrote to you from there and sent you some silver leaves. I had to throw the letters over the side to get them posted. We got into Cape Town on the Friday morning. We were taken off in the morning for a march. I was disappointed because we were not given leave. It is very pretty around Cape Town especially Table Mountain. We have had a lovely trip since we left the Cape, but had bad luck last night. We were travelling at full speed, when a blade of the propeller broke. The boat must have hit something as there was an awful jerk, and it shook for hours after. They think it must have hit a boat that was sunk about here. A lot of the men thought their last day had come. We were travelling very slow today, on account of the blade being off. A lot of the men never slept last night. As soon as the boat *hit. Some of the men rushed below and put their life belts on. We have to put our life belts on every Saturday. All the lights on deck are out at 7 p.m. and there is no smoking after dark. We are in the danger zone now. We are supposed to call in at a port called Dakar on Wednesday but we might not be there for a while now, and I suppose they will put a new blade on there. The tucker was rotten last week. We had a lot of S. African mutton on and it was as poor as bones, and half rotten, but it was not eaten. The tucker is better now. We get stew twice a day about 5 days of the week, but it is hardly ever eaten. We get porridge every morning. We passed a big boat an hour ago. There is a boat coming to tow us into port, so the yarn says. The boat is jerking like the devil. It is hard to write. Well Mum, it is my birthday today. It is Sunday, we had Church parade this morning. Well this is all this time. I don't suppose this will be posted till I get to England. I sent you a paper from Cape Town, called the Port Lincoln Lyre, it was printed in Durban. They are getting another paper out next week. I will send one home. Don't forget to keep them - Last Sat we were all paraded on deck in uniform to hear the sentences read out of the men that deserted at Durban. They were charged with desertion, striking an officer and N.C.O., swearing, drunkenness and resisted the guard. Three of them got 3 years penal servitude, and one got two years. We are duty company every Tuesday. I was on guard last Tuesday _____*

Dec 6th Well Mum since I wrote that we have had some shifting about. On the 28th Nov the boat altered her course 3 times and then stopped. It seems we were chased by submarines and had a narrow escape. We started again next morning and went for Freetown, the capital of Sierra Leone – At 10 am the ship ran into a sand bank about 5 miles from the harbour, and they tried all day to shift her. Next day the 3rd after a lot of messing about we were taken off the boat and put in barges and taken to the pier for 3 hours and then they marched us up to the Barracks on the top of Mount Aureol. We had our water proof sheet and two blankets to carry up. It was the stiffest climb I ever had. It is a lot higher than Pyramid Hill, and as Freetown is in the tropics, it was almost too hot to walk. We got to the top at dark, and wet through with sweat. A lot of the men fainted before they were half way up. We stayed up there two nights and had a good look around. The niggers were selling oranges, bananas and cocoanuts, almost for nothing.

By hell, we ate some fruit. The oranges were a lot bigger than cricket balls, and were just lovely. The bush is called jungle and is the prettiest place I ever saw. All around the barracks grow shrubs and flowers and some lovely roses. I never saw such lovely coloured leaves in my life before. There was dozens of different kinds, they grow wild. I packed up a lot to send home, but when we changed boats I had to leave them behind. The bush around the garrison would beat any Australian garden for flowers. I will never forget the lovely scenery. On the 2nd Dec we marched back to the boat, got all our equipment, and then went back to the pier and left all our kit bags in the goods shed. We marched up to the barracks again before dinner with our web equipment on which weighed about 50lbs, we stopped the night at the barracks and then got up at 5 next morning and marched back to the pier, then we went on board the New Zealand transport [Willochra] and left Sierra Leone that afternoon. We got a great reception on board. It is a lovely boat, and the tucker is great. There are 1 000 N. Zealand troops on board and they are all fine fellows. We reached a port called Dakar on the Wed 6th Dec where we took on a gun and some coal, left there the same day, and are now on the way to England. I forgot to say that Freetown has very few white people in it, as it is so hot. It was over 120 in the shade when we were there, and that was supposed to be cool. A lot of the men got a heat rash there, and I think a lot would get malarial fever if we stopped much longer. No doubt it is as near hell as I have ever been, the sweat just ran out of us there, and we were not sorry when we left there. We did not get off at Dakar, it seems a nice little place and not as hot as Freetown. I got some post cards of Dakar which I am sending to you. We have been 7 weeks on the trip now, and I don't think we will get to England before a fortnight. This is a fast boat, but she is altering her course a lot, and is going south now and instead of north. There are submarines about, and it is rumoured there is a naval battle and that some of the German ships got out. I was on submarine guard today. We had a rifle and ten cartridges. There is 120 men on guard with rifles, there must be something doing. The officers say that this is the most adventurous trip that troops ever had. We had a rough time on the Port Lincoln for the last fortnight. The tucker was awful and we couldn't eat it. It was no use making complaints they never took any notice of us, so we were all glad when we got on this boat. She has been a *passenger boat, and is fitted up lovely. The tucker is fit for a king, and I don't mind how long the voyage takes. We can get hot baths on board, we have our meals dished out to us, and it seems just like home. We have lime juice for dinner instead of the tea because of the hot weather. We are going to get soup when the weather gets colder. The New Zealanders are the finest lot of soldiers I ever saw, no kids among them. They are printing a magazine on board. It is going to be finished in London. I am sending one to you. Dont forget to keep it. We came on the boat too late to get our names printed in it. When we left the Port Lincoln there were 50 men in the hospital with the measles. That young Ross I told you about in another letter was left behind in the hospital at Freetown. He was very bad when I last saw him. Well Mum I think this is all this time so I will conclude hoping all are well as I am at present. I have been tip top ever since I left. I will write when I get to England, so goodbye*

From Your Loving Son
Albert
Remember me to all the Mologa people
Continued …

Albert did not finish the chronicle of his experiences on the *Port Lincoln* until his safe arrival in England. It would be at least another fortnight before the reinforcements would sight the mother country.

ENGLAND, NOVEMBER

Like his brothers, Charlie was immediately granted leave and quickly took the opportunity to meet his English relatives for the first time:

33 Green Lane Road Leicester
Nov 30th 1916
Dear Dad,

I am sending you a few lines, well I have got my four days leave, I was at Hurdcott Camp, Salisbury we took the train from Wilton to Waterloo, then I caught the train at St Pancras, London at 3.40 pm for Leicester I had written to Ida to tell her I was coming, the train took about 2 hours to get to Leicester from London, when I got out at the station a Y.M.C.A. man came to me

*and asked me if I was a stranger here and told me he would show me where I
wanted to go. I told him I had a cousin coming to meet me, and all Australian
soldiers wear their felt hats in England and the Tommies wear caps so it was
easy for Ida to find me as there was only another Australian soldier there. I was
walking to the gate and we recognised each other she said I was so much like
Allan, we walked home it is not far and I saw Auntie and Ethel and May,
May is a very pretty little girl she is ten years old, auntie has a nice place and
is very good to me it is just like being home I have to go back tonight by 12
oclock. I have written to all the aunties and got letters from them all. Ida took
me to Drayton yesterday I saw the following first of all I saw your father's grave
then saw the church he used to go to, and the place where he always used to sit.
I am sending you a photo of the church which you can have till I come back,
as I could not buy them here this time so auntie gave me this one for you, this
church was built by the Romans it is called St. Nicholas, the name of the parish
is Bringhurst. Another card is the bridge at Great Eastern [Easton] you cross
over this bridge to get to Drayton, also a photo of where your father lived and
another where Auntie said you used to go through going to work. I saw Auntie
C. Wilson Auntie E Patrick, Cousin Flo Wilson Cousin Alice Marlow 2*nd*
cousin Grand uncle Ted's girl, Uncle Walter Patrick Grand Uncle Ted Marlow
Uncle John Wilson, Cousins Annie Marlow and Grace Marlow you brother's
two girls. I also saw another little church at Drayton, but your father did not
go there very often it was called St Leonard's. I also saw Grandfather's old bible
which he said was for you, Auntie Wilson told me I was to bring it back with
me, he has all the dates when all the family were born, also when Jim and I
were born. Your father lived next door to where Auntie Charlotte lives and I
saw his old armchair. Ida sent word to Aunt Charlotte that we were coming
and also to Flo Wilson and to Aunt Edith and Aunt Charlotte sent for Alice
Marlow and Grand Uncle Ted Marlow they all came to Drayton to Aunt
Charlotte's place. Uncle Ted Marlow was very pleased to see me I think he is
about 73 but he looks real well and is a grand old chap. Al and Percy did not
see him Flo Wilson is a very nice girl and very good looking she got a letter
from Jim that day it was dated Oct 15*th* he said I sailed 3 weeks and told her
Albert was up on final leave, so he cannot have been long in camp, so when
I go back I expect to get letters from home and from Pearl, as I have had no
mails from Australia yet. I was afraid the mails went down on the Arabia but*

I think they must have saved them. I told them in another letter that I saw Al and Percy and gave them 3 pounds and sent a sovereign to Geordie as far as I know Al and Percy are in France I saw them on Sat Nov 18th and they were to go on the Wednesday Nov 22. I got a letter from Percy on the 20th Nov he said they were to go in the Wednesday they were camped 17 miles from me I have written to Geordie but so far have not got an answer as I told him to send the letters to the base as I would be sure of getting them there I sent him some cake and cigarettes and a pair of socks Pearl made for him and a handkerchief and some matches. Al and Percy hear from him regular. I am leaving some money here with auntie to send a tin of cake etc to Al and Percy before Christmas, she says she will only be too pleased to do anything for us … Your father is buried about two chains away from Bringhurst Church which I enclose. You can see just the top of a tree by the back of the church on the right hand side that is the cemetery it is very small covers about ¼ of an acre.

If at any time you want to know where we are or anything about us write to.

To
The Commandant
Administrative Headquarters
130 Horseferry Road
London S.W.

… Auntie Lizzie gave me a silver tie pin which your father used to wear as a keepsake. I will leave it here to when I come back

* * *

ENGLAND, 2011

In May 2011 we travelled to Salisbury and drove through Larkhill, today the home of the Royal School of Artillery and surrounded by green, rolling hills. It is a stunning albeit chilly day, the birds are singing and, in contrast to Percy's description, there is not a drop of rain. This is where the sons of Charles and Sarah prepared for their time in France. We had come from Salisbury where the boys visited the magnificent cathedral. Only a few minutes further from Larkhill, we arrive at Stonehenge and wander there for a while, contemplating the significance of the site as had our forebears before us. Among Albert's possessions which arrived home from the war was a copy of *Stonehenge: Today and Yesterday* by Frank Stevens, Curator of the Salisbury Museum in 1916, in which Albert had carefully recorded his name and company details. We stand at the ancient site; in the distance beyond a ridge is Larkhill.

We then travel on to Leicestershire, to find the tiny villages in which the sons of Charles and Sarah sought refuge in their brief moments of respite. With Charlie's letter in hand, we drive the narrow lanes of the English countryside to follow in his footsteps. We have previously found relatives living in Leicestershire and they meet us for lunch in the small village of Medbourne from which we know many of our relatives originated. We visit surrounding villages and the churches mentioned in family documents, the sites of weddings and of funerals and eventually we find Bringhurst, the tiniest and prettiest of villages on a gentle rise in lush green fields. It is here that Charlie writes that his grandfather was buried in 1910. There is no headstone; perhaps there was once a simple wooden cross, but it exists no longer. The local curator lends a hand and a few days later we discover the resting place of my great-great-grandfather in Bringhurst Cemetery. A headstone has been erected to honour our ancestor. At various times the sons of Charles and Sarah stood here and reflected on their heritage. They travelled by train from London to Leicester and trekked the lanes we drove along to find their family during their short periods of leave. They sat in the village churches and contemplated the history of the family that lived here centuries before. It was their footsteps that brought us here and incredibly, it felt remarkably like coming home.

EIGHT

... ONE GOES UP TO HIS HIPS IN MUCK AND WATER

MOLOGA, NOVEMBER

Despite his earlier attempt to enlist, Jim now sought an exemption from the compulsory home service enacted by Prime Minister Billy Hughes on 29 September. As the demand for men to take the places of the fallen had increased, the physical requirements had been relaxed and Jim is likely to have been considered fit for service. But he was fully aware that Sarah and Charles could not manage the farm on their own. He may also have decided that six sons at the front was beyond the call of duty for any family. Sarah's eldest son appeared before the local Exemption Court seeking release from compulsory home service — he was destined not to fight on the battlefields of Europe.

Three days later, the *Pyramid Hill Advertiser* published the long list of applications for exemption from the district. Jim, incorrectly named John in the report, was one of many who stood before the Police Magistrate.

EXEMPTION COURT

The court at Pyramid Hill continued its work on Friday, Saturday and Monday, and had completed the business at noon on the last named day. It was presided over by Mr Bevan, Police Magistrate and Lieut. Josephs represented the Defence department. Of the 109 cases heard, 81 were allowed temporary exemption, 11 absolute, 6 refused, 5 adjourned, 3 withdrawn by applicants, 3 struck out ...

Marlow, John W., 27, Mologa – Five brothers at the front, he being the only one left to manage the farm. Charles Marlow, the father, confirmed the statement. Lieut. Jacobs withdrew the objection. It was a good thing, he said, to see a family who had sent sons as in this case. The P.M. – You've done well, Mr Marlow. – The application was granted. [1]

In 1916, public pressure to enlist was enormous. The more sons a family could send to the front, the more accolades the fathers received. Those with similar family situations to the Marlows also received exemption. Most applicants were granted a temporary stay until 28 February when crops would be harvested and there was no excuse to keep men from home military service and, perhaps, ultimately from the fields of France. Very few letters remain of those sent from home to the front. A Christmas postcard from Sarah to George, who was often referred to as 'Ten', is among the few. While wishing her son a bright New Year, Sarah acknowledges that such brightness would be unlikely in yet another year of war. The distress she felt at Albert's rapid departure is clearly evident.

My dear Ten

Just a card Wishing you a Happy C and a bright New Year, but I don't suppose there is much brightness there, hoping all are well, Albert sailed without a minutes notice

Mother

Charles, Sarah and Jim were kept busy with the harvest. Fortunately, the family's relationship with Pearl had thawed following the wedding, as the letters between Sarah and her daughter-in-law indicate. It is unclear whether Pearl had yet shared her secret with her new family — she was carrying Charlie's baby.

Postcard Sarah to Pearl no date
Dear Pearl

I got a letter from Charlie, and he wished one to tell you in case you did not get one but I suppose you did he is well I am in a hurry to catch the mail

From mother with love

C/o Mrs A Rackham
South Morang
Post office
December 16ᵗʰ 1916
Dear Mother

Just a line I am sending you a letter that I received from Percy it was addressed to me, he must have made a mistake in the letters and sent me yours. I also have received one from Allan and Percy they are getting on fine Allan said "they would be going to France about the middle of November" so it will be only a chance if they see Charlie.

You can address my letters to the above address, I may go to Aunties on Wednesday or Saturday Syd will meet me at the station after his work so I think Saturday will suit him best. Now Mother dear I will draw this note to a close the children are going down to post it. Hoping you are well as we are,

I remain your loving child
Pearl

C/o Mrs Rackham
South Morang P.O
Dec 31ˢᵗ 1917
My dear Mother,

Just a line in answer to your letter which I was very pleased to receive, I am sure you must be kept busy with the harvest and it has been so very hot this last few days so suppose it will be very hot up there, most of the crops at S. Morang are spoilt with so much rain. Mother dear I am at Aunties at present but think I am going back to Non's this coming week, I have been here a week yesterday I have put the address to send any letters too. Have you had any word from Albert yet. Non has made the two Balaclava Caps for Charlie and Albert and I have been making socks I will send them one day soon. Now Mother dear I will draw this to a close as this is all the paper I have but I knew you would be anxious to get a letter, I am keeping well Thank you dear Mother give my love to all at Mologa not forgetting yourself dear Mother love from your affect child

Pearl

Myrtle Stone (right) and her sister Lillian (standing) with their friend Ruby Lee (Adams).

Myrtle Stone, Albert's romantic interest, also sent a message to Jim that her family would visit the Marlows just prior to Christmas. Her brothers, Joe and Jim, were soon to depart for the training camps of England. Joe was a mate of Jim Marlow and it seems important to Myrtle, with Albert so far away, to retain contact with the Marlow family.

14/12/16
Dear Jim

Just a line to let you know if it is not raining we will be over on Sunday Jim and Joe are home until the 3rd of next month so Joe is coming with us.

I had letters from Albert he was well when he wrote. Will close hoping you are all well.

Your affect friend
Myrtle Stone

FRANCE, DECEMBER

Percy and Allan arrived with the 38th Battalion in the old French port of Le Havre in the early hours of the morning of 23 November. Percy was promptly isolated as a companion had been diagnosed with mumps. He would not see active duty for six weeks. The rest of the battalion began a long uphill march to camp during which the Australians were greeted by women and children selling chocolate and fruit, and were entertained by their attempts to communicate. The following day the men boarded trains for the slow and tedious northward journey to Bailleul, a busy staging post behind British lines close to the Belgian border. They then travelled by bus to the village of Strazeele arriving on 26 November. Billets were soon found in the homes and barns of the farming community while General Monash established Divisional Headquarters in a chateau at Steenwerck. For the first time, the soldiers of the 3rd Division could hear the roar of the guns at the front and see the flares light the night sky. The central Victorian troops of the 38th Battalion, after months of training and delay, were anxious to do their bit; they were soon to experience war on the battlefields of Europe.[2]

Within days, the 38th was marching towards the industrial town of Armentieres, captured by the invading Germans in 1914 and later recaptured by the Allies. The battle-scarred town now served as a British base and place of recreation for resting troops. Close enough to be within range of enemy artillery fire, the people of the community continued their daily routine amid the chaos of war, welcoming the Australian soldiers into their cafes, their homes and their hearts. Armentieres was referred to as the 3rd Division's 'nursery'. In the German advance of April 1918, the town once again fell into enemy hands and was razed by the retreating Germans in October 1918.[3]

Under threat of enemy aircraft and artillery fire, the 38th moved into Armentieres where they spent three days preparing for the move to the front. On 1 December the troops were issued with gumboots and Allan began the arduous trek through the communication trenches en route to the line. Deep, sticky, black mud greeted the newcomers. Wading through a morass of mud to their thighs and in places to their waists where duckboards had given way, the men reached the front filthy and exhausted. Their homes for the next ten days afforded no protection from the freezing conditions. Dugouts were cut into the sides of trenches with rusty iron ceilings and walls of oozing mud. Rats, occasional artillery fire, enemy raids and the threat of sniper fire from the ravaged township of Frelinghien nearby combined to ensure that conditions during this relative period of quiet on the Western Front were truly appalling. Horse-drawn wagons carried supplies to the line, including food and hot tea for the troops. It was here that Allan was to celebrate his 21st birthday.[4]

Percy was the first to write to his family, although he made no mention of being quarantined and separated from Allan.

December 3
France
Dear Mum & Dad

Well Mum, we are in France, but where we are I cannot tell you, as it will be struck out. We had a quick trip over, there were a few sick on board I was not sick. It is fairly cold here at times but it will be nothing like it will be. How is the harvest going on, you will be short handed without Albert. Charlie ought to be over here soon. News is terrible scarce, so do not expect a long letter. The country looks very dreary now, we have not had much snow since we have been here. Well I will have to close as I have no more news, so I remain your loving son.

Percy

Somewhere in France
Dec 3
Dear Jim

Received your ever welcome letter, of the 21 Oct, you seem to be worried, why life is to short to worry; no doubt it is a terror to see such a lot of cold footed sods. My word Albert did go quick, you would miss him in the harvest, he ought to be in England now. You seem to have good crops this year Jim that compulsory training caused a stir. You seem to be talking a lot about girls, you have always got a fresh one, my word Jim you are lucky; do not forget to tell us the new one's name. Well Jim it is very cold over here, and it is raining nearly every day. Sunny France "I don't think" there has been a few casualties in the Battalion. You will be having Christmas now, I suppose at the spread in the hall. You will be cutting a dash Well Jim news is terrible scarce so I will have to close from your loving brother

Percy

While Percy remained at Le Havre, Allan had already experienced the tenuous nature of life on the Western Front. He described to his parents the terrible state of the trenches without revealing the terror of those first moments under artillery fire, the fear of snipers, and the death and destruction he had now witnessed. Typical of Allan he chose to lighten his situation with tales of the other enemy — the rats that were a curse to every soldier.

12.10.16 [10.12.16]
France
My Dear Mother & Father

Well mum we are in France at last and have just come out of the trenches. We had 12 days in there and now we are in our billets having a spell. The trenches are in a bad state. In places one goes up to his hips in muck and water. It is pretty cold, but not as cold as Lark Hill. We get splendid tucker and plenty of it. The only trouble is the rats, they are in 1 000's. The other night I went to bed for a couple of hours and as soon as I got to sleep they hauled me out and had taken full charge of the dug out. So you see that we have more than Fritz to fight. When we were coming over from England the mumps broke out and a terrible lot of our boys got isolated and were left at -- Percy and W Street were amongst them but I believe they will be joining us up in a week or two. I saw Charlie before we left England. I have got a lot of mail since we have been here. I never got the letters telling me about the floods and the parcel. But I was pleased to hear that you got it.

When we were in the trenches I got a lovely parcel of cigarettes and tobacco from Mick Grant. I hadn't had a smoke for 5 days I never knew they were coming. Thank Mick for me. I also got a parcel from Mrs J McKay. I will get yours this week.

We got a big mail tonight. It wont be long before Charlie will be over here. Albert had rotten luck to sail so soon. Was pleased to hear that the crops are good. Well dear mother I cannot tell you much news so I will close hoping all are well as it leaves us all at present.

I remain
Your Loving Son
Allan
Goodbye Mum

I celebrated my 21ˢᵗ birthday last Sunday.
Waiting anxiously for a letter from dad.

The 38th had been relieved but not without casualties. Allan was enjoying a return to the comfort of Armentieres and its estaminets where refreshments such as beer, wine, eggs, chips and coffee could be found amid the warm welcome of the local residents. Although the men were resting, fatigue parties were still required to carry supplies, ammunition, barbed wire, pickets and corrugated iron to the front line. Allan returned to the front on 16 December for five days and was then withdrawn to billets at Houplines where the Australians decorated their dwellings with greenery and celebrated Christmas with roast beef and plum pudding.[5]

Throughout December, George remained in the Gueudecourt sector, some ten kilometres north-east of Pozieres. Enemy shelling and low-flying enemy aircraft combined with fog, rain, snow and the bitter cold — which froze hot tea in less than one minute — were to dampen his spirits. A day of leave in Amiens was a pleasant interlude and perhaps the catalyst which triggered a longing for home. On Christmas Day he enjoyed an issue of rum and a Christmas billy. The yearning for the warmth of an Australian Christmas and the trimmings of a family celebration must have added a melancholy touch to the joy of Christmas, the coldest recorded for 40 years.

George sent his mother Christmas wishes from the trenches of France.

France
Dec 1st
Dear Jim

I received your letter and Mother's card today dated 21 Oct. and was surprised to hear that Albert has sailed they didn't keep him in camp long. I told you in my other letters that Charlie Fyffe was wounded well Hughie Johnson got a letter from him saying that he was in a hospital here in France and was hit in the arm and leg I think he will be in England by now. I was with Hughie tonight let his people know that he is well as he asked me to mention it. It is fairly cold now we don't see much sun it is foggy all day. It is rumoured here that Allan and Percy are over here now they saw Charlie in England. Fancy Eddie getting through his father will miss him for the harvest.[6] Well Jim I have no news as I wrote to you a few days ago, so will close hoping all are well.

I remain
Your affectionate Bro
George

France
Dec 14/ 1916
Dear Mother & Father

Just a few lines to let you know I am well hoping all are the same, we are in the firing line and is fairly cold and have had some more snow, it is cloudy here every day very seldom see the sun, the artillery is fairly active in this part of the line. Before we shifted up here we had a day's leave into a certain big city, and I can assure you I enjoyed myself very well, it put me in the mind of being back in Melbourne again to see the trams and all the nice shops. I received word a few days ago from the bank that there was some money there for me, it will come in very handy as I will just about get my leave to England in the beginning of February that is if they keep it going. I had a letter from Charlie saying that he was on leave and at the time of writing was at Payne's and was sending me a parcel which I suppose is waiting for me now but we cant get them till we go back from the line as they cant get them all up here at present. I suppose Albert will have arrived in England by now. I think Al and Percy are over here now but there isn't much chance of me meeting them. Ewan had a letter from Charlie Fyffe, he is badly wounded and is in a hospital in England, we haven't heard anything of Charlie Wales but I suppose he is over there too he got wounded just a few days before C.Fyffe. Ewan gave me a couple of Pyramid papers and noticed that there was one of my letters in it. I wish you wouldn't put them in the paper. You appear to have had great floods. I suppose you are very busy at present. Fancy Eddie Cheyne passing, his father will miss him. Well the guns are still nagging but nothing is dropping close here. I will now close as news is scarce.

I remain
Your Loving Son
George

Allan wrote to his family on Christmas Day:

France
Xmas Day
Dear Jim

Well Jim old boy I hope you had a merry Xmas. What a good time you must have had at the tea meeting & concert. We are having a merry xmas here. We are out in the billets now but we go back to the trenches to morrow. I think it is better in the trenches than out here, because here it is nothing but fatigue work. We are always situated up in the front line. It gets a bit exciting at times but one wants that to keep him warm. Well Jim I hope you have a good harvest. I suppose you are up to your dam neck in work now. It is a bit of a terror young Albert sailing so soon. He will just about land in England in the middle of winter and it is colder there than here. I have had letters from Charlie and Geordie also the relations. All are well. Percy has not joined us up yet and will not do so until another 3 weeks. Well Jim I have told you all the news so I will close hoping all are well.

I remain your loving bro
Allan

To his parents, Allan wrote:

… We have just finished our Christmas dinner of bread and butter but I believe we are going to get a good tea. I suppose you all had a quiet Christmas over there. I have not got our parcel yet, but may get it by New Year. There is a parcel here for Percy from L Sharp. He is not turned up yet. W. Street has got the mumps now and they are isolated for another 21 days. Where they are they are doing well. Charlie will soon be over here with us. I would like to run across Geordie but he is miles away from us …

After Christmas, Percy wrote to his parents:

… Well xmas is over, we had a fairly tame one, no ham and turkey for dinner, roast meat and so on. I was a little lucky, there were a few parcels sent from the comforts fund, and I won one of them in a kind of a raffle. There were 2 boxes matches, matchbox cover, pipe, 2 cigarette, 2 handkerchiefs, 2 packets of lollies, toothbrush & paste, it was a very handy win. The French people are very hard to understand, some words you can understand …

ENGLAND, DECEMBER 1916

Across the English Channel, Charlie had returned from leave and was preparing for his move to France. However, like his brother, he was soon isolated as a result of an outbreak of mumps. Nonetheless, he would leave for the front prior to Christmas. Four of the Marlow boys were to enjoy 25 December in the billets and camps of the Western Front.

3rd Dec 1916
Dear Mother,

… I have just got back from my four days leave, we took the train to London and then I got the train to Leicester I got there at about 6.15 p.m. I wrote to Ida and told her I was coming so she came and met me, we recognised each other on the spot, she said I was very much like Allan, she would have not had any trouble in finding me as there were only three Australian soldiers on the station, they do not see many Australians up there and when I was coming away all the children were coming out of school and the boys stood and looked at me and would say to themselves he is a Canadian he's an Australian he's from New Zealand. Auntie Payne is very nice and also the girls auntie and I had a waltz one night, she is very lively, whilst Ida played they are all good dancers the youngest one May, is such a nice little girl she is 10 years old auntie gave me a silver tiepin, and a glass tumbler it is very old and I never saw one before it was Grandfather Marlows. I left them there along with some other things I did not want, I sent Geordie a parcel I bought a cake and sent a pair of socks that Pearl knitted for him also some cigarettes and matches and a handkerchief. Geordie was out of the trenches with Amos when he wrote he is getting on alright I was surprised to hear that Albert sailed on the 21st Oct neither Jim nor you sent his No. but the 4/38 will find him. I will write to the base in London and find out what camp he will be in, I will give him money I have about £7 on me. I wrote to Dad last week about sending money to Paynes for Geordie and Al and Percy, they can send it over to Geordie anytime he wants it should he get leave auntie said they would be only too pleased to do anything for us as she knew we would do the same if Clem was in Australia, if you sent money in a registered letter, say notes they could change them here, I told Dad to cable it if it did not cost too much, but if it did a £5 note registered would be quite safe, I sent a sovereign to Geordie and gave Al and Percy £3 between them, they all say they have plenty but in case any of us should be short it is just as well to send over some and it can be left at Paynes, I will see that Albert has got enough. There are dozens of Australians here with hardly a shilling to their name, but it is their own fault, they drink all they have at the canteens …

While writing on the same day, Charlie does not mention to his mother that he has been ill with mumps, although he tells Jim that he had been admitted to hospital. The golden rule when writing to their mother was not to cause her worry. An astute mother, Sarah soon realised that her sons were protecting her from the truth, a situation which only added to her apprehension.

3rd Dec 1916
Dear Jim

Just a few lines to let you know that I am quite well although I am in a hospital, I came in here yesterday with the mumps along with 8 other mates from the 3/38 it is more of an isolation than anything else, it is said that the cold weather brings them on although mine is nearly alright now but some of the chaps are terrible they do not give us any medicine for them, there is no pain. I believe we will be here for a week but I don't mind as we get four meals a day and we don't get up till 8 or 9 oclock and do nothing all day, it is very catching that is why we are here ... I have no idea when we are going to France Geordie was alright when he wrote he said C Fyffe was wounded, I was up to Leicester I saw all the relations there. Flo Wilson got a letter from you the day I was there she is a lot better looking than the photo she is a lively girl. I saw Grand Uncle Ted Marlow he was very pleased to see me, he did not see Al and Percy I also saw his daughter and all the other relations I saw the Old family Bible and Grandfathers grave and the church he used to go to. I heard about the conscription being knocked and it was hard luck, but I hope it will come on again, I also heard of the great coal strike. Well the hospital Sergeant Major has just been round and told us when can go back to our own huts again so we have not been long here, as we came in yesterday, we will be leaving a good home here ...

12th December 1916
Lark Hill Salisbury Plains
Dear Mother,

... I have not heard from Al or Percy but got a letter from Geordie he asked me to send him a £1 which I did next day, he has been on a few days leave and was in the town of Amiens, he said he was a Lance

Corporal now so he will stand a good chance of being promoted when once he gets a start. I got a letter from Ida yesterday and was sorry to learn that the youngest little girl May fell in the school yard and broke two bones in her left for arm, they took her to their lodge doctor but he would not set it so they had to take her to the hospital to have it set and I believe she is getting on splendid she is I think 9 or 10 years old and such a nice little girl. I also got a letter from Flo Wilson last week. I have not got that parcel you sent but I will get it alright as they have not given out any parcels yet. Lark Hill is not as good a camp as Hurdcott it is nothing but mud here although it does not rain very much yesterday it was snowing, we have a nice fire in our hut and can get plenty of coal, we get good food here for breakfast we get stew about every second morning and bacon the rest, on Sundays we get bacon and sausages for tea we get bread jam and margarine which is just like butter in fact I cannot tell the difference, I have not heard anything of Albert yet I wrote again yesterday to the base in London to try and find out where he is, I also sent a letter there for him. I am getting on splendid and feel real well a lot of our chaps have got terrible colds so far I escaped. Wilsie Townsend was at Hurdcott camp also Bill Crossman and Jack Sinclair they were to go to France very soon I saw Alf Ferris at Hurdcott Wilsie Townsend and Jack Sinclair will be with him did you get the cable which I sent, the A.I.F. have a place in London where we can find out anything regarding the soldiers and their whereabouts. I wrote to Arthur yesterday and to Bernie Day. Tom Roberts is still with me. Also Les Cant, there is one of the Tailors from near Jim Cheynes place also in my company. There was one of the Humberts from Calivil with Wilsie Townsend he is such a nice fellow and has a brother killed at war. I suppose you will know that Charlie Fyffe was wounded, he was not far from Geordie when he was hit, it was in a bombing attack. Amos Haw was only about 100 yds from Geordie the first time he wrote to me, he has seen such a lot of the local boys over there. I suppose you will be finished harvest by the time this reaches you, wheat ought to be a good price as it is a good price here now I saw in the papers this morning that wheat was 80/- a quarter, I saw in the Bendigo paper which Pearl sent me, the fuss about conscription and the lads having to go and get examined …

17th Dec, 1916
Lark Hill
Salisbury Plains
Dear Mother, Father & Jim,

Just a few lines to let you know that I am quite well and got 7 letters from Australia and also your xmas box, I thank you very much for it the cake is real good also all the other things… They seem to be having some fun with the conscription, I was sorry it did not pass, it would shake a lot of them pro Germans up. I suppose you have heard of the germans offering peace to the Allies, I was surprised when I heard it, they must be about knocked out or they would never have offered it, at any rate I don't think it will last much longer, we get some lovely frosts here it lasts all day and part of the next day, it has not rained much since I have been here but it snows fairly often, I heard from Lorrie Taylor that Eddie Cheyne had been discharged, was he called up or did he volunteer and how about those who were in the camps will they have to go now conscription has failed, George and Arthur had a debate in Mitiamo with Spencer and Wells the Methodist parson they gave him a bad time so I believe.[7] Ida gave me a balaclava helmet and Flo Wilson knitted me a nice pair of mittens they will be alright this cold weather. Well I will ring off for this time. I write to you every week and hope you get my letters …

19th Dec, 1916
Lark Hill
Dear Jim

Just a few hurried lines to let you know that we are off to France any moment now, we have to train there, for how long I don't know. I have not seen Albert but sent £1 up to Paynes for him I have not heard from Al or Percy but no word has come across from any of the 38 I have got 3 letters from Geordie since I have been here he is alright. I am with Tom Roberts from the Ox we sleep together there is a lot of chaps that I knew before are off with us, Lorrie Taylor told me Eddie Cheyne got discharged and Auntie Florrie said Bert Gibson was called up again. I bet he did not like it. Auntie Payne sent me a box of cake yesterday. I have got No. 10 boots 3 pairs of socks on Flo Wilson knitted me a Balaclava helmet, I never felt better in my life before and weigh over 13 stone, I do not think the conscripts will be wanted after all what do you think of the Kaiser wanting peace and in todays paper it says the French took 11, 700 prisoners we get the war news straight out here, no bluff, the Allies have them on the go now, there will be peace very soon Lloyd George gives his speech today on the peace proposed they will suggest their terms to the Germans and I think they will make up some terms for a peace. I reckon all those fellows you spoke of in conscription wants hanging head downwards, I will write as often as I can when in France, so hope all are well as I am at present as I said before Al and Percy are in France now well goodbye for this time

I am your affect brother

C.E.

Charlie's optimism that the war would soon end was fuelled by newspaper reports of Allied successes and an offer of peace made in the German Reichstag. Moves to end the conflict would, however, come to naught. Belgium would not give up land currently occupied as Germany had proposed and what was an ambiguous and arrogant offer of peace was overwhelmingly rejected by Allied governments. In December David Lloyd George was elected British Prime Minister. He told the British people that he would not accept or negotiate the terms proposed by the Germans. The war would continue on its destructive path and Charlie's hope for peace would be crushed.

Charlie wrote his next letter after arriving in France:

Boxing Day, 1916
France
Dear Mother, Father & Brother

As you will already know I suppose, that I am [in] *France, we are in a training camp I have not seen the boys they have gone up to the lines some of the old battalion boys are here Jack McDonald from Pyramid is one of them I was talking to him, he is with us, Tom Roberts and all the boys from up about Pyramid are here. Les Cant did not come over from the old country he was isolated for mumps. I have written to the 3 boys since I have been here and wrote to Albert and sent the letter to Paynes for them to send on to him I also sent a £1 note there for him I have sent 2 letters to the base for him I also left a note with Les Cant for him he will join up with what was left out of our company. Well yesterday was Christmas day we had a very good dinner ham and beef, cheese, pickles and plum pudding, the pudding was a bonzer they also gave us dates, so you will see we have had nothing to complain of, we get plenty to eat over here and don't work over hard. I said before I received your very nice parcel the pudding was about the best I have ever tasted, I also got a parcel of cakes from Auntie Payne a few days before I left for France. I got a mail from Vic 2 days before I came away, I have answered all of them, but now I will not be able to write to all of them as I did before, but I will endeavour to send you a line as often as I can. It is not near as cold over here as England, but rains often, there has been no snow since we have been here. Well I will ring off for this time, I hope you are all well at home and getting on alright, I am quite well. And I believe the boys are alright. I will say goodbye with best wishes to all.*

I am your affect
Charlie

Charlie made the crossing to France but was soon isolated again as a result of the mumps epidemic that continued to plague the soldiers. He mentions seeing Jack McDonald of Pyramid Hill. Jack, who was married with eight children, signed up at the age of 39, leaving his job as an engine driver to sail on the *Runic* with Allan and Percy. Jack was awarded the Military Medal for his action at Buire sur l'Ancre in France on 4 April, 1918. Under heavy enemy shell fire for seven hours, Jack 'displayed an utter disregard of danger and untiring energy' to repair telephone lines. He was largely responsible for maintaining communication with Battalion headquarters.[9] On 29 September 1918 he was shot in the neck and shoulder which left him with limited movement. He returned to Australia but died soon after, another casualty of the war. The *Pyramid Hill Advertiser* reported:

> … After long strenuous, and brave service in the great war, Signaller Corpl. J R McDonald, of the 38th Battalion, returned with his comrades who had survived the great ordeal and rejoined

his family here and through suffering in health through being gassed he showed indomitable courage that marked his work in the war by setting up productive work, taking up part of the "Mangatt Hill" estate and growing wheat … Unfortunately his health continued to decline, and after a rather long illness, endured patiently with a courageous heart, he passed away on Monday night last at the comparatively early age of 46 years … He enlisted early in the war, and served for five years, three of which was spent in the field and marked by bravery and resourcefulness, a fact attested by his having been awarded the military medal for gallantry in the field…[10]

30 Dec 1916
France
Dear Mother Father & Jim

… I did not see Albert before I left but left a letter with Ida and a £1 for him I do not think they will take him into the firing line till the spring as he is too young … One of my mates got the mumps and was sent to the hospital and the rest of us were sent into an isolation camp and will be here for 25 days. I like France better than England for the cold it is not too bad over here at all, of course it is the middle of winter and out in Vic you will be dodging the sun. There is great talk of peace over here now and the Fritzs seemed to have turned Uncle Sam down I think that was a good thing, we get the English paper over here every day I saw by it there was to be a conference of premiers and Hughes was coming over. I think they will come to terms. I met one of the Piepers from near Clees he is in the same division as I am, I said before I got your parcel, I expect some more mail any day now. I have not got any letters since I have been here. I wrote to all the boys and told them I was over here, I will see them when I go up the line. I suppose you will be finished harvest by the time this reaches you I hope the crop turns out well, you can use that horse of mine any time. I was glad to hear that he looked so well it is very good of Mr Alford to leave him in his paddock. I have not heard anything of Tom Alford or Charlie Fyffe but I hope to see them, Tom Roberts from the ox is still with me also George Collison and Albert Sinclair I have not seen anything of Jack Sinclair since

I have been here. I met young Gardner yesterday from Pyramid. How are they getting on with the conscription now. I suppose they will just have to rely on volunteers now to back up the Australians. Well I will draw to a close for this time hoping you are all well at home as I am at present so goodbye.

I am yours affectionately
Charlie

As Charlie awaited the end of his time in isolation, Albert was soon to arrive in England after a long and eventful ten-week journey.

AT SEA AND IN ENGLAND, DECEMBER

At Sea
Dec 20th
Dear Mother, Father & Jim,

Just a few lines to let you know I am well, and still on the water. Since I last wrote our boat ran aground on a sand bank, so we were taken off and put on another boat. This is a lovely boat. Plenty of room, better tucker and bunks to sleep in. We expect to land a day or two after Xmas, we have been a terrible long time on the water, and have called at more places than I thought we would. We are not allowed to say where we have been, or anything about the trip. It gets a bit monotonous at times. We don't do much drill, but we get plenty of fatigue work to do. The sea has been very calm since I last wrote. I am still as fat as a fool, and feeling tip top ...

Albert also continued his lengthy, uncensored letter to his mother, originally dated 16 November, as his perilous journey to England rolled on. On reaching Larkhill he was looking forward to being reunited with Charlie. He was bitterly disappointed to discover that he had missed his big brother by a matter of days.

... Well mum since I wrote that we have been shifting a lot. We had left Dakar two days, when the boat turned back and went back to Freetown, we got there on Saturday the 10th Dec. When we turned we were within 10 miles of a German armed merchantmen. We travelled back at full speed (20 knots) Two British and one French cruisers left Freetown that day and

sunk the German boat. We left Freetown on the 14th with 4 other transports and a cruiser. We left some transports at Freetown. Two of them were taking nigger soldiers to France to do fatigue work. There were 32 boats in port when we left there. We have war news on this boat every day. The most important seems to be about peace. The Kaiser wants peace by Christmas. It was 8 weeks last Friday since we left, and I don't think we will get to England for Christmas now. We are having an exciting trip. The C.O. told us to be thankful we are not at the bottom of the sea_____

Dec 26 Well Mum it was Xmas Day yesterday. We had Church parade in the morning and a concert in the afternoon. We do not get meat on this boat for dinner so we only had pudding for dinner, and it was plum pudding. For tea we had raw meat and bread and jam, so we had a tame xmas. We expect to land tomorrow or next day. It is nearly 10 weeks since we left and the trip is getting tame, especially as the tucker is getting short. It is very cold now.

Dec 31st – Well Mother, we arrived at Plymouth on Thursday the 28th and disembarked at 6 am on Friday morning, and went on the train. We had no dinner and got a bun and a cup of tea at 2 oclock, which was given by the Mayoress of Exeter. We arrived at Amesbury at 7 oclock and marched 5 miles to the camp. We have done no drill yet. When I got there I expected to see Charlie, 50 of the 3/38 were left behind, and they told me that Charlie had gone to France. I was never so disappointed in all my life. He left a note behind with Cant, a chap from Milloo, to write to Mrs Payne, so I wrote yesterday. I sent a cable home last night. I hope you get it. I got 6 letters the night we got here, one from you, 1 from Jim, 1 from Ralph, 1 from Myrtle Saville and 1 from Myrtle, and I was glad to get them. I have not received the tin yet. You say you are cabling me money. You need not have sent me any as we draw £5 tomorrow for the trip over. Besides I don't spend much money. We expect to get leave soon I am going to Leicester. Well Mum I have no time to write any more so will ring off hoping all are well, as it leaves me at present.

I am Your Loving Son
Albert

PART THREE

1917

NINE

WE WERE FALLING IN SHELL HOLES AND SHELLS WERE FLYING ABOUT US …

THEATRES OF WAR

By the close of 1916, any celebration of Allied success had been tempered by the more sombre overall picture across the theatres of war. Under the leadership of General Robert Nivelle, the French had finally won ground at Verdun. In Egypt, the Allies were successfully defending the deserts from the advancing Turkish army. Allied forces occupied El Arish on the Sinai peninsula on 21 December and were now preparing to advance against the Turkish forces in Palestine. But elsewhere the situation looked bleak. Romania's support for the Allies ended in December with the deaths of 250,000 Romanian soldiers and the occupation of the little country. Russia had also suffered huge losses; the country was starving and was now teetering on the brink of a disastrous revolution. If Russia collapsed, German soldiers fighting to the east could be mobilised to bolster the Western Front.

The British Navy had achieved some notable successes, its blockade effectively cutting Germany's supply routes. Suffering severe shortages of vital food and supplies, Germany was struggling to produce the war materials to supply the demands of the battlefields. Over one million soldiers had now been killed and grieving families were also hungry. As Charlie had mentioned in his letters, American President Woodrow Wilson had attempted to negotiate a peace deal. But neither side could agree to the proposed terms and the talks failed. Wilson was soon to turn from attempting to negotiate peace to a declaration of war.

With the German fleet trapped in port, submarine attacks against Allied shipping increased. On 31 January 1917, Germany announced that it would begin attacking ships of neutral countries that continued to trade with the Allies — including the United States (US).[1] The final blow to American neutrality was struck in the early days of April when a cable from the German Foreign Minister was intercepted en route to Mexico. The Minister suggested that, should the United States declare war on Germany, Mexico should take up arms against its northern neighbour. Germany offered Mexico the sweetener of reclaiming Texas, Arizona and New Mexico. The Americans were outraged.[2] On 6 April, Woodrow Wilson declared war. The impact of his declaration would take time to be realised as the US army was small and ill-prepared to fight a war. With delays to mobilisation, it would be six months before American troops would fire their first shots on the Western Front and not until 1918 that the American policy of selective conscription brought troops in significant numbers.

THE WESTERN FRONT

On the Western Front, as a blanket of snow settled on the scarred land, the quagmire of previous months turned to ice and mud-filled shell holes quickly froze. Troops sleeping in their dugouts woke to find their sodden boots frozen solid. Dry blankets were more precious than gold and warm food just as valuable. Lambskin gloves, leather waistcoats and thigh boots were issued but did little to protect the soldiers from the bitter and relentless conditions. The men held the line during that dreadful winter while, in the warm, dry chateaus and around the negotiating tables in England, planning for a spring offensive was underway.

Newly elected British Prime Minister David Lloyd George was at loggerheads with General Haig who was eager to push through the German defences in the Flanders region to wrest the Belgian ports from enemy hands. The Prime Minister preferred the battle plans of the new Commander-in-Chief of the French forces, General Nivelle, who had replaced the hapless General Joffre, and was celebrated as the hero of recent successes at Verdun, won in the tough fighting that marked the last months of 1916. Nivelle believed he could end the stalemate using French troops to break through in the southern sector of the French front on the River Aisne, with English troops attacking to the north at Arras. Haig was overruled and British forces were placed under the overall command of Nivelle. An attack on the German 'bulge' between Arras and Soissons was to commence on 1 April.[3]

The 3rd Division remained in the north of France at Armentieres. At 1.00 am on the first day of 1917, simultaneous raids were launched on enemy lines. Raiding parties were charged with the task of collecting intelligence, destroying enemy morale and seeking to exert sufficient pressure to avoid the redirection of German troops to the Somme. Allan and 25-year-old Mallee farmer Jack Lockett were members of one of the four parties of between 12 and18 soldiers from the 38th Battalion who crept quietly towards the enemy under cover of darkness. Having reached the enemy defences, they began to cut through the barbed-wire entanglements. Allan's group was soon caught in the glare of German searchlights. A barrage of concentrated rifle and machine-gun fire, bombs and grenades pounded the sodden earth around them inflicting heavy losses. The surviving men lay in shell holes, pinned down by enemy fire. At 4.00 am five men, including Allan, crawled their way back towards the safety of the trenches. As the sun began to rise and hope of any further survivors faded, Jack Lockett dropped into the Allied trenches. The following night another wounded soldier was brought in by a relief party led by Lieutenant Peters. Peters was later awarded the Military Cross for the rescue of this man and for his courageous actions during the previous night's raid. [4]

Just six of the 17 men from Allan's raiding party had survived. At his home in Bendigo in 1984, Jack Lockett recalled his mate 'Ackers', a nickname derived from Allan's initials, and talked briefly of New Year's Day 1917. It was a moment he would rather have forgotten, rated as one of his worst memories of the Western Front. In December 1917 Private Lockett had sailed with Allan and Percy on the *Runic* and was later promoted to platoon sergeant when Allan was commissioned to second lieutenant.[5] Having left school at the age of nine, Jack recalled that his lack of education had prevented further promotion: '… it was the big words …' Jack passed away in 2002 with the distinction of being Australia's oldest man at 111 years of age; he was regarded as a national hero. He was awarded the Order of Australia in 2001 and France's highest decoration, the Legion of Honour, in 2002.

In October 1917, Jack was sent to a rest camp at Senlecques with Charlie. Both men sent a photo home to their families, Jack jotting on the back:

> … As you will see I have put the names down. We are all doing the same. If anything happens to any of us it might come in handy to ones who receive them …

Few of Charlie and Jack's mates would emerge unscathed. John Lewis, a 25-year-old horse-driver from Melbourne had sailed on the *Runic* with Allan and Percy. He was Mentioned in Despatches on 7 April 1917, wounded on 28 August 1918 and later awarded the Military Medal. He was invalided to Australia in January 1919.[6] Earnie Butler, a labourer from Melbourne, was 23 when he enlisted and sailed on the *Shropshire* with Charlie. He was shot in the face on 27 February 1917 and wounded again on 17 July 1918, this wound sufficiently serious to prevent him seeing further action on the front. Butler also returned to Australia in January 1919.[7] William Jones, a 21-year-old labourer from Mildura, was another who had sailed on the *Runic*. William was frequently hospitalised with illness but survived the war without serious wounds.[8] Edmond Jones was 18 when he enlisted from Melbourne where he had been working as a baker. He was wounded on 28 May 1917 and rejoined the battalion a few weeks later, eventually returning to Australia in August 1919.[9] Wren Teale was 24 years old when he sailed on the *Runic*. He had worked as a clerk in Melbourne prior to enlisting and, as noted by Jack on the back of the photo he sent home, Wren was an Australian champion cyclist. He was killed on 19 November 1917 in the vicinity of Ploegsteert Wood, north of Armentieres in Belgium.[10]

Left to right standing, John Charles Lewis, Charlie Marlow, Earnie Butler, William Lloyd Jones; seated, John Henry Lockett, Edmond Michael Jones, Wren Teale (image courtesy of the Bendigo RSL Museum).

Jack also sent a photo home which was taken in France on 3 November 1917. To the list of names Jack added the comment: 'This is the remains of 13 Platoon that left Aussie.' In World War I a platoon usually consisted of around 40 men. There are seven soldiers in this photo. These men had sailed together on the *Runic* on 20 June 1916 and miraculously survived the war. Sidney Maslen enlisted at the age of 22, having recently emigrated from England. He was wounded on three occasions and returned to Australia early in 1919.[11] Stanley Rumble was a 19-year-old labourer from near Bendigo. He was gassed on two occasions, but recovered and married in England in February 1919, returning to Australia in November.[12] William Wormald was born in New Zealand but had been working as a furnace-man in Melbourne when he enlisted at the age of 30. He was wounded twice and returned to Melbourne in April 1919.[13] Twenty-year-old John Fiven had worked as a cabinet-maker in Melbourne and married in England in February 1918. He was shot in the arm on 29 August 1918, eventually returning to Australia in December.[14] Like the remarkable Jack Lockett, John Adams and Goodsir Fowler managed to survive the war without serious wounds. Adams had enlisted as a 28-year-old farmer from near Ouyen, while Fowler had been a farm labourer working near Kerang when he enlisted at the age of 22.[15]

Original members of 13 Platoon, D Company, 38 Battalion, 3 November 1917. Standing, left to right: 1236 Private Sidney Maslen, 1322 Private William Wormald, 1639 Private Goodsir Fowler, Private Stanley Rumble; sitting, left to right: Sergeant John Fiven, Corporal John Adams, Sergeant Jack Lockett (names courtesy of the Bendigo RSL Museum).

Allan continued to reassure his mother, telling her again and again not to worry about him. Despite what must have been a narrow escape during the raid, he wrote home soon after, simply describing the perilous mission as a 'big turnout'. He wrote also of the other concerns he considered a mother might harbour: his state of health, his food, his clothing, did he have enough money? He intimates that he is enjoying the business of soldiering, comparing his early days of trepidation to his hardened approach just a few weeks later. Yet Allan had also lost a mate. In relating news of the death of his friend, we see a glimpse of the tough reality of life at the front as he expresses his grief.

France
New Years Day
3 oclock
My Dear Mum & Dad & Jim

Well dear mum I am writing this letter to you in my dugout. This is the first time I have been in my dugout for some number of hours as we have been that busy. We have had nothing but rain and cold winds but am used to muck and all this by now. We had been getting very little tucker but we got plenty at the start. We go out to our billets in a day or so thank God a man will be able to buy some tucker. I received your most welcome letters & was pleased to hear all are well and that the crops are good. I hope they yield well. I suppose you had a good time last night at the turnout. We had a big turnout too. I cant say anymore about it mum just think for yourselves. Mum you don't know how I have been looking out for my parcel but it hasn't turned up yet. I do hope it comes while I am out of the trenches. I have got 35 letters for Percy, 1 parcel from you and one from L Sharp I cant make it out why my one aint here. Percy has not come along yet and will not be along for a while yet. He is doing well and having a cosy time. He is very lucky. Charlie is over here but have not met him yet. He is not in action. Mum just after we came here our section was split up amongst the companies. I am still in D Company so have no bother with mail. I had 2 bonnie mates from Lake Boga. They have been getting parcels a treat so was rather lucky Mum but sorry to say one poor fellow got killed the other night. A sniper caught him while he was firing the gun. They are brothers. For all the world he was the dead image of Jim a bit bald in front too. Mum I used to look down upon him as a brother. I do feel sorry for the brother, but I cheer him up. I am writing to his mother when we go to the billet. I have not got any papers since being here, but if I keep getting the letters as I have been doing I am well pleased. Yes mum you would have a quiet Christmas, but we will all be home for the next. Tell Jim to set the duck eggs. Wont they get a doing ah. Mum you don't seem to believe me when I tell you that I am splendid. Really mum I never felt better in my life and am enjoying this. It is a bit solid at times but stand up to it well. We often laugh over the first day we came in. Oh dear mum if you had of seen us you would of too but have settled to it and brave as anything. Yes mum between Charlie & I we will look after Albert. Mum I have tons of money. I have over £5 and as soon as hear from Albert and can send him some I will do so. Well dear mum I hope this letter gets through alright. We are only supposed to write a little and be very careful what we do write. Our censor is very strict. Mum every time we go out of the trenches we get a hot bath and clean under clothing. Mum don't bother sending any socks as we get plenty. My relations & Charlie sent me parcels but never got them. It is a wonder they didnt want to send Jim to the war. Mum you must feel proud of having 5 of us here. You will want to get a store of tucker in when you hear of us coming home. I was sorry to hear about poor Mr Williams. Well dear mum dad & Jim I will say goodbye for the present. I wish you all a Happy & prosperous New Year. I also trust that you all are well as I am at present, but I may get sick when I get this parcel. Well dear mum don't worry over me I [will] always be safe & sound. It is now 4 oclock and I have to go on duty.

So goodbye
I remain
Your loving son
Allan

Allan's mate had been like a brother to him and he clearly felt the loss. His reassurance to his mother that he will look after Albert was offering her a guarantee he knew he simply could not keep. Allan could caution and advise, but keeping family safe from the reach of fate on the Western Front was beyond the love and care of a brother.

On 13 January, with the 38th back in the line, a heavy bombardment of *minenwerfer* (German trench mortar) hit the troops killing four men and wounding seven. A communication trench which connected rear areas to the front lines was destroyed. The following day the men of the 38th returned to their billets. As night fell, some 200 men were charged with the task of building another communication trench to connect the front line, a task they achieved in freezing conditions with searchlights exposing the working parties to deadly machine-gun fire, the bullets ripping the mud around them. From mid-January, the conditions turned colder, mud became ice and for four weeks snow covered the Western Front. The change brought some relief from the sticky morass of autumn and early winter. While the freezing conditions brought the added curse of frostbite, the men found it easier to remain dry, stamping their feet to promote circulation without creating a quagmire, rubbing whale oil without needing to balance on one foot planted in knee-deep mud. With their dugouts frozen and no longer collapsing about them, their health improved and their spirits lifted.[16]

The 38th was withdrawn from the line. Allan wrote a letter home from the comfort of his billet:

Jan 17-1-17

France
My Dear Mum & Dad

Well dear mum & dad I was pleased to get some more letters from you last mail I am getting the letter splendid. I was also pleased to hear that you are all well I am splendid and going strong. We are out in our billets now and all are supposed to go away for a spell. We have had some very funny weather here but one thing I never feel the cold as I did at Lark Hill. One soon gets seasoned to it. We had a pretty lively time of it but enjoy it. Well dear mum Percy and Will Street has not come along yet, they are very lucky to keep back where they are. Charlie is in France but not with us yet. I got my first letter from Auntie yesterday. She says Albert is in England, landed on the 30th. Well dear mum I got your parcel it was a beaut. That cake was the nicest ever I tasted. I cant tell you [how much] it was acceptable. I also got a parcel from L Sharp and M Gamble. Very decent ones too. I am writing to Mollie again you thank her too. Tell Jim just to shove a word or two in, and to give her that old hat of mine so that I will be able to go up and get it when I come back. Anyway tell him to leave something there. I got a bonnie parcel from Auntie in Eng. I have got 7 altogether. I have 5 parcels and 40 letters from Percy. Mum I have had some fun over here in the trenches since being here. We don't take any notice of the muck and water & cold. Young Mossop was killed the other night and A Brooks slightly wounded. We are getting treated well again now. I don't think we will ever get peace. I think Germany is about done for. Well dear mum you will be pretty near finished the harvest. I hope it yielded well. With good luck we all ought to be home for next Xmas. Mum tell dad to write a letter. I have only got one from him since leaving home. He will find a piece of pencil in this letter and the alphabet below. I was thinking that he must have forgot how to spell and had no pencil. Well dear mum & dad I have such a lot of letters to write so I will close hoping all are well.

I remain
Your Loving Son
Allan

Albert Brookes (image courtesy Pyramid Hill Historical Society).

Albert Brookes was a 23-year-old farm labourer who had sailed on the *Runic* with Allan and Percy and, like them, became a Lewis gunner. He was hit in the shoulder by a bullet on 3 January 1917, but recovered to return to the 38th Battalion on 2 September 1917. At Passchendaele, on 13 October, he was again hit in the arm and thigh. He was discharged from hospital in time to see the armistice declared on the front.[17] 'Young Mossop' as Allan refers to George Mossop, a farm labourer from Janiember East (Bears Lagoon), had also sailed on the *Runic*. He was 20 years old and arrived for duty near Armentieres on 4 January 1917. He was killed just nine days later. [18]

Throughout January, the 1st, 2nd, 4th and 5th divisions held a section of front line close to Bapaume, north-east of Pozieres, tasked with maintaining pressure on the German front. There had now been significant changes in the divisional commanders of the Australian forces. General Legge, in command of the 2nd Division during the disaster of Pozieres, had been replaced by Victoria Cross recipient Nevill Smyth. General McCay of the 5th Division, commander at Fromelles, was relieved of his duties and replaced by Australian General William Holmes. Yet another Australian,

Joseph Talbot Hobbs, assumed command of the 4th Division, replacing General Cox.[19]

In the front-line trenches, little could be achieved by the infantry given the prevailing weather conditions. Instead, pressure was maintained by sporadic artillery attacks. George moved with his brigade into the Albert area on the Somme, enjoying the break from the front line, participating in training activities, carefully noting details of his training in his notebook, but always aware of the relentless boom of artillery fire on the front line.

France
Jan 1ˢᵗ, 1917
Dear Jim

… I haven't met any of the boys yet, Charlie said in his last letter that he thought he would be sent over here before Xmas, I havent had any word from Albert yet he ought to be over by now. Both Ewin and Amos are well I often see them, Amos is Lance Corporal too, I was told that Archie Bailey is on his way back to his Battalion he has had a good spell in England. I suppose you went to the tea meeting and concert. I had my xmas in the firing line, not in the front line trenches but not far from it, we got our xmas boxes, they were N.S.W. ones, it must have been a quiet one at home only 3 of you. There is a chap in our unit who knows Dave Fyffe well, he came from where he was working. They seem to be going to a lot of trouble for nothing over this conscription business. I would like to see more of the shirkers sent over here, would do them the world of good. You will be up to your neck in work now. I hope the crop turns out successful …

France
Jan 5 1917
Dear Father

I am just writing a few lines to tell you I received a parcel yesterday I think it must be the one you thought had gone down on that boat it had a xmas cake, scarfe, tinned pudding and few other things in it so you know if it was the first one you sent, the tin was a little knocked about but the contents were as good as gold, the cake was splendid, we heard here about that boat and that all the mail was saved but was not certain about all the parcels. I don't think I have missed any of your letters for a long while now but don't get all the papers you send. I just wrote to Jim a few days ago so haven't any news, we cant say anything about war as the censor is very strict now. I got a letter from Allan yesterday he had just come out of the trenches he said that Percy and Bill Street were in isolation for mumps there is nothing serious about mumps, I had a letter from Johnny Price a little while ago, he was in the hospital with the same thing. I havent any of those mates with me that you saw one was in the 7 Batt. but I haven't seen him for a long while, some of the others are in the casualty list, there are two with me now that came over on the same boat but I didn't know them at the time. I often see Amos, Ewin and Harry Burrows they are all well. The weather for this month is very promising so far not as cold as I thought it would be. Well I ought to be in England on leave when you get this letter that is if it continues the way it is going now. I think Charlie is over here now I received a field card from him two days ago saying he was well. I have received the money you cabled over, it will come in very handy while on leave. Well I will now close hoping all are well.

I remain
Your loving son
George
L/Corp G.T. Marlow

After ten months of war, George had lost contact with many of the mates with whom he had trained. As he explained to his father, some were now casualties. Less than a fortnight later, George wrote to his mother of a chance meeting with Tom Alford, Jim's mate from Mologa. It was a little over 12 months since they had last seen each other, yet George remarks on how Tom has altered. Perhaps Tom thought the same of George. The young men of World War I had left their youth behind and had become hardened, many also haunted by their experiences.

France
Jan 19ᵗʰ 1917
Dear Mother

I received yours and Jim's letters dated Nov 26. You seem to be having funny weather, we had a heavy fall of snow a few nights ago, it is warm while it is snowing but after it gets cold. Albert has arrived in England after a very long time on the water I might get over on leave in time to see him there, Charlie is over here now but haven't seen him or the others yet, I had a letter from Allan he had been in the trenches and was out for Xmas. Percy is isolated for mumps. I met Tom Alford a few days ago but only had about 5 minutes to speak to him as he was marching up to the trenches and we were about to move, he looks well but seems to have altered a little. We are out of the trenches now but don't know how long …

While George was rotated through the trenches, to the north Charlie remained in the isolation camp. As his letters to his mother and uncle suggest, he and his comrades were anxious for mail to arrive with its news of home.

Jan 7th 1917
France
Dear Jim

… I am in an isolation camp still, we are not overburdened with drill and I suppose we will be going up the line soon after we come out, I have written to the boys twice since I have been here but so far I have not got any word from them, I have also written to Payne's in Leicester but have not got any reply as yet the mail do not run very often to England or I would get some letters as Ida said she would write to me, but I hope this week will bring me some news from there of Albert. We have French money over here we are paid in French money and hardly ever see British money, since we have been over here we get issued to us every week 4 packets of cigarettes and one box of matches so we don't do too bad as regards smokes, Alf Ferris is in this camp with us, also Ottery and Guinane I have not seen Wilson Townsend but I believe he is over here and Jack Sinclair also. Bill Crossman was in Hurdcott when I saw him last. I suppose you will be finished harvest by now how did the crop turn out how did Mahoneys crop yield and who took it off are they pooling the wheat this year the same as last wheat is a big price in England now …

To his uncle, Charlie wrote:

… We get the "Daily Mail" over here every day but there is not much news in it other than war. There is canteens here just the same as England and they sell every thing from beer upwards, we get issued every week with 4 packets of cigarettes and one box of matches since we have been in France and women come round selling fruit cakes lollies postcards etc. I suppose you will be finished up with the harvest by now I believe the crops yielded well in Australia this harvest, wheat is a great price over here. Is there any more young fellows about Calivil declared war yet I think a few more from around that could come and lend a hand …

11th January 1917
France
Dear Mother,

… it has been raining here a good deal lately and today it is snowing it is the first snow that I have been in since we have been in France, we have been confined to our tents this last three days with the wet, it rains over here more often than when we were in England but is not near as cold, I have not received any letters from you or from Pearl since I have been over here I have been expecting a letter from Ida but so far have not received any I write to them every week and also sent a letter to England for Albert but so far I have not heard anything of him the mails to England do not run very often but I hope to get a letter from Paynes this week. I am still in the isolation camp we go for a rout march one day and to the training camp the next so you will see that we are not over burdened with work, Jack McDonald from Pyramid is in here I also met one of the Jaspers from out Pine Grove way the other day he is in the same battalion as we are, we get the papers here every day at about 4 oclock so we see how things are going. I suppose they will have finished up with the harvest by now, wheat is a high price over here and bread is very dear, but I think on an average things are cheaper here than in England Capstan cigarettes were 4d a packet in Lark Hill and the same cigarettes over here are 3d and yet they are made in England and sent across, we are issued with 4 packets and a box of matches every week so we do not do too bad for smokes. I write to the boys every week and to you also …

A week later, he wrote to his mother again:

… I have not got any mail from Australia for a good while, but I believe Allan is getting his letters alright and perhaps my letters may have gone to the battalion so Al will perhaps get them for me. We get the paper here every day and there is Australian news in it at times I saw two Pyramid papers and a Bendigonian last week. Jack McDonald from Pyramid got them. All the news of the show was in it and I saw where the Gordon Shire and the Dimboola Shire were neutral and up to the time it was printed they had decided not to declare war. I am not fighting yet but suppose it will not be long before we will be going up the line, it has been very miserable weather over here this last two weeks raining and snowing nearly every day, but still it is better over here than at Lark Hill …

Charlie took the opportunity to read about the news from home, critical of reports indicating that the Gordon Shire, in which Mologa was located, had chosen not to promote conscription. The Federal government's recruitment scheme required local governments to be actively involved in recruitment campaigns to the point of quotas being issued. An article in *The Argus* of 25 December 1915 states that, of the 50,000 men then promised, the quota for the Gordon Shire was 32 men — nine soldiers per month.

France
21ˢᵗ Sunday Jan 1917
Dear Jim,

… I got another letter from Ida she said that Albert was up at their place, she said she would have known him from the rest of us, he did not go to Drayton as it was a terrible day and about a foot of snow on the ground, I was expecting a letter from him, but so far have not received any. I saw the Pyramid papers last week and the Bendigonian, they were sent to Jack McDonald I saw in one of them about the Gordon Shire deciding not to take any part in the conscription bill also Dimboola shire they are apparently the only two pro German shires in Victoria, they ought to change the name of Gordon Shire Councillors to German Shire Councillors for they are little better. We will be coming out of here some time this week and I suppose it

will not be long before we go up the line. I don't think Albert will be over here for a good while as he is too young for the winter fighting. It has been very cold over here lately but the winter is getting on and it will soon be getting into the warmer months. We get the paper here everyday the Anzacs are playing football in Paris today I would like to have seen it as I believe Paris is a grand place, I saw some very nice houses when on a route march yesterday they were a fair way out from the town …

Charlie and Percy were reunited just prior to making their way to the front-line trenches around Armentieres. One can only imagine the delight of meeting a family member on distant shores and Allan's pleasure at the arrival of his brothers in his own D Company although, as a later letter reveals, their arrival may well have been met with some reservation.

On 29 January, 800 men from all battalions of the 10th Brigade were selected for a raiding party to conduct a large-scale assault in February. Allan indicates in his letter of 8 February that his commanding officer had asked him if he wanted Percy 'on this stunt'. Allan had refused the offer, replying that 'one of us is quite enough'. Allan left Charlie and Percy at their billets and moved to nearby Erquinghem for training. Within days both Charlie and Percy were to gain their first experience of warfare in the trenches of Bois-Grenier to the south of Armentieres.[20]

Charlie penned a brief note before moving out to join his battalion:

France
24th Jan 1917
Dear Jim,

… Percy and I are leaving for the front we will be both together and will be with Allan, I have not heard from Albert but got a letter from Ida to say that he was up there on leave I also got a letter from Flo Wilson and one from May Payne they were all well.

I did not hear from Geordie but Paynes and Allan heard from him and he was alright, I have not much time so will have to ring off I will write whenever I can I am writing to Pearl tonight, I have not heard from you for a good while. Well I will say goodbye for this time again hoping you are all well so once again goodbye

I am your affect. brother
Charlie

Allan wrote to tell his mother that his brothers had arrived at their billets:

… Well dear mum we are out on a decent spell now and it is very acceptable too. We are having very cold weather now, but we are in nice warm billets & have a good fire going Charlie & Percy both joined up the battalion yesterday. They are both in D Company with me. They have had a good time especially Percy. My officer is going to get Charlie into the Lewis Gun. I have not heard from Geordie for a while now. He is fighting a long way from us…

ENGLAND, JANUARY

Albert soon settled into the training routine at Larkhill and was entertained by the many letters from home, some of which amused him, while others appeared somewhat disheartening:

Jan 4th 1917
Dear Jim

Just a few lines to say I have received two letters from you, rather interesting ones at that, I damn near died laughing at the one I got this morning. An Australian mail came in today, I got 10 letters, one each from you 1 from Mum, Myrtle Saville, Auntie Florrie, Mollie Gamble, Dolly Rowe, G. Price, Myrtle, and Will Stone, and one from Dolly Burgoyne that was addressed to Royal Park. When they were giving out the letters to me, all the boys said – the lucky devil. I also got two from Leicester today. One from Ida Payne, and one Charlie had left there for me. I was sorry to hear about those buggars you called traitors etc. I suppose they will all get out of going into camp now. I got a letter from M. Saville and she said, "I hope you have a good time in England before you go to the death-bed." Rather encouraging isn't it. I was sorry to hear you did not have a tart for the show. Why didn't you get Eva. By your letter you seem rather taken up by her, so I will not be surprised to hear anything now. Your letter was rather amusing about Tom Reigel. I fancy I can see him now, with the straw in his mouth and kicking the dirt with his hoof. I got those letters from J. Price they were a bit funny, especially about the saluting. If the M.P.'s see you pass an officer without saluting him, you are in for a warm time. I was glad to hear you got the photos. Don't forget to send one to Dolly Rowe. If you ever go to Bendigo, you ought to go into Brown's and see her. I got a very nice letter from her today. Well Jim you asked me how I liked the snow I have been here a week and haven't seen any yet. There is 4 blankets for every man in the huts and last night they issued us with another blanket, one that we take to the front with us, also a pair of black boots, that weigh about 9lbs and a pair of gloves. It is not cold at night as we have 5 blankets to sleep in, besides the waterproof sheet and the overcoat. Tell Mum not to worry about me being cold. I think it is colder in the day time than it is at night. Anyway we don't have time to get cold in the daytime. We drill with our overcoats on, and some days with the equipment on. They don't waste any time drilling here. Everything is at the double, meals and all. The tucker is good here. One doesn't care a damn how stiff the drill is, as long as the tucker is good. Aeroplanes are as thick as bees here. I counted 17 this morning. They sound like a harvester, when they are about 3 000 feet up. Harry Street applied for a transfer to the artillery but was refused. He is trying to get out of going into the trenches. Jimmy O'Hare is in this company. He is likely to get into trouble again. He got down on some of the kits, he is the biggest waster in the company. Les Cant from Pine Grove is camped about 50 yds from my hut …

Lark Hill Camp
Amesbury
Jan 5th
My Dear Mother

… Since I last wrote to you, we have been drilling fairly solid. We got inoculated again tonight. It is a dam nuisance. We get our 4 days leave on Monday. I was sorry to hear that the referendum was defeated, and that the shirkers are still at large. Well Mum, you seem to think that I will be cold here, but it is no colder than Australia so far. We have 5 blankets, and a waterproof sheet and an overcoat to sleep in. Also we drill in uniforms, and as they keep you moving we never get cold. They issued us with gloves yesterday also a pair of boots, that take all hour to up-end them. The tucker is very good here so far … It doesn't cost me much here, as I hardly ever

smoke and the only thing I get is a few buns sometimes. They are very cheap here. Well dear Mum, I suppose Mologa is busy with wheat carting. I was supposed to get teeth out today, but when I got to the dentist, he said he wouldn't bother, so I didn't bother either. Well dear Mum, news is very scarce here, so I will ring off, hoping all are well as it leaves me at present.

I am
Your Loving Son
Albert

Excuse the scribble as the light is bad. We had a dance in the hut a while ago. I have not received the tin yet.

Lark Hill
Jan 10th 17
Dear Dad,

Just a line to let you know I am still going strong. We got our 4 days leave on Tuesday, and got out to London at 2 o'clock. I then caught the train to Leicester. I sent a telegram to Ida Payne to tell her I was coming and she was out at the station to meet me. I got there at 6 oclock, They were all home except Clem. He is on the H.M.S. Fox and is at present in Bombay, where the Fox is getting repaired. Paynes have a very nice house. They were very nice to me, and I had a real good holiday, only it wasn't half long enough. On Wednesday Ethel and I went all over Leicester. We went to the Museum and saw a lot of old Roman war images that were dug up in the streets of Leicester. I have often heard you speak of Daniel Lambert. In the museum there is a photo [of] him, the chair he used to sit in, and a pair of his trousers and a waistcoat. He weighed 52 stone. I sent you some postcards of Leicester. I was under the St Mary's Gateway, and also saw the magazine. Then we went to the Church where Auntie was married in, St Martins, and also saw the other churches there. They look very old. I don't know if you remember the Drury wall, there is only a few feet left of it now. It is a wall that the Romans built around a part of Leicester, Auntie and I were going to Drayton on the Thursday to see Aunt Charlotte, but through the night there was a heavy fall of snow. Wilson's place is 3 miles from the station, so it was too far for Auntie to walk in the snow. It was no use me going on my own as they did not know I was coming. I would have liked to have gone over to see them, but it was too bad a day for Auntie. I left Leicester at 5 oclock on Friday night, and didn't get back to camp till half past two on sat morning. We had to get up at 6.30 and after breakfast went for a 10 mile march. Some of our fellows stopped 2 days over leave and got 28 days in clink with their pay stopped. One of the corporals has not come back yet. If they catch him he will most likely go up in front of a brick wall. They are very strict here. If you go on parade with a button undone they will crime you. The officer that was over us before is not with us now, and a damn good job. I said in my letters from the boat, that our officers were good, but we couldn't say anything else as they censored our letters. He used to try and bounce the men. He used to roar Harry Street up a treat. Harry applied for a transfer to the artillery but they wouldn't listen to him. Now he is going to try and get transferred to the Army Service Corps. He wants to get out of going into the trenches. His feet are very cold. There is 50 men going to France out of our company soon, and Harry will most likely have to go, as he has had a lot of drill. I got the tin that Mum sent on Saturday, also a box from the Australian War Contingent in London. This notepaper was in it. Well Dad, I have not heard from the other boys yet, but Ida got letters from all of them. I think Geordie will soon get his leave, as a lot are coming out of the trenches now on leave. Well Dad, I think I have told you all so I will close hoping you are all well as it leaves me at present,

I remain
Your Loving Son
Albert

Harry Marlow is still in the hospital and I think he will not be much good for anything, when he gets out. I got a Bendigo Advertiser yesterday, and it had our photos in it, I also saw in the Bendigonian where Jim is made president of the Farmers Union in Mologa.

An article entitled 'Mologa Family: Five Sons Serving the Empire' appeared in the *Bendigo Advertiser* in late November. The article included a photo of Sarah and images of each of her soldier sons. There was generous praise for the family:

... Only one son remains at home. All were members of the Mologa Football Club, and being thoroughly good sportsmen, it is small wonder that, one after the other, they are all finding their way to the front to fight the battles of their country. No small measure of satisfaction must be felt by both Mr and Mrs Marlow in the knowledge that their duty to their country has been well done ... [21]

The propaganda and pressure to enlist could be as overt as large coloured posters and the anonymous delivery of white feathers; it could also be as subtle as public tributes to a family shouldering a great burden for their country. To Albert the publicity meant little, he was a soldier and he had embarked on a wonderful adventure.

Albert made the most of his leave and enthusiastically wrote home to his father of the sights he had seen, particularly those with which his father was familiar. Prudently, Albert was not one of the many Australians who chose not to return from leave at the designated time, staying days, sometimes months past their return date. While Albert appears concerned that one such soldier may face the firing squad, this severest of penalties was never enforced against an Australian soldier in World War I. The Australian government refused to endorse the death penalty, much to the annoyance of British authorities who considered this attitude a factor in the lack of discipline for which the Australians were renowned. While the volunteers of the AIF may have been considered undisciplined given their contempt for military courtesies and rules, their initiative, staunchness, loyalty and sense of comradeship would later mark them as among the finest shock troops of the Allied forces.

Lark Hill
Jan 14th
My Dear Mother,

Just a few lines to let you know I received your parcel yesterday and was very pleased to get it. Many thanks for sending it. It is lovely to have some home made cake again, and the cheese is very nice, besides the other things. It is grand to get a parcel from home. We got our four days leave on Tuesday. I had to go to London first. I stopped there for about an hour and caught the train for Leicester. I stopped at Paynes all the time I was there. They were very nice to me and I had a real good time. I was going to go to Drayton, but there was a hell of a snowstorm so I did not go. I had to wait at London on the way back as we had to "fall in" there. The officer had a job to line the men up as a lot of them were drunk. The N.C.O.'s were nearly all drunk, and it was about 2 hours before we were ready to start. We got back to camp at 2.30 am on Sat. We got up at 6.30 and went for a route march of 10 miles, and then a holiday for the afternoon. I had just come back from the march when I got your box. I have not received any letters from home for over a week, but I think there will be some more handed out soon. Well Mum we were given a Christmas box today. It came from the Australian War Contingent in London, and in it there was 2 packets of cigarettes, 2 boxes matches, 1 match box cover, 2 boxes lollies, post cards, notepaper, envelopes and a handkerchief. We have straw mattresses to sleep on now. They are very strict on keeping your beds tidy here. Well dear Mum I got on the scales the other day and weighed 11 stone 12 lbs. I think I lost a bit of weight on the boat, so ought to be putting more on now. We get a great dinner here on Sundays. I met Dave Mullins here yesterday. He has been here a long time now. Charlie is in isolation for 28 days in France. Ida Payne got a letter from him last week. Percy is in isolation with mumps. I think Geordie will get his leave soon, as a lot are getting off now. I don't suppose I will have the luck to see him. I don't think we will be here a great time as they drill the men in France now. I saw a Bendigonian today, and I notice K Haw has enlisted. It wont be long before he's here, as they don't drill them much in Australia now. The drill here is much different to that in Australia. One of our Non-Coms and 3 men have not come back from their leave yet. They will catch it pretty hot. Well, my dear Mum, there is no news so will close, so once again thanking you for the box.

I am
Your Loving Son
Albert

We just got word that there is a mail from Australia coming here tomorrow.

Albert provided more detail to Jim:

… It is only a 2 ½ hours trip from London, and a lovely train to travel in, but it was dark going up and coming back, so I could not see any of the country going through. I was at Paynes all the time. They were very nice to me. Ida is a nice girl. Ethel is a bit quiet, and Little May is such a nice girl. She is only ten, but has more manners than a lot of girls have at 20 … I had a good time in Leicester. It is a very large town and seems very old. The museum has a lot of Roman figures in it, also a lot of badges and ammunition & rifles captured from the Germans in the present war. I left Leicester on Friday and got up to Waterloo station at 8. We had to wait till 10 oclock for the train to leave. A lot of our fellows were drunk and they had a hell of a job to line the men up. Some of our men are not back yet, and will get a rough time when they turn up. I was up to Amesbury this afternoon. It is a village about the size of Pyramid. The cockies about Amesbury are ploughing. There are some big fields about. The biggest crop paddock is about 40 acres. You see as many as 6, 2 horse teams ploughing in one field. I was over to Stonehenge last Sunday. It is only 2 miles from here, and you can see the blocks of rock from here quite easily. It is a mystery how they got there, as they are a hell of a size and there are no stones like them within 100 miles of here. Another place we used to read about when we were going to school is near here, the chestnut tree where the "village blacksmith" used to swing his sledge hammer. The village is only a mile from here and the chestnut tree is still there. I am going over to see it next Sunday. Well Jim, I got the box that Mum sent. It came in very handy. The cake is lovely. We got a Xmas box given to us today. This note paper was in it. You asked me how I liked the snow. We had it here one day, and it is a buggar drilling while it is snowing, with the blasted stuff running down your neck. I have not heard from the boys since I have been here, but Ida got a letter from them all. There is a mail coming here tomorrow from Australia. Well Jim how is Eva getting on. Next time you go to see her, remember me to her. I suppose you are nearly finished the harvest now. Well Jim, this is about all so I will close hoping you & yours are quite well.

I am
Your Loving Brother
Albert W. Marlow

The following week Albert wrote again to Jim. His words reveal the level of confidence with which Albert was approaching the task ahead. While at age 19 he was likely to be younger than his officers, yet he labels them 'kids'. His self-assured comments on his own strength and ability reveal something of the pluck that had seen him attempt to enlist on several occasions.

Sat Jan 20th 17
Dear Jim

... We had a little snow over here today. I looked at the thermometer today, it was 49 and it is not near as cold today as it is some days. One of my mates is in the hospital. I think his lungs are weak. His name is Stewart Dabb. He comes from Maldon and knows Mr & Mrs Stevenson of Mologa. He also knows Mrs Lister. He used to be in a bank at Bendigo, and he says he knows Geo Gibson well. I got a letter from Myrtle today, also a couple of photos. She is sending me a tin so my luck is in. The tin that Mum sent is finished, I'm sorry to say. Nearly every one that writes to me sends me some notepaper so I have plenty of paper in my pockets. I am writing letters nearly every night. We are drilling strong now. It is a cow of a parade ground. The frost sets it as hard as hell, and it is as rough as a wood-heap. We drill with our scarves on and also gloves. The C.O. that was over us before is not over us now, and no bluddy loss. He is only a damn kid. I could stand the buggar on his head in two ticks. The other officer is only a kid too, but is a decent chap. Well Jim, I suppose you spend Sundays on the <u>hill</u> now. I always thought there was <u>somethin doin</u> there.

Jim's love life continued to be the cause of much speculation by his younger brothers. Albert mentions Jim spending 'Sundays on the hill' which, in this case, is a reference to the home of Cr Richard Jones and his family of four girls and two boys. He appears to be hinting at a possible friendship between Jim and Eva Jones. The Jones family were very supportive of the Marlows during the war years — Eva made a habit of traipsing across the paddocks on washing day to lend Sarah a hand. Jim was never to marry, although while cleaning out the old house we found a receipt for a diamond ring. But, to the best of our knowledge, it was not intended for Eva as this relationship never blossomed and the intended recipient remains a mystery. A century on, Jim's love life is still the subject of speculation.

Sun Jan 21st 17

… Well Mum, the cake's finished. It was lovely I often used to put a piece in my pocket to eat on the parade ground. I never enjoyed cake so much before. I got a letter from Myrtle yesterday, and she said she is sending me a tin, so I will be right. I got a letter from Charlie, he is coming out of isolation tomorrow. Percy got about 50 days isolation altogether. Well Mum I am glad you got the ducks again. Fancy them getting so far away. That buggar on the hill had a neck to tell them he had to support his aged mother. I bet she would not like to be told she was aged. I'd like to see the crawler over here with a b on his coat. His feet would be cold here. There is talk of sending us all away to France as this camp is condemned. But I think we will be here a while yet. We have done nothing but squad drill yet. We had a half holiday yesterday. There was a church parade this morning. Every one is supposed to go, but I stopped behind to write letters … Well, dear Mum, I suppose Mologa is pretty quiet now, but the wheat carting will liven things up. All the men in the hut are making toast, so I think I will make some too …

Salisbury Plains
Jan 28th
My Dear Mother & Father,

… I have been here a month now, and have had 35 letters from Australia. I had a letter from Geordie yesterday. He expects to get leave next month, so I hope to see him. I am going to see the C.O. about leave when Geo. comes over. Charlie also wrote to me, but he hasn't got any of my letters yet. I haven't heard from Al or Percy yet, but Charlie said that he and Percy were in the same isolation camp. They both are out now, I believe. It has been very cold this week and to make things worse, we didn't have much marching to do. They gave us lectures about things, that we knew as much about as they do. There was a route march yesterday, but I was a hut orderly, and my mate and I did the hut extra clean, and took a long while over it, and so missed the march. I don't mind route marches, but don't see any sense in going on

one if you can get out of it. A fellow doesn't want to be too slow at this game. The ones that have the most cheek get on the best … We get good tucker so don't need to buy anything much to eat. Every morning & afternoon, we have a drink of tea out on the parade ground. This just started on Friday and is a good move. It comes out steaming hot so warms you up a bit. There is a draft going to France on Sat, but none of our coy. are going. We haven't had any shooting yet. I think they pick out the men from the drafts that do the best at the range. I met a chap here yesterday named Alf Wilson. He told me he knew you well, also all the Mahoneys. He is a fairly old chap, looks to old for this game. Well Mum, I haven't been on guard yet, but I suppose its my turn next. Tell Streets that Harry is well. He is not in my hut. News is scarce here so I will close hoping all are well, so with love,

I remain your aff son
Albert Wilfred

To Jim, Albert joked about military discipline:

… Well Jim, we are still buzzing away at the drill, it has been very cold here this week. They are very strict here on discipline. I don't suppose you know the meaning of discipline. It is a military word and means shaving every day, standing still while on parade, folding blankets in 3 folds, having the beds in line and various other things. It's going to make a big difference in the war how we keep our huts clean. This shaving once a day gets on my nerves, but I generally leave it until every 2nd day. I think I told you about one of our corporals staying A.W.L. He went on leave with us to London and on Sat. he was in a suit of civi clothes, and was in a consuls office getting a pass to some place, when the detectives grabbed him. Another hour and he would have been away to blazes. He is a bit of a Dutchman, and I think he was going to Holland. His trial is on now, and no doubt he will get a few years. If he had been caught in Khaki he would have got off, but the civies put the pot on. You seem to be having bad weather for the harvest, but I suppose its nearly finished now. I am glad to hear the garden is getting on alright. I don't fancy watermelon much here. Fruit is very dear here, grapes 1/-lb apples 2d each. Mum said that Jones' have had the influenza so I suppose Eva had it that Sunday. Hardly ever see a girl here, and wouldn't give a damn if I didn't. I have got plenty of girl correspondents and some

*of them write very affectionate letters too. I suppose I will have to knock off
writing to them when I get to France. Les Cant is in the draft that is going
to France on Sat … hoping all are well as it leaves me at present, I am*

Your Loving Brother
Albert Wilfred

Remember me to Eva
Don't forget to write, I will write again next Sunday

FRANCE, FEBRUARY

After the loss of Pozieres and Thiepval, the German High Command
revised its strategy. On 9 February German troops began a systematic
withdrawal to what was known as the Hindenburg Line. This heavily
fortified defensive line comprised a carefully positioned trench system
of solid concrete fortifications and pillboxes fronted by rolls of barbed
wire that, in places, towered above the heads of the tallest soldiers. The
line was positioned between six and 18 kilometres behind the former
German front, stretched 160 kilometres and, in some sections, was up
to seven kilometres deep. While intelligence from prisoners had warned
of the building of defensive positions, the snow and rain of the long
winter had hidden the extent of the line's construction. The withdrawal
effectively straightened the enemy front line which had bulged into
Allied territory both north and south of Bapaume, the same bulge that
Nivelle had planned to attack in the Spring Offensive. The withdrawal
to the Hindenburg Line, though initially dismissed by Allied soldiers as
a sign of weakening German resolve, had significantly strengthened the
enemy position, reducing the number of divisions required to protect
the front and dodging the expected Allied attacks on the bulging
salients from the north and south. The retreating German forces left
a trail of utter devastation in their wake, destroying homes, burning
barns, bombing wells and railways, contaminating water supplies,
decimating orchards, and leaving delayed-action mines in wait for their
pursuers. It was a strategy referred to as a 'scorched earth policy' and
only added to the view of the barbaric 'Hun' so effectively represented
in the propaganda of the time.[22]

George returned to the trenches of Gueudecourt to the south of Bapaume where the frozen earth had begun to thaw, the trenches gradually filling once again with the dreaded mud of early winter. The task of the Australian divisions in the Somme region was to maintain pressure on the German forces and, on 4 February, despite the icy conditions, Stormy Trench was seized by the 13th Battalion following an assault by the 15th Battalion three days prior. It was in this sector of the line that George was promoted to corporal early that month. Soon after, he was granted ten days' leave in England where Albert anxiously anticipated his arrival.

ENGLAND, FEBRUARY

Lark Hill Camp
Feb 5th 1917
My Dear Mother, Father & Jim,

… Well Mum, I got the tin tonight that Myrtle sent me, and it is a bonza one at that. I suppose its just as well to tell you whats in it. There was a cake, a tin of biscuits, tin of cheese, 4 tins lollies, 4 cakes chocolate, cigarettes, tobacco, nuts, chewing gum, tin of rexona, pack cards, dates, buttons, needles and cotton also a lot of bootlaces, so it was very acceptable. The cake is very nice, it has icing on it and kept lovely. There is enough eatables to last me a week. Ida Payne sent me a Balaclava helmet last week and it came in handy, as I was on guard Sat and Friday. When I was on leave Ethel gave me a scarf, so I have two now. We had a very busy week end. Went on a ten mile march Sat morning. Went on guard at 2 in the afternoon, and finished Sunday at 5 pm. Monday morning went on a 7 mile march, and at night we had a night march. It snowed here all day Sunday. It was about 5 inches deep. It isn't so very cold this week. One of our chaps died in the hospital last week. He was fairly old, too old for this game. I havent heard from the boys lately, in fact I haven't heard from Al or Percy yet. I haven't heard when we're likely to go to France, but I don't think it will be for a long while yet as we haven't been to the range yet. 20 of us were at the miniature range last Monday and I surprised the C.O. by getting top score with 10 bullseyes out of 10 shots. We do a lot of drill here [in] gas helmets they are very particular

about it. We have a fairly easy time now. Revielle is at 7.30 now it used to be ½ hour earlier. Well Mum, this is all this time, so I will close hoping all are well as it leaves me at present so goodbye from

Your Loving Son
Albert

Sun Feb 11th 17
My Dear Mother & Father,

… I got a telegram from Geordie yesterday from Walham Green, to say he was coming to see me today, but I waited here all day and he hasn't arrived yet. I was picked for guard today but got out of it. They seem to fancy me for guard, as I was on last Sunday, and on picket in at Durrington on Thursday night. We are known as B Coy. now and the C.O. is Lt. Collins. He used to be over Al and Percy at Bendigo. They used to say he was a fair buggar, well, that's praising him up, He comes round every morning, to see if we are clean-shaven and dressed properly. My mate was on guard today, and with a lot of others got crimed for having dirty rifles. When they told him that they had nothing to clean them with he said, "hold your tongue". He's one of these "stay-at-home" crawlers. No fear of him going to France. They say he's too frightened to go out at night, for fear someone will heave a lump of rock at him. If Geordie comes tomorrow, I am going to apply for leave, and if he wont give it, I'm going to get paraded to the Major. Just to show you what sort of a buggar Collins is, I went up to him this morning told him that I was on guard and that Geordie was coming to see me, and asked him to relieve me from guard. He didn't wait till I had finished but said No. I stood there, and he pointed to the door, so I saluted the waster and went to the Sergeant and got him to relieve me. I knew before I went to him that he wouldn't let me off. He'll get a good count out when we go to France …

After 16 months without seeing his brother, Albert was not about to allow the detested Collins to spoil his opportunity to see George, even to the point of risking punishment. George made the long journey from London to Larkhill and finally arrived at the AIF's training grounds to stay overnight with his younger brother. Their efforts to spend more time together prior to George's return to France would come to no avail, although this time Collins was not responsible. Illness was still ravaging the camps and, within days, Albert was hospitalised with mumps and any hope of leave was banished.

Lark Hill
Tuesday 13th Feb

Well Mum, Geordie got out here last night, and is looking real well on it. He stopped here with me last night. I have got half a day off, I took it, so might get a day or so in the clink. I was so pleased to see him. I am applying for weekend leave to London on Saturday, but don't know how I will get on. The soldiering life seems to agree with Geordie, as I never seen him looking so well before. He says it is not too bad over there, and seems to like it all right. Well Mum I gave Geordie £4. I had £5 and as he hasnt got too much, I did not like to see him short, he wants to have a good time while he has the chance. I don't need much here, and we will be paid again next week. Well Mum this is all so I will say goodbye

From Your Loving Son
Albert

George also wrote home to tell his family that he had been reunited with Albert:

England
Feb 13.2.17
Dear Mother, Father & Jim

Just a few lines to say I am on leave and came out here to Lark Hill yesterday to see Albert and stopped here with him last night, it is a terrible long way out here I thought he might be able to get leave to London but don't seem to have much chance he is going to try for weekend leave and in the meantime I am going to Leicester and then going back to London. It is bonzer in London I would like to put in a couple of months there, we only get 10 days. I met Gordon McKay he is on leave too but has gone back again to France. I came straight out of the trenches on leave from just in front of Bapaume on the Somme we have been about that part of the front for this last 5 months. I think Al & Percy's division are round in Belgium. I received another parcel from you just before I left France also some more letters dated

Dec 15, the crops seem to be going well. I received the Bendigo paper with the photos in they weren't too bad, I am getting mine taken over here and will send some over. The Military treat us rotten when we come over from France on leave, we have to pay for our own clothes, what do you think of that, the people over here treat us well they cant do enough for us, girls will stop you in the streets and invite you out to their places for tea. I am sending a cable to you. I will be sorry when my leave is over. Will write again when I get back so hoping all are well with best wishes.

I remain
Your loving son & brother
George

George's notebook, in which he carefully recorded the names and addresses of relatives, friends and comrades, also attests to the hospitality of the girls who stopped George on the streets of London. Whether these were innocent offers of friendship, or less honourable offers from the prostitutes who thronged the streets, is unclear. However George certainly added a number of addresses of the ladies of London to his notebook.

Lark Hill Camp
Amesbury
Feb 15th 17
Dear Jim

Just a few lines to say I am well. Geordie came down from London two days ago. He stopped the night with me and left here at 2 yesterday afternoon. I had the morning off with him. He looks real well, just the same Geordie, not altered a bit … I got a letter from Allan tonight. It's the first I've had from him and it took a month to get here. He was having a spell out of the trenches when he wrote. Well Jim, it is not too bad here just at present. We are having a fairly easy time here now, only this bludy Collins is a fair cow. We have to go out on a night manoeuvre tonight, all through him. He's the C.O. of B Coy, and he's always falling us in for some damn thing. He crimed my mate for having a dirty rifle. I think I'll miss the night manoeuvre as I've got some letters to write. We have been here over 6 weeks now and I believe we have to do 12 weeks training before we go to France, so according to that, we will be most likely leaving here at the beginning of April, just in time for the Spring offensive, so you know what that will be like. A few of our chaps got the mumps and nearly all the coy. is isolated. One lad out of this hut got the mumps, but we never got isolated. The snow that fell 10 days ago is just melting now, and the place is as muddy as blazes. This must be a cow of a place when it rains. There hasn't been a drop of rain since I've been here, it snows instead. I am sending home a few photos I got taken a while ago …

Albert had written too soon. According to a letter to his parents dated the same day, he had been isolated soon after. The following day he was hospitalised with mumps.

… Geordie came down from London to see me and went up to Leicester. I was going to apply for leave to go up to London on Saturday to see him, and had a good chance of getting it, when today, one chap out of my hut went to the hospital with mumps, and we are isolated now, and so the leave is cooked. We will be isolated for 3 weeks, and it's a fair devil, as we have to drill just the same, and yet cant go anywhere. We go for a route march every day instead of the ordinary drill, so its no fun being isolated. I was trench digging this morning, and the sweat ran out of me in spite of the cold …

Park House Hospital
Tuesday Feb 19th 1917
Dear Dad

Just a few lines to let you know I am in the hospital with mumps, I came here Saturday evening. Our hut was isolated and 6 of us out of it have got mumps. This hospital is about 8 miles from Lark Hill. It is just the same as being in camp only we have no drill. The huts are the same, 30 in a hut, and we have good beds to sleep in. I have got a lovely swollen jaw, but it isn't sore and I cant eat like a horse. I feel tip-top, and it's a holiday to be here, after being isolated. When we were isolated, we had all route marches. Go about 10 mile a day, so its no fun being in isolation. We will be here 3 weeks. The mumps stop in your neck for about 4 days. It is a great relief to be here for a while. It will do me for a holiday for a few weeks. When

*I left Lark Hill there was only 30 men not isolated out of 270 in our coy
and the 5/38, so its pretty bad over there. Anyway most of our chaps are
praying to God they all get them. They reckon your very lucky to get mumps
and 3 weeks holiday … We have had some rain lately and it makes a hell
of a mess on the parade ground. We were drilling the other day in about
4 inches mud. I never saw such a muddy shop in all my life. According to
the papers things are getting lively in France, and they seem to think the
Big Offensive has started already. The Dardanelles Inquiry is coming out
in a day or two and I will send a paper with it in home to you. I suppose it
is in the Australian papers about the food allowances here. The people are
rousing about only being allowed ¾ lb sugar a person a week. We never
see any in camp, but there is always a little in the porridge. We were just
given cigarettes and writing paper here, and before we leave here get a pair
of socks and soap, besides the usual cigarettes every second day. I got a letter
from Ida a few days ago and she says it is very cold up there. I saw in a paper
today where G. Mossop was killed in action. His number was 510. I think
it must be young George Mossop from Bears Lagoon, he was in the 38ᵗʰ
Batt, and that would be about his number. Well Dad, there is some pretty
places about here, no doubt it must look great in the summer. There is a lot
of villages about here, and everyone has a stream running through it. There
are very few hedgerows about here all fences. Well Dad, I think I have told
you all so will close hoping all are well, I am*

Your loving son
Albert

Contracting mumps with its resultant stay in hospital appears to have
made a welcome change from route marches and the mud of the parade
ground. Being sick but warm and dry in hospital brought Albert a
perverse sense of relief.

FRANCE, FEBRUARY

While Percy and Charlie remained in the trenches of Armentieres,
Allan spent three weeks in training for a major raid to be launched
from the trenches of Houplines to the north of Armentieres. On 17
February Charlie was admitted to hospital with bronchitis, the same

day that Albert, across the English Channel, had been admitted with mumps. Allan wrote:

France
Feb 8th 1917
My Dear Mum & Dad & Jim

Well dear mum I received your most welcome letters also dad's photo. I was pleased to hear all were well. You must have had a lot of work during harvest but my word it seems to be turning out splendid. It seems funny to hear about people harvesting and it is so cold over here, but one stands it well. Well mum I with a lot more of the boys are out of the trenches at present and are going through a special training. Percy & Charlie as I told you in a previous letter have joined up the battalion and are in the same company as me. They are both in the trenches at present. They will not be in this stunt with me.

Well dear mum we have seen a good deal of active service now and have been in some very nice bombardments. This is the first time Charlie & Percy have been in the trenches I went into them a fortnight before my birthday and I can tell you I have had some joy in that time. Well mum the ground here has been covered with snow for 3 weeks now and still it lays. Every canal is absolutely frozen. We had a great game of football on the ice today. I suppose you won't believe it. In places the ice is 3 feet thick and I suppose over there they sell it as fast as they make it. I have had a couple of letters from Albert. He is getting on first rate. I have not got a letter from Geordie for a good while now. I haven't got any letters from the relations for a good while and yet they write every week. Our mail don't close until the 20th so I am continuing this letter. I am still training mum and we are getting it solid. Well dear mum Charlie & Percy came out of the trenches for a spell and I went over to see them. They were splendid and getting on with the trenches they are in better trenches than we were in. I might tell you that the day we were leaving to go away on this training Mr Odonnel asked me if I would like Percy on this stunt with me and I told him no as I think one of us is quite enough on this stunt and I cannot tell you what it is. Well Mum a young chap by the name of Will Mowat is returning to Australia I was with him the night he was wounded so if you happen to

meet him he will be able to tell you where we are. He comes from Macorna.
He is very badly wounded.

Well mum I suppose you have finished the harvest by now and I hope you
all are away on a good holiday …

I remain
Your Loving Son
Allan S.

Dad drop a line or two when you get time. Thanks for the photo. The mail
closes tonight and I only hope you get the letters.

Will Mowat had sailed with Allan and Percy. His time on the Western Front
was short; on 8 December 1916, after just 16 days in the line, he suffered a
severe gunshot wound to his right leg, also sustaining damage to his lower
left leg. He returned to the family farm at Macorna in June 1917.[23]

Charlie wrote to his family:

France
12th Feb, 1917
Dear Mother Dad Jim,

… I have just come out of the trenches with Percy, He and I went in together
Al is away on special training but will be with us in a week or so the
trenches were nice and dry and not too cold, we get good food in there and
hot bacon and tea for breakfast tea bread and jam and butter for dinner
for tea stew and tea and tea again at about 11 o'clock at night so that is
not too bad, Hughie Martin was in with us and a lot of the local boys, we
are out now on a spell I have a lot of letters to write as I have received a
lot, Tom Roberts got a light tap on the head with a piece of shell but he is
nearly alright again, it is surprising that the French people take no notice of
the guns and it is a shame the way the houses are blown about, we get mail
in the trenches I got two letters from you and five from Pearl, Auntie Ettie
writes very often also Clee's girls …

I am your Affect son and brother
Charlie

On the same day Percy also put pen to paper:

Somewhere in France
Feb 12
Dear Mum & Dad

Well Mum, I am writing this in a hurry, we have just come out of the trenches; just before we went in I wrote a letter to you and forgot to post it, I never discovered it till we were in the trenches a while, so that would make a bit of a pause between the letters, I have got a lot of letters from you and Jim and I do my best to answer them but we have not much time. I was isolated for mumps for a while and Charlie came back with me and Allan and kept all the letters that came for me, so I had a pile when I arrived back. Charlie and I are together. Allan at present, with a lot of others are training, so he will not be with us for a while, the longer he is away the better for him, so do not worry at us being split up, we will be together soon. Your parcel was very good Mum, it was very good of you to send it … It was very good when we were in the trenches last time, there was no rain the nights put you in mind of some of the bright Australian nights. Well Mum there is no need to worry, even if you do not get a letter for a little time as it is hard to tell when the mails are going out. I write as often as I can to you and Jim. I have a pile of Jim's letters to answer now… I remain your loving son

Percy

Charlie, as the eldest brother on the front, now adopted the role of patriarch, writing to his family of monetary matters and the welfare of his brothers:

France
13-2-17
Dear Mother Father and Jim,

Today I received word from the Commonwealth Bank that there was £10 there for me all I have to do is get an order signed by my commanding officer and send to the bank and they will send it over in a registered letter to me, the bank was very prompt in sending the letter, the money will be very useful, of course I do not want it for myself I will divide it amongst the other brothers. I got a letter from Geordie to say that he had got word from

the same bank to the affect that there was £5 there for him and he expects
leave this month so the money will be handy to him, we generally want a
few things when we come out of the trenches and if they don't happen to be
paid it is rather awkward All was short on Sunday, but had a lot coming
to him but could not get it so I gave him a sovereign. I will give him his
share of the £10 when I get it, Albert wrote and said he did not want the
£1 I sent to Paynes for him but he has not been in France yet. I got a bonzer
parcel from Pearl today it was just the thing she sent me 5 handkerchiefs
and that was just what I wanted also a lot of other useful things including
a pocket writing pad it will be handy to write in the trenches also some cake
and pudding which we are taking to the trenches with us, she sent a tin of
milk and coffee which we are taking we have fires in the trenches and can
easily boil some water and make a drink. I wrote to you yesterday I got a lot
of letters yesterday and 12 today so I am doing alright, you asked me to tell
the truth about All and Percy well they both look well and are quite well
also myself, we are all well and hope you are the same. I will ring off for
now and say goodbye.

I am your loving son
Charlie

Allan wrote to Jim:

France
18-2-17
Dear Old Jim

… I am splendid I never felt better in my life. We are having some bonnie
weather now. I am not in the trenches now, but Charlie & Percy are, and
they are getting on well. I am out doing a special training and we get it
pretty solid. I cannot tell you what it is for. My boss asked me if I would like
Percy on this stunt with me but I told him no as one of us is quite enough
to go through it, but I have every confidence in getting through alright. Well
Jim you seem to be having a good harvest and I was pleased to hear it. No
doubt you must have had a lot of work to do but I suppose it is all over now
and that you are away on a holiday. I got a letter from Albert tonight and
he is getting on well. He said that they are having some nice weather there

too. He said that Geordie had been on leave and that he came down to see him. By jove I would like to see him too. But we are a long way away from him. Well Jim I ought to have some interesting news to tell you in a near date. Well Jim I think I have told you all the news so I will close hoping all are well as it leaves me at present. Goodbye Jim

I remain
Your Loving Brother
Allan

All the boys are well.

Their training completed, the men of the raiding party from the 37th and 38th battalions were well-prepared for the task before them. In an attempt to confuse enemy intelligence, the unit marched out from Erquinghem under cover of darkness on 24 February, returning a few hours later. The following night they once again appeared ready to enter the trenches as they left Erquinghem, but returned soon after, a move again designed to puzzle enemy observers. On the night of 27 February the raiders marched from their billets and were later picked up by lorry for the short journey to Armentieres. Here they quickly entered the communication trenches and moved forward to the front at Houplines. An Allied artillery bombardment at 10.00 pm, followed by relative quiet, was designed to further confuse the enemy. Two hours later, 650 Australian soldiers silently edged their way across no man's land, their faces blackened to avoid detection in the glare of searchlights, and making every effort to dodge the sporadic machine-gun bullets that whizzed above them. At 12.30 am the Australian artillery bombarded the enemy trenches with deadly accuracy, and the raiders rushed forward. The artillery then formed a box barrage of heavy fire to prevent counter-attacks from all sides. Wire that had not been blown apart in the barrage was cut through or mats thrown across to allow access, while enemy flares burst in the sky above them in the midst of the flashes of shell and the pungent smell of explosives. The men reached their objectives and, within 35 minutes, had decimated almost a kilometre of enemy trench lines. Ammunition and rifles were destroyed, dugouts blown apart, prisoners taken and intelligence gathered.

Eric Fairey, the 38th Battalion historian, estimates that 12 Germans were killed for every Australian. Of the men from the 38th who were involved, 45 men were wounded and 16 killed.[24] The action was hailed a complete success. Despite their losses, the men of the 38th were jubilant. Allan wrote home describing his experiences. This was one of the few occasions when he provided detail and described to his family the reality of what he had experienced. While addressed to his parents and Jim, the body of the letter refers only to his mother. Sarah wanted honesty from her boys and, unusually, Allan is more than forthcoming. But his words will have brought his mother little comfort.

Somewhere in France
6-3-17
My Dear Mum Dad & Jim

… Well dear mum in my last letter I told you we were training for a big stunt. Well mum it came off the other night. It was a big raid. There was 800 of us in it. They were not all out of my battalion but some out of the next one lower. Well dear mum I told you that Percy and Charlie were not in it and I am pleased too. Well mum I will try and tell you what it was like but no-one has any idea what we had to go through. It was the biggest raid and bombardment that has ever been on this front. It was just like hell. Well at 12.30 in the night we hopped our parapet and went across to Fritz's trenches under our own barrage of artillery. Immediately Fritz opened up with his artillery. Well mum my gun team had to get back to his third line and prevent a counter attack. Well mum just before we got to Fritz's first trench we had to cross a ditch which was full of water. We was up to our waist in it. Anyway we got out [of] that into his first trench. Then we had to get into his second trench. To get there we had to tear ourselves through his barb wire and fight our way. Anyway we got through that and still had to get to his 3rd trench. Well we were falling in shell holes and shells were flying around us and by hell it was good. Just before we got to his 3rd trench we had to go through another ditch full of water up to our waists again. Anyway we got through that and we met some strong opposition. They started to bomb us but we soon put them out of their trouble. But by hell we had a lively time. When we were coming back we had to come under our barrage. But in places in Fritz

trenches the muck was that deep that we had to pull one another out. No man could get through it on his own. Well Fritz shelled us all the way back. After we got into our own trench we volunteered to carry out the wounded. Well we were carrying them out Charlie Mills Corp Patterson Spuddy Kerr and 2 more of my mates were on ahead of me about 100 yds, They had a stretcher case too and Fritz put a shell right in amongst [all] of them. They were thrown all over the place. Corporal with 3 other lads were killed and the lad on the stretcher had his leg blown off. When I got up to them I got a terrible shock. Anyway we got them all away to the dressing station as fast as we could. After doing our job and helping with the wounded we crawled into bed at 4.30. They gave us a good drink of rum before going to bed. Frank Dee was wounded in our own trenches just before we hopped. A lot of boys from up our way got hit. You will see their names in the paper. But mum how on earth we came out alive I don't know. Well mum I am back in the trenches again and having a good time. I am in charge of a Lewis Gun at present but if it is for good I do not know. It gives me a lot of work. Well mum Charlie is in the hospital with [a] cold. I have not had a letter from him since. Had a letter from Geordie and Albert yesterday. They are getting on well. I also got letters from Leicester too. Well Mum you must have had a busy year with the harvest alright. Well dear mum I think I have told you all the news so I will close hoping all are well as it leaves me at present. Percy is with me the other boys are strangers. Well goodbye dear mum.

I remain
Your loving Son
Allan

Corporal Robert Paterson enlisted on 29 January 1916 leaving the farm at Buckrabanyule near Charlton, Victoria, to sail with Allan and Percy on the *Runic*. He was killed in the shell blast on 27 February.[25] Frank Dee had also sailed with Allan and Percy. He enlisted at the age of 23 at Pyramid Hill where he worked as a butcher. He sustained serious wounds to his abdomen, back and face and was lucky to survive as wounds to the abdomen often proved fatal. He returned to Pyramid Hill and was discharged on 5 November 1917. In 1941, he enlisted again to serve his country in World War II. [26]

Charlie Mills was a 30-year-old engineer whose family came from Lake Boga, Victoria. He survived the raid only to be hit by shrapnel on 8 June 1917 at Messines. In January 1918 he returned to the front and was wounded again on 28 March 1918 but remained on duty. He returned to Australia in July 1919. [27]

Edward 'Spuddy' Kerr was a labourer from Janiember East (Bears Lagoon) who enlisted with Allan and Percy on 1 March 1916. He survived the shell blast but was shot at Passchendaele on 13 October 1917. His leg was amputated when infection set in and he was repatriated in January 1918. [28]

On the Somme front to the south, George had returned from English leave to discover that the situation had changed dramatically. On 24 February raiding parties from the 2nd Brigade had discovered abandoned German trenches near Bapaume. The systematic withdrawal of German soldiers to the Hindenburg Line had been revealed. Patrols along the front line reported that pockets of enemy troops remained, their task to delay pursuing Allied forces. George's brigade encountered one such group in its raid of 25 February when a number of casualties were sustained. He wrote to his aunt the following day.

France
Feb 26/17
Dear Florrie

… I have just been on my leave to England and have been back two days I had the time of my life … While I was over there I met Gordon McKay he was on leave also. To walk about London you wouldn't think there was a war on, of course I struck it about the worst time of the year, it would be lovely over there in June or July. The worst part was coming back we were fooling about for days, the Channel wasn't too safe as there was a heavy fog every night we were held up at Southampton for 3 nights and 2 days and then again when we did cross. It is a bit sloppy again when I left here the ground was frozen hard this winter has been the coldest for over 20 years. Charlie is with Allan & Percy now, I had some letters from them they had just been in the trenches they are a long way from here. I never got the parcel

you sent me, there are 3 altogether that I haven't got. The enemy have fallen back here on our front this last few days I think it will be lively. I left the trenches to go on leave and are still in, a few of my mates have been knocked out here. I will now close with best wishes to all,

From George

At the age of 26, George Gordon McKay had enlisted in July 1915 as a driver in the artillery. On 21 October 1917 at Chateau Wood, east of Ypres, he was guiding his laden horse team through the Ypres battlefields when the team was struck by a shell. One horse was killed and another two were wounded. Under heavy fire, Gordon freed the remaining horses and led them to safety. He was awarded the Military Medal for his coolness and courage under fire. On 19 September 1918 he was severely wounded in the arm and leg. Gordon came from a distinguished family within the farming communities of Australia and had worked in his father's business, McKay's Store in Pyramid Hill, with Allan prior to his enlistment. His uncle, former local farmer Hugh V. McKay, became a leading industrialist. Hugh McKay was most famous for the invention and production of the Sunshine harvester. Throughout the war years the Sunshine Harvester Works was contracted to supply war materiel ranging from ammunition shells to horse stirrups. Gordon's leg was amputated in England and he returned to Australia in June 1919.[29]

TEN

... SORRY TO SAY THAT AL HAS BEEN INJURED.

FRANCE, MARCH

While planning for the Spring Offensive continued throughout March, Allied troops began their advance to the Hindenburg Line and villages which had remained under enemy control for months, if not years, were systematically captured. Early in March, the 1st Division was withdrawn to the region around the town of Albert where George began training in the techniques of open warfare which now characterised the division's front-line experience.

To the north, where Charlie remained in hospital, the 3rd Division was relieved from the front line and marched to Moringhem, west of St Omer, where training was hampered by heavy snow and rain. On 19 March Charlie rejoined his unit. Opportunities for the brothers to spend time together in the days leading up to his return were instead devoted to sourcing food from the French villagers. On 27 March Allan was promoted lance corporal and was given charge of his Lewis gun team.

Percy wrote to his parents:

Somewhere In France
1/3/17
Dear Mum & Dad

… Just a few lines to let you know we are as well as it leaves us at present. We are out of the trenches now I do not know for how long, there was not many killed last time we were in … I had a letter from Albert yesterday he was still in England he saw Geordie when he was on leave …

He added a note for Jim:

Smewhere in France
March 5
Dear Jim,

… You would not be sorry when the harvest is over, it would be a lot of work for you but you are expecting a good time with the new girl, my word Jim you are always changing, of course they say there is nothing like a change. Frank Dee got wounded the other night, I don't know whether it was serious or not. Well Charlie is in the hospital with a cold, he will soon be out. Allan and I on [are] together. I am in the trenches while writing this, we are having a quiet time this time …

Your loving
Brother
Percy

Charlie was progressing well, as he told his mother in his latest letter:

France
6th March 1917
Dear Mother,

… I got wet in the trenches and had a bit of a cold, the dugout that I had was very wet, so of course that did not improve matters, and I paraded sick and the doctor said that I had better go to the hospital, which is not a bad place either. Percy was with me when I left the trenches and I believe Allan joined him a few days after I left … Albert will be able to get with us as soon as he comes over. I suppose you will be done harvesting by now but the freight is so high which makes the price low in Australia. It is getting a lot warmer here now and will soon be springtime. I think the war will end this spring, or very soon, as our side seems to be giving them a 'go' now. Well dear mother I hope you are all well at home and not worrying over us, for we are alright, so I will say goodbye for this time with best wishes to all

I am your affectionate son
Charlie E

I do not know whether I told you that I saw Jack Price about 5 weeks ago, he was going to the mumps isolation camp.

George had much to tell Jim concerning his leave and visits to his relatives:

Somewhere in France

March 10 – 1917

Dear Jim

… I had a good look round London it was "Good o" I wish I could get back again, it was a bit stiff coming back but once I got back with the boys it was alright but am sorry to say one of my mates was killed while I was away he came from Australia the same time as me, he came from Gippsland, he had just come back from England on leave the night I left my unit. I met Gordon McKay in England he was on leave also, I was rather lucky getting leave as it has been stopped ever since I left to go and doubt whether it will start again. I left the trenches to go on leave and went in again when I arrived back, we advanced here and took 3 villages, Archie Bailey was wounded this is the second time, I don't know yet how Ewan got on, Amos was alright a few days before we came out because I met him while in there, I have been dash lucky, we are out having a spell now but don't know how long it lasts.[1] *I haven't met the others yet, they aint anywhere near us, they are in a much quieter part of the line. I received a parcel from Florrie a few days, tell her when you see her next, as I had wrote the day before receiving it, that I hadn't got it, it was in perfect order, I also received one from home just before I left to go on leave. Well the winter is not over yet some days it isn't too [bad] we had some snow yesterday but I don't think there will be much more. I think I told you about 3 months ago that I was a Lce / Corporal, now I am a Corporal and receive a Corporal's pay so you need not cable me any more money as I can draw 5/- a day if I like. Well Jim I will now close hoping all are well.*

I remain
Your Affectionate Bro
George

As George wrote to Jim, Charlie was also writing home from hospital. It is clear that the eldest brother at the front was anxious to have all five brothers reunited in the 38th Battalion. Charlie told his family that, once released from hospital, he would soon be back with Allan and Percy.

France
March 10th 1917
Dear Jim,

Just a few lines to say that I am getting on fine and will soon be leaving the hospital, my cold is just about alright … I have written a good few letters this last few days as we do not have much time in the trenches nor when we come out for a spell, I wrote to Geordie asking him if he would like to get with us as I think he would stand a good chance but I have not heard from him, but I told him not to come till he got his leave to England as he would miss it if he came to our Battalion … I saw an "Australian" here and see by it that the Government are giving 2/6 a bushel for the wheat on Jan 15 but last year's wheat seems to be out of the question now, I think we have got all we are going to get for that lot. I will answer your letters when I get back from the battalion which I am not very far away…

Two days later Charlie took the opportunity to write once more to his family, aware that his time in hospital was coming to an end.

March 12th 1917
Dear Mother, Father & Brother,

Just a few lines to say that I am getting on alright and will be leaving hospital in a day or so, Al and Percy are camped about a mile from here but I have not seen them, I met young Ken from Bear's Lagoon he said they were well I will be with them again in a few days, they are out for a rest, he thought for about 18 days. I hope to get a pile of letters when I go back as I told Percy to get my mail, we get a lot of Australian papers here in the hospital, also get the English papers nearly every day, so we can see how things are going. The French farmers are starting to work up their ground, they fallow their ground the same as we do and manure it very heavily with farmyard manure, they have their manure heaps right in front of their doors it is a common thing to see the manure pits in front of the houses, nearly every house sells beer and wine or coffee eggs and chips, I don't think they use much tea at all, I was in at one place back a bit from the firing line and had a plate of fried potatoes chips and 3 eggs and a cup of coffee they charged me 1/7. Fruit seems to be very scarce and what is here is very dear also vegetables are scarce. I don't think they go in for fruit and vegetables like we do in Australia. They say that it is grand here in the spring the grass grows a great height, the trees have no leaves on them now and look as they were dead. I saw a thrasher at work about a month ago thrashing a stack of wheat the whole concern was similar to what they have in Australia, it was worked by boys, old men, and women, and it was not very far away from the firing line. I have written a lot of letters this last few days I wrote to Geordie, it takes a good while to get an answer back from him. I can get word back from England quicker, I have written to all the relations in England this last few days …

Charlie reminded his family not to be concerned over the various rumours and tales from friends and family, particularly from their Aunt Etta who had earned herself quite a reputation within the family for exaggerating the truth:

… I am now out of the hospital and in a reinforcements camp for 3 days, and will then be with Allan and Percy, I saw them last night, they are camped about ½ mile from here Percy had my letters I got 24 altogether… I got the money alright from the bank they gave the letter to Percy, Geordie got his leave he got 10 days he went to Lark Hill and stopped a night with Albert and the next day with him also he then went to London and then to Leicester and saw some of the relations, I suppose he will tell you all about it when he writes. I would have liked to have seen him Albert says he looks real well, he is now a corporal, he met Gordon McKay while in London, he said he saw Amos a few days before he wrote also Tom Alford. Albert is still in Lark Hill, I will keep some of that money for him when he comes over I will divide the rest between Allan Percy and Geordie I do not want any myself as I have plenty and a lot to draw on my pay book. I was down with Allan and Percy tonight we went into a shop and had steak and eggs and coffee for tea, so that is not doing too bad, they are both well, I saw Les Townsend he is camped with them, Jim said he heard that the ship I came over on was chased by a submarine, well it was not, we saw nothing in the shape of enemy boats or subs, you do not want to take any notice of the tales you hear especially Auntie Etties, why I heard that when I was in the trenches last time that I was wounded then I heard Percy was; Allan heard

that he was on his way to Australia. They are only yarns, you do not want to believe any of those sort of things … Auntie Lee seemed a bit hurt because we did not go down to Devon, but I had no chance at all as I only got the one leave 4 days and two days of that went in travelling their place is a long way away from where I was, I could not possibly do the Leicester trip and there too, I thought Geordie would be able to go but he only got 10 days and I suppose half of that went in travelling, if I ever get back to England any time I will go and see them …

Charlie later wrote:

France
March 28th 1917
Dear Mother, Father & Jim,

… we are out of the trenches now and have been out for a good while and have shifted to another part of France but we will be going back again to somewhere we [censored]. We all sent a field card to you the other day, we were notified that there was a mail going to Australia and we had about five minutes to write in. I wrote to Pearl and sent you a card I got two letters from Geordie not long ago he is a corporal now Allan is a lance-corporal he was promoted today, I don't think Albert will be over here for a good while yet by what he says, Allan was away with Les Townsend and a lot more training but they are back with us again. I said before that I got the money alright from the bank, we can buy a decent feed here this last two nights we went to a place, and had coffee, three eggs and some bread and butter, they charged us one franc (10d) for it, that is cheap to most places in France, and in this same place there was a child about 3 years old smoking a pipe and another boy about 5 years old smoking a cigarette I thought it was the limit it is nothing to see children smoking over here and drinking beer, nearly every house over here sells beer eggs and coffee, we are camped in farm places sheds etc they are nice and warm the days are getting warmer but still we get snow at times this is a much nicer part than where we were I think there must be about six months of winter over here, the farmers are ploughing now there are a lot of women working in the fields about here, the war news seems to be very good lately I think there will be a big smash this spring. I suppose you will be busy with the crop now men will be scarce over there

now, is there any more about Mologa "declared war" I see Hughie Martin
and Bill Street Peter Owens and all those from up about Pyramid every day.
Well I will ring off for this time, I think Al and Percy will be writing also,
I hope you are all well as we are so I will say goodbye

I am your affect son & brother
C.E.

To the south, as the snows thawed and the rain fell, the thought of the
coming spring brought a touch of optimism for George, who freely
admitted that he had now 'had my share of it' and hoped to be back
in Australia for Christmas. As he wrote he queried the message he
had received from Albert regarding the men from the neighbouring
communities who were now casualties, asking his mother if there was
any truth in what he had been told. Such was the state of communication
on the front; family members and friends serving in different battalions
often relied on letters from Australia or newspaper reports to discover
that they had lost a brother or a mate.

France
March 29 1917
Dear Mother

… I think the cold weather will soon be over, this month is nearly out the
time is flying, the clocks have been put back an hour it is supposed to be
spring now. We are doing well on this front now, Fritz is being pushed back
if the weather had been suitable he would have got a much rougher time.
I am beginning to think we might be back in Australia for Xmas, well I
hope so I have had my share of it. I had my photo taken in London while
on leave and they have just arrived and am enclosing one in this letter it is
a good one of me. I haven't met the others yet they are a long way from here
we are still on the same part of the line as I told you in my letter that I wrote
from England. I sent a couple of brooches home from London I hope you
got them, one you will notice was made over here by the name on it. I was
fighting round there last year. Both Amos and Ewin are well, Albert was
saying in his letter that Bob Campbell is killed, is that true, he also said that
Frank Dee was wounded and Tracey killed, they are with Allan. I haven't

had a letter from Australia for about a fortnight the mails don't seem to be coming so well now, well I will now close hoping all are in the best of health.

I remain
Your Loving Son
George

I am enclosing a photo of the gun I use. Put it away for me. I think I told you some time ago I was a Lance Corporal well now I am a corporal.

To the north, Allan, Percy and Charlie remained billeted in the safety of Moringhem. The bitter winter conditions continued to hinder their training and brought illness and discomfort to the troops, although Allan again reassured his mother that he had never felt better.

France
31-3-17
My Dear Mum & dad

… Well mum we are out of the trenches at present but are going back in a day or so, then there will be something doing. Well mum we have had a lot of rain this last few days and we have been out in it all. I can not tell you the exact stop where we are but we had 40 mile march here. Full packs up too and the country very hilly too but we got through it all right. It took us 3 days to do it. I had a letter from Geordie the other day. He is getting on well too. He is a Corporal now. I also had a letter from Albert. He is doing well and having a good time. I am in charge of a Lewis Gun team now and am a Lance Corporal. Charlie and Percy are in my team. So everything is good oh. Well dear mum everything is looking better now. The war and France. Things are beginning to look green now and I really think that the war will end soon. We are all well. I myself never felt better in my life. I have never had a cold or a day's sickness of any sort. The winter will soon be over. Mum dear you have no idea what the winter was like. It was a fair terror. Charlie & Percy was lucky missing the worst of it.

I remain
Your Loving Son
Allan

We are getting a mail to night Hurrah.

ENGLAND, MARCH

As the new month began, Albert was enjoying his period in hospital recovering from mumps, although the English food shortages were causing him some concern. He was discharged from hospital on 7 April and promptly returned to the training fields of Salisbury Plain where he welcomed the letters from home and where news of his move to France was anxiously anticipated.

Salisbury Plain
Park House Hospital
Sunday, March 4ᵗʰ 17
My Dear Mother & Father,

… I have been out here for a fortnight now, and have still a weeks holiday. It is a great change out here, but the food is not quite as good as at the camp, still its good enough when your doing nothing. They have cut us down to a slice and ½ of bread a meal now for breakfast and tea, and for dinner 1 slice and a small one at that. Food seems to be very scarce over here, but I suppose you have read about it in the papers. Well Mum, it is a very pretty place out here, and must look lovely in summer, there are a lot of villages round about and we generally pass through one or two when we have route marches, and the kids run out yelling. Left, Right, Left, Right. We get a great welcome in the villages. We get Red + [Cross] stuff here every second day. Last day I got a pipe, tobacco, cigarettes, tooth powder and brush. We get a pair of socks before we leave, also a toilet bag. The weather is much warmer here now, so different to when we first came here. It is grand to have the sunshine …

Park House Hospital
Sunday March 4ᵗʰ
Dear Jim,

… My mate and 7 others out of my hut are out here with the mumps. The mumps only stopped on us about 5 days. Missed a pay-day by being out here, and might miss another yet, but it doesn't trouble me, as I've got enough to keep me going. I told you in my other letter that I gave Geordie £4. he needed it more than I did. Well Jim, I suppose now the harvest is over

you are busy with the garden. Think of all the tomatoes I am missing, not to mention water melons and other things. I often fancy tomatoes here. You could get them some time back at 7d a lb. I believe some of our chaps are going soon in the next draft, but don't know how we will get on, I think we will be put back 3 weeks in the drill. Well Jim I suppose you have read all about the <u>tucker scheme here.</u> They have cut down on our rations a lot. We get a slice and ½ of bread a meal now, and not a big slice at that. People in Australia don't realise how scarce food is over here. It is on account of the huns sinking all the boats …

Lark Hill Camp
Sat March 10th 17
My Dear Mother & Father,

… I had a good holiday at the hospital, and didn't like leaving except to get the letters. We had a heavy fall of snow yesterday, but I'm glad to say, its melting fast. They gave us an extra blanket, we have six now, so have a decent bed at night. It is not so cold here now, but when the snow melts it is as muddy as _____. I got a lot of red Cross stuff at the hospital, and before I came away was given a pair of socks, which happened to come from the Dingee Red cross, but did not have the name of the sender in it. When I got back here there was a parcel from Auntie. It was a box of mince pies, cakes and chocolate and was just the thing. I thought Ida would have written to say they sent it, but there was no letter. I had a great feed, I can tell you. When I came back, I had to go to the doctor, so I told him, I was terrible crook at the hospital, so he gave me two days no duty. I start drill on Monday. I never felt better in my life, but I had the chance of a few days off, so I took it. A fellow wants plenty of cheek at this game. One of the chaps in my hut got a Bendigonian yesterday, and I saw where Bob Campbell was killed, also young Hannasky from Pinegrove. I met him at Rankin's Barn … None of our coy have gone to France yet and I don't think any will be going till April. We are issued with waterproof capes now. They are very warm and look very flash. That Lt. Collins I told you about is supposed to go to France soon. He always gets sick when a draft goes, he should have gone 3 weeks ago …

I am, your loving son
Albert

A typical soldier's postcard sent home by Albert.

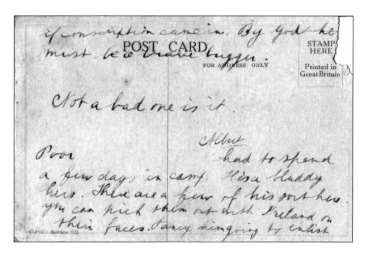

Albert made his feelings very clear about his neighbours who had not enlisted. The name has been censored.

The soldiers always derived great pleasure from the parcels they received from friends and family. Albert mentioned that he was surprised to discover he had been provided with socks by the Red Cross, knitted in the town of Dingee not far from Mologa. The coincidence was worth mentioning in his letter home.

Albert also mentions Mologa Central schoolteacher Bob Campbell, from the 57th Battalion, who was killed on 23 November. Only two weeks before, he had returned to action after four months recuperating from a head wound.[2] Fred Hannasky, also from the 57th Battalion, was a 21-year-old farmer from Pine Grove who had enlisted in January 1916. He was killed on 1 December 1916.[3] Ted Tracey was a member of the 38th Battalion.[4] He had enlisted from Janiember East (Bears Lagoon) and sailed on the *Runic* with Percy and Allan. He was listed as killed in action on 27 February 1917, the date of the Houplines raid after which Allan had written to his mother, '… how on earth we came out of it alive I don't know.'

The following day Albert replied to his father to explain why he had yet to rejoin his brothers. Sarah and Charles were anxious to ensure that their youngest son would soon be in the care of his older siblings. Albert was just keen to see the sights of England, many of which he had read about at school.

Lark Hill Camp
Sunday March 11th 1917
Dear Dad,

… I was glad to hear the harvest turned out so well and that you are getting a decent price for it. I think the farmers are lucky to get 2/6 as they are not importing much wheat from Australia on account of the U boats … I was glad to hear you got my cable. You told me to be sure and get in with Charlie, well, I told you when I wrote before that he had gone to France a week before I got here, so there was no chance of getting with him as we have to do 12 weeks training here, but I suppose I am better off here, and Mum says in every letter not to be in a hurry to go to France, so I think you will be pleased to hear that I am not with him. Anyway I will have no trouble in getting with them when I go to France, Charlie is in the same Coy. as Al and Percy. 8 chaps out of my hut got the mumps and we are in 6th week of training, while the rest are in the 9th week, so according to that we should do another 6 weeks at least. Well Dad it is not so cold here now, it is a bit on the rainy side, but I think it will be fine again soon. Anyway I don't notice the cold at all now, but about 6 weeks ago it was a fair devil I never want to see anything like it again. Tell Streets that Harry is still here and looking tip

top on it. I went into Amesbury this afternoon, and went to have a look at the Church of England church. It is a terrible age, but I forget when it was built. I will tell you next time I write. The key of the door is over 9 inches long and weighs ¾ lb and you could put a hen's egg through the key hole. All the tombstones are crumbling away with age, and the church has started to crumble in places. I will send you a photo of it when I get the chance to get some. The Sunday that I was going to see the Village Blacksmith's shop, we were isolated. It is in a village called Fighldean, and is about 4 miles from here. I never thought that when I was going to school, that I would ever see Stonehenge or the Village Blacksmith's shop. We have a bonza lot of fellows in my hut, 4 of them are from Bendigo. One of my special mates is from Bendigo. His name is Tom Dickinson, and he has an Uncle living between Mincha and Macorna. Another one is Gordon Swainston, he comes from Kyneton, and is a slight relation to Gamble's. I see the Bendigonian nearly every week. Well Dad, I have no more news so I will close hoping you are all well, as it leaves me at present,

I am
Your loving son
Albert

They won't tell us now when the mail leaves, I wonder what next.

March 14th
Dear Jim,

… Well Jim, General Sir Newton Moore inspected us yesterday.[5] *We marched 3 miles in mud up to our boot tops to a big review ground. It was a great sight to see the crowd of soldiers. The parade ground was a big paddock with two clumps of pine trees at the back, and as the ground was sloped, it looked very good. There was a hell of a crowd of soldiers, all from Lark Hill Camp. The Duke of Connaught is supposed to come over to see us on Friday, but as the duchess is very ill, I don't think he will come. Rumour has it that the King is coming next week. They say that the Duke will go back and tell the King that we're worth seeing. Anyway, I hope he does … The Allies seem to be doing well now. Things are getting a bit serious in the tucker line here. We cant get potatoes now, as there is a*

scarcity in England, but we don't do too bad all the same. You remember me telling you about one of our corporals who tried to desert and got caught. He got two years clink in the Isle of Wight …

Lark Hill Camp
Sunday March 25th 1917
My dear Mother, Father & Jim,

… The weather is much warmer here now, still we get plenty of snow. 50 of our coy are picked for the next draft. They are going tomorrow night I think. Harry Street is going, and all the other chaps that were in my hut, but the rest of us that had the mumps are left behind. We will have to do 3 weeks more training before we can leave here. Those that are going have only done 11 weeks drill. There is another draft going next week, but I don't think I will be in it. I forgot to tell you in my last letter that I got the £4 you sent me. Thanks very much for sending it. I sent a cable to you last night saying I had received the money and was well. It only cost 4/6 so I thought it as well to send one. I am sending a paper, it has a lot in it about the Russian Revolution. Things are getting pretty serious here in the food line. We get good tucker, but some days it is very scarce, anyway we get eggs and bacon every Sunday morning, besides the porridge. Potatoes are very scarce here and some days we have ½ one each. Every night at 8.30 we get a dixie of soup for each hut, and it is just the thing. Lt. Collins came round at 2.30 this morning, and roused all the coy out they had to get dressed and go out on parade, for 10 minutes. I didn't go out as I came off guard yesterday, and didn't have any sleep the night before. He came in the hut and poked each fellow in the ribs with his walking stick, and one fellow said, "Whats the bluddy time anyway". Collins is supposed to go to France soon, he has calmed down a lot lately …

Tell Streets that Harry is leaving here soon about the 20th March

… I had just finished this letter this morning, when 50 of us were called out and ordered to get our full marching order on (as if we were going to France) and were told to be ready in half an hour. So we went like the devil, and got all our things ready to go. After dinner, we were given field dressing, rifle & bayonet, iodine and had to fill our water bottles, and we thought

we were off. Anyway they gave us a bit of a lecture, and marched us in and found they had about 25 over strength, so all of us under the 9th week were told to stop behind. The rest are now waiting to be called out again at any time. We don't know what the game is, but I'm sure they are not going out of England. I think, myself that they are forming a battalion to guard the south coast of England, and so relieve an Aust. Batt that is there now. I may be called out again, but I don't think so. We don't know when they're leaving, and things were very excited this morning, as the men were called out so sudden, and all the officers had their revolvers in their belts. Harry Street was taken out of the draft and put in with this lot that was called out today. It was the biggest hurry up that I ever saw. It generally takes a week to fix a draft up and we took about ¾ of an hour. We were inspected this morning by a Brigadier-general. Well Mum I will say goodbye, I may be leaving here any day now

I am Your Loving Son
Albert

The anticipation of leaving for the front was building as the weeks of training in the English winter were drawing to a close. Albert's tension was palpable in the letters he wrote, as was the disappointment he felt when his mates departed before him. Albert sent home this photo postcard of his pals dated 26 March 1917. Seven months later, three of these men had been killed and another two wounded.

Lark Hill Camp
March 28th 1917
Dear Jim

… I have been on fatigue today and finished at 3 oclock, so thought I would write a few letters to pass the time. I told you in my last letter about us all being lined up. Well all those that were called up are not going anywhere. It was a mobilization order to see how quick they could get a mob of troops ready if they wanted them. But the other draft of our coy that were picked out last week, left here last night for France. Harry Street did not go as he was called out at the last moment. I hear they are picking out a draft again this week, so I may be in that. I got a letter

from Al last night, he had been in a scrap but was well when he wrote. There has not been any mail from Australia since I last wrote. The last I got was dated Jan 16ᵗʰ. Well Jim, how would you like to be limited to 6oz of potatoes a day, that's all we are allowed now, and I can tell you it's a fat lot too, we get plenty of haricot beans here but the meat is hard to find when there is beans on the plates. Some days we get plenty to eat, and other days get damn little. One slice of bread a meal. One thing the tucker is well cooked. There was great excitement here last night when the draft was leaving. Nearly all my old hut mates have gone, they are bonza chaps, and I would liked to have gone with them again in a few weeks ... How is Mologa and all the girls getting on. Remember me to Eva and any other of your favourites. Well Jim I am about beat for news, so will close hoping all are well as I am at present. I weigh 12 stone now, so am doing alright aint I, so goodbye, from your aff. brother

Albert
Have just heard that two boats with Australian mail on have been sunk.

Albert wrote: 'The one next to me [Albert is standing second from right] with the moustache is Pte Harnell on the right is Pte Dickinson and Pte Burt. The one in the front of me is Pte Swainston and the other Pte Duncan.'

THEATRES OF WAR, APRIL

News of the growing discontent in Russia had reached the far corners of the globe. Food shortages and the lack of basic supplies had led to desertion and mutiny within the Russian forces. Tsar Nicholas II abdicated and a provisional government was installed. In an atmosphere of unrest and discontent, support for Lenin's Revolutionary Bolshevik

Party was increasing while the military forces had virtually disintegrated. The failure of Russian forces in the east would release German battalions for deployment to the Western Front.

On the oceans, Germany's strategy of the domination of sea passages by submarines had now resulted in the loss of some 200 vessels. The news on 6 April 1917 that the United States had declared war brought relief for the Allies, although it was not until 1918 that a substantial force of two million conscripts would arrive on the Western Front. Early April 1917, however, would see the launch of the Allied Spring Offensive under the command of French General Nivelle.

BULLECOURT, APRIL

In France, the Australian divisions had continued to push forward towards the Hindenburg Line, clearing the sparsely occupied villages in their path. They were now positioned at the villages of Noreuil and Lagnicourt. The Spring Offensive was set to commence. On 9 April British and Canadian forces attacked to the north at Arras where tunnels and chambers had been dug by British and New Zealand tunnellers to allow the troops to approach the front unseen. The Allies suffered 150,000 casualties in their advance and held their newly won positions tenuously. The 4th and 12th brigades of the 4th Australian Division were to play a major role in maintaining pressure to the south. Their task was to attack the Hindenburg Line east of Bullecourt, a village embedded in the fortified German line. They soon discovered that the belts of German wire through which the Australians were to make their approach had not been cut by earlier artillery bombardments. The attack was briefly postponed until a tank officer suggested to the commander, General Gough, that his 12 tanks be used to spearhead the Australian approach, the tanks breaking through the defences and signalling once the way was clear for the advance. The Australians were sceptical. Victoria Cross recipient Captain Albert Jacka, now an intelligence officer in the 14th Battalion, was sent out on patrol to assess the enemy positions. The Australian brigades were to attack towards a re-entrant, a hollow in the German line exposed to enemy fire from three sides. The line was heavily fortified. Jacka returned and argued vehemently against the action. Despite additional objections from Australian commanders Birdwood and Brudenell White, General Gough ordered that the attack proceed the following day.[6]

A blizzard descended on the front. The lumbering tanks, with their poor visibility and manoeuvrability, failed to reach the line in time for zero hour. As dawn was about to break the weary Australians, having lain in the driving snow through the pre-dawn hours, were ordered to withdraw. To their left, British forces entrusted with a frontal attack on the village had not been informed of the withdrawal. They attacked as planned and came under heavy artillery fire. The retreating Australians of the 48th Battalion were caught in the bombardment, suffering 21 casualties. Later that day, with the tanks now in position at the rear, Gough ordered that the attack proceed the following day in accordance with the original plan. There was one change: the infantry would not wait for a signal from the tanks. The troops were ordered to follow 15 minutes after the tanks moved forward. It was to prove a fateful decision.

At 3.00 am the next morning the men were sent out to lie on the snow and await the arrival of the tanks. Young Jack Price of Mologa went forward with the 46th Battalion and lay shivering as he anxiously counted the seconds to zero hour.

Only four of the 12 tanks arrived, but the attack proceeded regardless. The infantry reached the wire before the failing tanks and without artillery support. The Australians were forced to break through the barbed-wire fortifications to capture two lines of trenches. Machine-gun fire from three sides cut through the gallant men of the 4th Division as they desperately tried to cross the wire, hacking at it with their bayonets, clambering across the top and becoming hopelessly entangled. Eventually they succeeded, breaching that section of the Hindenburg Line without support, the survivors assaulting the German trenches. This was an unlikely feat given the formidable defences they confronted. Under fire from all directions, they held their position while sending repeated messages calling for more supplies and artillery support. Neither came. Observers reported that the tanks had advanced through Bullecourt and the Allied artillery refused to fire on the village for fear of striking its own forces. The reports were incorrect; the tanks lay burning on the battlefield.

Running out of bombs and ammunition and suffering severe losses, the Australians were driven back, trying desperately to bring in their wounded as they retreated. Most had to be left. The 48th Battalion was now hit by Allied artillery fire. The reality of the situation had been verified by front-line reports and the artillery, following orders, was firing on the retreating men of the 48th. It was a complete debacle.

At 2.00 pm the bombardment ceased as German medical orderlies made their way onto the battlefield to assist the wounded, including the Australians who lay outside the defensive wire. Stretcher-bearers collected as many men as they could before the informal truce ended at 6.00 pm. Of the 3000 men of the 4th Brigade who had been caught in the maelstrom of enemy and friendly fire, 2339 were listed as casualties. The 12th Brigade lost 950 soldiers. Over 1000 men had been captured. Some 80% of the attacking force had been lost.[7] The First Battle of Bullecourt had ended in disaster.

Among those killed in the battle had been Albert's good friend Jack Price, who died on 11 April 1917.[8] His grieving parents later received a letter which appeared in the *Pyramid Hill Advertiser* on 28 September 1917.[9]

> … I feel it my duty to let you know how your son Jack lost his life. He had been wounded in the thigh and myself in the face and left fingers, on April 11th, at Bullecourt, when we both met, going back to the dressing station. I was hit a second time in the left arm, and indeed the chances are that I would have bled to death if it hadn't been for Jack bandaging my arm for me. We both went further back and a whiz bang (shrapnel) landed alongside of me. I lay there for an hour and a half and as no help was in sight I decided to get up. I went to Jack to tell him I was going, but he had died. I can assure you he suffered very little pain. I could not see where he had been hit. It must have been in a vital part. I,

myself, did not know that it has done any damage to me, except for being a bit shaky, until I arrived at the field ambulance, where two pieces of shrapnel were removed from behind my right knee, two from my left thigh, and one from my left shoulder. Jack went over in the same boat as I, in 3rd reinforcements to 46th Battalion. He went to C company and I to B. He died a brave soldier and I am sure a good son.

I am Yours faithfully
No. 1985 (Pte.) A.L. Rodger, B. Coy, 46th Battalion, A.I.F.
Home Address – Main Street, Bunyip, Vic
P.S. I arrived home last Tuesday.

Jack Price had just turned 19 when he was killed at Bullecourt.

It would be weeks before the Marlows discovered that their mate had been killed.

George was positioned to the south of Bullecourt where four battalions of the 1st Division, some 4000 soldiers, were spread along an 11-kilometre line in front of the nearby village of Lagnicourt. On 15 April a massive German force of 23 battalions attacked the 1st Division line. The Australians were driven from their advanced outposts, five guns were destroyed and the village of Lagnicourt captured, albeit only briefly. Within hours an Australian counter-attack had forced the enemy from their positions and the German troops retreated to the safety of the Hindenburg Line. While significantly outnumbered, the Australians had again achieved a singular victory. Courage, tenacity and the effective placement of skilled and deadly Lewis gun crews had seen the Australians prevail. The 1st Division lost 1010 men, 300 of whom were now prisoners. Germany had lost 2313, of whom 360 had been captured. [10]

George wrote to his family at home just days prior to the Lagnicourt counter-attack and also briefly described his experience in a letter the following week. Having now served over 12 months on the Western Front, George rejected the suggestion that he should attempt to transfer to the 38th Battalion. Not only would he lose his promotion, he is adamant that families serving together increased the risk of multiple casualties.

He later jotted in his notebook:

April & May 1917
Heavy Fighting
Bullecourt
Lagnicourt

France
April 12 1917
Dear Jim

… I had a couple of letters from Charlie yesterday, they are all well. Nearly all the chaps in Albert's reinforcements have been sent over here and one told Al that they wouldn't let Albert come away as he is too young, so he is lucky, I gave him some advice when I was over there, he said in his letters a few days ago that Harry Street was sent over here and said that Harry worries over going over here. Both Amos and Ewin were well when I last saw them. Harry Burrows, George Leed and Dave Kentish from Calival are in the same Battalion as Ewin. You remember the Jenners that used to play football with Macorna well there are two of them in the same unit as me now, Jim and Jack. I don't know whether you remember them they have

got fat, they used to be in the 7 Battalion. Charlie wrote to me asking if I would like to come in with them but I would rather stop where I am now it isn't a wise thing for all of us to be together, and if I joined them I would lose the stripes. Well Jim we weren't allowed to say anything in our letters about conscription, we certainly want the men. We have had a lot of snow this last few days also rain and has been very cold, we never had any snow this time last year. Well the fighting along here has been very successful lately, Fritz is getting a lively time of it … We are now in broken down houses that the Germans left in ruins as he went back, he even cut down the fruit trees and burnt chaff cutting and threshing machines that the French people left behind at the beginning of the war, they have been up to all sorts of tricks. Well I will now close hoping all are well as I am at present.

I remain
Your Affectionate Bro
George

Infantry soldiers were sceptical of the value of tanks on the battlefield and openly derided them. A newspaper article with the attention-grabbing header 'Those Wonderful Tanks' was carefully clipped and, despite its size, has survived the years among the collection of letters. It appeared in *The Argus* on 8 September 1917:

The accomplishments of the tanks are facetiously described by a private of the Bedforshire Regiment in a letter to his fiancée:-

"They can do up prisoners in bundles in straw binders, and, in addition, have an adaptation of a printing machine, which enable them to catch the Huns, fold, count, and deliver them in quires, every thirteenth man being thrown out a little further than the others.

"The tanks can truss refractory prisoners like fowls prepared for cooking, while their equipment renders it possible for them to charge into a crowd of Huns, and by shooting out spokes like porcupine quills carry out an opponent on each. Though 'stuck up', the prisoners are, needless to say, by no means proud of their position.

'They can chew up barbed wire, and turn it into munitions. As they run they slash their tails, and clear away trees, houses, howitzers, and anything else in the vicinity. They turn over on their backs, and catch live shells in their caterpillar feet, and they can easily be adapted as submarines; in fact, most of them crossed the channel in this guise.

"they loop the loop, travel forwards, sideways, and backwards, not only with equal speed, but at the same time. They spin round like a top, only far more quickly dig themselves in, bury themselves, scoop out a tunnel, and come out again 10 miles away in half an hour."

While at this point of the war the tank was much maligned, improvements to its design and employment over the coming months would see this monster of the industrial age become a valuable weapon of war.

Despite earlier thoughts of bringing the family together, both Allan and George now understood the nature of warfare on the Western Front. Sons, friends and neighbours were often together in the same battalion, frequently the same company, as was to be the case with Allan, Charlie, Percy and Albert — together in battle, together in support. One shell could destroy them all. George and Allan were steadfast in their decision that George should remain with the 1st Division.

France
3.4.17
Dear Jim

… Every letter I get you all say I must be sick and why don't I tell you so. Well I have never had a days sickness since being over here. I never felt better in my life. Every letter I get from anybody they say I hope you are quite well again after your mumps and I have never had mumps in my life. Percy was isolated for about 2 months but he never had them. If a man gets mumps and he sleeps next to you well then you are isolated for mumps because they are contagious. If any friends do not know what isolation is please explain to them. Auntie Florrie says in her letter to Percy that she hopes we are better again and we were never sick. There is no need for any body to worry over me. I am always right. Yes Jim I suppose you are glad the harvest is over. We are going back to the trenches in a few days.

Geordie is fighting a long way away from us so we cant see him. Mum says she would like us all to be together. Yes that is very nice in one way but Jim there is another way to look at it. It is the biggest mistake out because if a shell came it gets the lot of you. I used to think the same as mum but now I don't … I remain

Your loving brother
Allan

George also wrote to the family at home:

France
April 26/1917
Dear Mother, Father & Bro,

… We are in the line again, we get plenty of it too, Al's division seems to be having a good spell out so they say in their letters, I cant make it out, we have been fighting so long and never once have had a spell like them, and have held the worst part of the line of the whole British front through the winter in the bargain, anyway I feel just as fit as ever and have only been away from my unit once and that was on leave. Well where we are now is well into country what the enemy held a little while back they [Germans] have suffered heavy losses here, they attacked one morning with massed troops and were driven back with 1200 dead left behind, this was only a matter of a few hours fighting, I don't see how it can last much longer. I saw Ewin a couple of days ago he was quite well also young Charlie Wales he is back in the battalion again. Dave Fyffe is in England swinging it he hasn't heard a shot fired yet. Allan said in one of his letters that Frank Dee is wounded and that he saw Dave Glass's grave. I haven't seen Amos for a good while the last time I inquired for him he had gone away to some school and I don't know if he is back yet. This letter I am sending in a green envelope it doesn't be censored here but might be at the base, let me know if you have ever got any letters with green envelopes. I wouldn't mind helping to eat some of those tomatoes and water melons, such a lot of the men here break out in scabies it is for the want of fruit and vegetables, I havent had them yet, Jim said in his letter that he hoped I went to see Auntie Lee well I never had time and they live a long way from England [London] it took a good deal of my time going to see Albert

and Paynes. The <u>chats</u> [lice] as we call them are just as bad as ever I have only been free of them once and that was when I was in England. Well I must now close with love from

George

The green envelopes mentioned by George were issued by the army and were printed with a statement that restricted their contents:

> Correspondence in this envelope need not be censored regimentally. The contents are liable to examination at the Base. The following Certificate must be signed by the writer:

> I certify on my honour that the contents of this envelope refer to nothing but private and family matters.

All letters sent from the front were first read by an officer of the unit and censored if any of the contents were believed likely to betray the unit's location or contained other sensitive information. Sending a letter in an official green envelope and signing the declaration ensured that personal information would not be read by other members of the unit. Green envelopes were randomly opened at the base to ensure that soldiers were complying; there were penalties for those who did not and consequences varied according to the significance of the breach. Green envelopes were highly valued. The brothers often sent their letters home together in one very bulky green envelope.

The 38th Battalion had marched from its rest camp at Moringhem on 5 April in a tedious journey plagued by snow drifts, wind and driving sleet. Allan, in charge of a Lewis gun team, suffered in the harsh conditions. The hand carts on which the guns and ammunition were transported frequently stuck fast in the heavy snow. A 60-kilometre journey over two days laden with heavy packs and little rest left the Victorian boys exhausted, their feet blistered and bleeding as they reached Armentieres.[11]

France
7-4-17
My Dear Mum & Dad

… We have just come back from over a 40 mile march which took us 2 days. We all feel well on it too but a terrible lot of the boys are down to it with their feet. I had another letter from Albert yesterday. He is well and enjoying himself. Geordie too is splendid … it is a lovely day today and we are having a rest. We are going back to the trenches in a few days. I always have to go to the trenches a day before the rest of my team as I have to take up a position. I have been promoted to a Lance Corporal and am in charge of a Lewis Gun section. Charlie & Percy are in my section. Some of the boys have just come from the cemetery and they told me that Dave Glass's grave is there. I used to see Dave a good deal …

Like Allan, Charlie wrote to tell his family of the death of Dave Glass:

Somewhere in France
7 April 1917
Dear Mother, Father & Jim,

… I am in the Lewis gun section with Al and Percy my address will be 2123 Pte C.E.M. "D" Company machine Gun Section "_" Battalion A.I.F Abroad the reinforcements mail takes longer to get to us than the old battalion. Al and Percy got a lot of letters, you seem to think that Al has been sick, well he has had splendid health since he has been over here and he has not had a day's sickness in France, you must remember that we cannot always write and then the letters go astray. He wrote to Auntie Ettie the same time as you and she got her letter but yours has unfortunately been mislaid if he had been sick he or Percy would have told you. Percy did not get to the trenches with him as he was isolated, one of his mates got the mumps and as he slept next to him he was isolated so that was why he did not go in with Al. Percy and I went into the trenches for our first time together and Al did not go in that time but was away on special training for a raid which was successful and all the local boys got on alright. So Dave Glass [was] killed some of the boys came across a grave with Sergeant D. Glass and with the battalions number and he is in our division so we reckon it was him, it is hard luck for his wife, I got the Pyramid paper that Jim sent also got a Bendigonian that was sent to Albert but it was an old one, we are still out of the trenches and got a day off today, tomorrow is Easter Sunday and I hope you have got duck for dinner as we will be having "something" like that here.

Dave Glass was 32 years of age with three small children when he enlisted in the 41st Battalion in November 1915. By the time of his death he had risen to the rank of sergeant.[12] Dave had served in the Boer War in both an intelligence role and in the Natal Mounted Police. When he returned from South Africa he worked as a camel driver in Western Australia during the construction of the rabbit-proof fence. He married a local Mologa girl, Elizabeth Jones, sister of Richard and aunt of Eva. Dave and his young family had moved to Home Hill in Queensland where they owned a sugar plantation. Elizabeth occasionally wrote to Sarah Marlow during the long years of war, including the following undated letter:

Dear Mrs Marlow

No doubt you will wonder who this stranger is writing to you. I often think of you & all the anxiety you must have with your five boys at the front. You have truly reared a fighting family I do hope they will all return safely to you, but it seems a lot to hope now. I had a letter from Dave dated 22nd August he was then in England & very anxious to get to the firing line it seems no time since he was a little fellow going to school. I have a little boy now he is just 2 years & two little girls the eldest girl is going to school & promises to be rather clever I will not write too much & try again wishing you & your soldier sons all the good things you deserve I am one who too is anxious

Elizabeth Glass (nee Jones)
Riverdale
Home Hill
Via Townsville
Nth Queensland

Dave died of wounds on 3 March 1917 and was buried close to Armentieres. His widow and their children later returned to Mologa.

Charlie was enjoying a few days' rest as he wrote home:

April 8th 1917
Easter Sunday
Somewhere in France
Dear Mother Father & Jim,

...we are still out of the trenches and had a day off yesterday and today, I got a lot of news in Joe Pickle's letter his Mrs read it and pulled it to pieces she said it was a real old man's letter all about the weather and crops and nothing about the housewife it was real good. We had C of E church parade this morning there was a big crowd there, the boys are quite satisfied that that is D. Glass that has been killed. Tom Roberts is back again with the battalion we get plenty of Australians papers over here there is a great pile of them on the bench today. Pearl said she sent the Bendigo paper but I did not get it, it would go somewhere else, it is no good sending papers as they seldom reach their destination. I got a letter from [Uncle] Arthur saying that he reckoned to get 5/5 a bushel clear on his wheat I wish they would make that last years wheat the same, Arthur has had a fair crop by the number of bags he got. I have not got any letters from [Uncle] George or the Mrs for a good while. I was sorry to hear that Grandfather was not well but hope he is better by now ...

The letters Sarah sent to her sons clearly expressed her concern that the boys were not being truthful over such issues as the state of their health and were not writing regularly. Percy seems particularly frustrated ... they were consistently writing home and were not responsible for the failure of their letters to arrive, or the fact that their letters were occasionally brief when time was scarce. The missing correspondence was probably at the bottom of the sea, a casualty of the German submarine attacks that plagued the English coastline.

France
9 April
Dear Jim,

... Mum seems to think I am keeping some things quiet well I would tell you, if anything was the matter, I think I used [to] always mention Allan's name. Of course when I was isolated for the mumps, I could not mention Allan, because he was not with us. That would be the time we came to France, when you did not get any letters for, I know we did not have time to write for some time, I know I wrote a few lines and Mum was not satisfied with them, she seems to think it is an easy matter to write long letters, but it is not over here. Well Jim you must have been sick of the harvest, being on

your own, it would be a pleasure to get it over. Geordie has got two stripes now, so he will be all right now. Allan has got one stripe now, my word he does go crook if you call him Corporal. We have had a lot of snow lately, I am sick of the look of it. Charlie is all right again. We had a letter from Albert, he expects to come over soon. Well Jim I have no more news so I will have to close.

From your loving brother
Percy

Charlie also wrote to explain the absence of letters:

April 11th 1917
Just got 2 more letters from Pearl
Dear Jim,

… Albert is still in Lark Hill I got a letter from him this week. Harry Street has joined the battalion but Albert did [not] *come with him as he has not done the same amount of training … we are still out of the trenches it is a good while since I have been in on account of being in the hospital, I was sorry that you did not get any letters from Al & Percy of late but everybody has been in the same fix, don't think that because you have not got any letters that we have not written … When Albert comes over he and I will be together, and A and P will work together, we will be in the same company but different platoons, the officer spoke to me about fixing him up …*

On 15 April Percy and Charlie enjoyed their last night in the relative comfort of billets before returning to the trenches at Houplines on the border of France and Belgium. Allan, his second-in-command, and a senior officer, traversed the maze of trenches under cover of darkness. Artillery exchanges frequently bombarded the sector and, as the three men picked their way along the trenches, the roar of shells thundered around them. Now an experienced soldier, Allan knew when to take cover, but as the men moved forward through the muddy, twisting maze, the breastworks of sandbags that formed the parapet suddenly exploded, duckboards were thrown into the air and clods of earth rained down on the men. Allan was alive, but buried under the debris.

As his officer desperately dug beneath the soil, Allan fought hard to breathe against the crushing weight as he faced the terrifying realisation that his life hung in the balance. Moments later he was pulled from his tomb; he had cheated death, but was not unscathed.

With the casual air typical of Allan he refused to seek medical treatment. He was overruled. Allan was admitted to hospital with suspected internal injuries and would remain for a fortnight. As his body recovered, the notification that Allan had been wounded was received at Mologa from Base Records Office, Victoria Barracks, Melbourne, dated 3 May 1917. The letter advised that Allan had been wounded but provided no detail of his condition. It would be another five weeks before the letters of reassurance arrived in Mologa.

Charlie wrote:

The Trenches
France
April 20th 1917
Dear Jim,

Just a few lines to let you know that I am quite well also Percy but am sorry to say that Al has been injured, we were not with him when it happened, the no 1 and no 2 go in the trenches the night before the others and it was on the first night that he was injured, he was walking along the trench when a shell blew the parapet in on him, and an officer got him out and he was taken away to the hospital, I have not seen him since and whether he is hurt much or not I do not know but one of the sergeants told me that he did not want to go out of the trenches but that he would be alright by the Morning. I will try and find out how he is, I am expecting a letter from him anyday perhaps he will have written to you, it happened last Sunday night, he could not have been in the trenches more than two hours when it happened I will let you know later if I hear anything of him. Albert is still in Lark Hill I heard from him last week he did not know when he would be coming over, I heard from Geordie some time ago he was quite well. It has been miserable weather over here lately they say that this has been the coldest winter for 35 years. Flo Wilson says she saw in the paper that this is the coldest April for 60 years, so you will see that it has been a bit tough …

Fear gripped the family at Mologa as they waited for news. Charlie's letters of reassurance took over a month to arrive, during which time little more would be known of Allan's condition. There is no evidence that Allan wrote of his brush with death or of his hospital stay during the fortnight. If he did write, his letters were either lost in transit or perhaps Sarah kept them elsewhere. It was unlike Allan not to reassure his mother that he was recovering.

Charlie continued to write in an attempt to keep his family informed and to reduce their anxiety.

The Trenches in France
April 25th 1917
Dear Mother,

Just a few lines to say that I received your welcome letter that you sent to Leicester, I suppose you will have heard that Allan had been injured, but I am pleased to say that he is getting alright again, I got a letter from him two days ago he said he thought he would be back with us in about a week or so, he was struck with a duck board and the shell blew the trench on him, there were two other chaps with him at the time, he was taken straight away to the hospital, which is not far from here. You have no need to be anxious about him as he will be quite well long before this reaches you. As you will see by the above that we are in the trenches but going out tomorrow, I am pleased to say that we have had some very nice weather here this last week and I hope it continues so. Jim spoke about A & P not getting their parcels well so far they have got every one that has been sent to them, it takes about a fortnight longer for a parcel to reach us than a letter … Tom Roberts was only slightly wounded and is back here again it did not take long for them to get the word about. Geordie was quite well the last time I heard from him… I got a letter from Ida and one from Flo this week they said they had got letters from Australia. Harry Marlow expects to get his discharge Auntie Wilson sent me his address. I will write to him if I can find time. Percy is here with me we are both quite well and hope you are the same at home I wrote to Jim a few days ago, I have written a lot of letters to you all lately I never seem to be done writing. Well I hope you will not be worrying about Allan or any of us in fact …

On the day Allan returned to his unit, Charlie penned a brief note to reassure his mother.

April 27th 1917
Dear Mother,

I wrote to you while I was in the trenches but was unable to post it I told you about Allan being hurt well he has just arrived back and does not look too bad so you will know now that he is alright, we are out of the trenches now I got a letter from Geordie this morning he is quite well he says Amos is quite well, Albert is still in Lark Hill but expects to be over here any day. Well I will say goodbye for now with best wishes

I am your affect son
Charlie

ELEVEN
I AM LEAVING FOR FRANCE TOMORROW …

ENGLAND, APRIL

Throughout April, as George battled at Lagnicourt, Percy and Charlie held the front line at Armentieres and Allan recovered from his wounds, Albert was to remain at Larkhill where his training continued. The youngest brother knew how to shoot, he could drive a bayonet into a hapless dummy, survive a simulated gas attack and he could throw live bombs. He considered himself ready and anxiously awaited the news of his inclusion in the draft for the Western Front.

Lark Hill Camp
Sunday April 7th 17
My Dear Mother & Father,

… I have just come back from Church Parade, it is a lovely day today, we have had some awful weather, over a foot of snow Monday night. We went for a route march next morning and coming home got wet up to the knees. We went down to Figledean and saw the Spreading Chestnut tree, and the Village Blacksmiths Shop. It is a very pretty place around the village, and the river runs through it. We were out on a Review again yesterday, took our dinner out and were inspected by Brig Gen Sir Newton Moore. There was 20,000 of us, it looked tip-top. All the "heads" were there, and all the people from the villages around. It is rumoured that the King is coming tomorrow. I hope he does as I'd like to have a quiz at him. Harry Street left in a draft a few nights ago, and poor devil was crying when he left here. I nearly got isolated again. The corporal in our hut got mumps, so we thought we would shift out of the hut, so about 2 hours after we shifted the hut got isolated. All of us that had the mumps expect to be warned for draft this week. I met Sgt Jameison here a few days ago, he used to be school teacher at Bald Rock.

He knows Al well. Jim would remember him, he used to play football with Pyramid. Jimmie O'Hare is still here, he has been in the "clink" a good part of the time. I got a letter from Charlie this week, he has not been too well on it. Allan is a Lance-Corporal now. If the King comes tomorrow we may get 4 days Kings leave. I'd like to get leave to go up and see Auntie at Water Farm [Devon]. There was a concert here last night, any amount of amusements here. I got 5 letters from Australia this mail one from Auntie Etta. It's a wonder I got it as she put the wrong number. The Composite Batt that I told you I was in, has been knocked in the head. We heard here that the Port Lincoln was sunk a few weeks after we left her. No damn wonder. Well, Mum, I am beat for news, so I will close hoping you are well as it leaves me at present.

I am
Your Loving Son
Albert

Lark Hill Camp
April 9th 1917
Dear Jim,

… I stayed home to do some washing, and write letters. I used to take my washing to the laundry. They wash them lovely there & very cheap at that, but they take a week or ten days to do them so I did not take mine there, as a fellow don't know where he will be in 10 days time. There is a draft going tomorrow week, and I may be warned to go on it. I have done my shooting, and today went through the gas-chamber, which is a small air-proof hut, and into which about 30 men go in at once, and they turn on the gas, which is almost harmless, but not smell-less. I forgot to say we put the gas-helmets on before we go in. We stop in there about 2 minutes, come out, and keep the helmet on for an hour, and double for 5 minutes. We have to be able to put the gas-helmet on in 20 seconds; when we get to France, we get a box respirator, besides the helmet. Well Jim, it was a buggar of a day today, the cold wind nearly cut my face away, it is burning like blazes yet. I think there will be more snow tonight, we get more snow now than when we first came

here, but it isn't half as cold, I suppose I am used to it, and don't notice it. We are not allowed to have fires in the huts now. I don't miss them much, except for making toast. I think we have to throw live bombs tomorrow, supposed to [throw] 3 live bombs before we leave here. Each bomb weighs 22 ounces, and you have to throw a dummy bomb 30 yards before they let you throw a live one …

The following week, Albert wrote home:

Lark Hill Camp
Sunday April 15th 1917
My Dear Mother, Father & Jim,

… I have not been warned for draft yet, so I think I will be here for another fortnight, at least. All the 4th/38 have gone except the war-babies, and the ones who have been in hospital. I have not heard from the boys since I wrote to you, last Sunday. There has been some awful weather this week, rain, hail & snow, but it is a grand day today. We went to Church parade this morning and they put us on fatigue work as soon as we got back from church. My mate & I were eating an orange each the other day, and we threw a bit of peel in the gutter. Collins the O.C. (I told you about him before) saw us and gave us 7 days C.B. That shows you what sort of a buggar he is. Another chap got 5 days C.B. for not having his chin-strap on his chin. He's a cold-footed buggar, if I see him in Australia I'll break every bone he's got. He crimes a fellow for a thing like that, and then asks you to (play the game). All the other officers call him "Lizzie". There was a bad accident near here this morning. An aeroplane came down from a hell of a height and fell in Durington village, just missing a house. He was badly hurt, and they said he was dying at dinner time. We have not been getting too much tucker lately, and last night there was a bit of a row in the mess-room. We got two slices of bread and dripping for tea. Food seems to be getting short all over England, and I think the food shortage will end the war, if it ever ends. The British are capturing a lot of villages now, and by today's paper they are closing on Lens and St Quentin. I am sending a paper by this mail you may see some interesting articles in it about peace …

Lark Hill
April 18th
Dear Jim,

Just a few lines to say I am well. I am sending you a few photos of my mates.
The hut group are the chaps in my hut, but a lot of them are out of the 5th
Rfets. Well Jim, there was another review here yesterday, this time the King
was there. It was a grand affair about 30,000 Australians taking part.
When he first arrived we presented arms to him, while the massed bands
played the National Anthem, then he inspected us, followed by about 30
"heads". Then there was the "March Past" the saluting point, when we got
to where the King was, we got "Eyes right", so we all had a good look at
him. When he was leaving all the men gave him 3 cheers. By hell it was a
grand sight, I wouldn't have missed it for a fiver. I got a letter each from Al
& Charlie last night, they were all well. Well Jim. I am going in the next
draft, I think it leaves on the 24th. I should have been in the last one, but
the coy clerk is out of the 4th refts. and he wouldn't put me in it, because
Tom Dickinson & Alex Duncan had to stop till this one goes. The clerk is a
cobber of mine & he used to be in camp with the Stone boys.

Well Jim, I will say goodbye
From
Albert

Lark Hill Camp
Sunday April 22nd
My dear Mother & Father

…We are having some decent weather at present, and things look as if it
may last. It is supposed to be spring at present, the trees are just coming in
bud and the bulbs in the garden are in flower, so things look much better.
We went into Salisbury yesterday. It is rather a nice place & has a lovely
Cathedral in it. We were shown through the Cathedral, and I can tell you it
is worth seeing. It is an enormous size and the Cathedral at Leicester is like
Mologa Church in comparison to it … I put in for leave this week to go up
to Leicester again, but could not get it. I could have got two days, but that
was not worth the train-fare. I told Jim that I was on draft, and expected to

go on Tuesday, well I hear that the draft is not going till Tuesday next week, so I will be here another Sunday. The King was out to see us on Tuesday. It was a grand affair, 30,000 Australians being in the march past, and about 9 bands there. Then there was a host of Australian nurses. I got a good look at the King, as he rode past on horseback. There were about 20 Colonels etc. following him. I did not get to Church parade this morning as I have a lot of letters to write. Well Mum, I am putting the weight on here. I weighed 12 stone 4 yesterday, just a stone heavier than when I left Australia. This place seems to be agreeing with me, although it has been cold at times. I have not got any letters from Australia for some time, as they go to France. Charlie said a paper came there for me some time ago. I hope to get a heap of letters when I join up the battalion. I don't know if the Stone boys are here & could never find them if they were here unless I knew what coy they were in …

Albert visited a photographer while in Salisbury. On April 29 he sent his parents and George a copy of the photograph.

Monday – April 23rd
Dear Jim,

… I put in for leave to go to Leicester again but couldn't get it, because I am draft. I would liked to have got leave because I couldn't see Flo Wilson when I was there before, on account of the rotten weather, also I wanted to

see Auntie Lee at Water Farm. Anyway I hope some day to see them, if the war doesn't last too long. Well Jim, I have not done much drill lately except digging trenches & putting up wire entanglements. We had some new style of bayonet fighting this afternoon, it was damn hard work. We had to run about 100 yds and jump over 5 trenches and bayonet dummies, as we went, it was the hardest work I've done for a long time. The 7/38th are coming in tomorrow, I might happen to strike someone I know…

Salisbury Plains
April 30th
Dear Jim,

… It is glorious weather here now, it is quite warm here at present. The grass and crops are starting to grow & the hedges are beginning to look green, the place looks so different, to what it did a few weeks ago. My word the grass does grow here when it starts. I am leaving for France tomorrow, so have been busy all day getting ready to go. I nearly got kept back today on account of my teeth, we have to be medically examined tomorrow. We all got a clean change of clothing, plenty of socks and anything we liked. I met Neil Haw a few days ago, he is in this camp. His boat was torpedoed when a few hours sail of Plymouth. They all got off safe on to destroyers only one chap getting injured. The huns fired two torpedoes at her, the second one missing. The boat, the Ballarat, sank a few hours after. A destroyer was with her & I hear that it sank the submarine. The poor devils on the boat lost everything, some of them came here in blueys, some without boots & hardly any clothing, but they got plenty when they got here. I havent had any letters "except the one you sent to Paynes" since God knows when. I hope to get a pile when I get to France, well Jim it is very nearly "Lights out" so I will have to close hoping this finds you all well I am

Your Aff Brother
Albert

After four months of training on the windswept fields of Salisbury Plain, Albert was finally on notice that he was to leave for France. As Albert wrote with news of his neighbour Neil Haw, he appeared unaware that

Joe Stone, the brother of his girlfriend, Myrtle Stone, had also been aboard the *Ballarat*, a troopship torpedoed in the English Channel on 25 April 1917. Albert was keen to catch up with both Joe and Jim Stone but had been unable to trace their whereabouts. Joe wrote a lengthy description of his experiences aboard the *Ballarat* to his mate Jim Marlow.

Codford England
April 8/1917
Dear Jim,

Just a line in haste hoping it finds all in the Best of Health as it leaves us at present. Well Jim we arrived safely but under difficulties on (Anzac Day) & I don't think I will ever forget it as we were the first Australians to be torpedoed coming from Australia. The Voyage. After leaving Port Melbourne on the 19ᵗʰ Feb we had a pretty rough trip across the bight some of us were not half sick either I think I had my share of it. We called at Albany and we were the first lot to get leave there though it was only one night. We had a good time there as we got a few Tabs and had a dance in the YMCA till it was time to go back to our old lugger, next we called at Fremantle and spent our four days leave in Perth. After leaving there it took us three weeks to get to Cape Town (the dirty hole). We stayed there another four days, after leaving there we called at Sierra lieone in the North West of Africa, here we stayed another four days but we did not get off the boat, as, I suppose they thought we would interfere with the blacks as there is 50,000 blacks and 150 whites there. After leaving there things went all right till the 25 of April that was the day we had been longing for as we were to reach Plymouth about 10 that evening all was excitement on the old Boat, and our Quarter Master Sergeant was issuing us with our waterproof sheets and I was forming the Company up out side when all of a sudden the submarine Guard yelled run aft. I did not bother any more about the men but went to where they were running from and I could see the torpedo about 100 yards away of course we were on the move and the torpedo struck right aft where all of them had run too. Well I stood and watched it explode about 30 yds away. There was a loud report and the old ship gave a big lurch and a shiver then began to settle down. We all fell in at our tables and waited for the advance, then made for our boat stations. Well I had to report our boat all correct to the Heads, then go back and get down a rope ladder into the boat, it is rather an awkward job I can tell you although of 1700 men there was not one fell off the ladder. Our boat being full we pulled away, meanwhile the operator had been sending out S.O.S. signals. We had only been in the boat about an hour when on the horizon we could see little black specks of smoke. It was the Navy coming to our rescue, they turned out to be destroyers and after sighting them it was no time before they were there as they came at the rate of 40 miles an hour, after they got there they cruised around in hopes of finding the submarine also to prevent it from firing us another torpedo. Then one pulled in along side the ship and got off all the remaining men while some of the rest came around and picked up the little boats full of men, what a relief to be on board again after being in the little tubs for over 2 1/2 hours and though it was a calm day you had to look out as you might be capsized any minute. All the men picked up, the first boat left for Plymouth after 6 oclock it being 90 miles away it arrived there the same time as my boat the HMS Hardy at 10.30 that night it was terrible cold as on the destroyers we had to stand on top and travelling at 25 miles an hour on a cold night with hardly any clothes on it is no picnic. After arriving we were marched to the Big Naval Barracks at Devonport where we slept that night they gave some of them tea but I was too cold to wait for it and went to bed among about 100 Naval Guns I got in bed about 1 oclock. We got up next morning about 7 oclock and went around the place to have a look around it. Then we had a good breakfast my first meal on old Blighty, afterwards falling in and calling the roll to see who was missing, at noon every one was accounted for. Rumours were afloat about whether the ship sunk, But at 10.30 our feelings were relieved when it was officially announced that it had sunk at 4.30 that morning. After we strolled about awaiting our departure to our different training camps there to settle down and learn to uphold the traditions that the Anzacs had made for Australia. At 4 oclock we entrained and made our way to what is to be our homes for a few weeks. On the way the people of Exeter gave us a cup of coffee and a good big bun and I can tell you it was very acceptable as we felt the cold after being so long in the tropics. At 10 oclock we reached Codford and our Coy got out the others going on to Salisbury there was a band to meet us and bring us to our camp 2 miles away, a good lot of the lads turned out to see us as we came along, as, it is small camps all along the road. They gave us a good tea and we got to bed about 1 oclock and got up at 8 the next morning. Too much cannot be said about our gallant C.O. of troops Lt. Col. McVea V.D. he remained on the bridge till the last. He was as cool as a cucumber all the time. The troops on board the Ballarat found him a true soldier and a man and that is a good bit. They say the Australian troops have no discipline, but not that day the 25 April shows whether they have it or not and it was perfect all the time there was not a slightest bit of panic anywhere. Getting over 1700 troops off a sinking boat with out one getting wet through falling in is one of the things that will live in the history of discipline and it speaks well for the Australian soldiers. This is the first time that Australian soldiers have landed over the sea in a new land bootless and hatless. Here ends one of the biggest Dramas that has ever been played and came out without a scratch. The sinking of His Majestys Australian Troopship The Ballarat A70. May it rest in Peace. All on board at the time will have something in years to come to look back upon and think of the watery grave they would have had it not been for the efficiency of the British Navy, every man on board that ship is able to say The British Navy has saved my life. May it continue to do so, here the story ends. Well Jim you will notice a X on page 5 I got up to go out and see the 23ʳᵈ Reinforcements leave. We are next. Before you get this I may be there, no one knows. I wrote to Albert and Percy about a week ago I expect to hear from them any day. Lark Hill is only about 11 miles from here if Albert is there I will go and see him Sunday. Well Jim I have a beastly cold and it is getting late I think I will close.

With Best Wishes
I Remain
Yours Sincerely
Joe

Remember me to Father and Mother also tell them a Little that used to stay at the Stiffs Retreat that used to teach your Father to play patience is in our coy he came in the 23 refs but is on home service on account of bad eyesight. Remember me to all Mologa friends don't forget the nice girls as well. Joe

FRANCE AND BELGIUM, MAY

As the arrival of spring brightened the Western Front, Allan, Percy and Charlie made the most of their opportunities to enjoy its pleasures.

The 38th had been withdrawn as a reserve battalion to a farm west of Ploegsteert Wood, to the north of Armentieres, once the picturesque hunting ground of the King of Belgium. For two weeks, despite remaining within artillery range, they enjoyed the relative safety of the area while preparing gun pits and cable trenches.[1] To the south on the Somme, Nivelle's attack in the Aisne region had achieved limited success while further British attempts to push through at Arras had fared little better. At Bullecourt, George was once again to engage in bitter fighting as the Spring Offensive forged on in the face of fierce resistance and the fortified defences of the Hindenburg Line.

On 3 May, 17 weeks after arriving in England, Albert sailed for the battlefields of France. On the same day, the 2nd Division was ordered to attack in the same sector of the Hindenburg Line at Bullecourt that the 4th Division had breached, but had been unable to hold some two weeks prior. They were again to be asked to attack into a re-entrant. The battle raged for two weeks and involved the 2nd, 1st and later the weary 5th Division. Troops of the 1st Division were sent in on 4 May to relieve the 6th Brigade (2nd Division) which had successfully breached the line and was steadfastly holding a sector that bulged precariously into enemy lines. The dead lay all around them. The 5th Division arrived on 12 May. George, as a member of the 2nd Light Trench Mortar Battery of the 1st Division, would be witness to the bloody and brutal hand-to-hand combat and raging artillery duels that savaged the Australian forces as they fought off seven major counter-attacks and waves of minor assaults, until the German withdrawal from Bullecourt a fortnight later.

By 20 May, only two sectors had been captured along the 25-kilometre front between Arras and Bullecourt where 14 Allied divisions had advanced during the Battle of Arras. To the far north, Canadian forces had captured their objective, but were to hold it only briefly. To the south the Australians played a major role in the capture of Bullecourt which would remain part of the Allied front until March 1918. Breaching the Hindenburg Line had drawn accolades for the Australian forces. Through sheer tenacity they achieved an unlikely success despite appalling casualties; in addition to the enormous toll from First Bullecourt, the Australians lost

7000 men in the Second Battle of Bullecourt. The combined Bullecourt battles had cost the four Australian divisions 10,000 casualties, with over 1000 soldiers now prisoners of war.[2]

In between stints in the Bullecourt line, George took time to write to his family. His friend Amos Haw who, as George often wrote, was always just 100 yards further up the trench, had been wounded. Amos was a 24-year-old farmer from Mologa who had suffered a serious gunshot wound to his leg. He slowly recovered to rejoin the 5th Battalion on the front nine months later. In the last months of the war he returned to England to train others in the techniques of gas warfare.[3] George was unsure of the extent of Amos's wound and typically provided little detail of his own experiences other than describing the debacle as 'lively'. He focused on snippets of news he had received, including the loss of his potential love interest. George had been gone from Mologa for over 18 months, a considerable time for a young heart to wait.

France
May 8th 1917
Dear Jim

… I came out of the line a few nights ago but are still well in the range of shells, while I was in Amos's battalion was along with us so I enquired after him and found out that he had been wounded in the leg I don't know how the others got on it has been lively in this part of the line lately I will enquire after young Twigg. I had a letter from Allan saying he had been slightly wounded but is alright again and has joined his battalion up again so don't worry about him. I had a letter from Albert saying that N. Haw had arrived and that he met him his boat was torpedoed but all were saved … You are always asking about the conscription, we are not allowed to say anything about it, well I voted the same way as you, the answer to the other question is yes. You say Dick and the one that was promised to me the night of my sendoff have made a start, I don't think there will be any girls left when we all get back. I think I will bring one back from England there are plenty there and what about one for you. Dad said in his letter that Mrs Gamble had sent us cigarettes etc. well I have never received any of them. Well Jim we have had our voting day and I voted for the same ones as you would …

France
May 11th 1917
Dear Mother & father

… I wrote to you a few days ago, we had just come out of the line but went back again it was lively too, both Amos and Ewin were wounded I havent heard how any of the other local lads got on, I got out of it safely. I will inquire about young Twigg and will let you know in next letter as this mail closes in 10 minutes so have to cut it short I had a letter from Charlie yesterday Allan has joined them up again and all are well I will now close hoping all are well.

I remain
Your Loving Son
George

My Dear Mother

Just a card to let you know I am well all well hoping all are the same. I had a couple of letters from you and Jim a few days ago. That dream you had wasn't true I have been splendid. I haven't heard how Ewin & Amos are getting on. I told you in my last letter that I heard Jack Price was killed well it is true. I saw his name and number in the Anzac bulletin. Allan's was in the wounded list. I will write again soon. George

PS Am sending a small parcel today

The beautifully embroidered card that George sent to Sarah.

Ewin, often referred to as Hughie, was Alexander Ewen Johnson, a 25-year-old farmer from Mologa who served in the 6th Battalion. He was seriously wounded on three separate occasions, the first in May 1917. He recovered and returned to France on 20 September 1917, but was wounded again five weeks later on 28 October. He was once again sent to England to recover where, in March 1918, he married Christina Cameron of Ballachulish, Scotland. He rejoined his unit in France on 23 May 1918. Twenty days later he was shot in the chest and arm, sent to England and listed as dangerously ill for months. Ewen miraculously survived and returned to Australia in January 1919.[4]

Further north in France and across the border in Belgium, George's brothers were preparing for an attack in the Flanders region. Haig now had his opportunity to prove that his projected attack east of Ypres to capture the heights around Passchendaele and then assault the German flank was superior to Nivelle's failed attempt to the south in France.

Charlie wrote:

3rd May 1917
My dear Mother,

Just a few lines to say that I am quite well also Allan and Percy, Al is none the worse for his experience, he was only away about 12 days … Al got your parcel a few days ago and was pleased to get it. I got a lot of mail in the trenches last time also a parcel and papers from Pearl, we are out of the trenches at present, it is lovely weather here now the days are quite hot, it is such a change from the awful winter, they say that it was the severest winter that they have had in Europe for over 35 years and Flo Wilson says that she saw in the paper that it was the coldest April for 60 years. I got a letter from Geordie a few days ago and Al got one last night he is getting on fine we have not met him yet as we are a long way away from where he is. Albert is still in England but expects to be over here very soon. Percy had a letter from Joe Stone the other day, they had an exciting time coming over. I hope you have got my letters for I have written to you often. I get all your letters now since I have joined the battalion. The trees are beginning to look green over here now and the grass and crops are growing very fast, but they look as though they want rain …

As Charlie wrote his letter home, he was unaware that Albert had arrived in France the same day. It would be several weeks before they were reunited:

5th May
1917
Dear Jim,

… we are out of the trenches and the weather is grand, this week has been weather like we have in October in Australia, the last time in the trenches it was not too bad at all. I got a letter from Geordie a few days ago he is getting on fine, Albert is still in Lark Hill and expects to be over here very soon, all his company are over here …

Albert wrote to his family at the first opportunity:

France
Sunday May 6th 1917
Dear Jim,

Just a line to say I got here without being hit by any tin fish, we got here on Thursday and had to march [censored] miles with our full packs up from where we landed to this camp. The roads were rough as blazes and dusty & as the country is very hilly, it was a stiff march. We are camped near a town right on the sea-shore, have to do a few days training before we go up to join the batt. We are treated very well here & get well fed. We passed through a lot of towns on the road here & got a great welcome. The town is quite close here, but we are not allowed to go into it …

France
May 7th
My Dear Mother & Father,

Just a line to say I am quite well & hope you all are the same. I got here last Thursday to this camp. We were the first lot of troops that marched from where we landed to here, a distance of [censored] miles over hard dusty roads & hot as hell, just my luck as usual. But we got a great welcome coming through the towns, kids following us asking for pennies & selling chocolates & fruit. We expect to be here a few days before we go up to join the battalion, I haven't heard how the boys are getting on, but 5 of our company have been wounded. I hope to get some letters when I get over with the battalion. This place is on the coast & is all sandhills. We have a holiday this afternoon because we are going out tonight all night for manoeuvres. I got leave to go into town yesterday afternoon, but it is a very tame place. We get well treated here in the tucker line. Our parade ground is a 3 mile march from the camp, we drill in our steel helmets & carry our gas masks. I like here tip-top, we get treated far better and the O.C. doesn't come round to see if we are clean shaven etc ...

On 13 May the 38th Battalion relieved the 40th and moved up the line to support the 37th in trenches in front of Ploegsteert Wood, Belgium. On 22 May, as Albert arrived to take his place with his brothers, the battalion entered the front line. Six days later, on 28 May, members of the 38th were involved in a raid on the enemy line. It was on this night that Light Horseman Bert Wishart was to lose his brother Rex. Of the 221 men involved, 60 were killed or listed as missing, another 65 were wounded. Many of the casualties were caught in their own artillery barrage.[5]

AUSTRALIA, MAY

A local friend, Myrtle Forsyth, wrote to George while she holidayed at Corryong. Her familiarity hints that perhaps George had more than one love interest prior to his departure. Nonetheless, Myrtle provides a glimpse into life at home as they waited for news from their loved ones at the front. George would not have received this letter until July or later. Myrtle would later pen a rather bemusing letter to Allan.

Willow Bank
Towong P.O.
Near Corryong

May 23rd 1917
Dear Tenny

I received your most interesting letter last mail and was very pleased indeed to hear from you, I had been looking for a letter and was beginning to think that my letters hadn't interested you enough to answer them but of course your letter has reassured me in that respect. You have indeed seen numerous countries in your travels and I am glad to know that you think Australia equal to any of them. Yes Tenny there are many changes over here and things are not just what they used to be, but still compared to what the other countries are going through we are not so badly off, but oh the suspense of waiting for news of "one never knows what" is very depressing. You will see by the above address that I am still on holidays, I think I wrote you a short letter after I arrived here. I have been away for two months and intend returning home on 30th. I have enjoyed the change amongst the mountains very much and my friends have been most kind to me so that it would have been impossible for me to do anything else than enjoy my trip especially in such a pretty place. There are not many entertainments now to go to Tenny, in fact only patriotic ones, anyhow we don't feel inclined for frivolities. I went to hear the "blind soldier poet" lecturing in Corryong I don't remember if I wrote you since the lecture, or before, but the lecture was very interesting and it seemed such a pity for one so young and handsome as Signaller Tom Skeyhill to be blind for the rest of his life. He is touring the world lecturing and it is unusual for him to visit such a small township as Corryong but did so on account of it being such a splendid recruiting district. Fancy your three brothers being together in the trenches. Percy writes at times but he never said they were all together, the last letter I had from him he had just come out of isolation from the mumps, they are raging around here now, but I am hoping to escape them if for no other reason, because I have enough jaw of my own. So you see I am coming on since you seen me last, I see you still remember That Precious Dinner but you didn't say how you come to remember it I daresay it was as I said "enough to make me feel hungry for ever" By the way how do you fare over there for meals one hears ever so many tales of the Menu some seem to fare far from well to say nothing of the mud and "company" in the trenches. Did I tell you in my last letter that I was taking lessons in riding since coming up here and I'm sure Tenny you missed a "sight" worth seeing by not being present to see me having my lessons, but I had hard work to convince them here that I had never been on horseback before so I couldn't have been such an _Awful Sight_ after all and I think I shall be risking my neck on some of our own horses, when I return home. I have been doing some hill climbing on horseback and waded through the creek a few times so I consider myself quite professional now. I had a letter from May last week, she is having a treat by way of driving the kiddies to Sth Calivil School and by all accounts they are not going to be successful in having the North Cal, one opened in a hurry. Wonder if you have any mice over in France they are working great havoc amongst the wheat stacks, when I left home they were something dreadful and one used to be afraid to go to sleep at night for fear of being eaten _Do you believe that_. They are not so plentiful here as this is a dairying district, but one plague at a time is enough and the fleas here are most annoying though until this year the folk here never knew what it was to be worried by them. I myself had never seen the creatures before and I am in no hurry to see them again either. I am looking forward very much to my return journey by car, I am leaving at 6 a.m. and am hoping it will be fine so as I can have the full benefit of the drive. It has been raining here this last fortnight and I am thinking that I may have a wet trip back. But until this last fortnight the weather has been ideal. Now Tenny I am sure I have tried your patience to its utmost so I will draw this to a close hoping this finds you still going strong, with plenty of luck.

With kind remembrances from Yours very sincerely
Myrtle Forsyth

TWELVE

GOD ONLY KNOWS HOW THE THREE OF US GOT THROUGH …

THE WESTERN FRONT — MESSINES

The Spring Offensive had failed to achieve its objectives. The French army under Nivelle had begun to mutiny as Second Bullecourt raged on the Western Front. French casualties to the south along the Craonne Plateau were mounting, now around 120,000 men. With the failure of Nivelle's planned breakthrough, he was replaced by General Petain whose task it was to rebuild the largely ineffective French forces. It took five weeks for successive mutinies to be controlled during which time, and for some weeks afterwards, the task of holding back the German forces fell to the British. General Haig, despite the opposition of British Prime Minister Lloyd George, now had the opportunity to implement his plan of 1916 to drive the Germans from their stronghold in the Belgian coastal ports of Ostende and Zeebrugge from which aggressive submarine assaults were launched. Prime Minister Lloyd George preferred an attack on the eastern Italian front where enemy forces were weaker. The British War Cabinet eventually approved Haig's plan, despite the reluctance of the Prime Minister.

Haig's strategy involved tactical 'bite and hold' offensives to wear down enemy defences and gradually drive the German forces from their strongholds. Limited objectives were set. Heavy artillery bombardments would precede a line of advancing infantry who would remain behind the protective curtain of their own artillery fire. Once an objective was gained, the artillery would move forward and the manoeuvre would be repeated. The strike was planned initially at the broken city of Ypres in Belgium. Enemy lines on the high ground to the east of the city at Polygon Wood, Broodseinde and Passchendaele would be breached, allowing Allied forces to strike to the rear of enemy forces, cutting off the German garrison positioned on the coastline. To achieve this objective the German front to the south of Ypres, along the high ground between Messines and Wytschaete, had first to be taken in an attack involving British, New Zealand and Australian forces under the careful planning of General Hubert Plumer whose responsibility it had been to hold the Ypres salient for the past two years. Plumer was a meticulous planner and knew the area well; he calculated carefully and his secret weapon was hidden deep beneath the German front-line trenches.[1]

The 3rd Division was well prepared for the offensive, with Lieutenant General John Monash ensuring that his men were highly trained and well equipped for what was to be, apart from the series of successful raids in the Armentieres sector, their first major test. This was a test the battle-weary soldiers of the 1st, 2nd, 4th and 5th divisions awaited with anticipation. The mettle of the new Australian division would be tested in its attack on the Messines-Wytschaete ridgeline.

The 3rd had been nicknamed 'the neutrals', a reference to the division's late entry to the war, the length of its training and its occupation of the relatively quiet Armentieres sector. But these men were also the 'fair dinkums', men who had enlisted not so much with the spirit of adventure of earlier volunteers, but largely from a strong sense of duty. They had seen the casualty lists and the wounded and maimed soldiers who had returned to Australia. Under the command of the meticulous General Monash they had become disciplined fighters, but did not lack spirit. Outwardly they were also set apart as they wore their hats bashed flat by order of their commander — not necessarily a preference shared by his troops. Despite the fact that they were now considered an effective and experienced raiding team, the men knew that their next 'stunt' would prove their real worth. Well aware of what was to come, the brothers wrote home with anticipation and, in Allan's case, of another moment when luck proved on his side.

In the field
1-6-17
My Dear Mum & Dad & Jim

Well dear mum I am writing again today I hope you are all well as it leaves us at present. I believe there is another Aust mail coming in. No one knows how delighted we are to get it. Well dear mum we are still in the trenches and I won't be sorry when we get a bit of a rest. We have been in for a few weeks now without a blow. Things are very very lively here now. I have never seen anything like it before but it's nothing to what it will be in a few weeks. There is one thing we are having bonnie weather and everything is looking lovely and green. Well dear mum & Dad I had a shell come through my dugout last night and it blew everything to pieces. I lost my shaving kit and a few more things what Uncle Arthur and Dolly sent me. I had just gone out of it so I consider myself very lucky. The only thing I got out of it was my revolver. I got a parcel from Uncle Arthur & Dolly Mahoney the other day they were tra bon I can tell you. Albert came along about 10 days ago and he looks splendid he has grown such a lot. Percy is a lucky fellow. He and a lot more chaps went away about 3 days ago. I can't tell you where they are but they are out of the trenches to billyo. They will miss something that I won't. I was glad some of us went away I cant tell you what they will miss but you will hear about [it] soon enough. Some more of the boys from about Mincha & Macorna got knocked over the other night …

As Allan described to his family how significantly Albert had grown in the 12 months since they had last been together, Albert was writing his own letter. While he had yet to experience the front-line trenches, he was acquainted with the frailty of existence behind the line as many of his mates had already been wounded.

In the field
June 1st
My Dear Mother & Father

… Well Mum, I have had a very good time since I have been here, as I haven't been in the front line at present but my mates have been unlucky. Young Dabb was wounded two days after we got here and yesterday Duncan & Swainston were wounded also Alex Chisholm another of my mates. Harry Street had a narrow go the other night too. A fellow doesn't need to go to the front line to get hit. All those that I mentioned were wounded behind the

line. We are supposed to go out tonight for a spell. Fritz has been shelling the Y.M.C.A. canteens, so now we cannot get cigarettes, or anything else. Uncle Arthur sent me a parcel of cigarettes and socks last week. We get clean socks every day here, so we don't need to carry any about with us. We are having glorious weather here it has been so ever since I've been here. I have been busy lately writing letters. Auntie Etta writes every week, besides a number of others, so I have plenty of letters to answer. Well Mum, Mologa must be very quiet now the hall is closed. It's a pity Joey could not be patriotic enough to let the Red + [Cross] have it for nothing. Percy is away at present, he went away in a reserve company, I suppose he will be away for a few weeks. He will miss something too. It is pretty lively here at present but nothing to what it will be. It is amusing to watch the chaps hunting for <u>chats</u>. I have managed to dodge them so far, but Al & Charlie caught a few the other day. Well dear Mum & Dad, it is a job to find news here. All the boys are well & Geordie is also. I hope you all are the same. I will write again when I go out so I will say ta-ta for the time, with love from your loving son

Albert

I am writing this on my knee so excuse the scrawl.

Stewart Dabb had been 20 years old when he sailed with Albert on the *Port Lincoln*. He was wounded on 27 May 1915 but recovered and joined the 38th Battalion in September 1916. He returned to Australia in February 1919.[2]

Alex Duncan from Kyneton had left the farm to enlist in October 1916 and appears in the photo postcard Albert sent home in March.[3] He was shot in the back at Messines in the days leading up to the battle but survived his wounds to rejoin the battalion after Passchendaele in October 1917. He returned to Australia in August 1918.[4]

Alexander Chisholm was born in Scotland but enlisted in Melbourne in October 1916 at the age of 31. He also sailed on the *Port Lincoln* with Albert. He recovered from wounds sustained on 1 June to return to the front on 20 October following the Battle of Passchendaele. Alexander had married in Scotland in April 1917 and it is unclear whether he returned to Australia. His records indicate that he left for Australia in

1919, but did not disembark. Perhaps he jumped ship to return to his new wife. He was later cleared of being absent without leave. [5]

Gordon Swainston also sailed on the *Port Lincoln* and appears with Albert in the photo postcard sent home in March.[6] An 18-year-old farmer from Green Hill near Kyneton, he was wounded four times. He sustained his first wound on 31 May 1917, returning to his unit two weeks later just after Albert wrote home with news of his wounding. At Passchendaele on 13 October 1917 he was shot in the leg and was not fit to return to duty until May 1918. Four months later, on 10 August, he was wounded again, but returned to the front after a week in hospital. On 8 September 1918 he was shot in the hand and classified as unfit for active duty. This remarkably resilient young man returned to Kyneton in January 1919. He was one of four brothers serving in the AIF.[7]

Percy wrote to his aunt to tell her that Albert had arrived:

In the Field
June 2nd
Dear Auntie Florrie & All

… Albert has arrived here, he looks real well on it, I had a lot of letters for him. I received Uncle Arthur's parcel, a few days ago and was very pleased to get it, the cigarettes were just the thing, I got one from Dolly Mahoney not long before that, so I was set, I gave Allan his cigarettes and socks. Well, it's a lovely day, a pleasure to be out. It's a bit lively here at times, they give Fritz all the shells he wants, when he starts. The place is nice and green now, and it looks quite a change from a few months ago. The French people, a few miles back from the line, have a lot of potatoes and beans in, they look real well, they are always working with them, women as well as men. We are out of the trenches now, after a good long run in them, I suppose we will be going back in a few days. Today is Sunday, and our dinner consists of rabbit, I do not know what way, but I suppose the same old tale, stew. Well, I suppose you have just about finished the cropping now, it does not seem no time since last cropping season. How are Grandfather and Grandmother keeping. I saw a paper today, first for about two weeks there was fairly good news in it. Well news is terrible scarce, so I will have to close.

With love to all
I remain your loving nephew
Percy

Charlie also wrote:

June 4ᵗʰ 1917
Dear Mother, Father & Jim,

… I got a letter from Geordie last week he was out for a spell and has been out for a fair while he seemed to be enjoying things by the way he wrote, he had met Tom Alford. I saw in the Anzac Bulletin where Tom had been wounded, but Geordie wrote since then and did not say anything about it, so it must have been a mistake, Amos Haw was not wounded badly and I don't think Ewen Johnson was wounded badly. We are having grand weather over here now one would not know the place after the winter. I think it is the prettiest place I have ever seen the trees and hedges look grand every thing is so nice and green the crops of all kinds seem to grow very fast. I met Claude Piper the other day, he was up near the trenches he belongs to our division and enlisted in New South Wales there are two chaps that I know from Pine Grove Jim Hutching and Jasper. Percy has been picked out for a reserve or something of the sort at any rate not a bad job. I sent a parcel to Pearl last week I registered it so she ought to get it alright. I believe there is a chance of seeing Geordie shortly but only a chance. I would like to see him, Albert said he looked real well when he got to Salisbury Plains, he got his photo taken so I suppose he sent you one. I got a letter today from Flo Wilson I think I told you before that Flo's father met with a very bad accident, but Flo said today he was getting on splendid and was out of bed I was sorry for him as he seems a very nice fellow. Auntie Edith's little girl, her only girl, is very ill Ida said she thought it was meningitis and that there was not much hope for her she lost a little girl before with diptheria and Flo said today she was still very low …

Concerned after receiving the cable informing the family that Allan had been wounded, Jim wrote to the Red Cross. As the society penned its reply, Allan, now recovered from his wounds and considering himself fortunate having narrowly escaped another shell, was preparing to once again cheat death in the trenches and shell holes of Messines. The first phase of Haig's offensive, which aimed to take the heights surrounding Ypres, was set to begin. It would be Albert's first experience of battle.

Later, Albert wrote to Jim, having survived his initial foray into the line, and now writing with the confidence of the battle-hardened soldier:

In the field
June 5th
1917
Dear Jim

... We are out of the trenches now, but I don't think for long. Things were very lively when we left, but nothing to what it will be. Percy was lucky enough to go away in a reserve company, he will miss a damn lot too. Well Jim, I am not with the Lewis Gun Section yet, as we wont be long enough out to go through the training, but I believe I will be going in the section as soon as we come out again. I am in a bombing section now, and perhaps will have an opportunity soon of showing what I can do with them. Well Jim it is glorious weather here now, everything looks so pretty, the crops and grass are growing very fast, and I suppose they will be cutting before long. Charlie, Al & I went out last night for a feed of eggs, but I ate three and wasn't half satisfied then. The people here [censored] are [censored]. They wont come down a penny, but I managed the other night to beat one for a half penny. We went for a bath today, it was tra bon. Most of us are beginning to get a bit chatty. I have had a number of letters from England lately. I also had a letter from Geordie. There hasn't been any Australian mail in lately, we are all looking forward to some letters.

June 6th

Well Jim, I haven't got any mail today, we have been very busy all day, we will be leaving here before very long, I am going my hardest to try and get this letter finished before I go. I have just been told that I am going to the Lewis Gun Section after all, but don't know if I will be on for good or just this stunt. I am not going in Al's section. Al has just been made a corporal. Well Jim, I haven't time to write more, before you get this you will know, I suppose, all about it, hoping all are well, I will say goodbye with love to all from your loving brother

Albert

June 11ᵗʰ

I wrote this letter but did not have time to post it, so it went through the push with me.

Tell Streets that Harry and Bill are alright.

On 31 May, almost two weeks prior to Albert's letter, the Allied bombardment of the Messines line had commenced and lasted seven days. German forces were well aware of the impending attack owing to intelligence reports and their position on an elevated feature from which they could clearly view the massing of artillery behind the British lines. However, they were not prepared for the intensity of the artillery onslaught which decimated their own heavy guns and men. Nor were the German forces prepared for the devastating effect of the almost simultaneous detonation of 19 mines buried below their front lines. Deep beneath the network of surface trenches lay a complex system of German and Allied tunnels so close in places that the footsteps of enemy soldiers in nearby tunnels could be heard distinctly by both sides.[8]

In the early hours of 7 June, British, New Zealand and Australian soldiers commenced their advance along a 12-kilometre front. On the southern end of the attacking front, the 3rd Division, well prepared by General Monash for its task, now moved forward. Allan and Charlie and the Lewis gun team made their way across the pitted landscape, accompanied by the constant whine of the defensive gas bombardment raining down on Ploegsteert Wood. Albert also moved forward with another Lewis gun team. Percy had been withdrawn from the line to make up reinforcements and to maintain a nucleus of troops from which the battalion could be rebuilt in the event of heavy casualties. The men of the 4th Division, who had not returned to the front line since their mauling at Bullecourt, were less than impressed to be positioned for an attack.

For over two hours the advancing men choked behind the smoky haze of their masks as they groped their way through the wood. Five hundred men were lost from the Australian forces as gas shells rained on them and high explosives lit up the sky. By 3.00 am eight Allied divisions were in place. At 3.10 am the earth shuddered and then tore apart as massive blasts decimated the German lines. The roar of the colossal explosions were rumoured to be heard in distant London. Nineteen mines were detonated, including one beneath the infamous Hill 60 where the 1st Australian Tunnelling Company had been working since November 1916. The explosions shattered the enemy front, killing, burying, maiming and leaving very few survivors.[9]

The Allied infantry attacked as the deafening roar of the explosions shattered the countryside. Enormous clouds of crimson smoke and debris rose into the sky, throwing up a curtain of dust that shielded the attackers and left huge craters where once the German line had existed. British troops attacked to the north of Messines, the New Zealanders assaulted from the west, and the Australian 3rd Division attacked the German line from its position at Hill 63 on the edge of Ploegsteert Wood to the south of Messines. The role of the 38th Battalion was to capture 'Ungodly Trench' and Belthéem Farm and then connect the trenches captured by the New Zealanders to their left and the 39th Battalion on the right. Under cover of a 'jumping barrage' in which the troops moved forward under systematic artillery bursts and rests, the Australians fought their way to their objective. They captured demoralised German soldiers who chose to give themselves up and killed those who attempted to retreat. By 5.30 am all objectives, apart from those in the sector to the very north close to Ypres, had been achieved and positions were held in anticipation of the order to the 4th Division and the 37th Battalion, waiting in reserve, to move forward and advance to the Oosttaverne Line.

By late that afternoon, despite a series of German counter-attacks, the carefully planned Battle of Messines had been won. Much of the Oosttaverne Line was firmly held, apart from a sector in which the battle raged for the next four days. At its furthest point, the front line had been pushed back just over three kilometres. The battle continued for another week with artillery bombardments and fierce hand-to-hand fighting until the German troops withdrew. Allied casualties were reportedly around 26,000, with 6800 Australians killed or wounded.[10] Among the casualties were mates of the Marlow brothers.

The 38th held its position for 48 hours. When the relieving troops arrived, the proud soldiers wearily gathered their gear and independently made their way back to their billets. The action had been a success; the 3rd Division had proven itself in what became known as the Second Battle of Ypres (Messines).

The brothers were out of the line having survived the bitter fighting, but the reckoning had come. Anxious to tell their family that their luck had held, they began their letters home. Charlie sent a field postcard on the day they reached their billets. When time allowed and exhausted bodies were rested, they would write.

Sunday 10th June 1917
Dear Jim,

Just a few lines to say we are all safe and well we have just come out of a big battle Percy was not in it he along with others was kept on reserve. Albert was in it we all had several narrow escapes but managed to get out of it alright, I am very sorry to say that Tom Roberts was killed he was not with me as I was with the Lewis Gun, and Tom was carrying a bridge to cross a small stream, I have reason to believe he was killed near the stream between 3.30 am and 5 am on the morning of June 7th 1917 he had a wallet on him and had about £10 in English and French money in it, the Pioneers that buried him handed the wallet to the Adjutant, who will send it home to his people, Tom gave me an English Pound note to keep for him the night before I will send it home to his people when I write to them also some other cards I got his pack and took anything that was any good out of it but most of his things were in his wallet. I will write to his people today or tomorrow. George Collison that came over with us was wounded the same morning but I do not think it was serious, I believe Peter Owens was wounded but do not know if it is true, as far as I know all the rest of the local boys are all safe if you read the paper 22 days before my birthday you will get a fair idea of the fight. It is a fair while now since we had a mail from Australia I am hoping it will be here this week. Al was made a corporal the night before the advance young Spuddy Kerr from Bears Lagoon is a Lance Corporal Joe Reed from J Cheynes is a corporal Albert Sinclair is in England has been there for some time he went there sick and was likely to go home to Australia there is a lot more I would like to tell you about different things and things in general I could write a book on it, but will tell you when I go back. Geordie was quite well when he wrote, last week. I wrote to Pearl last night I have no idea when the mail goes out but hope this reaches you alright and finds you all well. I have got a lot of letters to write and not much time nor inclination to write.

Well Jim I will draw to a close for this time we are all well
I will say
Goodbye for the present with best wishes

I am
Your affect brother
Charlie E Marlow

As Charlie reflected on the first major battle in which he had fought, it is clear that the death and injury of his mates and the horrific experiences of battle had subdued the eldest son. His mate Tom had asked Charlie to keep an English pound note to send home to his family in the event he did not survive. An exchange of letters and valuables prior to battle was common as each soldier weighed his chances of survival.

Conversely, Allan writes with bravado; he is as euphoric following the success of the battle as Charlie is subdued. Every man's response to the chaos and carnage was unique; many hid their feelings with bravado and attempted to cheer themselves and their families with casual wit and nonchalance.

In the field
10-6-17
My Dear Mum, Dad & Jim

... Well dear mum I am a corporal now I was corporal on the 7-6-17 so you will get extra money now. We have just come out of a big battle which we

won. I never enjoyed anything better in all my life. We went over the top a few days back. We fairly mowed them down. Talk about a bombardment, it was terrific. Percy was not in it but Charlie and Albert were. Poor old Tom Roberts got killed different other lads got wounded but we three came through alright. Talk about narrow goes well one has to laugh. This pushing them back will do me. Mum I got some souvenirs and I hope to get them home to you all. I can tell [you] I had [to] fight for them, but they will do me. Well dear mum & dad I suppose we will be in more in the future. Old Geordie is still pushing along. I haven't had a spell since we landed over here but I am going to try for England leave one of our boys went today. Well dear mum & dad & Jim I will now close trusting all are well as it leaves us to day.

Goodbye
I remain
Your Loving Son
Allan S

Albert wrote with blunt honesty, freely admitting that his first time in a major attack had been akin to a trip to hell. He questions how he and his brothers had survived being buried and buffeted by artillery blasts and casually remarks that his wound was not bad enough to warrant his being sent to England. He is now a hardened soldier, casually commenting on the death of his mates and prepared to gather souvenirs from the dead, wounded or captured Germans. Albert had not bothered to take souvenirs, considering that there would be plenty of time to collect a few keepsakes.

In the field
June 11th 1917
My dear Mother, Father & Jim,

Just a few lines to let you know I am still alive & well. Since I last wrote to you, I have seen a bit of war. We left here the other night for the front line, and going up had to go through a gas-attack for over two hours, it was a fair buggar as Fritz shelled us all the time. You will have read about it before this how we hopped over the top and attacked the huns, we took our *objective in about 20 minutes, but it was a hot go. The worst part of it was holding the position, we were in it for two days and it was particular hell. A lot of my pals were [censored] wounded. God only knows how the three of us got through. Our section was the only one that got through without a casualty. I am in the Lewis Gun Section, and I was in the stunt with Joe Reids team. Al & Charlie were in another section. I got hit in the arm with a spare bullet & hit on the shoulder with a piece of shrapnel, but not bad enough for a <u>blighty</u>. The lot of us were buried a few times. By God it was a rough shop, but the worst was going up to the line through the gas. Poor old Tom Roberts got killed. Harry Harnell was also killed & Tom Burt was wounded. There is only Tom Dickinson & I left now out of the lot of us that left Royal Park together. We are out having a spell now but don't think we will be out long. There hasn't been any mail come in for some time now. Percy came back this morning, he got a couple of letters from England. I hope we get some letters before we go in again. Al got a lot of German souvenirs, I got a few but didn't bother much about them. I could have got plenty if I wanted them, but I suppose there is plenty of time yet. We had the <u>tanks</u> helping us in the attack, it was a great affair. I wouldn't have missed it for anything, although it was a rough affair. Well Mum, I will now close hoping you all are well as it leaves me at present, so with love I am*

Your Loving Son
Albert

In the field
June 11th 1917
My Dear Auntie

… We were in a big stunt the other day, and had a rather rough time, although we gave Fritz a hell of a doing. Going up to the trenches, Fritz sent some gas over and we were in it for over 2 hours. We went over the top at day break and attacked Fritz and took our objective in about 10 minutes. It was rather tough holding on to our positions, but we hung on for two days and were then relieved. You will have read before this of the capture of Messines, we were not far off that town whats left of it, and saw it taken. It was a great go, and was a great win for our side. The worst part of it was going up to the trenches

through the gas. It was worse than all the shells he threw at us. The three of us got through alright, although we all got hit a few times with shrapnel, but not bad enough to go out with. We are out now for a spell, which I hope will be fairly long, as when we were out last we only had a few days … Allan has two stripes now. Allan got a few souvenirs off dead Germans. I got a few little things but did not bother much. A lot of the boys got watches and revolvers … It is glorious weather here now the place looks so pretty and the roses are out in bloom in the gardens. There are a lot of vegetables growing near here, and the peas are out in flower, so before long we hope to have a good feed of them. Oranges are the only fruit here and they are very dear, you cant beat these people here for much. It was amusing to see Charlie the other day trying to cut the price down with an old woman, but she wouldn't come down a ½ d. I was in the stunt with the Lewis Gun Section but don't know if I am stopping in, if I do I will go in Spuddy Kerr's team. Well Auntie I have no news, so I will close hoping this finds you all well as it leaves us all here at present. I am

Your loving nephew
Albert

Albert began the task of replying to the mail he had received. By now he was aware that his mate Jack Price had lost his life at Bullecourt:

In the field
June 12th, 1917
Dear Jim,

… Mum says she sent me a tin, so it ought to be along soon, parcels come a few days after the mail, I am looking forward to getting it. I got 6 old letters this week, two were from Mollie Gamble, one of them had 9 pages in it so I had plenty of reading. I have had nearly 50 letters since I joined the boys. Its grand to get plenty of letters but its rather tiresome answering them all, still its better than getting none at all. I hope to get a pile of letters in a few days. Well Jim, it has been very warm today, we are still out having a spell. I wrote to you before telling you we were in the Battle of Messines and Hill 63. It was a great success and although it was rough at times, I am not sorry I was in it. The gas was a fair buggar. You will remember I sent you a photo of Bert Jeanes well he was killed early in the battle. Poor old Tom Roberts

was also killed. Alex Duncan is in a hospital in England. Things seem to be getting a lot livelier in Mologa. I'd like to have been at the dance in Jones's barn. I suppose you had your own way with the young lady. It's a damn shame that old Squires cant give the hall. He's worse than a German. Winnie Price sent me three Pyramid papers and a Weekly Times. I havent got any mail so I suppose she wrote to me too. Poor old Jack got killed. I thought something must have happened to him, as he never answered my last letter. It is hard luck for his people. According to letters the Australian people seem to think the war will be over soon. I think it would end much quicker if our aeroplanes would raid Germany. It would be a good thing if they did as it would demoralize his troops a bit. It doesn't take much to set them running, as we saw in the fight at Messines Ridge. We got great praise over that fight. I could tell you a lot about it but circumstances forbid. I got a few souvenirs, but if I liked could have got more than one could carry. I wasn't looking for souvenirs. There are plenty of Y.M.C.A.'s here and we often have a feed there. I don't care much about the French eggs, no guts in them. I ate 6 the other night and was still hungry. They are not like Australian eggs. Well Jim I have any amount of money, don't ever worry about me wanting money, I never spend any except on cigarettes and a feed sometimes. In fact I'm richer now than ever I was. It might come in handy soon, if ever I get to England … Charlie is busy here writing to the wife, so I am thinking of writing to a young lady as I haven't such a thing as a wife. I have just heard that today is Sunday and there is church on this evening, so I think I will go. It isn't dark here till nearly 10 o'clock. Did I tell you that I got a letter from Mrs Braddish. I also got a number of letters from Savilles girls, I don't think Pearl gives a damn for Tom or vice-versa. Anyway she is no good to me. I have had a number of letters from Myrtle lately she wears glasses, so will be some style. Joe and Jim are in Codford Camp in England …

The brothers continued to put pen to paper and with each letter they revealed more of their experiences at Messines. Charlie wrote:

13th June 1917
Dear Mother Father & Jim,

… I said before that Tom Roberts was killed I wrote to his brother a day or so ago and sent them a £1 which Tom gave me the night before he was

killed, the Adjutant has his wallet which he will send home to his people, I heard since that Lorrie Taylor from near Cheynes was also killed the same day and heard that Les Cant was wounded but I think it was only slight, we had several narrow escapes when we were going over. Al got hit on the back and was knocked down but after a while he was alright later on in the day we had several close shaves, Percy was not in it he was kept as a reserve with others. About two days afterwards the General that commands our Corps said that our brigade was the best and did the best work under his command later on he told our Colonel that our battalion was the best in the brigade and that he was proud to have us under his command, our Major told us that our battalion was the first battalion in the A.I.F. to capture a field gun which I understand will be brought back to Australia. We have not had a mail from Australia for a good while but they say there is a mail at the brigade P.O. and I hope so this is not a very long letter but I will answer your letters when they come. Albert met one of Jack Price's battalion and he said that Jack was killed on 11 April Geordie wrote some time ago and said he heard Jack was either killed or missing, it is hard luck for his people. I saw Jack when I landed in France.

The roll call of mates who fell at Messines is sobering:

Tom Roberts, who had handed Charlie the pound note before they went into battle, had left the farm at Durham Ox to enlist in April 1916 at the age of 25. In February 1917 he was wounded, hit in the forehead by a bullet. A month later, on 1 March, he returned to the front. He was listed as missing sometime between 7 and 9 June and, a week later, reported killed in action. His mother wrote numerous letters but received no official report of his death, although her letters explain that his mates wrote to her. His name appears on the Menin Gate Memorial at Ypres.[11]

Harry Harnell was a labourer from Heathcote and is pictured in the postcard Albert sent home in March.[12] He enlisted on 12 May 1916 at the age of 40, joining the 38th on the Western Front in March 1917. He was killed by machine-gun fire sometime between 7 and 9 June. Official documents report that he was buried in a large shell hole 1500 yards south-south-west of Messines. His body was never recovered and his name also appears on the Menin Gate Memorial. [13]

Lorrie Taylor was also buried in a shell hole in the same area as Harry Harnell. His death occurred sometime between the blowing of the mines and the withdrawal. He was 20 years old and an orchardist from Shepparton. According to one report, 'whilst asleep in a shell hole which he had previously fortified, he was killed by shell fire'. Menin Gate is also his memorial, his grave a lost shell hole at Messines. [14]

Tom Burt was 27 when he left the farm at Heathcote; he is also pictured in Albert's postcard.[15] He was wounded by gunfire at Messines but survived to rejoin his unit in September for the disaster of Passchendaele. An official telegram home to Tom's family listed him as missing on 13 October 1917. After a Court of Enquiry hearing in 1918 the family was told that he had been killed, lost in the mud of Flanders Fields. His name also appears on the Menin Gate. [16]

Bert Jeanes had enlisted at the age of 21 and sailed with Albert, but had not been killed as Albert had thought. Bert sustained multiple wounds to his face, arm and leg, but had survived. He returned to Australia in November 1917. Whether he lived much longer given the severity of his wounds is uncertain.[17]

Les Cant lived on a farm a short distance from the Marlows at Pine Grove. He was 25 years old and was shot on the day the mines exploded. He recovered to rejoin his unit in August and survive the carnage of Passchendaele, returning to Australia in May 1919. [18]

Peter Owens, another farmer from Pyramid Hill, was 34 years old when he enlisted on 13 January 1916. He was wounded by gunfire on the second day of the battle but recovered and returned in December 1917. A bullet found him again on 14 June 1918 and he never returned to the Western Front. He was repatriated in January 1919.[19]

George Collison of Bealiba had sailed on the *Shropshire* with Charlie. He sustained a gunshot wound to the chest but returned to the front in October. He was wounded again on 11 June 1918 and his leg was amputated. He returned to Australia in January 1919.[20]

Other mates were more fortunate, as were the Marlows:

Tom Dickinson was a 26-year-old farmer from Nhill who also appears in Albert's postcard.[21] His war service records indicate that he survived the war years without serious physical wounds. He returned to Australia in May 1919.[22]

Corporal Joe Reid was a 22-year-old Irishman; his father's home was in County Cork. He listed his occupation as a labourer on enlistment and joined the 38th and later the machine-gun section which he led into Messines. In August 1917 he left for several months of training in England, returning in February 1918. He was discharged from service in November 1919.[23]

In Allan's following letter he predicts that the Battle of Messines would long be remembered as a significant battle in the 'history of the world'. It certainly proved its significance in the history of the war.

In the field
13.6.17
Dear Old Jim,

Just a few lines to let [you know] *that I am still standing on the ground and am well so are the other boys. We are still having bonnie weather and I hope it continues as we are taking part in some big jobs. We have just come out of the battle of Messines which I don't think will be forgotten in the history of* [the] *world. As you know the troops have taken it twice before but lost it again anyway we succeeded in holding it. For 2 solid hours before we hopped it, he rocked the gas into us but anyway the lads stuck to it well and then we went over the top. We had some hard fighting at times and the bombardment was terrific. Well after we had taken our objective 2 ½ divisions of Fritzy attacked our brigade but without success. I believe the bombardment for that was the worst ever in the whole war. Well Jim now we are out for a spell for a few days and it is lovely to get a rest. We were supposed to go back to the trenches the other* [day] *but after the good performance we put up, they are giving us a few days spell. I have put in for Blighty leave and if I get* [it] *well I am going down to Devon. I think I stand a good chance I hope I am there by the time you get this letter. Think*

I wont have a good time. Well Jim I am corporal now I was made that a day before we hopped the top so I am satisfied now. Percy was not in the advance. Well Jim I think I have told you all the news so I will close with best love to all.

I remain
Your Loving Brother
Allan

Albert wrote home to his mother when a chance meeting confirmed that his mate had been killed:

In the field
June 19ᵗʰ 1917
My Dear Mother

… I wrote to you before telling you we were in the fight at Messines and got through alright. Since we came out we have had an easy time. It has been very warm lately and yesterday and today it has been raining a bit, the first rain since I've been here. The country looks grand now, all the crops are coming out in ear now. Well dear Mum, things seem to be getting a bit livelier in Mologa, everybody round there seems to be getting married. Fancy old Joey not giving the hall. I reckon they ought to kick him out of the district … Since I've been out this time I've wrote such a lot of letters. We can always fill in our spare time writing. Well Mum, I suppose it is getting a bit cold in "Aussie" now. Everybody that writes to me thinks that the war will be over soon, but I am afraid it will go a bit longer yet. Dolly Rowe's brother and two step brothers are over here. They are very decent chaps. A fellow feels quite at home here now with all the local boys. We only heard here last week that Jack Price was killed. I met some chaps out of his company the other day and as I hadn't heard from him for a long time I asked them and one of them showed me a list with Jack's name and number on it. He told me that Jack was killed on or about the 11ᵗʰ April. Then two days after Geordie wrote and told me about it. It's sad for his people …

He added in a note to his father:

… The country looks grand now and the crops are all coming out in ear, the cockies will be cutting them soon. The farmers here have a lot of potatoes,

beans and peas in and they will soon be ready for eating. They are great ones for weeding in the crops, women, kids and old men are at it from daylight till dark. We often go to the farm houses and get a feed of eggs and coffee, but the eggs wont satisfy you unless you eat about half a dozen. They charge pretty hot for anything they sell. Well Dad, I got a letter from Joe Stone today, it took over two months to come from England [to] here, I suppose he and Jim will be over here soon. Bill McKinnon is sitting near me at present writing letters, he is a Sergeant now. Bill Street is a Corporal and Eddie Kerr a L. Corporal. There is a lot of our district boys here, but I havent met any other local boys other than those in the battalion. I get a lot of letters from England. Flo Wilson's father had a bad accident but is getting on alright now. I had a letter from my Auntie in Devon a while back. I sent them all a photo. Well Dad it was pretty hot about old Joey not giving them the hall. I heard that Mrs Gamble gave him a bit of a talking to. Its easy seen he hasnt got any relations at the war. I am in the same platoon as the boys. I am supposed to be in the Lewis Gun section, but have not had any training on it yet. The officer doesnt want four of us in the one section, so if I do join the Lewis Gun I will have to go with Eddie Kerr in another platoon. Anyway we will always be together whatever I am in. Percy was not in the stunt we were in, he was away for a spell, but has been back with us some time now. I suppose you have read about the Battle of Messines. We were very lucky as usual to get through alright, the worst part of it being the gas that Fritz sent over. There is talk of air raids on Germany, so that will put the wind up the huns a bit and perhaps help to end the war sooner…

Bill McKinnon was 39 years old when he left the farm at Pyramid Hill. He was farewelled by the townsfolk at the same evening function as Allan. He was allotted to B Company of the 38th Battalion. Bill survived the war without serious wounds to eventually return to Australia.[24]

On the same day that Albert wrote to his parents, Allan was providing a very precise prediction of when the war was to end. Just where this date came from is a mystery, perhaps it was yet another furphy. What we do know is that the war did not end on 3 November 1917 as Allan had predicted.

In the field
20.6.17
My Dear Mum & Dad,

... I told you in my other letters about the great battle of Messines, but I never told you why Percy and a lot more of the boys were sent back. The boys that were sent back were old original battalion boys and it was because if we were smashed up, they would have something to form the battalion on again. But we had the good luck to get through pretty right. We are out of the trenches at present but I am afraid not for long. When we go over the top again there will be one of the boys go back again it is a splendid idea, but I will never have the luck to go back. Well Mum I told you in my last letter that you will be getting extra pay but it wont be a while yet I got a pleasant surprise the day when I got my pay book back that I have £18 in the bank. On the 6.6.1917 the Major read out that I was to be corporal so you can see what back pay I got. I made a new allotment but it is no good until another corporal is struck off strength but the pay is still running on in my pay book. I have not heard anything of my blighty leave yet. I am anxious to get down to Devon. Auntie says things are lively there. I get any amount of letters from our relations and Geordie. I got a parcel from Auntie Lizzie it was tra bon. I am sending home souvenirs what I got in the battle. I do hope you get them alright, I am registering the parcel. Well Mum I suppose you have finished cropping by now everything is look[ing] lovely over here but things are very lively.

Well Mum the war will end about November third I think. All the boys are well. Les Townsend has gone down on 14 days leave to a part in France which I cannot mention. He put in for Blighty leave but this is where he was sent. In the letter you will find some German notes and a photo. The German on the right is the one that was stonkered in the big push. He is an officer. I got some useful information papers off him and handed them into our officer the rest of the souvenirs I got off him too which you will get later on. He was a Doctor. Well dear mum I will let you know when my new allotment comes through. I am satisfied now that I am a corporal but I don't know if I will get any blightie.

Well dear mum dad & Jim I will close with best love and say goodbye for the present.

I remain
Your Loving Son
Allan S.

All the boys have wrote. I hope you have got my letters by now.

A photo of German soldiers which Allan 'souvenired', possibly during the Battle of Messines.

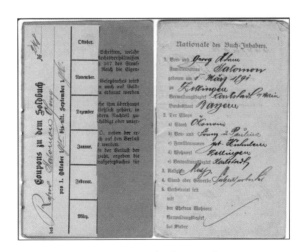

The soldbuch (paybook) of Georg Salomon.

Whether the above items are related to those Allan mentions is unclear. He appears to be referring to an additional photo which is not in the collection. A paybook and identification book, known as a *Soldbuch*, belonging to a German soldier, Georg Salomon, recipient of the Iron

Cross 2nd Class, was also found with these photos. Allan and his brothers frequently sent home 'souvenired' items from front-line engagements.

Percy wrote home to Jim:

In the field
June 21st
Dear Jim

Well Old Sport, once again I am writing in answer to your most welcome letter, which I received by the last mail, was glad to hear you were well. Well Jim, as regards the girls, I am like yourself Jim, you know we have a lot to think of at times, especially when there is a lot of shells flying about. I suppose the elections would cause some fun, as they generally do. You would be set at Jones party, they tell me you are a little fond of Eva, her age is the only trouble Jim, isn't it. Old Squires is a real nark, what is his idea for not giving you the hall. You are having a terrible time with the mice Jim, they are a real pest. Charlie has not got the tin yet, but it will be along soon, it never comes as quick as letters. There was a bit of a go, a little time back, all the boys came out all right, you ought to have seen the place after it, there was shell holes every where, our artillery done great work, old Fritz is getting the worst of things now Jim. Some of our Battalion are getting leave. Les Townsend has got it, not out of France, you ought to have seen him, he was pleased. I have put in for English leave, but it will be some time before I get it, as there is only one a week getting it. Well Jim, I suppose you will be finished with the cropping now, and be having a spell, before ploughing. The crops over here look real well, they are out in head in most places you ought to see them working in the fields, they only have one horse teams; in some cases two the plots are very small; there are a lot of peas about here Jim, none fit for eating. Allan has got two stripes now, there has been a lot flying lately. Peter Owens got wounded not serious, he will get to England. I suppose Frank Dee will be back to Australia soon, Spuddy Kerr has got a stripe, and also Bill Street got another. We are out of the trenches now, for a spell we are on fatigue work every day, fairly easy Jim. It was sad about Jack Price getting killed, his people will feel it; most of his Battalion have been near us lately, Geordie is at a school, he says it is a good spell, its about time he had a good one, he ought to get further promotion I believe Amos Haw and Uwin Johnson are wounded, Geordie did not hear whether it was very serious … Fritz shelled us out of our billets last night, it was funny to see them getting out, men everywhere! I had a Bendigonian sent to me from a girl, in Bendigo, a bit of a fancy of yours, well she was when I was in Australia, you might think of her, you remember you and I met her and another girl near the Fountain opposite the fish shop, and you said after we left, what a pity we did not ask them to the pictures …

He added in a note to his parents:

… there was a hot time here a bit back, about the 7ᵗʰ. I was not in it, I and a lot of others were sent back, so many were sent back out of each battalion, well they got through it all right, our artillery cut the Germans up, it done great work, it was a big set back to Fritz, he has gone back a long way and they are still on to him. Our Battalion had 48 hours of it, and then they came out for a rest, and all of us that were away joined them up. Charlie, Allan and Albert came out all right. Peter Owens got wounded, not very serious, he has gone to England, I think he got hit in the head. You knew Tom Roberts from The Ox, well he got killed it was a pity, he seemed to have had bad luck ever since he came here … There is a terrible lot getting married over in Australia, something seems to be urging them on …

Charlie also wrote:

… I got a letter from Geordie last week, he is getting on fine and was quite well when he wrote … Geordie did not say how Amos or Ewin Johnson were getting on, I was expecting a letter from George Collison who was wounded on the 7ᵗʰ but so far nothing has turned up. Albert Sinclair is in England and was likely to go home. I wrote to the Roberts again and hope they get their letters if you see them you can tell them that I wrote to them, Les Cant from Milloo was wounded and I believe he is in England. Young Hill from Calivil is camped about a mile from here, he came over one night but I did not see him, Percy says he is a corporal, Les Townsend is a Lance-Corporal on the M Gun … Well I will ring off for this time we are getting on fine and get plenty to eat. I will say goodbye with love and best wishes, I will remain

Your loving son & brother
Charlie E Marlow

Albert Sinclair was a 29-year-old married farmer from Durham Ox who had enlisted on 13 March 1916 and sailed on the *Shropshire*. When he arrived in France he became ill and returned to England where he convalesced until September 1917. On 13 October he was gassed at Passchendaele but recovered and returned a week later. He was wounded by gunfire on 17 July 1918. No longer fit for battle, he left England for Australia on 20 November 1918.[25] His brother, Jack Sinclair, was a 23-year-old farmer who had also sailed on the *Shropshire*. On 22 October 1917 he sustained a gunshot wound to the head and returned to Australia in January 1918.[26]

Percy now penned a letter to Jim in which he enclosed a note marked 'Private'. He felt it was time he asked his family to overcome their disapproval of Charlie's sudden marriage:

In the field
June 30
Dear Jim

… Glad to hear you had a good time at the fair Jim, I dare say you had a girl or two, you saw Alice, I suppose you had a bit of fun. Well Jim, we are further back from the line now, we are drilling, have to go fairly solid, we had a half day off Saturday, but it was too wet to go anywhere, so we stayed in the tent, there are thirteen of us in a tent, round tents its fairly warm. The weather is a lot cooler than it has been, we have had a fair bit of rain lately. There is going to be sports here soon, it will be a bit of a change from drill, one item that will be interesting that is a Mule race, bare back they are tricks to ride. There is a cricket match on tonight between the 38 and 37 it is going on now. Yesterday was Sunday, we were to have church parade in the morning, but Fritz put a few shells over so they put it off, great idea church parade in the morning, and drill in the afternoon. Well Jim I have no more news so I will ring off hoping you are well I remain your loving brother

Percy

Private
Dear Jim

Well Jim old sport, you are a bit solid on Charlie, don't you think, in one letter he got from you today you were letting things fly, you ought to know that it hurts especially when you are so far away, he has been going off a bit about it. I had to hide two letters I got from you I knew if I showed him he would have went off pop. Charlie broke the news about the new arrival, just fancy you being Uncle Jim.

On the day Percy wrote to Jim, Charlie received a cable with news of the birth of his daughter, Beatrice Eva, on 6 June. The message arrived in London on 11 June but took almost three weeks to reach Charlie. His joy must have been diminished by the criticism he continued to receive over his marriage and now also his fatherhood. Some exchanges hint at both financial concerns and political differences as the cause of some tension. In Australia at the time, political and religious divisions had deepened as the conscription debate polarised the community, perhaps also a symptom of broader social issues that lay at the core of the divide. Nonetheless, Percy admonished his brother Jim, telling him that such letters were harsh and distressing for Charlie; a lack of family support when life was so tenuous was callous and unfeeling, particularly since this was a young man who had simply followed his heart.

It unclear whether the brothers were aware that they were soon to become uncles, nor is there any evidence that the family at home had any idea, for the letters reveal no hint of Pearl's pregnancy prior to the arrival of Eva, as was her preferred name. Later letters from his brothers would suggest that Charlie had kept the news of the pregnancy to himself. Nonetheless, it would be difficult to imagine, at least for her paternal grandmother, that the arrival of Eva had not been cause for celebration. For Charlie, like so many young Australian fathers serving their country in foreign fields, the birth of a child would bring great joy tempered by the anxiety imposed by distance and the uncertainty of life inherent in war.

As Charlie received his joyful news, the 38th remained under fire while occupying the rear areas at Regina Camp behind Ploegsteert Wood. Long-range enemy artillery could reach up to 25 kilometres and periods of rest were rarely completely safe. The Germans were well aware of the location of the camp and, as the incidence of artillery fire increased, the men were relocated — fortunately just prior to heavy shelling of the camp. The 38th moved to the foot of Mount Kemmel on the banks of the Douve River close to the location of General Plumer's headquarters which, for the duration of the Messines Offensive, was buried deep in The Lettenberg, a 97-metre-high rise which formed part of the side of Mount Kemmel. This point was a significant observation post providing a commanding view of the front line from Messines over Wytschaete to Ypres. It was here that the men rested, competed in sports competitions and enjoyed the relative quiet while Haig's preparations for the next phase of the Flanders campaign continued.

* * *

BELGIUM 2011

It is a glorious spring day as we traverse the area around Messines and Mount Kemmel and, with the sun on a southerly path, I struggle with my sense of direction and wonder how the Australians adjusted to the change in 1916. We find our way to Hill 60, today a poignant memorial to those who perished in the blowing of the mines and the subsequent fighting that erupted all along the Messines Ridge on 7 June 1917. Hill 60 rises, as its name suggests, just 60 metres above sea level and was formed from the spoil of the deep railway cutting that runs along its side. The rise provides a clear view across to Ypres in the west. Little wonder the Germans fought so fiercely to hold the feature. They would have no need for intelligence, balloons or aircraft to tell them what the Allies were planning, they need only peer over the parapet. Little wonder then that Haig was compelled to push the Germans off the ridge to ensure the success of his Flanders plan.

The memorial to the 1st Australian Tunnelling Company at Hill 60. Bullet holes from the fighting during World War II pit the surface (author photo 22 April 2011).

My father and husband stand alongside the remains of German fortifications on Hill 60 (author photo 22 April 2011).

We move towards Hill 60, past the memorial to the 1st Australian Tunnelling Company. The scars of World War II are clearly evident in the bullet holes that pit the surface. We walk through the massive crater some 18 metres deep and 79 metres wide, testament to the force of the explosion. Surrounding it are undulating dips and rises, lumps of concrete left where they fell after they were blasted to the sky. We stand in awe of the remains of a menacing pillbox and examine the rusting steel reinforcement protruding from concrete close to a metre thick in places. Today Hill 60 is green and quiet. Under the soil along the ridge where 19 mines exploded at 3.10 am on 7 June, 10,000 German soldiers lie, their bodies never recovered.

Just ten minutes' drive south-west of Hill 60 are the excavated remains of Bayernwald trenches (Bavarian Wood) close to Wijtscahte. These were fortified German trenches that included the entrance to a tunnel and concrete bunkers. It is an eerie feeling walking in the footsteps of the soldiers and looking out across the fields from the top of the shallow trenches. Beyond the farmland, perhaps only three kilometres away, is Lettenberg Hill, a spur of the larger Mount Kemmel and the site of General Plumer's headquarters during the Battle of Messines. Four large bunkers are set into the hill, the entrance to the tunnel system that was the headquarters. The exterior is pocked with bullet holes, many a legacy of World War II. One bunker is marked with a red cross while another has communication wire protruding from the thick concrete. It is at the base of these hills, on the Douve River, that the 38th rested following the battle of Messines.

Bayernwald trenches (author photo 22 April 2011).

On our way to Ypres, some ten kilometres from Kemmel, we drive through a roundabout which was once Hellfire Corner, heavily and relentlessly shelled by German artillery. This intersection lay on the main route through which Allied soldiers approached the front, rushing through with transports and supplies, praying that God was on their side that day. I recall a conversation with retired Lieutenant Colonel Jack Swatton who had commanded the 38th Battalion post-World War I. Jack had been a transport driver responsible for delivering ammunition and supplies to the front line. He described the route as hell; he would leave for the front with a team of horses and he would never return with the same number.

A first aid post in the Lettenberg bunkers, built into the side of Mount Kemmel. The bunkers served as Allied Headquarters (author photo 23 April 2011).

We had come to Ypres to visit the Menin Gate Memorial at the eastern entrance to the city where the names of close to 60,000 Commonwealth soldiers are commemorated, soldiers lost in the mud, missing, with no known grave. When the imposing memorial was constructed in 1927 it was not large enough to contain the names of all those who had been lost in the Ypres salient. Some 35,000 missing from 15 August 1917 are inscribed on the wall at Tyne Cot Cemetery near Passchendaele, including all those from the New Zealand and Newfoundland forces. The numbers are staggering. The gate stands over the Menin Road in the old walls of the fortified city where ramparts and two stone lions once guarded the entrance. The restored lions of the original ramparts guard the entrance to the Australian War Memorial in Canberra. They were briefly returned to Ypres for the commemorative period of the World War I centenary.

The historic Menin Gate at Ypres (author photo 22 April 2011).

Australian soldiers trudged through the ruined city, past the decimated Cloth Hall and cathedral and past the lions, on their way to the battlefield, or through Lille Gate further to the south. We wander through Grote Markt. Like the thousands of visitors every year, we eat ice-cream in the square, buy Belgian chocolate and later have a Belgian beer in a sidewalk café. We are amazed by the enormity, medieval design and symmetry of the Cloth Hall and cathedral, both reduced to shells in the war but rebuilt on the original foundations. Inside the thirteenth-century Cloth Hall, so named for its function in centuries past, is the sombre Flanders Field Museum.

As evening draws near, we walk to the gate with throngs of others. We are all here for the moving Last Post ceremony. Since the memorial was unveiled in 1927, uniformed firemen from Ypres have played the Last Post here every evening at 8.00 pm. The ritual was briefly interrupted during the years of German occupation when Belgium fell to the invading forces. Tonight the police arrive and close the busy road for the gathering crowd. It is just three days until Anzac Day. The Australian naval cadets march in, Australian schoolchildren lay wreaths and Australian veterans read the Ode. As always, the haunting Last Post triggers emotion as, in the shadow of the gate, I reflect on lives cut short, futures lost and the thousands of husbands, brothers and sons who were never found. As dusk falls and the Last Post echoes I stand in silence; the enormity of the tragedy that unfolded here is overwhelming.

THIRTEEN
HE HAS DIED A HERO AND NOT A COWARD …

FRANCE, JUNE AND JULY

George remained in the south around Amiens and the village of Albert during June and enjoyed a period of relative quiet. In the fine weather, various sporting events were held while training continued, including lectures on the prevention of venereal disease, the rate of which was alarmingly high among Australian troops. George does not mention such lectures although he will almost certainly have encountered these at the school where he was currently being instructed.

France
June 15 1917
Dear Jim

… I have been away from the unit for about 10 days I am at a school of instruction and wont be going back for a few days yet. I haven't heard from Amos or Ewin yet but there might be a letter from them when I get back. My word its red hot giving that fellow a send off and only being in Mologa such a short time, they ought to use their brains a little and give it to the red cross instead of throwing money away like that. I sent a small parcel home by the last mail I hope you get it. The other lads have been in an attack so I see by the paper and seems to have been a great success, I was in that part of the line 12 months ago and it used to be lively there then, I have an idea that I will meet them soon. I suppose the Price's will be cut up on hearing that Jack is killed, I was in the same part of the line where he was killed, we went in after them it was the worst fighting that I have been in, that[s] where Ewin was wounded although he was half a mile behind where I was and Amos was hit before we went in there, in a much quieter part, I was buried but didn't affect me in any way …

George wrote home again a few days after King George V arrived to inspect his dominion troops on 12 July. Within a week, George would be preparing for a move north in preparation for the next stage of Haig's Flanders plan. After 19 months of absence from home, this was, as he remarked in his letter to Jim, his opportunity to finally see his brothers.

France
July 16 1917

Dear Mother Father & Brother

A few lines to let you know I am still going strong and hoping all are well. I received my last letter from you about a week ago dated the 28 April, there has been some from Australia sunk since then and we were notified some our mail that we sent away from the 21 to 31 May have been sunk. I wrote two in that time I sent a small parcel at about the first of June so I think it will be safe I am sending another one soon with a belt with badges of different regiments also some other little things. I got a letter from Charlie a few days ago saying that he got a cable to say he had a daughter fancy being an uncle now, they were all well. Archie Bailey is back with the battalion again I am going to see him tonight as his unit is not far away. I saw a letter from Ewin Johnson this morning he is out of hospital now and has had his furlough he went to Scotland he is now in camp out at Lark Hill, I suppose he will soon be back as they don't leave them over there long now as they want the men over here different to when we first came to France they used to leave them in England a long time when they got wounded, you will understand what I mean when I answer this question that Jim asked me in his last letter about what they are going to do with some of the N.S.W. troops, the answer is yes I cant put it any plainer as the censor will only cross it out, and for Poziers I cant tell him any experiences of it or it will also be crossed out and as for the other question, well I have been in every battle that my brigade has been in since we came here. I met a mate of Amos's he said that he was in England and has a big wound in the leg I think he said there was a hole right through and that he thought Amos would not do any more fighting. Mother asked me in her letter if I had enough money while in England yes I had plenty I brought some back with me. I was glad you got the brooches, don't loose the one of Ypres as it is a good souvenir. We were inspected by the

King a few days ago. I am sending a photo of 8 of us we were at a school of instruction and had them taken they are not good but keep it as a memento of some of the lads that fought with me. Well I will now close hoping all are in the best of health.

Your Loving Son & Brother
George

Written on the back of the photo: 'Top row l to r Bert Hawkesworth, Harry Hoskins, Charlie Edwards, Syd James, George, Joe Steel, (Buff) Braithwaite, George Brittain.'

The details of all of the men in Charlie's photo have been difficult to confirm. Certainly Joe Steele and George Brittain were members of the 2nd Light Trench Mortar Battery and both survived. Joe was an Englishman working as a sheep farmer near Melbourne, his parents still living in England. He was 20 when he enlisted. He was wounded in August 1916 and returned to his unit but was then frequently hospitalised with scabies and influenza. He returned to Australia in May 1919.[1] George Brittain was 19 years old and working as a draper at Numurkah. He was shot in the head and knee on 25 April 1918 and was repatriated in December 1918.[2]

Harry Hoskins, a 33-year-old metallurgist from Geelong, landed at Gallipoli on 1 June 1915. He fought there until September when he was hospitalised with gastroenteritis. He joined the 2nd Light Trench Mortar Battery in France in September 1916. Harry was shot in Belgium on 4 October 1917, but recovered from his wound. He was hospitalised again with a badly wounded finger in May 1918 and was admitted once more in October. This time he did not recover, dying from influenza on 27 October 1918.[3]

AUSTRALIA, JULY

Letters from Australia written to George in July reveal something of family affairs and broader social matters. The brothers' cousin, Eddie Cheyne, describes his eighth unsuccessful attempt to enlist and highlights the debate over conscription and the religious basis for the various attitudes to this contentious issue. Newspaper reports of the situation in Russia were initially encouraging and, on 1 July, a successful offensive against the Austrians brought short-lived hope. However the Russian army was eventually defeated by German reserves and, by August, the collapse of Tsarist Russia was all but complete. Russian forces were in retreat with many units mutinying. The German High Command would be quick to turn the revolution to its advantage.

In the local Mologa community, fundraising events for the Red Cross brought fierce competition as young ladies and their sponsors vied for the crown of 'Queen'. Pearl was unwell and Sarah's trip to Bendigo to visit her sick daughter-in-law must surely have been a positive sign from Pearl's new family, although Jim's letter to George also tells of the bitter division that remained.

8 July 17
Wattle Park
Junortoun
Dear George

I thought that I would write you a line or two, as I no that always a letter comes in handy, as you don't have much amusement over there in the trenches, I have had one or two letters from the boys especially Percy, and *also one from Charlie. I suppose you heard by this that his wife has got a daughter and she is very proud of it. I suppose you never see the boys at all and you won't have much time. I don't suppose you heard that poor Lorrie Taylor is killed in action, it was a hard blow for his parents, but of course they were expecting something like that, and also Mrs Taylor's two nephews were killed there seems to be a lot getting killed now and wounded. How are you getting on over there I haven't had a letter from you this long time but I suppose that they go astray. This is the last time that I am going to enlist, and it is the eighth time George but it was no good. I am strong enough but it is my legs that puts me out. I might be called up for home service but that is no good to me I want to be over there with the boys. There seems to be a lot of boy kicking around in Bendigo on a Friday but they don't seem to enlist I don't know what they are thinking of. If they would only go the war might end more quickly than what it is. I don't think that they are going to bring in <u>Conscription</u> it seems a pity if they don't as the <u>R.C.'s</u> wont go not unless it does come in. They are all finished putting in their crops and thinking about fallowing, some have made a start. We are ploughing up more new ground it is the only thing that a man wants to get a lift but wheat is not much good as they cant get it away on account of the shortage of boats and the Germans are making them less every day. I think that I will now close from your loving cousin*

Eddie

Jim also wrote to George:

Mologa
July 8ᵗʰ
Dear George,

There is no sign of the mail going out but I will write a few lines today, have not long had dinner after being to Church this morning. Mum went to Bendigo yesterday, Pearl has been very bad she caught a chill, I have not heard what it really is, they did not tell us much. It was a great mistake Charlie ever got married look what it will cost him, he will want all his money when he comes back. So we are batching today, not a bad game I got 3 cows to milk and 3 calves to feed the latter are a damn curse, I have also got the young ducks to feed. We have a lot of fowls some of them ought to be in the pot there are not many "clucks" which you used to be so fond of looking after. I started fallowing a few days ago, it sticks of course, we have had about an inch of rain and it might work better now the crops are looking well, I notice there is a lot coming up in between the drills. The season is shaping well, every indication of a good one. The concert and dance came off the other night and I was very disappointed in not being able to go, I had a bad headache and had to go to bed, I never can go anywhere. The concert was real good, the best for a long time. There was a good crowd there even though it rained as usual. Florrie Gibson is up at Mahoneys, Florrie sang. Most of the young crowd around here went down to S Calivil to the crowning of the Queen, it was good so they say. Queen of soldiers won easily £ 271- to £201 you will see that things were humming. Uncle George was running the Q of S with D. Bell. Dave Gow & S McCrea was running Miss Lowe. The town crowd were very cocky of winning, I was glad they got beat. About that girl, you can bring one home for me, of course I was thinking of going to England and France after the war, so need not bother if it is any trouble. That's if I don't go to the war. I think T. Alford has tossed over Pearl Saville, I had a letter from him the other day and he hinted at it. I have no Mologa news just at present, so hoping you are well as we are at present.

Your aff bro
Jim

Sarah wrote to tell George the news of the baby and of events in the local area:

July 10th 17
My Dear Ten

Well Ten there has been 2 mails gone down one was coming out here and the other was going over hard luck is it not I was sending parcels over but I think it escaped that or I hope it has. I was very sorry to hear of the boys coming out in scabs for want of fruit and vegetables I am sending you a tin next mail and will put some preserved fruit in it there is one gone to you that you ought to get soon now the Russians are doing well. Well dear Ten I was down to Bendigo to see the baby it is a pretty little thing and so good. Poor Mrs Ogilvie is dead I told you in another letter that she was terribly burnt she suffered terrible agony for a week and then died it was very sad. That Barber girl that works in McKay as been arrested for stealing they searched her box and found a pair of boots and heaps of other things they told her to write out on paper what she took and she had a list as long as your arm. Well Georgie it is bitterly cold and raining half the time and we still have the mice plague we get very little notice when the mail are going out I hope this one get[s] over safe I don't feel too good on it to night I think I caught a cold in Bendigo. Well dear Ten I suppose you are sick and tired of the blessed war I do wish it was over. They got a Queen Competition in Calivil and they got nearly 500 pound it is in aid of the British red cross it caused a lot of jealousy. I think it cost Uncle George a good bit he was working strong for the Crathurs [Carruthers?] Queen. Well dear Ten I must ring off as I have five to write and I am not too good so I will say goodbye and good luck from your loving Mother

BELGIUM, JULY

In early July the 38th returned to the support trenches of Messines where enemy pillboxes provided shelter for company headquarters and dugouts had been rapidly constructed from scavenged materials. Support trenches were generally some two to three kilometres behind the front but well within range of enemy artillery fire. Working parties from the 38th were sent to the front-line trenches under cover of darkness and under threat of mustard gas attack to assist with the construction of a trench system capable of thwarting enemy attempts to regain their lost ground.

During the weeks between the attack on Messines and their return to the trenches they had won, Charlie, Allan and Albert spent time with Percy, enjoying the contact with family members. They enjoyed feasting on the coffee, eggs and fresh fruit that local farmers were happy to sell. They participated in battalion sports and exchanged news of home from the many welcome letters that managed to reach them despite the threat of loss at sea. Parcels from home were most welcome of all and the sharing of fruit cake, lollies, cigarettes and cheese was a favourite pastime and a tangible link to family and friends.

Charlie wrote:

Sunday, July 1st 1917
My Dear Mother,

… I received a cable yesterday from Bendigo to say that our baby is born and that Pearl was well, it took a long time to reach me, I do not know when it left Bendigo but by what I can make out it arrived in London on June 11th and landed here June 30th thus took 19 days to reach me, however I am glad that when it did come the news was of the best. We are out of the trenches yet and will be out for at least a fortnight, we are all well, and having a good time at present, we can buy a feed of eggs and coffee at a reasonable price, the fruit will soon be ripe over here but I think it will be very dear, it will soon be harvest time, there are some nice crops around this camp of course they do not use harvesters but thrash their crops, they grow a lot of peas and potatoes which grow to some order. Pearl said in her letter that Dad paid my insurance, I will give him the money when I come back. I think Jim was a bit hard in his last letter, regarding Clees and elections, well if I had a vote in Bendigo I would have certainly not vote for Hughes, and if Jim was over here he would say the same. I cannot say much about it here as it is subject to censor and we would get into trouble, there were very few soldiers who did vote for him out of our battalion. Well mother I am putting this in a green envelope which I am sending along with a note from Percy. I am sorry to hear that your eyes are not well, but I hope that next mail will say they are quite well again. Geordie wrote last week he is all right. I will say goodbye with love and best wishes from your loving

Charlie

On the same day that Charlie wrote of his news, Percy also penned a letter to his parents:

In the field
July 1st
My Dear Mother & Father

… We have shifted to different billets, to what we were in last time I wrote to you, back further from the line, he does not put as many shells over near us: today is the first time we have had any close and we were just going on church parade when he started, so they dismissed us, its Sunday and the first church parade for a long time, we were drilling in the afternoon. We are drilling all the time back here, no fatigue work. We go back for drill after a certain time in. They gave us Saturday afternoon off, but it was too wet to go anywhere. We have had some wet weather lately, the first for a long time. Well Mum, I have written a lot of letters to you lately, this one is a very short, better than none. Charlie has got a cable from Pearl, with the good news, that he is a father …

Albert wrote to Sarah to thank her for the tin packed with treats that she had sent him. Sarah will have gained some reassurance from knowing that her boys were together and sharing what she had prepared with such love. Unfortunately, the delay in communication meant that Albert's heartfelt words did not reach home for six weeks. Time was rare and precious given the tempo of life on the Western Front.

In the field
July 3rd
1917
My Dear Mother,

Just a line to say I received the tin you sent me this evening and I can tell you I was very glad to get it. It has been a fair while coming but it got here safely. The cake is just lovely. The three boys are here and it seemed like home again when the four of us set to work on the cake. It would have done you a world of good to see how we enjoyed the cake, to say nothing of the cigarettes, cheese, and lollies etc. Well Mum I thank you very much for sending it, because its grand to get something nice from home. There was a bit more of my mail come in yesterday. I got 8 letters altogether, I have got 18 letters by this mail, so did not do bad. I got a letter from Miss Sherlock also one from Mollie and Winnie and a few more around. I also got one from Jim which I am answering tonight. By the way, Charlie got a cable the other night and it seems that I am an Uncle. It makes me feel a lot older. Well dear Mum, we are still out of the trenches, it's a nice spot where we are now. Plenty of sport here, football and cricket being the main things. We had two good concerts here last week, and this week there is to be a sports meeting. Stewart Dabb and G Swainston are back from the hospital. Alex Duncan is in England, he got a pretty bad crack. Well dear Mum, how is Mologa getting on. I suppose its as quiet as ever. I believe Mrs Gamble gave old Joey a pretty rough time of it. Allan is not in the Lewis Gun Section now. He is in charge of another section so I may go in with him. So far, I am in with Percy and Charlie. Les Townsend is a Lance Corp … The mice still seem to be bad over in Australia. We have a few rats here at times and also a few chats. Its not uncommon to see a chap with his shirt off hunting for them. I have been lucky enough to dodge them so far. I got a bonzer shirt at the baths last week, that came from the Australian Comforts Fund. Hugh Martin and a lot more of the local boys are playing football at present. Bert Gibson was lucky getting a job at Cape Town. Did I tell you that Dave Hill from Calivil came over to see us the other night. He has had a pretty long go of it now … It would be nice over in England now. I'd like to be over there now on my four days leave. Well my dear Mother I have no more news so I will close this letter hoping you all are well as it leaves us all here at present, once again thanking you, dear mum for the bonza tin. I am

Your loving son
Albert

Writing to Jim, Albert describes with almost childish delight seeing the King for a second time, although he had managed only a fleeting glimpse. He also expresses the hope that he will one day have the opportunity to visit his relatives in Devon.

In the field
July 4ᵗʰ 1917
Dear Jim

…I also received the most welcome of all, the tin that Mum sent me. I received it two days [ago] and the cigarettes you sent me were very welcome. We had a good time with the cake. Charlie received his tin tonight. They are having sports here, they will last a day or two. Allan is in the Siamese race. Well Jim, the war news is getting a bit better lately, the Russians seem to be

shaking Fritz up a bit. Allan got a letter from Geordie today, he was well. You seem to have had a good time in Bendigo. Everybody said the Easter Fair was very good. The photos ought to look very good. I had a letter from Flo today, she is sending me a photo. I had a nice long letter from my Auntie in Devon yesterday. It must be a very pretty place down where she lives. I hope to get down there some day. Well Jim, the King was travelling past this way yesterday, so a lot of us went out and lined the road as he went past, and gave him 3 cheers. But he went past that fast in his motor, that all we saw was a cloud of dust. That's the second time I've seen him. We had some good concerts here last week. A couple of soldiers done up as tarts, they were got up well too …

Charlie wrote to thank his family for the parcel he had received:

Sunday
8th July 1917
My dear Mother, Father & Jim,

… I received your very nice parcel on Thursday and thank you very much for it, the things were very acceptable & the cake was very nice…We went for a walk yesterday and got some fruit but it is very dear over here cherries are the cheapest being about 10d a lb. I saw some peaches they wanted 10d each for them, grapes are worth about 3 francs an ordinary bunch (a franc is worth about 10) they are much cheaper in the south, as they are grown under glass in this part. I have not heard how Les Cant is getting on nor George Collison. I do not know their address or I would write to them, I wrote to Albert Sinclair but have not got an answer he must have shifted to another hospital or sailed for Australia, I think I told you before that he was in England. Geordie did not know how Amos or Ewin were when he wrote but he thought their wounds were slight …

As Charlie was writing, Allan was likewise penning a letter. It was Sunday and the boys, now in a rest area, had the luxury of time to reply to their welcome mail:

…Oh mum we do have such fun with the chats. They are brutes of things and very thick over here. I enjoy killing them but they take some catching. Everybody has them on them and it is funny to see the boys with their shirts

off looking for the brutes. We are out of the trenches at present but will be back again in a few days. Tomorrow we hold our sports which out [ought] to break the monotony a little. Charlie got your parcel the [other] day which was bonzer. I got one from Auntie at Leicester the other day which was lovely. I often get letters from them all also Geordie. All are splendid. Charlie got a very surprising cable the [other] night. I believe we are all uncles now. I feel about 20 years older now…

Percy also put pen to paper. Within a couple of days the brothers knew they would be back in the line and opportunities to write would be few:

In the field
July 8th
My Dear Mother & Father

… we are still in the same place as we were last time I wrote, but I think we will be going in soon again. There is sports here, starting tomorrow they will be fairly good, it will be a change from drill. Charlie got your parcel the other day. The cake was real good, I must thank you very much for the cigarettes, they will be very handy. We are expecting a mail in soon, it's a long time since we had a mail, I hope it comes before we go into the trenches, They are playing cricket here every night, some good games. Les Townsend has come back from his leave, he had a good time. They had a lot of the guns captured by the [censored] in one of the towns near here, there were a lot of Machine Guns. We had some rain today, it was Sunday, we had church parade in the morning. Well Mum the Russians are making a bit of a move now, they have taken a lot of prisoners. I will have to close now, as I have run out of news, which is very scarce just now, so I remain your loving son

Percy

HOLDING MESSINES

By mid-July the men of the 38th were back in the trenches near Messines holding the front they had won earlier in June. The battalion found cover from the elements and from German observation in the ruined homes of Messines, in the remains of German pillboxes and in makeshift shelters.[4] From the precarious shelter of a dugout Allan took a moment to write to his mother of the warm weather and its effect on the rotting bodies of the dead that could not be recovered from no man's land. He suggested that recent Allied success had effectively destroyed the might of the German forces; in his opinion, the war would soon be over.

In my little dugout
13-7-17
My Dear Mother,

Just another few lines to let you know that we are all well and hope you are the same. We are back in the trenches now and things are pretty lively at times. We are in the trenches what we took a little while ago. It is pretty warm weather here at present and the smell about here is not the best. Charlie got a letter from Geordie today. He is splendid and is out of trenches still. He is having a long run out. Mum I had stiff luck the other day. There was 8 Corporals and Sergeants nominated for an officer school at Oxford, England. In the finish there was only 2 of us left in. I happened to be away just at the time and the other chap got it. It was [a] 6 or 7 months school. I was wild with my self. Well dear mum the war is nearly finished now we absolutely got old Fritz stonkered. He is getting particular hell. Mum I sent you a parcel of souvenirs and I hope you get them alright I registered the parcel. In the letter you will find a little card and hanky. When we get out of the trenches I will send you something better. Well dear mum dad & Jim I will say goodbye for the present.

I remain
Your Loving Son
Allan

Allan rose early on the morning of 16 July. He dashed off a note to Jim as he made his preparations to leave for two weeks of training; as usual his war predictions had proven optimistic.

Two days prior, Percy had presented with enlarged glands. He was now on his way to St Omer General Hospital in the north-west of France on the railway line to Calais. He was isolated with mumps and would not rejoin the unit until 10 August. Albert and Charlie remained together as the Allies continued to hold the front line at Messines.

In the field

16-7-17
Dear Old Jim

Just a few lines to let you know that we are all well and hope you are the same. We are having lovely weather and are in the trenches at present. All the other boys are in bed yet, but I had to get up early as I am going away for a school for a fortnight. It will do me. Well Jim I think I will get my blighty leave soon wont that be bon. Things are pretty lively at present well plenty live enough. I think we have old Fritz stonkered. The Russians are doing splendid work now. I would like to see what the Age or Argus says about it. Harry Street was wounded the other night but not badly. He is lucky. I often wonder what old Mologa is like she must be pretty quiet now but I suppose you hit up a pretty fair time. I heard that your old girl Chrissie was going to be married. Jim how did you come to let that happen. Well Jim what do you think we are all Uncles now. Charlie got the cable about a week ago. I could have laughed at myself being an uncle. Oh well such as things do happen, we always look for the best. I had a letter from Geordie the other night he is splendid and is still out of the trenches. We will make a final dash one of these days I think, I hope so. I [will] enjoy meeting him face to face. Well Jim I think I have told you all the news so I will close with best love to all. I must have some breakfast (Bacon, bread and tea) and then get away. Hurray

I remain
Your Loving Bro
Uncle Allan
I hope you get the souvenirs
Tell mum we will be home for next easter
The war is going to end in November

Albert also wrote home on the same day hopeful of seeing George who had now received word that his unit would be moving north to take part in the coming offensive, the Third Battle of Ypres. Albert's letter, written as he rested the paper on his knee, is mud-stained and covered in a fine dust which still rises from its surface.

The Trenches
Belgium

July 16th
My dear Mother, Father & Jim

Just a few lines to say I am quite well, and hope you all are the same. We have just come into the trenches again. We were out for over a month and had a good spell while we were out. We have been in three days now, it is a fairly quiet spot where we are. Geordie wrote to us yesterday he was still out of the trenches, and was quite well. He thought he may be coming over this way shortly, so we may see him soon. There hasn't been any Australian mail in for some time now, but I have had a few letters from England lately. Some of our mails home were sunk. The letters that were written between the 23rd and the 31st of May were the ones lost. Well Mum Harry Street was wounded two days ago, but I don't think it was a serious wound. I heard that he got hit in the elbow. Jimmy O'Hare the chap that used to be in Pyramid, came up to trenches for the first time this week. He was fooling about with a German Grenade and it exploded and gave him a nasty hit in the leg. I believe he was badly wounded. We are having a fairly good time since we've been in. It is grand weather here at present, we had some rain a few day ago. The new potatoes are in here now, so it seems like home to get some new spuds. A nice piece of mutton would be very acceptable. Well dear Mother, I am sending you a card in this letter. I hope you get it alright. I hope you can read this scribble as I am writing it on my knee. There is very little news here. Hoping this finds you all in the best of health, as it leaves us all here at present. I will say tata with love to all,

from your loving son & brother
Albert

With thoughts of new potatoes and a nice piece of mutton, Albert tucked his pencilled and dusty letter into his coat pocket and went about his duties as the war thundered on around him: standing to as the sun rose and set, mounting gas guard, shoring up trenches, listening for the distinctive sounds of enemy shells, hunting the endless 'chats' that burrowed into clothing seams and caused constant irritation. He had been on the Western Front for close to two months and was used to the routine.

The following day, on the afternoon of 17 July, a German artillery burst sent the troops diving for cover. Albert was positioned in the support lines in a dugout serving as company headquarters with Lieutenants Abbey and Wyndham and Sergeants Onians and Cunningham. The last shell of the volley was accurately sighted. The dugout in which the men sheltered took a direct hit. All five men were killed instantly. The life of Albert, the youngest son of Charles and Sarah, had abruptly ended at the age of 19.

Just 100 metres away, Charlie rushed through the shellfire to dig out his youngest brother. There was nothing he could do, no chance to console or reassure, no chance to say goodbye. After just 11 weeks on the Western Front the last son to reach the battlefields had made the greatest sacrifice.

Charlie searched Albert's pockets, removing his final letters, including the one he had written just the day before. Charlie would ensure that the family received his final words. He watched as Albert's body was placed on a stretcher to be carried from the front line, then on to a cart heading to Neuve Eglise, some five or six kilometres to the rear. It was then Charlie's task to tell George, Allan and Percy and to write home with the tragic news. Struggling with his own grief and aware that the family will have received the dreaded telegram long before his letter reached them, he tried to find some words of consolation:

In the field
July 17th 1917
My Dear Mother, Father & Jim,

I suppose long before this reaches you you will have received the sad news of Albert being killed we came in to the trenches last Thursday and I believe are to go out on Friday next, and today between 1.45 pm and 2.25 the Germans were shelling us it was not in the front line but what is called supports. Albert was on gas guard near our company office I was about 5 chains away from him at the time in my dugout Albert and two officers and two sergeants were taking shelter behind a big dugout when a shell came over and killed the lot of them instantly, a sergeant came and told me Albert was gone and I went to him as quick as I could but he was dead and they had him on a stretcher. Joe Reed helped to carry him out, he was killed instantly as I said before and knew nothing. I know it will be a hard blow to you as it is to me, Allan went away this morning to a military school at about 8 oclock and will be there for about 12 days. Percy had a lump come up on his jaw like mumps and the doctor sent him to the hospital about 2 days ago, I have just wrote and told them I expect Percy back next week I have wrote to them all in England and wrote to Geordie, poor Albert's watch was broken he had his coat off at the time there was a letter in it addressed to you and one to Myrtle Stone I am sending them on there is also a card for mother I got all his things and his money he has been paid by the military the sum of £23/14/5 and up to the 30th June he had £25/8/- which left a balance of £1-13-7 which the military owed him on the 30th June. I cannot realise that he is gone but we will feel it, and will miss him very much, it is hard luck to be killed so far back from the front line which is about 2 1/2 miles away from here and only his second time under fire I know it is doubly hard on you so far away and to us here it is a hard blow under the circumstances I do not know where they will be buried but I think it will be near here, up to the present they have not buried them but I think it will be this evening they take great care of every man's grave and place a nice cross over it with the name and number and battalion etc. it is near where we made the push I cannot tell you the name of the place or country but I think you will know. I am writing a few lines to Pearl and will put them in with this so will you send them on to her as I have not got many of these envelopes Albert and I used to always sleep together and go out together I can tell you I will miss him very much I will keep whatever things I can of his for you and I think Allan will get leave to England shortly so will either leave them at auntie's or send them home. I suppose you will think this letter is never coming but I can't write somehow I will try and write you a line on Sunday I can guess how you will all feel at home and I can tell you we all share in your grief of our sad and sudden loss and I trust the rest of us will be spared to come home once again, you will be comforted to know that he died without pain and had no fear of shells or bullets, he died doing his duty to his country. I will say goodbye for this time there is nothing that I can say I know, that would relieve you of the awful blow, but let us hope that the rest of us will soon be home again, so goodbye with love to you all

I will remain your loving son and brother Charlie E Marlow

The next day Charlie's grief was further compounded. Despite desperate efforts to reach the cemetery in time for the funeral, he missed the little service and Albert's burial took place without him. He had promised to take care of Albert but had been powerless to keep his promise — now he had missed the final farewell.

18th July 1917
My Dear Mother,

I have just got back from Albert's grave he was buried this morning at 11.30, of course being in the line it is hard to get leave at any rate I managed to get leave to the cemetery I hurried as much as I could but the Chaplain had just finished the service and had gone but there were 7 of our officers still there one of them was Mr Bowden who was officer in charge of the Coy that Albert was in. I went to his grave and the men had just started to fill it in the cemetery is well out of the reach of the shells and there are a lot of Australians buried there, they are all buried in a row and each man by himself, it is a nice little cemetery and will eventually be fenced off and well cared for, the English Government put a small cross over each man but very plain, so I thought I would have a nice one made and have it erected, I tried the pioneers and several others but did no good so then I decided I would wait till we came out which will be on Friday, and on my way back I called to see the Chaplain about it and he told me that our brigade has a special cross made and will allow no other to be erected he said it is a special cross made like [drawing] it stands about 3 feet high and is about 2 feet wide with full name number battalion and date of death I will be able to see it when it is put up the chaplain said there may be a chance of getting a photo taken but that is very hard as no soldier is allowed to take photos. Captain Chaplain Hayden was the minister who buried Albert, he belongs to the C of E and is attached to our battalion, he is going to write to you with regard to the name of the place it is Kandahar Farm British Cemetery and is about 1 mile from Neuve Eglise I am not sure if that is the correct way to spell it but I will make certain later, Albert was killed about 1 mile north of Messines and was taken back last night to the cemetery which as I said before was near Neuve Eglise which is about 4 or 5 miles from Ballieul (I am not sure of the spelling but will find out) that place you will find on the map, and it is in Belgium the grave run as follows Lt Wyndham, Lt Abbey, Sgt Onains, Albert, Sgt Cunningham first 2 officers 1 sergeant Albert and then another sergeant, I sent word to Geordie today also to Al and Percy it was hard Al or Percy not being able to see him but I am going to see them if I can on Saturday. Well Mother I have told you as much as I could about poor Albert and I feel it very much I am on my own at present, but poor fellow he died without pain in fact they all did, Mr Bowden the Lieutenant that brought Albert over told me that he was a good boy and always did his best, he said he was sorry for you and told me to tell you that he was given a good and proper funeral and buried with military honours there were 7 officers there including Major Hurry 2nd in command of the battalion and Mr Bowden, he has just joined us and so far has only been up in the line for an hour or so, when I was in Bendigo I was in his company and when I went out today he knew me at once. Well mother I will draw to a close for this time I will write again on Sunday. I can tell you I share with you the loss of our dear Albert. Enclosed is a note to Pearl you will send it to her, I will say goodbye to you all with love and best wishes I will remain

Your Loving Son
Charlie E

18.7.17
Dear Mrs Marlow

It is with the greatest regret that I write because it is to offer our deep sympathy in the sad loss of your son. It seems so hard when you have four sons at the front & your anxiety cannot be realized by us who are in it. Your son was in a dugout which was hit direct by a big shell & it killed and buried five men. We have been subjected to severe bombardment during the past week and I am sorry to say yesterday one shell snatched from us two officers, two sergeants & your boy who were taking refuge from flying fragments of shell. It is the most awful calamity which has befallen us since we came to France. Accept the sympathy of us all in this your sad bereavement. What else can we offer? We also express our determination to go on & revenge the death of our mates & your son which this war has so cruelly taken from you. He was a good brave lad & is sadly missed by all who knew him. Your other boys are feeling the loss but taking it bravely.

I beg to remain
Yours Respectfully
RW Gollan Lieut

Long before Charlie's letters arrived at Mologa, the cable from AIF Headquarters in London reached Albert's parents. It was dated 26 July; records indicate that confirmation of the cable was received by Headquarters from Mologa on 30 July. Charlie's letter may not have reached the farm for another four or five weeks. It would be four days before Charlie was able to make the long trek to find Allan, still training behind the line, to break the devastating news. George received Charlie's letter the same day; four days later Percy was also to hear of the loss of his youngest brother.

George wrote to his family and, while clearly distressed, he also appears almost emotionally disconnected. He had survived Pozieres and Second Bullecourt. He had been on the front long enough to expect that such news was likely at any time. All the brothers could hope in the future was that luck would be on their side.

France
July 22nd 1917
My Dear Mother, Father and Brother

I suppose long before this letter reaches you, you will have heard of the sad news about Albert being killed I got word from Charlie yesterday saying that he was killed on the 17 of this month it was a terrible shock to me when I opened the letter he was doing gas guard on the company headquarters when the germans started shelling and one killed him outright Charlie said he was not far away and a sergeant came and told him but when he got there he was dead, it is very hard on us all but we must cheer up and hope for the best. He had just joined them up before that big fight in Belguim and was in it, Charlie said he was very game, so cheer up he has died a hero and not a coward. I am glad I met him while on leave I didn't think that would be the last time I would see him. Well Dear Parents and Brother it is very hard on us all but it is no use being down on it as it wont improve matters but we must hope for better luck in future well dear Mother Father and Brother I will now close hoping all are well.

I remain
Your Loving Son
George

I cant write any more you will quite understand why. Geo

Two days after he wrote, on 24 July, George left the horrors of Pozieres and Bullecourt behind him to deal with the personal tragedy that had now traumatised his family. A train took the 2nd Brigade to Caestre in northern France and, following a lengthy march, they reached their billets close to the village of Sainte-Marie-Cappell, seven kilometres north of the rail junction of Hazebrouck. Other than his brief meeting with Albert in England, this was the closest George had been to his brothers since he had left Australia's shores. Determined to find his brothers as soon as possible and personally farewell his youngest brother, George had written the details of Albert's burial in his notebook:

> July 18th at 11.30am
> "Kandahar Farm"
> British Cemetery
> Neuve Eglise

Allan wrote home to console his family and to reassure them that there was honour in the loss of their son and brother. For the first time he addresses his letter to his 'Darling Mother' and, despite including his father and Jim as recipients, the letter is truly written to his mother alone.

In the field
22.7.1917
My Darling Mother, Father & Brother

It is with the greatest sorrow that I have to write you this letter. It absolutely breaks my heart everytime I think of it, and it is how poor Albert was killed. No doubt you will have heard that he was killed but that would be all. Well mum it was on the same ground as what we took some little time back and in which he took part in. And on this particular sector the artillery is very active, and at times you would wonder how it was possible for a man to live. The lads [are] having a rough time, and we must expect some one to go, and dear Albert along with 2 officers & 2 sergeants were the unfortunate ones to fall from the explosion of one shell. He was on gas guard at our company office not up in the front line but in support. Fritz had been shelling the trenches pretty heavy. A shell came and killed him by concussion. The boys tell me he was not hit at all. Concussion from a shell kills one instantly. Dear mum there is one thing we will never forget and that is that he was one that played a great part in the taking of M - which we got a week or two ago. This ground on 3 previous occasions was taken by other troops but lost again and dear mum we are one of the overseas troops that help to capture it and to day we hold it. In that battle which was actually the first one he had been in, he played the part of a good soldier. Dear Mum I had just gone away to a school that morning at which I am now and I only knew yesterday (Sunday) that dear Albert was killed. Charlie came down and told me. Mum I could have died and went back with Charlie and we went up to the cemetery and I saw dear Albert's grave. Charlie told me he got buried with full military honors and he is buried in a very pretty place. Dear Mum I know it is hard on us all, but do try and look at it on the bright side. Mother try & forget it and don't worry as I think we will be home soon. Dear Mum things are very lively here and we must expect some to go. Percy is away in the hospital with mumps he will have a lovely time because they are not serious illness. We had a letter from him and he is getting on well. We have absolutely everything of dear Albert's. I go back to the battalion to morrow I have had a lovely time here. I believe we are getting our blighty leave soon and it will be a few days rest for us. Well dear mum, dad & Jim I think I will close with best love to all.

I remain
Your Loving Son
Allan S

I had just sent those souvenirs just before we went to the trenches

Written on the back of Allan's letter was a note from Charlie:

In the field
From Charlie
Dear Mother,

I have only got one green envelope so Al and I are using it between us, we are getting issued tomorrow or next day so will write to you then I am sending a letter in this for Pearl will you send it on to her. Well dear Mother it is just a week ago today that we lost our dear brother and I can tell you I feel it very much, I know how you will all be at home and will think our letters are never coming I have written to you two or three times telling you all about it I also wrote to Arthur, Florrie, Gibsons and G. Mahoneys so if you did not get my other letters, ask Mahoney's for theirs, I took Al down to the grave on Sunday I got a day's leave from the Adjutant to go and see him as he was away at the bombing school, he did not know a word about it and he got leave to come back with me to see the grave, the English Government have erected their cross with a plate with Albert's name number, battalion date on which he was killed etc, Jack McDonald and I went down to it last Saturday he wanted to see it so I took him down he says that if we are here and can manage it he will get a shrub to put on the grave. There was a letter come from Geordie last night he is still out of the trenches I think he has been out for near 2 1/2 months, he had not got the sad news of poor Albert then, I also got a note from Percy he has got the mumps but that is nothing, he of course, did not know then I wrote again and told him. Well dear mother it is getting dark and I want to post this tonight so will draw to a close. I can tell you I share and mourn with you the sad loss of our dear Albert, I trust you are all well as can be expected as we are here so goodbye with love from

Your Loving Son
Charlie E.M

It was over a week before Percy received the dreadful news that Albert had been killed. During this time he wrote to his family of his daily routine in hospital and his pleasure in having missed a 'little trip to the trenches':

In the field
July 25
My Dear Mum & Dad

Well Mum, I suppose you have been expecting a letter from me, but I have been in the trenches, and from there to the hospital with the Mumps. I have been here ten days. I will be going out soon, this is the first trip I have had to the hospital. I missed a little trip in the trenches. I am having a good time here, there are a lot here, we are a long way back from the line. Well Mum, we have had some rain lately, they could do without rain here now, they are cutting the crops. Before we went in to the trenches we had sports, they were fairly good, a mule race was funny. I suppose you are busy ploughing now, we have not had a mail for a long time, I suppose there will be one waiting for me, when I get back. There seems to be a bit of trouble in Russia now, its be hoped it soon ends. Well Mum, news is terrible scarce here. The Hospital is in a nice place, a big avenue of trees all round. There are three nurses, one at night, two in the day. Well I think I have told you all the news so I will close, hoping all are well I remain

Your loving Son
Percy

Percy added a note to Jim:

… Well Jim, how do you feel now you are an uncle. I droped [dropped?] *to the joke, as soon as I saw the cable come. Charlie went outside the tent and opened it, and we got the good news about half an hour after. I think Fritz must have sunk some of the mail boats, we have not had a mail for a long time, there ought to be some mail waiting for me when I get back. The French here are cutting their crops. We have had some rain lately, it does not improve things now. What do you think of Russia*

it's a terror to see them playing up in such a critical time as this. There are a lot in here, every sort, very few Australians. How's the girl Jim, not married yet …

Percy received Charlie's letter later that evening. Overcome with grief he attempted to write to his mother but abandoned his attempt, writing to Jim instead. He does not suggest that 'cheering up' is possible, but rather implores Jim to do his best for his mother. With the enormous distance between the family at home and the men on the front it was not easy to find a way to provide comfort: a smile, a hug, the companionship of just being there, none of these was possible. Each brother attempted to write the most comforting words he could find.

In the Hospital
July 26
Dear Jim

Well Jim, its hard to write, after hearing the sad news about poor Albert, which I received from Charlie last night, I tell you, I felt it very much, poor Mother must feel it terrible, you must do your best for her. Charlie could tell you all about it, he would get a terrible shock being there. I know he used to shell the place, before I left, it was really only his second time in. I wrote a little note to Mother, but I cannot write, perhaps just as well not to say much it only makes her worse. Allan was away at the time at a bombing school for twelve days so there would be only Charlie there. I believe the one shell got five of them, including two officers. Well Jim, it's a good job, when the war is over. I feel awful sorry for Mother, she would feel it worse than we. Well Jim I will close and share with you the loss of our loving brother

I remain your
Loving brother
Percy

Charlie wrote to his mother:

July 27ᵗʰ 1917
My Dear Mother,

… I trust that you are all well but I know the sad news of poor Albert will be a terrible shock to you I got a letter from Geordie saying that he had received the sad news which came as a great shock to him, I have told you all about it in one of my letters and hope that you have received them all safely, I can tell you we miss him very much, I wrote to you a few nights ago and told you Allan was back, but Percy is still away with the mumps, but that is nothing, we are out of the trenches at present and not far away from where Albert is buried, Geordie says he hopes to be round this way shortly and hopes to see the grave. There has been a lot of your letters lost at sea as I can tell by what you write and then we have had no mail for about 6 weeks, I can tell you the mail was very acceptable, you seem to be having a bad time with mice over there but this is not as bad as the chats and lice over here, also rats, the lice would drive you mad but we manage to get a bath about every fortnight and a clean change of clothes you asked me about the parcel, yes mum I got it alright and thank you very much for it, I forgot to tell you before that Albert had £2/10/- in English and 60 francs in money on him a franc is worth 10d. I kept the money as I thought it was no good sending it home and we can divide it amongst us, all his other things I have kept and as I said before I will keep them all for you, his watch had the glass broken but I think it could be easily mended, the case was slightly knocked about but a jeweller could fix it, I think it is best to send them to Auntie Payne for a while till the boats are more certain of getting home. I am sending this little note with Allan he has written so I suppose he has told you all the news, what there is to tell. Well mother I know you will worry your heart out over Albert but that will do no good so try and look more to the bright side and cheer up and let us hope for the best. I will draw to a close for this time and will say goodbye with love and best wishes to you all

I will remain
Your Loving Son
Charlie

Allan also penned a note to try to lift his mother's spirits:

In the field
28-7-17

My Dear Mum & Dad,

Well dear mum & dad I hope you are all well as it leaves Charlie & I at present. Percy is still in hospital with the mumps. Thank goodness it will be a spell for him. I would not mind the mumps just for the spell. Well dear mum I know you will be worried after dear Albert but mum try and look at it on the bright side, wont you mum. We know it is hard, but one is taking such risks over here. We are out of the trenches at present & are camped a little way from Albert grave. We had a letter from Geordie last night. He is splendid & is still out of the trenches. Isnt that bon. We are going in again and then we are coming out for a long spell. So they tell us. Then I hope to get down to Devon. Mum, what do you think, we got an Ausy mail yesterday. We were all pleased because it was about 6 weeks since we had one … We are having great weather over here now & everything is a picture. I told you we were out of the trenches but we have to [do] a lot of day & night fatigues. We are always working. I came back from the school last Tuesday & brought back good results with me. Well dear mum this is the third letter that I have wrote to you this week so news is scarce so I will close with best love & wishes to all.

I remain
Your Loving Son
Allan

In late July the 38th was relieved from the support trenches by the 40th Battalion. For a fortnight Allan and Charlie were camped at Neuve Eglise (now Nieuwkerke), a short distance from where Albert was buried. Percy remained in hospital. Two days had passed since he had received the news of Albert's death and he again attempted to write to his parents.

In the field
28 July
My Dear Mother & Father

Well Dear Mother, I am still in the hospital, but will be out in a few days, I received a letter from Charlie with the sad news of Albert's death. I am awful sorry for you poor Mother, for you must feel it worse than we do.

I cannot realise that he has gone; poor Charlie must have got a terrible shock. Allan was away for twelve days, at a bombing school. Well Dear Mother I will not say any more as it will only make things worse, in fact I cannot write. I feel it so much. Once again I express my sympathy for you dear Mother and share the loss of our dear brother.

I remain your ever loving son
Percy

* * *

BELGIUM, 2011

The sun is shining, the breeze is warm and the fields are green as we drive through the lush Belgian countryside to find the cemetery where Albert is buried. Kandahar Farm is a small cemetery that contains the graves of 443 Commonwealth soldiers. It sits around one kilometre from Wulverghem on the road to Nieuwkerke. Both these villages fell into German hands in April 1918 but were recovered the following September. The cemetery is in a beautiful location; the land is covered with thick, green grass and dotted with the brown brick farmhouses and barns of the people who reclaimed this area at the end of the war. Fat, contented cattle casually survey their visitors. We open the iron gate and walk into the cemetery as the sunlight catches the blossoms that fall from the trees above the headstones; they float like snowflakes, twisting and twirling on the breeze. The tranquillity of the rural surrounds makes this an ideal resting place for a young farmer who did not come home. Albert desperately wanted to join his brothers at the front and delighted in the great adventure, in the sights he had seen and in his experiences in the line. He felt he had grown up and had proven to all that he could do his duty. We stand here, thousands of kilometres from home, and reflect on this young man and what could have been had the war not claimed his life. Next to Albert's grave are those of the soldiers who died with him that day, buried in a row, side by side, their futures also lost in the great calamity that was 'the war to end all wars'.

The cross Charlie organised to mark Albert's grave.

Albert's grave at Kandahar Farm Cemetery, Belgium (author photo 22 April 2011).

We place a cross of remembrance on Albert's grave in a moment made poignant by our knowledge that we are the first members of his Australian family to have visited since 1924, possibly the only relatives since then to have brushed his headstone and placed a little cross in his memory. I think of Sarah and the moment in the midst of the conscription debate, when she and her husband Charles signed Albert's consent form. The burden of that decision was an overwhelming one to carry.

We find it very difficult to say goodbye to Albert, a young Anzac so desperate to do his duty.

Kandahar Farm Cemetery, a peaceful resting place for a young man who loved the farm. To the right of this photo was the busy dressing station to which Albert's body was brought (see AWM E00482) page 430 and cover image). The building stands today (author photo 22 April 2011).

FOURTEEN
I HOPE THE REST OF US WILL BE SPARED TO RETURN

ENGLAND

Across the channel in the tiny village of Drayton, the death of Albert was also felt by his relatives as they wrote to their family in Australia:

Drayton
Uppingham
July 25ᵗʰ 1917
My Dear Auntie, Uncle & Jim,

We were all very sorry to hear from Charlie this morning telling us of poor Albert's death, it really does not seem possible to think the poor boy has really gone. I had several letters from him while he was in France & he always wrote so cheerful, it seems so hard to lose them when they are so young. I cannot find words to say how sorry we are, I must close this short note. Trusting you are all quite well during this your great trouble.

With our very deepest sympathy to you all.
With love from mother & myself

I remain
Your loving niece & cousin Flo

Drayton
Nr Uppingham
31ˢᵗ July
My Dear Brother & Sister

I cannot tell you how sorry I was when I received Charlie letter telling us of poor Alberts death we were sorry when he had his leave that we were not able to see him it seem so hard him being so young I am sure it must be a great trial to you all, it must be an anxious time for you both with all the other boys in France to i do hope they will be spared to you we were please to hear the news that Charlie had got a daughter I am sure you would all be pleased it's a girl I hope they are getting on nicely well my dear brother I must thank you very much for the ten shillings it is very good of you I wonder weather you get my letter as I wrote a long time ago as I haven't heard from you for some time we have about finished hay time here and have had some very good crops & the corn looks well. Harry Marlow has got his discharge & he is back at The [indecipherable] *at his work & he looks very well he is a fine big fellow not much like his Father I don't think Fred his at Harboro* [Market Harborough] *he is not old enough to join up he been twice to see if they will have him well my Dear Brother I haven't much news to tell you this time Uncle Ted sends his love he is quite well Fred his son has been home for ten days we given him Charley address so praps he may meet with them I hope he will I think I will now close hopeing this will find you all well with love to all*

I remain your ever loving sister
C Wilson XXX

Edith is quite well

THE PASSCHENDAELE CAMPAIGN, BELGIUM (THE THIRD BATTLE OF YPRES)

Throughout June and much of July, Allied High Command continued to debate Haig's proposed plans of attack at Ypres. The Germans, sited high on the ridges encircling Ypres, could clearly monitor Allied movements and preparation. It was now obvious to the German High Command that the Allies were planning an offensive and their intelligence only served to confirm what was laid out like a map before them. German preparations to repel the offensive intensified: reinforcements were brought in from the Eastern Front where Russia was in the final stages of collapse, additional pillboxes were constructed, barbed wire rolled out and more guns hauled in. In some sectors the fortifications were over ten kilometres deep. The Allied conferences continued, with Prime Minister Lloyd George remaining staunchly opposed to the Ypres attack, asserting yet again his preference to advance on the weaker Italian front. Regardless,

Haig forged ahead with his preparations until, on 25 July, he received approval to proceed. Three days earlier, on 22 July, he had launched a massive bombardment in preparation for an advance on the German-held high ground that he believed would open the way to the capture of the coastal ports. General Hubert Gough would lead the advance, the more experienced General Plumer, who had been on the Ypres salient for two years and was responsible for the success at Messines, was overlooked. General Gough had no experience in the Flanders region.

Apart from the small pockets of high ground held by enemy forces, Flanders is generally flat, consisting of reclaimed land with a series of ditches and dikes that form a complex drainage system. It is easily flooded. Under the topsoil lies thick clay. The ground over which the advance was to be made had been blown apart in previous artillery bombardments and was now being pulverised anew. With recent rainfall, it would soon be a quagmire.

On 31 July the Third Battle of Ypres commenced. Seventeen divisions of British and French infantry advanced on a 27-kilometre front from Pilckem Ridge in the north to the Gheluvelt Plateau to the east of Ypres.[1]

By the end of the opening day, British and French soldiers, supported by the artillery of I Anzac, had gained ground, although losses had been heavy. Despite Allied casualties totalling 27,000, the vital Gheluvelt Plateau remained in German hands. The well-prepared German forces had repelled the Allied advance. Heavy enemy artillery fire fell not only on the front line, but also in rear areas hitting roads, bivouacs and battery positions. The rain arrived in the afternoon and continued for days. The battlefield turned to a sticky morass; shell holes filled with water, and heavy fog reduced visibility. The wounded died where they fell, drowning in shell holes or falling victim to infection, their gangrenous wounds left to fester. It was close to impossible to evacuate them from the battlefield. Six stretcher-bearers took one hour to carry a man less than two kilometres, hopelessly bogged in the Flanders mud. Despite the conditions, the attack pushed on through its various stages. The rain continued throughout the month of August.

Kandahar Farm dressing station, the 3rd Australian Division field dressing station, on the afternoon of 7 June 1917 during the Battle of Messines as described by Charlie. The building stands today (AWM E00482).

Charlie wrote from behind the line the day after the battle commenced:

1ˢᵗ August 1917
My Dear Mother,

I am sending you a few lines in a note to Pearl which she will send on to you I have not got many envelopes we are out of the trenches and have not been in since our dear Albert has been killed, I got a note from Percy he is getting alright again and will be back soon he got an awful shock when he got my letter about the sad news. I also got a letter from Geordie he was alright when he wrote Allan was made a Temporary Sergeant the other day, a lot of the N.C.O, have been hit and they were short of Sergeants I don't know how long he will be temporary if some of the wounded sergeants return he will go back to Corporal. Geordie ought to be a sergeant now if he had been in the infantry like us and had good luck all through he would have went close to a commission of a second Lieutenant, but I think the trench mortars are safer and that is better, it would be better to come back a private than be buried a captain, we are camped close to where Albert is buried I often go and see his grave, there was a photo of the dressing station alongside where Albert is buried in the

Anzac bulletin I think Al sent one home to you I have got one for myself I am sending it home to Pearl if you have not seen it ask Pearl for it his grave is the other side of the building. I would get a photo of the grave but the military will not allow you to take photos or have them taken by any one else. I got letters from them in England they are shocked to hear of the sad news of Albert Ida said she got letters from you at home I wrote to you the other day and sent it with a letter of Als, I said I got your letter also some from Pearl and them all up there. I got your parcel and Ida got the money you sent. I think we will be out of the line for a good while this trip, Geordie has been out a good while, I was surprised to hear that Archie Turner had returned also Fred King and Garnet Whitfield had enlisted I did not think his mother would let him go. I got a letter from Auntie Etta last night she said Bert was in South Africa, what is he doing over there is he a private or what. Auntie Etta never says what he is doing over there or anything about him bar that they have not heard from him for a long time. Well mother I have no news I have written to you a lot lately and hope you have got the letters alright. I hope you are all well and that you are not worrying your heart out over us I know that it is hard on you but let us hope for the best and that we are spared to return. I will say goodbye for the present

With love and best wishes
I will remain your
Loving son
Charlie

Percy was discharged from hospital and rejoined his brothers on 9 August at their camp at Neuve Eglise. Just 12 kilometres across the border in France, George had reached Bailleul. The mobilisation of the 1st Division in preparation for its role in the attack on the high ground at Ypres was now underway. The men had settled into billets where the threat of enemy aircraft fire was ever present. Fortunately, George found his way to his brothers and arrived the same day as Percy returned from hospital. The four young Australians spent an afternoon together, a reunion saddened by the loss of their youngest brother.

Percy wrote:

In the field
August 10
My Dear Mother & Father

Just a few lines to let you know that we are all well, I am out of the hospital now, came back a day ago, there was some letters for me, from you and Jim, which I was very pleased to get, it was the first mail we had for a long time, there were two mails sunk and I think there is another sunk since this last one came it's a terror to see them sinking the mails. I put a little over three weeks in the hospital, it was a good rest. Geordie came over yesterday, he is not such a long way from us, I never saw him look better, his unit has been out for three months, he did not have much news he says Uwin Johnson is in Lark Hill Amos Haw got hit in the leg, he will be away for some time. We have had a lot of rain lately, it has done a lot of damage to the crops, they are knocked about a lot. We had a bit of a march today to be inspected by one of the heads, it did not rain as it generally does when there is anything like that on. Harry Street and Bill Stephens got wounded. Harry got hit in the elbow, I do not know where Bill got hit. Allan is a sergeant now, there has been a lot of stripes flying about lately. I saw Fred Smith and Dave Mullens after I came out of the hospital, Fred was saying he saw Alf Ferris the day before.[2] I do not know why you do not get any letters, I am always writing. I mention in one of my other letters about getting the tin which we thanked you very much for, there has been one or two of the mail going to Australia sunk, so that would account for you not getting letters at times. George Johnston is hot on teachers, they must take up all his time. There is a terrible lot of marriages coming off over there, they will be all married by the time we get back …

The following day he added a note to Jim:

… Geordie came over day before yesterday, he looks real well, he is not such a great way from us. Alf Ferris, and Young Baker came over today we have saw quite a lot lately. I saw Fred Smith and Dave Mullens when I came out of the hospital. Allan is a sergeant now, there has been a lot of stripes flying lately. Well Jim, I see you are out at the bush, you have some company. I would have liked to heard you when you got the fox. You need not worry about the French girl. Jim, I have not too much time for them, so I am neutral …

In mid-August the 38th travelled west by train from Bailleul and detrained at Wizernes to the south of St Omer. There they commenced a long march south-west to billets in the small villages of La Calique and Senlecques, some 15 kilometres from the French coastline close to the town of Devres. Although it was midnight when they arrived, the villagers welcomed them and throughout August the 38th remained in the relative comfort of French barns with beds of straw. Training continued, sports days were held and the Australian soldiers endeared themselves to the locals as they helped in the fields and with the daily routine of farm life. It was a welcome touch of normality.

Allan wrote of meeting George and his delight that he had been granted leave to England:

In the field
18-8-1917
My Dear Mother & Father

… Well dear mum we are along way from the line at present supposed to be having a rest, well it is a rest compared with the line but we are drilling. We met dear old Geordie at last. He looks well on it. I spent one afternoon with him but he is a long way from us now. But when we go back we will be near him. I also seen Jim Baker & Alf Ferris Jim Grath. They all look well on it. Geordie has been out of the trenches 3 1/2 months. Well dear mum I am going on leave to England next Thursday. I am terrible delighted to get away for 10 days. I am going down to Devon first and then to Leicester. I have got about £20. We got a few comforts funds today and they were all from Bears Lagoon. We are billeted in a French joint now and the people are bonza. The best I have struck yet and we are having good weather now too. Well dear mum I think the war will end when I said. Well dear mum when I go to Blighty I will write you a good long letter … Geordie is going to see dear old Albert's grave…

Two days later he wrote:

… Just before we left we met dear old Geordie he looks well on it. I can tell you we had an interesting talk and compared our battles. He has been out of the line for 3 1/2 months. Well Jim we got another Ausy mail last night

I only got 2 letters. The ones from home. I don't get many letters at all now I can't make out what has come over my letter writers. They seem to have gone to the dogs. Oh well if they don't write they can't expect any from me. You seem to be very busy over there. I hope the crops come up allright. Where we are now we are in a pretty spot in France, where everything looks lovely. Well Jim old boy I am going away to Blighty on Thursday. It will be a bit of a rest for me, but I won't be able to enjoy it as is nothing had happened to dear old Albert. My word Jim we do miss him. I don't know what it will be like when we get home. But Jim we must look at it on the bright side. These things are to happen. Well Jim old man I am going down to Devon when I get over to Blighty & am going to have my photo taken so I will send them on. When I get over there I will write you a good long letter about things. I have a few postcards that I will send over. I am orderly sergeant today so I have a good chance to write letters …

While Allan was clearly looking forward to his leave, his letter also conveys how much the brothers missed Albert. Just prior to leaving for England, Allan was promoted in the field to corporal and then immediately promoted to temporary sergeant after Sergeant Burroughs was evacuated to England with shrapnel wounds sustained at Messines in June.

With Allan on his way to England, Percy jotted a quick note to Jim:

… Well Jim, we are out of the trenches now, having a bit of a spell, we are a long way back from the line, had a ride in the train some of the way, and a nice long march the rest. Allan has got his Blighty leave, he went yesterday, it was a lovely weather but it is raining today. I was mentioning in Mums letter about being lovely weather and so it was yesterday but it has taken a change like it generally does. We are in a farm house, its to wet to drill, so I am writing this. Charlie is cleaning his ammunition, for the sports, which comes off soon, there is a show platoon in it and Charlie is in it I missed it, no dam good to me I had a go in one the last sports that was enough for me. Well Jim, I would like to be in Allan place fancy 10 days clear in Blighty, Bon "eh" Bon means good well I will close now no more news hoping this reaches you …

Away from the line and at a bayonet fighting school, George found time to write to Jim:

France
August 26/17
Sunday
Dear Jim

… We have been having splendid weather but today was sultry and now it is raining like the devil, it is generally a sure thing to rain when it gets sultry here, it is a pity for us and a godsend to the Germans as it stops our attack, at present they are hammering at Lens and the French and Italians are making great progress, a little while back it rained for a week and the British had just started a big push then it started to rain so fritz got off lucky. You don't seem to think we see much crop here well around here it is nothing else but crop and very good too, the people are working hard at their harvest now, it is hard to see them old men and women, they have been getting assistance from our chaps, plenty of them out in the fields working away, they cut all their crops here and do nearly all of it by hand very few reapers and binders here they thresh it in the winter with those old time threshers worked with a horse. I am glad you got that photo also those other things, that parcel mother sent I think went to the bottom we never got any of the mail either there has been a lot of mails gone down. I don't think you ought to send any more parcels as I only get half of them. I am at a bayonet fighting school at present it lasts a fortnight. This morning we had church parade and this afternoon went into a village close by and had pork chops, eggs and chips for tea, it was a bit of a luxury …

Having received a big mail delivery from home, Charlie penned a letter in reply:

… I got the parcel you sent for my birthday and thank you very much for it. I hope you get all my letters I have written regular to you since Albert was killed, I told Geordie where he was buried he knows the place well and will go and see it, I said before that I sent a cable to you and hope that you get it alright. I wrote to you all last week and am sending this with Percy. The mice plague must be very serious over there and will make it bad for the wheat pool business, I hope that they have died out by now. I wrote to Auntie Florrie today and to Pearl, we are having a grand time here, today it is raining, so we have a half day off, we have a splendid Chaplain now. We

are having sports shortly between the brigade, I am in a platoon (about 30 men) drilling for a competition there is a great keenness between the heads, if we win each officer in our company is going to give us 100 francs (a franc is 10d) and if we win in the divisional show, they say they will double it, we are doing our best, you should see my equipment, I have got a new tunic and it is a splendid one, I will let you know how we get on later. This is a very pretty place, the best I have seen for a long time. I think we will be here for a long time, we are camped in a large barn, and sleep on straw. Al and Percy got those tins you spoke about. Poor Albert got one a bit before we went in last time, I feel it very much when the mails come in and he is not here to get his letters, there has been a lot of mail come in for him. I feel sorry for you at home so far away and so long before you would get my letters, but I hope the rest of us will be spared to return. I will draw to a close for this time and will say goodbye with love and sympathy to you all

From your loving son and brother
Charlie

While Charlie wrote of the grief he felt when letters for Albert arrived he was all too aware of the impact of the communication gap on those at home. It was just six weeks since Albert's death. It is likely that the letter Charlie wrote to his family on that fateful day had only just arrived in Mologa.

Throughout the wettest August in 30 years, a series of pointless, desultory attacks and counter-attacks continued in the Ypres sector on the Gheluvelt Plateau and at Langemarck to the north. Haig's grand plan was stalling, his move to push through now becoming a matter of wearing down the enemy. Australian troops moved up to help break the stalemate. The 4th Division, some 2000 men below strength, was justifiably unhappy to be sent back into the line. For the Australian soldiers, the welcome rest had come to an end.

MOLOGA

In Australia, the congregation of St Luke's Church at Mologa gathered in August to farewell one of their youngest, a likeable young man who had gone to war with youthful idealism and enthusiasm and whose life had been cut short. Reverend Plumtree decided that Matthew 26.8 'To What Purpose Is This Waste?' would represent the most fitting tribute to Albert.

August 24, 1917

Last Sunday a large congregation assembled in St Luke's Church at an In Memoriam service to Private Albert Marlow, who was killed in France on July 19. The church was draped in black and white and the service was most impressive.

I doubt the Reverend Plumtree's words provided much comfort to Albert's parents who had permitted their son to go to war:

It is the spirit of love for country, home and dear ones, which makes such men as Private A. Marlow say "Here I am, send me; and neither father or mother can hold him back …"[3]

While in the churches the tributes flowed, letters and messages of condolence were choking the postal services all over the Western world. They now flowed to the Marlows of Mologa:

Argyle St
St Kilda
1.8.17
Dear Florrie

I was very upset, on reading in the "Argus" this morning, the account of the death while on active service of one of Mrs Marlow's sons. Please convey to Mr & Mrs Marlow & Family my very deepest sympathy. I would write to her myself but feel that I do not know her well enough. This war seems dreadfully cruel, doesn't it?

[Author Unknown]

ENGLAND, SEPTEMBER

The time had passed too quickly for Allan who had enjoyed visiting his relatives in England. They were a tangible link to the rest of his family so far away in Australia and provided some comfort at this dreadful time. For a brief period Allan had returned to something akin to normality and he had delighted in the peaceful serenity of the English countryside. On 2 September he crossed the channel to return to his battalion. On arrival, he reverted to the rank of corporal as reinforcements had arrived.

London
1ˢᵗ Sept 1917
Dear Jim,

… Well Jim I have just had 10 days Blighty leave which was just tra bon but the time flies. Well Jim I went down to Devon and had a glorious time. It is the prettiest little place ever I seen, but it rained pretty well all the time I was there. I saw Uncle John auntie Grace May & all the children. They are all splendid. I think they are in a fairly comfortable way. They have a very nice home. They are bonnie people. It takes a day to get down there & a day to get back after spending 5 days with them I went up to Leicester and seen all the Paynes bar Clem & Flo Wilson. It rained while I was there. I go back to France at 5 o'clock in the morning. So I will be with the boys again on Monday night I don't think it will be long before Percy will get away now I was the first out of our company to get leave so I consider myself lucky. All the boys were well when I left them I don't think they are in the line. Geordie has been out of the trenches 4 1/2 months now. I believe there has been another Australian mail in so there is something to look forward to when I get back … The people seem to think that the war is going to end about the end October. Things are jolly lively up the line now. The last place we were at was Messines and it wasn't fit to live in there. I never saw anything like it in my life. I hope you got my souvenirs alright I am sending you home a few postcards what I missed last time. I have still a beautiful revolver but how to get it home I don't know. I think I had better wait until I go myself. Well Jim old man this is all the news this time so I will close with best love & wishes to all.

I remain
Your loving Brother
Allan

Never publish a letter of mine unless <u>I say so.</u>

Allan added in a note to his parents:

… I wish my leave was starting again. One loses so much time getting across from France and then it took me a day to get to Devon and a day to get back. I hope there is an Australian mail for me when I get back. We are having an awful lot of rain over here. The people are held up with the crops and the biggest part of them are ruined. Well dear mum I believe the war will end about the end of October well every body says so …

Perhaps the death of Albert had crushed some of Allan's earlier confidence. His predictions of the war's end are now qualified as being those of 'the people'. He also insists that his letters not be sent to the local newspaper for publication without his approval. His bravado appears to have been shaken. Nevertheless, he had lost none of his good humour and charm as Allan's cousins explained to his brother; his visit to his relatives was enjoyed by all.

33 Green Lane Rd
Leicester
2.9.17
My Dear George
I am almost ashamed to write to you after keeping you so long for a letter. I hope you will forgive me and I'll promise to write oftener in the future. I was away on my holidays when I got your last letter and that is why I was so long sending your parcel. I hope you got it safely and liked the contents. I sent it last Thursday. I began a letter to you on Thurs and some thing or other put me off. We had Allan here on Friday. We were finely pleased to see him. He had to go away again on Saturday so it was a short stay. He looks well but thinner than when we saw him twelve months ago. How the time flies. We hope to see Percy soon. Allan says he will be sure to have leave before long. When shall you be having leave again? It's about time you did. We should love to see you again. Cousin Flo was here so she saw him this time too. She missed him last year as she was away at the time. He didn't half tease her. We were glad to hear in your last letter you had been to see the boys. I can guess how pleased you all were to meet again. Allan says Charlie is much thinner. Clem has been in a rest camp in India again. He sounded rather doleful when we heard last. He said he was not lucky enough to get

"winged". Allan made us laugh. He said he would like a nice little wound that would mean Blighty for a bit. He spoke as if he could get one to order. We are having a terrible lot of wet here lately. The harvest will spoil, I fear. We hope this will find you still quite safe and well. Have you had a mail from home lately?

Mother and the girls all send their love and say they hope to see you soon.

With best love
I remain your affectionate cousin
Ida

Drayton
Uppingham
September 8th
My Dear George

I was pleased to hear from you again & to hear that you were well. It would be quite a treat not being in the trenches for so long wasn't it? Have you gone in yet? It would be very nice to see your brothers, it was nearly 2 years since you had seen them wasn't it? I was staying at Leicester when Allan came, so of course I was able to see him, he had a very short stay with us, but it was very nice to see him. I am thinking of going to Leicester to live on the 1st of October, so will give you my address when I write you again. I am not quite sure if I shall go, but shall know on Wednesday. At last we are having some decent weather, it rained nearly every day I was at Leicester. It was the wettest August for 50 years. You haven't had very good weather either have you. It has made the harvest very late here but have been getting on well these last few days. I had a letter from Jim about a fortnight ago so expect you have a mail in. I have no news of interest so will close Trusting this finds you quite well.

With love & best wishes
Your Loving Cousin Flo

George appears to have met a young lady during his stay in England and was now corresponding with her. Maudie was one of four ladies whose names and addresses appear in his notebook, although he never mentions her in his letters home. The Australians were often stopped in the street and asked home to dine; they were so far from loved ones, many with no English relatives to visit, that such offers of hospitality were welcomed with alacrity.

325 Wilmot Street
Bethnal Green
London E2
12/9/17
Dear George

Received your ever welcome letter, & was pleased to hear you are still in the pink.

I am glad to hear that the weather is keeping fine over there, as it must be much better for you, the weather is just lovely in London, in fact everything in the garden would be A1 if it were not for those beastly air raids, last week we had a big moonlight raid & I can tell you it was a bit OT [hot?] I think I shall have to go out to Australia where they don't get air raids. Well George at last I have had my photo taken, & as soon as I get them I will forward one on to you, that is if they are good. Have no more news so will conclude wishing you the best of luck.

With Fond Love
Sincerely Yours
Maudie xxxxxx [Miss Maude Mealing]

Of course some invitations were not as well-intentioned as others, as Tom Alford's letter to his mate Jim may suggest. Tom was enjoying his leave in Brighton, although he was clearly shocked by the number of maimed soldiers who were recovering in hospitals in the area:

London
Sept 26th 1917
Dear Old Jimmy

Expect you will be wondering what the 'ell I'm doing over here. Well I'm on my leave & I'll give you the oil its just the thing. I got it a bit before I expected it but it is just as well as the weather has been real tip-top. I'm due to go back tomorrow but am going to take a day or so extra if all goes well. We just came back from a week at Brighton at the seaside. Had a real ripping time. You know the seaside air etc, & there's plenty of little brides about. Talk about females. This country is just full of them. I don't know what half of them will do for a man. I've not been sight-seeing much used to spend most of the day on the beach & go to the theatre at night. Any amount of Music along the beach, perriots, orchestras etc. It is one of England's premier watering places. So you can guess what it was like. We were staying at a place overlooking the sea. Didn't go in Bathing as it was a bit cold. Talk about getting lazy I'd hardly stand up. Don't know how I'm going to cotton on to work again. Brighton was full of wounded principally legless and armless. By God it was pitiful to see them, thousands with only one leg or one arm & it was not an uncommon sight to see one with no legs at all. Yet the poor buggars seem happy. I expect they'll feel it later on all the same. There was an air-raid here last night, but they kept them off London itself pretty well. Only three killed I think. Look Jim our aircraft is absolutely up to shit along side of Fritz. He has done pretty well as he liked up till lately. It used to make me rave and curse the way he carried on last winter in France. Our buggars were never about when they were wanted. Well Jim old sport I was so sorry to hear of poor Alberts death. I heard a long while ago but I didn't know which one. Poor little buggar he didn't reign long. Bear up old cock and remember me to your people. I know how you will feel it especially as some of the buggars around Mologa show scant sympathy in their actions. I wish to Christ it was over. Must say I've had a very lucky run so far & I am missing a big stunt now. My Fabby just tells me not to put too many lies I stayed at her flat last night & am writing in the sitting room. She is buzzing about so you will have to excuse mistakes. She is a bonzer little girl. Pesters the bludie life out of me. I tell you if a man can get through this war it is an experience. I know you would like to be in it and take the risk. Expect by the time this reaches you harvest will be near at hand again. Time soon goes. It was a poor harvest here and in France this year too much wet. Well must close this now hoping you are all well

I am your old pal
Tom Alford.

Tell G. Johnson if he wants a girl he better come to London & he can have his pick of a lot.

FRANCE, SEPTEMBER

As Allan crossed the channel, Charlie was writing to his mother:

2ⁿᵈ Sept. 1917
My dear Mother,

… I got a post card last week from Geordie he was quite well he is near that place where poor Albert is buried. We are still out of the trenches and having a splendid time, it is the easiest time I have ever had since I have been in the army, and we get plenty to eat, we are camped in a big barn which belongs to the Mayor of the village, we can buy coffee, bread, milk, and anything that we want, they are very fine people. I cut one of the old lady's son's hair yesterday and she gave me a lovely drink of coffee and scalded milk I can tell you I enjoyed it tip top, there are a terrible lot of apple trees about here, the trees grow a great height, but some of the fruit is not very nice, there are also pear trees here and the pears are grand. Well mother I have no news as I don't see much and I wrote to you last week, I am sending this note with a letter for Pearl, she will send it on to you, I hope you are all well and that you are not worrying too much over us, I will say goodbye for this time with love and sympathy.

I remain
Your Loving Son
Charlie E

Percy is here and is quite well he may be writing to you today.

George replied to his mother who had written to warn him that he had lost the young lady Sarah had considered promised to her son. As George had commented in May, he was not concerned that Winnie Price was being courted by another local man. Somewhat defensively, he added that there were plenty of options for him abroad.

France
September 4ᵗʰ 1917
My Dear Mother

A few lines to let you know I am sending a small parcel home hoping that you will get it alright. I have received two letters from you lately dated the 19 and 26 June. They were the only two I got from Ausie. You say I have lost Winnie Price well I didn't know that I had her anyway there are plenty in England and here too. One of our chaps have just come back from leave to England he told me he met Allan over there I didn't know he had gone he told me when I met them that he expected it soon. Yes I used to hear from Miss Lowrie but haven't had a letter from her for a long time. I met Tommy Gray a few nights ago he looks well he is a saddler in the Light Horse and a good job too never has to go in the firing line, he is expecting leave to England again soon, he's lucky don't you think. Some of our chaps are getting a few days leave to Paris I would like to see the place, they say it is better than London. Well we are still out of the line we have had a long spell now. It has been lovely this last two days I hope it continues for awhile we wont have much more good weather …

Charlie wrote to George:

Monday
September 10ᵗʰ 1917
My Dear Geordie,

Just a few lines to say we are all well we have received no word from you for some time the only word I have had was a post card which came some time ago. I hope you are well I wrote to you last week and I think Allan wrote when he was in England … I heard that your division had gone to the line, we are having a grand time here and having real good weather this last week …

Two days later, Charlie wrote to his mother with the news that he had received a letter from George:

Sept. 12ᵗʰ 1917
My dear Mother,

... we are all well and out of the trenches I got a letter from Geordie last night he is still out of the line and is quite well, Allan is back from England I suppose he told you all about his trip, he had to give up one stripe as there were a lot of N.C.O. come over out of another division and there were to many for the company, he being a temporary sergeant had to go back to corporal ... We are still in the same place, I think I told you about being in a show Platoon the other day, well we won it easy the officers gave me great praise for the way in which my rifle and equipment etc was cleaned, we are going before the Colonel on Friday he is giving us a decent prize also the officers out of our company. I will tell you what we get next time I write. I will close for this time with love and my sympathy.

I am Your Loving Son
Charlie

Percy wrote:

In the field
September
My Dear Mother, Father & Jim

Just a few lines to let you know we are all well still in the same place, I think we will be shifting soon. Allan is back from leave, he had a good time, he did not like coming back. Well Mum, we were out on a route march yesterday we were going nearly all day. I was glad when it was finished, we get plenty of route marches here. They seem to delight in giving us route marches. We had a letter from Geordie the other night he was not in the trenches when he wrote, he has had a long run out this time. They are busy carting in their hay here now, the women have to do a lot of work, there are very few young men about here. We ought to be getting another mail soon, it's a good while since we had the last. Well Mum, its very amusing trying to understand some of the people. The sports that was supposed to come off are knocked in the head. I will have to close now no more news hoping all are well.

I remain Your Loving Son
Percy

Following another delivery of mail, Charlie penned a reply to his mother:

… I was very sorry to hear that Pearl has been so ill, in her last letters she was getting on splendid and the baby was splendid, but she must have taken a bad turn, according to their letters. Poor Pearl has had a very severe time, I feel sorry for her. I hope that by this she is quite well and that they are both getting on alright. I was glad to hear that there was another payment on the wheat and I hope it will be followed up with a little more. There seems to have been a great go in with the Queen business, so the Mayor's Queen won easily, I bet he would spend a few pounds to win. I believe Billy Jones and Nellie Gamble are engaged they has started young enough … I got a letter from Geordie the other night he was well and out of the line. Do not at any time put my letters in the papers as I do not care about it. I will write a longer letter tomorrow so I will close for now as I am in a hurry, we are having a grand time here …

Allan was finally promoted to sergeant, having briefly reverted to corporal. His rank was now permanent, a fact that he was clearly pleased to report to his family. He also described his pleasure at the sight of the lovely French countryside:

In the field
13-9-17
My Dear Mum & Dad

… I received your most welcome letter & no one knows how delighted I was. No doubt you are glad you have finished your cropping but it wont be long before you are cutting it down again. Well dear mum I am pleased to hear you are getting my letters now. We get yours pretty often well you know there is no use growling. We are still out of the trenches but for how long we don't know but hope for the best. I was terrible surprised to hear that about the Barber girl but as for D Smith I am not. I use to see him doing things when I was there and always told him to give it up, but don't say anything …Well Auntie Florrie tells me in her letter about Myrtle Stone and Lowe but I know better mum you don't [know] as much about that as me. Where we are now the French people are very busy with the harvest and different lads are helping them after parade. Percy has just come in on a big load of

hay. The other night a big load came in and I thought I would give a hand well I got up and threw off a few sheaves and blisters started to rise so Allan got down. Where we are now it is just like home. We have a bonza time. The best I have had since being in the army. We had a letter from Geordie the other night he is well as it still out of the trenches. What a fine spell he has had. But good luck to him. Well mum I am going to a school on Sunday it lasts a month. I was pleased as punch as I was made temporary sergeant about 2 months ago and so reinforcements came in and I was reverted to Corporal but to morrow I will have my three stripes back again and will be of permanent rank so that is good. It was only for a week that I was reverted. I am sending you three photo. I hope you like them alright. Well dear mum & dad I think I have told you a lot of news this time so will say goodbye for the present. I don't think we will be home for Xmas but may get home for the proceeding one.

I remain
Your Loving Son
Allan

Charlie wrote to Sarah:

… I was sorry to hear that Pearl had been so ill I hope that she is better by now, I thank you for sending the fowl to her, I am glad that the little baby is fine. Percy and Al got a good few letters Al got a parcel from Ida with a nice cake and some lollies it was tip top, we have not received your last parcels yet but we will get them alright as we have got all the parcels you have sent so far … We are still out of the line and will be out for some time we are having a grand time here the best we have ever had. I got a letter from Geordie through the week he was quite well and was out of the line. Percy and Al are quite well. Percy got a letter from Auntie Florrie saying that Mrs Ogilvie died, she must have had an awful death.[4] *Well dear mother I have no news much this time so will draw to a close with love and sympathy to you all. I will write to Jim tomorrow so goodbye for this time.*

I remain
Your loving son
C.E.

The 38th Battalion remained billeted close to the French town of Devres near the coast where the men enjoyed rest, the pleasant countryside and opportunities to help the French villagers with their daily routine. Training continued with the 3rd Division preparing for the role it would play in Third Ypres.

By late September the men were once again moved forward to the support areas of the front line. Unlike George, they would not take part in the battles of September.

FIFTEEN
I WAS 15 YDS FROM MARLOW WHEN HE WAS HIT …

MENIN ROAD PUSH, BELGIUM

In an effort to reinvigorate his plan for the capture of the high ground surrounding Ypres, Haig now placed General Plumer in command of the southern Gheluvelt sector, just to the north of Messines where Plumer and Monash had been successful two months earlier. General Gough was to continue to lead the advance on the battlefields to the north of Ypres. Plumer decided to take the Gheluvelt Plateau in a series of 'bites', not unlike his successful Messines campaign in which the infantry would advance no more than 1500 yards (1370 metres) per day under cover of an intense artillery barrage. This approach was designed to provide maximum protection for the attacking troops; it allowed regrouping and reorganisation under a screen of smoke and dust created by the dense bombardment. However, success was reliant on dry weather.

In the few days of preparation prior to the attack George hastily penned a field postcard to tell his mother he had received her letter and would reply as soon as time permitted.

George found a moment to send a field card to his mother before the Battle of Menin Road.

449

On 20 September the 1st and 2nd Australian divisions were to go into battle side by side for the first time in an attack involving 11 divisions on a 13-kilometre front. To the north was Gough's British infantry with Plumer's to the south. The prospect of going into battle with fellow Australians elated the troops who marched by night through the devastated town of Ypres, past the shattered ruins of the once magnificent Cloth Hall, along the Menin Road then on to rough roads constructed of logs to occupy their positions. Three and a half million shells were fired in the week prior to and on the opening day of the Menin Road 'push'. The weather was mercifully dry, the only water lying in shell holes. As the men waited, it began to rain, although by early morning the rain had ceased.[1]

Troops of the 1st Division, passing along the Menin Road, in the Ypres sector, from Hooge Crater to the front line to take part in the attack opened earlier in the day 20 September 1917. (AWM E00850).

At 5.40 am on 20 September the men were ordered to advance. The German defences proved difficult to breach; the enemy front line was not a systematic trench system but rather a collection of machine-gun outposts and concrete pillboxes with the strongest points to the rear. The artillery could no longer fire along a clear line of trenches. The 1st Division was tasked with clearing the ravaged area of Glencorse Wood and Nonne Boschen (Nun's Wood) immediately west of Polygon Wood. George had moved into position under cover of darkness. He had been in reserve but was called in at the last minute. He waited as the showers came, trench mortar ready, mist covering the battlefield. Precisely on zero hour the Australians rose in unison through a wall of dust and fumes as the British and Australian artillery opened fire in a deafening barrage.

Less than an hour after the battle commenced George fell, hit by gunfire on the approach to Polygon Wood, wounded but alive.

Red Cross records contain a report by No. 3431 Private Robertson, also of the 2nd Light Trench Mortar Battery, who wrote an account of what happened next:

> I was 15 yds from Marlow when he was hit. He received two bullet wounds in the stomach. I saw him carried away to Dressing Station. I recognised him. That was the last I saw of him. Height 5ft. 6ins, stout build. Cleanshaved and fair. Age about 26. This happened at Polygon Wood, September 20th 1917[2]

Stretcher-bearers carried George from the battlefield, the 6th Field Ambulance transporting him to the 3rd Canadian Casualty Clearing Station near Poperinghe.

The following day, at 11.50 am, George succumbed to his wound. He was 24 years old. The officer in command of the clearing station recorded that George had died as a result of a bullet entering his left hip then penetrating his abdomen. The war had taken the life of another of Sarah and Charles' sons.

Despite the many casualties that day, the battle was regarded by Allied commanders as a success. Objectives had been taken. Plumer had pushed forward over one kilometre and taken around 13 square kilometres of enemy territory. The cost was high: 20,000 Allied troops, of whom 5000 were Australian, were now dead or wounded. [3] George was just one of so many casualties.

The 4th and 5th divisions relieved the 1st and 2nd in the advanced front line and continued the push to Polygon Wood on 26 September along an eight-kilometre front. While the offensive's military objectives were achieved, the human cost had been enormous; in just a few days Australia had suffered 10,000 casualties in the battles of Menin Road and Polygon Wood.

MOLOGA, OCTOBER

Military records indicate that Sarah, Charles and Jim received the news of George's death sometime before 8 October. It was on this date that they confirmed receipt of the official cable containing those few short words — 'killed in action' — the words that daily brought devastating news to so many.

Six weeks were to pass before the surviving brothers received word that their 'dear Geordie' had been killed fighting only a few kilometres from where they were positioned. They continued to write home with optimistic accounts of George's health, messages that must have been starkly incongruous with the sympathy cards that flowed to the family at Mologa, cards that reinforced the reality that their son and brother was truly gone. A few days later, on 13 October, Jim wrote to the Minister for Defence seeking a copy of George's will and death certificate. Jim had now taken responsibility for dealing with the legalities and military communication associated with the death of his brothers.

The *Pyramid Hill Advertiser* wrote of the family's second loss:

> We learned yesterday of the regretful news that Mr. C. Marlow of Mologa, has lost the second of his four sons on active service.

> October 12, 1917

> Corporal G.T. Marlow ... was born in Mologa, and was the first to leave here for the front ... He saw fighting on a large portion of the British front, the notable places being Armentieres, Ypres, Pozieres, Bapaume, Bullecourt, and Ypres again. He fought in every action his brigade was in, was never wounded and never sick since the day he left Australia ... A returned soldier spoke of him as being a cool soldier in action and popular with the men. He did many brave deeds and never spoke of them, and never complained of hardship.[4]

George's personal effects were sent home in December, the family receiving his belongings in April 1918. The package included the items he carried with him at the time he was hit: letters, pocket case, cards, souvenir brooch, safety razor, blades and holdall. In his kit were: a metal cigarette case, seven coins, three watches (one silver, two damaged), scissors, notebook, a letter and photos. At the time he died, George was carrying letters he had received from cousin Eddie, his mother and Jim.[5] They are fragile and appear stained. They had been carefully stored in a tin containing souvenirs George had collected and sent home.

The original cross placed over George's grave.

* * *

LIJSSENTHOEK MILITARY CEMETERY, 2011

George was buried at Lijssenthoek Military Cemetery, just south-west of Poperinghe where he was taken the day he was wounded. As the crow flies, he is no further than 15 kilometres from the final resting place of his youngest brother, Albert. This cemetery is overwhelming in its size, containing rows and rows of men whose lives were prematurely snatched from them. In this patch of land, 9901 Commonwealth soldiers are buried, with an additional 883 men from Germany, France and the United States. The cemetery constructed in this location was originally sited in a hop field close to the hospitals and casualty clearing stations which, safe from artillery fire, were spread throughout the busy soldiers' place of respite, the town of Poperinghe. Almost all those buried here died under medical care and are identified.

George's grave today (author photo 22 April 2011).

Two graves down from George lies Second Lieutenant William Seabrook of the 17th Battalion who also died of wounds in the Menin Road advance on 21 September. Both his brothers had been killed at Menin Road on 20 September. They have no known grave. The appalling cost of war is measured in tragedy on this scale — three sons lost to their family in the space of one day.

Major Frederick Tubb of the 7th Battalion, a Gallipoli VC winner, is also buried here, having been killed on 20 September. Like George he was killed by gunfire, but not before his company had achieved their objectives, overpowering nine pillboxes to reach the southern side of Polygon Wood.

We place a cross of remembrance and some poppies on the grave of George Tennyson Marlow. We have not forgotten, nor will we forget. The short time we have to pay our respects to this young soldier buried so far from his home is insufficient to honour the sacrifice he has made. As I look out over the sea of headstones the scale of the tragedy of the First World War is apparent, each marker a heartbreaking reminder of the senseless slaughter of young men who died doing their duty.

Lijssenthoek Military Cemetery, Poperinghe. The tragedy of war is apparent to the visitor in the sea of white headstones.

SIXTEEN
GOOD GOD, DID WE REALLY SEND MEN TO FIGHT IN THAT?

FRANCE, SEPTEMBER

Within three days of his death, Allan, Percy and Charlie had received word that George had been wounded. They continued to write home for weeks, unaware of the death of their brother.

Sunday Sept 23rd 1917
My Dear Mother,

… we are still in the same place and having a good time, we were reviewed yesterday by Sir Douglas Haig, the whole of our division was inspected by him it seemed a tremendous crowd of men. I got two letters from Cheynes's during the week and I am pleased to say that Percy got your parcel yesterday and dear Mother I thank you very much for it we have got all your parcels so far I got a letter from Ida a few days ago they were all well she said that Flo Wilson was coming to work in Leicester. Allan is away at a school but I think he is coming back during the week he is now a full sergeant. I will be sending you a card for Christmas during the week which I hope you receive safely. I am sending you this note with a letter for Pearl, Geordie was quite well the last time he wrote, we get a letter from him every week …

Charlie later added in a note to his father:

… Today is writing day I have been writing near all day I wrote to mother this afternoon and just as I had finished news came of an Australian mail I got six letters … I think Percy will get his leave any day now and I may get leave at Christmas or after I have about £10 on me and my pay book, but if I get leave I will want that, and then when I go back to where Albert is buried if the Brigade have not put the cross up I intend

to put one up myself. I am going to see the Chaplain again and find out if it has been done, it is part of his duty to find out those things I think it will be up, but we are a long way away at present. Well I am cabling to you for £5 one day this week, I do not like sending to Pearl as she is so ill I will give it back to you when I get back. I said I got Mother and Jim['s] letter I will write to them during the week Geordie is alright …

On the same day, Allan wrote from his army school:

In the field
23-9-1917
My Dear Mum, Dad & Jim

… We are still out of the trenches but it is not for much longer. I think we will soon be in something good. We had a letter from George the other night he is splendid & is still out of the trenches. We are having glorious weather at present. I suppose it is the same in Ausy. Well dear mum I am a sergeant again and am pleased too. It doesn't matter how many reinforcement sergeants come along I cannot be reduced. Well I have some good news to tell you and if I get the job Allan will be pleased. I have been nominated for a musketry school in England I think it is 3 or 4 months job. There are about 15 of us in for it so if I get it I will be terrible lucky. Anyway there is a chance for me. Well dear mum I am at a school. It is supposed to last a month but I am afraid it will break up before then. I am about 4 miles away from the boys. One of the lads has just come in and told us there is an Ausy mail in so I will go up to the boys to day (Sunday) and get mine. It is a half holiday. There was a Church parade this morning. Well dear mum I am sending you a few silk handkerchiefs today. They are not much but I hope you [get] them all right …

At around this time Allan sent photos home to Jim and his parents. To his mother he provided some detail, writing on the back:

Dear Mum

We had these taken for a joke. I think they are good. Can you see Allan with the boxes on. He looks lovely. The other 3 lads are mates. Allan S

Allan standing on left in a light-hearted photo he sent to his mother.

Allan and his mate Spuddy Kerr.

Dear Mum

This is a very cheap and poor photo. It is Spuddy Kerr and I. Allan S

…. We have shifted back near the line again. Geordie was wounded in a stunt the other day but I believe it is not serious. They tell me he will get to Blighty with it so that is tra bon. There is plenty doing up our way now. Charlie is going away to a rest camp for 14 days. He goes tomorrow. Well dear mum & dad I am going over the top again at any time now. I will be able to get a little of mine back. I am looking forward to it. Well dear Mum I am putting a couple of handkerchiefs in the letter & I hope you get them

alright. Well dear this will be the 4ᵗʰ stunt I have been in. So I am having my share of it. Well dear mum I don't think I have any more news to day but will have some after the stunt so goodbye dear

I remain
Your Loving Son
Allan

Percy got your parcel alright. It was lovely.
This a very hurried note.

Percy (seated, right) photographed with his mates.

Charlie wrote:

Sept 29ᵗʰ 17
My Dear Mother, Father & Jim

Again it is my hard lot to write and tell you that Geordie is wounded. I went out to see him yesterday as his unit is close at hand, and to my great surprise they told me he was wounded and they believed he was in England as he had got through the Casualty Clearing Station and that is the first step to "Blighty". He was reserved for the stunt but at the last moment he had to go, he was hit in the stomach with a machine gun bullet his equipment saved him the bullet went in and came out the wound is not too deep so there is no need to worry he will be alright over there, he was wounded on Sept 20ᵗʰ at about 6.30 am, his things were sent on to the base and will be forwarded on to him later, the sergeant has sent all his private belongings, his men done all they could for him and they said

458

he did not seem to have much pain. If the military do not send you any more word, you will know he is getting on alright I will write later I am in a hurry now. I may get word from Geordie, and will then write and let you know how he is getting on, they said the wound is not serious so do not worry.

I will say goodbye with love and sympathy
I remain
Your Loving Son
Charlie

From a rest camp which would keep him from the coming battles, Charlie wrote home to his aunt with continued optimism that George was recovering and would soon write to tell his brothers that he had survived.

October 3rd 1917
My Dear Auntie Florrie

Just a line to say that I am quite well and trust that you are all the same at Hayanmi. You will have heard that Geordie has been wounded, we have moved up where his unit was camped and I went one afternoon to see him and to my great surprise his mate told me that he had been wounded and that was at about 6.30am on the morning of Sept 20 in the push, he was reserved for the stunt and at the last minute one of the other corporals took ill and Geordie had to go, the sergeant told me that his wound was not serious and that he thought Geordie was in England so if he is he will be alright he will get 16 days sick leave when he comes out of the hospital if he had not been wounded he would have now been in Paris as the sergeant said he was next to go. I have written home and told them about it. I have not heard from Geordie yet it is hardly time. I am now at a rest camp for 14 days so you will see I am not doing too bad well dear Auntie I will draw to a close I trust you can read this but the wind is awful today, we are on the beach. I will say goodbye with love and best wishes I remain Your loving nephew

Charlie E M

On the same day, Tom Alford wrote to Jim to offer his condolences over the loss of Albert:

France
Oct 3rd 1917
Dear Jimmy

Just a line in answer to your [letter] of the 7th August which I've just got today & also had one from you a few days ago. Sorry you are not getting any from me but I write to you easily once a month & sometimes oftener. I've just come back from leave to England. I wrote to you while I was over there so haven't any fresh news much. The Australians have had another pretty big slap up I was lucky enough to miss it but suppose there will be plenty more stunts. Sorry to hear about Albert, but hope you are bearing up as well as you can. Poor little beggar he didn't reign long. I saw the two Stone boys a few days ago. They had not long been in France. They are in the 17th Battalion. I haven't heard how Wilson Townsend or Charlie Cockcroft in the last mixup. Well Jim have nothing to write about so hoping all are well

From your old pal
Tom Alford

Charlie put pen to paper on the day that Allan and Percy were sent in to battle. He explained that he had received word that George had been wounded:

Army Rest Camp
Oct 4th 1917
My dear Mother, Father & Jim

Just a few lines to say I am quite well, we have shifted from where I wrote about a fortnight ago, I wrote telling you poor Geordie was wounded. I suppose you have got a cable saying he was wounded if you do not hear any more from the military you will know he is getting on alright and there will be no need to worry, first I will tell you that I have been sent to a rest camp by the sea for 14 days leave, Allan and Percy will be in the line for a few days and then will be coming out, I may say I have not been in since Albert was killed, well we shifted up near where Geordie's unit was and one day I got leave to go and see him, I had a long way to walk and had a hard job to find his unit, and when I got there to my sorry they told me he had been wounded on the Menin Road push on Sept 20th at about 6.15 am. The sergeant said he would now be in England he was hit in the stomach with a machine gun bullet the equipment saved him, the bullet did not go deep but the men said it seemed to go in and then come out again almost at the same place, and they said it was not serious so there is no need to worry he will be well looked after and will be away for a long time and if he is in England he will get 16 days sick leave. I am cabling home next week for some money I may get leave early next year…

BROODSEINDE RIDGE, BELGIUM

On 4 October the 1st, 2nd and 3rd Australian divisions and the New Zealand Division advanced on the German stronghold of Broodseinde Ridge to the east of Ypres. The ridge was regarded as one of the most strategic positions on the Western Front from which enemy observation posts readily observed the movements of the Allies below. To all appearances it is just a slope rising above the flat Belgian fields. The taking of Broodseinde Ridge would clear the way for the advance to the village of Passchendaele. As the official war historian Charles Bean later wrote: 'Never before or since did four Anzac divisions attack side-by-side, and the already high spirit of these troops was greatly enhanced by this concentration.'[1] General Plumer was to employ his 'bite and hold' strategy once more. To the north, Gough was to advance on the village of Poelcappelle. At 6.00 am, the Allied forces were scheduled to move forward simultaneously.

Allan and Percy were well prepared for the role they would play in the taking of Broodseinde. For two nights the battalion had been camped in a field on the edge of the busy Ypres-Zonnebeke Road. During the day they had received additional ammunition, flares and water. All were familiar with the terrain and the objectives of the planned assault. The 10th Brigade, comprising the 37th, 38th, 39th and 40th battalions, was to attack along a 500-metre front. The 37th was to take the first objective and the 38th would then leap-frog and take the second objective, followed by the 39th taking the third. The 40th was responsible for the final objective.[2]

As darkness fell on 3 October the battalions began the single-file march forward along the duckboards to the front line. Sporadic enemy artillery fire caused heavy losses as the men moved up to their positions. From midnight the area was relatively quiet. By 2.00 am the men were in position. As light rain fell, they waited under the cover of waterproof capes along the white tape of the jumping-off line that traversed the shell holes.

Just 40 minutes before the scheduled attack German artillery opened fire on the Allied troops. It was immediately assumed that the Allied plan of attack had been revealed. In fact, the enemy artillery fire signalled a German attack on the village of Zonnebeke, immediately to the west of Broodseinde, scheduled for exactly the same hour as the Allied assault. The enemy bombardment was ferocious. Stretcher-bearers carried wounded to the rear as the troops waited. There was little the men could do but pray as shells rained down all around. Approximately one-seventh of the attacking force was hit prior to zero hour, although the 38th Battalion diary indicates that it suffered few casualties.[3]

At 6.00 am and under the protection of their own artillery, the Allied troops clambered from their shell holes. Many paused to light a cigarette before beginning their approach to no man's land, relieved to be released from the bombardment of their line. The leading 37th Battalion had crept forward during the German barrage to avoid the heavy artillery fire; they were now within 30 metres of the German pillboxes on the summit. Despite being under heavy fire, the German infantry almost simultaneously commenced their approach. The German soldiers hesitated, perplexed by the sight of the approaching troops. Australian Lewis gun teams opened fire. In the resulting confusion fierce hand-to-hand fighting erupted as enemy machine-gun posts fell to the advancing Australians. The 10th Brigade was subjected to heavy fire but continued its advance through the valley. German machine-gun fire burst from the ruins of a farm; bombs and grenades took out the enemy post and the diggers continued their advance as the battalion diary describes:

In the centre a machine gun post at Israel House gave trouble for a time. On the right the main opposition came from concrete pill boxes about Judah House and Springfield Farm; the latter yielding several Machine Guns and about 150 prisoners. In almost every case opposition was overcome by working round to the rear of the pill-boxes and throwing in a "P" bomb or Mill's grenade. Rifle grenades were little used. Generally speaking our men kept so close to the barrage that they were on the enemy before he could recover from it. [4]

Along the front the assault pushed forward. By 7.30 am the 38th Battalion had reached its first objective.[5] Prisoners were taken in droves. The next move forward commenced at 8.10 am. Under cover of heavy artillery, the 39th and 40th battalions reached the ridge where they could see the green fields of farmland in the distance and the rear areas of German-held Belgium. By 9.12 am, both I and II Anzac had reached their objectives. While intense German shelling continued, the Australians fortified their positions, repairing and improving trenches and constructing new front lines and support areas.[6]

On 4 October, 12 divisions attacked on a 13-kilometre front and, despite fierce resistance, the Broodseinde attack succeeded, described as 'the most complete yet won'. Five thousand German soldiers were taken prisoner. Official German records described the battle as 'the black day of October 4th'.[7] They had been driven from one of the most strategic positions on the Western Front. From the ridge to the east of Ypres, British forces had victory in their sights. Yet the sacrifice had been enormous. The three Australian divisions suffered 6500 casualties.[8] The 38th Battalion War Diary records 184 casualties with 34 killed, 143 wounded and seven missing.[9]

On the night of 5/6 October the 38th was relieved soon after a heavy enemy barrage had opened on the exhausted soldiers. They marched wearily through the night to Ypres and then on to Vlamertinghe, just east of Poperinghe. It had been a hard-won victory. Within a few days they would be back to face an ordeal which was to become their own living hell.

FRANCE, OCTOBER

In France, some 600 kilometres away from the scene of Allied victory, Charlie was preoccupied with finding his wounded brother. He had searched the nearby hospitals and continued to make inquiries. He wrote from the rest camp at Boulogne on the French coast of the willingness of the Australian nurses to help and their concern for those attempting to trace missing friends and relatives.

9th Oct 1917
My Dear Mother,

… Of course I have not heard how Geordie is getting on as I will not get any mail while I am here, I hope to hear when I get back how he is getting on also to get some mail from you I wrote to Pearl last Sunday and to you a few days before that, I hope you are getting my mail regular for I write to you regular. There are a lot of Australian Hospitals about here and a lot of our wounded come here, I have inquired at a lot of places if Geordie was there, but there was no one of our name in them. I am sure he has gone to England, the nurses are only too pleased to help anyone looking for wounded friends and the Australian nurses are only too pleased to do anything they can for us, one of them the other day asked me if we were getting plenty to eat and if I had plenty of money as she would give me some but of course I had plenty and thanked her very much. There are 6 out of my company along with me and we are having a very pleasant time. I bought a little Christmas present for Pearl yesterday and have sent it to her I hope she gets it alright. I do not know yet if she got the parcel we sent her about last May, there were some boats sunk about that time but I hope the parcel was not on any of them. I weighed myself yesterday and went 12 stone 8lbs so I still hold out, I got my photo taken last week they were to be done today but I only got two of them and they are hardly dry enough to send but I will send you another one later, the people over here are not the best at taking photos …

PASSCHENDAELE — BELGIUM, OCTOBER

While Charlie was preoccupied with finding George, his brothers were preparing for the next phase of the Ypres campaign: the taking of the village of Passchendaele, visible from Broodseinde Ridge. Continual rain since 4 October had transformed the Ypres battlefield into a sinister morass of thick, sticky mud — the Battle of Passchendaele was doomed from its inception. On 9 October, in Gough's sector at Poelcappelle, two British divisions and the 2nd Australian Division launched their initial assault on the village. They met fierce resistance — the Germans had sent in fresh troops. The Allies were exhausted from their Broodseinde attack and from the effort it took just to reach the front line through the fields of mud. Little time had been allowed for preparation and the infamous enemy pillbox defences appeared virtually impregnable. Allied artillery was bogged in rear areas and what was available was insufficient to shatter the German defences and shield the advancing troops. Swift advances such as those of Messines and Broodseinde which were ideal for overpowering such defensive positions were now impossible in the muddy morass. Shell holes filled with mud claimed the lives of those unlucky enough to slip from duckboards: men, horses and mules. The landscape was devoid of all vegetation. Stunted, blasted stumps of trees were all that remained in a sea of deep, black mud and shell holes filled with putrid water.

Given the conditions, little ground was taken on 9 October apart from some gains at the northern point of Poelcappelle. The order to continue forward was given heedless of the conditions. The taking of Passchendaele and beyond was the objective of the 3rd and 4th Australian divisions combined with the New Zealand Division and five British divisions. The 38th was to reach the third objective, a line just beyond the village. Inexplicably, the 38th had been ordered to push forward over a much greater distance than the troops at nearby Poelcappelle. On 10 October the 3rd Division found itself preparing to attack yet again. Depleted divisions had been reinforced, new equipment issued. But it was not enough.

As darkness fell on the evening of 11 October, the Australians filed forward into their positions, moving along congested tracks, each man grasping the pack of the man in front in an effort to maintain contact in the gloom. Rain fell in an unremitting deluge. They huddled under their greatcoats and waterproof sheets as best they could as the German artillery mercilessly shelled the Allied positions.

At 5.25 am on 12 October the advance commenced. Allan and Percy went over the top with the 38th. Heavy enemy shelling had already reduced the attacking force. Rifles and machine-guns were clogged. Artillery bombardments were ineffective as shells fell into the sticky mess, failing to explode or smothered by thick mud. The great guns became bogged on impassable tracks or sank beneath their own weight as they fired. German troops rushed to the ridge, fortifying pillboxes and trenches and firing down on the advancing soldiers. Allied casualties were heavy.

At 8.40 am Major Giblin of the 40th Battalion reported that he could not continue; he could only find 200 men for the advance from his position in the swamp of the Ravebeek Valley below Passchendaele. Above him on Bellevue Spur, the Germans were decimating his men. By early afternoon he had received no reply, such was the state of communications. Further messages were sent by lamp and pigeon. Reinforcements eventually arrived but the position was hopeless. They were being gradually destroyed by the intense artillery fire.

A small party of the 38th managed to make its way to Passchendaele after the surrender of German troops in an enemy pillbox at the point known as Crest Farm on the outskirts of the village. Allan and Percy could have been members of the party. Finding no German troops and lacking support, the team withdrew.[10] As they moved back the men were targeted by heavy fire. Crest Farm had been reoccupied by enemy forces and fire from Bellevue Spur rained down on the Australians. The New Zealand Division to the left on the spur had not been able to capture the formidable pillboxes protected by uncut wire along the ridge.

The remaining troops of the 37th, 38th and 40th battalions, under the command of Major Giblin, formed a line close to their first objective. The situation was impossible. Giblin ordered the men to retire to their start point. By 3.00 pm, those who could had retreated, others lay dead or wounded in the Flanders mud.

On the night of 13/14 October the surviving men of the 38th Battalion were relieved.[11] The Allied operation had failed and the name Passchendaele became synonymous with the horror and futility of war. It was here that the Australian 3rd Division suffered its highest casualties of the entire war. Of the men of the 38th Battalion who went over the top that day, 62% were now casualties with 381 men killed, wounded or missing.[12] The 3rd Division lost over 3000 men. The New Zealand losses also totalled around 3000 while the 4th Division had lost 1000.[13]

There were few reinforcements to replace the Australian casualties. The once eager volunteers were no longer streaming onto the ships which would carry them to the great adventure. The casualty lists and the maimed returned soldiers were testimony to the reality of this war. The conscription bill had failed. The Australian forces, having lost 38,000 men in eight weeks, would depend on the return of the sick and wounded to reinforce their severely depleted ranks.[14]

In total, there would be 11 battles in the third Ypres campaign which stretched through the months of June until November 1917. Of these battles, the Australians were called on to spearhead five, the third through to the seventh.[15] Three of these attacks were made in conditions which encouraged success and were regarded as such despite massive losses. The final two battles of October would forever mark Passchendaele as a bloody, senseless slaughter.

Canadian forces relieved the remains of the Australian battalions. Haig continued to press ahead with his plan. While there was little hope of a breakthrough before the onset of winter, the capture of Passchendaele Ridge remained a priority. By mid-November the Canadians had achieved Haig's objective and had taken Passchendaele, effectively creating a dangerous salient on the top of the ridge where they could be enfiladed from three sides. It was here at Passchendaele, after the Canadians had broken through to the village, that Haig's Chief of staff, Lancelot Kiggell, is reported to have covered his face with his hands and cried as he surveyed the scene from his car: 'Good God, did we really send men to fight in that?'[16]

* * *

PASSCHENDAELE, 2011

Tyne Cot Cemetery, Broodseinde Ridge. The Cross of Sacrifice and memorial to the 3rd Division sits above the remains of a German blockhouse that looked down on the valley (author photo 21 April 2011).

The remains of one of two German blockhouses inside the cemetery gates (author photo 21 April 2011). 21.04.2011

Today, Tyne Cot Cemetery, the largest Commonwealth cemetery in the world, sits atop Broodseinde Ridge where the Australian troops halted on 4 October after reaching their objectives. It is the last resting place of close to 12,000 men. The remains of the German strongpoints can still be seen in the area from Ypres to Tyne Cot; the rubble of Israel House and farm buildings at the site of Judah House where the 38th Battalion established its headquarters and then further on to Springfield Farm. Most formidable are the two pillboxes that guard the entrance to Tyne Cot Cemetery. Looking out from these at the Allies' avenue of approach is sobering. They are just two of many from which the soldiers were raked with machine-gun fire as they fought their way through barbed wire, shell holes and enemy artillery.

The memorial to the 3rd Australian Division, which captured the pillboxes on this small area of land, lies within the grounds of the cemetery. The Cross of Sacrifice sits atop a German blockhouse, its inscription recording that the 3rd Division captured the blockhouse on 4 October. It was then transformed into an advanced dressing station. Surrounding the inscription is a laurel wreath behind which the original pillbox can be seen. The memorial looks out over the rows and rows of Allied crosses and towards the approach that the men took through the valley.

My father stands at the marker of 'The Road to Passchendaele Australia Walk' (author photo, 21 April 2011).

The railway cutting and the remains of the line (author photo, 21 April 2011).

We walk to Dash Crossing, the point marked as 'The Road to Passchendaele, Australia Walk, 4 October 1917', just below Tyne Cot Cemetery. It is an old railway cutting, peaceful and green in early spring. Australian soldiers advanced along this cutting on 4 October. We stop at the point where the men of the 44th Battalion halted, where the uncovered remains of a section of the Ypres-Roullers railway line can now be seen, trying to visualise the battle. We stand along the 3rd Division start line where the men formed up on 12 October just outside Tyne Cot Cemetery. We look across the ploughed fields trying to visualise the mud, the shell holes, explosions, the roar of artillery, the inescapable horror. This was the site of some of the bloodiest fighting in the attempt to take Passchendaele. I recall a photograph (AWM E03864) of Australian soldiers resting in this railway cutting taken by an unknown official war photographer. Austin Garnet Henderson is one of two men watching the photographer. The exhausted soldiers rest among the dead. Austin was a signaller with the 38th Battalion, originally a member of D Company along with Percy, Allan, Charlie and Albert and had sailed on the *Runic* with Allan and Percy. He had been shot at Messines but returned a few weeks later and, by late October, was attached to the postal service of the 10th Brigade. He returned to Australia aboard the *Rio Padro* in June 1919.[17] Though we cannot be sure, my father has often looked at the face of the other man and wondered whether the haunted soldier was Allan Marlow — it could well have been him. But, while there is a definite likeness, there are no insignia or other identifiers to confirm that the exhausted man is Allan.

Photographer Frank Hurley kept a detailed diary of his front-line experiences. His diary entry for 12 October describes the scene in the cutting:

> Every 20 paces or less lay a body. Some frightfully mutilated, without legs, arms and hands and half covered in mud and slime. I could not help thinking as Wilkins and I trudging along this inferno and soaked to the skin, talking and living beings, might not be the next moment one of these things — it puts the wind up one at times. We pushed on through the old Zonnebeke station (now absolutely swept away) up to Broodseinde and entered the railway cutting near the ridge crest … I noticed one awful sight: a party of, ten or so, telephone men all blown to bits. Under a questionably sheltered bank lay a group of dead men. Sitting by them in little scooped out recesses sat a few living; but so emaciated by fatigue and shell shock that it was hard to differentiate. Still the whole way was just another of the many byways to hell one sees out here, and which are so strewn with ghastliness that the only comment is: "that poor beggar copped it thick", or else nothing at all.[18]

Dead and wounded in the railway cutting, Broodseinde Ridge, 12 October 1917. On the far right facing the camera is Austin Henderson. The man we believe could be Allan is in the middle of the photograph also facing the camera (AWM E03864).

* * *

2011

In Passchendaele we sit opposite the rebuilt church which the men of the 38th reached on 12 October; we eat some pastries from the local bakery and watch the villagers go about their daily life. Aerial images of the pulverised village present a stark testimony to the resilience of the Belgian communities who rebuilt their physical surrounds and their spirit, only to be crushed a few decades later in the German occupation and then to rally once more. We walk along Canadastraat, the road the men of the 38th took to reach the church. We arrive at the Canadian memorial which marks the Canadian capture of Passchendaele on 6 November 1917. This was the site of Crest Farm, the massive blockhouse that rained murderous fire on the Australian and later the Canadian forces. We look across the fields in which the Australians were slaughtered, where many remain, the final resting place of the men whose names are etched on the walls of the Menin Gate or at Tyne Cot.

While tracing the footsteps of our forebears we have taken up residence at Varlet Farm, nine kilometres from Ypres at Poelcappelle on the Passchendaele battlefield. The farm was named by British soldiers in 1916 and formed part of the German defensive line. It was liberated by British soldiers on 26 October 1917. The ruined farm was rebuilt some 50 to 100 metres from the original in the 1920s. Piles of war debris sit in a corner of the farmyard and unexploded ordinance is frequently uncovered and defused by the Belgian army bomb disposal team stationed nearby.

It is Anzac Day on the Western Front. In darkness we drive from Varlet Farm to Zonnebeke and take a five-minute bus journey to Polygon Wood and the Buttes New British Cemetery which sits in a north-eastern corner of the wood. The pathway to the butte of the old rifle range is illuminated by candle light. Mist twists its way among the trees and we shiver in the early morning chill. Atop the rebuilt remains of the Butte the memorial to the 5th Division rises majestically to overlook the cemetery. On either side stand buglers, a Scottish bagpiper and soldiers of the Belgian army, all silhouetted by the morning sky. The poignancy of the service is profound, particularly as George was shot only a short distance from where we stand. Only a few kilometres away, Allan and Percy were ordered to do the impossible. I struggle to hold back the tears and I am not alone.

My father and I lay a wreath at the Australian service, Polygon Wood, Belgium, on Anzac Day 2011 (author photo).

SEVENTEEN
IT BREAKS MY HEART BEYOND WORDS TO THINK THAT I SHALL NEVER SEE HIM AGAIN

FRANCE, OCTOBER

In the aftermath of the Third Battle of Ypres, the depleted 38th Battalion was loaded onto buses and transported back to the small village of Senlecques from which it had earlier departed. It was 15 October. The villagers welcomed their Australian friends and joined them in their grief for those they had lost.

Days after, when the traumatised men had been rested, Percy and Allan wrote home to reassure their family of their safety and also that of George, as the news of his death had yet to reach them. Allan seemed aware only of localised successes, celebrating what was achieved at Broodseinde and his own good luck, perhaps choosing not to acknowledge the enormous losses of Passchendaele, possibly unaware of the roll call that told the real story.

In the field
20-Oct 1917
My dear Mum Dad & Jim

Well my dear mum we are back out of the line once again and I am very thankful too. We are back miles and miles away from the line too they tell us we are back for 3 months we are due for a spell now. We have had a terrible rough time lately something awful if I was to tell I know you would not believe me. We are back in the same place as we were before we moved up to the line. We went over the top twice in a fortnight. Charlie had the good luck to get away to a rest camp for a fortnight & he missed both stunts how Percy and I both came out without getting a knock I don't know simply marvellous. It rained and it hailed while we were taking our objectives and talk about mud it was up to our hips in places. We lived in shell holes half filled with water absolutely the only things we had to live in. I can tell [you] we killed thousands of Fritz's and [took a] jolly sight [more] prisoners. It was in this battle that [we] made such a success. I shot more in this stunt than I have ever done so before. I give the b- no mercy all our boys are the same. Les Townsend was very lucky he got slightly wounded I had a letter from him and he says he is having a tip top time. A man that's got wounded is very lucky. Percy and I was not lucky enough to get a nice little wound. The wounded have a bonnie time and 9 times out of 10 they are slight wounds. Spuddy Kerr has been wounded also Bill Street. Percy & I are the only ones left out of the local boys from Pyramid & Mologa & Calival all the rest have been killed or wounded. I cant mention anything about the stunts but I will never forget it so you will hear it one of these fine days. Oh dear mum it is lively back here and a bonnie time we are having a rattling time. We are in for a good time here I can tell you. I was offered further promotion the other day but I refused it. I have something better in view. I am not going to tell you what it is but if I have the good luck to get it, it will mean 6 months in England for me. Well dear mum you seem to be terrible worried don't worry mum as these things are to happen. Poor old Albert was to go so don't worry yourself to death. We expect a letter from George any day now. He will be in England now. I told you in a previous letter that the war was going to end today but I am afraid not. But all the same Fritz is done. Well dear mum I am going to a nice little town to morrow & hope to get a few little things. Well dear mum & dad & Jim this is all the news this time so will close with best love to all. Oh mum I forgot to tell that we got a bonnie Ausy mail about a week ago also the beautiful parcel for which we thank you for. It was a beautiful one. It was in tip top order when it arrived but Percy & I soon disordered it. Charlie had gone to a rest camp and we just got it in time as we were going to advance next morning so we had some of it with us. Well dear mum dad & Jim I will say goodbye this time.

*I remain
Your Loving Son
Allan S Sgt*

I think Percy will be going to Blighty soon. I am going to try for todays Paris leave.

Percy's letter was more subdued:

In the field
October 22
My Dear Mother & Father & Jim

Just a few lines to let you know we are all well as it leaves us at present. I suppose you will have been expecting to hear from me before, we have been very busy, had a couple of stunts pushed Fritz back a bit. Charlie got 14 days leave to a rest camp on the coast, and he missed both stunts, he was lucky. I went over in both, got through all right, it was very wet for the last stunt, he tried [to] gas us, when we were going up, to go over, but it was too wet as luck happened that mustard gas [is] terrible stuff if you get it. When we got to the jumping off trench he shelled us while waiting to go over; he had plenty of machine guns we were all over mud when we came out. I was lucky to come out, it was pretty hot I tell you. We are back in the same place, as we were before the stunt, not very often you come back to the same billets. It rained today, so we had no parade, do me. I am never anxious to go on parade. Got Charlie's parcel it came when he was away, just before the last stunt, I carried the tin of crabs over with me, went allright. I must thank you very much for it. Well Mum I will close now hoping all are well I remain

Your Loving Son
Percy

While Allan writes of the virtues of being wounded and a trip to Blighty, perhaps his words are also an effort to reassure his parents that George was safe. While a wound might bring a welcome trip to England and a chance to live in safety, even briefly, many wounds brought incapacity, long-term illness, permanent disfigurement and death. A welcome wound appears contrary to all reason — although reason does not abound in war.

Of those neighbours and new friends the brothers mention in their letters home, there were few who had survived Passchendaele unscathed. Allan and Percy were yet to fully realise the true cost of the battle.

Will (Bill) Street was a farmer who lived near Mologa. He enlisted in February 1916 with Allan and Percy at the age of 23. Allan had earlier written home expressing his concern that Will now regretted his decision to enlist. Clearly Will had overcome his fears as he had been promoted corporal. Will was severely wounded on 12 October 1917 during the battle to take Passchendaele. He died two weeks later and is buried near Poperinghe.[1] His brother, Harry Street, was a 36-year-old single farmer who had sailed on the *Port Lincoln* with Albert. Harry also expressed some regret that he had enlisted. Albert wrote from Larkhill that Harry had cried when leaving for France. He had been wounded earlier in July 1917, but returned to the front and survived to reach Australia in March 1919.[2]

Hughie Martin returned to Australia in April 1918. He had enlisted in March 1916 with so many of the Mologa men. He was wounded on 4 October at Passchendaele as the 38th Battalion rushed the Broodseinde Ridge towards where the Tyne Cot Cemetery now sits. As the wound to his femur healed, his leg was permanently shortened and he was later invalided to Australia.[3]

Les Townsend was a labourer from Mologa. He was 21 years old when he enlisted with Allan and Percy and, like them, became a member of the 38th Battalion's Machine-Gun Section. He sailed on the *Runic* with the twins and was wounded at Broodseinde on 4 October 1917. He rejoined his unit on 12 January 1918.[4] Another ten long months of war remained.

Spuddy (Edward) Kerr was a labourer from Janiember East who had also sailed on the *Runic* with the men from Mologa and was a Lewis gunner. He survived a shell blast during the Warneton raid in February 1917 and was shot in the leg at Passchendaele on 13 October 1917, lying in the morass of the battlefield for two days before being rescued. Infection took hold and Spuddy's leg was amputated. He was repatriated in January 1918.[5] At his welcome home gathering, Sarah Marlow's brother, George Mahoney, presented a purse of 100 pounds to Spuddy. The locals had raised the money for Spuddy to purchase a prosthetic leg. As he made the presentation George explained that his nephew had sent a letter describing how Spuddy had dug him out under fire when his nephew had been buried alive. Which nephew sent the letter is unknown, the action likely to have been at Messines after which Albert remarks that they were all buried a number of times. Spuddy later worked as a valuer with the Loddon Shire Council. After his marriage in 1921 he moved to Frankston, had two children and was active in the local football club and RSL. He passed away in 1970.

A number of men who were casualties were not mentioned in the brothers' initial letters home after Passchendaele. Their names would gradually appear over the subsequent weeks.

David Mullen was a 20-year-old farmer from Mitiamo who served with the 2nd Pioneer Battalion. He was killed on 13 October 1917.[6] His brother Hugh landed with the first wave at Gallipoli, was shot three days later and sent to England. Hugh died of septicaemia in Birmingham, England, on 15 May 1915.[7] The *Pyramid Hill Advertiser* reported on 13 August 1915 that Hugh was the first Australian soldier to be buried in England.[8]

Tom Burt was 27 when he left the farm at Heathcote and sailed with Albert on the *Port Lincoln*. He appears in the photo postcard Albert sent home.[9] He was shot at Messines but rejoined his unit in September 1917. The official telegram told his family that he had been listed as missing on 13 October 1917. After a Court of Enquiry hearing in 1918, the family was informed that he had been killed, lost in the mud of Flanders Fields.[10] His name appears on the Menin Gate.

Like Tom, Gordon Swainston had sailed on the *Port Lincoln* and also appears in Albert's photo postcard.[11] An 18-year-old farmer from Green Hill near Kyneton, he was one of four brothers serving on the Western Front. He was wounded on 31 May 1917, but had returned to his unit two weeks later. At Passchendaele on 13 October 1917 he was shot in the leg and was not fit for duty until May 1918. He would be wounded twice more before he returned to Australia.

Albert Brookes was a 23-year-old farm labourer who sailed with Allan and Percy on the *Runic* and also became a Lewis gunner. He was hit in the shoulder by a bullet on 3 January 1917 but recovered to return

to the 38th Battalion on 2 September 1917. At Passchendaele on 13
October he was again hit in the arm and thigh. He survived to rejoin
his unit.[12]

Albert Sinclair was a 29-year-old married farmer from Durham Ox who
had enlisted on 13 March 1916 and later sailed on the *Shropshire* with
Charlie. On 13 October he was gassed at Passchendaele but recovered
and returned a week later. He suffered a gunshot wound on 17 July
1918 and returned to Australia on 20 November 1918.[13]

With over 60% of the battalion killed or wounded, Charlie could count
himself very fortunate that he had been moved to a rest camp prior
to the battles of 4 and 12 October. He was reunited with his brothers
soon after their return to Senlecques. The delay in communication
meant that the surviving brothers were now receiving letters from home
seeking information about Albert's death.

Oct 17th 1917
My Dear Mother, Father & Jim

*… we are now at the same place as we were some time ago it is a long way
back from the line and I think we will be up here for a long time I think
till after Christmas, so you will have no need to worry over us. I have not
heard any word of Geordie, it takes a long time to get a letter when they
are wounded. I wrote to the Officer commanding his unit and to the base
in London so hope to hear very soon. I wrote and told them in England.
You have received the sad news about Albert. I wrote to you the day he was
killed and told you how it happened. You asked if he said anything before he
died. Well I said before that he did not he was killed instantly and I think
by concussion, I ran to where he was as soon as they told me but when I
got there he was dead. Yes, he had plenty of money and before we went into
the line we always used to go every night and get something to eat. I got his
breakfast for him the morning he was killed and he got up about 10 oclock
and then he went on guard which was about 100 yards away from where
I was, that was the last time I saw him alive, our work at that time was at
night carrying war material up to the line at times it was so hot but Albert
was not on any of that, or Percy. Allan was out a few nights. Albert was*

left behind on gas guard. He is buried in a nice cemetery. I told you before where it is. He died without fear I know he did not have any fear at all of shells or bullets, it was in the <u>push</u> that he was with Spud Kerr, but he was not far from me and when we got our objective. Spud Kerr Les Townsend U Martin Bill Street were wounded in the pushes the other day …

It was now close to four weeks since Charlie had received the news that George had been wounded and, without a letter from his brother, his anxiety was increasing. He wrote to his family in the hope that George had written home.

Oct 23rd 1917

… I was sorry that when you wrote you had not got the letters telling you about Albert for I wrote the same time as Mr Gollan I am sorry to say that he was wounded the other day but I can get his address I will write to him and thank him for you, he told me at the time that he wrote and I thanked him and when I see him again or get his address I will thank him for you. I told you all about poor Albert in a lot of letters how it happened and all about it, so there is no need to tell you again, but if you did not get the letters tell me and I will tell you everything again. Percy has written to you today and we are sending this with a letter to Pearl this note will be very short but I will write again I hope to get some more mail tonight or tomorrow, tomorrow morning I am going to a N.C.O. school Allan went this morning I have to get my kit ready tonight, I will be there for 3 weeks or a month it is about 4 miles away from here. I will get my mail just the same, I am not too keen on going, we are out of the line till after Xmas so that is not too bad. I have not heard about Geordie, but expect word next week I will let you know as soon as I can perhaps he has written to you. I am glad you got the cable I sent. Percy has told you about the local boys being hit I have not been in the line since Albert was killed. I am glad to hear that Pearl and our Baby are getting on well again. I sent you my photo which I hope you got alright …

Soon after, Charlie arrived at the school for non-commissioned officers where he was reunited with Allan.

Oct 27th 1917
My Dear Mother, Father & Jim,

... I am now at a Brigade N.C.O. School it is 3 miles from here I come back here every Wed. Sat. Sun half days off. Allan is there instructing he is now a sergeant. I think the school last 3 week or a month when I left to go I had to put on one stripe. I was made an acting Lance Corporal how long I will last at that I do not know but I will draw a Corporal's pay that is about the best part of it a corporal get 10/-. I have not heard word from Geordie but hope to do so this week from Base Headquarters and from the officer. I feel confident that he will be all right. I will write as soon as I hear from him, we will be out of the line for a long time so there is no need to worry. We are starting on the winter now the trees are beginning to loose their leaves. The parcels you are sending will turn up alright we are getting our mail regular now it is alright to get the mail so often. Percy met Wilson Townsend he was alright I did not see him I was at the rest camp at the time, Spud Kerr wrote to Allan tonight he has had his leg taken off at the knee it is hard luck for him he will be going home now Les Townsend will soon be alright, Bill Street was also hit I do not think his wound was serious. Hughie Martin was also hit ...

The following day Charlie wrote to his Aunt Florrie. He was still uncertain of the whereabouts of George and unaware that Bill Street had died two days earlier. It is in this letter that he first expresses his real concern for George. For four weeks he had written to his parents with optimism in an attempt to boost their spirit, unaware of the obituary notice that had already appeared in the *Pyramid Hill Advertiser* and surmising that George must be badly wounded or worse. While Charlie continues to reassure his parents, he reveals his true thoughts to Sarah's sister:

... I am sorry to say that I have not heard anything more about Geordie I wrote to the Base in London and to the O.C. I cannot understand why I have not heard anything about him he must be badly wounded. I do not know how things will be at home. I am going to cable home when I hear. Allan got a letter from Spud Kerr last night he has had his leg taken off at the knee and is getting on alright Les Townsend has a slight wound Bill Street is also wounded also Hughie Martin but as fas as I know their wounds are light. Percy may get leave to England soon, some of the boys are getting leave now...

As Charlie expressed his concern to his aunt, Allan wrote to Jim. It was a fortnight since Passchendaele and the reality of the casualty list had dampened Allan's initial reaction:

In the field
28-10-1917
Dear Jim

Just a few lines to let you know we are all well & hope you are the same Jim we are back in bonnie place. It is the same place as we were in before we went up to the line. There is an Australian mail in & I am anxiously awaiting for mine. I'm down at brigade instructing my junior N.C.O.'s. There is 14 of us here. Charlie is of the junior N.C.O. and he is getting on well. I expect to get something good soon I have a fair chance of going to Blighty to a school if I don't get that I am putting in for leave for Paris. So I am thinking seriously of cabling for a £10 if I don't you tell mum to take anything like that out of account. There seems to be nothing but dam strikes in Ausy lately. They ought to send them over here & give them a taste of what we have had lately and I'll bet they would not strike again. I won't forget to thank the Jones' for their kindness to me. I have had a lot of letters to write lately. We had two buggars of stunt Jim as long as I live I will never forget them you really don't know what it like here under bad conditions. Different lads were wounded and they wrote to me to fix things up for them. I had a letter [from] *my cobber last night Spuddy Kerr. He was bad wounded & he lay out in the battlefield for 2 night & days in the cold & rain. He had his leg taken off above the knee. He is a fine fellow. If he ever comes up our way fetch him home and get him to stop a night. He can tell you all about us and poor Albert. Jim there is nothing doing up the* [meaning Pyramid Hill] *now. No four finish* [finally].[14]

On the same day he also wrote to his parents:

… We [are] *still in the same old place and my word mum it is tra bon. We are likely to be here for some time… I had a letter from my best cobber last night & he is Spuddy Kerr. He has had his leg taken off above the right knee. I am terrible sorry. He is such a fine fellow. He is cert for Ausy. Mum if*

he come up our way at all you must get him to stop a night with you he can tell you all about us and dear old Albert. He is such fine bright lad. I know you will do this mum. There is only Percy and I left out of that Pyramid & Mologa mob, all our cobbers are killed or wounded. I think we all will be home for Easter. Well my dear mum & Dad I will say goodbye for the present trusting you are all well. Mum I have not had a days sickness since I left Australia.

Well goodbye all
I remain
Your Loving Son
Allan S

Myrtle Stone's brother Joe briefly wrote to Jim of his wound, 'a bit of shrap' which had pierced his finger:

Somewhere in France
October 30th 17
Dear Jim

… I suppose by the time you get this you will be well on with the harvest I suppose they will be long and tangled this year on account of it being a very [good] season. I have not heard from Percy lately expect a letter any time now I have saw none of the Mologa lads only T Alford since I came over I received your last letter up the line, came out all right got a small bit of shrap through one of my fingers it is about healed up now. It is getting a bit on the cool side over here now we have had no snow yet but I think they have had it in Blighty according to the Papers. Has Charlie Fyffe gone home I heard he had. I have had a bit of a touch of Rhuematics this last few days I suppose it will be hard to get men for the harvest this year. Well Jim news are scarce so I think I will ring off

I remain
Yours Sincerely
Joe [Stone]
7326

It was now close to six weeks since George had been killed. Charlie wrote:

Oct 31st 1917
My Dear Mother Father and Jim,

… I have not had any word from Geordie but perhaps he has written to you before this, I have not heard anything about him from the base in London nor from his unit although I wrote last week, but I believe he will be alright and there is no need to worry. I am still at the school, Percy went to a Lewis Gun School this morning I believe he will be away about 12 or 14 days. The weather has not been the best here lately of course we can expect as much, but still it is not very cold. I wrote to you last Sunday also to Pearl, I only got one letter from you this mail but I think there is more to come in. We had a note from Les Townsend he is getting on alright …

As October drew to a close, American forces were now being sent in limited numbers to the stalemated war on the Western Front. By the end of the war two million American soldiers would have arrived in Europe. To the east, Italy was experiencing grave difficulty. The might of the German and Austro-Hungarian forces was rapidly eroding the Italian defences. However Allied forces celebrated some successes in the battles fought in Palestine. On 3 October in the Third Battle of Gaza, the 4th Light Horse famously charged Beersheba in what is regarded as one of the last great cavalry charges. Effectively the Australians cleared the way for the capture of Gaza on 7 November. By December Allied forces had reached Jerusalem.

BENDIGO, OCTOBER

In Bendigo, life continued as Pearl recovered from her illness and settled into life with baby Eva. She wrote to Sarah of her concern for Tom Alford, the friend and neighbour of the brothers who had written very candid letters to Jim. His records do not indicate that he had been listed as missing, although close to this time he had been withdrawn from the front due to illness.

208 Barnard St
Bendigo
27th 1917
Dear Mother,

Just a line as I am sending a letter on from Charl also a photo he sent for you, he does not look well in it by any means. He said in my letter Tom Alford was missing I am sorry for his people it is hard on them. Charl sent a photo for Mr Walker. I went to see him the other day he think baby is a real Marlow, he kissed her and made a fuss of her she liked it. She had a bad turn Xmas night with her teeth. Mrs Grant came in and put the cloths on her she soon got alright again, she is fine again today she has another tooth through that is two at the bottom. I will close now dear Mother hoping all are well as we are with love to all and best wishes for the New Year, with love from

Pearl and baby Eva

Mother & Dad are going to Melbourne later on it is too hot now for them to enjoy it.

MOLOGA, NOVEMBER

As winter approached on the Western Front, at home in Mologa preparations were commencing to begin the harvest. The death of George was now widely known and Sarah, Charles and Jim received letters of condolence as they struggled to come to terms with the deaths of two sons. Lizzie Glass, widow of Dave who had been killed in March 1917, wrote to Sarah from Queensland:

Riverdale
Nov 2nd 17

Dear Mrs Marlow

It is with regret that I now write to say how very sorry I am to hear of your second great loss, I'm sure you must have a terrible anxious time let us hope that the other three boys will return safely, I have received all of Dave's little things back & it all opens afresh the wound. I hope you will excuse the shortness of this Mrs Marlow & someday when you feel inclined I would like to hear from you with sincere sympathy

From Lizzie Glass

News of George's death also reached some members of the family in England before his brothers could be informed. The length of time it took for word to reach them almost certainly exacerbated their grief.

Drayton
Nr Uppingham
Nov 6 1917
My Dear Brother & Sister

i cannot tell you how sorry we are to hear of your great loss & pain what a blow it would be to you both i hope his dear Mother will bear it as well as she can i am so sorry for her i have not seen him but she said what a dear boy he was i should have liked to have seen him but i was to poorly when he came to Leicester i could not go i did not see Albert either i do hope i trust that the other will be spared to you this war is dreadful isn't it i do wish it would end Ted youngest boy went up last week but they sent him back he not big enough Harry has got his discharge but i think I told you dear brother give my love to my dear sister & Jim & except the same your dear self i know you will excuse a short letter this time hoping you are all well as it leaves us all well Thank God we are having a lot of rain here & the potoes are going very bad i am sorry to say well my Dear Brother & sister i will now close with love from us all i remain your ever loving sister

C Wilson XXXXX

In the south of England the Lee family had yet to hear of George's death, although Annie, sister of Charles senior, appears resigned to the worst:

Water Farm
Manaton
Moretonhampstead
Nov 8 1917

My Dear Sister & Brother I feel I must write you a few lines to tell you how very pleased we were to see dear Allan he is a dear boy We all fell in love with him Since seeing him we feel very anxious about them all the enclose snapshot was taken while with us I thought you might like one and one for Jim with my love I heard from Allan on the 6th he said they were quite well we are very sorry about Poor George as they have yet no news of him you have our sincerest sympathy in your loss of loss of Poor Albert he wrote me several nice letters although we did not see him we knew he was very nice by his letters We are looking forward to seeing Percy & Charlie I do hope they will be spared to you it is a awful war their seems no ending yet and the weather is very hard for them it is nearly always raining it will be nearly Christmas by the time you get this I am writing to ask Charlie to try & get leave for Christmas if he does not get it before he says Percy may get his any time now I am afraid my letter will not be of much interest to you I hope you will excuse a short one Trusting you are all quite well with love to all from your loving sister

A Lee

Allan on leave in England — a photo his aunt sent to Sarah and Charles.

THE WESTERN FRONT, NOVEMBER

In France, Charlie, Percy and Allan remained in training. Charlie wrote:

November 3rd 1917
My Dear Mother, Father and Jim,

… I am still at the school Allan is there Percy is at a Lewis Gun School. I was talking to the Lewis Gun officer this afternoon he says he will get a stripe out of it, it was the officer who sent him there. I told you that I was a temporary Corporal. I can now draw 4/6 a day over here as I cannot make

an allowance while I am temporary rank of course Pearl's money goes on the same she draws 4/- 1/6 deferred 4/6 goes into my pay book which makes 10/- a day. I was going to cable home to you for some money but now I will have a good bit in my book, I am promoted a Corporal via a wounded man if he returns inside 3 months I will go back to Lance Corporal, but I think I am pretty safe. Allan was a temporary Corporal right up to the time he was made a temporary sergeant, he is now a sergeant and will stand a good chance of getting a commission as a second Lieutenant there are always a certain number of sergeants get commissions and he will stand a good chance, if he does, he will very likely got to a school in England for 4 months and then 2 months at the training battalion in Lark Hill. I will not be a Lewis Gunner now but will be in charge of another section, Percy will be in charge of the Lewis Gun section, if Geordie had been in the infantry he would have had a commission by now or he would have stood a good chance. I expect a letter next week to say how he is and I will let you know at once …

Percy penned a letter to his aunt:

In the field
Nov 3rd
My Dear Auntie Florrie & All

I am at a Lewis Gun School, and we have plenty of writing, and learning to do, it is a good way from the Battalion, they are still in the same place. We get a lot of lectures, and have to take notes, and write them up at night. Charlie & Allan were still at the school when I left, which was three days ago. We have a nice little camp, huts to sleep in, and good meals, work from nine till one, two till five two smoko ¼ hour each. I will be here twelve days. There is a fairly large town about two miles away, but I never bother to go in. Poor Spuddy Kerr, got his leg taken off above the knee, blood poisoning set in, it was a pity for him he was a good fellow, one of the best in a stunt. He will go to England later on, when fit to travel. Have not heard yet from Bill Street or Albert Brooks either Hugh Martin.

There is some heavy fighting in Italy just now. Fritz has pushed them back a bit. You will be well into harvest by now. Just about twelve months since we came to France. The weather is very miserable & I suppose it will remain so for a while now. I had a terrible slow train ride to get here, started 9 am got here at 10 pm, quite no distance, was in a carriage with a New Zealand chaplin, he was saying it would make a parson swear, the trains are always slow here. There is a chap in my Company that was relieving the station master at Mitiamo about four years ago, named O'Brien knows Uncle Jim Mahoney well …

Allan's next letter to his parents lacked his earlier buoyancy and his bravado has clearly been shaken — he admits he has had enough of war:

In the field
6-11-1917
My Dear Mum & Dad,

… It is a fair while since we had a letter from Ausy I can [can't] make it out but we always hope for the best. Well dear mum it is raining a treat now but thank God we are out of the line for Xmas, anyway we have done our share of fighting for a while. Twelve months solid fighting without a spell is pretty solid. This will be the first spell we have had since being in France. We situated in a nice quiet little place. Free from shells & gas. Tra bon mum. The last two stunts are enough for me especially the last. Well dear mum I am now sure we will not be home for Xmas but cheer up there is a good time coming. I don't know whether I told you my last letter that I was an instructor at brigade NCO school. Charlie is here is getting on well. Percy has gone away to a lewis gun school. He is lucky. When this school ends I am going to hit the captain up for a school. I have had one school since I enlisted and it lasted 6 days. Well dear mum I say in every letter that I am going to cable for money but I havent done so yet. I believe I can get to Paris for 10 days anytime I like after the school breaks up. If I do I will cable but if not I won't cable. I get plenty of letters from England. Mum you all are worrying a terrible lot over dear Albert. Do look at it at the bright side. When I sit for a while it nearly breaks me up and when I know that you all are worrying it makes it worse so cheer up. Just take note of the date of this letters & I might have good news for you one of these fine day. Keep these letters. Well I suppose you all are busy with the harvest. I think I would make a good lunch boy. In fact I could sew the bags. I was never too good at it. Well dear mum hows bobs I could do a night camp there. Well dear

mum dad & Jim I will say goodnight wishing you all as brighter Xmas as circumstances will permit,

I remain
Your Loving Son
Allan S. M.

P.S. I hope you get the few little things I sent home

While choosing not to mention George to his parents, he is clearly Allan's first concern in his letter written to Jim on the same day:

In the field
6-11-17
Dear old Jim,

… We have not any word from Geordie. It is terrible to get letters at times over here. Well Jim it has been very wet lately but thank God we are out of the line. I am still instructing at brigade. Charlie is here getting instruction as a N.C.O. He is doing well Percy is away a Lewis Gun school. He is very lucky … I'm afraid we will not be home [for] Xmas but I hope you have a good one. Have a little extra duck for me. I say in every letter I am going to cable home for a tenna but haven't done so yet. They tell me I can go to Paris anytime I like after the school. So that is tra bon it would be lovely to see it. Well Jim I might have some good news for you very soon. Just take note of this letter the date. I tell you I wont forget to thank Mrs & Eva Jones for the parcel tra bon ah. Have you got a girl yet. Eva is a beaut is she Jim. Is Bill Jones married yet. Let me know when it is coming off. Im finished now with so & so up the road. Well Jim old man I think I have you or mum all the news so with best love to all

Your loving bro
Allan

Their hopes that George had recovered were now shattered as the truth was clearly spelt out to the surviving brothers. Officially, AIF Headquarters responded to Charlie's inquiries on 6 November. By the time he received the standard letter he had also heard from George's commanding officer in a brief note received from the trenches on 8 November.

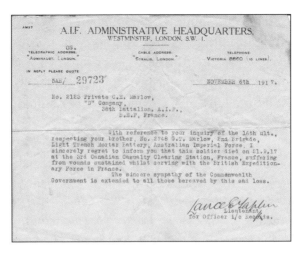

The letter Charlie received confirming the death of George.

AIF ADMINISTRATIVE HEADQUARTERS
WESTMINSTER LONDON
5AR/29723 Nov 6ᵗʰ 1917
No. 2123 Private C.E. Marlow,
"D" Company
38ᵗʰ Battalion, A.I.F,
B.E.F, France

With reference to your inquiry of the 16ᵗʰ ult., respecting your brother, No. 2748 G.T. Marlow, 2ⁿᵈ Brigade, Light Trench Mortar Battery, Australian Imperial Force. I sincerely regret to inform you that this soldier died on 21.9.17 at the 3ʳᵈ Canadian Casualty Clearing Station, France, suffering from wounds sustained whilst serving with the British Expeditionary Force in France.

The sincere sympathy of the Commonwealth Government is extended to all those bereaved by this sad loss.

Lance E Laplin
Lieutenant for Officer i/c Records

Charlie and Allan were together when the news finally arrived. They knew that George had cheated death at the disasters of Pozieres and Mouquet Farm and in the battles that raged at Lagnicourt and

Bullecourt. But, after 19 months of fighting on the Western Front, his luck had finally run out; good luck charms were no match for cold, hard steel. Seven weeks after the death of his brother, it was the eldest son who composed the words of consolation to his family, his anguish as palpable as his pride for George which he expresses in his letter.

8th Nov 1917
My Dear Mother, Father & Jim,

Again you will have received the awful sad news that our dear Geordie is gone, it breaks my heart beyond words to think that I shall never see him again, I wrote and told you that when we were camped near his unit I went one afternoon on my own to try and find him. I walked miles and miles but would not give up till I found him at last I found his unit and they told me that he was wounded and that it was not serious since then I had not received any word from him so I wrote to England and to his officer and today I received the very sad news from the Captain of his unit that poor Geordie died of wounds at one of the Casualty Clearing Stations I think in France, the note I got was short as they were in the line, the Captain is writing again telling me where he is buried, if possible I will go and see his grave, he did not state when Geordie died but it must have been soon after he was wounded, generally speaking in one of those stunts if a wounded man got out to the dressing station he will get on alright but the stomach is a very bad place, his mates dressed his wound and said that he was in good spirits and was not in any pain, his wound was not deep as the equipment saved him, they carried him behind a big concrete dugout and got a stretcher bearer, who brought him out, and the unit received word that he had passed through the Casualty Clearing Station, and they thought he would be alright when I heard that I was confident that he would be alright as he was not a fellow who would go down in spirits. Geordie was reserved for the stunt he and his team but at the last minute one of the other Corporals took ill and Geordie had to go, his mates told me what a fine fellow he was, and that when he was told that he was not to go over he was quite disappointed he wanted to go, he was not a bit frightened. I could see from what he told me when I met him that he was not frightened, I can honestly tell you that I don't believe there is another Australian living who has done as much for his country than Geordie, he has done many things worthy of a Military Medal and a Distinguished Conduct

Medal. I will find out all I can, how he died where he is buried and everything about his last moments, the Captain is writing again to me as he as in the line when he wrote he is going to write and tell me where he is buried, I will write to the Chaplain and nurses of the hospital and find out all I can, I am very glad that we met over here he was just the same as always, he had that same smile on his face and looked splendid, I was out with him two days, I worked a point one day to see him, I broke my teeth and said I wanted them mended so parade for the Dentist at the same time I made arrangements to meet me in a certain town I shouted him a splendid tea, it seemed like home to be with him, I also gave him a £1 note that was poor Albert's I divided Albert's money up amongst us, I asked Geordie if he wanted money when I left he said no that he had a good bit in his book. I often sent him a /- note, of course it was not mine it was some of that £10 which you sent, still I would give him what he wanted if he was short. I do feel it terribly he was an ideal brother nothing was any trouble to him, I was to meet him another day, but we shifted here, little did I think that was the last time that I should ever see him again poor fellow he died doing his bit for his country and whatever he done it was done as a soldier should do it. The Captain said he was one of the best N.C.O. that he ever had. Percy is away at a Lewis Gun School, he was away when Albert was killed I have written to him today, Allan is here with me, we are both at the school, and we came here today you get the mail and that is the sadness I got, I suppose Allan will be writing to you but he does not know as much about it as I do. I do not know how you will ever stand it, but I feel broken up to think that we have lost such fine fellows as Albert and Geordie, we are out of the line for how long I do not know, but please God we will be spared to return to you as we have done our share in this war, however I trust that their lives will not have been given in vain, but it is hard to part with them. I am a Corporal now, I will take care of myself for your sake, and trust that the day is not far distant when we will be home again, I will write a line to Pearl and send it with this, I share with you the loss of our dear Geordie and deeply mourn his loss, I know you will feel it I can tell you I feel it very much, I will say goodbye for the present with love and sympathy to you all.

I will write again shortly.
I remain
Your loving
Charlie

While Charlie promises his family that he would take care of himself and ask God to spare the brothers, he knew that such promises and prayers were no defence against the destructive might of artillery and machine-guns. A sense of regret also pervades his words; they had done their share, yet without an end to the war in sight, the Marlow family would not be immune from the threat of another casualty.

Soon after Charlie wrote his anguished letter to his family, the men of the 38th were informed that their 'rest' period had come to an end. On 10 November Allan and Charlie were again on their way to the front line near Ypres, this time to hold the Warneton sector near Messines from 13 to 21 November. On the darkest of nights they made their way along broken duckboards through the network of damaged and waterlogged trenches to the front line where they began repairing the defences, a task they continued for eight days until they were relieved. They then made their way through the shattered remains of Ploegsteert Wood and camped a few kilometres to the rear at Romarin in reserve.[15]

A week after receiving the letter that brought the dreadful news, Charlie wrote to his family from the trenches near Messines.

Trenches
Thursday 15 November, 1917
My Dear Mother Father & Jim,

I received two most welcome letters from you today and your bonzer parcel. We are in the line again near where Albert is buried, dear mother I got the very sad news about dear Geordie only last Wednesday, you will have heard at home before I did, I wrote to the Captain of the Trench Mortars and I got the very sad news I wrote a short letter to you but since then I have been unable to write as we were on the march and then we came in the line. I did not think we would be in so soon. Ida wrote to the War Office about poor Geordie and I got her letter the day after I got the word from the Captain on the card she got was that Geordie died of wounds on Sept 21st that was the day after he was wounded, he died at the 3rd Canadian Casualty Clearing Station so he will be buried there, I will find out where that is and will let you know, I had no idea that the poor fellow would die from what his mates told me, it is terrible hard luck to lose and I feel it very much it breaks my heart to think that that we have lost both Geordie and Albert I feel it very much and cannot get it out of my mind I would dearly loved to have seen him before he died, I would have liked to have got both Geordie and Albert buried together, but there is no chance, I sent a cable home to you about a week ago, I also got word from London that there was money there for me I will get it alright, Percy is still away at a school I am with Allan he has got his commission as a Second Lieutenant so he has got on well he will be a First Lieutenant in 3 months they always get their second star after 3 months on Active Service. I am a Corporal as I told you before. Al called home to you that he was a second Lieutenant. He has got on well I think Percy will get a stripe when he comes back from the school he should have had one long ago but they put someone else over him, he should have got one before me as he has been in the army longer than I have and had a lot more training. Well Mother I got your Christmas box, that cake was the best I have ever eaten it was not dry or broken up it was just splendid George Collison and A. Sinclair were with me are in the same dug out I gave them some they said it was splendid Allan also got his box from you, I gave him some of my cake he thought it was very good, the parcel could not have come at a better time than now as we were in the line. Abe Sinclair also got one so we are well off today, living high, I got a letter from Bill Roberts and a letter came from Miss Roberts for Collison [and] Sinclair and I [think] she is sending a parcel each to the 3 of us for Christmas. Abe Sinclair said to tell you that we had quite a picnic today, dear mother do not send tea as we cannot get hot water very well what is best of all is cake lollies and cigarettes … Well dear Mother I know how you will be when you heard about dear Geordie it is terrible beyond words. I am writing this in my dugout I have plenty to do now as a Corporal I have to take a party out each night for rations and plenty of other work to do I will write again shortly. Well dear Mother I will say goodbye I share with you all in the sad loss of our dear Geordie, but hope that we may be spared to return to you once again. I will say goodbye with love and sympathy.

I am your loving
Charlie

While the field postcards were dashed off in haste, a week later, when the 38th was withdrawn from the front line, Charlie had a chance to write at length:

Nov 22ⁿᵈ 1917
My Dear Mother, Father & Jim,

I got a lot of mail again tonight, we came out of the line last night after 8 days, we are close to where poor Albert and Tom Roberts are buried I intend to go to Albert's grave, so far I have not found out where dear Geordie is buried, beyond 3ʳᵈ Casualty Clearing Station I think it is near Ypres I cannot help thinking about the poor fellow, it is awful to lose him and Albert I feel it terrible I wrote to you when I was in the line, of late I have not been able to write much owing to marching and being in the line and then being a Corporal I have a little more to do … you asked why A.S. was out of the machine Gun he was taken out as to get promotion I am now out of it they took me out to make me a corporal, but we are all still in the same platoon and company Percy is in charge of the machine gun section I am in charge of a section, but when we were in the line this time I was in charge of the rations when they came up the line, I had to see that it was dealt out to the whole company fair and square it was a good job, but next time I suppose I will have a different job, as we have different jobs at times and it does not make any difference to our promotion, when I was at the school I believe I got a good report so that goes a long way. Al will be going to an officers school, I believe soon. When we came out last night, about 3 miles from the front we got a hot drink of cocoa a packet of biscuits and two cigarettes, I think it was given by the YMCA and the comforts fund, it was like giving me £1, I can tell you I did enjoy it. I got your parcel for Xmas mother I thank you very much for it the cake, pudding and all the rest was splendid if you had seen us when we were eating it you would have thought the same. Percy got yours tonight also one from Auntie Florrie and a small one from Mrs G. Mahoney Percy's cake from you was just like mine, bonzer, he has not opened Auntie Florries yet, Al got his parcel too we all thank you very much for the very nice cake and all the nice things, it must have been hard for you in your sad trouble to get them ready. I do feel sorry for you all at home at our sad losses for I know and feel it myself I know what it is over here and then Geordie has done so much it is hard luck, as he was an ideal brother without doubt, when I saw him he was just the same as he always was, his mates told me he was a fine soldier without a doubt I am trying to find out all I can about him, if there is anything you want to know about Albert or Geordie let me know and I will try and find it out, I will only be too pleased to do anything I can to relieve your anxious feelings I will write again soon, this is two mails in a fortnight but this has been delayed I will write to Pearl tonight, I will say goodbye for tonight with love and best wishes to you all, I share with you the loss of our dear Albert and Geordie.

I am your loving
Charlie

Back from the front line and housed in huts, each son had time in between unloading ammunition, repairing tracks and carrying supplies to the front to think of home, to unwrap parcels and to reply to letters. Allan wrote of his initial refusal to accept that George had gone. He complained to his mother that he would like his father to write and that there were some with whom he would rather not communicate. His letters reveal a sense of bitterness towards those men remaining in Australia and his views on conscription are abundantly clear, the death of his brothers fuelling his anger. In the chaos of battle, the capture of prisoners was not always the preferred option. After the death of two brothers, Allan had decided it was no longer the option he would choose, as he wrote to his parents: 'I never intend to take any more prisoners.' He proudly reports being commissioned, the first in his battalion to have risen from the rank of private to officer, and describes a watch 'given' to him by a Prussian Guard officer. Australian soldiers were notorious for collecting souvenirs from German prisoners, a pastime that, for some, proved quite profitable.

Allan delighted in the parcels that friends and family packaged and sent to the line, also mentioning Eva Jones, his neighbour across the paddocks, who was now a young lady and frequently referred to by the brothers in their letters to Jim as one of his latest love interests. Eva would watch for Sarah's washing day from high on the hill and traipse across the paddocks, through the fences and down the dirt track to lend

Sarah a hand. The boys never forgot her generosity and her support for their mother.

France [Belgium]
23-11-17
My Dear Mum & Dad,

… I have just come out of the trenches but things were fairly good there. Well dear mum there seems nothing of trouble lately. We got word the other day that poor old Geordie has died of wounds. It is awful to think that he is gone. I cant believe it yet not until I see his name published in the paper. Mum you people over there would [have] heard more about [it] and when he died than we did. It [is] no good mum I cant believe it so I will say no more about [it] not until I hear further. I have most tremendous mail to answer. I got 35 letters this mail practically all were got when I was in the line. Mum dear I got your lovely parcel. I must thank you it was a beaut. It was absolutely the best parcel that ever I got and once more what makes one appreciate it more was because I was in the trenches. Percy has been away to a school and he just came back in time to put a few days in the front line. That parcel was lovely next time you send me anything mum send a parcel like that, with plenty of smokes in it to. You don't know how I appreciated that parcel. Well I said I got about 35 letters and then of them I would not give a tenny if I never got. I have not got any time for them. I wont mention any names but guess for yourself. Somebody is always hitting me up for not writing they forget what conditions we are living under and I reckon they think we do anything but writing and a man ought to send them a line saying never expect a letter from me. I am not so much terribly obliged by their letters. They might think I am but that's not what I think. Now dad never writes to me he writes to Charlie and sometimes Percy. I cant make it out at all it has me absolutely beat. Mum do tell him to write to me I have had only two letters from him since being on service about 20 months. Mum when you write again do tell me why Mick Grant got the sack. I cant make it out at all. Dear Mum you seem to worry a terrible lot but give it up. Look as best you can on the bright side of things. Well dear mum it is 10 oclock so I think that I will go to bed so goodnight dear

Best love to all

I remain
Your Loving Son
Allan XXXXX

(I have no pencil so I am writing this with a very bad pen)

Allan wrote twice on the same day — the death of George had now been confirmed. In his second letter, Allan writes of his acceptance that another brother has been taken from them:

Belgium
23-11-17
My Dear Mum & Dad

… Well mum I received your welcome parcel about a week ago and it was lovely you don't know how much I appreciate it and once more I got it when we were in the trenches. That cake of Eva was lovely Mollie chocolate also. Eva put a short note in. It was very good of her. I will write to her to night also Mollie. Well dear mum & dad also Jim poor old Geordie is gone alright it is awful I cant help thinking about our two boys, yet others will stand back, the cowards. We are terrible short of men at the present time. Us lads that are here are doing about 3 mens work & what thanks will we get when we get back. I do hope conscription comes in. No body in Ausy can credit what operations have been put before the Australian lately and such a lot of them too. The ground we have had to take lately was most difficult & when we have done it, they say well done you brave lads, but how many are in it? If I was some of those fellows over in Ausy I would feel ashamed to poke my nose out of the door. I could not tell any one that I was Australian born. The cowards. Well dear mum I have some good news to tell you & that is I am a 2nd Lieutenant now. I was promoted to that rank on 3-11-17. I am simply delighted I cannot offer my allotment for awhile. I am the first one in my battalion that left Ausy as private to become an officer. Each officer has a batman & he cleans the boots look after my clothes and bed etc. It is tra bon. Well mum my next move is to become a 1st Lieut and I reckon within 3 months I will get it I hope so anyway and then after that it goes by seniority. Some few letter back I was talking about cabling for money but I will not now.

Mum one of these days I will send you home one of my stars for a keepsake and if I get [more] I will get them made into a brooch. I do hope you get my souvenirs that I sent a long time ago. I have another German watch which a Prussian Guard officer gave me. I took him prisoner he was a bit close to shoot. I never intend to take any more prisoners. I will [bring] the watch home one of these fine days. We are close to dear old Albert's grave again & we are going up to see it one of these nights. You ask if Mr Gollan is still going strong. Well mum he was pretty badly wounded in first stunt he is over in blighty. I am glad you are going to have a good harvest. Fancy such a lot of floods. I would enjoy them if I was there I will never forget the big one. Everybody seemed terrible disturbed and one thing & another but I was having a time of my life. I often think of the good old time we used to have together ah what Mum remember that pretty little thing I bought at the △ [Pyramid Hill] show and dad went crook. Wasn't it funny. I could tell you lots of little things I say mum do you remember the quilting I got for swearing. Well mum I have to get up at 6 in the morning to take a party out on fatigue very nice aint it. She seems to be getting a bit breezy again. I think we will have the winter on us again before we know it. Yes mum you seem to be having a lot of visitors. I will be writing to Stones again. How's Bobs that a jolly fine place. Well dear mum & dad I think I have told you all the news so I will close with love to all.

I remain Your Loving Son
Allan XXXXX

I sent you a cable about me getting my commission address 2ⁿᵈ Lieut A.S. Marlow

D Company 38ᵗʰ Batt 10ᵗʰ Inf Brigade AIF Abroad

Lieutenant Robert Gollan had written to the Marlows after Albert had been killed. Robert sailed on the *Runic* with Allan and Percy and was a member of D Company. He was wounded in the head on 7 June 1917 and his hearing had been affected. He was deemed fit to return to the 38th only to be shot at Passchendaele in the back and left leg. On 6 May 1918 he was back with the unit when he sustained his third head wound. He recovered to be wounded once more on 24 August

1918 as the Australians pushed the German troops from the villages on the Somme at Bray and Curlu. His medical records state that he was hit by a piece of aeroplane debris which pierced his right leg. Robert Gollan returned to Australia in July 1919. He never fully recovered his hearing.[16]

Allan wrote to Jim:

Belgium
24-11-17
Dear Jim,

… Well Jim we are out of trenches at present but we go up everyday on fatigue work. I was up there yesterday things were fairly quiet. We will be holding the line in a few days. I received your welcome letters last week. I got 35 last mail some answering today ah what. Well Jim poor old Geordie has died of wounds alright oh it is terrible. For godsake Jim don't let poor old mum worry to much. Cheer her up as best you can. Well Jim I am a 2nd Lieutenant now I was promoted on the 3rd 11-17. That is not to bad for me is it. I hope to get another star within about 3 months. I cannot alter my allotment for a while yet but will let you know as soon as I do so. Well Jim the cold weather is setting in again and I am afraid it will be a pretty [severe] winter. I hope it wont be like the one we had last year. I suppose you will soon be on the old harvester now. I suppose you don't want a bag sewer. I do hope you have a good harvest. Tell mum I received her lovely parcel. I also wrote M.G and your Eva. Things are not bad down in the vally where the blue birds sings. I don't write to the girl in Δ [Pyramid Hill]. No pour fini. Well Jim old man I think the war will [end] this year, next year, sometime never. Honestly I don't think it will end for another couple of years. I do hope they get conscription in. I would love to see some conscripts looking over the top. Well Jim I think I have told you all the news so will close with best love.

I remain
Your Loving Brother
Allan

Never publish any of my letters

Allan's earlier optimism concerning an end to the war had been dampened as he implored Jim to do his best to ease their mother's sorrow and reminded his brother once again that he should not publish any of his letters in the local newspaper. Percy wrote home on the same day. It is clear that they had yet to hear that Bill Street had died of his wounds.

In the field
Nov 24
My Dear Mother Father & Jim

Just a few lines to let you know we are all well. I received your ever welcome parcel it came while I was in the trenches and they kept it till we came out. The cake was lovely and the other things were very useful and I thank you very much for it I must write and thank Mollie Gamble for the tin. Well Mum, you would have heard the terrible sad news of poor Geordie it was such a sad thing for us all, especially for you I feel so sorry. I was at a Lewis Gun School went [when] the sad news came, and I wrote to you then. Charlie wrote when we got no word from him. We are writing now to find out where he is buried. Well Dear Mother we have just come out for eight days, but we are doing fatigues up the line, I am lucky being number one on the Lewis Gun, I have to stop home and clean the gun, it does me I will do my best to make it flash, I have done my share of fatigues. We have had a fairly quiet [time] in the trenches, sometimes it was a bit warm, the trenches were a bit muddy and wet, they are not very old trenches, it is ground that has not long been taken from Fritz so there is not many dugouts so we did not get too much sleep, the nights are terrible long, nearly 14 hours, especially when you have to sit up. You will be surprised to hear that Allan has a star he got it a week or two ago, he was lucky. We are in huts, they are very warm, it is too cold for tents now. I don't think it will be as cold this winter as last. Last year at this time we had snow it has been very good up to yet. We have a canteen here in one of the huts and there is tables in it, so I am making use of them. I have received a lot of letters from you and Jim lately a lot came while I was at the school. I had twelve days at a Lewis Gun school, it was a good stunt. I came back in time to catch them going in the trenches. You have been having a lot of wet weather over there, it would make it bad for ploughing. Well Mum, you was asking about Les Townsend, he is in England on leave now, he was not badly wounded. We have not heard from Bill Street or Albert Brooks, Spuddy Kerr lost his leg, it was stiff luck for him. Well Mum, I will close now hoping all are well, and sharing with you the loss of our dear brother.

I remain
Your Loving Son
Percy

As Christmas approached each son sent home cards with messages of greeting and Christmas wishes. They hoped these cheery greetings would arrive in Mologa in time to help ease the burden of the first Christmas since the death of George and Albert.

Charlie wrote home after visiting Albert's grave:

27ᵗʰ Nov 1917
My Dear Mother, Father and Jim

I am writing you a few lines tonight, at present we are out of the line, I wrote to you while I was in the trenches telling you what I could about Geordie, I got another letter from the Captain of the Trench Mortars but he was unable to tell me where Geordie is buried bar 3ʳᵈ Canadian Casualty Clearing Station, so I have written to that place and hope to hear next week I will write and tell you as near as possible when I hear I have written a lot of letters inquiring about Geordie and have asked the Clearing Station for information, it is very sad indeed, being unable to find out anything about him makes it worse. Percy and I went to Albert's grave on Saturday I was very pleased with the way it is looked after and kept so well, the grave is in perfect order and the cemetery is in a grand place and is already partly fenced in, it will be well cared for so you have no need to worry, the cross that I spoke about is not yet erected, I spoke to the Chaplain about it he said it would be done in time, at present there is a small cross with number name battalion etc. on a tin plate. Geordie grave will be similar as that Station mentioned above will be well back from the line … I am not in the Lewis Gun Section now, as I could not hold two stripes and be in it at the same time. Percy is the No 1 on the Gun it does not make any difference being out of it, I think you misunderstand the Lewis Gun for Machine Gun Company which is attached to the Brigade. I am in the same Platoon as Percy but attached to a different section. Well I will close for this time, I share with you the sad loss of our dear brothers which I feel sure you feel the same as I do. I will say goodbye with love and my sympathy, I am

Your Loving
Charlie

On 29 November the 38th Battalion was sent back to the front line in the Warneton sector. Unlike the previous stint just eight days prior, the line was now battered by artillery fire. The Allied response was to greet same with same. The pounding of the big guns was relentless. Holding the line as the winter approached became increasingly difficult and the men prayed that the winter would not be as severe as that of their first year on the Western Front, remembering the bitter cold of 1916.

THEATRES OF WAR

In France, Allied preparations for a surprise attack on the Hindenburg Line were underway. On 24 November at Cambrai, 80 kilometres north-east of Amiens, the Allies sent 324 tanks across a ten-kilometre front advancing on an unwary enemy. The use of tanks was generally scorned by the infantry who had witnessed their failings in previous battles.[17] However, the employment of tanks on such a large scale had not been attempted to date. The tanks rapidly broke through the Hindenburg Line and were followed by infantry and cavalry. The attack was heralded a great success and celebrated across Britain. The elation was premature. Many tanks were hit and soon out of action and the Germans quickly brought up reinforcements. By 7 December much of what had been gained was lost; a small section of the Hindenburg Line remained in Allied hands, but a sector of the Allied front had been lost. While Cambrai revealed that tanks could be successfully employed, the battle had ended in yet another stalemate.

To the east, Lenin's Bolsheviks had taken over Petrograd on 7 November. Russian forces had collapsed. Lenin now sought an armistice with Germany and German troops fighting on the Russian front were rushed to France and Belgium. On the Italian front, in the northern mountain ranges, the two and a half year stalemate between the Italians and the attacking Austro-Hungarian forces had been broken with the use of highly trained German storm troopers on 24 October. The Battle of Caporetto saw 180,000 Italians captured along with 1500 guns. The remaining Italian forces, nearing collapse, retreated 100 kilometres to the Piave River near Venice and, remarkably, held off the attacking force.[18]

MOLOGA, DECEMBER

In Australia, a second conscription referendum was more convincingly defeated than the first. Australia was to remain one of the few Allied countries that did not rely on conscription. The controversy continued to divide the country between those who believed that Australia had sent enough of its young men to the front and those who believed that the soldiers needed support and that others should do their bit. Catholic and Anglican divisions deepened as the rhetoric of Prime Minister Billy Hughes and that of his opponent, the Catholic Archbishop of Melbourne, Daniel Mannix, resounded throughout communities across Australia. Australian soldiers abroad once again voted for conscription but by a narrow margin. Some wanted the 'shirkers' to have their turn, while many soldiers could not send others against their will into the hell that they were experiencing.

As social divisions deepened so did the fear of the 'enemy within'. Many towns and geographical features that bore German names were renamed. Initially, those from countries with which Australia was at war were interned in camps which also held prisoners of war; these were mostly German sailors who had the misfortune to be in Australian ports when war was declared. As the war continued, the list of enemy aliens expanded to include those who had been born in enemy countries but had later become naturalised British subjects, along with Australian-born descendants of migrants from those countries. Many of those who were detained were later to be deported when the war finally reached its weary conclusion.

At Mologa, Charles Snr, Sarah and Jim were busy with the harvest. Their answer to the conscription question almost certainly will have been 'Yes' although, having lost two sons, I am not entirely convinced that Sarah would have voted for other sons to have been committed to the war. Anglican ministers generally encouraged their parishioners with patriotic fervour and their sons and brothers at the front all appear to have voted in favour. These were difficult times for Sarah who not only struggled to cope with the death of her two sons but also the passing of her father on 4 October. Cards and letters of condolence and this report from the *Pyramid Hill Advertiser* did little to ease her grief. Letters of congratulation on Allan's promotion may have briefly provided some brighter moments.

CORPORAL GEORGE MARLOW

ROLL OF HONOR

Mologa

Mrs. Marlow, Mologa, has received the following letter from Capt. James D Johnston concerning the death of her son, Cpl. George Marlow.

Long before you receive this you will have heard of the death from wounds of your son No. 2748, Cpl. George Marlow, of this unit, but I know you will want to know something of the manner in which he met his death. We were making one of the biggest attacks of the year, and George was in charge of one of our teams. All went splendidly until he happened to be struck by a spare bullet. He was taken away immediately by the stretcher-bearers and we were confident that he would be quite safe. However, we were very sorry to hear that he had succumbed at one of the hospitals; at which one I do not myself yet know. No loss had been so much deplored by the boys in the battle as that of your son. He was one of the best N.C.O.s I ever had, and most popular. The men under him would go anywhere with him. The men have asked me to send you their sympathy, and asked me to say how much they deplore his loss. With the deepest sympathy of all the officers, N.C.O.s and men of the battery in your bereavement,

I am sincerely yours,

James D Johnston

Commander 2 A Light Trench Mortar Battery[19]

4 Comts
Parkhouse
Salisbury
England
Dec 1ˢᵗ 17
Dear Mrs Marlow,

I trust you will pardon me if I am doing wrong in writing to you. I saw in an Australian paper here AW Marlow had been killed in action, as I heard Albert had made the supreme sacrifice from one of our 4/38 Batt boys. I used to hear from Albert regularly & when no news came through I thought something was wrong. What I knew of him he was a good living boy, it takes something to play the game. I sincerely hope your sons have been spared to come through the heavy fighting of late. I was transferred to A.S.C. [Army Service Corps] having had a lot of sickness in the Infantry. My brother Aiken was killed in action on Oct 1ˢᵗ so I am left to represent one family. We are both single & I am thankful for it. We live near Bairnsdale-Vic. I do pity all you dear home folk it is not so bad for us here in England – We have not the worry you have at home but trust and pray the much talked end of the war will come to pass. Believe one to remain Dear Mrs Marlow

Yours fraternally
Harold Scott 2392[20]

"The Lord giveth & the Lord taketh away"

P.S. Please do not bother replying

9-12-17
6 Hotham Grove
Elstenwick

Dear Mrs Marlow

We have twice written to you to express our sympathy with you in your bereavement, losing your two brave boys. Now, it is up to us to express our joy at seeing that your son Alan has won his commission. It is a grand thing for a young soldier to get especially as he has won it on the field. We are proud and delighted to be allowed to join in congratulating you on your boy's promotion and hope that he will win much more and that the rest of the war will be to you a time free from trouble or fresh sorrow. May God bless & keep all your brave boys & send them safe home again.

Yours sincerely
A.W. Williams

Pyramid
Dec 10ᵗʰ 1917

I wish to convey to you my sincerest congratulations on the promotion of your brave son Allan. He was the only one of your noble sons I knew personally, but I do earnestly hope that at some future date we will have the pleasure & honour of welcoming Allan & his gallant Brothers home again. You have every reason to be proud of such fine sons & we Australians are proud of you in having reared such noble men who are willing to give their lives for their country.

With kindest regards from Mrs Wood my sisters and myself.

I remain yours sincerely
C.E. Wood

BELGIUM AND FRANCE, DECEMBER

The 38th remained in the Flanders region throughout December as Allied soldiers rotated through the line. On 6 December they were relieved and made their way to Hill 63 and 'Red Lodge', a site a few kilometres behind the front line at Messines where the troops were treated to the luxury of powered dugouts nestled in the side of a hill, complete with bunks. While out of the line, fatigue duty required frequent treks to the front and brought the weary troops back within range of the enemy artillery. Being out of the line did not always guarantee safety.

Soon after, the battalion moved to Aldershot Camp on Waterloo Road, a position behind Neuve Eglise and to the west of Warneton. Percy was promoted lance corporal and was now in charge of the Lewis gun team, his promotion long overdue in the opinion of his brothers. On 20 December the 38th moved further back to Hollebeke Farm (Jesus Farm) near Steinwerch close to the familiar Armentieres.[21] They spent Christmas here and, judging from their accounts, enjoyed the offerings supplied by their battalion cooks. Charlie had additional cause to celebrate, as he was promoted to the rank of lance sergeant just three days before Christmas. He now enjoyed the luxury of turkey for dinner on Christmas Day.

Early in December, as winter descended on the battlefields, Allan wrote to his neighbour Eva Jones as he had promised his mother, a letter Eva chose to keep (although the first page is missing).

… The second one was fought in the same sector but without a complete success, we suffered very heavily which was due to not enough artillery support on account of the lads not being able to get their guns forward on account of many different conditions. It was absolutely the worst time we have had yet. For slush and water also machine gun fire and shellfire we found it almost impossible to make good progress. Anyway we got out of that place with a few men. From there we went back a few miles for a spell of about 3 weeks, then we went up into the trenches again and at [present] we are out but will be returning in a couple of days. The weather is getting very cold again and I am afraid we are in for a severe winter but we will have to put up with it. I believe Charlie Fyffe has landed home. By jove he is lucky. We have been in France about 15 months now and they tell us we will be getting a long spell soon. I hope to be going over to Paris next month. I got leave to England about 3 months again [ago]. Well Eva I think I have told you all the news so will close with kind regards to all.

I remain your Loving Friend
Allan. S. M.

Many thanks for the parcel.

P.S. I forgot to tell you that I was promoted to 2nd Lieutenant last month. I will send you a photo one of these fine days. Eva I think the war will end this year, next year, sometime never. Tell them in Mologa to keep the old flag flying. ASM

Charlie wrote to his mother with sadness as he described Albert's prediction when visiting his English relatives and of receiving word that Bill Street and Bill Crossman had died:

... When I was in England Auntie Payne told me about poor Albert saying that he would get knocked he said :- Auntie I will leave these things here for Charlie as I suppose I will get knocked, but he never at anytime was frightened he went all through the battle of Messines with us and took it as an every day occurrence, he never said anything to me about being knocked, he was very game. Harry Street has not heard much about Bill's death, I saw in the paper where Bill Crossman had been killed ...

Bill Crossman was 32 when he left the farm at Milloo to enlist in February 1916. He was discovered to have poor eyesight and was discharged a few months later. There his war records inexplicably end. Bill later sailed with Charlie in September 1916. He was allotted to the 59th Battalion and was killed on 29 September 1917, one of the many lost to the fields of Flanders. His name is etched on the Menin Gate. [22] His brother Samuel had enlisted in July 1915 and was a gunner with the 4th Field Artillery. He survived and returned to Australia in March 1919. [23]

Charlie wrote:

9th Dec 1917
My Dear Mother, Father & Jim,

Yesterday I received the money you cabled to London, I had it sent on to Ida and she sent it to me. I thank you very much for it and will give it back to you when I get back. Today I got a photo for each of us of Geordie and when I look at it it breaks my heart to think that I will never see him again and to think that he should die of wounds like he did. I wrote to the 3rd Canadian Casualty Clearing Station to find out all I could about his death later on I will send you the letter also a letter that the sergeant of the Trench Mortars wrote I want you to keep them for me, the first note said he was hit in the stomach and left hip and died on the 22 Sept but this is wrong he died on the 21 Sept the note said he received every consolation at the time of his death and where he is buried I will look up the map and will give you the exact place I am writing again to the burial people and if I get near I will try and put a cross over him. I told you before that I went and saw Albert's grave that was about a fortnight ago, the cross is not erected and now to my mind it will not be done, so I am going to see what I can do myself, of course it is hard to get away but if I have the money I will get the Pioneers or Engineers to do it and the same with Geordie's. I would like to put a nice cross over them both, and would have liked to have had them both buried together, it seems hard to think that they are gone, I cannot get any information as to how Geordie died, or whether he was conscious or if he said anything, I think I will write to the Chaplain of the 3rd Canadian CCA. Percy may get leave to England shortly he was very cut up over Grandfather dying but I partly expected it, as he was so old and could not last much longer but still I was very sorry to hear the sad news I would have very much liked to have seen him again. I heard that one of Pearl's brothers have died, we seem to be having our share of bad luck. I hope that it will change for the better now and that we will have no more bad luck. We are out of the line again and will be out for Christmas and I believe a rest, but this Christmas will be a sad one for us all and I hope for better days to come and that the three of us will be spared to return again. There is to be another referendum on the war business over here. I am sending one of the letters that the Sergeant wrote to me about Geordie, you may show it to anybody or put it in the paper but keep the letter for me. And about the photos of Geordie I got Ida to send them home to you I want you to send one to Pearl for me Geordie told me he did not make a will in Victoria but I understood him to tell me that he made one while he was on leave in England and I think that will be sent on to you from Horseferry Road London or from the base in Victoria. Every soldier over here is issued with a will form to make a will if he pleases whether Geordie made it on that I do not know, the form they give us is useless to make a will on as it is too brief, but if he made it on that, it will be sent on to you. Albert, I think made a will on the issued form, he also made a will in his paybook, but if he made one on the issued form the paybook one would be cancelled, the forms were given to us the day before the advance on 7 June. You asked who was killed with Albert, Lieut, A.G. Abbey, Lieut Windham, Serg N. Onians, Serg P.J. Cunningham. I hope you will be able to read this but I am writing this in an uncomfortable place. Last night I wrote the Chaplain of the Canadian C.C.S. for information I will let you know as soon as I can what he has to say. I am sending this with a letter to Pearl she will send it on to you let me know if you get it, we are near where Albert is buried. Well I will close for this time I will write soon, I share with you all the sad loss of dear Geordie and I know you will feel it the same as I do.

I will say goodbye
With love to all
I am your loving
Charlie

A letter received by Charlie appeared in the January edition of the *Pyramid Hill Advertiser*. The article began with an introduction:

Sergeant Chas E Marlow. Who has recently gained promotion from temporary corporal and corporal has recently received the following letter in the field:

France

1.12.17

Dear Charles

Your letter of Oct 31st to hand. The delay was caused by me being at a school and the letters being sent on after I had left, so they had a trot round until they landed back here again. Your letter also reached the C.O. of the Battery and I believe he wrote to you recently. I am sorry indeed to have to tell you that George was wounded 20.9.17 and died of wounds 21.9.17 at 3rd Canadian Casualty Clearing Station. The wounds were Gun Shot wound in the Stomach and right Leg. I cannot give you the place of burial, but if you wrote to the O.C. Anzac Section, 3rd Echelon GHQ. BEF. I think he would be able to give you it. I had known George for nearly 18 months and he was a fine type of manhood. Quiet going, honest and as straight as anyone I know. He was well liked and highly thought of by all the Battery, and to gain the respect and admiration of your comrades is something to be proud of, which I think you know only too well. I cannot express my feelings I have for you and those of your home — words seem empty — but I want you to know that your late Brother George has left a name behind him in this Unit which you should be proud of. Please accept these words and thoughts of mine in your great loss.

Yours very sincerely

Norman Day

Lieutenant Norman Day served in the 2nd Light Trench Mortar Battery with George, having signed up in June 1915. He was shot near Herleville Wood on the Somme on 25 August 1918 and died from his wounds in a London hospital on 21 September 1918, exactly 12 months to the day after the death of George.[24]

At Mologa, Jim received word from his mate, Tom Alford, who had earlier been listed as missing. He appears completely unaware that there was any question over his whereabouts. What is certain, however, is that, for Tom, the excitement of the grand adventure is over …

December 10th 1917
Dear Jimmy

Well how is the old sport going along. Expect you will be looking for another letter. Haven't done much writing lately as things have been up to shit judging by this last few days rain will be worst but so far this winter has been a king to last not near as cold as last but it is young yet. Haven't had any letters lately but expect they are lying about somewhere. Suppose you will be up to your neck in work by this. What sort of a year have you had. I don't seem to have heard anything about the prospects at all lately. Haven't been fortunate enough to strike any of the boys lately. I thought I might when we all got on the same front. I have had a lot of pals killed lately, am just getting that way that I don't give a damn. Wish to God it would finish. Didn't like going back after having leave. Don't know if I told you before but I met the two Stone boys. They hadn't been on the line then but expect

they have had a gut full before now. I say Jimmy what is doing at the P.O.
I still get letters from that way but they are mostly about Fred Bramley &
Myrtle doings. Is he got a leg in with her now. Well good luck to 'em. Your
only young once is about all I can see in it. Well don't know what to write
about damn me if I do, so with best regards to your people from you old pal

Tom Alford

Allan wrote two letters to his parents on the same day, the second after
receiving news that his grandfather had passed away. The letter conveys
his sense of melancholy as thoughts of home on his birthday and the
prospect of Christmas spark a longing for the life he once knew at
Mologa. He asks his mother and father to pass a message regarding
'minnies and pineapples' to Frank Dee who had now arrived back in
Australia after suffering a gunshot wound to his abdomen. A German
'minnie' or *minenwerfer* was a medium trench mortar. A 'pineapple'
was a light German trench mortar shell that was grooved into sections
and would fragment on bursting. Both had distinctive sounds and both
were deadly.

Belgium
10.12.1917
My Darling Mum & Dad,

… I have had 3 parcels from you in 3 weeks. They were all bonzers. Well
mum I got a terrible shock just now. I asked the captain what was the date
and when he said the 10ᵗʰ I said why hell I am 22 today. I am getting old
now. I have had 2 birthdays in France now. Well dear Mum we have just
came out of the trenches again, we had a pretty rough run. We have had our
first snow for the winter. This time last year it was dreadfully cold but now
its not bad at all. Last night I was up in the trenches with a fatigue party
of 50 men we were repairing trenches. It was a brute of a job. Tonight I am
not going up 2 other officers go up. In a few days we go back for about a
month. So that means we will be out for Xmas (Hurrah). We will be soon
having a vote for the Refer-. A big yes from me. Fancy old Frank Dee being
back. Remember me to him when you see him. Tell him we are still getting
Minnies & Pineapples. Charlie Fyffe is back too. Some boys are lucky. Tell

Jim I have another Fritz watch to send home also a bonzer revolver. I have not got my Paris leave yet but I am trying to work it in for Xmas. Do you remember the team meeting at the hall. Weren't they tra bon. I suppose you don't have them now. I met Wilson Townsend a few days ago. He looks well. I had letter from Les too. He is in England on leave. He got slightly wounded in our first stunt at Pashendale. I cant find out anything about Bill Street. I think he is gone. But mum dont say a word about until I get official news. I got a letter from poor old Geordies officer. He wrote such a nice letter. Mum don't worry so much. It is terrible hard you know. Fancy Mick Grant ah. It is awful about him I cant hardly believe it you know. Mum I have some photo of different people cousins & so forth They are only getting broken & ruined so I am going to send them home will you keep them until I <u>return</u>. It makes me laugh when I hear anyone use the underlined word I think the only way we will end the struggle is by peace. Well dear mum this is all the news to day so I will close with best love to all.

From your loving
22 year old son
Allan

… I suppose Jim is on the old harvester and you can't see him for dust. Dad on the bags and mum on the lunch. Just picture me at the lunch. Well I hope the crops turn out well I think we will be home for next Xmas so keep an extra bag of wheat for the fowl. Mum get those ducks in good order. I think we will have the old black rooster last. We will have some rabbit and hare sausages to. Ask Jim does he remember the ones we made on Sunday when you was in Bendigo & Dad said, "None to much fat in them now Jim". By jove I have laughter at times when I have thought of our little incidents.

Well hurrah dear mum

… Just another few lines to let you know how very sorry I am to hear about poor old Grandad's death. I got [a] terrible shock when I heard the news from Percy. But you know mum he was a big age. We seem to have our share of trouble lately, but I sincerely hope it is ended now. So mum cheer up dear. Lets have a cheery letter now. We [will] all soon be home again eating those ducks etc. We are out of the line at present but we go up every night

on fatigue work but in a few days we will be moving back again. I hope to be able to get a few little things to send home to you I wrote you a letter this morning and told you all the news…

Allan's following letter to Jim illustrates the intensity of his hatred for the enemy; 'for King and Country' is now secondary to avenging the deaths of his brothers. He is pessimistic at the prospect of an end to the war and his reflections of home are tinged with the melancholy of longing for the life he once enjoyed.

Belgium
10.12.17
Dear Jim,

…We have just come out of the trenches. We had a pretty ruff turn too. Now we go up every night on fatigue, repairing trenches so forth. In a few days we will be moving back clear of the line for a little while. We had our first snow the other day. This time last year it was brutal cold but now its not to bad. I received your welcome letters the other day. I was terribly sorry to hear about grandfather but you know Jim he was a big age. Percy is taking it pretty bad. We had some letters from poor old Geordies officer. Oh Jim it is awful to think that both him and dear Albert have gone. We will realise it more when we get back. We have had a terrible bad run. I have given Fritz no mercy since dear Albert was killed and I can tell you we have been in pretty close quarters at times too and I have had the good luck to come off best. Our boys absolutely stonker them all now. They will never do us any good I have seen [a] good many of his tricks on the battle field and seen lads lose their lives through being too easy with them. I have seen some of their doing with the poor women of Belgium and when they tell you about it, [it] would break your heart. So when you think of it what are we here for. To kill. No doubt Jim you will be pleased to hear that I am a 2nd Lieutenant now and I hope to get higher too. Jim tell mum all will soon be home cheer her up as much as you can. I had a letter from Les Townsend the other day. He is on furlough in England having a great time. He was slightly wounded in our first stunt at Pashendaele. That is where we had terrible fighting. Fancy Tom Gibson enlisting. His people are dam fools to let him go. We hold our referendum to morrow. I am one of the authorised witnesses. I am cursing it as I wanted to

write letters. I hope it goes through. How are the Johnson's. I would like to see u u u in the front line. It would take all the dancing out of him. Well Jim I suppose you are terrible busy with the harvest now I suppose you cant see your self for dust. How is it for a job of bag sewing. I bet you get some lunches ah. A man ought to be there even if it only for the lunch …

It was Allan's day for letter-writing with three letters home, while twin brother Percy wrote an unusually long letter to Jim:

In the field
Dec 10ᵗʰ
Dear Jim,

Received your ever welcome letter, with the sad news about Poor Grandad, of which I was very sorry to hear about, it gave me a great shock especially not long before hearing about Poor Geordie. Well Jim, things are going just the same, the war seems no nearer an end than ever it was. I suppose you heard before this that Allan has a star, some boy now eh. We are out of the trenches now, just behind the line doing fatigue work at night. I miss it, being number one on the Lewis Gun, have to clean the gun in the day time, does me Jim, I have had my share of fatigue. The night work is a sod of a job, a long way to walk to it, and when you get there, its so dark to see what you are doing. We had a livelier spin in the trenches this time than before, he gave us a bit of hurry up with shells at times he can make it feel very uncomfortable for you if he likes. The nights were terrible long, about fourteen hours and a nice frost in the bargain. The trenches we were in are not very old and there are not many dugouts in fact where we were there was not any and when we have to sit up all night, you wish for morning. We had two raids in one night on our sector, not our Battalion went over, a raiding party from two of the other Battalions of the Brigade they wake old Fritz up. I see by your letter you have had a visit from Mrs Stone who brought with her a couple of girl friends well known to me especially the latter Selina "don't quite get you Jim". Well, I will admit I know her Jim, but that is about all. Better give you the good oil. You remember that turnout at Stones before we left; well I could not get rid of her and I did my best. She could not see who I was paying the best regards to for the night I don't know why. The first dance she thought I was going to have with her, only one thought it. Never want to take any notice of Mrs Stone, she would tell you anything, so as not to stop talking. Ruby Lee is a hard case Jim. We had snow the other week first for the winter. I think we are going to have a better winter than last. I suppose you will be well on with the harvest now. Like to get to England for Xmas Jim, I ought to get leave soon. I have had a fair run …

In the field
Dec 11ᵗʰ
My Dear Mother & Father,

Well Mum, its terrible sad about Poor Grandad. It gave me a great shock I never thought such sad news would come so soon. It breaks me up to think that I will not see him anymore, my sympathy is with you Dear Mother in this time of sorrow… We have not heard from Bill Street since he has been wounded. Harry Street who is back with the battalion was trying to find out he has written to England. I am expecting leave anytime now I would like to get it for Xmas it ought to be good in England Xmas time. We have had some lovely frosts this last night or two, when you get a frost here it is one. I suppose you are well on with the harvest now you will be having hot weather while we will be having just the opposite. I don't think this winter will be as bad as last. I think I told you in my last letter that Allan has a star some head now. Some of Fritz aeroplanes came over today and our planes set on to one and set it alight. Fritz dived for the ground but did not reach it before the plane fell to pieces there were two men in it they got a terrible fall. When it caught alight he tried to get to his lines but he did not succeed. Well Mum I have run out of news so I will close hoping this finds you all well as we are at present.

I remain your ever loving son
Percy

Charlie wrote a detailed letter describing his promotion to lance sergeant and Percy's to lance corporal.

In the field
15-12-17
My Dear Mother Father & Jim

… You will be pleased to hear that I have been promoted from Temporary Corporal to Corporal and from Corporal to Lance Sergeant. I do not know whether you know what a Lance Sergeant is but a L Sgt does not get Sgts pay like a Temporary Sgt, but is entitled to wear 3 stripes and sgts mess and cannot be reverted to Corporal like a Temporary Sgt. If a Temp Sgt goes to hospital sick or wounded or if reinforcement NCO's come in he goes back to Corporal, A.S. was a Temp Sgt once and reinforcement Sgt came in and he had to go back to Cpl, but I will not be reverted if the above was the case. Address my letters Sergeant C.E. etc they never mention the lance. Percy was made a Lance Corporal the same day 12.12.17, he should have been a lot higher, they put some shady work in and sent a chap that was below him on the gun away to a school and made him a LCpl the same fellow is now a Temp Sgt, it was through the Lewis Gun Officer then that P.P. got his stripe. A.S. will be a First Lieut after he has had his first star 3 months. We have been out of the line about a week and will be here for some time so there is no need for you to worry. I have written again to the 3rd Canadian Casualty Clearing Station this time to the Chaplain to try and get information about poor Geordie. I feel it very much not being able to find out anything about him I wrote to the sergeant who wrote to me from the Trench Mortars. I sent the letter home to you through Pearl. When I get the reply from the Chaplain I will send you word…

20th Dec 1917
Dear Jim,

… We are expecting a mail soon we got a letter last mail from Auntie Florrie to say that Grandfather had died, and soon after that you will have got the sad news of Geordie, I have written to you all before and told you all about it. I wrote to the Clearing Station and asked where Geordie's grave was, the C.O. sent the Map Reference and the name of the Cemetery, so far I have not been able to get hold of the map but I saw a French map and was able to trace the place. I cannot tell you where it is owing to Censor, it is a hard blow to all of us and it is hard that he should die so suddenly. Harry Street got word the other day that Bill had died of wounds. I wrote to the Streets yesterday he lived about a fortnight after he was wounded, Harry did not hear where Bill was buried. Well I will close for this time and will be writing again soon, I will say goodbye with sympathy to all.

I remain
Your loving Brother
Charles

Harry Street had also suffered the agonising wait to hear news of his brother. He wrote to his parents in a letter which later appeared in the local newspaper:

Harry Street, writing to his parents from France, where his brother met his death in action there towards the close of last year, said: I suppose you have heard of Will's death long before this. As nobody here seemed to know where he was and none of his mates got any word of him, I decided to write to Military Headquarters, London, and to my surprise received word saying that he died of wounds in the head and side, penetrating the abdomen. He was wounded on 12th October and died on the 26th, so I fancy he must have had a very bad time, as he lingered a fortnight before death. I suppose blood poisoning set in. The last time I saw him was the day before I was wounded myself. That was about June. I can just imagine that you folks feel it very much, as I can tell you I do, away in the wilderness, and no friends, but anyway I feel that we have given the best, and I hope that I shall be spared to return home to tell the tale of this terrible war. I am trying to find out where he was buried so that I may get the chance to have some little bordering put around his grave and get a photo to send to you, but there are others that are broken hearted as well. If he was buried in England I would have got someone to visit his grave, but of course I do not know yet where he is buried. Some of his mates tell me that our Battalion was marching up to the front line to go into action; that Will was at the head of his gun team, when a big shell from the German heavy artillery landed just in front of him, with the result that a good number of the men were put out. Alb. Sinclair told me he saw Will in the dark not long afterwards, and he said he felt very ill. He was walking back to the dressing station, so I had hopes after hearing that that when he could walk a bit he would not be so bad; but as no word came from him I felt anxious. I will not say more about it at present. It is dreadfully cold here now (17 Dec.) It has been snowing all the morning and we have been out doing fatigue work. We are short of men and of course: get a lot of extra work to do and we don't get much rest. I am well at present and hope you are the same. I know the bad news will spoil your Christmas, but you must cheer up. I will be out of the line for Christmas, and will certainly think of you all, as I do every day. I will enclose the letter I got from London.[25]

With the death of Bill Street now confirmed, on Christmas Eve Charlie's thoughts turned to home and the grief he felt over the loss of his brothers:

Christmas Eve
In the field
My Dear Mother, Father and Jim,

A few lines tonight to say we are all well, Allan is at a junior officers school, it is not far away he was here yesterday and I saw some of the officers today, I think he will be back here tomorrow. Tomorrow of course is Christmas day and under the circumstances we will have an excellent dinner we Sergeants have got two turkeys, pork, beans, nuts, chocolate, plum pudding, cake, cigarettes and numerous other things, the men I think will have a splendid dinner of something the same as us bar turkeys we have got an excellent cook. I will tell you tomorrow what it is like, but there is to me a sadness tonight when I think that Albert and Geordie are gone ... I have partly found out where Geordie is buried and I will make certain next week, he is buried In Lyssenloek [Lijssenthoek] Cemetery I will, in my next letter, give you the town which that is near I will just write the name of the town so you will know what it means, and later on I will give you fuller details, get hold of a map of two countries, it is in the same country as where Albert is buried, well I will close for tonight and will write again tomorrow and tell you about our Christmas. Percy is here and is quite well ...

Charlie wrote again on Christmas Day:

25th Dec 1917
My Dear Mother Father Jim

Just a few more lines tonight we had a splendid dinner, it will no doubt interest you to hear what we had, I mean sergeants, well we had two turkeys, pork, plum pudding, custard with the turkey, we had onions, potatoes seasoning some sweets of all descriptions, bread, coffee cigarettes, and for those who wanted it beer wine champane I did not partake in the last 3 items, but the turkey was my height it was splendid beyond words and the best feed I have had since I left home we had our dinner at about 5 oclock, the men had dinner at 1 oclock and the sergeants waited on them, I was Orderly Sergeant for today it was my job to see that the men were all fed etc, the men had roast beef carrots potatoes and plenty of it plum pudding tinned fruit custard and beer cigarettes they had a splendid dinner, of course ours was much better but we paid for the turkeys we have a sergeants mess, the turkeys were young and fairly dear. Allan is at a junior officers school but he comes here every Sunday etc he was here today. I do not know if I told you the YMCA gave every soldier a nice little writing wallet this is the paper I am writing on. Well I am looking out for a mail from you, we will be out of the line for a long time so do not worry. I share you feelings today in the loss of dear Geordie and Albert, it sets a sadness to it all. I will say goodbye with sympathy to all

I remain
Your loving Charlie

A few days later, Percy described his Christmas dinner to his family:

In the field
Dec 28
My Dear Mother Father & Jim

Just a few lines to let you know we are all well hoping you are the same. Well we have had xmas, no turkey for dinner, roast beef, carrots, and potatoes, plum pudding to follow, it was a fairly good dinner. We were out of the line, that was one thing, it was snowing part of the day, the place was white. It is very cold over here now, some nights you would nearly freeze. We have some lovely frosts, and I suppose you are nearly roasting over there. How are you getting on with the harvest, were you finished by Xmas.

We are expecting a mail anytime now, it's a good while since we had one. I suppose there is a lot of traffic and they cannot get the mail over the channel. I suppose you heard about Bill Street, it was bad luck, he died on the 26th Oct of wounds, received on the 12 Oct. I believe Dave Mullens, from Terricks, was killed. I saw some of the chaps that was in his Company. Gordan McKay is not far from us, Charlie and I went to look for him yesterday, we did not see him. Les Townsend will be back soon, he is in England at present. We are in huts now, they are not too bad, they are warmer than tents.

Well Mum , I will ring off now, I will be writing again in a few days, so I am your

Loving son
Percy

As promised, Charlie wrote to his family and included the name 'Poperinghe' to tell them where George was buried:

Sat 29ᵗʰ Dec
In the field
My Dear Mother, Father & Jim,

… I have not gained any more information regarding Geordie. I wrote to the Sergeant of the T.M. and he was at a school and could not give me the information I required but said that all Geordie's private things would be sent home to you I do not know about his watch when I last saw him it was not going I do not know if he had it on him at the time he was hit, but I wrote to the Sergeant about it, however I think it will go home if it was on him. I would very much like to get it. I hope you got those photos safely and will you send one of them to Pearl for us. I wrote to the Chaplain of the Clearing Station but so far I have not got an answer.

Popperinge.

We are camped near where Albert is buried Allan is at a junior officers school, I think Percy will be going on leave to England next week he was asked about it today so I think he will get it alright. Gordon McKay is camped about a mile away from us but I have not seen him. Bill McKinnon told me he was there, all the Australians are in the one corps now and we wear our hats up at the side like the others. I do not know if you know that our division at first wore the hat down all round and the badge in the front, none of the men cared about it and were very pleased when it was altered. We are a long time getting a mail I was very sorry to hear of grandfather's death but it could only be expected on account of his great age. We heard that Dave Mullens was killed so inquired and found that it was only too true, I wrote a letter of sympathy to the Mullens'... I see by the paper the Hughes Conscription Bill failed again I wonder what he will do next ... I suppose you will be finished harvest by now, the time seems to go so quick I have been 12 months in France, we are well out of the line. Well I will draw to a close for this time I trust that you are all well but I know how you will all feel at the terrible blow which we have received through this war, but trust that there are better days to come. I will say goodbye with love and sympathy to all. I am your loving

Charlie

Allan found time to scribble a quick line:

Belgium
29-12-1917

...Well we had a very decent Xmas & I hope you had the same. It snowed all day but that was nothing. Well dear mum we are out of the line at present and I think we are going to get a bit of a spell and I hope it is true. Well dear mum we are having a pretty decent winter this year not near so bad as last. Well dear mum I am at a brigade officers school and we are having a pretty decent time. I believe Percy is going to Blighty soon. I have not got away to Paris yet but hope to get away as soon as we finish up the school ... Well dear mum I suppose you are terribly busy [with] the harvest yet I hope it turns out well. I believe you have a good year over there ... I don't think the war will last much longer now...

THE MIDDLE EAST AND EASTERN EUROPE

As 1917 drew to a close across the theatres of war, the overall position of the Allies provided little cause for jubilation. In the Middle East, the famed Light Horse charge at Beersheba on 31 October had paved the way for the Allied forces to gain control of Jerusalem and Baghdad. By late December, Germany and her Turkish ally had effectively lost control of the Middle East. But the good news was tempered by sombre reports arriving from the Eastern Front. The Russian army had ceased to exist. German forces were making their way en masse to the battlegrounds of France and Belgium while the Kaiser boasted that his storm troopers would be invincible. By spring 1918, the concentration of German soldiers on the Western Front would create a formidable force.

PART FOUR
1918

EIGHTEEN
WE SHOULD BE HOME FOR
THE NEXT HARVEST

THE WESTERN FRONT

As winter set in, fighting on the Western Front stalled and, as the troops shivered in the front line, the Allied commanders continued to plan the Spring Offensive. There was no unified strategy. The French demanded that the British take over more of the front line — indeed Paul Painlevé, the French Minister for War, recommended that all forces be combined under French command. Haig insisted that more reinforcements be sent to Flanders, a demand rejected by Lloyd George, who argued that it was futile to send more men into the fray. Six divisions of British and French troops were instead sent to Italy to prevent the collapse of Italian forces following the disastrous Battle of Caporetto. At the same time, 35 German divisions were rapidly making their way to France and Belgium to launch a major offensive.

The great battles of 1917 had inflicted massive losses on I and II Anzac Corps, with some 55,000 men becoming casualties. The Third Battle of Ypres alone had cost the Australians over 38,000 men. By the end of the year General Birdwood was becoming increasingly anxious that losses of such magnitude would render the five Australian divisions untenable. With the fall in reinforcement numbers arriving from Australia, Birdwood estimated that his shortfall in men would amount to some 18,000 by the end of the year. The only real solution was to combine all five Australian divisions on the Western Front into one Australian corps, a proposal that had been floated as early as 1916, but which had been resisted until now. The Australian Corps, under command of General Birdwood, was formally established in November 1917. The men of the corps were no longer regarded as British troops but as members of an

Australian force with Australian officers, albeit a severely depleted force without a sustainable supply of recruits and reliant on the return of sick and wounded to reinforce their ranks. As Charlie had written previously, the 3rd Division was also entitled to wear the iconic hat of the Australian forces in a manner that no longer identified them as late arrivals. They had done their time.[1]

The corps remained in a quiet sector at Messines resting and reorganising. The repair of the trenches and breastworks and the nightly patrols continued, but heavy fighting had stalled with the winter rains, reducing the likelihood of major offensives. The 38th Battalion history records that, on the last day of December, the battalion moved to Aldershot camp, a short distance from where Albert was buried at Neuve Eglise. Here the men endured rain, followed by frosts and snow. In the wet and mud, the battalion continued training, the men also involved in the constant maintenance of the support trenches. Fatigue parties were detailed to dig up the shallow water pipes and rebury them at a greater depth to prevent the water freezing in the icy conditions and bursting the pipes.[2]

The beginning of the month saw Percy on leave in England for 14 days. Charlie followed one week later and organised a few days' leave with Percy in Devon at Water Farm near Manaton, home to their aunt, Annie Lee, and her family. Both also spent time with another aunt, Lizzie Payne, and her family in Leicestershire. Percy rejoined the battalion in mid-January while Charlie returned a few days later on 24 January. Allan was sent to officers' school not far from their Belgian camp, but then briefly returned to the trenches before being sent to another school, some two days' travel away 'on a famous battlefield near where the Australians made the first push'. He was probably referring to Amiens. This was a bombing school, and Allan was completing refresher training so that he could instruct others once he returned to the line.

MESSINES

On 27 January the battalion left Aldershot camp to move to the familiar Warneton sector south of Messines close to 'Grey Farm' on the Douve River. The four companies rotated through the line with one company in reserve, sheltered in the series of tunnels known as the Catacombs deep beneath Hill 63, a short distance from Ploegsteert Wood. The Catacombs had been constructed throughout 1916–17 by men from a Canadian Tunnelling Company and the 1st Australian Tunnelling Company of Hill 60 fame. The deep, intricate dugout accommodated around 1500 men in a series of chambers containing sleeping quarters complete with bunks and a small hospital.[3] The main entrance was a busy junction aptly named Hyde Park Corner.

As the weather improved the men began repairing the trenches, draining the knee-deep mud and fortifying defences for the expected Spring Offensive. While the sector was relatively quiet, they were still subject to bombardment by German trench mortars and the threat of German patrols, snipers and machine-gun fire remained ever-present.[4]

Charlie received his first letter from his parents following the death of George and replied with a carefully constructed missive.

In the field
4-1-18
My Dear Mother Father & Jim,

… Percy went on leave to England 2 days ago he has got 14 days. Your letter was dated Oct 22nd, so you will have heard the sad news about dear Geordie before I did, it came a sudden blow to me I have been writing to different ones to try and find out all I can about him but cannot get hold of much information I have had no answer from the Chaplain of the Canadian Clearing Station but hope to get a reply soon. We are camped not far from Albert's grave Allan and I are going to see it on Sunday, I am getting the Pioneers to make a cross and getting a brass plate with the name on it, I do not know if we will be here long enough to get it finished, the trouble is to get the wood but I think we will be able to manage it at any rate I am going to have a hard try, and will do the same with Geordie's grave if I can manage it. When I get Albert's finished Vincent Kelly said he would go and have a look at it and would write to you. I may get leave to England shortly they are sending a lot away on leave now. We are out of the line yet there were some American Generals having a look around our camp the other

day they will be a big help in the war which I think will wind up any day now… I share with you all the sad loss of our dear Albert and Geordie. Your parcel will come in about a fortnight.

I am
Your Loving
Charles

Allan also wrote of visiting Albert's grave:

…Well dear mum Percy is away on leave in England & Charlie expects to go this week so everything is good oh. You don't know what a few days holiday is to us especially at present. I don't think I will be able to get away for awhile yet. Yesterday (Sunday) Charlie & I went up to where dear Albert is buried. We are erecting a cross over him. They are making a very nice cemetery of it. Well dear mum I am still at the school but will finish about next Saturday. Then I am afraid we will be going back into the line. Well mum you seem to be having a lot of visitors. Fancy that telegram you sent to Sharps ah what. You never mentioned any about the crops. I hope you have a good harvest. Well conscription never got through. I was afraid it wouldn't you mention about that time I can tell you we was fair into it. I am hoping to get my photo taken one of these day but the Frogies never take a good photo so you needn't look forward to it. Just wait until I get to Blighty. We have had a fair amount of snow lately. The winter is nothing to compare with last so far. I have been playing football these last few Saturdays and you can tell Jim I am getting back my old dash again and will stir them up <u>when I get back</u>. Note the underlined it makes me laugh. Tell Mollie G it is her turn to write. I am also writing to her. I say is N.G. & WJ married yet. They tell me er er er is doing good work too. I am afraid by the time some of us get back we will be pretty old don't you know. Mum I must say I have received all your lovely parcels and I must thank [you]. Well dear mum, dad & Jim I think I have told you all the news so will close with best love to all.

I remain
Your Loving Son & Bro
Allan

While Allan is now amused by his earlier predictions of coming home soon, the following day, having heard of a mass mutiny by German soldiers, he is less sceptical. Perhaps he would be home by next Christmas after all.

Belgium
8-1-18
Dear Jim,

… Well Jim we had a very decent Xmas considering. I hope you all had a nice one. I know it would not be too happy. The winter is with us again but honestly it is nothing to compare with last. The good old snow just streamed down all day today. It is not at all cold when it is falling. To night after parade we had a lovely snow fight and by the time I was finished I was perfectly white. Well Jim by the war news we got tonight things are not to bad at all. There is a wireless came through that 25000 Germans have refused to fight on the western front. They reckon they wont be slaughtered. Percy is away in Blighty on leave & Charlie expects to get away this week. I don't know when I will get away now. At present we are still at the officers school but we expect to finish our course next Saturday. I am rather sorry in a way because we are having a jolly decent time.

Last Sunday Charlie & I went up to the cemetery where dear Albert is buried. They are making a very nice cemetery of it. We are erecting a cross over Albert. At present it is a toss up whether we are going in the line or not. The other day I met Joe Cocking he looks the same old I think I told you in a previous letter that poor old Bill Street had died of wounds I can tell you I am very sorry. I often get letters from my old cobber Spuddy Kerr. He will be going home to Ausy soon. Well Jim you never mention anything in your letter about the crops. I do hope they turn out excellent. Jim I often wonder if you have still got Linker. I hope you have … You seem to have a lot of visitors. Keep your eye out for a nice girl. They say we will be home for next Xmas

Hurrah …

Having received Jim's letter informing him of the death of George, Tom Alford wrote to express his condolences:

France
20/1/18
Dear Jim

Just a P.C. as I wrote to you not very long ago to say that I received your of Oct 21 containing the sad new[s] of poor old Geordie. It was the first I heard of it. Convey my sympathy to your mother & accept the same yourself. I wish I could have a bit of a yarn to you. It must be very hard on your mother & the anxiety of the others on top of it all. Tom Richards said he saw Alan & that he had a star up. Well good luck to him. It might help to keep him out of the line a bit as a young officer gets a lot of schools. I'm still on the same job, but have lost a lot of my old pals in this last smash up. Well good luck Jim old Man & bear up as well as you can. It is a -- of a time for everyone.

Your old pal
Tom

This is the only card I have. It seems rather a silly one to send to a man but expect I must have been a bit magnoon when I bought it.

On his return to France, Percy penned an unusually long letter to Jim:

In the field
Jan 21.1.18
Dear Jim

… Well Jim old sport. I have had leave to Blighty, fourteen days, it was good quite a pleasure to get away from the frogies to where they can understand what you are talking about. I went to Leicester first, stopped at Paynes, they were very pleased to see me, and treated me well [they are] very nice girls, saw Flo, she is in Leicester, I got there on the Friday, and Flo came down Sunday, so we had a nice afternoon and night, Flo is a real nice girl, and so lively Jim <u>do me</u> I took quite a fancy to her, I get some nice letters since say no more, Jim. Well Flo came over on Tuesday, gave her a kiss for you and I went away on Wednesday to Devon at 8.20 AM, and got to Lec at 7 o'clock PM. Grace and May were home, and the kiddies besides Uncle Auntie and Connie, I suppose you would not know who she is. One of Uncle Ted girls she is about 16 a very nice girl. There was quite a house full of us. They have a very big house Grace and May are very nice girls. Charlie came two

days after I was there, so we were together a couple of days. Their place is out in the country, a pretty place, I would like to see it in the Summer time, it would look lovely. It is in among the hills. May went home the day after Charlie came. We had a good time there. Grace and Auntie did not like me leaving. I hope I get a chance to go and see them again, also to Leicester. Charlie did not leave till after me then he was going to Leicester. Oh Jim the coming back to France it was hard. It rained and snowed the day I arrived, a nice welcome it was not. We have had a fair lot of rain lately thank goodness we are not in the trenches. Yes Jim, this Mrs St_____ amuses me, always got some tales, she put a good one into Mum, about Selina of course. Mum believed her. You were talking about coming to Blighty after the war, I think I will come with you, and we will live there, I ought to get a job as bootblack, I have had fair experience of that kind, since I joined the army. I would like to see England again before going back. I've got that what you put in the letter, you know, yes I dare say there is something in it, as you said "enough said"…

Charlie also wrote:

24-1-18
My Dear Mother Father & Jim,

… You seemed to think that Geordie was lying on the battlefield wounded, well that is wrong, he was taken out shortly after he was hit and I got a letter today from the Chaplain of the 3rd C.C.S. who said that he died a peaceful death and every thing possible was done for him, he said he wrote home to you the Captain of the Trench Mortars also wrote and said he wrote home to you and told you all about poor Geordie. Well I had a grand holiday in England, it was very rough going across to England but coming back it was grand. I wrote to you when I was at Devon. Well I will describe a little I got to London at about 5.30 P.M. and got to Horseferry Road got a new set of clothes and got paid next day I stayed in London and went down to Devon the following day Uncle met me at Boney Station at Water Farm I met Auntie Annie and Connie Marlow, Grace Hallam and May Maddaford and Grace and May children. I stayed there about 5 or 6 day and then went to Leicester. Devon is a very nice place I liked being down there very much and had a real fine time. Uncle John took me all round the farm it is a very

fine one and in a very pretty place. I went up to Leicester and stayed there the remainder of the time, when I was at Devon they, Paynes sent word to Aunt Charlotte and she came to 33 Green the day after I did. I was going to Drayton but the trains are so awkward now but as they sent for Aunt Charlotte I could not go in any case. I sent Aunt Annie Edith Charlotte Uncle Ted a photo of Geordie. I thought Ida had sent them home but she did not on account of so many ships going down. I am getting another dozen of another photo of Geordie later and will send some of them to you. I will say goodbye for tonight as I am tired after the trip. I had no sleep last night …

He added in a note to Jim:

… I have just got back from leave to England where I had a real good time I went down to Devon and to Leicester, none of the relations have received any of your photos from you, they are anxious to get them. I gave them all one of Geordie's and will give them one of mine when they are finished and will send some of them home to you. I got another dozen of Geordie's taken it was with his hat off, he gave Auntie one and I got it done off that. I thought it was very good. Mother seemed to think that Geordie was laying on the Battle Field for days well that is wrong, he was carried out by stretcher bearers soon after he was hit and taken in a motor to the dressing station where he [died] next day at about 10 P.M. I got a letter yesterday from the Chaplain of the 3rd Canadian Clearing Station he wrote a similar letter to you at home but addressed it Victoria New South Wales Australia so I doubt if you will get it. I will send you the one I got later…

The details of George's death which Sarah had accepted as truth did not alleviate her distress. Allan now wrote to reassure her:

France
26-1-17 [1918]
My dear Mother & Father

.. Percy was well when I left him and Charlie was away on leave. Well dear mum in my last letter I told [you] I was going away to a bombing school and here I am sitting down by [a] nice fire writing this letter to you. I am billeted in a very nice building and just beside me is a very comfortable bunk absolutely the best I have had since I left that place called Ausy. We

get splendid tucker and a good batman to look after me. Well now mum what better do you want than that. Now I had a pretty good time coming here which took me 2 days. I am situated in a camp on a famous battlefield where the Australians made the first push. Of course Fritz is miles back now. This bombing is very interesting work. I like it. Of course I have hundreds turn but this is a refresher course and when I go back to my battalion perhaps I will have to instruct the men on them. Well dear mum you seem to think that Geordie was killed by the bayonet because he attended a school. Nothing of the sort mum I guarantee that no Ausy will be beat with the bayonet. The germans wont use them. Well dear mum we have had quite a lot of Australian mail lately. I have got a lot of letters from home and Aunt Etta and Liz. Well mum I got that postcard of you, dad, Pearl & the baby. It is very nice, everything looks lovely, but I don't think there is anything that touched me more than that postcard. Well I hope to get my photo taken in my officer's uniform and I bet you a penny none of you will know me. Oh by the way you never said whether you got my photo which I sent you when I came back from leave. I do hope you got it but anyway it was very poor. My battalion will be in the line now but by the time I get back they will be out. This is the first time I have missed. You cannot believe the weather we are having now it is just like spring and I think we will have an early spring. This time last year it was brutal, but anyway that is over now. Well dear mum, dad & Jim I think I have told you all the news so will close with best love to all, and I do hope that you all are well.

I remain
Your loving son & brother
AS Marlow

Charlie wrote to Jim a few days later, describing further casualties:

I believe K. Haw is over here and in the battalion next below us I think R Hercus was wounded some little time back but only slight. It was hard luck for the Mullen's losing the only two boys who came over here. I got a lot of letters from you but I think there is some more out yet ... Allan is away at another school Percy is here with me. I told you in my other letters that I had been to England on leave Percy was over there part of the time with me. Those snapshots were very good that Crissie A took, will you send me Tom A address ...

Rupert Hercus was born in Mologa and left the area to join the 37th Battalion in March 1916. He was wounded at Passchendaele on 4 October 1917 but rejoined his unit once his wound had healed sufficiently. He survived to return to Australia in 1919.[5]

FEBRUARY

Percy had returned to France by mid-January but, as his brothers explain in their letters, he became ill soon after. Army records initially referred to his condition as nephritis (inflamed kidneys). He was hospitalised on 2 February and was back in England 15 days later, admitted to the Kitchener Military Hospital at Brighton. Percy was later diagnosed with trench fever, a common illness causing fever, headaches, muscle pain and inflamed eyes. In 1918 the cause of trench fever was found to be a bacteria carried by lice. Recovery could be slow and the illness often recurred. Percy spent much of his time in the trenches cursing the dreaded 'chats', but ultimately he may have thanked this tiny enemy for keeping him from the dangers of the front line. He had his 'Blighty'. Percy was not to rejoin his unit until August 1918, spending some six weeks in hospital and, from late March until mid-August, in camp at Hurdcott in England while he regained his strength.

Early in February, soon after Allan had been promoted lieutenant, 100 men were selected from the 38th Battalion to train with troops from the 37th for a raid on enemy trenches in the Warneton sector south-east of Messines scheduled for 10 February. It is unclear whether the raiding party included either Allan or Charlie. However, Jack Lockett vividly remembered the February raid some 70 years after he had crossed no man's land to assault the German front line. He proudly described what he dubbed 'the most successful raid of the 38th'. The enemy was deceived by the stealth of the soldiers and the 'Chinese Party', a contingent of dummy troops positioned half a mile to the north of the actual point of attack. With the pull of a cord, each dummy rose from the ground to attract fire from the German lines. As the enemy sprayed fire on the fake attackers, the soldiers moved forward under cover of fire from their own artillery, machine-guns and trench mortars.

An estimated 100 enemy soldiers were killed and 30 prisoners taken. The Australians incurred 39 casualties; the unprecedented nature of the raid had taken the enemy completely by surprise.[6]

Prior to the raid, Allan wrote a letter home:

In the Field
Sunday
2-2-18
My Dear Mum & Dad,

… Well dear mum I am still at the bombing school and having a good time. To morrow I go up for my exam and I hope I get a good pass and on Wednesday I go back to my battalion and then I hope to get a lot of mail and parcels. Well dear mum & dad we are having magnificent weather one would hardly realise that it is winter time. This weather will do me to a tee and I suppose you all are saying those poor soldiers in trenches must be having a terrible time but that is not so at present. Well dear mum & dad by the time you get this letter I suppose I will have had my 14 days blighty leave. I will be going to Devon & Leicester. There is only one relative who I haven't seen and that is Uncle Ted but I will see him this time. Now I wonder how the crops turned out. I hope they were the best we should be home for the next harvest. In fact you can tell dad to put plenty in and I expect to go straight in with the stooking when I get back, but I won't guarantee to load the load on the wagon, but I will be up to time when the lunches come out. Just leave that to me. I am afraid everybody will be married when I get back in fact it will be a good job because we all will be to late for presents. Andy Blow getting married beats me.

Now dear mum & dad I don't want you to worry over me in the least. I am enjoying this and [when] the time comes for the old Swan Hill Kerang train to pull into Mologa I'll be there. I often get a letter from Ben Johnson. Well dear mum & dad Jim I think I have told you all the news so will close with best love & wishes to all.

I remain
Your Loving Son & Brother
Allan

Charlie will be back from Blighty now I have some views of towns that are just close to me and I have been in them.

While Allan wrote to his family of his eventual return home, Joe Stone, recovering in a convalescent camp in France, acknowledged with some pessimism in a letter to Jim that he felt resigned to an uncertain fate:

France
5/2/18
Dear Jim

Just a line in haste hoping it finds all in the Best of health as it leaves me at present. Well Jim there is nothing new over here to my knowledge things are very quiet where I am. I am still in Con Camp will be leaving shortly for the Base. Sorry to hear about Poor Old George it comes hard to think he was over here so long & then to go near the finish. But we never know what to expect here you never know when your turn is coming. But we are just hoping and trusting for the Best & are quite resolved to our fate. I am sending a parcel home with some walking sticks one in for Father they will send it across from home I made them here in my spare time. They are not very brilliant but are all right as a souvenir. Well Jim it is lovely weather here now & as news are scarce I think I will ring off.

I remain
Your Old Cobber
Joe [Stone]
Love to the Mologa girls

Charlie continued to answer his family's questions over the circumstances in which George and Albert had been killed:

The Field
7.2.18
My Dear Mother,

… You asked about whether Geordie said anything when he died, well I have written to everyone who I thought would know but could get nothing out of them, he would get every possible attention especially at a Clearing Station. I wrote to the Colonel of the Station he said he died peaceful and

received a decent burial. There is one thing we should be thankful for and that is that both Albert and Geordie are buried in decent cemeterys well out of the line of fire, and not like so many of our poor fellows, I told you in my letter this morning that I did not cable for that five pounds but thought the letter would reach just as quick as I was unable to cable at the time owing to shifting. I met Knowlson Haw two nights ago he looked well and said Amos was back here again but was at an N.C.O. school. I was very sorry to hear about Dave Mullens he was a fine fellow. I wrote a note of sympathy to his mother. I believe Bill Crossman was killed he came over on the same boat as I did. I was sorry to hear that he was killed he was a very nice fellow. I have never met Sam Crossman but if I knew his address I might be able to find him. I have not met very many of the boys I know over here except Wingfield. I told you that I got a parcel from Mrs Stone, Jim asked why I was sent to a Refts Camp well the reason was, to escape two "advances" or stunts as they are called, one was the one Bill Street was killed in the other Les Townsend was wounded in, it was a good thing for me and good of the Captain in sending me, they send so many every few months there were 6 others with me under Lieut Langley the Bishops son, he was a fine fellow we had a good time. Well dear Mother I will close for tonight with love to all I will say goodbye

I remain Your loving
Charlie

Allan also wrote a brief note from the trenches:

16-1 19 -18 [16.2.18]

Just a few lines to let you know that Charlie and I are splendid. Percy is away with trench fever he is lucky it is not a serious affair. Well dear mum I am back in the trenches and it is good. We are having magnificent weather. I expect to go to Blighty at the end of the month. I received 36 letters when I got back from the school also 5 parcels. I have not opened the parcels yet as I was hurried away up to the trenches but will have a good time when I get out. You must excuse this short note I will write a long letter when I get out. Trench life is as good as ever still. The weather we are having is magnificent. I can't make it [out] at all. It is just like spring time …

Once he had further news of Percy, Charlie wrote to his family:

In the Field
20th Feb 1918
My Dear Mother, Father & Jim

... I got a letter from Percy two days ago, first he was at the Field Ambulance he was getting on alright and was sent to the Casualty Clearing Station, it is another hospital, he says he did not feel so well there and they sent him on to another hospital near where our base used to be from there I think he will get to England for some months. I met the Dr and he asked me if I heard from him he said he thought it was Trench fever but could not tell for sure the difference between influenza and trench fever for a few days. I told him that I heard and how he was it said it was fever but nothing anyway serious, he will be lucky if he gets to England. I have told you exactly how he is and there is no need to worry. I see I have his last letter here I will send it to you and you will see for yourself... I should have had my photos to send you but I am waiting for Ida to send them I got a letter from Auntie Wilson she said they turned out well I weighed myself in England and went 13 stone 3 lbs so you will see I am not doing too bad. We came out of the line last night and I believe we are going back for a decent spell ...

A few days later Charlie was on his way to a training facility at Poperinghe. There he would have the opportunity to visit George's grave which was less than an hour's walk from the busy town. He wrote to his family assuring them that Percy was well; he was safer in hospital than in the front line.

Feb 25th 1918
In the Field
My Dear Father Mother & Jim,

Just a line to say I am quite well, you will perhaps have heard that Percy is in England with Trench Fever, I wrote to you last week saying that I thought he would get to England. Well he landed at Kitchener Hospital Brighton on Feb 17th I think you will get a cable to say that he is ill but it is not serious, the Dr told me it takes a long time to get over and they keep them in England for a long time as it is likely to come on again if they are sent back to the line, some of the men that get it bad are often sent to Australia for six months, it would be grand if he were to get home but he has not got it that bad, there is no need for you to be anxious he will be better there than in the line, I am at present at a school I will be here for five weeks, I am not doing a course but I have to look after the officer's servants I have not done anything yet I landed here yesterday, our adjutant told me he was sending me there for a spell out of the line and said to be sure and have a good time out of it, I am about four miles away from where Geordie is buried I am going to see it one day this week I will not have much to do and will be able to get leave I am sending you my photo tell me what you think of it I wrote to Pearl last night. Allan is back from the school again he was away about a month. When I get to see Geordie's grave I will try and find out anything I can about him from the nurses and chaplain I was very pleased when the adjutant told me he was sending me there, and will be able to go and see the grave. We just came out of the line a few days ago, they are in reserve now behind the line …

ENGLAND

With his symptoms showing no sign of improvement, Percy was sent to England and admitted to Kitchener Hospital at Brighton. He wrote home to tell his family of his illness:

20ᵗʰ Feb
England
My Dear Mother, Father & Jim

Just a few lines to let you know I am going on well, I am in Blighty now good eh its to hard to take, I have Trench Fever, at first they thought I had nephritis, but now they find out I have Trench Fever, that is practically nothing I have pains in my legs now, they are fairly bad just now, but it will not last long. With Nephritis it's a three month stunt at the least, I am under observation for it, for a few days, but I know I have not got it. I am quite different to the other patients. I had about two weeks in hospital in France before coming across. I have been here three days, it's a Canadian hospital on the coast about fifty miles from London, a very nice place in the Summer time. I have not had any mail for a long time, there will be a lot of mail for me at the Battalion I have written to Charlie to send it across so I will be set in a few days. We have had good weather lately, for this time of the year this was our worst month last year. We were up round Messines way, when I left, they are supposed to go back for a spell when they come out this time …

A few days later Percy put pen to paper to provide Jim his rather candid impression of France:

22.2.18
England
Dear Jim,

Going on well Jim, got up yesterday, quite a change to being in bed. I have only got pain in the legs now. I am still on light diet, I have not had meat for three weeks, so you see I have had a few meatless days, I won't be sorry when they give me a bit of meat. When I came here I was supposed to have Nephritis, suppose you have never heard of it, its one of the army names, I think it's a kind of kidney complaint, well you get three months hospital, at the least, and if lucky discharge. But two mornings after I had been here, a new doctor came round and he says I have not got Nephritis, but Trench Fever, they are not certain about it, so they are waiting for a few days, so Jim you see I am unlucky in one way perhaps lucky in another. Have not heard from Charlie yet, he will get a surprise when he gets my letter. I am anxiously awaiting the mail to come across from France, it ought to be here any day now. Well Jim, how are things going on, pretty same I suppose. I would like to hang out here in the spring, to miss the <u>races</u> in France, not a bit anxious to go back to sunny France, as you hear about, do you know I hate the people, it's a dirty place. In the farm places their stables, pigs cows are right joining the house, in a kind of a square, and they put all the manure in the centre of the yard, about ten yards from their door, just fancy that in Australia. If they had found out in France I had only Trench Fever I would never had got over here, its round a lot Jim, but it isn't really much, nothing like any other fever. This is a Canadian hospital, its not a bad hospital, its on the coast at a place called Brighton, about fifty miles from London, a very nice place in the summer and spring some of the patients go down the town, you have to be up a certain time, they get a pass from 2 to 5, and late pass till seven. The bread *is very dark we get here, you know it is all like that now, the Government has ordered it so. Out in France the bread we get is very white and always good, never seems to alter. I have heard from Flo and the others since I have been here, the letters go very quick from here and they are not censored. My word Jim the people are rationed down very light here now, you could not believe it; you would wonder how they live. Its been very good weather considering the time of the year, this was our worst month last year ...*

25.2.18
England
My Dear Mother, Father & Jim

Just a short note to let you know I am getting on well. I am feeling all right. I will be able to go for a walk in a few days. I am still in the nephritis ward, they must think I have still got it, as for me I feel sure I have not it will mean a longer spell if they keep me in here. I have not got any mail yet, been expecting it any day now, it takes a fair time for letters to go and from France. Another nice day, the weather seems to change so quickly, the mornings will be nice and sunny and the afternoons cloudy and cold. We have blue clothes, long trousers, seems like a civilian again. Well Mum, did they notify you I was in hospital they did so with another Australian, that is in this ward, they said he was a lot worse than he realy was. Mrs Stone had any more tales, she ought to have been an author. There were some visitors in here yesterday, there is one lady comes in about twice a week, I think she is on behalf of the church, for she has always some nice little books as she calls them, the one I got yesterday was "how you can be saved"...

Percy appears to have enjoyed the irony in the title of the book left by his regular visitor.

As the ground thawed and the mud dried on the Western Front, the spirits of the Australian troops began to lift after the relative quiet of winter. There was an air of expectancy, as Percy commented from across the English Channel. With the arrival of spring they were waiting for the 'races', an event he had no desire to attend. A German attack was imminent and the brothers felt sure that their contribution would be vital to the Allied defence.

On leave in England, Allan wrote home of the expected German offensive. Only three months before, he had written: 'think the only way we will end the struggle is by peace'. His attitude reflected the revival of the flagging Australian spirit — his bravado had returned and honour and glory were paramount once again. He admitted for the first time that he did not describe his battle experiences to his family so as to protect them from the tough reality of the war.

The Alexandra Hotel
Hyde Park Corner, S.W.I
3-3.18
My Dear Mum & Dad

I am writing you a few lines to let you know that I am in Blighty I came over 4 days ago and I went up to Brighton to see Percy. I stayed the 4 days with him, he does look pretty well but I feel sure you [will] have him back in Australia. I reckon he will get his ticket. Such a lot are going back with it. To night I am going to Devon and will stay there 5 days and then go back to Brighton and see Percy before I return to France. I have not time to go to Leicester too but I think I will be over England again within a couple of months. Well dear mum I received such a lot of letters from you all before I came over. I can tell you I was delighted to hear from you again. I trust that the crops turned out well. I think we will have a decent harvest here too. I mean the hun. The wretch is going to push and oh mum we will have such fun. He will get such a doing. It will do me for a bit of sport. It is the only way to end the war. We have had us most glorious weather over in France. The winter will soon be over. When I left Charlie was going away to school for 4 or 6 weeks to look after batmen. It will be a beautiful rest for him. It is not the best weather here to have but it is a pleasure to get away from the battlefield for a few days. Dear Mum & Dad you seem to be having a lot of worry. You don't need to worry yourselves so much. It is hard to loose two brothers but mum they have died for King & Country. It is a glorious death compared to the cold footers who are remaining back in Ausy [who] are not game to risk their lives for King & Country. Those fellows will not be able to [look] a soldier in the face when they get back and what must the people think of them. So dear mum & dad do not worry so much I find it hard to enjoy myself here but one must think that he is away from the front. You said you were disappointed in not getting a good letter from me about the battles. Well mum it will do you no good if you were to hear it now but you will hear it all when I get back and if Percy gets back he will be able to tell you where we are and where we have been. I suppose Charlie Fyffe & Frank Dee were glad to get their discharge but mum I would not like to get mine to [till] the job is over. I am not anxious to get home till it is all over but all the same I would like to see Charlie & Percy out of it. I have plenty of clothes and money if ever I wanted money I would send for it, Well dear mum I will write again before I go to France so Cheerio.

I remain
Your Loving Son
Allan S M
XXXXX

Never publish any [of] my letters in the paper

Allan wrote to Jim the same day:

… I think we will have some fun soon with the hun … Well Jim I cant tell you anything about the fighting in France only that it is pretty hot. I came straight out of the trenches to go on leave and I can tell you I appreciate It …

Percy wrote from Brighton where he was content to remain for the present. Reading about the expected offensive was preferable to engaging in battle:

March 3rd
England
My Dear Mother, Father & Jim

Received your welcome letter 26 Dec, and am sorry to hear Grandmother has not been well, the hot weather makes it bad for her. I am feeling pretty well. I have been going out this last day or two, it's a very nice place here; yesterday was a very cold day a cold wind blowing, being so close to the sea accounts for it. I got a parcel from you before Xmas, there are three or four parcels in France now for me, I must ask Charlie who they are from. I got two little parcels since being here. I wrote to London to the Base Post office

*to send all my mail here and I have had a good few letters come here, and
two parcels. One of them from Auntie Florrie sent had about five pairs of
socks. I notice some of them have been knitted in Bendigo, so I [have] a few
more letters to write. It puts in the time here, writing letters, and reading.
I am hot stuff at making beds Mum, got a certain way here to make them.
Had a letter from Nelly Gamble, she was saying she never heard from me
for a long time, well a lot of others have said the same, there must have been
a mail or two sunk, for I often write to them. Got a letter from Eddie the
other day, it's the first one he has put the right address on generally used to
get hold of somebody else number then Machine Gun Section, France, the
letter I got before this was written 23 of last March, and I got it a month
ago then he could not make out why I was not answering his letters. Eddie
must be in a bad way with that girl of his, its hard to tell whether he or
Hilda is the worst. Today, is Sunday, just two weeks since I came in, it looks
very much like rain. I have some mail to come from France yet, expecting a
letter any day now from either Charlie or Allan. Charlie was expecting to
go for six weeks to a school, he just got back in time to go to the trenches. We
get paid ten shillings tomorrow, every month they give you that. By the look
of the papers, there will be something doing in France soon, it will do me to
read about it, not a bit anxious to cross the channel again …*

Percy was soon moved to Harefield Hospital, a country manor home
near London that had been converted to a hospital for Australian
soldiers for the duration of the war.[7] Initially, Harefield was modified
to accommodate 150 convalescent soldiers, but quickly burgeoned to
a 1000-bed hospital. The children of the village liked to gather flowers
for the wounded soldiers, a tradition that continues today with villagers
gathering flowers to place on the graves of Australians at the local
cemetery each Anzac Day.[8]

From Harefield, Percy wrote to express his hope that his illness would
mean that he had seen the last of France.

Harefield
England
15 March 1918
My Dear Mother Father & Jim,

Just a few lines to let you know I am going on good you will see by the top I am in a new home. I came up here two days ago, I did not like leaving Brighton, it was a nice place. This is an Australian hospital, ten miles from London, seems a fairly good hospital not near as warm here as Brighton. The doctor came to me today, he did not examine me just asked how I felt, he says he will wait for a few days to see if anything comes out of it, that is one of the main symptoms, I have. I will get a board and very likely get back to Australia, or not see France again, its not good looking so far ahead. I had a couple of letters from you they were sent from France so they are old letters, one had a photo of you Dad and Pearl, poor photo of Pearl I would hardly know her. Allan has been over on leave, he was at Brighton with me for four days, then he went to Devon and came back to me, before he went to France he did not go to Leicester it was not worth his while, half of his time left, would have been taken travelling. Well Mum, its been cold this last two days, raining last night, the sisters here are very good, all Australian. Had a letter from Charlie, he is at a school near Ypres, about four miles from where Geordie is buried, getting a cross put up over him. There seems to be a good few going back to Australia from here. Spose you are finished with the harvest now …

Within a few days Percy was disappointed to discover that a return to Australia was unlikely. He was on his way to a convalescent camp at Hurdcott, a further step in the process of rehabilitation prior to returning to the front line:

Harefield
England
19 March 1918
Dear Jim

Well Jim old man, very short note this time, feeling pretty good on the b_ move again, we might not have much money Jim but we do see life, it's a dam nuisance just get the mail coming to one place and then got to go, they do not keep you here long, a lot go to Aussy and a lot going to camp for France, I think I am very near one of them. I am going to a convalescent camp, at a place called Hurdcott, a most delightful place "I don't think" not a great way from Lark Hill and that is the last place God made I am going there under observation, will most likely get a board, to see if I am fit for France, the doctor here has not examined me much. I know I am not right yet, caught a bit of a cold shifting this being a lot colder than Brighton, I seem to be a little worse, but it has not proved in, the doctor tests; pain across the back. Had a letter from Charlie, he was having a good time at the school. I told Mum in the last letter Allan was across. I am expecting to hear from him, spose there will be a few of those words you often use when you are driving the team. I have an idea what it is like to go back from leave. Getting a few shillings in the pay book, we can draw 3/6 a week here, its very handy. I am putting in a photo of the ward taken a few days ago, turned out very good for the price threepence, you will notice my hard face there, in the blues, not a bad uniform Jim, it would do me to fight in them this spring, in the hospital. I should not say that, ought to be breaking my neck to get back at the hun, course I am "I don't think". Well Jim, will close now hoping it finds you all well

I am your loving brother
Percy
Hows the new or old girl

Percy (front 2nd from right) in hospital in England.

548

MOLOGA, MARCH

Among the letters from his brothers, Jim kept one he had received from the father of his mate, Tom Alford. The letter provides some insight into the social divisions of the time. The letter also reveals that life on the farm has not been easy. Jim appears to have been ill, although the nature of his illness is not specified. Throughout his lifetime Jim suffered from severe headaches; perhaps these were now causing him problems.

134 Victoria Avenue
Albert Park
March 12 1918

Dear Jim you will no doubt be a bit surprised a [at] getting a note from me but I have just got a letter from Ella, telling me you were very ill & she said I ought to write you one of my newsey letters but I can tell you for a start that I don't feel in the best of trim for writing, especially to a sick person. In the first place I am very sorry to hear that you have been so ill & I sincerely hope that you will soon be quite well again, I know you must have had a tough time of it through the summer with your long harvest. I know you must feel a bit lonely too with all your brothers away so long & the loss of two fine boys but cheer up Jim, it makes any one feel very proud of what our boys are doing over at the Front when we see so much rotten flashness and laziness as there is going on this side of the world. I feel as though I would like to get my No 11 in to some of their bread baskets. Melbourne fairly stinks of flashness and spungers (both sexes). We are having a fairly long holiday but cant say as I am enjoying it much as I begrulle [begrudge] both the time & the money but it as [has] done Mrs Alford a lot of good so far & we have seen a lot of old friends & we have a very nice place to stay & it is not very expensive living, we are boarding ourselves & we get things very much cheaper (in most cases) than we can in Mologa & we can always get nice fruit & vegetables & plenty fish & nice meat & ice cream & Kola beer galore. I have had a few days work each week for the last 3 weeks wood cutting, draining & fruit picking out at a place called Mitcham & Ringwood about 16 miles from here we get up about 5 am Mum gets my bit of breakfast in a few minutes we have everything nice and handy. Electric light in the three front rooms & gas stove for the cooking so it is quick & easy & we have a very clean place & nice people just a couple in the house beside ourselves & we are very close to the train & beach & traveling is cheap & go from the door to Ringwood & back (33 miles) for ½ [d]. So you see town traveling is far cheaper than country traveling. I have been getting 1/- an hour & dinner & fair bit of fruit. I like going out it is a great chance after the north, in fact if Tom come back all right I think I will try & get down Mitcham or Ringwood for the balance of my term of life. There are some very fine gardens out that way & some very nice homes & some pretty scenery. I keep the house well stocked with fruit and flowers (Gum leaves). I was over at Williamstown yesterday having a look at the wheat stacks that they are pulling down & I can tell you it would make your back ache to see the waste & destruction with wet weavel & rats & the way the men work beat cock fighting. Generally about 6 or 7 in a batch about an average of two working & the balance looking on we tried to get a look at the shipping but you get a bayonet poked at you at every gate way I suppose it is quite right as there are a lot of sneakes prowling round they say. Well Jim this is rather a ramblin sort of note & I don't seem to have any very cheery news so will close remember us to your Mother & Father & I do hope you will soon be well again.

Yours respectfully
Thos Alford

C/o Mr St Clair
134 Victoria Avenue
Albert Park
P.S. Hope you have had letters from the boys & that they are alright. I had a nice letter from our Tom

NINETEEN
I HAVE SEEN TOO MUCH OF BROTHERS BEING TOGETHER IN THESE BATTLES

BELGIUM, MARCH

Charlie was still at a training facility near Poperinghe and took the opportunity to visit George's grave. He wrote to his family to describe his brother's final resting place:

3rd March 1918
My Dear Mother, Father & Jim

This morning I went to the Lyssenthoek Military Cemetery and found poor Geordie's grave, the cemetery is about ¾ of a hours walk from here, it is a tremendous size of a cemetery there are all battalions and regiments of the British Empire buried there and rank from a private to a major general. There is a party of men who do nothing else but look after the graves, it is on a nice piece of high ground and is a great number of miles behind the line, it could never be disturbed by shell fire. There are Australians of the same Brigade as Geordie buried in the same row. There is a place in England who takes photos of the graves, this I did not know before, but the Corporal in charge told me, so I have written and am getting a photo taken of Geordie's grave and also of Albert's. I also made arrangements to have a cross erected similar to Alberts, it will also have a plate on it, the words are - In loving memory of our dear Brother No 2748 Cpl. G. T. Marlow 2 A.L.T.M.B. AIF Died of Wounds 21-9-1917 Erected by his loving Brothers/ The cross is costing me 40 francs (a franc is worth 10d). The cemetery is at the 2nd Canadian C.C.S., the place where Geordie died was the 3rd Canadian C.C.S. which is about 200 yds further up the road I could not find out anything regarding his death only that all his personal things will be sent home to you, the Chaplain who buried him was Major Ambrose C of E who is at present away. Well I do not know if there is anything else I can tell you about it if there is anything you want to know write and ask me and I will answer it. It opened my eye to see such a large cemetery and to know the number buried there. I am still at the school I do not have much to do, I have not heard from Percy yet but there is no need to be anxious about him …

A few days later he wrote again:

March 7th 1918
In the Field
My Dear Mother, Father and Jim,

I am writing a few lines to Pearl so I will send a line or two to you at the same time I have not got too many green envelopes so have to make the most use of them they issue us with them about once a month. I am still at the school having an easy time. I told you before I would be here for about five weeks, I heard this morning that our battalion is moving back for a rest so that is not too bad. Since I have been here I have not had any mail, but I hope to get some next week from Percy and from them in England. I also hope to get some Australian mail in I believe there is another mail in. I wrote to our Quarter Master to send on my mail. I told you that I went and saw Geordie's grave last Sunday and that I am getting a cross erected over the grave, it will be similar to the one I put over Albert it is costing 40 francs (10d) is the value of a franc, it will also have a plate with the name etc. When I landed here we were having rotten weather but this last two days the weather has been lovely, we are camped on a hill and when the winds blow it blows. There were some parcels come up for Percy but I think they have sent then on to him there is a new arrangement about parcels now, we have to sign for them and they will not give them to anyone else …

10th March 1918
In the Field
My Dear Mother, Father & Jim,

… Percy is getting on alright he will get his mail about a week after the rest of us as his mail will come to the battalion and then readdressed on to

him, he gets a lot of mail from the relations in England. I am still at the school our battalion has gone back for a rest, so that is not too bad. I told you in my last letter that I made arrangements to have a cross erected over Geordie's grave it is to be finished next Tuesday I am going down one day this week to see it, I have also written about having a photo taken of both Albert and Geordie Grave which I will send on to you when I get it, it will take some time to get the photos done as I think there is a party comes out to France twice a year, to do this work. Pearl said in her letter that Tom Alford was missing well I think he has since turned up there are some of his battalion here I will try and find out from them. We are having lovely weather over here, this last few days, I think the winter has gone it was nothing like as severe as it was last year we did not have near as much snow and rain this year as we did last year. I suppose by the time this reaches you you will have finished cropping again, there must be a terrible amount of wheat in Australia now, it would be a great thing if they could send half of it to England where it is needed so badly, the food question is going to be a big thing with England we are not cut down at all we get splendid food and plenty of it of course we pay for a few extras when we are out of the line, and at this school we pay two francs a week for extras. The daylight Savings Bill is in force over here the clock was put on one hour last night. I reckon it is a silly idea they have it in all these countries the Huns time is one hour ahead of us, some of our chaps have got watches from prisoners which are one hour in advance of ours …

He added a note to his mother the following day:

… I suppose you will be anxious about Percy but there is nothing seriously wrong with him, I think he will be there for some time yet as trench fever is likely to come on again, at any rate he is safer there … There was a parcel sent to Allan from the Trench Mortars it was one that had been sent to Geordie I think it was from Stones, there were two parcels for Percy, they would not give them to me but I think they will be sent on to him. Our battalion is out for a rest at present, will be here another three weeks …

In the field
Sunday 17ᵗʰ March 1918

My Dear Mother, Father & Jim

... I got a letter from Ida today she said that Allan had had leave and he was down to Brighton to see Percy I got a letter from Percy during the early part of last week he was getting on alright. Flo said in a letter to me that he was likely to be shifted to another hospital but I have not heard anything more about it. Today I went to Geordie's grave the cross that I ordered was finished and put up it looks very nice I have also ordered a metal plate which is going to be finished this week. There are some of our battalion men buried in the same cemetery Major Tubb V.C. is buried a few yards from Geordie's grave, he was killed the same day as Geordie was wounded, there is a lot I could tell you about the place but I fear it would be stopped by censor. We are having lovely weather over here now the trees and hedges are beginning to show signs of Spring. I am still at the school and will be here for another fortnight. I am hoping to get a letter from Allan this week to hear about his trip to England he was lucky to get leave so soon after his other leave, when I go back I think I can get leave to Paris it would be for about 8 days. I have not got any more mail from you since I wrote last which was about the middle of last week. Did you get Albert's and Geordie's deferred pay and let me know if you got Geordie's things, in one lot there should have been a safety razor, wallet, and photos, they would be sent from the base. I do not know what became of his watch I think he always wore it and I suppose he would have it on him when he got to the hospital, when I last saw him it would not go, let me know if you got [it]. I got some photos of Geordie taken off one he gave to Paynes, they are finished and Ida said she would send them across this week, so when I get them I will send them home to you. I think I told you before that Hughie Martin is likely to be sent back home, he was badly wounded and one of his legs is an inch shorter than the other, I think Spuddie Kerr is on his way home. Well I have no more news this time so will draw to a close, again hoping you are all well as this leaves me.

I will say goodbye with best wishes to all
I remain
Your Loving
Charlie

FRANCE, MARCH

Allan had now returned to France, rejoining his unit on 16 March. The battalion had moved from the Warneton line to the Lumbres area near St Omer and the men were now billeted throughout the district. Allan returned to the battalion via Le Touquet, a popular holiday destination on the coast of France.

20.3.1918
My Dear Mum & dad

At present we are out resting in a very nice place. We are having glorious weather. I received your lovely parcels. I also got a lovely billy of butter from Mrs J McKay. It was beautiful. I don't think I ever tasted any nicer. I am writing a letter so Cheerio with best love … Please keep these views I send you till I get home & I will tell you all about them …

Le Touquet
20.3.18
Dear Mum

This is one of the prettiest little places I have seen. I spent a couple of days here when I was coming back from school. We have had a glorious winter. It has been sunny every day. Hope you had a glorious harvest …

Lumbre
20.3.18
Dear Mum,

Just a few lines to let you know I am O.C. 38th Batt football team and we are playing a big match today …

Allan may not have had the opportunity to write his promised letter as there is a gap in his letters until 4 April, a fortnight later. His period of rest and comparative tranquillity was about to come to an abrupt end.

As Allan wrote home on 20 March, German forces, bolstered by troops redeployed from the Eastern Front, were ready to launch General Ludendorff's *Die Kaiserschlatt*, the Kaiser's Battle, comprising four attacks along the front. The first and largest of these, 'Operation Michael', was to be launched on the old Somme battlefields. Ludendorff knew that American soldiers would soon arrive in force and his numerical advantage would be lost. The following day, 21 March, a concentration of German forces, some half a million men, launched an attack along a 90-kilometre front from Arras in the north to La Fere in the south. The British Third and Fifth armies, some 160,000 soldiers, were thinly spread along what was a weak point in the Somme front line, an area just north of Cambrai and to the south of St Quentin where they protected the vital rail junction of Amiens. A German breakthrough here would sever the British and French lines, push the British north toward the ports and, ultimately, perhaps even force their withdrawal across the English Channel.[1]

Ludendorff's Operation Michael commenced at 4.40 am on the foggy morning of 21 March. The Allied front line was shattered as the full force of German artillery opened up in a massive barrage. For five hours the German guns pounded the Allied line and its support areas. The bombardment concentrated on supply and communication lines, artillery formations and machine-gun posts. Gas overcame many troops as they raced to defend their lines. The bombardment lifted and the storm troopers — elite soldiers trained to assault defences and destroy communication lines — charged what remained of the British troops. The outposts were soon overwhelmed and German forces rushed forward in pursuit of the retreating British. The nature of the war had now changed from stagnation to momentum as the German infantry raced across fields the Allies had held since 1916. The heavy artillery followed and rapidly overran those troops who had gallantly remained at their posts. Losses on both sides were heavy. Close to 80,000 men were killed or wounded with 21,000 British soldiers taken prisoner. Two hundred and fifty square kilometres of ground was captured by German forces.[2]

Much of the land that Allied forces had claimed and defended for two years with staggering loss of life had been recaptured in just five days by the rapidly advancing Germans. The English and French lines had been breached. The road to Paris was all but open and the channel ports vulnerable to the rapid enemy advance.

As the disaster began to unfold, the majority of Australian forces were positioned 170 kilometres north of Amiens in the Flanders region. By 26 March they were moving, on their way to reinforce the 60 kilometres of broken line south of Amiens. Along the congested roads they met fleeing civilians and panicked troops withdrawing in the face of the German onslaught. With dogged determination, the men marched forward despite the chaos that now enveloped an area so familiar to many of the Australian troops. They were marching to defend the land they had helped protect since 1916. As Charles Bean wrote:

> Again and again the Diggers were told by the passers-by, "You can't hold them!" and some of the leaders were a little anxious as to how all this advice and the depressing sights would affect their men. They need have had no worry; it was immediately evident – as was constantly found in the coming months – that the confidence of these troops was overflowing. Each man knew that every blow now counted; this, they felt was what they had come from Australia for – and the sight of their cheerful, grim faces and confident gait put new heart into French and British alike. "They were the first cheerful stubborn people we had met in retreat," said a British major of artillery. In the French villages whenever during those weeks these hearty, stalwart battalions marched in they were met by striking demonstrations of affection and trust – and this, too, reacted strongly on them. [3]

The 3rd Division was to fight on the Somme battlefield for the first time. Allan was to assist in defending the countryside for which, just under two years before, his brother George had courageously fought. To the north in Belgium, Charlie was writing home as Allan was moving forward to meet the advancing foe. Charlie appears unaware of events unfolding to the south.

In the Field
24th March 1918

My Dear Mother Father & Jim,

... I am still at the school but will be going back to the battalion one day this week ... I got a nice cake and some cigarettes today from Auntie Charlotte Wilson it was very good of her to send it, she often sends me a cake I have just written to her thanking her for it. I also got a letter from Devon they were all well ... I went down to poor Geordie's grave this morning to see if the plate I ordered was put up, but the corporal told me they were unable to finish it as they had been so busy at the hospital, he said he would see that it was fixed up alright. I did not hear anything from the people in England who were to take the photos, so I spoke to the Chaplain of the school he said he would see to it for me as he did a lot of that work I gave him my address also yours, one photo will come to me and one will go to you, so you will get one alright I think it will take some time as they have a lot to take, but it will be done in time. We are having lovely weather over here now today was a perfect day, I have had a splendid time here and feel the benefit of the rest. I do not think Percy will be over here for some months, he is better where he is ...

On 23 March, as the Germans began shelling Paris, the 38th Battalion was resting to the north at Lumbres near St Omer. The battalion was now ordered to the Ypres sector; over the next 24 hours the men received various orders for movement, marching and bussing north towards the Belgian border, then returning to St Omer where trains waited to take them to the Somme battlefields.[4] Orders were frequently changed as confused reports of enemy movement arrived. The rail system was chaotic and some main roads were clogged and impassable; the German advance had wreaked havoc.

By 26 March the 38th had reached the Somme, arriving at Mondicourt station to be greeted by the news that enemy forces were just over four kilometres away. The battalion began a march of some eight kilometres to the village of Authie along roads crowded with terrified refugees and disorganised Allied troops retreating in disarray. They reached Authie at 7.00 pm and rested briefly. The battalion diary entry the following day carried a note of urgency:

2am Orders received that Bn. to proceed at once by route march to MARIEUM where Bn. embussed at 5 a.m. for FRANVILLERS. Arrived FRANVILLERS 1.30pm. Immediately proceeded by route march to HEILLY – Germans reported to have reached vicinity – Moved forward in open order to village MERICOURT and a previously selected position was taken over from 43rd. Battn. A.I.F. just beyond Village - No enemy yet encountered. A. & B. Coys holding line from MERICOURT Le-ABBE Station to about cross-roads at D.11.b. [Map reference difficult to read] C. Coy in support – D. Coy in reserve.[5]

By 8.00 am the following morning — 28 March — the 38th's encounter with the enemy had begun. German soldiers were sighted on a ridgeline less than one kilometre from the battalion's line in Marrett Wood, close to the tiny village of Treux on the Ancre River between Amiens and Albert. The German troops fired into the wood and advanced. The men of the 38th resisted stoically and the Germans retreated taking heavy casualties. Enemy artillery fire intensified. For the next 24 hours the battalion watched and waited. If German forces broke through, they would have a clear run to Amiens, the vital rail junction central to the movement of troops and artillery to the Somme battlefields. From Amiens, enemy forces could readily reach the coast, open up the supply lines to Germany and advance on Paris.

On 26 March the 4th Division had arrived at Doullens where a hastily convened meeting of Allied commanders was underway. The New Zealanders were moved to Amiens and both divisions positioned to form a line north of the 3rd Division in an area with which they were very familiar — the hard-fought battlegrounds of 1916. Pozieres, Mouquet Farm and Albert had now fallen in the face of the German advance. In Doullens the Allies agreed that a coordinated defence was the only way to halt the German advance. French commander General Foch was appointed Supreme Commander on the Western Front, uniting all Allied forces under one commander for the first time.[6] General Gough, whose command of the past two years had included the devastating battles of Pozieres, Bullecourt and Passchendaele, was relieved of his duties and returned to England on 28 March.

During the final days of March, the 3rd Division artillery moved in to support the infantry as they beat back German attacks on their position. On 30 March the Germans advanced south of the Somme. To the north the 3rd Division held the line above Hamel as the enemy pushed forward. [7]

The 3rd Division Memorial crowns the ridge at Sailly-le-Sec (author photo 27 April 2011).

The events that unfolded that day are described on the memorial to the men who fought courageously to stem the advance. High on a ridge just south of the Ancre River at Sailly-le-Sec sits the memorial to the 3rd Division. The inscription reads:

Sailly-le-Sec
March 1918

At dusk in front of the [Australian positions] the Germans were seen retiring from whatever shelter their broken waves had reached. The cries of their wounded for stretcher bearers could be heard all night.

(Charles Bean, Australia's official historian)

The soldiers of the Third Division arrived on these heights overlooking the Somme on 27 March 1918. The next day the Australians pushed further eastwards only to be met by stiff German opposition as the enemy's forces also tried to advance. Approaching the village of Sailly-Laurette on the Somme River east of Sailly-le-Sec an Australian unit was ambushed by massed German machine gunners. However, the Third Division consolidated its positions and held firm. On 30 March 1918 the

Germans began a general advance mainly to the south of the Somme but one division attacked above Sailly-le-Sec. Three times during that day waves of German infantry tried to come up the valleys and slopes east of the Third Division Memorial. Each time they were beaten back with heavy losses caused by intense rifle, machine gun and artillery fire. No further attempt to break the Australian line here was ever made. To the Third Division this was the place for the memorial – the fighting ... called a halt to the German offensive ... [and] it was natural in choosing a site for a memorial it [the 3rd Division] would select a position on the line which it first occupied under such historic circumstances...

According to Charles Bean, by the end of March, Ludendorff knew that 'the offensive had failed; in crossing the desolation of the old Somme battlefields the Germans had outrun their communications. Guns and shells could not be brought up in the quantities necessary for breaking down the new Allied line, drawn around the wide salient made by this thrust.'[8] The storm troopers could go no further; vital support had failed to arrive. Ludendorff would not abandon the offensive, but the assault paused as communications were restored and artillery hauled to the front. He was determined to strike again.

BELGIUM, MARCH

As the situation to the south rapidly developed, Charlie wrote to his family from close to Neuve Eglise. He had initially been ordered to travel south to return to his battalion but fortune had smiled on him and the order had suddenly been cancelled. The race to stem the German offensive saw units move with such rapidity that Charlie had no idea where the main body of the 38th Battalion was now positioned.

In the field
28th March 1918
My Dear Mother, Father & Jim

... I have left the school, we were all recalled a few days before the school was to finish and ordered to join our battalions, but we were stopped

before we got back and put on another job behind the line, so I am not with Allan I wrote to him about my mail, I have no idea where they are. I saw Albert's grave today and got the Caretaker to look after it and level it up and plant some flowers I will be getting a photo of it for you. I do not know how long I will be here, you will see by the papers that there is a big fight on, there are more of my battalion here, I got another letter from the Commonwealth Bank re another remittance which I think is from Pearl I wrote to the Bank asking them to forward it on to Ida for the present. I wrote to you the day before I left the school. I got a letter from Devon and a nice cake from Auntie Wilson also a letter from Percy he was getting on alright. We have been having grand weather over here lately the trees and hedges are starting to look green. I have a platoon on putting up barbed wire entanglements behind the line, it is not a bad job. I am hoping to hear from Allan next week and hope to get some of your mail which is there, we can buy anything we want here and there is a fine YMCA not far away so we don't do too bad. Well I have no news so will close for this time with love and best wishes to all.

I remain
Your loving
Charlie

Charlie wrote to his mother on Easter Sunday — just a day after the 3rd Division had courageously held the ridges of Sailly-le-Sec. He had paid another visit to Albert's grave. He appears relieved as he writes, believing that it is unlikely he will be recalled to the 38th.

In the field
Easter Sunday
31st March 1918
My Dear Mother,

Just a few lines to say I am getting on alright I am not with Allan but I am in charge of a platoon putting up barbed wire entanglements we are working near where Albert is buried, I saw his grave today also two days ago when I asked the caretaker to fix it up for me and put some flowers on it and when I saw it today I was so pleased to see that he had done it. I wrote to

England, as I told you before, to get a photo of it, which will take time but you will get it. We were recalled from the school a few days before it finished and ordered to join our units as you will know long before this reaches you that there is a big battle on but I do not think I will see any of it as we are ordered to stay here for some time yet …

ENGLAND, MARCH

In England the news of the German offensive spread rapidly and the familiar village names of two years ago began to reappear in the newspapers. The situation was clearly desperate. Holding Amiens was critical, but the villages to the east of the rail junction were now falling with alarming speed. Percy wrote home; he was improving and was now at the convalescent camp at Hurdcott on Salisbury Plain. The news of the German advance soon reached the soldiers recovering from illness or wounds.

March 26th 1918
Hurdcott
Dear Jim

Well Jim, just a few lines to let you know I am still alive and well I am in a new home again, a convalescent camp at Hurdcott, don't think I will be here long, they will be sending them across to France quick now this big push is on. I have not seen anything in the paper about the Australians, so I don't think they can be in it yet if all goes well I ought to be a month in England, yet there is some rumours about cutting out the sick leave, that will be a terrible [indecipherable]. *I am waiting on a mail anytime now, there is one in, but I have not got any yet. I was at Harefield when I wrote to you last, they soon shift you out of there if there is not to much wrong. There is a concert on here tonight, they have some pretty good turnouts. I saw Charlie & Albert Cockcroft Uwin Johnson had just gone on leave the day I got here, he went to Scotland struck oil there I believe. I am thinking of going to Leicester and Scotland. Its hard to get meat in England, you have to have a pocket full of ticket, sugar, meat tickets & so on. Well Jim I will close hoping it finds you all well I am your loving Brother.*

Percy

FRANCE, APRIL

Allan wrote: 4/4/18 This is a photo of D Company cooks & Quarter Master.

On the final day of March, the 38th moved into forward trenches between Mericourt and Treux, south-west of Albert, to relieve the 39th Battalion. Heavy rain was falling and continued intermittently over the next fortnight as the battalion moved in and out of the line around Buire. German forces continued to rake the area with machine-gun fire and heavy artillery barrages while the Australians secured the trenches and laid more wire. Enemy aircraft and observation balloons ranged in the sky above. Even in the rear areas, in billets at Ribemont, the soldiers were not safe from the German artillery as it set its sights on the village.[9]

On 4 April German forces thrust forward along a 34-kilometre front taking the village of Hamel, but were repulsed at Villers-Bretonneux by the Australian 9th Brigade of the 3rd Division which suffered 660 casualties in its defence of the strategic position.[10] The following day, in a battle Charles Bean described as 'the strongest attack made against the Australians in the war', the 12th and 13th brigades of the 4th Division lost 1100 men as they defended the village of Dernancourt just beyond Buire on the railway line between Amiens and the town of

Albert, which was now in enemy hands. Battalion historian Eric Fairey estimates that, on 9 April, 1000 shells fell in the area around the villages of Buire and Treux and along the railway line which the battalion was holding. That night the 38th Battalion was relieved and moved into the support trenches of Mericourt where battalion headquarters had been established in a nearby chateau.[11]

Allan was promoted lieutenant on 2 April and promptly sent for a two-day 'rest' during which he was finally able to write home after two weeks of movement and fighting the 'fray ... and having the time of my life'. Typically laconic, he forgets to mention his promotion in a letter to his mother.

Dear Mum

This is one of my brother officers of my company. He is a little bonza ASMarlow (To another D Coy "Knit" Joe Poole)

Lieutenant Joe Poole.

Joe (Harold Frederick) Poole had sailed on the *Runic* with Allan and Percy. Like Allan he had been promoted in the field to lieutenant. He suffered a severe gunshot wound to his jaw on 20 August 1918 and returned to Australia in July 1919.[12]

4-4-18

My Dear Jim,

... I received your letters safely & was delighted over same what a stunner harvest you must have had and it was a good one too. What a pity I was not home for the bag sewing & the lunches. Bill Jones would be great company

alright. When is he getting married you might ask him to wait till I get home. I believe Bob Leed is winning MG now that is [indecipherable]. You seem to have had a wet harvest. Ill bet the boyscouts would put the wind up you with their fires. I have told you in previous letters about Bill Street that he died of wounds about a fortnight after he received them. We cant find his grave. I was also disappointed with the conscription. I am in favour of conscription. Men are very short at times very few coming in now. There were never 6 divisions in France. No division has been cut up to reinforce another. Very few Australians have been resting. No we had a most glorious winter this year is the most pleasant year I have ever spent. Fancy Billy Williams breaking it off. Well Jim you may not get a letter for a week so don't worry because we were travelling and I had a minute to write. Well Jim I am well [in] the fray which is going on at present and having the time of my life. Percy is still in Blighty & doing well. Charlie is still away at the school so I am happy as they are both away. Sometimes when the guns open up one would think hell had open up. I will be sending you some photos in a day or two so I hope you get them …

After days in the field, paper was in short supply and Allan was writing on a series of postcards from England. He appears pleased that Charlie and Percy were not with him as he played his part in the defence of the Somme; his relief was to last just a few days longer. Limited by the censor, he clearly hints to his father of his whereabouts by underlining the word 'some'.

Postcards of Manaton, England

In the field
4-4-1918
My Dear Dad

Just a few lines to let you know that I am well & was terribly pleased to get your letter. What a good harvest you had. By jove wouldn't you miss me at the bag sewing or at the lunch table, mostly at the latter I am afraid. Well dear dad you will see by the papers what has taken place and we are well in it. I never had such an experience in all my life. By jove we were hurried down here. My captain sent me out for two days rest & I am billeted in a lovely French house, a cosy bed & plenty to eat but I return to the line to night. I *had a letter from Percy he is getting on well and is still in Blighty. Charlie is still away at the school. So I am as happy as old Dick because the two boys are away. I like to be in the fighting on my own. I have seen too much of brothers being together in these battles. Well dear dad I cant tell you where we are but it is a new sector. I can tell you it is <u>some</u> place. Well cheerio dear dad & all I am happy. Don't worry it is better than the combined Sunday school picnics.*

I remain
Your Loving Son
Allan S

All the <u>lads</u> are well and in great <u>spirits</u>

ENGLAND, APRIL

Still recuperating, Percy wrote to Jim from Hurdcott; he had been granted leave to visit his relatives and was looking forward to heading further north to Scotland:

England
April 7 1918
Dear Jim

Well old boy got a couple of -- pesting me, Albert Cockcroft U Johnson they are talking and I am writing. Uwin got married up in Scotland, I suppose you can hardly believe it. Its been a bad day raining and blowing all day we had church parade in the morning half holiday in the afternoon. Got a letter from Mum the other day, it was the first I have had for a long time. I am going on leave Thursday, going to Leicester and to Scotland. I expect to get four days leave after I am back for a while, then I am going to Devon.

Charlie Cockcroft went away from here yesterday, to Sutton Veny he will soon be over.

Well Jim I will close
Hoping it finds you all well
I remain your
aff brother
Percy

The following letter is written on the back of a photo. Lieutenant Leslie Roberts, MM, was a member of the 38th Battalion, later signing up to serve in World War II. At the time he wrote he was in Cambridge recovering from a fractured ankle. He describes the AIF's desperation to find men to bolster the defences on the Western Front.

Lieutenant Leslie Roberts wrote to Allan from hospital in England.

12 Ward
1ˢᵗ E.S. Hosp
Cambridge
15-4-18
Dear Allan,

I am not going to dare wangle an excuse for not writing before, therefore must get away from that line of thought. I did send you a card while I was at Morbecque congratulating you on the pip but got no reply. Well old sport I suppose Perc has told you how I got in this place. I am now in the 5ᵗʰ week of bed (Did I hear you saying lucky dog) may be I am after what you are going through. I should sit for the final on the 30ᵗʰ of this month but, can see myself well in this place, it will mean I will be put in another coy. with a short time to go after I get clear of this place. I have heard rumours of the 3ʳᵈ Div + 12ᵗʰ Bgde of 4ᵗʰ Div being cut to hell and am afraid this time as it came from A.I.F. H.Q. Did you know they cleared about 200 out of A.I.F. H.Qrs & sent them over, some of them have never handled a rifle, left Vic with "Army Post Office Corps" what a gutser, up to coming in here I had a good time in Cambridge. Well old sport trusting this finds self, brothers & fellow officers in the best of health.

Good luck
Your Old Pal
L.A. Roberts

I sent your photo home & it arrived safely L.A. Roberts [13]

Now visiting relatives in Leicestershire, Percy wrote to Jim:

C/o Mrs Payne
33 Green Lane Rd
Leicester
17-4-18
Dear Jim

Well old boy how are you going on. You will see by the top I am in Leicester having a good time Jim. Last Saturday Flo and another girl friend of Paynes were here, well it was lively Jim, I wish you were here. Flo, as you know, works in Leicester she is a lively girl, Auntie is a hard case, so when they are all together things are very lively. The weather is terrible just now its raining every day makes things very disagreeable. I will be off to Scotland in a few days, they say Glasgow is a nice place. Ida had a letter from Charlie this morning; he and Allan were well when he wrote. My word Jim, Fritz is exceeding himself isn't he; but we will stop him if it only takes two years now that we got the "god dam Yanks" I guess. I hope to have a lot of mail when I get back. Well Jim hope this finds you all well.

Your aff brother
Percy
Love from all

Percy remained in England while Charlie was positioned to the north in Belgium where Ludendorff was set to unleash the next stage of his plan: 'Operation Georgette'.

TWENTY

... IT BREAKS MY HEART
TO WRITE THIS LETTER

On 9 April German forces attacked south of Armentieres sending Portuguese troops fleeing from their positions in a headlong retreat to the coast. Armentieres fell. The enemy was now heading for Hazebrouck, a key transport centre, with St Omer and the channel ports in their sights. Mount Kemmel fell and Messines and Passchendaele were lost with little resistance. Only a few months before, Allied troops had suffered enormous casualties capturing and holding the same villages that had now fallen into enemy hands.[1]

The 1st Australian Division, which had just arrived on the Somme, was turned around under shellfire at Amiens and sent back to the Flanders region. The men arrived at Hazebrouck on 12 April and immediately began digging new trenches which soon became the front line. A few days later, as waves of German troops advanced toward them, the men of the 1st Division mowed them down with withering machine-gun and rifle fire; the Australians held the line. Against the odds, the vital rail centre of Hazebrouck had been secured.[2]

On the same day that the 1st Australian Division arrived at Hazebrouck in the north, the 38th Battalion was moving into the front line at Buire to relieve the 40th. A and B companies were positioned on the left of the River Ancre while Allan's D Company was on the right along the Buire-Ville-sur-Ancre Road. C Company remained in reserve in Buire. The area was under constant German artillery fire.

Charlie had received his orders to return to the 38th. Before he reached the line he dashed off a card to his mother:

7th April 1918
My Dear Mother

Just a few lines to say that I am quite well and not in the line I hope you are all well at home. I am not with Allan yet but may see him this week, I have not heard from Percy as I have not got any mail since I left the school but he will be getting on alright. We are having nice weather over here now and not much to do this last week. Well I will close for this time with love to all. I wrote to you a few days ago. Goodbye with love

From your loving
Charlie xxxxxxxx

All the lads are well and are in great spirits

Charlie's card to his mother before returning to the 38th Battalion.

As Allan wrote to his aunt and to Jim, he remained unaware that Charlie was about to return to the battalion:

France
12-4-18
My Dear Auntie Florrie

This is the first time I have written to you since being in France. I never used to write because Percy & I have been together all the time and he done the writing. Well dear Auntie I had a letter from Percy last night and he is doing well. I spent 4 days with him when I was on leave. I am well in the present offensive and having a time of my life. Thank God Charlie is still at the school. All the Mologa boys are going strong. I was promoted to First Lieutenant about 2 months ago & I forget to tell them at home. I get my letters regular & was very pleased to hear that they had a good harvest. I often get letters from Gibsons about Milne and for me to look him up. Well I don't know his address nor know him from a bar of soap. Bert is surviving it well. I will say goodbye dear Auntie I remain your loving nephew.

Allan S M XXXX

In the field
14-4-18
Dear Old Jim

Another few lines to let you know that I am excellent & I do hope that you all are the same. Well old boy I am well in it and enjoying the fun. It is absolutely the most exciting time ever I had. Talk about a football match between Pyramid & Mologa well it is nothing to it. One could easily buy a fight those days and it is the same here. Thank God that Charlie & Percy are not in it. I am as happy as happy can be. Mind you she gets awful willing and on my right at present there is a terrific go. We expect it here any minute. The Australians have the Bosch absolutely b- You ought to hear what the French people say about us. There is no doubt about it the boys are standing it gallantly. My lads will do me. We are getting splendid tucker, practically no sleep but everything is OK. We are on a jolly warm front. It is where poor old Geordie had all his severe fighting. It is disgraceful to think that we have to fight for the same ground again. Well Jim I suppose you are not sorry that the harvest is over. What lovely crops you had. No doubt you had a terrific lot of work. But it is worth it. What sort of a crop did Johnson have … Some of these cold footers must be having a hell of a good time over there. I think with a bit of good luck we ought to be home by New Year. What a rejoicing there will be when we get home. Some with wives and some without. I suppose you know that E Johnson is married and Charlie Cockcroft is just about. That is the way to do it. It will teach some those Ausy girls to flirt. I suppose you know that Ewen Johnson's girl turned him down also Charlie Cockcrofts. Hughie's wife is a Scotch lassie. I believe she is some girl too. Well Jim old boy between Mums & your letter I had told you all the available news so will close with best wishes to all

I remain
Your Loving Brother

I nearly forgot to tell you again that I was promoted to Lieutenant on the 3-2-28. I [am] well satisfied now

Cheerio Jim
ASM

Allan's relief at being the only Marlow brother in the line of fire was not to last. As he wrote, Charlie was moving into the line to fight alongside his brother. Together they awaited the expected German attack as Charlie took a moment to write home:

14th April 1918
In the field
Dear Jim

Just a few lines to say that I am quite well also Allan, I got back to the battalion 2 days ago and got over 30 letters I wrote home last night. I got a letter from Percy to say that he was going on furlough, I think he was going to Leicester and perhaps to Devon, and then I suppose it will not be long before he will be over here again. I got about six letters from you, I missed a lot of mail when I was at the school, they sent it to the wrong school so they came back to the unit again. You asked me in your last letter if I thought Geordie got proper attention at the hospital and if he said anything before he died well I think, in fact I am sure he received the very best attention as the hospital is well behind the line and very up to date, I was unable to find out if he said anything in his last moments as it was too long after that I got word, (that was on the 7th Nov) if I had got word within a few days I would have stood a good chance of finding out ... Allan ... thought he would be going to an officers school but he was given his commission in France instead I missed a chance through being away on leave, since then all officer's schools and commissions given in France have been cancelled till further notice as they have such a lot of officers on hand. We are getting on O.K. here there has been a fight on but we are alright there is no need to be anxious, I will be writing home in a day or so, so will close for tonight. With best wishes to all I will say goodbye.

I remain
Your loving brother
Charles

The following day Allan wrote with his characteristic candour to Jim:

In the field
Monday 15-4-18
Dear Jim,

… Charlie just rejoined us 2 days ago from the school. He had a splendid time there, but had a lot of travelling about before he got here. He looks real well. He said he had an easy time at the school. I think he must have because he is terrible fat. Well Jim old boy I am still plodding along the same as usual. Enjoying life first rate. I think I told you in my last that I was sent out for another rest. Well I am busy letter writing I have wrote about 8 letters to you all home this week you will wonder what has happened. I believe there is another Australian mail in and we are all anxiously waiting for the news. I had a letter from Percy the other night he is in camp in England & expects leave soon. I was wishing he would not have to come back here. I wish we could get Charlie or Percy out of it. Well I suppose you are busy cropping now. No doubt you must have a lot of work to do. I suppose mum did not have much of a holiday. You people seem to be working a terrible lot but you should try and look on the bright side of things. Mum said in one of her letters that Geordie should have been with us. Well Jim it is the greatest mistake out for brothers to get together I have to much of it. Brothers are always together and if a shell comes it gets the lot of you …

The next day the battalion was relieved and the troops marched out to nearby Ribemont for a few days of rest. Charlie was pleased to receive a copious amount of letters which included the news of the Australian government's decision to allocate land to returned soldiers. He had hopes of securing a block close to the forest at Mologa where, on his return, he could begin his new life with Pearl and their baby. Once again he tried hard to reassure the family that all was well despite the shock of the German advance.

In the field
19ᵗʰ April 1918
My Dear Mother, Father and Jim,

I got a big mail this morning 15 letters … I was so pleased to get them all so soon after my other big mail which I got from A.S. when I joined the battalion after being at the school. A.S. got about 9 letters this morning also so we are not doing too bad. I was surprised to hear of G Johnson buying a motor car also J Squire things must be looking up in Mologa lately. That seems a good move on the part of the "heads" in anticipation purchasing Crown and Major Anderson's lands for returned soldiers, I saw by the Pyramid paper that they were having a look at the Terrick forest, I would like a slice of it myself and I hope they reserve it for the "Defenders" of the "Country". I suppose you will all be in a great way at present over us on account of the war news but Allan and I are quite well and everything is alright Percy is still in England and on leave at present, I do not know how long it will be before he will be sent back here again. Jim said we never say anything about Bill Street well all that I know is that he died of wounds. I spoke to Harry about it but he was unable to find out much. I can tell you it is a hard matter to find out anything about anyone over here. We are having good weather over here at present we cannot buy any notepaper I got this off another chap but it answers the purpose. I heard that one of the Miles boys got a Military medal but I do not know how he got it …

Writing to his father, Charlie describes how much he is looking forward to visiting Paris once leave arrangements are reinstated and suggests that another trip to England would not be far away. He regrets the need for Percy to return to the front. Preventing another death was paramount to both Charlie and Allan.

In the field
April 22ⁿᵈ 1918
Dear Dad,

… Allan is here we are both quite well, I got a letter from Percy the night before last he was on leave at Payne's I do not think he will be over here for about a month or more yet I was in hopes that he would get home but I think the offensive which is now on has caused a lot to have to return to their units. Les Townsend is here with us also Harry Street, I met Amos Haw about a fortnight ago he looked real well I spent the evening with him. I also saw Knowlson Haw he had just come from Hospital with a bad

eye he is in the battalion next below us I saw Rupert Hercus, he was along with Knowlson, he was wounded last October and is now alright again. I got a letter from Hughie Martin sometime ago he was likely to go home but I have not heard if he has gone. Ewen Johnson and Charlie Cockcroft are in England and will be over here shortly. The crop at home turned out real well I think, and you seem to be getting a fair advance on it. There seems to be a lot of people selling out up Mologa way lately. I was surprised to hear that Gordon Carey had enlisted and one of the Coutts. I got that Money which you sent to the Commonwealth Bank £10 I got them to send it on to Ida she sends it on to me as I want it. I am looking forward to going to Paris when leave starts again and my turn to go on English leave again will not be long coming round. We are having good weather over here now the days are like the spring in Victoria and the nights are very short, at present it is light up till 9 P.M. and is light at about 3.30 A.M. I cannot say anything of where we are or what is doing but we are both well and getting on alright. I got a parcel from Mrs Bray last week I will get the parcels that Mother sends alright. Well I will draw to a close for this time with love and best wishes to all

I will say goodbye
I remain
Your Loving Son
Charles

On Anzac Day Allan wrote to Jim, his opinion on Percy's return quite different to Charlie's:

France
25-4-1918
Dear Jim

... Yes Jim I am First Lieutenant but I will bet you 100 £ that Miss B never got a letter from me saying so because I have never written her for 8 or 9 months. Well Jim I was sorry to hear that you had been sick but glad to hear that you were better again. You seem to be having a rotten time with headaches. Well you would not better them if you were here, and for God's sake don't ever think of coming here. There is enough of us here now. Myrtle

Stone seems a jolly nice little girl I am glad she is with you all. Percy is still in England and I don't think he will ever come back here. I am doing my best and of course I have a little weight now. Tell Mum that Major Maudsley is writing to her. He told me this the other night. Yes Mannix & his crowd seem a dirty rotten lot. Yes Jim we have been well in the offensive and no one knows what it is like. Well Jim old boy I wrote to you last night so news is scarce. Glad I got all your letters so good night old boy.

I remain
Your Loving Brother
Allan

In the early hours of 26 April, Charlie set off to collect breakfast and deliver it to his platoon, positioned in the forward trenches at Buire. It had been a long night. Enemy artillery fire had fallen heavily along the railway line. After four days in the front line, the exhausted men of the 38th looked forward to their relief later that day. On his way Charlie spoke to his brother at company headquarters and chatted with mates along the lines.

Between 5.30 am and 6.00 am, laden with breakfast for his men, Charlie picked his way through the network of trenches as he returned to the front line. He had just been warned to keep his head down, as a sniper was active in the area. The warning came too late.

With a palpable sorrow which he struggles to express, Allan wrote to Jim:

France
27-4-1918

My Dear Jim, Well dear Jim it breaks my heart to write this letter. Our dear Charlie was killed yesterday morning at 5.30. The bullet killed him instantly and he never spoke a word. I had just left him and gone down the trench to see the other lads when I was called back. Oh Jim it is awful. He is buried in a nice cemetery a good way behind the line I attended the burial with a lot more. It is awful to think that poor old Charlie has gone now. Oh I do hope he is the last. What awful lot of trouble we have had in a few months. Jim I do hope you all bear it the best you can. It has broke me up properly. I am out of the line. It is awful losing 3 good lads like this but Jim you know someone must go. It is impossible for it to go on without somebody going. I am doing my best to get Percy home. Everybody tell me that it is a cert for one to go home so he can go. I am writing to heads in London. Jack Angus, MLA Angus' son is doing a lot for me too.[3] I do hope it works. Jim I will tell you in a later letter where our dear Charlie is buried. I am having a nice cross put up over him like we had put over Geordie & Albert. Dear Jim he was buried with full military honors. Tell dear mum & dad to try and bear up as well as they can. As it worries me I was never so broken up in all my life but Jim you know we have to keep going. Well dear old boy I can't write anymore so will close with best love to all.

I remain
Your Loving Brother
Allan S.M.

Allan's distress is clear as he writes to Jim.

Charlie had lost his life at the age of 26. He was never to hold his baby daughter and his wife was now just another young widow. Sarah and Charles Marlow had lost three sons to the relentless carnage of the Western Front. They did not have the opportunity to say goodbye, nor to grieve at a graveside. Jim, Allan and Percy had lost three brothers in nine months.

Later letters explain that Allan wrote home to Sarah and Charles on the day their eldest son was killed and wrote further letters throughout the month, although only those written to Jim were found in the collection. Perhaps Sarah kept the letters she received elsewhere and they have now been lost; perhaps her grief was so great she could no longer hold on to what had given her hope. Others also wrote home of Charlie's death. The author of this letter is unknown; it was possibly sent to Myrtle Stone's sister Lilly.

In the field
27/4/18
Dear Lilly

As I have a few spare moments I want to give you some news which is very sad to us here I can well imagine what your district will feel, when you get the sad news of the death of Serg Charlie Marlow he was killed on 26 April at 6 oclock in the morning, shot through the nose by a sniper and was dead almost instantly for he never spoke a word, no one got a bigger surprise than I did, for it was only 3 minutes before it happened, that he came to my dug out and gave me my breakfast, and we were joking with each other, and it was a few minutes after that I heard a cry for a stretcher bearer and was on the spot in about 2 minutes but he had passed away by then. We got him on the stretcher right away and had him down to the Dr in twenty minutes for we had to carry him some about 2 1/2 to 3 miles to the R.a.p. some of the track we had to travel was very rough, and as the country is so level, we ran a big risk getting him out in day light, but we chanced it, and got through allright of course it was our luck. His two brothers were away at the time, Pips [Percy] is in Blighty and Allan was back somewhere (where I can't say) I know Allan Lieut will take it very bad, and his poor mother & wife will. I can't say how I feel for them, it will be a terrible blow when they receive the news, and every lad in the Coy and also other Coys nearly cried when it happened; Charlie was so well liked when we were getting him out there was of course enquirers from every one for miles along who it was and when we would say Serg Marlow there would be all sorts of comments. One Serg of C Coy asked the said question, and when he was told he wouldn't believe it, for he had been in the trench with him making some arrangements not long before. Poor Charlie is and will be missed very much for a better N.C.O. among his men there never was and as for Allan well he is very near worshipped among his platoon as he comes from up your way I just thought I would let you know a little about it as I was on the spot and practically seen it all happened…

While others mourned the death of a mate, Allan's grief had led to an expression of his own fragile sense of mortality. To live every day under threat of death had hardened this young soldier. Allan shared his fatalistic sentiment with Jim, revealing that, in the darkest moments of coping with the death of yet another much-loved brother, he could see the time when destiny would end his own life. The hand of fate was ever-present. As Jack Lockett would explain years later, '… if a bullet had your name on it you were gone'.

France
30-4-1918
Dear Jim,

Well dear Jim by the time you get this letter you will have heard of the death of our dear Charlie. Well Jim it is terrible to think that those three boys are gone but that saying What must be will be. Well I attended dear Charlies service it was very very sad indeed. All of the boys were there also Mr Angus and Harry Street. Poor old Harry was terribly broken up but Jim know one knows how I feel it. I can just picture my time, oh my dear mum & dad. Jim do try & cheer them up. Jim do what you can to brace them up a little. I am doing my best to get Percy sent home you do your best that end. Dear Jim I received your loving letter to night also the one dear mum wrote when she was in Bendigo. I do hope dear dad is better now. What trouble we have had. I hope that is the last of it. Dear Jim I am out of the line at present but don't know how long for. I am only about 500 yds away from dear Charlie grave. He is buried along way from the line. Well dear Jim try & cheer up a little. Percy is still in England. Well dear old boy I will say good bye and best love to all

I remain
Your Loving Brother
Allan S

Albert Sinclair wrote home to his wife with news of Charlie's death. He was also about to suffer at the hands of fate. He was wounded just three days after his wife wrote to Sarah. He survived his wound but saw no further action.

Roselin Farm
Durham Ox
July 14ᵗʰ 18
Dear Mrs Marlow,

A few lines as promised. I had letters from my husband on Thursday. The one dated 29.4.18 he told me of your sons death. This is how he wrote it. Charlie came up to our post, which was an advanced one, as he regularly did every morning, to see us and have a chat with us all and this morning a sniper had been at work on us and made us keep our heads under cover. The trench was very shallow & one either had to sit or crouch down when in it. Charlie was talking to us & just had his head above the trench & he had a word half uttered, when the bullet hit him about ¾ inch below the eye & the poor fellow just dropped dead & didn't even breathe so it was a painless death. It was a terrible shock to us all & I thought a great deal of Charlie. I hope this will be a comfort to you to know he did not suffer. So trusting you and all are well.

I remain
Yours sincerely
Daphne Sinclair

Further accounts from the men who witnessed Charlie's death arrived months later via the Red Cross. Their recollections varied as some were written over six months since Charlie's death. I doubt they provided much comfort to Sarah, whose grief must have been overwhelming.

Australian Red Cross Society
Information Bureau
Melbourne
28th August, 1918
Mr J. W. Marlow
Mologa P.O.
Via Bendigo
Dear Sir

Re L/Sgt C.E. Marlow No. 2123 38th Battalion

We have now received from our London Agents the following reports in regard to the above named soldier who is officially stated killed on the 26th April, 1918.

Pte. W. McMillan No. 2605, 38th Battalion on the 27th June stated – He was a Sgt. And in D. Company. I saw him killed at Mericourt, on the Somme, when death was instantaneous, he having been hit through the head by a bullet, in early morning. He was going up to a post he was in charge of, and just as he reached it he was hit. I knew him well, and he came from Victoria. I did not see his grave, but he was buried I'm sure, for his body was taken back to Heilly for burial. He had a brother a Lieutenant in the same company who knows all the particulars.

Pte. W. Anderson No 3021 on the 27th June stated – he was killed instantly about 100 yards from me by a bullet between his eyes from a German sniper while carrying rations to the front line one evening about the end of April or the beginning of May. It happened about ¼ mile in front of Ribemont. I saw his body which was taken back and buried. He had a brother Akers Marlow who is now Lieutenant in 38th A.I.F. Hqrs. Lewis Gun and who was very much cut up about it. He has all the particulars. Marlow's initials were C.E. and name Charlie. He was a Sgt. In D. Coy. A very nice man who would do anything for another. All the boys loved him. He was about 25 and 5'81/2" broad and darkish.

Mr J. W. Marlow

Our Agents have written to Lieut. Marlow asking him to let us have all the information he is able to supply in regard to the death of the above named soldier, but you will no doubt have heard from him in the meantime and be in possession of all details.

Yours faithfully
Beacham Kiddle
Hon. Secretary

Australian Red Cross Society
Victorian Division
Information Bureau
Melbourne
2ⁿᵈ October 1918
Mr J.W. Marlow
Mologa Post Office
Via Bendigo
Dear Sir

   Re L/Sgt. C.E. Marlow, No. 2123, 38ᵗʰ Btn.

Since writing to you on the 28ᵗʰ August we have received from our agents the following further reports concerning the above named soldier who was killed in action on the 26ᵗʰ April, 1918

Cpl. Whipp, No 1329, has stated:- " That is Sgt. Marlow of D. Coy. He is one of five brothers who have been sent out there and he is the third to be killed. He was taking out rations from the Dump to the front line at Buire. He just looked over the parapet and was shot dead through the head. I was in charge of the next post at the time and so did not see him. His brother Lt. A.S. Marlow now at the base was with the Battalion at the time and has the full particulars."

Pte. P. Owens, No. 116, has stated:- "He was a Sergeant. I have lived alongside of him all my life, at Pyramid Hill, Victoria, and I knew him well. He was visiting pals in the early morning before breakfast at Buire when he was sniped through the head. He was the brother of an Officer D. Coy. with the Battalion now. He told me when we were talking afterwards that he had been at his brother's funeral. I am not certain where the Sgt. was buried.

Pte. G. Collison, No. 2183, has stated:- "I was with Sgt. Charlie E. Marlow, 2123 (38.D.) when he was killed instantly by a bullet in April at Ribemont near L'Ancre. Just at Break of day he came round just to see how we were getting on and walked into our bay – a L.G. Post.[Lewis Gun Post] *There were a few bullets about so we told him to keep down. He was going to sit down when he was hit in the eye. He never spoke a word. I was quite close to him, we were sitting down and he was standing up. I think he was taken away by the stretcher bearers to Battalion Headquarters. There were 4 brothers in the same Coy. Percy Marlow was away with Trench Fever, but another brother Alan Marlow was at Battalion Headquarters and I think he went up to bury him. He would know all about it. Description :- Mologa, married, one child, out about 18 months."*

Pte. J. Flower, No 2214, has stated:- "I saw Charlie Marlow who was a Sgt. being carried out he having been killed on the right of the R. Ancre to the right of Buire. I was told by one of the chaps in the line that he was killed by a bullet early in the morning, it was about lunch time when I saw him. I can't say where he is buried but probably about Heilly. I came over in same reinforcements 3/30th leaving … [page missing]

Pte. Cameron, No. 2540, has stated: "I think Marlow was in B.Coy, he lived somewhere near Melbourne, had another brother in the same Battalion as a Lt. And was the third brother to be killed. He was killed about April when we were in the line, in the Amiens district near a place Buire. We were holding the front line, and he was skilled by a Sniper being hit by a bullet, which went through his nose. I did not see him killed but I saw his body later, and put him on a cart to go to burial. I am not sure, but I think he was buried at Heilly…

* * *

FRANCE, 2011

It is 26 April 2011. Ninety-three years ago, on this day, Charlie Marlow was killed. It is a crisp, clear and breezy spring morning; it is easy to imagine that, on the day Charlie died, the weather was not dissimilar to the glorious day of our pilgrimage. We join our Somme battlefields guide Martin Pegler and drive some 30 kilometres to Ribemont

Communal Cemetery Extension where Charlie is buried. It is small in size and attached to a local cemetery. Charlie was originally buried at Heilly No 2 Cemetery in the grounds of Heilly Chateau. His body was exhumed after the Armistice as the Commonwealth War Graves Commission began consolidating the hundreds of small cemeteries scattered the length of the Western Front. We search for his grave and, to our consternation, Charlie is not buried in the plot as listed. We continue to search and, with relief, soon find that his resting place has been recorded incorrectly. It is only a matter of the difference between Row A and Row H; possibly an error between the handwritten records made on site and later records compiled during the exhumation process.

Ribemont Community Cemetery Extension, France (author photo 26 April 2011).

The final resting place of Charlie Marlow.

As we stand by Charlie's grave, we reflect on a life cut short and the sacrifice he made. He left behind his young wife and the daughter he never knew, a little girl who would never meet her father.

Later, the Red Cross reports in hand, Martin drives us a few kilometres to Buire-sur-Ancre. Somewhere to the east of the village is the place where Charlie lost his life. Today it is green and lush, grasses shimmer in the breeze and tall trees line a stream which makes its way to the nearby Ancre River. It is remarkably peaceful. There are no cars, the only sounds the trees rustling in the breeze and the low calls of contented cattle on a land long healed.

I try to imagine the early morning of 26 April. I picture Charlie joking with his mates on his route through the trenches and yarning with his brother, Allan, at headquarters. He gathers the morning's rations, carted in before dawn from the Quartermaster's Store at Heilly. He makes his way back through the crowded lines to the welcome greetings of his platoon. These were shallow trenches and the sniper was alert. For just a few seconds Charlie forgot to keep his head down. Then the shot, the cries from his mates for the stretcher-bearers, the dangerous journey in broad daylight to the aid post in a cellar west of the village, someone racing through the trenches to find Allan. Then comes the moment when Allan has to say goodbye to his brother who was his mate, his confidant, his keeper. The pain of another loss was crushing.

The simple cross that marked Charlie's original burial place at Heilly.

***

South-west of where Charlie lies buried is the village of Villers-Bretonneux. This village was strategically important to the German forces as a vantage point in the taking of Amiens. On Anzac Day 2011 we drive from the dawn service at Polygon Wood and the later service at Tyne Cot Cemetery in Belgium to the French village of Villers-Bretonneux to commemorate the great sacrifice that the Australians, including the Marlow family, made in this region of France. We are surprised by the rolling hills, the patchwork of yellow canola, lush green grasses and the blended browns of fallow. My father, who farmed the Mologa land, remarked how similar it was to the countryside around Mologa in a favourable season. He thought the boys would have felt at home. Of course by 1918 this country had been much fought over, churned to dust and mud, pockmarked with shell holes and scarred by a maze of trenches. Perhaps in the rear areas in the early spring of 1918 there may have been moments when the similarity with home provided comfort.

The Australian Memorial, commanding the high ground just a few kilometres from Villers-Bretonneux, is an imposing white stone tower that has stood sentinel across the valley since 1938. We take some photos and look across the fields in an attempt to envisage the battles that had taken place on the ground where we stand. Then we arrive at the memorial. Hundreds of floral tributes form a bright sea at the base of the Cross of Sacrifice as we walk forward to lay our wreath. The dawn ceremony is long over.

We linger for a while and look down the seemingly never-ending list of soldiers who have no known grave. We raise our eyes to study the tower, riddled with bullet holes, the scars of World War II. Further down the valley, just 15 kilometres or so, lies Amiens and its magnificent cathedral. We stand on the ground that German forces sought to capture, to pave their way to Amiens and onward to victory. The Australians fought a desperate battle here, bloody and brutal, to ensure that their enemy would not attain his objective. German forces captured Villers-Bretonneux on 24 April and, that very night, the 13th and 15th brigades stormed the burning village and pushed the Germans back to their starting line. It was a turning point. The Australians, with courage, determination and aggression, had halted the enemy advance and prevented a potential catastrophe. Ludendorff's Operation Michael had failed.

Charlie Marlow had died as the Australians doggedly held the line that protected Amiens. In the defence of the city, Sarah and Charles had lost another son. Allan, Percy and Jim lost another brother. Pearl would no longer feel the loving touch of her husband and baby Beatrice Eva would never know her father.

Pearl Marlow and baby Eva.

TWENTY ONE
I HAVE LOST A REAL FRIEND AND COMPANION, TO SAY NOTHING OF THE BEST N.C.O. I EVER KNEW.

APRIL, ENGLAND

In England, Percy had returned from leave and wrote a lengthy letter to Jim. Percy had yet to hear that Charlie had been killed just two days before. It would be some weeks before he received the dreadful news that yet another brother had given his life. Percy's letter displays little of the enthusiasm with which he had departed Australian shores. He had mentally finished with the war, preferring instead to consider his prospects on his return.

Hurdcott
England
28-4-18
Dear Jim

I received three letters from you, two of them came while I was on leave, glad to hear you are well, but sorry you did not have a holiday for I am sure you would need one, I fully thought Mum & Dad, would have a month or two at the coast, that is what Mum wants after so much trouble. I have just come back from leave; the weather was terrible all the time I was away but all the same I had a good time. I went to Leicester first; put in most of the time there, it's a very nice place; was at Paynes saw Flo pretty often Jim, a real nice girl, while I was there Ida had a letter from you dated March, it came a lot quicker than ours. I went to Drayton & Middleton Corby, so had a little riding about, they were very pleased to see me. I intended to going to Scotland but the weather was so wet. We used to have some fun at Leicester; there were three or four girls here at times of course me being so shy, had to take a back seat. It was hard coming back from leave to sleep on boards again, and the first mornings breakfast was stew, a bit hard to take. We get good meals here as a rule. I don't expect to be here much longer; spose I will be shifting to Sutton Veny in a few days; that's the last stage. The last time I heard from the boys they were well. You seem to reckon you are on the shelf, make a strong one and both of us will be able to get on it. As you were mentioning that all the girls were booked I had better look for one for myself as well as for you. If I should send one back for you, see you have a strong body of police on the pier to see that she gets a safe landing, what I have heard of others, they have fared badly. You want a motor car Jim, that takes their eye, see the office [offers] you got from one. But wait a minute Jim, you had a nice tea at the Jones didn't you, that right get in with the old Lady first. This last few days it has been quite warm, was just my luck to strike bad weather while away. There is very few here I know. Fred Perry is the only one from up our way, you would know him dare I say, he played football for Lagoon, one of their best players; at present he is marked C.I. home service in England he had a bullet through the hand, left some of his fingers stiff. The war news has not been the best, but I think we [will] stop him, I hope he takes a tumble before I get there, I have not too much of the fighting spirit left. I tell the boys I am only going over just to see them; if I stop as long there, as I did when I went back from leave, it will do me; should not talk like that should I make you think I don't like playing soldiers, which you know I do, after a twelve month or so in France. When I was at Paynes, I was a little social, and a girl's friend of Paynes gave me a half penny for luck, it was bent about a bit. I believe it was true, wouldn't part with it for something. I got a 1918 farthing in the YMCA but lost it, I was going to send it to you. Things are getting a little dear now, and one of them appeals, "note the mistakes Jim" that's cigarettes a packet of ten ordinary, are 5 1/2 used to be 4 1/2 a week ago in France 2 1/2 now, there is no duty to pay over there funny isn't it, made in England sold cheaper in France, well it's a good thing for as regards myself I smoke more over there, they are like a comfortor when shells are playing a tune over your head. Today is Sunday, I was on a job, washing spuds we never peel the spuds now mash them skins and all allright, as long as there is not too much dirt on them; and to night I am on picket, in a little village near by; about ten of us I think. Yes Jim, Mrs Stone can spin a fair tale, I wonder can she sing, never want to take any notice of the tales. Was at a good concert here in the YMCA last night that's all there is to go to here …

To his aunt, Percy wrote:

… Mum said I ought to write to grandmother, but I think it would be better not to, she would only worry. There was a good concert here last night in the Y.M.C.A, it's the only thing to go to here. Fully thought Mum & Dad would have gone to the coast for a holiday it is what Mum wants after so much trouble. Yes things must be looking up out there, all buying motor cars, they don't know the wars on yet, in regards foodstuff and other ways; if Fritz dropped a few of his bombs near some of them they might wake up. See some very funny letters in the papers from soldiers, some of them makes the people think we are on a bit of a picnic. I would not like to see any of mine there. We get good meals here, not such a lot of stew as there generally is …

It is not apparent from the chain of letters precisely when Percy was told of Charlie's death, as some of his letters are missing. A regular writer, it is unlikely that he had failed to communicate with his family. It is clear however, that problems with communication not only contributed to disastrous outcomes on the battlefield, but made personal grief even more difficult to bear.

Hurdcott, England
2.5.18
Dear old Jim

Many thanks for your welcome letter of the 3ʳᵈ March, yes Jim news takes a lot of getting now, its only the other day I wrote to you, so do not expect much. I dare say Jim, you like going to the Easter fair, it breaks the monotony of Mologa, so you are going to have visitors, you will be set now Jim. Mrs Stone putting in a good word for Ruby "eh", she can spin a fair tale, I know she had a fair one, about me and the other you mentioned, but I hardly spoke to her. So Eddie would like to do it in, he was going strong when I left, spose he has caught that fever that is flying about. You were asking about those D.S.O and so on, Henderson got his for a stunt at Ypres, and he deserved it, the bar he got for another soon after, he is a real good in a stunt, always with the boys, I happened to be near him in the stunt; and he stopped with us all night and he had no occasion to. Davis got his for a raid in February, twelve months ago, he organised the raid, and it was a great success. Yes Jim, I'll take your advice and be on the look out for a girl for both of us; spose you want one that can knock a bag of wheat about. Expect to be moving Saturday for Sutton Veny, so I will not be long out of France. Just had to leave your letter to go on parade, that [is] what I hate when its nearly finished, to have to leave it. Had a letter from Flo yesterday, she says the last letter from Charlie he was allright also Allan.

Well Jim old boy, must close
Hoping it finds you all well
I am your loving brother
Percy

Lieutenant Colonel Robert Henderson, DSO, was an officer from the 39th Battalion. He had sailed on the *Runic* as a major in the 38th Battalion and was awarded the Distinguished Service Order for his calm leadership in the dreadful days of Passchendaele. His citation describes the actions of a man who was highly respected throughout the 3rd Division:

East of Ypres, both during operations of the 4/5th and 12/13th Octr. 1917, this Officer stood out conspicuously on account of his absolute indifference to danger and of his leadership. On the 4th when he and his Battalion had reached their objective he personally supervised the digging in and re-organisation. He then remained in the shell holes with his men – his cheerfulness and high spirits having a wonderful effect in keeping up their courage and spirits. On the 12th his Battalion was in Reserve but was quickly absorbed as reinforcements owing to very heavy casualties. The various units had become mixed up and many Officers had become casualties so that it needed vigorous action by a senior Officer on the spot to re-organise. This task was carried out admirably by Lt. Col.

HENDERSON in spite of the great difficulty due to the marshy nature of the ground and to the heavy enemy shell fire and perfect hail of machine gun bullets which were enfilading the position.

His example was a great incentive to all troops not only of his own but of other units.[1]

Lieutenant Colonel C.H. Davis of the 38th Battalion was also awarded the DSO in June 1917 for organising a composite battalion of men from the 10th Infantry Brigade to raid enemy lines at Houplines, north of Armentieres on 24 February 1917. This was the raid for which both Allan and Jack Lockett had trained and in which a shell blast had killed Corporal Paterson and wounded their mates, Charlie Mills and Spuddy Kerr. Frank Dee was also wounded in this raid.

MOLOGA

At home, letters and cards of condolence were once again arriving at the farm. These would do little to ease the overwhelming grief of losing three sons. Cousin Eddie, who had attempted to enlist on numerous occasions, wrote to suggest that the family should demand that the AIF return Allan and Percy to the safety of Australia.

12-5-18
Wattle Park
Junortoun
Dear Uncle, Auntie & Jim

I received a great shock on Friday evening to hear that poor Charlie is killed.

They saw it in the paper on Friday. Charlie wrote a letter to Mum and Hilda opened it. He said he was doing up poor Georgey grave, and he was going to have a Photo taken, and send it home. I think that it is up to Uncle & Auntie to cable over to France, or the Headquarters, and send Percy & Al back again. I will now close from your

loving cousin
Eddie

P.S
Please express my deepest sympathy. I will be sending a card along in a few days.

The *Pyramid Hill Advertiser* reported on the enormous loss the family had suffered:

> The sad news was conveyed to this district on Wednesday 8th inst, that another of our brave soldiers had paid the supreme sacrifice, that soldier being Sgt C E Marlow, of this district and husband of Mrs C Marlow, of 208 Barnard St Bendigo. Sergt Marlow left with the 3rd reinforcements for the 38th Batt. in September 1916. He was rejected twice previously owing to teeth regulations. He had been at the front for 18 months, and fought in the great battle of Messines with two other brothers and has taken part in other engagements. Sergt. Marlow, like three of his brothers won promotion in the field. He rose rapidly when the chance came to him and was recommended by his Captain and an officer of his Company for training in an officers school in England. He was unfortunately away on leave and lost his chance, which occurred a short time ago.
>
> In a competition a few months back Sgt Marlow was paraded before a Staff Captain and complimented on his perfect order in which his equipment, kit, clothes etc. Prior to leaving for the front he was hard working, industrious young man, and for a short time had worked on the share system with his uncle in the farming line, and he made a big sacrifice in going to the war. He was a popular young man, and, like his two brothers who have been killed, was well built and a typical soldier. He was a member of St Luke's Church of England, Mologa and was well known as a footballer …[2]
>
> On Sunday night a large congregation attended as St Luke's Church of England, Mologa, to pay tribute to the memory of Sergeant C.E. Marlow, who was killed in France on April 26th. The deceased soldier was one of five sons of Mr. and Mrs. C. Marlow serving the Empire and the third who has paid the

supreme sacrifice. He was a regular worshipper at the church up to the time of going on service, and was very much esteemed by all. The Rev. Mr. Nichols, writes a correspondent, preached a most impressive sermon in memoriam ...[3]

The following month the *Pyramid Hill Advertiser* published a letter of condolence sent to Sarah from Captain William Orchard of the 38th Battalion. Orchard was an accountant from Geelong who had married just prior to his departure. He had rapidly risen from the rank of private and had been wounded twice, shot in the face in March 1917 and then suffering an accidental bayonet wound in August 1918. He was awarded the Military Cross for 'conspicuous bravery and devotion to duty in action east of Ypres on 4th October, 1917'. Faced with the loss of all his officers who had been killed or wounded, he took charge under heavy fire. He was admired by all his men. [4]

Mrs Marlow has received the following letter regarding the death of her son, Charles:-

I cannot help putting pen to paper on account of the latest bereavement you have had and because of the very high esteem I had and have for your Charlie. I want to let you know that he was one of your boys whom I knew and he was held in the highest esteem by everybody. I know too well how futile words are but ask permission under the circumstances to say how sorry I am that such a grand chap should be killed by an insignificant and filthy Hun. I have known him intimately for twelve months and more and know his work. Many of the men in his ranks are better than their officers, to say nothing of the sergeants. I can tell you truthfully that I have often said to myself – The Marlow's are better men than I am. They ought to be leading me instead of the other way about. You have lost in him one of those few real white men we know and again hear of, and I have lost a real friend and companion, to say nothing of the best N.C.O. I ever knew. I always felt safer myself and happier in nasty places when the Marlows were about. Please express my sympathy to Charlie's wife. I thought it better to write to you. I think I understand how she will be feeling now, as I left Australia in the same circumstances as he did.

Yours truly,
W.H. ORCHARD [5]

Company Commander Major Arthur Maudsley also wrote to Sarah, promising that, with Percy's return to the front now imminent, he would endeavour to keep her son from danger:

In France
8ᵗʰ May 1918
Dear Mrs Marlow

It was with much sorrow and regret that I learnt of your dear son Sergeant C E Marlow being killed on the morning of 26ᵗʰ April. I had not been away from the line more than a couple of hours when I heard of the sad occurrence & had been talking to him for a few minutes when I had been up inspecting the line – it evidently was a stray bullet that killed him – still these things will be and Gods Will be Done. He and his brothers were ideal fellows & respected by all as an ideal man. Your four boys have all served under me in my Company and no praise was or is too high for them. Lieut AS Marlow is doing exceedingly well and your other boy is expected back to the battalion any day & I will do what I can to keep him out of harm's way. Please accept my deepest sympathy

Yours sincerely
A.J. Maudsley Major

Major Maudsley was himself killed a few months after writing to Sarah. He was Mentioned in Despatches on 28 May 1918 and died under shellfire on 31 August at Clery-sur-Somme.[6]

FRANCE, MAY

As the Allied forces waited expectantly for a further German attempt to breach the line, the Australians began to engage in their own private war with the enemy. From April to July, the tactic of 'peaceful penetration' became infamous along the fronts held by the Australians and New

Zealanders. This tactic suited the Australian character as it involved the men in ingenious acts of stealth which developed spontaneously but soon became carefully planned sorties occurring daily along the line. The Australians' aggression and their success as they moved along the German front, capturing entire posts and taking hundreds of prisoners, dealt enemy morale a severe blow.[7] Prisoners, once relieved of their possessions by their captors, were known to reveal that the German soldier did not want to fight against Australians.

In mid-May 1918, the commander of the 3rd Division, Lieutenant General John Monash, was appointed to command the Australian Corps, with Birdwood moving to command of the Fifth Army. Major General John Gellibrand took over the 3rd Division. All Australian divisions were now commanded by Australians. This army of volunteers was spirited, tough and fiercely loyal to their battalions; but with every battle they won, and every day in the front line, they were running out of men.

The Australians had spent seven weeks moving in and out the trenches. They were exhausted, having received little rest for their shattered nerves and tired bodies. The 38th marched out to Allonville some 15 kilometres to the west of Ribemont and remained there for a fortnight. They left just prior to a German bombardment of their camp that killed 18 men from the 14th Battalion.

For Allan, the opportunity to rest and write home came as a welcome relief, an escape from the furore and uncertainty of life in the trenches:

France
Sunday
12-5-18
Dear Jim,

Just a few lines to let you know that I am in the best of health & I hope that you are all the same. I heard from K. Haw that you had been very ill, I can tell you I was very sorry to hear it & I hope that your are better ere this. Well dear old Jim we came out of the line a couple of days ago after a strenuous go, I can tell you it is a well earned rest. Our boys fought gallantly and have gained a high reputation over here. Well dear Jim I do miss dear old Charlie. I wonder how things are at home. It is a terror to loose 3 brothers. I suppose dear mum is broken up completely. Do your best to cheer them up a little I am doing my best to get Percy home I hope it works alright. I had a letter last night from him. He [is] still in England. I suppose you are very busy over there with the crops again. I think we will be home for the next harvest alright. Well Jim I met Dave Smith, Joe Walls, K Haw yesterday. They all look well & I was dam pleased to have a yarn with them. Well dear Jim I got 3 or 4 letters from you the other day & they were about 4 or 5 months old but still there was news in them. We have been very lucky for mail lately. In fact we have been lucky right through. I sent you all my photo before Charlie was killed I hope you get them all. Well dear Jim I am in the best of health and have not had a day away from the battalion though I am only telling you this in case you think I have been sick. Well dear Jim I am having a nice cross put up over Charlie like we put up over Geordie & Albert. I have plenty of money. No need to send any over. I have got £6 mum sent me. And many thanks for sending it. Well dear Jim I think I have told you all the news so will close with best to all.

I remain
Your Loving Brother
Allan SM

Allan continued his attempts to have Percy repatriated to Australia despite the military machinations that seemed intent on sending his brother back to the killing fields of France. The death of three members of the family in the space of nine months had taken its toll on those at home and the surviving sons abroad. Allan was determined that Percy should not return to the battlefields of Europe; the risk of another death was too great. But Allan could control neither the might of the military nor the workings of fate.

As Allan was writing to Jim, so was Tom Alford who wrote describing his involvement in the defence of Villers-Bretonneux. Like Allan, he had become fatalistic and his talk of receiving a 'full issue', while tragic, was simply now the soldiers' reality. They had witnessed enormous destruction, brutality and death and now carried that burden every minute of their time at the front.

France
Sunday May 12th
Dear Old Jimmy,

Expect you will be looking for a letter from me before this reaches you. I've pretty nearly given up writing letters altogether now. A few home and an odd one to you is about all I write. Your latest one was dated March 3rd. Glad to hear from you again & that you were all fairly well. As usual it is raining again not heavy but just enough to make things miserable especially if your damn dug-out leaks like ours. It never rains very heavy in France. Your just about right Jim I've pretty well forgot about crops etc. & it is about sickening this job day after day. We [have] been in hot and strong again this last 8 weeks but I still dodge the hun. It makes you feel a bit off to see the chaps getting nice little "Blightys" & hear of the times they have in Hospitals & leave in England. I think I have had as much continuous service as most & would not mind a spell out of France for a while but I suppose I must consider myself lucky to be alive after what we've been through. You only seem to come out of one stunt to catch another. It's a moral one can't go on for ever. I suppose a man will get a full issue one of these days. Expect you will not think this letter very cheering but you get sick of it not so much the actual fighting but the bloody bullshit known as red-tape & discipline. They reckon discipline is the main thing but I notice the Ausys, tho are supposed to have very little discipline, generally come out on top. The poor bleeding Tommies are hounded down that much that they get very little encouragement to act on their on initiative if placed in a tight place. Your boys Division have been close to us but I haven't come across their Brigade yet. I suppose you will know before this that we are down on the old Somme again only a damn sight further back than ever. It seems damn hard to think that a bit earlier than this last year we were going past Bapaume & about this time just coming out of Bullecourt but its all the same I don't care a damn. I worry about nothing now, just take the good with the bad. It is wonderful how the troop knock the hun out at times. Our Brigade got great praise in the retaking of Villiers Bretoneaux in conjunction with a 4th Divy Brigade. She was a pretty hot joint I give you the oil. I tell you Fritz had me thinking a few times. The troops put the bayonets into him thick and heavy. It would make you laugh to hear some of the tales the lads tell. Mologa seems to be doing well in loves affairs lately. I saw photos of Peter Cox wedding *in a Bendigonian. It must be funny with Bob & Mollie. There is no doubt she wants a man badly. What the hell are you doing? to see a nice tab like her wanting. She is the pick of the district. God bless my soul it makes you feel like standing on your head to hear about it. There won't be many left single by all accounts directly. I expect you will have heard that Wilson Townsend was wounded in this last stunt. I saw their doctor & he said he didn't think it was serious, although the back is a nasty place to get hurt in. Good luck to him I hope it takes him home. There seems to be a good many soldiers returning to Ausy lately by the papers. A good many have gone from this Batt.*

Well think this is all this time, so will close, hoping you are all well
From your old pal
Tom Alford

Wilson Townsend was a farmer from Mologa who had enlisted in May 1916 at the age of 22. Wilson had joined the 60th Battalion while his cousin Leslie was serving with the 38th. Wilson's battalion was later amalgamated with the 59th in which Tom Alford served. Wilson was hit in the back by shrapnel and returned to Australia in June 1919. His mother had passed away 12 months earlier.[8]

On 20 May Allan sent a photo postcard to Eva Jones, the young lady who lived near the Marlow homestead at Mologa and was often mentioned in letters home to Jim.

The now damaged photo that Allan sent to Eva Jones.

France 20-5-
Dear Eva

Just a few lines to let you know I am well and hope that you all are too

We are having magnificent weather … and of course things are all terrible willing

The hun is getting a very rough time [though] *not as rough as I would like to see him. Percy is still in England and I hope* [he stays] *there. We lost dear old Charlie a few weeks back and I do miss him. It is awful … loosing 3 brothers. Well Eva on the other side you will notice somebody you may know. Cheerio I remain your loving friend Allan*

Joe Stone, brother of Myrtle, who was now staying with and assisting the Marlows on the farm, wrote to Jim from hospital in France. He was recovering from a gas attack in May. He, too, shared the fatalistic attitude of the hardened soldier.

Hospital
France
24/5/18
Dear Old Sport

Just a line in haste hoping it finds all in the best of health. Well Jim I suppose you will know long before you get this I got a whiff of Jerry's Gas I have had it 14 days I cant talk yet but I suppose I will make up for lost time when I start. I met Harry Street as I came through Field Ambulance he had a poisoned finger. He was telling me about Poor Old Charlie that was the first I heard about it. My word Jim your boys are having hard luck But one never knows when his turn is coming in this game. Well Jim there is practically no news here only it is like Spring at Home plenty of Grass &
Flowers and [censored] *to eat it.*

Well Jim I think I will ring off

I remain
Your Sincere Pal
Joe

Love to all Mologa Girls

Now back in the line, Allan wrote to his family:

France
25-5-1918
Dear Jim

Just a few lines to let you know that I am well & I do hope that you all are the same. We are situated in a most beautiful part of France and the weather is magnificent so what is wrong with that. Well Jim we are back in the line about [not completed – near Blangy-Tronville eight kilometres west of Villers-Bretonneux]. *We have just had about 10 days rest after over 50 days in the line. It is pretty strenuous going still but we are winning so that is the main thing. Well Jim you will have heard of the bad news about dear old Charlie. It is a terror and I do miss him. It is a terrible blow to me. Percy is still in England and is doing well I don't think he will ever come back here. I have done my best to get him home and I think it will work. Let us hope so anyway. Well Jim I heard from H Haw that you was very bad. I have not had any letters about it and I hope it is not so. I sent you all some photos of mine a little while ago and I hope you got them alright. They were not much good but still they were better than none. Well Jim I suppose you all are up to your neck in work again now as you would be busy with the crops. I received a very nice parcel from Dolly Mahoney last week and a parcel of socks from Miss Opie it was jolly good of them. Well Jim old boy I think I have told you all the news so will close with best love to all*

I remain
Your Loving Brother
Allan

All the Mologa boys are well.

I am writing this in a dugout and the shells are flying about.
Never publish any of my letters.

Allan wrote to his father on a series of postcards of the Royal Mews, Buckingham Palace, London:

CHAPTER 21

France
25-5-1918
My Dear Dad

I am writing a few lines to let you know that I am well and am glad to hear that you all are the same. I received your welcome letter tonight and I was so delighted I got 6 from you all and one each from Aunt Liz & Etta and no doubt I will get more to morrow. Well dad I am always pleased to get yours. I know how difficult it is to always write. Well dear dad it is awful losing dear old Charlie & I do miss him. I have had a nice cross put up over him like dear old Geordie & Albert. Dad it is awfully hard. But we must expect someone to go. No one knows what things are like. I can tell you we have had a terrible ruff spin this last few months and [the] boys fight gallantly. We have gained a high reputation amongst the French people. We get great letters of praise from the French people. We just finished a 50 day tour in the front line and then we had 10 days rest and now we are back in it again. We are fighting in a most beautiful part of France and the weather is magnificent. All the Mologa boys are doing well. All leave has been stopped since the Bosch opened his little stunt up. But as soon as it opens I am off to Paris for a few days leave. Well dear dad you seem to be having pretty wet weather over there again. It is very nice of M. Stone to come over and stay with you. She is a jolly good girl. I often get letters from her and she has sent parcels beauties too I can tell you. I do appreciate those sort of people kindness. I got a parcel of socks from Miss Opie and a parcel from Dolly Mahoney. I get letters regular from all relatives in England. What a bonnie welcome Spuddy Kerr got. He deserves every bit of it. Well dear dad the views are some I got while on leave in England and I have all the places & people concerned. I have a number of them so I will send them along to you. I have also some Fritz souvenirs which I will also send along. Well dear dad I think I have told you all the news so will close with best love to you all.

So goodbye dear dad
I remain
Your Loving Son
Allan XXX

Percy is still in England and have a decent time. He has been there about 5 months now. I am doing my best to have him returned and I hope it works. Goodbye dear Dad

Allan XXXXX

The 38th was bivouacked on the Somme River at Blangy-Tronville between Amiens and Villers-Bretonneux. The men were involved in the dangerous task of laying cable to forward areas under cover of darkness. Between spasmodic enemy bombardments, they also took the opportunity to bathe in the cool water of the river and go fishing, which usually involved throwing grenades into the water and gathering the stunned fish.

Postcard of Royal Footman & Letter
France 27-5-18
Dear Jim

Well old boy I wonder how you are now. I am in the best of health and we are just waiting for the hun to attack. Yes that is true about the Aussies anxiously waiting for him. I never seen the boys more anxious. Our lads hoe into line right and left. It is a beautiful day and at 4 oclock I am taking my boys down to the river for a swim. Remember the days when we used to swim in the old creek. We are fighting beside the French now and I met a couple of French officers the other day. They asked me out to tea so I went and I had a royal tea. The French soldiers are splendid fighters. Well Jim if you don't get plenty of letters from me well I don't know what is wrong. I have wrote about 12 letters & postcards this last few days. I sent home a little parcel of souvenirs again I hope you get them. Do you ever get the Anzac bulletin I send you. I send one every week. If you don't get [them] well I will cut them out … Percy is still in England having a decent rest. I am doing my best to have him sent home & I hope it works …

The following day Allan wrote again to Jim:

… I received a most beautiful parcel from [home] last night. It was addressed Charlie but worst luck dear old Charlie is not here to receive it. The cakes arrived in splendid order and they are beautiful. Last night

the Adjutant of the Battalion and I were asked out to tea to the 59ᵗʰ Batt. and I got a very pleasant shock when I met Tom Alford by jove I was pleased. He looks well and is going to have tea with us to night so we will have some of mums cake. He told me Wilson Townsend was wounded. I am sending you a letter I got from M Forsyth it is the first and I don't know her at all. Percy was writing to her and I put a footnote on his letter. Well Jim old boy I have told you all the news so will close with best love to all.

I remain
Your Loving Brother
Allan SM

Myrtle Forsyth had written to Percy and to George prior to his death. Her earlier letter to George and the following to Allan suggest that it was in her nature to write flirtatiously to those soldiers with whom she corresponded. Allan was amused enough to enclose her letter with his own to Jim.

"Brookleigh"
Milloo P.O.
Via Prairie
Australia
Jan 30ᵗʰ 1918

My Dearest Ducky Darling Allan,
Beg Pardon, Hardly the way to address a real live Lieutenant, that, I'll make a fresh start,

"To Lieutenant Allan Marlow, I.D.",
Dear Sir

Don't quite appreciate that style either so I shall try again by addressing you as "Dear Allan", First of all please accept my congratulations on your promotion, not on your promotion to Censor though, for I consider that is just a little too much of a promotion, well when its my letters you are censoring anyway. Talk about girls being inquisitive "they are not in it" when compared with you. No doubt you quite enjoy reading the poor old boys love letters, "thank goodness I don't receive such things", or know what they are , just imagine you knowing all my secrets, it would be too awful to think of. Tell me? Do you always add a postcript to all the letters you censor. At anyrate Allan you should be well versed in the subject of love letters when your present role is over. I presume you find not a few love letters amongst the correspondence. And you should be an adept at the game of writing them when "occasion" demands them, but a little bird whispers you are not a stranger in that respect. But oh I do think you are an "inquisitive" little "devil" to go and read your brother's letter to me (You will no doubt "comprey" the meaning of "I.D" after your name) And if ever I have the chance of reading any of your letters I shall certainly avail myself of that pleasure. Now to answer your question, I certainly do wish they were real and I know it is only a case of "sour grapes" with you and as I am sending Percy a few paper ones and expressing a wish that they were real ones. I shall also send you some and express the same wish so as you won't be jealous of your little brother. You inquisitive devil. But I spose I had better cease my nonsense as not being very well acquainted with you I may offend you but it would serve you right (I don't think). I believe I have met you once may have been twice at Mahoneys, I remember I was playing football with you one Sunday, but it is hardly likely you will remember such a thing as that now (too high up in the world). I am enclosing this in Percy's letter, not knowing your number, and am going to ask him to deliver it to you (I hope he reads it first). Now I think I have told you just how mean I think you are so will close with

Best Wishes and XXXXXXXXXXXXXXXXXXXXXXXXXXXXXXXXX
From your sincere friend XXXXXXXXXXXXXXXXXXXXXXXXXXXXXXXX
Myrtle Forsyth XXXXXXXXXXXXXXXXXXXXXXXXXXXXXXXX
I wish they were real also that there was room to add a few more Allan

Be good
MF

Though a playful letter from Myrtle was not what Allan had expected, he looked forward to the parcels and letters that Eva Jones and her family were sending and continued to write to Eva at Mologa — letters she chose to keep:

France
29-5-1918
Dear Eva,

Just a few lines to let you know that I am still going strong and in the best of health and spirits. I received a very nice Ausy mail three nights ago and was delighted with same. All at home seem to be pretty well although Jim had been sick, but I heard that unofficially. Well Eva we are having [a] very strenuous time since the Hun offered up his offensive we are kept very busy in the front line since the opera opened. Now we are anxiously waiting for him to attack again. He has had quite a number of minor attacks at us but between the artillery, machine gun and rifle fire he finds it impossible to succeed. Last night was the most anxious night we ever put in. He was supposed to attack on the whole front but unfortunately he never. We put a tremendous bombardment down on him and I'll bet there was a good number of huns gone west. We are fighting down in a most beautiful part of France. The scenery is glorious and the weather is glorious so there is nothing wrong with that. Well Eva you will have heard by this time that dear old Charlie has been killed. It is awful to think that 3 brothers have gone. Poor old Mother will be in a terrible state again. There is one thing that Percy is out of it for awhile he is still in Blighty and has had 5 months of it now. Well Eva I have no more news to night so will close with kind regards to all.

I remain
Your Sincere Friend
Allan S Marlow

TWENTY TWO
HE WAS A GALLANT
YOUNG SOLDIER

THE WESTERN FRONT, JUNE

By June, the German forces were exhausted. To the north in Flanders
the Allies had held the line, beating back the German offensive. South
of the Somme, American forces had arrived and fought off a German
attack on the Marne and there were additional American troops
arriving daily. Australian battalions, usually at around 1000 men, were
now down, in some cases to 300; there were no reinforcements arriving
from Australia.

Allan's war records indicate that he was appointed Battalion Lewis
Gun Officer on 8 June 1918. Two days later he was seconded for
duty with the 1st Australian Convalescent Depot at Le Havre on the
French coast for duty as censor. Three weeks earlier, the commanding
officer of the 38th Battalion, Lieutenant Colonel Davis, had been
promoted colonel and appointed to a leadership position at Le
Havre. It would be interesting to know who made the decision to
remove Allan from the line. Was it Davis, the commanding officer
who had been with his men from the battalion's inception, or Major
Maudsley who, in his letter of condolence, had promised Sarah that
he would do his best to keep Percy from harm? For Allan the decision
was met with mixed emotions; to leave the family of his battalion
and his cobbers from D Company was difficult as they had been
through so much. But his parents had lost three sons. The Marlow
family had sacrificed enough.

Allan did not reveal the reasons for his base duties in his letters home.
Years later, Jack Lockett provided an explanation when he described
the order 'Akers' received to leave the front. Allan had almost certainly

been posted as a result of the losses to the family. With three brothers killed, the AIF moved to limit the chances of yet another Marlow death. While Allan's attempts to have Percy repatriated had yet to bear fruit, he now found himself removed from the line. His duties presented a stark contrast to his earlier role at the front and, despite the safety of his position, his later letters reveal his eagerness to return to the line and to his 'boys'. His frustration is clearly evident.

During this period, the 38th Battalion had been moving in and out of the line around the shattered village of Villers-Bretonneux. Good friend and neighbour, Peter Owens, was wounded on 4 June, along with George Collison, whose wounding on 11 June resulted in the loss of his leg. Ewen Johnson of the 60th Battalion, who had married in England only a few weeks earlier, suffered his third serious wound. Despite the severity of this wound, he survived to return to Australia.

From June there are few letters, perhaps because a number of ships were lost from June to August 1918. HMAT A69 *Warilda*, carrying wounded soldiers and emblazoned with the red cross of a hospital ship, was torpedoed and sunk while crossing the channel on 3 August with the loss of 123 lives. HMAT A43 *Barunga* was also torpedoed and sunk on 15 July while en route to Australia with 855 invalided soldiers, all of whom survived. It is highly likely that Australian mail was lost as the family at Mologa did not receive any correspondence from Allan during the months of June and July. Writing to Jim in December, Allan could not provide a reason for the failure of his letters to reach home. I suspect they were lost somewhere in the North Atlantic.

But the family at Mologa did receive a letter from Percy in England dated 23 June. This letter provides some clue to the movements of the brothers, but nothing of Allan's experiences as he made the transition to Le Havre. While Percy does not mention the death of Charlie, he is likely to have received the letters from Allan informing him of the death of their brother.

Warminster
England
23.6.18
Dear Jim

… I will be pleased to get that snap of you, I have not got a photo of you. I put a photo in I had taken when on sick leave, it's the best I have ever had taken. I heard from Allan the other day he was detailed for Base Duties, so he is at L'Havre now, so he will have a bit of a spell out of the trenches, he needs it too. We are having nice weather now; its about the best time in England now. I am still working in the sergeants mess, it will do me for a stunt. Well Jim, old boy, I spose you are up to your eyes in work now.

Well Jim, I must ring off now, hoping you are all well.
I remain your loving brother
Percy

JULY

July was the month that Australian Lieutenant General John Monash was to make his mark on the battlefields of World War I. Between Villers-Bretonneux and Albert lies the village of Le Hamel which remained in German hands. Monash, in his first major action as a corps commander, combined artillery, tanks, infantry and aircraft to take the village in 93 minutes in one of the best-planned attacks of World War I. He had hoped it would take 90. The enemy line was bombarded and gassed then, as brigades from the 2nd, 3rd and 4th divisions and some American companies moved forward, aircraft bombed Le Hamel. The roar of the bombing masked the sound of 60 rumbling Mark V tanks, a faster, more robust version of its predecessors. As the tanks protected the infantry, aircraft destroyed German machine-gun nests. Monash's moment arrived on 4 July 1918. His combined arms battle plan became a model for further Allied offensives in 1918.[1] French Prime Minister Georges Clemenceau was so delighted by the Australians' success that he rushed to the front to offer his thanks. He addressed a group of the troops who had taken Le Hamel:

When the Australians came to France, the French people expected a great deal from you … We knew that you would fight a real fight, but we did not know that from the very beginning you would astonish the whole continent … I shall go back tomorrow and say to my countrymen: "I have seen the Australians. I have looked in their faces. I know that these men … will fight alongside of us again until the cause for which we are all fighting is safe for us and our children."

The fighting during July had taken a further toll on the mates of the Marlow brothers. Jim Stone, brother of Joe and Myrtle, was wounded on 9 July but would return to his battalion in October. Charlie Cockcroft was badly wounded on 29 July; he recovered to be married in England in November and to return to Australia in December. Tom Alford was wounded on 5 July; his wound was listed as slight and he continued on duty. Tom did not get the 'Blighty' he so desperately wanted.

AUGUST

Rumours of a 'big push' were to become reality. On 8 August, at 4.20 am, with the British advancing in the north, the 2nd, 3rd, 4th and 5th Australian divisions and the Canadian Corps advanced together in the Amiens Offensive. This was the beginning of what became known as the Hundred Days Offensive, a series of Allied victories from August until November which saw German forces pushed back and villages reclaimed in an advance of extraordinary rapidity. The offensive was launched on 8 August, the soldiers tasked with destroying the enemy positions south of the Somme; the French attacked still further to the south. Under the veil of dense river fog and a barrage of artillery fire, the men pushed forward to take the German line in the most significant advance made by Allied troops to that point. By nightfall, the Australians alone had advanced over 11 kilometres, taken 8000 prisoners and 173 guns. By 12 August, Australia had suffered another 5991 casualties, but had advanced 20 kilometres towards the Hindenburg Line and taken 10,000 German prisoners.[2] The success of the offensive forced the German General Ludendorff to admit that '… the 8th August was the black day of the German Army in the war … The war must be ended.'[3] American forces had arrived on the front and German troops would soon be outnumbered. At home, the German people were starving. Ludendorff knew it was time to negotiate. The Kaiser did not.

The advance across the 1916 Somme battlefields continued. Series after series of shattering blows hit the enemy as village defences crumbled. The morale of the Allied troops soared and those not in the 'big push' were considered to have missed something remarkable. Allan wrote briefly of the advance and his disappointment at not being involved as the relentless advance pushed the German army back to the defences of the Hindenburg Line.

France
15-8-18
Dear Jim

I have just received a lovely lot of mail from Ausy and am awfully delighted. I was very pleased to hear that you all were well and that dear old grannie is on the mend. You all seem terribly worried according to letters you had only got word I have told you in previous letters how dear old Charlie was killed. Mum asked in her letter if Charlie ever regretted coming away. Well Jim not once did he. Many a talk we [had] over all the business and he never regretted it once. Those dear boys were to go but it is awfully hard on us but we must cheer up a little you need not worry over us as I am at the base and Percy is in England. There is some awful heavy fighting going on up the line I wish I was back with my boys. I have had several letters from my captain and the boys wishing that I was back with them. My Captain [Orchard] was the [best] man ever I met and the boys simply worship him. You seem awfully busy over there. Well Jim I hope you have a good harvest. I just received you & mums lovely parcel and I must thank you it is simply beautiful. None of the other boys are here to get the cigs. Well dear Jim this is all the news to night so will close with best love to all.

I remain
Your Loving Brother
Allan

On the day Allan wrote home he was unaware that Percy was crossing the channel, arriving back in France on the same day, perhaps in time to share the cigarettes. Percy's time in Blighty had come to an end. He left Longbridge Deverill and boarded his ship at Folkestone on 14 August. After some seven months, Allan had a brief opportunity to see his brother at Le Havre before embarking for England; he was on duty but also looking forward to taking some leave to visit his cousins. By 18 August Percy was back with his unit.

From London, Allan wrote to Jim:

Hyde Park Corner S.W.I
21-8-1918
Dear Jim

Just a few lines to let you know that I arrived here safely with the draft but have to take them to Fovant to morrow. I am getting a few days leave so will be going to Leicester this time only about 4 days leave but it will do me. Well Jim old boy we are having glorious weather and I ought to have a nice time to Leicester. I'll be going to see Aunt Charlotte and Uncle Ted. I have not seen Uncle Ted yet. Well Jim old boy I suppose [you] are awfully busy over there now. I do hope you have a good harvest. They have had record harvests over here. Just before I left France I had a beautiful parcel & a lot of letters from home. I am very pleased you are getting my mail alright. There seems to be a lot of old people dying. Well Jim the war news is splendid now. Our boys are doing well. Just before I left I met Percy he was looking well he was at the base. Yes Jim it is awful loosing those 3 dear boys & I find it awfully hard I do miss them. Yes poor Charlie was killed right out. He never spoke a word. He had a very nice burial & I had put a nice cross over him. In London now there is a big strike on, no buses running at all and I hear that the underground train people are going to strike. It is b- awful. Well Jim old [boy] I might be returning for 6 months shortly. I would like to get home for a few months just see how you all are but I won't be staying. Well Jim old boy I can't write anymore. I want to go to bed as I have to get up early in the morning.

Well goodbye Jim old boy and best love to all
I remain Your loving brother
Allan SM

The Alexandra Hotel
London
26-8-1918
Dear Jim

Just a few lines to let you know that I came down from Leicester to night. I had a very nice time indeed. All up there were splendid. I never saw them looking better. Uncle John Wilson was awfully busy with the harvests. They are having record harvests over here so I hope you have the same over there. Well Jim old boy what do you think of the war news now. Isn't it splendid I think we will have the hun defeated by February. Let us hope so anyway. He is getting an awful towelling up now....

On the same day, Allan penned another letter to Eva Jones:

The Alexandra Hotel
Hyde Park Corner, S.W.I.
London
26-8-1918
Dear Eva

Just a few lines to let you know that I am splendid & sincerely hope that you all are the same. Many thanks for the lovely cake you sent me it was lovely. Well Eva you will see by the above address that I am in Blighty. I brought a draft of men over here and then they gave me a few days leave. I go back tomorrow morning. I spent my leave in Leceister with relatives & had a very nice time. The people over here are having record harvests and are awfully busy as they are not given much time to get them up. Well Eva I suppose you all are pleased with the war news now. I think we will have the rotter beaten by new year, let us hope so anyway. Eva I am always looking for one of those nice long letters of yours and I know there must be one on the water on its way across. Well Eva this is all the news tonight so cheerio and kind regards to all.

I remain
Your old Friend
Allan S

FRANCE, AUGUST

Now recovered from the effects of gas, Joe Stone had returned to his battalion. He wrote to Jim of the emotional impact of being in the line and of his thoughts on 'catching a bride' in Scotland:

France
30/8/18
Dear Jim

Just a line in haste hoping it finds all in the Best of health as it leaves me at present. Well Jim you will have to excuse me for not writing before but we have been pretty busy of late as you will have seen by the papers but we are out for a bit of a Breather at present & I can tell you we can do with it a constant going makes ones nerves <u>pretty</u> strung up & the only way is have a good spell. I had a letter from brother Jim the other day he had met Percy in Blighty I hope to be over there in a fortnights time as I have not had Blighty leave for 16 months and it won't do any harm to see the old place again. I am going to spend part of my leave in Scotland & see if I can leave it without catching a <u>bride</u>. They say it is hard to do. I say Jim how are all those Bonnie Wee Lassies in Mologa getting on. I suppose they are all caught by now. I suppose you will be doing your dash one of these days. I don't see anything over here that catches my eye so far. They tell me Pearly [Saville] and Tom have dissolved partnership & she is going with a guy up Pyramid way. Well Jim news are scarce so I will write a longer one when I get Blighty.

I remain
Your Old Cobber
Joe

Remember me to all

The 'breather' was not to last. The Australians were ordered to continue to push towards the Hindenburg Line, the 38th taking the village of Curlu on 28 August. On 31 August Monash sent the 2nd and 5th divisions to capture Mont St Quentin and the old moated fortress of Peronne. The 3rd Division was to attack Clery-sur-Somme just a few kilometres to the north-west of Mont St Quentin and then advance to Bouchavesnes Spur. In a fast-moving fight, the under-strength and exhausted but spirited Australian soldiers continued to move forward against enormous odds. By 2 September they had taken Mont St Quentin, an apparently impregnable German stronghold, which had been captured in one of the greatest single feats of the war.

Of the 38th Battalion, Charles Bean wrote:

> … the 3rd Division day after day had forced its way along the slopes and valleys north of the river, seizing Bray, Susanne and Curlu. The staff of the 38th Battalion, after seventy-one hours continuous work was just settling to sleep when Brig.-General W. R. Nicoll arrived with the order to push on immediately to Clery, at the actual [Somme] river bend; after dark on the 29th, at the end of eighty-nine hours of almost continuous effort, the battalion reached the eastern edge of that village.[4]

This period of the fighting saw astounding acts of personal bravery with men displaying indomitable courage and inspiring others. Corporal Albert Grinton of Tragowel, Victoria, won the Distinguished Conduct Medal on 31 August 1918, his citation describing his extraordinary pluck:

> For conspicuous gallantry and devotion to duty near Clery on 31st August, 1918. He became detached from his company and joined another party for the advance. Mainly through his assistance with a Lewis Gun, they cleared an enemy trench, killing about thirty men and capturing several machine guns. He got on top of the trench, and, under heavy fire, silenced a field gun which was firing over open sights.[5]

Grinton returned to Australia with his older brother, Jack, to farm on the northern outskirts of Bendigo. Almost 90 years on, when cleaning out a shed on the farm, Jack's daughter found an old tin with postcards, letters and unexposed film, some 896 photos of the movements of the 38th Battalion during its time on the Western Front. While soldiers were banned from possessing cameras, an offence punishable by court martial, the men always found a way to circumvent the rules.[6]

It is not clear exactly where Percy was as the Australians pushed forward. From later correspondence it appears that he was with the battalion but not in the front line; he was acting as a guide, responsible for directing troops to their positions in the line. What we do know is that Major Maudsley, the officer who had promised to keep Sarah's son from harm, had now become a casualty himself, killed by a shell on 31 August during the push to Clery-sur-Somme.

Knowlson Haw.

Other friends and neighbours of the Marlow brothers had also fared badly. Charlie's mate Knowlson Haw of the 37th Battalion had left the farm at Mologa and had arrived in France in January 1918. He was wounded on 23 August. Archie Bailey of the 7th Battalion was shot in the arm on 9 August in the action at Lihons for which he was awarded the Military Medal; it was the fourth time he had been seriously wounded. Charlie Wales of the 6th Battalion was killed near Lihons on 9 August; he had also been shot the previous September. Gordon Swainston had been shot on 10 August but returned a week later. He was shot again in the hand on 8 September in his final action; he would return to Australia in January 1919.

Most devastating of all was the news that Allan and Percy had lost their close neighbour, family friend and one of their best mates. Lance Corporal David (Les) Townsend had enlisted with Allan and Percy in the 38th Battalion and was a machine-gunner in D Company. He had sailed with the twins on the *Runic*. At Mologa they had been at school together, played football in the same team and also attended church as members of the congregation of St Luke's Church of England. Les had fought with the Marlows at Messines and had been wounded at Passchendaele on 4 October in the rush to take the area where Tyne Cot Cemetery now sits. He returned to the front three months later. He was killed by a sniper at Curlu on 28 August.

Allan described Les Townsend as being like a brother. This photo was taken in Bendigo in the same studio in which Allan and Percy had their photos taken prior to embarking.

Letters from the local boys arrived home and appeared in the *Pyramid Hill Advertiser.* Harry Street, who had cried when leaving Larkhill for France and whose brother Will had been killed, was now an experienced veteran.

Dear Friends,

No doubt you will have heard of Leslie's death long before you get this letter … The bullet was from a sniper and it hit Les in the centre of the forehead. German machine guns and snipers have a strong outpost and were giving our lads much annoyance. So Leslie's Company (D) and my own (C) were trying to capture the post or put Fritz out of action, and Leslie probably exposed himself too much and Fritz got him. I was talking to Les just a few minutes before and he was looking very well on it. However, he has had a decent burial. I was there, and his grave is only about two chains from where I am writing this. You have my greatest sympathy in regard to Leslie's death. He was well liked in his company. We have lost some fine lads lately. We have just finished 7 days of almost continuous fighting and I am almost knocked up. We have driven the Germans a long way back, but I fear peace will not come this year. The weather is fairly fine. I trust that I shall return to good old Aussie safely and give you all the news.

Yours truly,
H STREET

Private Bennett also wrote:

… We had been following up the river for five days. Les was at the right of the advancing troops at the place where he and three others fell. It was a very nasty place to take – steep hills on three sides; the Somme with its low lying, swampy ground, covered with tall reeds and trees; on the other the Huns had a machine gun hidden. I was there a few minutes afterwards and heard what had occurred, but did not see or hear who had fallen. It was a great shock two days afterwards on going round to see how my friends had fared. Les and his mates sleep on a gentle rise overlooking the Somme, only a few hundred yards from where they fell. A wooden cross with name, age and other particulars marks the spot – 29/8/18 in his case. God rest his gallant soul…[7]

Albie Brookes wrote to Les's parents, telling a poignant tale of comradeship:

… I must express my greatest sympathy in your son Les being killed. Through his death I have lost one of my best pals, and I can assure you that the company to which he belonged, D.Coy., have lost one of the best and bravest of lads. I came away with a great number of the Pyramid lads, as you remember. We were all machine gunners, but on proceeding to France we were split up and put into different companies. For all that, when out of the line, we were always together. Our little crew has gradually got smaller and at the time of poor Les' death only he and I were with the Batt. It was our custom when coming out of a stunt or trip in the line to look around for each other to see how we had fared, and many were the talks we had of old folks and times at Yarrawalla. Just before we went into the last stunt, I was round congratulating Les, on getting his second stripe, which he had earned months before receiving. The military authorities have notified you, no doubt, and perhaps you have heard from H. Street, but I thought you might like a little detail as to Les' death. As you know, the tables have turned in our favour lately and we have been pushing the enemy well back, the Australians taking a great part in it. Our Batt. had a rough spin and we were expecting a relief but were required to take a village called Curlu during the day, and A. and B. to follow the next morning. While they were advancing D. Coy. was held up by the enemy with machine gun fire and sniping. It was almost impossible to proceed, so the head of the column, made for the machine gun and Les. being amongst them and always ready to do his bit got sniped through the head. There is little consolation in knowing that the poor fellow suffered no pain, death being instantaneous. I received the news just as we were starting up ourselves and it fair knocked me. We breakfasted at the spot next morning and I learned where Les. had fallen, and immediately made for the spot, but was just too late, which did not make me feel any better for the day's work. But I was a little more at ease when I learned that the stretcher-bearers had carried him away. After coming out of the trenches I learned where his grave was and visited it. One cross is erected; on same are the words "In memory of Corpl. Les. Townsend, killed in action."At the time of writing this I am in a pokey dugout, barely room to move, so you will excuse the writing. We are looking for relief, which is expected tonight …[8]

Allan also wrote to the Townsend family:

… I wrote to you immediately after the death of our dear old Les., but have since heard that the mail had gone down, so thought it my duty to write again. Words alone cannot express my greatest sympathy towards you all in the loss of dear old Les., who was killed by a bullet near Curlu in one of our advances on the Bosch. He was killed instantly along with three other boys, and a cross has been erected over his grave. I know exactly how you will miss dear old Les., but believe me no one could miss him more than I do. Les. was always a great friend of mine, but I never knew what a great pal he was until we joined the army. He was just like a brother to me, as we were in camp together, sailed together, and fought together; and I am sorry I was not close to him at the fatal moment. He was a gallant young soldier, always a great pal of everybody in the battalion. Many a great time we spent together, and some very rough ones, but Les. never lost his smile. I don't think it will be long before we are home, and then I can tell you of some of his good work and our experience together. Dear old Les., who nobly did his bit, lost his life in the hour of a great struggle, in fighting for King and Country. In your sad loss I convey to you the deepest sympathy of all the officers, non-commissioned officers and men of the battalion …

The battle for Mont St Quentin had cost the community around Mologa dearly. Australian forces had suffered another 3000 casualties.[9] The numbers of Australians left to fight on the Western Front were rapidly diminishing. The battalions were now at one-fifth of their full strength.

SEPTEMBER 1918
FRANCE

Allan had enjoyed his short period of leave in England, spending time with relatives and relishing the opportunity to experience some normality away from the front. He returned to Le Havre on 7 September. The following day he wrote home to reassure his brother that, while Percy was in France with the battalion, he was not in danger:

Sunday 8-9-18
Dear Jim

Just a few lines to let you know that I am splendid & do hope that you all are the same. Percy is also ok. Just before I went to England I met Percy and he was going up the line. Well I had a letter from him today and he is away back out [of] the fighting. The adj and Major said if he came back they would keep him out of it so everything [is] ok. Well Jim I got back from England alright and had a very nice time. I wrote you a lot of letters from England and told you about my trip in Leicester. Well when I got back from Leicester I went to Headquarters and they gave me another 4 days leave. Mr Gollan was always wanting me to go and see his friend in Scotland and they have wrote and asked me to go at several times so I spent the few days with them and I had a glorious time. They [are] bonnie people and so awfully good. I will enclose some little snaps they gave so Jim will you keep them until I get back. Well old boy what do you think of the war news now. Aint it glorious but we are losing a lot of men. Jim I am not a bit surprised at what you say about the certain class. I am absolutely full up of them. They are disgraceful. When I got back from England there were 35 letters waiting for me. What a treat what letters from everybody. I got 2 very nice letters of sympathy from Mrs Braddish. I generally get a letter or two every mail from Eileen. Yes old boy I know how you all feel about 3 dear boys. I feel just [the] same but as you know Jim we must keep going. I believe now that poor old Les Townsend is killed it is awful. But don't say anything until you [have] heard definitely. No doubt you are all very busy but perhaps the days will come when I will be back to give a hand. Fancy Bill Johnson getting married and Edgar Saville, oh well…

I am sending home a couple of little parcels of things that I collected off the battle field some time ago. Well Jim old boy this is all the news so will close with best love to all.

I remain
Your Loving Brother
Allan

THE RACE TO THE HINDENBURG LINE

German forces continued their retreat to the Hindenburg Line and the old British trenches which faced it. The Allies pursued the German soldiers with speed and vengeance; villages burned while bridges and roads were destroyed in the retreat. The Australians, in desperate need of rest, were instead to be thrust against the final bastion of German defence, an extensive three-trench system some six kilometres deep, fortified by barbed wire and machine-guns and built along the deep St Quentin Canal.

The men were exhausted. The lack of reinforcements on the front necessitated lengthy stays holding recaptured ground often subjected to repeated counter-attack. The Australian casualty rate in proportion to their numbers was higher than that of any other units of the British Empire. They had been consistently thrown into the most costly battles. Others were spurred on by their successes. The ominous Hindenburg Line loomed as Monash sent the 3rd, 5th and British 23rd divisions to clear the villages and German outposts close to the old British trenches.[10] On 18 September a total of ten divisions, including the 1st and 4th Australian and a number of British and American divisions, finally pushed through, taking over 12,000 German prisoners. The two Australian divisions took 4300 of these alone.[11]

Allan wrote to Jim, but with obvious signs of frustration as he answered queries over missing letters and his missive home to inform his parents that they had lost another son. Dealing with a lack of understanding and sense of criticism delivered from the safety of Australia was difficult and Allan made sure his brother knew exactly how he felt.

Sunday
France
22-9-18
Dear Jim

I have just returned from church parade so I think I will drop you a few lines. I received about 12 letters from Ausy yesterday 2 from home 1 each from Mrs & M Stone one each from Eva & Elsie Jones one each from Nell Sherlock & M Gamble. I was very pleased to hear that you are all well and that you are getting the letters alright you said in your letters that it was 7 weeks since I wrote well I write every week and if you don't get [them] that is not my fault. You say you don't know how poor Charlie could have got shot. Well Jim you have no idea what the game is like or of what conditions or circumstances we have to fight against. It is quite possible for anyone to be killed with a bullet at any time when poor Charlie was killed certainly he was in a trench it was only shallow though and he put his head up and a sniper got him through the top part of the nose and it went into his head. He died instantly. You said Mum was disappointed with my letter, well that was the morning it occurred that I wrote and you ought to know how it affected me. I wrote the next day and told you all about it. Well Jim it is raining like billy o today. The winter is beginning to creep in on us but I don't think it will be like the 1916 one anyway I hope not. I never want to witness another one like that one. I am glad there is every indication of a good harvest. Well Jim what do you think of the war news now. Aint the b- hun getting hell and that is nothing to what he will get directly. I think we ought to be home Xmas 12 months. Let us hope so anyway. The way the RC are behaving is absolutely rotten. Mrs Stone gave me the full strength of it all. Well Jim I will say cheerio for the present and best love to all.

I remain
Your Loving Bro
Allan SM

Postcard of North Inch and Boating Station Perth [Scotland]
France
Sunday

22-9-19
My Dear Mum,

I have written already this morning I have just come from Church parade and we had a very nice service. It is raining like billy o. These two bits of paper don't look much but will be able to tell a good half day story about the one written in pencil. SO please keep them till I get back. I have lots of little things like these.

I remain your loving son
Allan XXXX

Postcard Tay Street, Perth
France
24-9-18
Dear Jim

Just received a letter from Percy he is splendid and away back out of the line. So there is no need to worry. Poor old Les Townsend has been killed and I feel awfully sorry. Have written to Mrs Townsend & Rene. Well old boy no news as I wrote on Sunday so cheerio and best love to all

Loving Bro
Allan

All along the Western Front, German troops were retreating. To the north of the Somme, the British and Belgian forces were attacking towards Ghent. Passchendaele had been reclaimed. To the south, American, French and British troops were advancing. Monash and his Australians were to take the line at Bellicourt, east of Peronne, although there were few Australians left to complete the task. The battalions had been decimated by enormous casualties and, for the first time, original Anzac troops were being granted two months' leave to return to their families in Australia. Some of the most experienced and courageous men were at last going home for a brief period of respite that had always been available to British and French soldiers but not to the distant dominion troops. With the strength of the battalions severely compromised, seven of the Australian battalions were scheduled to be disbanded to form reinforcements for their sister battalions. In the 10th Brigade, the 37th Battalion was ordered to disband. The troops refused, as they did in other battalions and, on their last parade, stubbornly declined to complete the order to move off to their new battalions. Instead, for several days they continued their routine duties without their officers.[12]

This was effectively a mutiny but no Australian soldiers were punished. This was not about refusing to fight. There was no mass uprising. These battle-weary troops simply sought to preserve the identity under which they had fought and lived — their battalion name and their colours. Monash chose not to punish the dissidents in his army of volunteer citizen soldiers.

On 29 September American forces advanced on the Hindenburg Line at Bellicourt. Once their objectives had been reached, the troops of the Australian 3rd and 5th divisions were to leap-frog the Americans. But the inexperienced Americans were no match for the defenders of the mighty Hindenburg Line and took heavy casualties. Australian troops moved in and, over two days of bitter fighting in freezing rain, they pushed forward.

On the same day, 29 September, at the age of 40, father of eight and Military Medal winner Jack McDonald was shot in the neck. He returned to Pyramid Hill but passed away just two years later from lung disease, a result of the effects of an earlier gas attack.

OCTOBER

On 1 October the 3rd Division seized the village of Bony. The Australian infantry had captured the first and second trench systems on their front.[13] The 2nd Division moved in to relieve the remaining men of the 1st and 3rd. The Hindenburg Line was crumbling. The final line was breached on 3 October. Two days later, after the 2nd Division captured the village of Montbrehain, the last of the Australian battalions was withdrawn and replaced by American units. Since 8 August the 'diggers' had been continuously in the line for two months. They had advanced some 50 kilometres, liberated scores of villages and taken thousands of prisoners. The cost was heavy; close to 27,000 Australian soldiers had been killed or wounded.[14] There were few reinforcements. The Australian forces were almost spent.

Percy wrote to Jim from behind the line. It seems there was now some concern within the family over Charlie's will and estate. Over the next few months the concerns would escalate, perhaps fuelled by rumours circulated by a meddling relative. Fortunately, later letters reveal that the rift had been healed.

In the Field
1-10-18
Dear Jim

Well Jim how are things going, I have received several letters from you lately, which I was very pleased to get, and glad to hear you are well. I am not with the Batt at present, at a Reinforcement Wing, behind the line not a great way from the line. I think I told you in my last letter Les Townsend was killed. He was shot through the head, it was stiff luck, he was so game. It has been very cold weather lately, and a little rain on and off. I got that little slip of paper, with the inquiry, I was surprised Jim. Very nice isn't it what [is] going on at 208 Barnard St, if the little kiddie got it instead of her, it would be allright, she [is] not entitled to a penny. Heard from Allan the other day, he was still at the Base, and going on well. So you have a piano in the house now Jim, it will make you feel quite young again Jim. Fritz comes over here bombing at times. Well Jim, it ought to soon be over now, by the way things are going, they are knocking old Fritz about now. Yes, Uwen Johnson has had his share of wounds, I believe this last one was pretty bad, his wife was over to see him. Albert Brookes was going strong last time I saw him. I met Tom Alford not long ago, he looked real well also Amos Haw, he was going to Blighty to the I.B. for six months. Well Jim I must close, hoping [this] finds you all well

I am your loving brother
Percy

A week later, Allan wrote to Jim:

Monday
7-10-18
Dear Jim

Just a few lines to let you know that I am [well] & hope that you all are the same. We are just dwelling on a big Ausy mail which ought to reach us today or tomorrow. I can tell you we do look forward for these. Well Jim old boy it is raining like hell again and things are now beginning to feel a bit chilly but I don't think it will be a severe winter. Poor old Les Townsend has been killed alright and I have written to his people and told them everything I could find out about him. It will be a terrible shock to his people. He was a good soldier and well liked. Col. Henderson has also been killed.[15] *He was a gallant leader of men and holds a high reputation over here. Well Jim old boy I suppose you are up to your neck in work as the harvest must be coming on now. I hope it turns out successful. Well old boy cheerio for the present.*

Your loving Brother
Allan

As Percy wrote to Jim, the end of the war was closer than either man realised. The Central Powers were now faltering in all the theatres of war. In Flanders to the north, along the Somme and to the south at Verdun, the Allies continued their rapid advance to the east. Bulgaria and Turkey were defeated and Austria-Hungary was soon to seek peace. The German fleet mutinied on 29 October. On the home front Germany was on the verge of revolution. The people were hungry. They were desperate for an end to the relentless slaughter.

Percy wrote to reassure Jim that he would not have to return to front-line duties:

In the Field
22.10.18
Dear Jim

… Well I am going good, we are out of the line just now, for a little time. I was very sorry to hear Mother was not well, she needs a good spell away.

Myrtle is still with you Jim, you are set now. I had a letter from Allan, he was going good at the Base got a good job, it will last till the shoot is over from what I hear. Its been a bit cold lately, of course we must expect it now, its getting late in the year. I am at present a guide at a station, for men coming in, its not a bad stunt, I sleep in a little hut every second night on the station, with some English chaps, that are on the station duty we have a fire and it is "bon". I tell you I am kept busy writing, get a lot of letters from the relations in England. Well Jim, its drawing near Xmas, I can see another one in France, I would like to get to Blighty for Xmas, the last two have been here. Well Jim, I will not have to go in the line again, might be close to it, for the wing move up when the Battalions are in, but one would be very stiff if he got hit then.

Well Old boy Must close now
With love To all

I am your loving brother
Percy

Jim's mate, Tom Alford, wrote after enjoying some leave in England. He was as frank and laconic as ever:

France
October 23rd 16
Dear Jimmy

Just a line in answer to your welcome letter dated July 14th & I think I had another one written out at the bush since I last wrote. I was pleased to hear from you again. I don't get so many letters now I expect because I've dropped most of my correspondence. I know Jim it must be very galling to you the way a certain crowd are carrying on out their but buggar them. One will know what to do when the next war is on. A friend of mine who lives in a suburb of Melbourne had a letter from his mother & she wanted to know of him: How it was that all the lads of that place who were returning were all the wasters etc. By what I can make of it the bigger lead-swinger & bloody nuisance you make of yourself the better you get on in the Army. Not that I've anything to go crook about but by just what you see. Well since I last wrote I've had fourteen days leave in England.

Had a real ding-dong time. Went to Wales. Stayed in Cardiff & Aberdare. Got in with some real good people in the latter place & they couldn't do enough for us. There were not many Aussies in the place so people used to get us off a bit. Talk about sitters you could catch a different one every hour of the day. Of course you know I don't bother the fair sex much. Had a night in Bristol & finished up with a few days in London. I had a real little Beauty in London. Saw Joe Stone in London & Jimmy in Boulougne on his way back. Jim had a bullet through his chin. It will be nice for you all to have Myrtle over with you for a while. Well we are out having our long promised spell but we are in a very quiet place. Yesterday I had leave to Abbeyville for the day. There is really nothing to see but you seem to be your own boss for the day. Well this is all this time so will conclude by wishing you all a Happy Xmas & trusting you are all well with kind regards to Ma & Dad from your old Pal Tom

TWENTY THREE
... ITS ABOUT OVER NOW

NOVEMBER

In France, the Australians remained out of the line. Joe Stone wrote to Jim with optimism that the war would soon end. He could not have envisaged that the end to the dreadful slaughter was just days away.

France
November 4-18

Dear Jim Just a --- in haste hoping it finds all in the best of health as it leaves me at present. Well Jim it is getting a little on the cold side again now but I have not put on a flannel yet you do not feel the cold so much if you don't put them on until you feel it a bit. I had a few letters from Aussy a few days a go. All the beginning of Aug so you see they take a good while to reach here. The war looks good now only Jerry *left in it I think we can lead him a pretty good dance on it. I suppose Mologa is just as quiet as ever. I hear all the girls are getting caught. So I think I will do my dash over here. Well Jim it is tea time & I am short of news. So I will Ring Off*

I Remain
As Ever
Joe [Stone]

On 9 November, as the Australians were preparing to return to the front, the Kaiser abdicated. Revolution and the proclamation of a republic had ended his reign as Emperor of Germany and King of Prussia. He fled to the Netherlands and never returned to Germany.

On the night of 9 October the German armistice delegation crossed the line in northern France. On 11 November, in a railway carriage at a forested siding at Compiegne, the armistice was signed. It was 5.00 am. In six hours all hostilities were to cease. The armistice marked the end of a global catastrophe.

At 11.00 am the armistice took effect. All operations on the Western Front abruptly halted. An eerie silence fell on the killing fields. The slaughter was over. The Australian soldiers, expecting soon to return to the front line, remained where they were. An air of disbelief pervaded the ranks.

For the troops who had been consumed by the grinding slaughter of the war, peace appeared beyond comprehension. Many could not understand what peace really meant. A deathly silence hung in the air that for four long years had reverberated with the roar of artillery, the chatter of machine-guns and the cries of the wounded and dying. The reality of peace for many was difficult to comprehend. Allan wrote home, continuing to reassure his family that Percy would remain out of the line. Perhaps for Allan an end to the war was simply too good to be true. He had heard stories of the war coming to an end before, and may have assumed that this was yet another wild furphy.

The 38th Battalion diary simply recorded:

> Telegram received from Brigade at 7.45 stating that the Armistice had been signed. Training proceeds.

The following day, little had changed:

> Training as per syllabus [1]

The telegram with the news that the war had ended arrived a little later at the 1st Australian Convalescent Depot at Le Havre where Allan continued in his role as censor. The 1600 men who were fit to parade were assembled and the news was read to them. The Convalescent Depot War Diary records that the proclamation was 'received enthusiastically' but that discipline was maintained. The soldiers were marched to the parade ground and then dismissed to continue with their routine. At 5.00 pm that afternoon, the Depot Band marched through Le Havre where the residents cheered the musicians warmly. They marched and played until 9.00 pm, a crowd following them through the town. The diary attributed the 'maintenance of good order and discipline' to the impromptu concert. Any concerns that the troops would become 'unsettled' remained unrealised. [2]

While the devastating war had truly ended, it left the darkest of legacies in its wake. The number of lives lost could never be accurately determined. Historian John Terraine suggests that the estimates of 12 million lives fall far short of the actual number.[3] Another 20 million were listed as wounded. This was a tragedy on a scale that beggars belief. What is certain is that, of the total Allied battle casualties, Australia suffered 64.8% killed or wounded, proportionally the highest of all Allied fighting forces. According to Charles Bean, of the 416,809 men who enlisted, 331,781 fought and of these 59,342 were killed with another 152,171 men wounded, many with long-term and life-limiting consequences.[4] Some were wounded time and again. Many had sustained wounds that were not visible to the eye, emotional and psychological scars which no treatment could ever erase.

The portion of a group photo taken on Armistice Day near Le Havre. The inscription reads: 'Taken on 11.11.18 at Rouelles, France 1st ACD.' Allan is seated far left, middle row with arms folded.

Allan's first letter to Jim following the end of the war contains little euphoria. Rather, there are signs of confusion. His reassurance to his family that Percy would not go back to the line, that 'everything is fixed for him to keep out', could imply that he thought there was more fighting to come, yet he also acknowledges that there are now excellent opportunities for the Australians to travel.

France

13-11-18

Dear Jim

Just a few lines to let you know both Percy & I are excellent & trust that you all are the same. I received such a lovely lot of letters (24) from Aussy the other day and was so awfully delighted. I received 8 or 9 from you all. I also got the photos they are dam fine and Jim believe me they made me think for awhile. Well Jim I was very pleased to hear that there are every indications of a good year. You must have found it dam lonely out yonder but it is nice to have visitors out there. Jim I think I told you I had a letter from Pearl at last. In my last letter I told you that Bosch would turn it in and of course you will have heard that by now. What rejoicing there will be in Aussy now wont those cold footers be pleased. Oh it is a pity we never got conscription over there and some of those damned cold footers would have had a taste of it. They will get a hell of a lively time when all of the boys get back. The Bramly boys have had hard luck. Well Jim someone has to go but unfortunately they all seem to go from one family. Well now Jim I suppose you are awfully busy over there, there is no doubt you all have had a lot of work since we all came away but I honestly believe that we will be home about next August or Sept well anyway let us hope so. Yes I am still at the base and I believe I will be here until the finish. I was so awfully pleased to hear that you got 14 letters from me I tell you I am always writing but I cannot understand why you never got any from Percy. I always hear from him. Fancy them dam fools arguing over a soldier's parcel I cannot make them out at all. It seems petty and ridiculous. I will get a lot of parcels this week. Mrs Stone has sent me more by jove they are awfully good to us. I say you all may rest assured that Percy does not go back to line. He has not been in the trenches since January and everything is fixed for him to keep out you might tell mum & dad that I was so pleased to hear Myrtle was still over there and it is awfully good of her mother to let her stay. No doubt she is great company for mum. Jim every letter I get from Etta is about Milne so I just wrote back & told her that he was in the trenches but was in England. She is always talking about Pearl and of course I don't know whether it is true or not and I don't think she should say anything to us about it. I don't mind if it comes from home because then I know it is true… There are lots of things I could tell you but it does [not] do [to] put it in letters as you never know where they go. Yes I was awfully pleased to meet

Tommy A. I have just sent home some photos and will be sending home some later on. I cabled for money as I am going to Paris just before Xmas and may go on to Italy. It is a great opportunity for us now. Jim I think I told you before that I had finished with the girl at P.H. about 12 months ago. It was getting too hot for me anyway I bet I get a stir from them when I return. Dam the girls Jim I will use my head next time. You might tell me if Dad & mum know that. Don't forget Jim. The boss always had the spike in me over that I will never forget the last to [of] leaves I had at home the boss gave me a dam hard time especially the last time you may remember that anyway don't forget. Well now Jim I have sent home a lot more Anzacs [Anzac Bulletins] hope you get them alright. The French people have gone fairly silly over here now but they have good reason to do so. Billy Hughes is shaking them up in England over the sums. Well now Jim this is all the news tonight so will close trusting all are well.

I remain
Your Loving Son [brother]
Jim there is a note in here for mum but give to her privately
I have put it in a separate envelope. [not found]

The Bramly boys, who had 'hard luck' as Allan describes, had both once lived at nearby Mincha West, their parents pioneers in the district. Lance Corporal Horace Bramley was killed in action in early 1918.[5] His younger brother, Private Charles Bramley, returned to the front after 14 months' convalescence and was killed on 10 August 1918.[6] Small townships all over Australia had lost so many of their young men.

Allan standing far left; photo taken on Armistice Day.

France
December 1ˢᵗ 1918
Dear Jim,

Just a rough photo of two pals & self which was taken the day the armistice was signed so it has rather an historical touch with it. One of the officers is an Adelaide boy & the other a Sydney boy I think I came out best of the lot.

Cheerio old boy
From AS Marlow

Allan was now turning his thoughts to home. He expresses unease over his lack of letters to the family of his earlier romantic interest in Pyramid Hill, while his concern for Pearl is clearly troubling him.

Postmarked Nov 14- 18
Dear Jim

I very seldom hear from Pearl as a matter of fact only once since dear old Charlie was killed, she take it dam cold. I am afraid anyway. I sent you that letter to see for your self Jim tell me all you know about the people at hill don't forget I am rather anxious to see how things are.

ASM

Allan included the letter from Pearl in which she appears to be seeking reassurance that Charlie's personal belongings would be returned to her and baby Eva. Allan had sent them home to his mother and they may have eventually been passed to Pearl. The diary which Pearl mentions was not with the collection of letters and personal items.

208 Barnard St
Bendigo
August 6ᵗʰ 1918
Dear Allan,

Just a line in answer to your letters, I received one this morning so thought I would answer it at once, not put it off as I have done the other letters. Allan I got your kind letters telling me about my dear one, it was good of you to write and tell me and I thank you very much. Allan dear no one knows how much I feel my loss, words are useless to describe how I miss my dear husband although we were parted I knew he was always thinking of me and his baby Eva, how I do miss his letters. I am so pleased to know his personal belongings are safe I will value them more than anything. Allan dear Charl told me that he was keeping a diary that will be lovely for baby to have, when she is older she will value her father's things very much. I would be pleased to know you was well out of the firing line Allan it is terrible for your Mother dear to know you are there. I have not seen your Mother only for a few minutes the day I came home from Kerang. I got your cable Allan thank you for sending it. I suppose Allan your people will have told you how Charlie made his will. Allan all our people are well, Annie received your letter also Percy's.

I can't write any more Allan dear so will close, from your loving sister Pearl.

Allan wrote on the bottom of Pearl's letter:

13-11-18
Dear Jim

This is the first letter [I] have had from Pearl since Charlie was killed I have sent home some of his personal belongings to Mum. The war is practically finished Jim I am writing you a long letter and a note for mum & you.

So Cheerio
Your Loving Bro
Allan

Percy wrote his first letter home since the signing of the armistice, simply indicating that there had been 'some joy' when the news was announced. It seems the Australians were being cautious in case the announcement was later revealed as simply another rumour. A few days on, and with time to contemplate, Percy was hopeful of returning home soon.

In the field
15.11.18
Dear Jim, Mother & Father,

.... Well the news is good; it's about over now, there was some joy here when the news came over so in the course of the next twelve months or so, we ought to be home. Having a pretty good time here now, at the Div Wing, good meals and not a great lot to do. Did you cable five pounds over. I was notified from the bank that there was five pounds there for me, which I am getting put in my pay book for the next blighty leave. Well Jim, I spose you are busy with the harvest now. Over here the weather has been good, for this time of the year, had no snow so far, a few nice frosts, the nights are a bit cold, but I have plenty of blankets, so am set. Well Jim, there is no news at present, expecting an Ausy mail.

Well goodbye for the present hoping all are well your loving brother
Percy

On 19 November Allan was admitted to the hospital at Le Havre suffering from tonsillitis. He remained there for ten days before he recovered and returned to his duties at the base where keeping the troops meaningfully occupied was now paramount. Lectures in mathematics, French, history, English, book-keeping and shorthand along with regular concerts, dances and sporting events were all on offer. Later in the month, with the constant stream of sick and wounded now abating, the depot had an abundance of beds available. All sick or wounded Australians who had been discharged from hospital spent their convalescence at the depot in Le Havre.[7]

France
27-11-18
Dear Jim

Well old boy I am dropping you a few lines to let you know that I am progressing very well indeed. I wrote to mum the other day told her I was in hospital with toncilitus. Of course I suppose you have received a cable about it. But don't get the wind up. I am alright it was just a swelling under the jaws. In ordinary life one would not take any notice of it. But Jim I am in the army and the armistice has been signed & they are awfully good to us and will give us rest for toothache now. You know what I mean. Well I am in a dam nice hospital, right on the beach in Havre, We get plenty of good food & there are very nice sisters here. So everything is ok. I will be going back to my depot about Saturday. Well Jim everything is at a standstill over here now & there are great rumours that we are going to Egypt. It will be a dam good job if we do as we will be nearer home & when we do sail it will not take us so long. Well Jim old boy it has been raining a treat this last few days. It is getting very close to Xmas now. I hope you have a good harvest I believe you have every prospects of it. Jim I was just wondering whether that block of Reily is sold yet. I think we will buy that when I get back. What do you say. I received a very nice parcel from Lily Stone just before I came into hospital. They are awfully good people. They have sent quite a number of parcels to me & post the same to the other boys. Well Jim old boy I will close with best love to all & trust all are well.

I remain
Your Loving Brother
Allan

I had another letter from Percy the other day. He is splendid and having a good time.

PYRAMID HILL, NOVEMBER

At home the celebrations reverberated across the country as Australians thronged the streets in an outburst of public jubilation. For others, the armistice did little to ease the heartache, the dreadful gaping hole left by the loss of their loved ones now in graves on the other side of the world. In Pyramid Hill the celebrations were reported in detail by the local newspaper:

THE ARMISTICE

The news of the most significant event of the past four years was telegraphed to Pyramid Hill on Monday night, and it transformed the quiet township into a centre of hilarious rejoicing and harmless noise. The clang of the church and fire bells roused the people from their slumbers and soon the streets were thronged by the crowd, who with band instruments, bells, beating of tins and other means greatly accentuated the feelings of rejoicing and thankfulness … The fire bell was rung with such vigour that the bolt broke and bell fell the forty feet to the ground, and fortunately the ringers were on the outside of the tower and no one was hurt … A copy of the telegram from the Governor-General, stating that the armistice had been signed, was read; and the people stood in silent respect for those who sorrowed for fallen ones. On Tuesday morning flags were hoisted, and school-boys, revelling in unusual liberty, paraded the town, beating tins and ringing bells, only stopping for the several ice-cream "shouts" which were offered in appreciation of their efforts …[8]

LE HAVRE, DECEMBER

While nations the world over celebrated, Allan's reaction was more muted. With Christmas and his birthday approaching, he wrote to his parents and Jim on a series of postcards and photos. His letters home had tended to spare the family descriptions of the worst moments of the war, and Allan had written of the daily routine: the weather, the harvest, how many letters and parcels he had received. However, with thoughts of home as his birthday and Christmas approached, he was clearly struggling with his grief.

5 Postcards of Perth
Havre
1-12-18
My Dear Dad & Mum

Just another few lines to let you know that I am absolutely better again now. I am back in my depot again I was not to go out until tomorrow but I have to go to Rouen tomorrow on duty I will be there 3 days. It will be a nice little spell for me. Well dear dad it is a "awful day" with cold wind & showers. I think it is going to snow I hope so anyway because it is much warmer when it is snowing. This is the first cold spell we have had & it is not bad at all. There will never be a winter like we had in 1916, by jove that was terror. I would sooner be dead than have to stand another like that, especially with the mud up to your waists. Well dad it is nearing Xmas again, those dear boys gone. This time last year dear old Charlie & I were trying to get to Paris but they stopped all leave. Oh dad I miss those dear boys but not as much as you at home do as the whole time I think they are still with me. Sometimes I cannot realize they are gone, but they are. When I leave France and the going home and when I get home will be the time I feel it. No doubt the war has brought sadness on our little home. I never like to mention about the boys as I am afraid it worries you all [the] more but today I cannot help it as there has been a big discussion of the going home & I cannot help thinking about the boys. There is no doubt Mologa has suffered badly. Well dear dad I suppose you are all awfully busy with the harvest now. I hope everything turns out well. I am sure we will be home for the next. I am going to send home some of my books a few odds and ends. I will be in Paris for Xmas and will send you all a little present from there. Well dear dad & mum I will say goodbye now with best love from your loving son.

Allan
XXX

Postcard of Le Havre
France
December 1ˢᵗ 1918
Dear Mum,

This is the first time we have [been] allowed to send views of Havre. It is not a bad little place, but not as nice as it looks. I had a nice letter from my Colonel yesterday. I have been writing letters all day and I will get a cup of cocoa directly. It would be very [nice] if you made it mum but cheer up dear we'll be home soon. The dam hun is knocked out thank God. Well dear mum goodbye and best love.

From your loving son
Allan XXX

Postcards of Le Havre
France Dec 1ˢᵗ 1918
Dear Jim

Just a few lines to let you know that I am well again and out of hospital. I was not supposed to come out until tomorrow but I asked to get out as I have to go to Rouen to morrow on duty. It will be a very nice trip for me. I do not come back until Wednesday. We are having brutal weather at present with cold winds & rain. I think it is going to snow anyway I hope so as it is much warmer when it snows. Mind you it is not cold yet and I don't think it is going to be too bad. I am going to Paris on the 23ʳᵈ I will be there for Xmas that [is] if the money comes along in time. I received two lovely parcels from home to day. There is also a big Aussy [mail] in. I will get mine to morrow. I have written a terrible lot of letters home again sent parcel, photos and goodness [knows] what. I hope you get them all. Well Jim old boy I will say goodbye for the present.

Your loving bro
Allan

On the same day, Allan wrote again to Eva, whose kindness and cooking skills he had always appreciated:

France Dec 1ˢᵗ 1918

Just another few lines to let you know that I received a very welcome letter from both you and Grace. I was very sorry to hear that you had not been well but trust that you are well once again. As a matter of fact I have just spent a lovely fortnight in hospital myself with tonsillitis. I was not very bad in ordinary times you would not take any notice of it. I just received two parcels from home & in one of them was a beautiful cake from you. I had some of it for tea tonight and it was simply delicious. I have not had anything so tasty for ages and I must thank you ever so much for your kindness towards me. The good work that is done and the kindness that is displayed to us by you all in Aussy is highly appreciated and is beyond praise and we all have realised thoroughly was [what] true friends we have in the distant little Aussy. Well now Eva this jolly old war is just about finished, in fact there will be no more fighting and I don't think it will be long before we all are home …

Allan's letter ends here. The final page is missing as are some of the numbered postcards and photos on which Allan wrote to his parents.

France
Dec 1ˢᵗ 1918
Dear Jim,

Just another rough snap of my premier hockey team & self, it is a very rough one I look awfully but not as bad as I look. The centre boy in the back row is Rumble from Mitiamo. I think you know him. Cheerio Jim old boy

Allan SM

Allan also describes the gifts and souvenirs he had sent home:

2/ … There [They] are very neat. One is a pipe lighter which will be just the thing for dad also a match box. I have also some views to send you which I got of different places up the line and down here. They stopped us from sending them when the bosch made his attack but now we are allowed to send them again. They will be…

4/ …but I am afraid to send them as they should go astray on me and they are battle beauties. I have a lot of little things I am going to send home to you. Well dear mum I have no more news to put on this as I have letters to write so will close with best love to all.

I remain
Your Loving Son
Allan

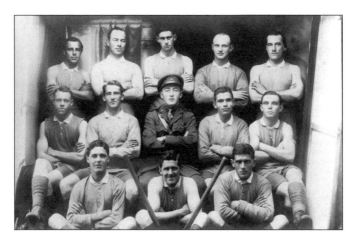

Allan's hockey team at the 1st Australian Convalescent Depot, Le Havre.

A game of hockey on the parade ground, 1st ACD, Le Havre.

2/ ... This is one of the parade ground & a game of hockey in play. The building on the right is another YMCA where boys get cocoa etc, then a military church (C of E) & then the men's mess huts. This camp is recognised as the best camp in France. It is where they do their convalescing after hospital they are well treated and cared for...

Havre

7-12-18

1/ My Dear Mum & Dad

... Do not be a bit surprised to see Percy come home shortly. I am doing my best. There are a lot of B Class men going home now that left here today for England it will not be long before we all are home.[9] I suppose there was great excitement in Aussy when the news came through about the armistice being signed. I can tell you the French people nearly went mad.

Allan's photo of the 1st ACD at Le Havre.

France
Sunday 8-12-18
Dear Jim,

… I was awfully pleased with those photos. I think they were very good. By jove they brought back old memories alright anyway it won't be long before we are home with you again. They seemed to have had a very successful night at Jones barn alright. G.J. seemed to have donated his money very nicely. I am [afraid] he and I will never hit it when I get back. Yes you will have your work cut out with the young horses I suppose they are pulling away at the old harvester now. I hope the crop turns out successful dont forget to let me know how it goes. No doubt you felt it lonely out at Bobs especially when the dear old boys have gone. Jim it is awfully hard alright. I am feeling it more than ever now as I know it wont be long before we go home. I have had only one letter from Pearl then people say they never hear from you and I have written dozens, it makes me sick. I cannot make out why you never got any from last mail you should have. I wish you will tell me exactly how many letters you get each mail. I had a very enjoyable trip to Rouen. One of our big hospitals there was shifting to England and I had to go up on duty. Anyway I met a lot of our bonnie Aussy nurses. No doubt Jim they are great girls & have to work awfully hard. I had some very interesting yarns. I was asked to dinner with them several times but could only get once. I felt a bit shy as I was the only officer there, anyway I had a good dinner. Well Jim old boy I will have to close now with best love to all. Trust all are well

I remain
Your loving brother
Allan

Percy wrote to Jim as he was experiencing his last Christmas on the Western Front:

29.12.18
France
Dear Jim

Well Old boy I received your letter of the 4 Oct, yes this time last year we were hopping over the bags at Ypres. Well Xmas is over again, had a good Xmas dinner Jim, best I have had for some time fowl and ham plum pudding, fruit and so on, very nice to, about thirty of us here on the staff, things are very easy. Having some very bad weather lately plenty of wind and rain, but no snow up to yet, I am not a bit anxious to see any either. Got a letter from Allan the other day, he was going on good, still at the Base. Yes Jim, I got the five pound allright, might happen to get leave shortly to Blighty. Got a parcel from Lilly Sharp, day before Xmas, very good too. Do not seem to be getting many letters from me Jim, although I write a lot. Well Jim, news is very scarce here, so I must close, hoping all are well.

I am your loving brother

Percy.

The last Christmas card Percy was to send from the Western Front.

TWENTY FOUR
EVA DON'T TELL ANYBODY BUT I WILL BE HOME IN TIME FOR THE HARVEST

FRANCE

As the new year began, repatriation was in full swing. The men of the 38th Battalion were now at Abbeville in France where opportunities for leave were frequent. Training was now simply a means of keeping fit and the men were fully occupied with sports meetings, lectures, concerts and dances in which young ladies from England, dressed in khaki, arrived to partner the Australian soldiers.[1]

There are only two surviving letters from Percy from January until May. We know little of his movements during this time, except that, at some point, he was sent for duty at the 3rd Division Headquarters. Allan remained at Le Havre and continued to express his disappointment at the lack of communication from home. He was clearly pleased that Aunt Etta's stories had proved to be just that; any ill-feeling towards Pearl was now dismissed as unjustified and had been relegated to the past. For the first time Allan reveals to Jim that he has harboured another far greater disappointment than a lack of letters.

6-1-1919
Dear Jim

… A lot of the officers have had letters since you heard the armistice was signed but I have not and am rather anxious to get them as no doubt that would cheer you all up a lot. Well Jim old boy it is dinner time so will finish it after dinner. I have finished a dinner of roast beef vegetables & pudding so I have not done too badly. This last mail which arrived a few days ago well yours was the only letter I got and it was a beauty. I was very pleased to hear that Pearl was up home and that was all lies in regard to what Etta

was saying. I was always saying exactly what you say about them. Now in regard to the relatives this side. Well Jim I have given them a lot of money and if dad is sending money he ought to send it to Wilsons. They are great people and awfully hard working. I suppose I have given them all about 35. The girls are awfully nice little things. There are a lot of things I could tell you but one never knows where this letter may get too. In regard to my recommendation. The first one was on June 7ʰ Messines 1917 and the other one Ypres Oct 4 Paessondale show. The boys all knew about [it] Spuddy Kerr can tell you about [it] but for Gods sake Jim don't tell I told you. Say that you heard it from one of the boys. But Jim don't tell anyone about as I don't want anyone to know I never got them and was disappointed so say nothing. Jim tell me all you know or heard about the Pyramid girl. Does mum or dad still think we are going strong. I did not play the game too well you know. But Jim tell me all you know about it & Jim if you ever meet her speak to her. She is dam good girl and they are dam good people and they thought the world of me. I have not written for 15 months and I think I should write but Jim be a sport and tell me all about things. Well Jim I don't think it will be long before we are home as they are sending a lot back now. We are kept busy down here. I will not rise any higher now than I am here but Jim I am lucky to be here. I told you some of my narrow squeaks I have had you say liar but I never tell anyone about the war no-one will ever get much out of me. Well old boy this is all the news today so cheerio & best love to all.

I remain

Your Loving Brother

Allan SM

The issue of military decorations and awards was often controversial and, in some cases, remains so today. What the men of World War I endured and what they were tasked to achieve in the most horrendous of circumstances and in the face of almost certain death or the possibility of terrible wounds, defies belief. These were all courageous men who gave so much: their youth, their innocence, their mental health — sometimes, their lives.

France
7-1-19
Dear Jim

Just a few lines today to let you know that I am splendid & trust that you all are the same. We are having nice weather indeed today as a matter of fact remarkable day, just like an Aussie spring day. I received 3 lovely parcels today from the following Aunt Florrie Dolly Mahoney & Mum. They were proper beauties. I have received an awful lot this Xmas, but it is not advisable to send anymore because we might go home at any time. Personally I think every Aussie will be out of France by June, but we may have to wait in England a while for a transport. There are 55 boat loads going home this next month so that will be a [all] full. I was having a long yarn to Alf Ferris and his brother the other day. They came around and had supper in my room. His brother Stan has just left for Aussie, so I told him to call & see you all. Well Jim I came a bit of a gutzer for not many at all, but I am always writing myself. I have written 22 letters this last couple of days. I suppose you have finished harvesting now & having a bit of a rest …

14-1-19
Dear Jim

…Well Jim we had a 5 mile cross country race the other day. There were 16 in for it and some of them were professionals. Anyway I gave them a good go for it and had I been in training I would have won. The winner done it in 26min – 45 sec and I done it in 27min coming an easy second anyway I get a medal out of it. I will send you the digger paper with the full account of the race. Well I am that stiff now that I can hardly walk. Well Jim in my last letters I told you I only got one letter last mail but expected that I would get more but have come a gutzer. Well never mind I got another parcel yesterday from Annie Clee from Wakool. It was a very good one indeed. I have had an awful lot of parcels lately. Well Jim there was a lot of boys just come down from the line to go home they are going over to England now like wild fire so I don't think it will be long before we are all home. I don't want to land back in Aussy in the summer time not after being so well seasoned here …

Sunday
19-1-19
Dear Jim

... I'll bet there were great jubilation when you heard of the armistice especially with the cold footers. The boys are going home very quickly now they seem quite contented too. I met little Joe Cocking the other yesterday he is leaving here today for England then Ausy. I had a letter from Perc the other day he is splendid and having a good time. The boys are doing very little now. Tom Gibson is still over in England he seems fed up.[2] Well old boy this is just a short note so cheerio & best love to all.

I remain
Your loving Brother
Allan

Requests for leave were now increasingly granted as the demobilisation and repatriation of troops continued. Allan left for England on 20 January and took the opportunity to once again visit relatives in Leicestershire.

From England Allan sent Jim a series of personal postcards for which I can find no explanation. Most are dated prior to the war and belong to Mademoiselle Lucie Duvauchel from the town of Albert. There are others addressed to residents of Amiens and from Ribemont, the village where Charlie is buried. How Allan acquired these we will never know. Were they given to him by the recipients as mementoes of their villages? Did Allan form a friendship with Lucie? Did he pocket them as souvenirs from the broken homes of former residents? There is no-one left to ask. Today they remind us of gaps in the accounts of the war, battles and circumstances of which the Marlow brothers did not write — their actions, events and relationships, their nightmares and their fears; the secrets they took to the grave.

Leicester
29-1-19
My Dear Mum & Dad

Just a card to let you know that I am at the above and am quite well and having a good time. It has been snowing and raining. I got an awful shock when I came over to England to find snow and so much rain as we were having glorious weather over there. All here are quite well & send their best love to you all. I am leaving here & going back to France on Monday that is if we cannot get an extension …

He added later:

… the boys home very quickly now I am afraid we will land home in the midst of next summer & by jove wont we feel it too. Anyway it will be a blessing to get home. I believe there is a big draft going home from the 3ʳᵈ Division this month so am wondering if Percy is in it. I have not heard from him for 4 days. Well dear mum & dad I will say goodbye & best love to all

from
Your loving son
Allan XXXX

FEBRUARY

Allan wrote to Jim from London:

United Forces Club
14 Belgrave Square, S.W.1.
London
Monday 3-2-19
Dear Jim

Just a few lines to let you know that I am excellent & trust that you all are the same. I have written to mum this morning and told her that I was trying for an extension of a week. Well Jim I gathered together a brave heart and asked them. I had to make a statement which they are going to verify. I told them that I had 3 brothers killed and I had a lot of business to fix up so I think I will get it alright anyway I will know to morrow morning. Well Jim I have had an excellent time but it snowed and rained practically all the time there is 1 000 men from my brigade going home in a couple of weeks. Percy may be in the mob. I have just had news of the 1 000 going home. Well Jim I suppose you will be back from Tassy by now …

Allan's attempts to remain in England a little longer before returning to Le Havre proved fruitless. He wrote from France just two days later. Perhaps the imminent closure of the 1st Australian Convalescent Depot ensured that his application was rejected.

France
Friday 14-2-19
Dear Jim

… I think I told you in one of my previous letters that I ran second in a 5 mile cross country race. I did it in 27 min and the winner done it in 15 sec faster than me. All the fellows had time training. There were 3 officers in it and we only went in it to give the boys a start. The winner is a professional. Anyway I got my medal alright and am sending it home. There is another one coming off on Monday and I am starting in that. I also had the proofs of my photos back so will be sending the photos shortly. We are kept very busy at present getting the men turning. A very big draft marched out for England tonight. It is believed that there is going to be a big strike in England shortly so that will affect our demobilisation a lot …

A week later he reassured Jim that he would be home for the next harvest, a time that had never been too far from his thoughts since his departure from Australia:

… No doubt you are pleased that the harvest is over. It was not such a success this year. Well Jim old boy I will give you the good oil and that is that I will be well home for the next. There is a big draft from the 38th down here now. Percy should have been on it but somehow missed anyway he will be on the next. George Wilson from Macorna is on the draft and he would like to see you all. He is a fine lad and has been a great pal of mine …

Just two days later, Allan replied to Jim's letter:

France
Monday
24-2-19
Dear Jim

Just a few lines to let you know that I am quite well & trust you all are the same. I received a very nice mail of 13 letters from Aussy a few days ago and needless to mention I was awfully delighted. It was between 7 & 8 weeks since we had received one. The letters were dated from Nov 14 to Dec 27ᵗʰ. Glad to hear the harvest was finished but what I heard I thought it would have turned out better, anyway that is far better than a drought ... Well Jim the troops are coming down very quickly now. There is a big draft of 3ʳᵈ Div here now and will be leaving here on Friday for Blighty then Aussy. I thought Percy would have been on the draft but somehow missed I have written up the demobilization officer to have him put on the next. Geo Wilson from Macorna is on it. He's a Lieut now, got his commission in October ... Please give my very kind regards to Myrtle and tell her that I am writing tomorrow. When you write next time I want you to tell me what parcels you have received since June. I have sent an awful lot since and you don't seem to get any at all.

Cheerio Allan

MARCH

With over 180,000 Australian men to be repatriated, many with new wives and children, the return to Australia proved a slow process. Ships were in high demand and were scarce. The repatriation was a mammoth task. As the waiting continued, Percy wrote from France. He was no longer with the 38th Battalion but attached to the 3rd Division Headquarters in a position he clearly enjoyed.

8-3-19
Dear Jim

Well old boy, I suppose you have been expecting to hear from me again; I received two letters from you, a short time ago. Still at the Div Wing on Mail man now Jim, some job, do me for a steady job better than with the Battalion. You have finished early with the harvest this year, don't suppose you are sorry either. Hope you get over to Tasy for your holidays. So Myrtle Saville is engaged, another girl you are going to loose Jim, spose you got one booked Jim, sooner have a nice little Scotch girl Jim, very nice too. Getting a fair share of rain lately, but it is not very cold and I think the snow has finished thank goodness. How is Mum, Dad and Myrtle keeping? Well Jim, I will send those cuttings out of the papers on to Allan. Close now Jim, hoping it finds you all well. I am your loving brother

Percy

MOLOGA

Names of soldiers appearing in the newspapers often sparked curiosity. There were few Marlows living in Australia at the time, certainly as far as the Marlows of Mologa were aware. In total, 28 Marlows enlisted from various locations across the country, including the five sons of Charles and Sarah. Jim wrote to the family of George. H. Marlow who was returning after being listed as a prisoner of war. Reading his name in the newspaper may have sparked some momentary hope for the family. Jim received the following reply:

8 Salisbury Grove
Northcote
17-3-19
Dear Mr Marlow

I received your letter last week have waited to see Father. He lives at Preston Reservoir. The G.H. Marlow you mention is my brother. He arrives home next week after 1 year 8 months in the German's hands. He was only 17 when he sailed. Father comes from Berkshire England his people were bakers in business Wakingham and Reading. He has one brother and one sister so I don't know if we can claim relationship or not Father's parents died when he was a boy he came to Australia coming on 40 years ago. During my leave in England I saw my Uncle. My Aunt came to Australia seven years ago. That is the only relations that Dad knows of. I am very sorry to hear that you have lost three brothers. But trust it will not be long before the other two return home fit and well Your family have done more than their share. I arrived home Xmas Eve and was discharged last month, I have started work at my old trade Painting and Papering not so easy as my last four years job. The reason of different address. My wife and little boy lived with her Mother while I was away at Fenwick St. We are now in our own home I thank you for congratulations on the M.M. I am to get it Wednesday.

I don't know if you will be able to trace any relationship between us. We may be 42ⁿᵈ cousins anyhow there are not many Marlow's that we know of. Trusting you will let me know if your people know of my father

I will now conclude
Yours Sincerely
Ern Marlow

Ernest Marlow enlisted in August 1914 at the age of 22 and was awarded the Military Medal in December 1917.[3] His brother, George Herbert, was just 17 when he signed up in February 1916. He was captured at Riencourt (near Bullecourt) in April 1917 and interned at Dulmen in Germany for the remainder of the war. His records indicate that he returned to England on 7 December 1918 where he was granted leave until 11 January 1919. He arrived back two days late and was promptly docked two days' pay. It would seem that some higher authority later saw sense — further documents listing his absence without leave are marked in red 'in error'.[4] I hope George had his pay restored.

FRANCE

France
Wednesday 17-3-19
My Dear Dad

Just a few lines to let you know that I am quite well & trust that you all are the same. It is raining a treat today but not a bit cold. This is just a ruff snap of myself which I had taken when I was in Leicester. It was a bitterly cold snowy day so I didn't bother to take my coat off. Well dear dad it should not be long before we all get home and then will be time. I met Tom Gray the other day he is splendid & is on his way back.

Well goodbye dear dad
Your Loving Son
Allan

While Allan was anxious to leave for Australia, his priority lay with visiting the graves of his mates and brothers. His departure from France was to be his final farewell:

France
Tuesday 17-3-19
Dear Jim,

… We are having very nice weather here and the trees are getting their foliage back again and the flowers are beginning to bloom. Anyway in a few weeks it will be lovely. I received an Aussy mail a few days ago but only got 1 letter from you & you were at the seaside when writing. It was dam hard luck not being able to get to Tassy. Well Jim old boy I don't think it will be long before I am home. They are getting them away very fast now. There was another big draft from my div today but were all 9th Brigade. Percy should be on the next one from the tenth away I should be too but I know I wont. I met Tom Gray a couple of days ago. He was going home. I am going to see all the boys graves before I go & have them fixed up. I am also going to Les Townsend & Bill Streets. Jim I am sending you a bit of a ruff photo with this letter. News is not too plentiful so will close with best love to all.

From
Your Loving Brother
Allan SM

While on leave in Leicestershire, Allan had a photo taken to send to his family.

APRIL

Allan's next letter to Jim is tinged with melancholy. Percy and Allan had been reunited at Le Havre as Percy arrived in the latest draft en route to England and then onward to Australia:

France
12-4-19
Dear Jim,

… Percy arrived down on the 10th Brigade quota a couple of days ago & will be sailing to England about Monday afternoon. He is looking real well. I only wish I could get home with him as all my old boys are on the draft. Tom Alford & Tom Gray are over in England on their way home. I think I am last of the Mologa boys now. By hell I will soon be on my way believe me. Ida [Payne] is getting married on the 24th and she wants me to go over and give her away but I cant possibly get away. I think Percy will be there for it. Ida is jolly fine girl and I have got a lot of time for her. She is marrying a very nice man & he is very clever. Well Jim I hope you had a decent trip, it would be rather disappointing not getting over to Tassy. I hope mum went for her trip, it would do her the world of good. I met Joe Stone yesterday, he is looking tip top, and is on his way home. Is Myrtle still at our place. It is jolly good of her to stay there. What a great assistance she must be to mum. We are sending out of here 1 000 men a week so the whole of the AIF should soon be out of it. Well Jim news is not too plentiful so will close with best wishes to all…

Leaving Le Havre — quota of 45 men leaving France in 1919, comprising 10 Officers 12 Sergeants and 98 ORs (image courtesy of the Grinton Collection, Bendigo RSL and Eaglehawk Heritage Society).

At some point Allan purchased a camera, perhaps while on leave in England, and sent home photos taken both during his leave and of his last weeks in France at Le Havre. There were also several from the journey he made to farewell his brothers.

Photos Allan took while at 1 ACD, Le Havre. Allan is second from the left in the above image.

Possibly a photo of Allan's quarters which he shared at Le Havre. The officer is admiring a photo.

MAY

Percy had now begun the long journey home. Men of the 38th Battalion had been crossing the channel from Le Havre since February. While married men and those serving the longest had been given priority, Percy's time to say farewell had now come. He would never return. He departed on the *Rio Padro* with Knowlson Haw, Tom Dickinson and Austin Henderson on 27 May 1919 and arrived in Australia on 7 July. He had spent just short of three years away from his homeland.

Codford
England
14-5-19
My Dear Jim, Mother & Father

Just a few lines to let you know I am well, and am on my way home. I have had the fourteen days leave and it will not be long now before we will be sailing so I ought not to be long after you get this. Its lovely here now, in fact its getting quite warm. Very sorry to hear Mother has not been too well lately, she wants a good holiday. Expect to get another four days leave before we go. Well Jim I spose you have plenty of work to do just now. News is terrible scarce so I must close with love to all.

I am your loving brother
Percy

MOLOGA, MAY

At home, letters from the Red Cross and those who served alongside Charlie continued to arrive, describing the circumstances of his death. Sarah actively sought more information, writing to a friend of the neighbouring Haw family who obligingly replied and who shared his story of Charlie's death and of his own narrow escapes. He candidly wrote of his disapproval of the actions of his brother, the cause of the rift between brothers not uncommon — a side effect of war which continued to affect families everywhere.

20-5-19
Roughead St
Leongatha
Dear Mrs Marlow

Your welcome letter to hand Saturday dinner-time. We all regret very much to know that 3 of your sons out of the five have paid the price & we all at home send you our deepest sympathy. Sgt Marlow of D Coy. 38th Battn I cant think of his Christian name Frank is it not. It was about middle of April last year 1918 in the morning serving out rations to the lads on his post at about 7 am when he was caught by a bullet from an enemy sniper just in centre of his forehead death being instantaneous. The place being on railway embankment between Mericourt-Ribemount & Albert Somme on main line from Amiens to Bapaume. He is buried just close by with a very nice cross inscribed in white letter black border. My brother Allan is still in England Sgt Major he was on the "Ballarat" when it was torpedoed in the Medderinean Sea. His wife has not had a letter from him for close on 12 month 14th June last year was her last letter he is not playing the game at all she is only [a] young girl not very strong but she is still managing the 5 little children. It seem a down right shame on his part in not writing to her; don't you think. I suppose it [is] because he wont take the time or trouble if it was on a post card I've sent a cable over month now asking for reply but nothing has come through yet. My sister husband is still over there expected home any time now last heard [from] him he was in Belguim (Charlerio) expecting to get to board for home that was in March. I know that Polygon Wood too well. In fact I escape my life by a very narrow margin there at that time October 1917. Yes thank you I am in splendid health. I had trench feet at Xmas 1916 & also received a very nasty gun shot wound at Perrone on 30th Aug 1918 in head just missing my right temple of forehead I have still got the piece the doctor took out of my head in hospital in France so if you or when you happen to be coming up to Leongatha to visit Mr Haw whom I know very well I'll be able to show it to you. I don't know when I'll be able to pay you a visit I am very busy getting my own ground ready, I'm starting to settle down about Oct or Nov just became engaged about fortnight ago so I've got to set to hard work now. Thank you very much for your kind invitation to your place.

*Well Mr & Mrs Marlow & rest of your family hoping this finds you all well
I will now close.*

With best of health & wishes to all

*I remain
Yours Sincerely
Bruce Nelson*

THE WESTERN FRONT, JUNE

Allan knew that his time to bid farewell to the Western Front and his beloved brothers was now close. He took leave before travelling to London and paid his final respects to his brothers, farewelling also those friends both old and new who had survived the Great War. Like Percy, he was never to return.

*Postcard of Lille
Lille
13-6-19
My Dear Mum & Dad*

Just a few lines to let you know that I am in Lille. I landed at Paris last night & came through Brulles to here today. I am on leave with a Padre from the demobilization depot. I am on my way to Messines tomorrow to see Alberts grave then going to see Georges at Popperinghe and then down on to the Somme to see Charlie also to take a photo of them. Then I am returning through Germany back to Paris and then to England. Well dear mum 2 1/2 years ago we were fighting just behind this place. Cheerio dear mum & Dad & best love

Allan XXXX

*Postcard Paris
Paris
18-6-19
My dear Mum & Dad*

Just a few lines to let you know that I am quite well & trust that you all are the same. I am leaving Paris to day for Havre and on Friday I sail to England. I have had a wonderful trip I went and seen all the boys graves and took a photo of them. I will tell you all about the trip when I get home. So goodbye & best love from

Allan XXXX

Allan standing beside George's grave. Allan visited the resting place of each of his brothers prior to leaving France.

MOLOGA, JULY

As Allan prepared to leave France, Percy arrived home and the local communities welcomed their brave sons who had survived the carnage, holding gala evenings with songs, dance and speeches. At Mologa, Amos Haw, who George often mentioned as close by in the trenches, was welcomed home, as was Tom Alford. Tom, Jim's laconic mate, disembarked on 21 July 1919. His family tells the story of the day he marched down the gangplank onto the wharf. A representative of the fledgling Returned Sailor's and Soldier's Imperial League of Australia stopped Tom and suggested he sign up as a member. Tom asked, 'Is it compulsory?' Having been told it was not, Tom replied, 'Well get out of my way then.' Tom was home and it was time to forget the war; he rarely spoke of his experiences, did not attend an RSL meeting or an Anzac Day service. He later married the sister of Les Townsend who had lost his life in the closing stages of the war. Tom's daughter married my uncle, Allen Marlow Junior. The local newspaper reported:

CORPORALS J RYAN AND T. GRAY; LANCE-CORPORAL P MARLOW AND PRIVATES. T. ALFORD, AMOS HAW

MOLOGA. On Thursday 24th inst., residents of Mologa and surrounding districts assembled in full force at C Jones' barn to welcome home the following soldiers.—Corporals J Ryan and T. Gray ; L-Corpl P Marlow and Ptes. T. Alford, Amos Haw. The president of the Patriotic League, Mr. W. Fyffe, occupied the chair. The barn was very tastefully decorated with flags and bunting, and as the soldiers took their seats they were loudly applauded and the chairman then welcomed them back. If I were to write down all the speeches and all the good things that were said of the "Diggers" by the many speakers it would take up a lot of space in this paper. It is almost needless to mention that every speaker warmly welcomed them home and praised them for their gallant work at the front. After the chairman had welcomed the men, all present sang Home, Sweet Home, which was followed by the National Anthem. The concert which followed was much appreciated ... [5]

Percy received another warm welcome from the community of Calivil North where he had spent some time at school:

LANCE- CORPORAL PERCY MARLOW

Calivil North.

A welcome home was accorded to Lance-Corporal Percy Marlow on Wednesday evening 6th inst, in Mr George Mahoney's barn, which was nicely decorated for the occasion. Lance-Corporal Marlow is the first of Mr and Mrs C. Marlow's five sons to return to his native land, three of whom have made the supreme sacrifice for King and country …

L.-Corpl. Marlow on rising to respond was received with great cheering. He thanked them all, his friends for their kind words and the gifts, which he said he did not deserve, as he had simply done his duty. The Chairman then said they had another duty to perform that night, that of presenting to Mr. and Mrs. D. Townsend a framed memorial of their son Leslie, who was killed in action in August, 1918, and he asked the Rev. Nichols to make the presentation. In doing so Mr. Nichols said the occasion was of necessity a sad one, for the residents were paying a tribute of loving sympathy to the memory of one whom they held in high esteem. Mr. David Townsend feelingly responded and thanked the residents for their kindness …[6]

ENGLAND, JULY

In July, Allan arrived in England on the first stage of his journey home. Like Percy a few months before, he took time to farewell the relatives who had opened their homes and their hearts to their young nephews and cousins from Australia.

Postcard of Leicester
Leicester
Sunday 6-7-19
Dear Jim

…Well Jim I go back to Camp tomorrow and hope to get away shortly. Percy will be pretty well at home now. I hope you are not writing any more letters as I will not get [them] *and I have not had any for some time which is due to the shifting about from place to place. Well Jim will see you shortly.*

Cheerio & best luck
Allan

Postcard of Leicester
Sunday 6-7-19
My Dear Dad & Mum

Just another few lines to let you know that I am at the above and enjoying myself. Well dear dad I have been down to Devon and said goodbye to Ida & Jim also Uncle Walter & Edith Went to Middleton to see Uncle Ted. He is well also to Drayton to see Aunt & Uncle also the girls that Auntie brought. All send their very best love. Tomorrow I leave here for camp and hope to get on a boat at the port. We have had rotten weather it rained every day but Sunday. Well dad I seen your sister Edith and she looks fearfully bad certainly will not ever get up again and I think she will pass away very shortly.⁷ I had a hour or more by her bedside talking and she sends her best love. Well dear they are all expecting you over here you would have a nice time if you came. Well dear dad & mum I will be home very shortly now. Percy ought to be landing in 2 or 3 days. Well goodbye dear dad & mum & best love

Your loving son
Allan SM

Allan boarded the *Ajana* on 19 August 1919. He had been away from his family for over three years. There are no other letters to his parents or to Jim. On 1 September he wrote to Eva Jones from the coast of the United States at Newport News in Virginia. He ends his letter with a poignant statement, a confidence he asks her to keep. His AIF appointment was terminated on 25 November 1919 — he had come home in time for the harvest. Perhaps he was back on the job of sewing the wheat bags and eagerly devouring his mother's lunches.

Newport News
New Norfolk
America
Dear Eva,

Just a few lines to let you know that I am at the above and having a good time. We arrived here yesterday morning after 12 days travelling from Liverpool on the HMAS Ajana. The boat is 10440 tons and is a beautiful sailing boat. Up to the present I have not been the least bit seasick and I think I am right for the rest of the journey. We have had a few ruff nights but on the whole it has been lovely. The food and accommodation is wonderful. There are only 20 officers on board therefore we get plenty of duty. Today has been a wonderful day for two of us. This morning quite early an American colonel came down to the boat to inspect it and we were the only two officers on duty and we had to conduct him all over the boat. Anyway after the inspection he took us out in his car all over Newport News and Norfolk and several other places of interest finally finishing up at one of the biggest hotel in Virginia for dinner. Tomorrow morning at 8 o'clock he is coming for us again and we are going to Washington for the day. Up to the present we do not know when we are leaving here but we still have a lot of coal, food and fresh water to go on. Anyway after here we go to Colen [Colon] then through the Panama Canal and then I believe we are going to Sydney and then to Melbourne and Mologa for me. We expect to land about the first week in October and won't I be pleased. I have taken a lot of photos of the different places I have been to and will have a good collection by the time I get home to Aussy and one rainy day when I am home I will show them to you. Well Eva I don't know whether this will get home before me or not anyway it will be a good race. Well Eva there is no more news so will close with kind regards to all.

I remain
Your old friend
Allan S Marlow

1-9-19
Today is Labor Day and it has been a public holiday all over the United States. I saw the procession here and it was some procession too. Half the population of these towns here are of the nigger type but well educated & good living and very respectable people.
Cheerio Allan S M

Eva don't tell anybody but I will be home in time for the harvest.

Composite badge photo of Charlie, George and Albert

Give me your hand, my brother, search my face;
Look in these eyes lest I should think of shame;
For we have made an end to all things base.
We are returning by the road we came.

Siegfried Sassoon, *To My Brother*[8]

PART FIVE
EPILOGUE

EPILOGUE:
WE WILL REMEMBER THEM

An age of Death and Agony and Tears,
A cruel age of woe unguessed before —
Then peace to close the weary storm-wrecked years,
And broken hearts that bleed for evermore.[1]

For the men who returned it was a different world. Old values were gone. Their youth had been stripped from them. They had seen so many men killed and maimed. They had lived in filth with the threat of death ever-present. They had killed. They had developed a comradeship that few civilians could understand. To return to the familiar yet changed world from which they had come was not easy; for some it would prove all too challenging.

For Allan and Percy, returning home was made more difficult by the loss of their three brothers. Their world had been torn apart and their lives transformed; leaving their brothers behind was the most difficult task of all. They returned to a home torn apart by war, to shattered dreams and broken hearts. They had to learn to live in peace, to sleep under a roof at night, possibly to relive the horrors of war in that sleep and to confront the realisation that honour and glory fade quickly. The bonds the family shared eased the process of adjustment, as did the continued comradeship and understanding of the few neighbours and friends who had also served and survived.

For a short time, Allan remained on the family farm at Mologa. Percy returned to 'Hayanmi', a property a few kilometres south-west of Mologa which belonged to his aunt and uncle, Florence and Arthur Mahoney, the brother and sister of Sarah Marlow. He would farm there for the rest of his life.

On 24 March 1920, the men of the Gordon Shire (east of the Loddon River) who served Australia were officially recognised and honoured for their courage and sacrifice with the unveiling of a handsome memorial. The event was reported in the *Pyramid Hill Advertiser*:

> The residents of this district have worthily placed on record their estimation of their soldiers by erecting a handsome stone column, which was unveiled on Wednesday 24th, by Mrs C. Marlow, to whom the honour was justly due, as is well known, by the fact that five of her sons volunteered, of whom three are in soldier's graves in France … In the unveiling ceremony Lieut. A. Marlow escorted his mother on to the platform and the large assemblage stood bareheaded as the cords were cut and the covering Union Jack removed from the pedestal. [2]

Allan and Sarah Marlow unveil the Mologa War Memorial.

Every city, town and hamlet in Australia has its own memorial, erected in recognition of those who served their country, particularly those who died. So much hope rested on the shoulders of this young generation of soldiers. Each family's loss was also a loss to the entire community.

After the unveiling of the memorial, the family continued to receive letters concerning the loss of their sons for some time, a few from family, some from complete strangers.

Water Farm
Sept 15
Manaton
Moretonhampstead
My Dear Nephew

Very many thanks for your kind letter I received this morning please forgive me for not writing sooner to thank you for the papers also the photos you sent me I received them quite safely it was nice [of] them giving your mother the honour of unveiling the memorial but it must have been a very trying day for her to think of her Dear boys lyeing so far away I should like to have known George & Albert we often think of poor Charlie I did think Allan would have sent us a line before now we hope both he & Percy are quite well. We are very sorry to hear your mother has been so ill I hope by now you have her at home again. Well you would all miss her very much I am very glad the operation has turned out so well. It does seem so funny to us for you to write about it being winter. I hope you have had some rain by now. We and people around here have had very poor crops of oats and wheat but of course this land is not suited for growing heavy crops ... I hope you will leave & see it some day but I don't expect you will this country is in a very funny state I can tell you every thing is very Dear I am afraid their will be a lot of suffering amongst the poor people in the towns this winter we had your Aunt Lizzie & her son Clem for 10 days a short time ago he is in Ireland now there is tough work going on their give our love to your father & mother Allan & Percy. I am afraid Dear Jim my letter will not be of much interest to you not knowing the place. I will close with love to all from your loving Aunt A Lee

Over 12 months after the end of the war, Sarah received a letter from one of Charlie's mates. The author, John Wright, writes with some reluctance, afraid of causing Sarah further grief. But he is keen to fulfil a promise made to Charlie:

72 Fawcett St
Mayfield
Newcastle
18-1-20

Mrs C. Marlow,
Mologa Post Office
Dear Madam,

As this is a very sad and delicate subject I wish to write about, I hope you will forgive me if I reopen any partially healed wound in so doing. When in France in March 1918, I was with your son, Sgt. CE Marlow, near the village of Neuve Eglise, and as we mated together we exchanged numerous confidences. He knew that I had my camera with me, and, as we were near the cemetery of Kandahar he asked me if I would photograph the grave of your Son, and, if possible send it to you. This I did with the enclosed results. You will be able to have an enlargement taken from the negative, as it is pretty clear. You will, I am sure, realise the spirit with which I send this souvenir to you. My Mother, had the positions been reversed, would have only been too pleased to have a photograph of the last resting place of her Son. I did not know this boy of yours, as I was in the 35th Battalion, but Charlie, I found was a thorough gentleman in every respect, and any one that knew him will bear out my statement. Mother, father, my wife and I, join in sympathising with you for the loss of a brave son who answered his country's call.

I remain
Yous sincerely
John G Wright

The photo Charlie asked John Wright to take of Albert's grave.

On 18 March 1921, the *Pyramid Hill Advertiser* published a letter sent to the Marlows from England:

Mologa Soldier's Grave

English author's kind thought – Mr C Marlow of Mologa who is father of the late Cpl. G.T. Marlow, who lies buried in Belgium. – The well known English novelist and poet, John Oxenham, and his daughter, recently visited an Australian graveyard in Belgium and seeing the grave of Cpl. Marlow have sent to Mr Marlow the following touching letter:

Woodfield House

Ealing London

Dear Mr Marlow,

You do not know us nor we you, but we are full of gratitude for the great sacrifice you made in the great war, and so, as the distance may prevent you from coming yourself, we have been across to Belgium to visit the Australian graves, including the grave of your son, and to tell you a little about the place where he lies. We hope it may be comforting for you to think that an English girl and her father have visited it on your behalf. Cpl G. T. Marlow, No. 2748, 2nd A.L.T.M.B. lies in plot 23, Row B, in Lijssenthoek cemetery just outside Poperinghe, some 9 miles north of Ypres. It is a place of restful beauty with green trees and a stream on one side, and hop fields and rolling meadows and ploughed lands with red-roofed farms beyond. At times there is not a sound to be heard. The body of your loved one rests in perfect peace after the hardships and trials of war. But we know – as we are sure you know – that he himself, his real self, is infinitely happier where he is than ever he could have been on earth at its best. The graves are planted with roses, violas, pansies, wallflowers, lupins, clarkia and marigolds, with trim grass walks between, and all are most carefully tended by a staff of gardeners, who also keep a large nursery for the sole purpose of supplying the graves with fresh plants. Nothing is wanting in loving regard for those who have gone. We enclose a photograph of a part of the cemetery and with sympathy and love remain

Yours sincerely
Erica Oxenham
John Oxenham[3]

John Oxenham was a prolific English writer, poet and journalist whose real name was William A. Dunkerley. Erica was also a writer. Their kindness in writing to the families of fallen soldiers is extraordinary. One wonders just how many letters they wrote to bereaved families all over the Commonwealth.

'Passchendaele', Mologa, 1985.

Some four years after the unveiling of the memorial, Allan married Eva Jones on a rainy 24 September 1924. They are my grandparents. The bond formed in their letters blossomed into a loving relationship following Allan's return. Grandma once told me that, on the day she opened the letter containing Grandpa's photo, she knew he was the man she would marry.

Their new mud-brick home on the railway line between Mologa and Mitiamo was not completed until April the following year. It took some time to construct as Allan made the mud bricks and built the home himself. The kitchen sported a grand pantry in which Eva kept the baking which Allan had so appreciated, a welcome comfort in the appalling trenches of the Western Front. The cakes and biscuits were neatly stored in rows of tins.

Allan named his new home 'Passchendaele', scribed lovingly in stained glass above the front door. His house represented his own monument to a dreadful carnage, the home a haven which provided a stark contrast to his memories of the horrific Battle of Passchendaele. The remains of the house today exist as a haunting reminder of an experience that only my grandfather and other veterans of that terrible conflict can truly appreciate and understand. Each man emerged from the war with his own unique reflections and recollections. Perhaps 'Passchendaele' stood to remind us all of the tragedy of war and the peace we should fiercely protect.

Despite the name he gave his house, Allan appeared determined to forget and to live in peace with his family, although forgetting was never really possible. He chose to sleep in a purpose-built sleep-out of screened walls attached to the main family home; he struggled with enclosed spaces, a legacy of being buried alive in April 1917. He rarely spoke of the horrors he had witnessed and chose not to attend RSL meetings. During the Second World War he joined the Volunteer Defence Corps, an organisation of volunteers, largely trained by World War I veterans, who would assist in the defence of the homeland of Australia, should it prove necessary. My father remembers the targets at Mitiamo Rock in the Terrick Terrick Forest above Mologa. There Allan and other returned soldiers would instruct the volunteers, preparing them for what could have been a crucial role in the war.

Eva Marlow aged 16 in a photo dated 9 July 1916.

After his mother's death in 1935, Allan no longer attended Anzac Day ceremonies. Sarah, like others, had not recovered from the anguish and loss of the horrific years of war. Albert's girlfriend, Myrtle Stone, would recount to her family how Sarah collapsed to the ground upon learning of the death of another son. For Allan, the memory was just too painful to dwell upon; irrespective, the war had taken yet another member of the Marlow family. When asked, the family always told me that Sarah had died from a broken heart. Having followed her journey through the war, I now understand what they meant. It truly was an age of broken hearts that bleed for evermore.

Allan and Eva Marlow on their wedding day, 24 September 1924.

The *Pyramid Hill Advertiser* reported Sarah's death:

> The blows of bereavement undermined the health of this mother of warrior sons, and later years there were recurring attacks of weakening indisposition. As late as yesterday week the late Mrs Marlow was attending to her regular duties about the home and afterwards complained of general weakness, but none thought she would never arise from her bed again ...[4]

The day Sarah Marlow was buried at Pyramid Hill, returned soldiers formed up at the cemetery gates and marched ahead of the pallbearers.

Charles senior died 15 years later on 18 April 1950 at the age of 93. He was buried with Sarah at Pyramid Hill.

As it shattered the heart of Sarah, the war also hastened the demise of the township of Mologa. Prior to World War I, the town had been a thriving community. But the lifeblood of many of these small towns had been spilt on the soil of France and Belgium. The Great Depression saw the town slump further and it never recovered. As a child, I recall passing the dilapidated hall and school, post office, railway siding and war memorial. Today, the memorial and decaying school are all that remain. But Mologa is not forgotten, nor are the soldiers who fought so gallantly so far from home. In recent years, my Uncle Allen and Gwen Gamble of Mologa, whose father was veteran Amos Haw, reinvigorated the memory of Mologa's lost sons. Anzac Day and Remembrance Day services at the memorial recommenced some years ago and the numbers who gather are growing every year. The memorial is now maintained by the Mologa and District Landcare Group who continue to develop the surrounding landscape and organise commemorative services. In 2015, I was honoured to provide the Anzac Day address for the community. The greatest honour was to also deliver the address in 2021 for the belated commemoration of the centenary of the memorial's unveiling by Sarah and Allan. The planning, fundraising and construction of the memorial was achieved in the midst of a global pandemic. One hundred years on, and with some irony, the planned 2020 commemorative service was delayed owing to COVID-19 restrictions.

A gathering of descendants (and their partners) of Allan and Eva Marlow at Mologa, Anzac Day 2015.

The author with her son Daniel Marlow Gray and granddaughter Marlow June Gray at the Mologa War Memorial Anzac Day Centenary Service, 2021.

The Mologa Memorial in 1984. Little remains of the township of Mologa today.

The older Allan in his twilight years (left). Percy later in life (right).

Allan and Eva had four children, of whom he was exceptionally proud. Allan died of lung cancer in Bendigo on 29 August 1968. He was 73 years of age. While there is no official medical record, Allan often expressed a fear of developing the illness as a result of being gassed in 1917. Despite respiratory distress, many soldiers did not report as injured after a gas attack. Allan regularly attended the lung examination services provided for returned soldiers. Upon receiving word that the tests were negative he would express his relief: 'Thank God for that!'. I have few memories of my grandfather for I was only four when he died. But I do remember 'Passchendaele' and Grandma's pantry.

Percy died after a short illness on 20 October 1973 at the age of 78. His brother Jim, the eldest son, suffered a stroke and died five years later on 9 June 1978; he was 88 years of age. In 1924 he had travelled to Europe to pay his respects to his brothers. Neither Jim nor Percy ever married. I am told that Percy once argued with the love of his life and they were never reconciled. Of six sons who reached adulthood, only two went on to create a new generation. One of those, Charlie, would never meet his daughter. When Jim passed away, the family gradually lost contact with Pearl and Eva.

On Anzac Day in 2015, Charlie's granddaughter made contact with me after discovering the 2015 publication of the children's version of *Anzac Sons: Five Brothers on the Western Front*. Our family remain in touch today. Eva passed away in 2016, at the age of 99 years.

* * *

The deeds of the Australian soldiers of the Great War transformed a nation. They established a tradition, creating a unique identity and giving a young nation its soul. But this came at an unimaginable cost. The spirit of those who never came home lives on in their legacy. Those who survived are no longer with us to tell their stories, but their memories are very much alive in their letters and their words. May they and their stories live on in the hearts of those they leave behind, for they forged a legend that we can never forget.

Have you forgotten yet?
Look up and swear by the green of the Spring that you'll never forget.

Siegfried Sassoon, *Aftermath*, March 1919

ABOUT THE AUTHOR

Allison grew up on a farm near Pyramid Hill, the small Victorian town where she was born. Her interest in the service of her ancestors began when she was studying to become a teacher. Allison used a selection of their letters to complete an assignment, a task which consequently ignited the dream to honour her family. She undertook the writing of this story from a sense of empathy with her great-grandmother, whom she never met, and a deep conviction that this story needs to be shared with others. *Anzac Sons: Mateship, Bravery and Sacrifice* is her undertaking that the sacrifices her family made will never be forgotten. It is also a testament to all those who served in World War I, and the families who supported them. She hopes readers will be inspired to research their own families and share their knowledge with others.

Allison is the author of the 2016 ABIA and CBCA longlisted title *Anzac Sons: Five Brothers on the Western Front*, the children's version of *Anzac Sons*. She has written five other children's books, *Granny's Place* and *Shearing Time*, two books in the highly successful *Australia Remembers* series regarding Australia's military history and *I Wonder*, a picture book for children inspired by the lovely beaches of the Sunshine Coast which she calls home. Allison was a recipient of a 2017 May Gibbs Children's Literature Trust Creative Time Fellowship. The resulting young adult manuscript *Follow After Me*, a fictionalised account of the story of the Marlow brothers, was published in 2019.

A teacher-librarian for over twenty years, Allison now works as a writer, publishing consultant and presenter in schools.

ENDNOTES

Chapter 1

1. C.E.W. Bean, *Anzac to Amiens, Australian War Memorial, Canberra, 1946, p. 23.*
2. *Not be confused with the infamous Hill 60 of the Western Front. Hills were routinely named for their height above sea level.*
3. *Interview with Albert Wishart, 'Northaven', Kerang, Victoria, 1985.*
4. *The Cheyne, Mahoney and Gibson families are all relatives of the Marlow family.*
5. *Zeitoun — throughout George's letters it is spelt Yeitoun.*
6. *See P. Stanley, Bad Characters: sex, crime, mutiny, murder and the Australian Imperial Force,* Pier Nine, Sydney, 2010.
7. 'CB' — 'confined to barracks' was a form of military punishment for minor misdemeanours in which the miscreant was literally confined to the barracks area and all local leave cancelled.
8. A pictorial magazine of the time which later evolved to become the *Australasian Post.*
9. *The Dripps were residents of Pyramid Hill.*
10. *Pearl Clee of Bendigo — Charlie Marlow's girlfriend.*
11. Eddie Cheyne was a cousin of the Marlows. Eddie enlisted on eight separate occasions but was refused each time. He suffered an unspecified condition which affected his legs.

Chapter 2

1. G.J. Downie, NAA B2455.
2. Bean, *Anzac to Amiens*, p. 213.
3. *Pyramid Hill Advertiser*, 18 February 1916.
4. The fountain is a well-known landmark in the centre of Bendigo.

Chapter 3

1. Bean, *Anzac to Amiens*, pp. 197–98.
2. Les Carlyon, *The Great War, Macmillan, Sydney, 2006, p. 35.*
3. The German salient at Fromelles covered an area of higher ground facing north-west known as the Sugarloaf which provided excellent observation of no man's land on either flank. A salient is a position which bulges into enemy territory. While salients were often vulnerable from enfilading fire and sometimes at risk of being cut off, those which included high ground presented a major advantage. Salients existed all along the Western Front, most infamously around the beleaguered cities of Verdun and Ypres.
4. Bean, *Anzac to Amiens*, p. 202.
5. *Pyramid Hill Advertiser*, 28 April 1916.
6. From 6 May 1918, recruits between the ages of 18 and 21 could enlist without parental approval.
7. *The Pyramid Hill Advertiser*, 28 April 1916.
8. Kalma was a Bendigo photographer.
9. Bill Gammage, *The Broken Years*, Penguin, Ringwood, 1982 (1974), pp. 133–55.
10. C.E.W. Bean, *Official History of Australia in the War 1914-18,* Vol. III, *The A.I.F. in France 1916,* Angus & Robertson, Sydney, 1941, p. 203.
11. The families of the sisters of Charles senior who had remained in England.
12. *The Anzac Book was a trench publication produced at Gallipoli which was first released to the public in 1916.*

Chapter 4

1. Edgar Rule, 1916, quoted in Bean, *Anzac to Amiens*, p. 249.
2. Camps were at Perham Downs (eight camps for the 1st Division), Larkhill (19 camps for the 5th Division and artillery), Rollestone (four camps for the 2nd and 4th divisions) and Parkhouse (four camps). A Machine-Gun Depot was located at Tidworth.
3. Les Carlyon, *The Great War, Macmillan, Sydney, 2006, p. 120.*
4. *Pyramid Hill Advertiser, 4 August 1916.*
5. *J. Stone, NAA B2455.*

6. *J.F. Stone, NAA B2455.*
7. *The Pyramid Hill Advertiser*, 21 July 1916.
8. Sarah Marlow's brother Arthur Mahoney served in the Boer War and remained in South Africa for some years before returning to Australia. It is likely that he had already returned to Australia and this reference is possibly to beat the censor. Allan had sent an earlier letter that mentions Durban and Cape Town and this letter may not have been passed by the censor. Indeed many soldiers paid locals to post their letters while in port.
9. Carlyon, *The Great War, pp. 26–27.*
10. Bean, *Anzac to Amiens*, p. 225.
11. Ron Austin, *Our Dear Old Battalion: The Story of the 7th Battalion, AIF 1914-1919,* Slouch Hat Publications, Rosebud, Victoria, 2004, p. 133.
12. Bean, *Anzac to Amiens*, p. 238.
13. Bean, *Official History,* Vol. III, *The A.I.F. in France 1916,* p. 590.
14. Bean , *Anzac to Amiens*, p. 24.
15. The British 48th Division attacked to the west of Pozieres.
16. Bean, *Official History,* Vol. III, *The A.I.F. in France 1916, p. 593.*
17. *Ibid., p.724.*
18. *Austin, Our Dear Old Battalion,* p. 238.
19. A.D. Bailey, NAA B2455.
20. H.G. Burrows, NAA B2455.
21. A.H. Haw, NAA B2455.
22. W.T. Alford, NAA B2455.
23. Bean, *Official History,* Vol. III, *The A.I.F. in France 1916, p. 787.*
24. *Bean, Anzac to Amiens*, p. 262.
25. Jonathan King, *Great Battles in Australian History, Allen & Unwin, Crows Nest, 2011, p. 110.*
26. *Bean, Anzac to Amiens*, p. 264.

Chapter 5
1. D.R. Leed, NAA B2455.
2. C.H. Cockroft, NAA B2455.
3. *The Pyramid Hill Advertiser*, 4 August 1916.
4. Ibid., 26 August 1916.
5. Grandfather William Marlow was buried at Bringhurst and 'Aunty' was living in one of the nearby villages — either Uppingham or Corby.
6. 'Bobs' was a block of land the Marlow family had purchased east of the Terrick Terrick Forest.
7. K. Laird, NAA B2455.
8. *Pyramid Hill Advertiser, 2 July 1916, 'Profiles of our Past –Obituaries from the Pyramid Hill Advertiser 1910-1919'.*
9. *A.J. Gibson, NAA B2455.*
10. *R.W. Campbell, NAA B2455.*
11. Allan would have been surprised to discover that Albert Jacka had not died of the wounds he received in his astonishing act of courage at Pozieres. While in hospital in England, Jacka sent a reporter away, asking another patient to tell the reporter he was dead. His fellow soldier obliged and suddenly, according to newspaper reports, Albert Jacka VC had passed away. Allan also mentions learning that 2700 Australians had been put out of action the day prior to his letter. He refers to the final action of the 4th Division in its attack on Mouquet Farm before its withdrawal on 5 September. See Carlyon, *The Great War,* p. 205.
12. Bean, *Anzac to Amiens*, p. 289.
13. Hughes was expelled from the Labor Party in New South Wales in September 1916.
14. Bean, *Anzac to Amiens*, p. 293.
15. The Saville family managed the Mologa Post Office.
16. A.G. Ferris, NAA B2455.
17. W.E. Guinane, NAA B2455.
18. W.T. Stevens, NAA B2455.

Chapter 6
1. P.J. Ryan, NAA B2455.

2. *The Argus* (n.d.), newspaper clipping found among the letters.

3. Will Hare was a local from Mologa; he was not an enlisted soldier but had passed away in Melbourne in 1916.

4. The 3rd Division was initially required to wear the slouch hat with the brim down and the rising sun badge at the front. To their great relief the order was reversed in November 1917 when the Australian Corps was formed. The 3rd Division no longer stood out from the other four divisions and could wear their hats with the brim up and the badge on the side.

5. Lighter clothing issued for the sea journey.

6. *Pyramid Hill Advertiser, 3 November 16.*

Chapter 7

1. The Ox refers to the town of Durham Ox, Victoria.

2. Bean, *Anzac to Amiens*, p. 294.

3. Ibid., p. 267.

4. Ibid., p. 268.

5. C.L. Fyffe, NAA B2455.

6. C.S. Wales, NAA B2455.

7. J. Cocking, NAA B2455.

Chapter 8

1. *Pyramid Hill Advertiser, 17 November 1916.*

2. Eric Fairey, *The 38th Battalion A.I.F.: The Story and Official History of the 38th Battalion A.I.F.,* Bendigo Advertiser Pty Ltd and Cambridge Press, 1920, pp. 7–9.

3. *Ibid.*

4. *Ibid., p. 10.*

5. Ibid., pp. 11–12.

6. Cousin Eddie Cheyne, who had attempted to enlist eight times, had now been accepted. He was discharged within weeks.

7. George and Arthur Mahoney, relatives of Sarah.

8. *J.R McDonald, NAA B2455.*

9. *J.R. McDonald, NAA B2455.*

10. *Pyramid Hill Advertiser, 9 September 1921.*

Chapter 9

1. Bean, *Anzac to Amiens, p. 316.*

2. Carlyon, *The Great War, p. 319.*

3. Bean, *Anzac to Amiens, p. 315.*

4. Fairey, *The 38th Battalion A.I.F, p. 12.*

5. *J.H. Lockett, NAA B2455.*

6. *J.C. Lewis, NAA B2455.*

7. *E. Butler, NAA B2455.*

8. *W.L. Jones, NAA B2455.*

9. *E.M. Jones, NAA B2455.*

10. *W. Teale, NAA B2455.*

11. *S.F. Maslen, NAA B2455.*

12. *H.S. Rumble, NAA B2455.*

13. *W.E. Wormald, NAA B2455.*

14. *J.E. Fiven, NAA B2455.*

15. *J.E. Adams, NAA B2455; G.T. Fowler, NAA B2455.*

16. Fairey, *The 38th Battalion A.I.F*, p. 13.

17. A.E. Brookes, NAA B2455.

18. G. Mossop, NAA B2455.

19. Carlyon, *The Great War*, pp. 296–97.

20. *Fairey, The 38th Battalion A.I.F, pp.14–15.*

21. 'A Mologa Family', *Bendigo Advertiser, 25 November 1916, p. 4.*

22. Bean, *Anzac to Amiens*, p. 317.

23. W.P. Mowat, NAA B2455.

24. Fairey, *The 38th Battalion A.I.F, p. 18.*

25. *R. Paterson, NAA B2455.*
26. *F. Dee, NAA B884, V13043.*
27. *C.A. Mills. NAA B2455.*
28. *E. Kerr, NAA B2455.*
29. *G.G. McKay, NAA B2455.*

Chapter 10

1. Archie was now on his way to England having been shot in his left leg, the second time he had been wounded. He recovered and returned to the front in July.
2. R.W. Campbell, NAA B2455.
3. F.M. Hannasky, NAA B2455.
4. E. Tracey, NAA B2455.
5. Commander of AIF Depots in England.
6. Lawrinsky, *Hard Jacka, pp. 260–90.*
7. *Bean, Anzac to Amiens, p. 334.*
8. *J.T. Price, NAA B2455.*
9. *Pyramid Hill Advertiser,* 2 July 1916, 'Profiles of our Past –Obituaries from the Pyramid Hill Advertiser 1910-1919'.
10. Bean, *Anzac to Amiens, p. 336.*
11. *Fairey, The 38th Battalion A.I.F, p. 19.*
12. *D. Glass, NAA B2455.*

Chapter 11

1. Fairey, *The 38th Battalion A.I.F, p. 20.*
2. *Bean, Anzac to Amiens, p. 334.*
3. *A.H. Haw, NAA B2455.*
4. *A.E. Johnson, NAA B2455.*
5. *Fairey, The 38th Battalion A.I.F, pp. 20–21.*

Chapter 12

1. Bean, *Anzac to Amiens, pp. 345–49.*
2. *H.T.S. Dabb, NAA B2455.*
3. *Chapter 10 third Image.*
4. *A. Duncan, NAA B2455.*
5. *A. Chisolm, NAA B2455.*
6. *Chapter 10. Third image.*
7. *E.G. Swainston, NAA B2455.*
8. *Bean, Anzac to Amiens, pp. 351–52.*
9. *Ibid., pp. 352–53.*
10. *Carlyon, The Great War, p. 421.*
11. *T.S. Roberts, NAA B2455.*
12. *Chapter 10. Third image.*
13. *H. Harnell, NAA B2455.*
14. *L.C. Taylor, NAA B2455.*
15. *Chapter 10. Third image.*
16. *T.C. Burt, NAA B2455.*
17. *H.J. Jeanes, NAA B2455.*
18. *L.W.H. Cant, NAA B2455.*
19. *P. Owens, NAA B2455.*
20. *G.H. Collison, NAA B2455.*
21. *Chapter 10. Third image.*
22. *T.W. Dickinson, NAA B2455.*
23. *J. Reid, NAA B2455.*
24. W.S. McKinnon, NAA B2455.
25. A. Sinclair, NAA B2455.
26. J. Sinclair, NAA B2455.

Chapter 13

1. J.F. Steele, NAA B2455.
2. G. Brittain, NAA B2455.
3. H.E. Hawkesworth, NAA B2455.
4. Fairey, *The 38th Battalion A.I.F, p. 28.*

Chapter 14

1. Bean, *Anzac to Amiens, p. 361.*
2. *Fred Smith was a member of the 38th Battalion. He was 30 years old, married and working as a clerk in Sydney when he enlisted in September 1916. He was wounded on 7 June 1917 but returned to the battalion in November that year. He was wounded again on 29 November 1917 and returned to Australia in April 1918.*
3. *Pyramid Hill Advertiser,* 2 July 1916, 'Profiles of our Past –Obituaries from the Pyramid Hill Advertiser 1910-1919', p. 75.
4. The death of Mrs Ogilvie, mentioned by the boys, was a tragic accident which reverberated throughout the local Mologa community. *The Pyramid Hill Advertiser* (29 June and 6 July 1917) reported that 30-year-old Alice Ogilvie of Yarrawalla was tending a fire in the open when her clothing caught fire. She was burned so extensively that she passed away a week later. She left behind a husband and two children.

Chapter 15

1. Carlyon, *The Great War, p. 447.*
2. *G.T. Marlow, NAA B2455.*
3. *Bean, Anzac to Amiens, p. 367.*
4. *Pyramid Hill Advertiser,* 12 October 1917, 'Profiles of our Past –Obituaries from the Pyramid Hill Advertiser 1910-1919'.
5. Letters dated 8 to 10 July.

Chapter 16

1. Bean, *Anzac to Amiens, p. 369.*
2. *Fairey, The 38th Battalion A.I.F, pp. 33–34.*
3. *C.E.W. Bean , Official History of Australia in the War 1914-18, Vol. IV, The A.I.F. in France 1917, Angus and Robertson, Sydney, 1938, p. 884; AWM 23-55-1 Part1, p. 6.*
4. *AWM 23-55-1 Part1, p. 6.*
5. *Fairey, The 38th Battalion A.I.F, p. 34.*
6. *Bean, Official History, Vol. IV, The A.I.F. in France 1917, pp. 870–74.*
7. *Bean, Anzac to Amiens, p. 372.*
8. *Ibid., p. 371.*
9. *AWM 4-23-55-1 Part1, p. 7.*
10. *Bean, Official History, Vol. IV, The A.I.F. in France 1917, p. 917.*
11. *Fairey, The 38th Battalion A.I.F, p. 36.*
12. *Ibid.*
13. *Bean, Anzac to Amiens, p. 374.*
14. *Ibid., p. 375.*
15. *Ibid., pp. 375–76.*
16. *Carlyon, The Great War, p. 510.*
17. *A.G. Henderson, NAA B2455.*
18. MS 883 Papers of Frank Hurley, 1912–1962 [manuscript] Series 1: Diaries, 1912–1961 Item 5 : My diary, official War Photographer Commonwealth Military Forces, from 21 August 1917 to 31 August 1918 http://www.nla.gove.au/apps/cdview?pi=nla.ms-ms883-1-5-s71-v and s72.

Chapter 17

1. W. Street, NAA B2455.
2. H. Street, NAA B2455.
3. H. Martin, NAA B2455.
4. D.L. Townsend, NAA B2455.
5. E. Kerr, NAA B2455.
6. D. Mullen, NAA B2455.
7. H.J. Mullen, NAA B2455.

8. *Pyramid Hill Advertiser, 13 August 1917.*
9. *Chapter 10 third Image.*
10. *T.C. Burt, NAA B2455.*
11. *E.G. Swainston, NAA B2455; Chapter 10 third Image.*
12. *A.E. Brookes, NAA B2455.*
13. *A. Sinclair, NAA B2455.*
14. *No Four finish* and later written *No pour fini* would refer to the French *pour finir* meaning 'finally'. I suspect Allan is answering a query from Jim regarding his romantic interest in Pyramid Hill which, it would seem, had now come to an end.
15. Fairey, *The 38th Battalion A.I.F, pp. 38–39.*
16. *R.W. Gollan, NAA B2455.*
17. *Bean, Anzac to Amiens, p. 375.*
18. *Ibid.*
19. *Pyramid Hill Advertiser, 21 December 1917.*
20. *Harold Scott had sailed with Albert on the Port Lincoln.*
21. *Fairey, The 38th Battalion A.I.F, p. 40.*
22. W.R. Crossman, NAA B2455.
23. T.S. Crossman, NAA B2455.
24. N.F. Day, NAA B2455.
25. *Pyramid Hill Advertiser, 5 April 1918.*

Chapter 18
1. C.E.W. Bean, *The Official History of Australia in the War of 1914–1918, Vol. V, The A.I.F. in France 1918,* Angus & Robertson, Sydney, 1941, pp. 1–13.
2. Fairey, *The 38th Battalion A.I.F, p. 41.*
3. *Bean, Official History, Vol. IV, The A.I.F. in France 1917, p. 951.*
4. *AWM 4-23-55-1 Part 1, p. 17.*
5. *R.J. Hercus, NAA B2455.*
6. C.E.W. Bean, *Official History of Australia in the War of 1914-1918, Vol. V, The A.I.F. in France December 1917-May 1918,* Angus & Robertson, Sydney, 1938, p. 47.
7. The owners, Mr and Mrs Charles Billyard-Leake, were originally from Sydney.
8. 'Anzac Traditions continues in Harefield, UK, site of WWI hospital', *Herald Sun*, 21 April 2009 at: http://www.heraldsun.com.au/news/victoria/anzac-tradition-in-englands-heart/story-e6frf7lf-1225700428960

Chapter 19
1. Bean, *Anzac to Amiens,* pp. 406–09.
2. Carlyon, *The Great War, p. 563.*
3. Bean, *Anzac to Amiens, p. 415.*
4. *AWM 4-23-55-1 Part 1, p. 21.*
5. *Ibid.*
6. *Bean, Anzac to Amiens, pp. 410–14.*
7. Ibid., p. 420.
8. Ibid., p. 422.
9. Fairey, *The 38th Battalion A.I.F, p. 50.*
10. *Bean, Anzac to Amiens, pp. 423–26.*
11. *Fairey, The 38th Battalion A.I.F, p. 52.*
12. H.F. Poole, NAA B2455.
13. L.A. Roberts, NAA B884.

Chapter 20
1. Bean, *Anzac to Amiens, p. 427.*
2. Ibid., p. 428.
3. Member of the Legislative Assembly.

Chapter 21
1. NAA, Honours and Awards: Robert Oswald Henderson.
2. *Pyramid Hill Advertiser,* 17 May 1918.
3. Ibid., 24 May 1918.

4. W.H. Orchard, NAA B2455.
5. *Pyramid Hill Advertiser*, 24 May 1918.
6. A.J.A. Maudsley, NAA B2455.
7. Bean, *Anzac to Amiens, pp. 453–54.*
8. D.W. Townsend, NAA B2455.

Chapter 22
1. Bean, *Anzac to Amiens, pp. 458–62.*
2. *Gammage, The Broken Years, pp. 220–21.*
3. *Bean, Anzac to Amiens, pp. 470–73.*
4. Ibid., p. 479.
5. A.V. Grinton, NAA B2455.
6. The photos have since toured the country in an exhibition entitled 'A Camera on the Somme 1916-1919' and are available for viewing at the Bendigo RSL Museum.
7. *Pyramid Hill Advertiser,* 1 November 1918.
8. *Pyramid Hill Advertiser,* 3 January 1919.
9. Carlyon, *The Great War,* p. 692.
10. Ibid., p. 696.
11. Bean, *Anzac to Amiens, p. 486.*
12. *Carlyon, The Great War,* p. 701.
13. Bean, *Anzac to Amiens, pp. 492–93.*
14. *Gammage, The Broken Years, p. 202.*
15. Lieutenant Colonel Robert Henderson, DSO, who had sailed with Allan and Percy on the *Runic* and who Percy had earlier praised for his leadership at Passchendaele, was killed at Bony on 1 October. He commanded the 39th Battalion, having initially served as a major in the 38th Battalion.

Chapter 23
1. AWM 4 23-55-1 Part 1, p. 61.
2. Convalescent Depot War Diary, AWM 4-26-84-8.
3. John Terraine, *The First World War,* Leo Cooper, London, 1983, p. 184.
4. Bean, *Anzac to Amiens, p. 532.*
5. *Pyramid Hill Advertiser, 17 May 1918.*
6. *Pyramid Hill Advertiser, 6 September 1918.*
7. Convalescent Depot War Diary, AWM 4-26-84-8.
8. *Pyramid Hill Advertiser, 15 November 1918.*
9. *'B' class troops were convalescent men fit for physical training, marching etc.*

Chapter 24
1. Fairey, *The 38th Battalion A.I.F, p. 86.*
2. Tom Gibson was a railway porter at Mologa and a relative of the Marlows. His brother Bert had been invalided back to Australia and then later sent to an AIF depot in South Africa. Tom enlisted on 11 September 1917. His mother wrote on his consent form 'on condition my son J.L. Gibson is kept in Victoria for 4 months'; he had just turned 18. Tom did not see the fighting on the Western Front. He arrived in England late in September 1918 and sailed home to Australia in May the following year. J.L. Gibson, NAA B2455.
3. E.E. Marlow, NAA B2455.
4. G.H. Marlow, NAA B2455.
5. *Pyramid Hill Advertiser, 1 August 1919.*
6. *Pyramid Hill Advertiser, 15 August 1919.*
7. *Edith died on 27 August 1919.*
8. *Siegfried Sassoon , Selected Poems, Faber & Faber, London, 1982 (1961), p. 14.*

Epilogue
1. V. Brittain, 'War (The Great German Offensive, March-May 1918)' in M. Bostridge (ed), *Because you Died: Poetry and Prose of the First World War and After,* Virago Press, United Kingdom, 2008.
2. *Pyramid Hill Advertiser, n.d.*
3. *Pyramid Hill Advertiser, 18 March 1921.*
4. *Pyramid Hill Advertiser, 10 July 1935.*

RECOMMENDED READING

Adam-Smith, Patsy, *The Anzacs*, Thomas Nelson, Melbourne, 1981.

——, *Australian Women at War*, Sphere Books, Melbourne, 1984.

Arthur, Max, *Forgotten Voices of the Great War*, Ebury Press, Sydney, 2002.

Austin, Ronald J., *Our Dear Old Battalion: The Story of the 7th Battalion, AIF 1914-1919*, Slouch Hat Publications, Rosebud, Victoria, 2004.

Bean, C.E.W, *Official History of Australia in the War 1914-18*, Vol. III, *The A.I.F. in France 1916*, Angus & Robertson, Sydney, 1942.

——, *Official History of Australia in the War 1914-18*, Vol. IV, *The A.I.F. in France 1917*, Angus & Robertson, Sydney, 1938.

——, *Official History of Australia in the War 1914-18*, Vol. V, *The A.I.F. in France December 1917-May 1918*, Angus & Robertson, Sydney, 1938.

——, *Official History of Australia in the War 1914-18*, Vol VI, *The A.I.F. in France May 1918 – The Armistice*, Angus & Robertson, Sydney, 1941.

——, *Anzac to Amiens*, Australian War Memorial, Canberra, 1938.

Bean, C.E.W. and Gullett, H.S., *Official History of Australia in the War*, Vol. XII : *Photographic Record of the War: Reproductions of Pictures Taken By The Australian Official Photographers (captains G.H. Wilkins, M.C., and J.F. Hurley, Lieutenants H.F. Baldwin and J.P. Campbell) and Others*, Angus & Robertson, Sydney, 1938.

Brittain, V., 'War (The Great German Offensive, March-May 1918)' in *Because you Died: Poetry and Prose of the First World War and After*, M. Bostridge (ed), Virago Press, United Kingdom, 2008.

Carlyon, Les, *Gallipoli*, Macmillan, Sydney, 2002.

——, *The Great War*, Macmillan, Sydney, 2006.

Carthew, Noel, *Voices from the Trenches: Letters to Home*, New Holland, Sydney, 2002.

Dando-Collins, Stephen, *Crack Hardy: From Gallipoli to Flanders to the Somme, the true story of three Australian brothers at war*, Vintage, North Sydney, 2011.

Davies, Will (ed), *Somme Mud: the war experiences of an infantryman in France 1916-1919*, Random House, Sydney, 2006.

Davies, Will, *In the Footsteps of Private Lynch*, Vintage Books, Sydney, 2008.

De Vries, Susannah, *Heroic Australian Women in War: Astonishing Tales of Bravery From Gallipoli to Kokoda*, HarperCollins, Sydney, 2004.

Fairey, Eric, *The 38th Battalion A.I.F.: The Story and Official History of the 38th Battalion A.I.F.*, Bendigo Advertiser Pty Ltd & Cambridge Press, 1920.

Fewster, Kevin, *Gallipoli Correspondent: The Frontline Diary of C.E.W. Bean*, George Allen and Unwin, Sydney, 1985.

Foley, Robert and McCartney, Helen (eds), *The Somme: An Eyewitness History*, The Folio Society, London, 2006.

Gammage, Bill, *The Broken Years*, Penguin, Ringwood, 1982.

Hamilton, John, *Goodbye Cobber, God Bless You*, Macmillan, Sydney, 2004.

King, Jonathan, *Great Battles in Australian History*, Allen & Unwin, Crows Nest, 2011.

Lindsay, Patrick, *The Spirit of the Digger: Then & Now,* Macmillan, Sydney, 2003.

Lawrinsky, Michael, *Hard Jacka*, Mira Books, Chatswood, 2010.

——, *Return of the Gallipoli Legend: Jacka VC,* Mira Books, Chatswood, 2010.

McDonald, Lyn, *They Called it Passchendaele: The Story of the Third Battle of Ypres and the Men Who Fought In It*, Penguin, London, 1993.

McKernan, Michael, *The Australian People and the Great War*, Collins, Sydney, 1984.

McLachlan, Matt, *Walking with the Anzacs: A Guide to Australian Battlefields on the Western Front,* Hachette Australia, Sydney, 2008.

Nott, David, *Somewhere in France: the Collected Letters of Lewis Windermere Nott January – December 1916,* Harper Perennial, Sydney, 1996.

Pedersen, Peter, *Anzacs on the Western Front: The Australian War Memorial Battlefield Guide,* John Wiley & Sons Australia, Milton, 2012.

——, *The Anzacs: Gallipoli to the Western Front*, Viking, Camberwell, 2007.

Pegler, Martin, *Attack on the Somme: Haig's Offensive 1916*, Pen & Sword, Military, Barnsley, South Yorkshire, 2006.

——, *Sniping in the Great War*, Pen & Sword, Military, Barnsley, South Yorkshire, 2008.

Poole, Phillipa, *Of Love and War; The Letters and Diaries of Captain Adrian Curlewis and his Family 1939-1945,* Century Publishing, London, 1983.

Prior, Robin and Wilson, Trevor, *Passchendaele: the Untold Story*, Yale University Press, New Haven, 1996.

Sassoon, Siegfried, *Selected Poems*, Faber & Faber, London, 1982.

Stanley, Peter, *Bad Characters: Sex, Crime, Mutiny, Murder and the Australian Imperial Force,* Pier 9, Millers Point, 2010.

Terraine, John, *The First World War*, Leo Cooper, London, 1983.

Travers, Richard, *Diggers in France: Australian Soldiers on the Western Front,* ABC Books, Sydney, 2008.

Walsh, Michael, *Brothers in War*, Ebury Press, 2006.

Wolff, Leon, *In Flanders Fields: The 1917 Campaign*, The Folio Society, London, 2003.

AVAILABLE NOW ONLINE OR AT ALL GOOD BOOKSTORES

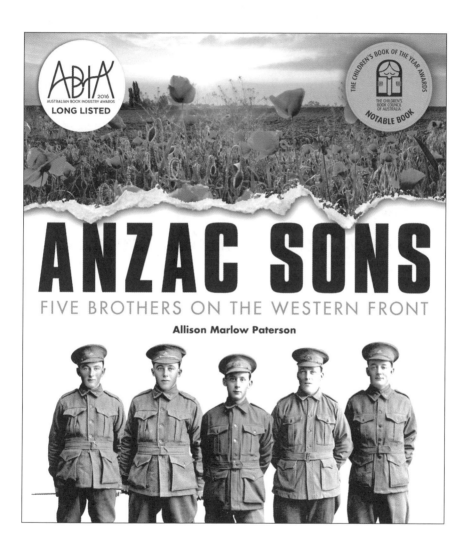

For more great titles visit
www.bigskypublishing.com.au